DEVELOPING AND MAINTAINING PRACTICAL ARCHIVES

A How-To-Do-It Manual
Second Edition

Gregory S. Hunter

HOW-TO-DO-IT MANUALS
FOR LIBRARIANS

NUMBER 122

NEAL–SCHUMAN PUBLISHERS, INC.
New York, London

Published by Neal-Schuman Publishers, Inc.
100 William Street, Suite 2004
New York, NY 10038

The paper used in this publication meets the minimum require-
ments of American National Standard for Informational Sciences—
Permanence of Paper for Printed Library Materials, ANSI
Z39.48—1992

Printed and bound in the United States of America.

Library of Congress Cataloging-in-Publication Data

Hunter, Gregory S.
    Developing and maintaining practical archives : a how-to-do-it
manual / Gregory S. Hunter.—2nd ed.
            p. cm.—(How-to-do-it manuals for librarians; no. 122)
    Includes bibliographical references and index.
    ISBN 1-55570-467-0 (alk. paper)
    1. Archives—Handbooks, manuals, etc. I. Title. II. Series.

CD950.H86 2003
027—dc21
                                                            2003059930

DEDICATION

To my wonderful daughters, Beth and Kate. May the past be a prologue to happy and healthy lives.

CONTENTS

FIGURES

PHOTOGRAPHS

PREFACE

Both the world and the archival profession have experienced tremendous change since the first edition of *Developing and Maintaining Practical Archives: A How-To Do-It Manual* was published in 1996. September 11, 2001 brought terrorism to our doorstep, fear to our hearts, and an immediate need to preserve records of an historic event. Nations have suffered "ethnic cleansing" accompanied by destruction of cultural artifacts and historical records. The "electronic revolution"—embodied by the transforming effects of the Internet—has altered society in massive and minute ways.

Change in the profession has created a twin need for maintaining and improving archival materials while expanding key areas of innovation. The archival educators who used the first edition of *Developing and Maintaining Practical Archives* as a textbook encouraged me to keep the core content for a second edition, but to add new topics and include international perspectives and literature. I have tried to balance theory and practice by summarizing the best thinking on archival theory and methodology while combining it with practical advice.

The first two chapters cover essential background and steps needed before opening an archives.

Chapter 1, **"Introduction to Archives and Manuscripts,"** discusses what an archives is and provides basic definitions.

Chapter 2, **"Conducting a Survey and Starting an Archival Program,"** details the steps needed to plan and implement an archival program for any type of organization.

Chapters 3 to 9 cover the basics of day-to-day operations:

Chapter 3, **"Selection and Appraisal,"** explores the best ways to decide which materials to destroy and which to add to an archives. This edition includes new sections on international perspectives on appraisal and refinements to U.S. theories.

Chapter 4, **"Acquisitions and Accessioning,"** discusses the acquisition of records and papers not generated by the parent institution. There is also an important update on the issue of documentation strategies.

Chapter 5, **"Arrangement,"** is the bridge between records and their use by researchers. This chapter explores the "processing" of the collection through organizing records to reveal their content and significance—the heart of arrangement.

Chapter 6, **"Description,"** examines the establishment of administrative and intellectual control over archival holdings through the preparation of finding aids. This chapter has new sections dealing with Encoded Archival Description (EAD) and the Internet.

Chapter 7, **"Preservation,"** considers the variety of interrelated activities designed to prolong the usable life of archives and manuscripts. It features the latest research on preservation storage and handling.

Chapter 8, **"Security and Disaster Planning,"** deals with potential problems caused by natural elements as well as human beings. This chapter updates security and disaster planning post September 11th.

Chapter 9, **"Access, Reference, and Outreach,"** balances the dual archival responsibilities of preservation and use. New sections discuss the Digital Millennium Copyright Act and the Sonny Bono Copyright Term Extension Act.

Once the basics covered in the above nine chapters are in place, an archivist is ready to address some advanced topics: digital records, audiovisual archives, management, and the nature of the archival profession.

Chapter 10, **"Digital Records,"** explores aspects of archiving electronic records, from policies to system dependence. This chapter includes major revisions and expansion to address today's rapidly changing digital landscape.

Three new chapters make their debut in this second edition:

Chapter 11, **"Audiovisual Archives,"** covers the unique challenges presented by photographs, films, videotapes, and sound recordings.

Chapter 12, **"Management,"** summarizes the best thinking about managing an archival program, including staff, finances, facilities, and technology.

Chapter 13, **"The Archival Profession,"** examines the nature of professionalism, archival education, individual certification, and professional ethics.

The wide-ranging bibliography offers hundreds of useful resources. In addition to updates, I have expanded it by including literature from Canada and Australia. Finally, the appendices feature three helpful additions. Appendix A is called "North Fork University: Institutional Background." To assist readers new to the topic, I use this case study throughout the book in which an archives is envisioned, planned, and begun. Appendixes B and C contain the full text of two important professional documents: The Society of American Archivists' "Code of Ethics for Archivists" and the Academy of Certified Archivists' "Role Delineation Statement for Professional Archivists."

In each chapter, I include references to literature published after the first edition of *Developing and Maintaining Practical Archives* and also integrate international scholarship. I have incorporated many new photographs and quotes from popular newspapers and magazines that demonstrate the importance of archives in different walks of life. Readers can use these materials to show administrators and others what I once tried to explain to a group of children: why do we need archives and archivists?

Years ago, I visited my daughter's sixth grade classroom during "career week" in order to describe my job. The children knew about lawyers, doctors…but only my daughter had ever heard of an archivist. How could what I do seem "practical" to these boys and girls? "What is past is prologue" may be a nice quote but I needed something less abstract to impress eleven-year-olds with the virtues of records preservation.

It happened to be Black History Month, so I chose to bring copies of relevant primary sources: a transcript from an oral history interview with a freed slave; the questionnaire used to limit black voting in the South; a flyer announcing a rally which Dr. Martin Luther King, Jr. attended. Presented with concrete evidence of the past, the children saw how compelling history can be. We even discussed sources they would preserve if they were their school's archivists—sources that future generations would use to understand the school as it once existed.

And so the phrase "Practical Archives" in *Developing and Maintaining Practical Archives* has two meanings. First, it involves showing people today how much their lives depend upon archives and the information they contain. This is what I tried to do in my daughter's school, and it accounts for the book's numerous real-life examples of the value of records. Second, managing archives can never be an abstract process. This has been brought home to me again and again in my teaching career. While professionals working with archives have a body of theory and methodology to guide them, it is the actual practice of the archival craft that enables society to benefit from the records preserved. I am always pleased when graduates tell me how the things we discussed made a difference in their working lives—that class was both theoretical *and* practical.

Responsibility for archival records can be a daunting task. Thus *Developing and Maintaining Practical Archives* is intended to be a companion for the professional journey and a balm for the frazzled archival psyche. The response to the first edition was very gratifying. My hope is that this updated book will similarly help archivists face the new millennium's challenges in our field.

ACKNOWLEDGMENTS

This book is the culmination of almost twenty-five years' education, experience, and professional activity. Therefore, there are many people to thank.

I was introduced to archives in the mid-1970s while a graduate student in New York University's History Department. Tom Bender, Mike Lutzker, and Carl Prince were my first archives teachers and also role models for my own academic career. I benefited from a year of working with Linda Edgerly in the Chase Manhattan Archives in New York City. Linda remains a consummate professional especially concerned with the ethical aspects of archival work.

I was very fortunate to have two remarkable professional working experiences. In 1978, the United Negro College, Fund, Inc. (UNCF) hired me to establish an archives for its headquarters and to work with the forty-one UNCF member colleges in improving their archives. Chris Edley and Turner Battle were excellent superiors, always very supportive of the mission of the archives. Even more, I will forever be in UNCF's debt for offering the opportunity for an Irish kid from the Bronx to meet some of this century's legendary black educators; I have been forever touched by Frederick Patterson, Benjamin Mays, Hollis Price, Albert Dent, and Harry Richardson, to name just a few. As a first generation college graduate, I remain in awe of the accomplishments of the men and women who pursued higher education early in this century and founded UNCF in the 1940s.

In 1984, I left UNCF to become Manager of Corporate Records at ITT's World Headquarters. Phil Coombe and Barry Kalen encouraged my professional growth, made it easier for me to finish my doctorate, and permitted me to teach as an adjunct. God put no better boss on this earth than Barry Kalen—and he certainly is one of the world's top ten people as well!

It was Mildred Lowe, the director of the Division of Library and Information Science at St. John's University, who arranged for me to get bitten by the teaching bug. I can never thank her enough for opening up this new world to me. Lucienne Maillet, the Dean of the Palmer School of Library and Information Science at Long Island University in 1990, worked long and hard to add me to the full-time faculty. My current dean, Michael Koenig, has continued to make the Palmer School a hospitable place for the study of archives and records management.

In terms of this book, I want to thank Michael Kelley, an editor at Neal-Schuman Publishers, for his patience with me and for his persistence in seeing the project through.

Above all else, I have been blessed with an extraordinary family. My mother, Isabelle Hunter, was a liberated woman before her time, who always encouraged me to follow my dreams. My wife, JoAnn Heaney-Hunter, is a nationally-recognized scholar in her own right—and "Dr. Mom" in our house. Few men are blessed with a wife who is also a friend and colleague. Her energy and courage never cease to amaze me.

Finally, I have dedicated this book to my daughters, Beth and Kate. Both of them have grown up hearing about archives and other strange things. Years ago Beth, who now is a sophomore in college, took great pride in telling me a joke she heard on Mr. Rogers: "Where did Noah keep the bees? In the ark-hives!" Kate, who is a sophomore in high school, helped me design logos for my consulting firm when she was ten years old. May you both always know how much I love you.

1

INTRODUCTION TO ARCHIVES AND MANUSCRIPTS

"I have drove Fords exclusively when I could get away with one," wrote a satisfied customer to Henry Ford in 1934. "For sustained speed and freedom from trouble the Ford has got ever other car skinned." The Ford Motor Company has received thousands of similar letters over the years. Why was this one preserved? Because a trained eye caught the play on words above and associated it with a famous (or infamous) author: "... even if my business hasn't been strictly legal it don't hurt anything to tell you what a fine car you got in the V8. Yours truly, Clyde Champion Barrow." There is no record of whether or not Bonnie agreed with Clyde's judgment.[1]

Archivists and manuscript curators are the ones whose eyes are trained to recognize such hidden values. Archivists work in many different settings: government agencies, colleges and universities, profit-making and nonprofit corporations, religious communities and institutions, labor unions, and fraternal and similar organizations. All of these institutions have one thing in common: they recognize the value of an historical perspective for daily operations and the importance of having a trained professional maintain their historical resources.[2]

Though the settings may vary, the mission of the archivist is the same: to identify, preserve, and make available records and papers of enduring value.[3] This three-part mission directs archival activities outward, toward the researchers we serve; just identifying and preserving records is not enough. Though the methods of serving researchers may change in the third millennium, archival outreach will not decrease in importance.[4]

Practical Archives is intended as a one-volume introduction to archives and manuscripts—a first step in the training of an archival eye. It will cover all aspects of the archivist's work, combining theory with practice.[5] As will become clear, archival management is as much an art as a science.

BASIC DEFINITIONS

Before proceeding further, it is necessary to define some basic terms. In the past, it was easier to understand the meaning of archives. There was a general sense that archives were items retained for a long period of time. The information age, however, has led to confusion. "Archiving" a word-processing document, for example, now means saving it on a floppy disk, perhaps only for a day or two. The distinction between long- and short-term retention has been blurred.

As used in this book, "archives" has three possible meanings:

- *Materials*: the noncurrent records of an organization or institution preserved because of their enduring value
- *Place*: the building or part of a building where archival materials are located (also referred to as an archival repository)
- *Agency*: the program office or agency responsible for identifying, preserving, and making available records of enduring value (also referred to as an archival agency, archival institution, or archival program)[6]

Archives is a collective noun, correctly used in the plural, though one may see the singular form used by some repositories.

Photograph 1.1 A selection of archival materials. Photograph courtesy of the Saint Benedict Center, Sisters of Saint Benedict of Madison, Wisconsin, Inc.

In common parlance, a manuscript is either a handwritten document or the first draft of a book or article. Though correct, there is a third meaning of the term in the context of this manual. While archives are generated by organizations or institutions, manuscripts are generated by individuals or families.

The holdings of an archival repository are called "records." An example would be the records of the Ford Motor Company. By contrast, the holdings of a manuscript repository are called "papers"—for example, the Papers of Thomas Jefferson, or the Rockefeller Family Papers. It is correct, however, to refer to both records and papers as "collections." Finally, the custodian of organizational records is called an archivist, while the custodian of personal papers is called a manuscript curator. Figure 1.1 summarizes these distinctions.

Figure 1.1 Distinctions Between Archives and Manuscripts

Category	Archives	Manuscripts
Source	Organization or institution	Individual or family
Specific terminology for holdings	Records	Papers
General terminology for holdings	Collections	Collections
Title for custodian	Archivist	Manuscript curator

Almost all organizations have records of enduring value; many have a place for the storage of these records (the place may even be *suitable* for storage); fewer organizations, however, have a department or program to manage the records effectively. This book is intended for the information professional who is responsible for archival records and wants to handle them responsibly, but must do so on a limited budget and with modest staffing. It presents as much defensive archives as practical archives.

THE ARCHIVAL MISSION

Let's look at the mission of the archivist in greater detail. The archival mission has three elements:

- to identify records and papers of enduring value
- to preserve them
- to make them available to patrons

Were you surprised that the definition of archives did not mention permanence? Why did I use enduring—rather than permanent—value as the mark of archival records?

This subtle change of wording is relatively recent. Archivists know that most records will not last forever, despite our best intentions. Atmospheric pollutants, improper handling, and similar factors take their toll on the often fragile physical media contained in archives. More importantly, the research value of the records may change over time, making them expendable for historical purposes. If we define archival records as having permanent value, we have bestowed sainthood on them—and have limited our ability to condemn them at a later date. Records of enduring value are beatified—a state below sainthood. Archivists maintain future flexibility while still treating the records with reverential care.[7]

Archivists used to think of the elements of their mission in a linear fashion: from identification, through preservation, to reference and access (see figure 1.2). This reflects the order in which archival tasks usually are accomplished. Today, however, archivists increasingly are taking a cyclical view of their work, focusing more on the ultimate purpose (use of the collections) than on the progression of activities (see figure 1.3).[8]

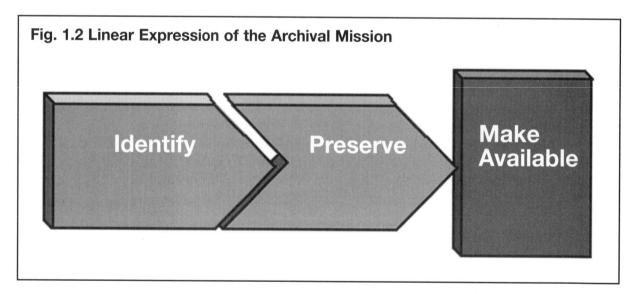

Fig. 1.2 Linear Expression of the Archival Mission

Identify **Preserve** **Make Available**

A cyclical model of the archival mission also permits one to locate the various archival functions and to relate them to one another. As part of *identifying* records and papers of enduring value, archivists conduct surveys and appraise records. A survey is a systematic procedure used to locate items of possible archival value. Appraisal is the process of determining the value, and thus the disposition (retention or destruction), of records.[9]

The bridge between identifying records of enduring value and preserving them is represented by two archival functions: acquisition and accessioning. Acquisition covers such areas as donor relations and contacts, and policies for collecting records and papers. Accessioning involves the actual transfer of records or papers to an archives or manuscript repository, along with the transfer of legal rights to the physical and intellectual property.

The mission of *preserving* historically valuable items encompasses three archival functions: arrangement, preservation, and security. Arrangement is the organization of archives or manuscripts in accordance with accepted professional principles.[10] Preservation involves both the protection of records from physical deterioration and damage and the restoration of previously damaged items.[11] Security is the safeguarding of records from natural and human disasters.[12]

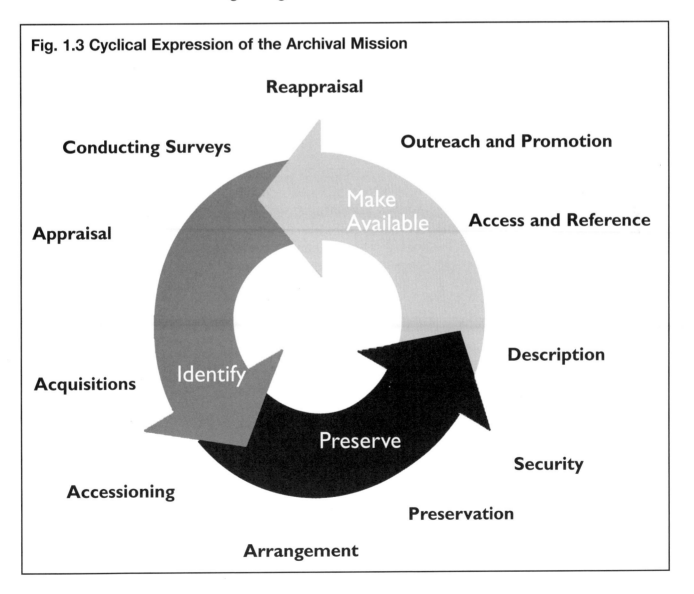

Fig. 1.3 Cyclical Expression of the Archival Mission

Reappraisal

Conducting Surveys

Outreach and Promotion

Appraisal

Make Available

Access and Reference

Identify

Acquisitions

Description

Preserve

Accessioning

Security

Preservation

Arrangement

Description is the bridge between preserving records and making them available; it is the opportunity for the archivist to record what is known about the collection and its arrangement in a way that will facilitate access by researchers. Description requires both clear and concise writing skills and a feel for the research questions archival patrons ask.

The third part of the archival mission, *making records available*, focuses on two sets of archival functions: access and reference, and outreach and promotion. Access and reference involve more than just presenting a box of records to a researcher. Rather, archivists employ a number of policies and procedures to ensure that use of the records involves neither physical damage to the items nor violations of copyright and the right to privacy. Outreach and promotion are attempts to make people aware of archival records and the valuable information they contain. To this end, archivists use exhibits, audiovisual presentations, and Web sites as well as the more traditional press releases and newspaper feature articles.[13]

"On any given day, a dozen or so people can be found huddled over vintage metal table lamps in the hushed reading room of the Communist Party's main archive... culling the millions of files for pieces to the vast puzzle of Soviet history.

"Now called the Storage Center for Contemporary Documentation, the building in the old Central Committee complex on Staraya Square is only one depository for 204 million separate files now controlled by the Russian Government.

"In the 18 months since President Boris N. Yeltsin placed all K.G.B. and Communist archives under Russia's control, a steady stream of revelations large and small has already come out....Yet for every piece fitted into the puzzle, another gap becomes more glaring....Many answers may never be known. Untold volumes of files have been destroyed."

—*New York Times*, February 8, 1993.

In a cyclical view, the archival mission does not end with making records available. On the contrary, archivists today use research trends and reference statistics when identifying additional records for preservation. And in a radical departure caused by the bulk and complexity of modern records, some archivists are using past reference activity as a basis for *reappraising* records already in archival institutions.[14]

And so the archival mission comes full circle. It is a continuous process of determining which records have archival value, preserving them in a professional way, and making them available to a wide variety of researchers. As with a three-legged stool, no one part of the mission is more important than the other two—unless all three legs are in place, the stool will fall. A well-balanced archival program will rest firmly on the three strong legs of the archival mission.

DIFFERENCES BETWEEN LIBRARIES AND ARCHIVES

Libraries and archives have been closely related for decades. In fact, many archives' collections are located within library structures, especially on college and university campuses. This does not mean, however, that libraries and archives are the same or that the theories and practices of one are transferable to the other. It is important to understand the differences in order to manage an archives or manuscript repository properly.[15]

The nature of the items in a library and those in archives differs. The fundamental difference is that library materials are published, while archival materials are, by and large, unpublished. Furthermore, libraries collect discrete items—books, journals, videotapes, and slides—usually one at a time. The books or other items are judged individually, on a case-by-case basis. In addition, most of the items collected by one library are also collected by other libraries. Therefore, a particular book usually is available in more than one location. In contrast, archives collect groups of related items: the records of a particular company or institution, for example. These items do not stand alone; they gain significance and importance from their relationship to other items. Archival and manuscript collections also are unique. While occasionally two or more archival institutions may have parts of the same collection, seldom do they completely duplicate one another.[16]

"In April 1945, more than 30 years before Love Canal became a synonym for toxic-chemical disaster, a manufacturing analyst at the Hooker Chemical Company wrote in an internal report that he worried about a 'potential future hazard' and a 'quagmire at Love Canal which will be a potential source of lawsuits.'

"In a Buffalo courtroom this week, R. H. Van Horne's prophetic memorandum, along with other yellowing documents from the company's archives, will be at the center of a $250 million trial of Hooker Chemical that lawyers on both sides agree will measure the company's conduct for history."

—*New York Times*, October 22, 1990.

There also is a difference in the creators or originators of the items collected by libraries and archives. The books, journals, videotapes, CDs, and other items acquired by a library are created by many different individuals and organizations, ranging from a lone novelist to agencies of the federal government. Archives, on the other hand, usually collect only the records generated by the parent organization or institution; there is one creator as opposed to thousands.[17]

The method of creation similarly varies. Library materials are created as the result of separate independent actions by a wide variety of authors or compilers. Archival materials, however, are never explicitly created—no one in an institution says, "Today I think I'll create some archival records." Archives grow organically as part of the creation of records in the normal course of an institution's business. Only at a later date are records judged to be of archival interest and properly preserved for future generations.

"On page 156 of a manuscript compiled by one of Louis XIV's chief music librarians, there is a slight, wispy arc of a line that has sat there for more than 300 years, probably confusing no one. It is apparently a comma, a simple stroke of the pen dividing two words. But for Jeffrey Cohan, a baroque flutist who will perform music from the Library of Congress manuscript at the Capital Hill Chamber Music Festival this evening, it is also an enigma, or worse.

"'That disgusting little comma,' he says. At issue, depending on which way that comma blows, is a tantalizing insight into the early history of an instrument he knows and loves well, the baroque transverse flute."

—*Washington Post*, July 28, 2002.

"The leader of Hitler's atomic bomb program, Werner Heisenberg, portrayed himself after World War II as a kind of scientific resistance hero who sabotaged Hitler's effort to build a nuclear weapon.

"But in a series of letters and other documents made public yesterday, his friends and onetime mentor, the Danish physicist Niels Bohr, said that is not so."

—*New York Times*, February 7, 2002.

There is a difference as well in the receipt of items. Libraries usually select items one at a time, though they may buy a number of books at once from a single source. Library acquisition decisions usually are revocable—if a book is not purchased this year, it often will be available next year (unless it is a rare or out-of-print item). An archivist appraises materials in aggregate and adds them to the collection—accessions them—in a group. Archival decisions are irrevocable—destruction is forever. The appraisal of materials is thus one of the most important duties an archivist performs.

Library materials are arranged according to a predetermined subject classification system. The Library of Congress classification system is the most widely used today, replacing such earlier classification schemes as the Dewey Decimal system. The bases for archival arrangement are two closely related principles, provenance and original order. Since chapter 5 defines and explains these terms, suffice it to say at this point that archival principles stipulate that records created by different organizations or entities not be mingled and that the order given the records by their creators be preserved as much as possible.

Description is different in libraries and archives. First of all, the published nature of library books and periodicals means that they come with built-in descriptive media: title pages, tables of contents, indexes, and other bibliographic access points. In contrast, archivists must build their own descriptive media for the unpublished materials under their control.

Second, since library materials are acquired one at a time, it is logical that they also are described individually. Most often this is done with a catalog, either manual or computerized. In keeping with their nature, archival materials are not described individually, but rather in the aggregate. Archival description explains the particular group of records, their relationship to other records, and their significance for research. Though many archives use a catalog as a secondary index, the principal descriptive devices are inventories of specific collections and guides to the general holdings of a repository.[18]

Photograph 1.2 A reading room for archival materials Photograph courtesy of the Joint Archives of Holland.

Access is also different for library and archival materials. Library materials (except for very rare, fragile, or expensive items) are stored on open shelves. Researchers locate the items they require and often are permitted to borrow them from the library. Because of their uniqueness, archival stack areas are closed to researchers. Staff members retrieve requested items and carefully observe researchers while they use the items. Archival materials do not circulate, but some repositories will provide copies (either paper, microfilm, or digital) for the private use of researchers.

Figure 1.4 summarizes the differences between libraries and archives in the area of the materials they contain. As subsequent chapters will indicate, these core differences affect all aspects of institutional administration.

Fig. 1.4 Differences Between Materials in Libraries and Archives

Category	Libraries	Archives
Nature	• published • discrete items • independent significance • available elsewhere	• unpublished • groups of related items • significance from relationship to other items • unique

Creator	many different individuals
	   or organizations
		parent organization
		   or institution

Method of creation	separate, independent actions	organic: normal course of business
Method of receipt	• selected as single items • decisions revocable	• appraised in aggregate • decisions irrevocable (destruction is forever)
Arrangement	predetermined subject classification	provenance and original order (relation to structure and function)
Level of description	individual items	aggregate (record group or series)

Descriptive media	• built into the published item
	   (title page, table of contents,
	   index)
	• card catalog, online public
	   access system (OPAC)
		• must be prepared by the archivist
		
		• guides and inventories,
		   online systems

Access	• open stacks • items circulate	• closed stacks • items do not circulate

Despite these many differences, it would be wrong to assume that libraries and archives have nothing in common. They share the mission of making knowledge available to a wide variety of patrons. They share a concern about the preservation of existing materials, especially those produced on paper in the last one hundred years. They share a belief that what has gone before can benefit generations still to come.

And, curiously enough, they also share a saint. Lawrence the Librarian was a church archives official in Rome. In the year A.D. 258, as part of Roman persecution of Christians, imperial guards searching for membership lists demanded the surrender of the church's archives. Lawrence previously had hidden the archives and refused to divulge their location. The guards tied him to a grid iron over a charcoal fire, but Lawrence still refused to relinquish the archives, telling his tormentors, "I am roasted enough on this side, turn me over and eat." In subsequent years, a cult grew up around Lawrence. Numerous churches were dedicated to him and he was the subject of artwork by Rubens, Titian, Ribera, and Fra Angelico. Even today, pilgrims still visit the basilica over the tomb of this librarian who died to defend the archives in his custody.[19]

A BRIEF HISTORY OF ARCHIVES

Archives are as old as civilization. As long as there have been records to preserve, people have preserved them. A brief history of archives highlights this fact.

The ancient world preserved records on a variety of media. Clay tablets have survived from 690 B.C. documenting the Egibi family of Babylon's trade in slaves and real estate. Records dating to the fifth century B.C., composed on papyrus in imperial Aramaic, were discovered at Elephantine, a Persian military post on the Egyptian frontier garrisoned by Jewish mercenaries. These records document all aspects of community life and financial dealings.

The dual seats of Western civilization, Athens and Rome, also preserved records. In Athens, valuable papyrus documents were kept in the temple of the mother of the gods. In addition to such official records as treaties, laws, and minutes, important cultural documents—what we would call manuscripts—were also maintained. Among these cultural documents were the statement Socrates wrote in his defense, plays by Sophocles and Euripides, and the lists of victors in the Olympic games. Since ancient times, then, archives and manuscripts have often gone hand-in-hand.

Rome had no official archives until the time of Cicero (first century B.C.). Catallus built the tabularium, the state archives of Rome, between 121 and 60 B.C.; however, not all official records reached the archives. Magistrates kept commentarii, which they took with them when they left office. Archivists today still face this problem of separating official records from personal papers.

Archives in Rome went beyond government records. Business people kept daybooks, called *adversaria*, in which they recorded daily transactions. Many prominent Roman families went so far as to keep their own "house archives," called *tablinum*. For example, the papers of the Flavius family document their own prisons, postal service, racing stables, public baths, counting houses, and Nile boats. By modern standards, the Flavius family would have been a conglomerate.[20]

"Since he was captured five months ago in Pakistan, al-Qaeda chief Abu Zubaydah has been cast as the biggest catch in the worldwide terrorism investigation that began Sept. 11. His hints about future attacks have led U.S. officials to issue several terrorism alerts, even though they weren't sure he was telling the truth.

"Now it's clear that Zubaydah's real importance stems not from what he has said but from the computer hard drives, CD-ROMs and documents the FBI and CIA found in his rented house in Faisalabad, Pakistan. The records have reshaped the terrorism investigation in the United States, where at least 200 people with suspected ties to al-Qaeda are under surveillance.

"More than any other evidence, Zubaydah's stockpile of records has moved the investigation beyond U.S. official's random roundup of more than 1,200 people, mostly Middle Easterners accused of immigration violations."

—*USA Today*, August 29, 2002.

Modern archives began in 1543 at Simancas in Spain. In fact, the principles developed at Simancas still remain useful to this day. Modern archives really developed, however, as a by-product of the French Revolution. France established the first of the modern national archives in order to document newly won freedoms and to protect the rights of citizens. Though some radicals wanted to destroy the records of the old order, calmer heads saw the value of these records for documenting the shortcomings of the monarchy and the need for revolution. France also was the first nation to pass a law guaranteeing citizens the right of access to archival records. After the French Revolution, government archives were considered public, not private, property.[21]

In 1838, fifty years after the French Revolution, England established its first central archives, the Public Records Office. At that time, England's badly decaying archival records were scattered in fifty repositories all over London. The historical community, in particular, pushed for the recognition of the importance of archival records and the establishment of a repository that reflected this importance. In contrast to the situation in France, the Public Records Office was a separate department, not part of a larger ministry. This independence of the archival function was later to become a key part of archival development in the United States.

The United States did not have a national archival repository until 1934, 100 years after England. This does not mean, however, that there was no lobbying before this time. President Rutherford B. Hayes recommended a national archives in his annual messages of 1878 and 1879. The American Historical Association began pushing for a national archives in 1884. While Congress authorized the building of the National Archives in 1913, there was no construction for twenty years. For its first few years, the National Archives was an independent agency. After World War II, however, the National Archives was made a part of the General Services Administration, the agency responsible for the government's buildings and supplies. Historians and archivists fought a long battle to restore the independence of the National Archives, only achieving success in 1984.

"Wells Fargo & Co. was once confronted with a $480 million suit alleging that it had misappropriated an idea to start a credit-card operation. Using materials from the bank's archives dating back to the 1960s, lawyers were able to prove that Wells Fargo had developed the idea itself."

—*Wall Street Journal*, December 21, 1987.

Archives in the United States, however, go far beyond the government setting. As mentioned at the beginning of this chapter, there are archives in a wide variety of institutions and organizations. The first business archives, for example, was started in 1943 at the Firestone Tire and Rubber Company.[22] Each institutional setting will also have a story of its archives development.

A BRIEF HISTORY OF MANUSCRIPT COLLECTING

As with archives, manuscript collecting has been pursued since antiquity. In Rome, both Cicero and Pliny had collections. Caesar kept his personal papers, called *sacrarium*, separate from the state archives. His successors followed suit. Constantine moved the *sacrarium* to Constantinople in A.D. 300, where it was destroyed by fire during the reign of Justinian, two hundred and fifty years later.[23]

During the medieval period, manuscripts were seldom collected except by religious groups. The efforts of monks in carefully copying and preserving key documents and books helped to preserve Western civilization.

The modern era of manuscript collecting began in the fifteenth century with the founding of such institutions as the Vatican Library and the Bibliothèque Nationale in France. Autograph collecting by individuals began around 1600; in England by the 1800s it was an avidly pursued, middle-class hobby.

In the United States, there were four strains of manuscript collectors: historians, institutions, editors, and autograph seekers. The earliest of the historian-collectors were Harvard-educated ministers. Their love of history led them to identify and preserve items of enduring value. Thomas Prince (1687–1758) collected the records of Plymouth plantation and the Increase Mather papers. One of Prince's students, Jeremy Belknap, was an aggressive collector. He also was instrumental in the 1791 founding of the first collecting institution, the Massachusetts Historical Society. In Belknap's view, "There is nothing like having a *good repository*, and keeping a *good look-out*, not waiting at home for things to fall into the lap, but prowling about like a wolf for the prey." Except for the rapacious analogy, this view has endured.[24]

"The information was gathered in April 1930, six months after the historic 1929 stock market crash and the dawn of the Great Depression. Homes were valued at $3,000 to $5,000 and rent averaged $25 to $30 a month. A scroll through some of the records showed that most homes still didn't have radios.

"Genealogists who showed up at the Minnesota History Center on Sunday afternoon to pore over just-released 1930 Census data were as pleased as gold miners who had just unearthed a shiny nugget....

"The data, stored on 59 rolls of microfilm, was carefully handwritten by enumerators who went door-to-door to collect it."

—*Twin Cities Pioneer Press*, April 22, 2002.

The Massachusetts Historical Society began the era of the institutional collector. Other states gradually followed Massachusetts's lead. Between 1830 and 1850, thirty-five state and local historical societies were founded. It was in the Midwest, however, that the historical society movement flourished. Lyman Draper, a private collector turned institutional collector, started the program in Wisconsin by collecting the papers of Revolutionary War heroes and trans-Allegheny pioneers. By the mid-1880s there were more than two hundred state, local, and regional historical societies, though few were as active as those in Massachusetts or Wisconsin.

After 1880 there was a shift in the focus of collectors spurred by a new type of researcher—even then, responding to the changing needs of researchers and modifying collecting programs to meet those needs was part of the archival mission. The end of the nineteenth century saw the rise of academic historians trained in the German tradition at such institutions as Johns Hopkins and Harvard. The German method, which is still in use today in graduate schools, relied heavily on seminars and the "scientific" use of evidence found in original records. This new breed of historian criticized the local collecting focus of most historical societies. The result was the growth of manuscript collections on university campuses for educational and research purposes.

"When Mount St. Helens erupted in Washington in 1980, Weyerhaeuser was faced with the enormous task of salvaging downed timber. The extent of the damage reminded old-timers at Weyerhaeuser of Typhoon Frieda in 1962, when even more timber was downed.

"Fortunately, the company had established archives in 1974, and documents relating to the earlier disaster's salvage operations were readily available. Weyerhaeuser based its Mount St. Helens operations on this information, and employed 650 loggers and 600 trucks over three years to complete the job."

—*Wall Street Journal*, January 16, 1989.

The third major strain of manuscript collecting was that of the editor-collector. These individuals acquired papers with the intention of publishing them, thereby making historical items more widely available to the public. The first of the great editor-collectors was Peter Force, who began to collect state papers in 1822. By 1853 he had published over a dozen volumes of documents in series called *American Archives* and *Tracts and Other Papers*. In 1867, the Library of Congress paid Force $100,000 for his collection of 429 volumes of original manuscripts and 360 volumes of transcriptions. Jared Sparks, another editor-collector and future president of Harvard, published twelve volumes of diplomatic correspondence. He also devoted seven years to a multivolume biography and the writings of George Washington.

The final manuscript tradition is that of the autograph collector. Yale graduate William B. Sprague was America's first major autograph collector. He was fascinated by the European hobby of collecting signatures of royalty. He decided to collect the signatures of "American royalty": the signers of the Declaration of Independence and the Constitution. After Sprague, autograph collecting grew in popularity in the United States. The first sale of a major autograph collection was in 1867 in Savannah, Georgia. Autograph collecting reached its peak in the United States and Britain in the 1890s. While autograph collecting still continues, most manuscript curators today are more interested in the contents and research value of an acquisition rather than just its signature value.

THE ARCHIVAL PROFESSION TODAY

Today's archivists draw upon their professional tradition to meet the challenges posed by new records media and new institutional settings. Archival education takes place at the graduate level, which is the case with most professions. Archival education programs are found in history departments and schools of library and information science. The Society of American Archivists (SAA), the national association of archivists, has established education guidelines for the profession. Unlike library education, there is no accreditation of archival education programs.

In addition to SAA, archivists have numerous regional and local professional organizations. Meeting several times each year, these organizations offer professional discourse in smaller settings.

In 1989, archivists established a separate national organization to certify individual practitioners. The Academy of Certified Archivists (ACA) administers a certification examination that tests the full range of archival knowledge, skills, and attitudes. There also is a national organization for government archivists—NAGARA, the National Association of Government Archives and Records Administrators.

Befitting the electronic age, archival professional community and discourse also happen on the Internet. People interested in record-keeping issues have more than one discussion group or "listserv" to access. Using these discussion groups, archivists can get almost immediate answers to work-related questions as well as insights into professional issues. More information about the profession today can be found in chapter 13.[25]

CONCLUSION

Archives and manuscripts are not something of value only in the past. Archives are important for many aspects of contemporary life; they affect us on a daily basis. Without archival records, both business transactions and personal endeavors would be more difficult, if not impossible, to complete. A young couple would not be able to close on their first home unless a search of government records confirmed a clear title to the property. A mid-career professional enrolling for an advanced degree would be rejected without a transcript of twenty-year-old grades from an undergraduate institution. A recent senior citizen awaiting a pension check from a long-term employer would wait a long time if the corporation did not maintain adequate payroll records.

Sometimes, however, we do not realize or appreciate the centrality of records. This book reinforces the centrality of records through a series of stories drawn from the news media. These real-world examples have a common theme—each situation would have been very different had relevant records not existed. Today's archivists help guarantee that future generations will have the records they need to function in society.[26]

Building upon a long tradition and using the strengths of such related disciplines as library science and history, archivists and manuscript curators daily try to fulfill their mission of identifying, preserving, and making available records and papers of enduring value. The rest of this book will discuss in greater detail how this is done.

NOTES

1. Letter dated April 10, 1934, from the collections of the Archives and Research Library, Henry Ford Museum, reprinted in the *American Archivist* 45, no. 3 (Summer 1982): 283.

2. For a recent overview of the importance of archives in a business environment, see James M. O'Toole, ed., *The Records of American Business* (Chicago: Society of American Archivists, 1997).

3. This statement of the archivist's mission is adapted from *Planning for the Archival Profession: A Report of the SAA Task Force on Goals and Priorities* (Chicago: Society of American Archivists, 1986).

4. For a sampling of articles dealing with the effect of the Internet, see Kathleen Feeney, "Retrieval of Archival Finding Aids Using World-Wide-Web Search Engines," *American Archivist* 62, no. 2 (fall 1999): 206—228; Anne J. Gilliland-Swetland, "Popularizing the Finding Aid: Exploring EAD to Enhance Online Discovery and Retrieval in Archival Information Systems by Diverse User Groups," in *Encoded Archival Description on the Internet*, ed. Daniel V. Pitti and Wendy Duff (New York: Haworth Information Press, 2001), 199–226; Helen R. Tibbo and Lokman I. Meho, "Finding Aids on the World Wide Web," *American Archivist* 64, no. 1 (spring/summer 2001): 61–78; William E. Landis, "Archival Outreach on the World Wide Web," *Archival Issues* 20, no. 2 (1995): 129–48. Catherine Nicholls and Jon-Paul Williams, "Identifying Roadkill on the Information Superhighway: A Website Appraisal Case Study," *Archives and Manuscripts* 30, no. 2 (November 2002): 96–111.

5. For readability, I often will use "archivist" when referring to both archivists and curators of manuscripts. While there are important distinctions, archivists and curators have enough in common to permit the use of a single term.

6. This and subsequent definitions are adapted from two archival glossaries: Lewis J. Bellardo and Lynn Lady Bellardo, *A Glossary for Archivists, Manuscript Curators, and Records Managers* (Chicago: Society of American Archivists, 1992); Frank B. Evans, et al., *A Basic*

Glossary for Archivists, Manuscript Curators, and Records Managers (Chicago: Society of American Archivists, 1974).

7. See Leonard Rapport, "No Grandfather Clause: Reappraising Accessioned Records," *American Archivist* 44, no. 2 (spring 1981): 143–50; James M. O'Toole, "On the Idea of Permanence," *American Archivist* 52, no. 1 (winter 1989): 10–25. For the universality of the concept of record, see Luciana Duranti, "The Records: Where Archival Universality Resides," *Archival Issues* 19, no. 2 (1994): 83–94. For a discussion of the larger role of archivists, see Francis X. Blouin, Jr., "Archivists, Mediation, and Constructs of Social Memory," *Archival Issues* 24, no. 2 (1999): 101–12.

8. For an example, see Elsie T. Freeman, "In the Eye of the Beholder: Archives Administration from the User's Point of View," *American Archivist* 47, no. 2 (spring 1984): 111–23.

9. Again, for convenience throughout this book I often will use the term "records" in place of the more cumbersome "records and papers." I will, however, employ both terms when manuscript practice differs from archival practice.

10. For more information about arrangement, see Fredric M. Miller, *Arranging and Describing Archives and Manuscripts* (Chicago: Society of American Archivists, 1992); Laura Millar, "The Death of the Fonds and the Resurrection of Provenance: Archival Context in Space and Time," *Archivaria* 53 (spring 2002): 1–15.

11. Paul N. Banks and Roberta Pilette, eds., *Preservation: Issues and Planning* (Chicago: American Library Association, 2000).

12. Johanna Wellheiser and Jude Scott, *An Ounce of Prevention: Integrated Disaster Planning for Archives, Libraries, and Records Centres*, 2d ed. (Lanham, Md.: Scarecrow Press and the Canadian Archives Foundation, 2002).

13. For some recent perspectives, see Tamar G. Chute, "Selling the College and University Archives," *Archival Issues* 25, nos. 1–2 (2000): 33–48; Wendy Duff and Catherine A. Johnson, "A Virtual Expression of Need: An Analysis of E-Mail Reference Questions," *American Archivist* 64, no. 1 (spring/summer 2001): 43–60; Kathleen Epp, "Telling Stories Around the 'Electric Campfire': The Use of Archives in Television Productions," *Archivaria* 49 (spring 2000): 53–83; Gabrielle Hyslop, "For Many Audiences: Developing Public Programs at the National Archives of Australia," *Archives and Manuscripts* 30, no. 1 (May 2002): 48–59; Angelika Menne-Haritz,. "Access—the Reformulation of an Archival Paradigm," *Archival Science* 1, no. 1 (2001): 57–82; Andrea Rosenbusch, "Are Our Users Being Served? A Report on Online Archival Databases," *Archives and Manuscripts* 29, no. 1 (May 2001): 44–61; Elizabeth Yakel, "Thinking Inside and Outside the Boxes: Archival Reference Services at the Turn of the Century," *Archivaria* 49 (spring 2000): 140–60.

14. The best expression of this view is found in Rapport, "No Grandfather Clause." See also Fredrick M. Miller, "Use, Appraisal, and Research: A Case Study of Social History," *American Archivist* 49, no. 4 (fall 1986): 371–92.

15. A fuller discussion of these issues is found in *Archives and Library Administration: Divergent Traditions and Common Concerns*, ed. Lawrence J. McCrank (New York: Haworth Press, 1986). See also Theodore R. Schellenberg, *Modern Archives: Principles and Techniques* (Chicago: University of Chicago Press, 1956), 17–25. Naturally, rare book libraries (that collect unique materials for their artifact value) are closer to archives than are public libraries. The differences presented here are at the ends of a wide spectrum.

16. The best discussion of the nature of archival materials is found in *Understanding Archives and Manuscripts*, ed. James M. O'Toole (Chicago: Society of American Archivists, 1992).

17. As noted above, manuscript repositories or special collections departments will acquire materials from multiple organizations or individuals, but the various collections still will be unique.

18. For some recent articles on archival description, see Toby Burrows, "Using Encoded Archival Description with Manuscript Collections: The Guide to Australian Literary Manuscripts," *Archives and Manuscripts* 30, no. 2 (November 2002): 82–95; Diana Dack, "Encoded Archival Description in the National Library of Australia," *Archives and Manuscripts* 30, no. 2 (November 2002): 60–71; Daniel V. Pitti and Wendy M. Duff, eds., *Encoded Archival Description on the Internet* (New York: Haworth Information Press, 2001); James M. Roth, "Serving Up EAD: An Exploratory Study on the Deployment and Utilization of Encoded Archival Description Finding Aids," *American Archivist* 64, no. 2 (fall/winter 2001): 214–37.

19. *SAA Newsletter* (September 1984): 6. Not all sources confirm this legend. *Butler's Lives of the Saints* has the story of St. Lawrence being roasted, but does not mention that it was because of archival records. Michael Walsh, *Butler's Lives of the Saints, Concise Edition Revised and Updated* (New York: Harper Collins, 1991), 245–46.

20. For more on ancient archives, see Ernst Posner, *Archives in the Ancient World* (Cambridge, Mass.: Harvard University Press, 1972); and Luciana Duranti, "The Odyssey of the Records Managers" (two parts), *ARMA Records Management Quarterly* 23 (July 1989): 3–11, and 23 (October 1989): 3–11 {Q}. For Greece, see James Sickinger, "Literacy, Documents, and Archives in the Ancient Athenian Democracy," *American Archivist* 62, no. 2 (fall 1999): 229–46. For the middle ages, see M.T. Clanchy, "'Tenacious Letters:' Archives and Memory in the Middle Ages," *Archivaria* 11 (winter 1980–81): 115–26.

21. For more on the French Revolution, see Judith M. Panitch, "Liberty, Equality, Posterity? Some Archival Lessons from the Case of

the French Revolution," *American Archivist* 59, no. 1 (winter 1996): 30–47.

22. For more on the history of business archives, see David R. Smith, "An Historical Look at Business Archives," *American Archivist* 45, no. 3 (summer 1982):273–78; and Gary D. Saretzky, "North American Business Archives: A Developmental Perspective" (unpublished paper delivered at the annual meeting of the Society of American Archivists, August 30, 1986).

23. Most of this discussion is taken from Kenneth W. Duckett, *Modern Manuscripts: A Practical Manual for Their Management, Care and Use* (Nashville: American Association for State and Local History, 1975).

24. See, for example, the influential article by F. Gerald Ham, "The Archival Edge," *American Archivist*, 38, no. 1 (January 1975): 5–13. Kenneth W. Duckett, *Modern Manuscripts: A Practical Manual for Their Management, Care, and Use* (Nashville: AASLH, 1975), 8–9.

25. The easiest way to learn more about national and regional archival associations, archival education programs, and Internet discussion groups is through the Society of American Archivists (http://www.archivists.org).

26. I am indebted to my students at Long Island University for many of these stories—the discussion of "archives in the news" is a weekly part of my introductory archives class. The Archives Listserv also features the regular posting of "Records and Archives in the News" (RAIN) by Peter Kurilecz.

2 CONDUCTING A SURVEY AND STARTING AN ARCHIVAL PROGRAM

Starting an archival program can be an intimidating task. Where does one begin when faced with boxes of all sizes stacked in piles of questionable stability? Should our first priority be purchasing acid-free boxes or miner's helmets? How will we handle requests from anxious patrons who just cannot wait to use the records we have not yet even identified? Unless we have a plan in mind, we will waste a great deal of time and energy.

Starting an archives involves two major activities: conducting a survey of the universe of records available within an organization or institution, and establishing basic policies and structures for the nascent archives. These tasks usually happen simultaneously: while conducting a records survey, the archivist is also drafting basic policies and shepherding them through the administrative hierarchy.[1] Therefore, the topics could be discussed in either order. This chapter, however, will look first at the records and then turn to the structure of the archives. This order reflects the fact that archivists must often begin the work for which they were hired even when the formalities of policy statements and other organizational basics are not yet in place.[2]

INSTITUTIONAL CONTEXT

The real-world nature of archival work makes it difficult to discuss conducting a survey—and indeed any of the topics in this book—in the abstract. To help make concepts more concrete, I will use a fictitious institution, North Fork University (NFU), for many of the examples.

NFU is a fictitious, private institution that collects both university archives and non-university papers and records in a department of Archives and Special Collections. Since the department was recently created, much remains to be done. Appendix A provides background information on NFU.

SURVEYS: AN INTRODUCTION

A survey is formally defined as a systematic procedure used by archivists, manuscript curators, and records managers to gather information about records and papers not in their immediate custody.[3] The key points are that a survey is *systematic* rather than haphazard or piecemeal, and that a survey is for records *not under the immediate control* of the archivist. Depending on the type of survey, the records might be elsewhere in the organization or they might be in another archival repository.

Surveying records is an important archival skill, but one which does not receive enough emphasis within the profession. Everything else an archivist does—appraisal, arrangement, description, reference, and outreach—presupposes the ability to locate and identify records. Informed appraisal decisions, in particular, require detailed knowledge of all relevant records.

Perhaps surveys lost their glamour when they lost their grant funds. During the 1970s and early 1980s, several large surveys were conducted under federal and other grants. An example is the Women's History Sources Survey, funded by the National Endowment for the Humanities. While such large-scale projects may be less likely in the present economic climate, surveying needs to be reemphasized as a basic skill applicable to and essential for any archival situation.

Photograph 2.1 During a survey archivists will encounter a variety of storage media. Photograph courtesy of the Roman Catholic Diocese of Amarillo (Texas).

Surveys can be a key part of the archivist's active role of consciously choosing records and papers for preservation, rather than waiting for the fallout from the modern paper explosion to land upon the archival repository. Any survey, large or small, expands the archivist's vision beyond the walls of the archives office and beyond the present holdings of the repository.

TYPES OF SURVEYS

There are four types of surveys with which an archivist may be involved:

- records management survey (single repository)
- archival records survey (single repository)
- multi-repository survey
- non-repository survey

Though there are differences among these types of surveys, many of the skills required to conduct them are interchangeable.[4]

RECORDS MANAGEMENT SURVEY

A records management survey covers a well-defined body of records—those for which the surveyor has administrative responsibility and authority. Such a survey is intended to identify *all* the records of an organization or institution, usually the parent institution of the archives. This kind of all-inclusive survey is a basic part of any records management program.

Records managers are interested in records from the time of their creation through their ultimate disposition (either permanent preservation or destruction). Therefore a records management survey tries to be as complete as possible—including active as well as inactive records, records in the offices as well as those in storage, and records of short-term value as well as those of enduring value.

A records management survey usually results in the creation of a "records retention schedule" (see figure 2.1 for an example). This document lists all the records of an organization and identifies retention periods and storage locations for each. The schedules are signed by all responsible parties (the department that created the records, legal counsel, tax and financial experts, and the archivist) and become the approved plan for the management of the organization's records.[5]

Fig. 2.1 Sample Records Retention Schedule

General Records Schedule No. 10
Motor Vehicles Maintenance and Operation Records

Item Number and Description of Records	Authorized Disposition
1. Motor Vehicle Correspondence Files.	
Correspondence in the operating unit responsible for maintenance and operation of motor vehicles not otherwise covered in this schedule.	Destroy when 2 years old.
2. Motor Vehicle Operating and Maintenance Files.	
a. Operating records including those relating to gas and oil consumption, dispatching, and scheduling.	Destroy when 3 months old.
b. Maintenance records, including those relating to service and repair.	Destroy when 1 year old.
3. Motor Vehicle Cost Files.	
Motor vehicle ledger and work sheets providing cost and expense data.	Destroy 3 years after discontinuance of ledger or date of work sheet.
4. Motor Vehicle Report Files.	
Reports on motor vehicles (other than accident, operating, and maintenance reports), including SF 82, Agency Report of Motor Vehicle Data, and SF 82-D, Agency Report of Sedan Data.	Destroy 3 years after date of report.
5. Motor Vehicle Accident Files.	
Records relating to motor vehicle accidents, maintained by transportation offices, including SF 91, Operator's Report of Motor Vehicle Accident; SF 91A, Investigation Report of Motor Vehicle Accident; and SF 94, Statement of Witness.	Destroy 6 years after case is closed.
6. Motor Vehicle Release Files.	
Records relating to transfer, sale, donation, or exchange of vehicles, including SF 97A, Agency Record Copy of U.S. Government Certificate of Release of Motor Vehicle.	Destroy 4 years after vehicle leaves agency custody.
7. Motor Vehicle Operator Files.	
Records relating to individual employee operations of Government-owned vehicles, including driver tests, authorization to use, safe driving awards, and related correspondence.	Destroy 3 years after separation of employees or 3 years after recision of authorization to operate Government-owned vehicle, whichever is sooner.

Disposition of Federal Records: A Records Management Handbook (Washington, D.C.: National Archives and Records Administration, 1992)

ARCHIVAL RECORDS SURVEY

An archival records survey also deals with records for which the surveyor has administrative responsibility and authority. Unlike a full-scale records management survey, however, this is a quick-fix approach when faced with severe time constraints. The object of this type of survey is quickly to separate archival from non-archival records.

An example may clarify the situation. Very often an archivist beginning a program faces a challenge similar to the one at NFU (see Appendix A):

> The new archivist received a call from Plant Operations one morning. A crew renovating a basement boiler room discovered some boxes of old records. The space must be cleared immediately so that the renovation can continue. The archivist must select the historically valuable records quickly; the rest will be destroyed.

Clearly it is not possible to prepare detailed retention schedules in the brief time allotted—this will have to wait until later in the life of the archival program. All that is possible now is a quick sort of the inactive records.[6] It is best, however, not to destroy any records until all records have been surveyed. Until the archivist has a thorough grasp of the entire universe of available records, it will be difficult to determine, for example, if these are duplicate copies. Records discovered later in the survey may affect the appraisal decisions: remember that archivists appraise records in groups.

> "Hundreds of unpublished songs, some previously unknown, by George Gershwin, Jerome Kern, Victor Herbert, Richard Rodgers and other composers have been identified in a treasure-trove of musical manuscripts stored in a Warner Brothers warehouse in Manhattan.
> "The music—80 crates of it—was discovered in Secaucus, N.J., nearly five years ago. But because of the value of the material and the copyrights involved, the manuscripts were immediately moved to a vault in Manhattan, where they have remained virtually inaccessible ever since.
> "Now the music has finally been examined and an inventory has been prepared. The contents are more bountiful than anybody had dared dream."
> —*New York Times*, March 10, 1987.

There are two final points about an archival records survey. First, a quick sort is not necessarily haphazard. The survey should still be systematic, at a minimum keeping detailed lists of records saved and destroyed. Second, an archival records survey should have a conservative bias. Though the archivist at NFU will attempt to reduce volume quickly, it should not be done at the expense of records of possible enduring value. If in doubt, it is better to retain a particular record until it can be appraised in detail at a later date. With a smaller volume of records and fewer time constraints, a final decision can be reached.

MULTI-REPOSITORY SURVEY

A multi-repository survey, the third major type of survey, deals with materials in more than one archival agency or institution. Unlike the previous two types of surveys, this one involves records or papers over which the surveyor does not have administrative control. The survey usually is intended to identify materials united in some way: by subject, type of record, or geographical region, for example. Very often these surveys are funded with outside grants and result in a published guide to aid researchers—the previously mentioned Women's History Sources Survey is an example. Beginning archivists usually will not be involved in administering this type of survey, although they may be asked to participate by completing questionnaires about their repositories and collections.

"Where do the business plans of the sock puppet, the grocery delivery services, the teen e-zines go when those dot-com businesses die? If the University of Maryland's Robert H. Smith School of Business and San Francisco's Webmergers.com succeed, those business plans will go into a business plan archive, a Web-based initiative designed to create a permanent record of the historic dot-com era."

—*Sacramento Business Journal*, July 5, 2002.

NON-REPOSITORY SURVEY

Beginning archivists also may have little involvement with the fourth type of survey, the non-repository survey. This survey is directed at records outside of archival custody. The survey usually has one or more of the following purposes:

- to make the creators and custodians of records more aware of the historical value of materials
- to improve access to materials not in archives
- to identify records or papers for possible acquisition by the surveying institution

An example of a non-repository survey is the "Brooklyn Rediscovery" project of the Brooklyn Educational and Cultural

Alliance. This 1970s grant-funded project identified records of historical value not already in archival custody.

A non-repository survey can be tricky, especially if it is intended as a precursor to acquisitions. The surveyor must tread a fine line: a records custodian who fears loss of the records may choose not to participate in the survey at all. The ill will created may even have the undesired effect of *reducing* access to the records in the future. As the next section will discuss, it is important to define the goals of a survey and to design the survey to meet these goals.

"An archaeologist's search of a desert cave yielded a wooden chest filled with gold and silver coins, apparently hidden 149 years ago during an ill-fated Gold Rush expedition across the harsh California desert.

"Among the treasures were journals documenting the wagon train trek of '49er William Robinson, who was among some 100 men, women and children seeking the gold-laden foothills of the Sierra Nevada but ending up in the merciless valley."

—*San Jose Mercury News*, January 19, 1999.

SURVEY GOALS

Any survey, even a small one, is a complex task. It will require a great deal of time and effort, resulting in the diversion of staff time from other activities. In order to have an effective survey, it is necessary to define the survey's goals—what it is intended to accomplish.

There is a difference between an *efficient* and an *effective* survey. An efficient survey gets the work done: there are procedures to report and summarize information about records. An effective survey, however, gets the *right* work done: it collects information to meet the survey's goals. It is possible to have an efficient survey without having an effective one—it is similar to an airline baggage operation that safely and smoothly delivers your suitcase to the wrong continent.[7]

The way to ensure effectiveness is to focus on the goals of the survey and to monitor constantly the progress toward these goals. There are six possible goals of a records survey, each of which will be discussed in detail. While many surveys will have more than one goal, usually one predominates. The goals of a survey are

- to aid researchers
- to foster administrative efficiency
- to promote preservation of archival materials

- to further a collecting program
- to improve planning for archival programs
- to educate and train

TO AID RESEARCHERS

Aiding researchers is a natural extension of the archivist's mission of identifying, preserving, and *making available* for research records of enduring value. This goal usually applies to all types of records surveys, with the possible exception of a records management survey. A good example is the New York Historical Documents Inventory (HDI), which produced county-by-county guides to historical records across the state.

If a survey is intended to aid research, it should be designed for the broad benefit of as many researchers as possible. However, as chapter 9 shows, identifying "the researcher" in archives is not as easy as it sounds. Researchers come from a broad range of backgrounds and interests: academics, genealogists, lawyers, students, and reporters, to name a few. In many cases, archivists and manuscript curators have incorrectly assumed that they understood the needs of researchers. This has led to surveys of questionable value.[8]

"New York City has faced urban crises, fiscal crises, even crises of confidence. But today, says Cooper Union architecture professor Kevin Bone, it faces an archival crisis.

"The city, he says, has hundreds of thousands of historical documents crammed in warehouses, closets, and basements—and many are in peril. Bone's own students helped discover an enormous cache of rare drawings, maps, and blueprints of the city's waterfront tucked away in the leaky, rodent-infested ground floor of the Battery Maritime Building on South Street...."

—*New York*, January 17, 1994.

TO FOSTER ADMINISTRATIVE EFFICIENCY

Fostering administrative efficiency applies particularly to a records management survey—economy and efficiency are basic goals of any records management program. The records manager tries to reduce the use of expensive office space and equipment, substituting lower-cost options like storage in a records center, microfilming, or digitizing.

But administrative efficiency will also benefit the archivist. Better administration of current and noncurrent records permits easier identification and transfer of archival records. Microfilming also can be of value by substituting a more permanent storage medium for modern, highly acidic papers. A survey is the important first step toward improving the efficiency of records administration.

TO PROMOTE PRESERVATION OF ARCHIVAL MATERIALS

The immediate result of many surveys is the transfer of valuable materials to better storage conditions, if not to a formal archives repository. By carefully documenting the poor quality of records storage, it is possible to build institutional support for improvement. If the survey report is combined with reasonable suggestions for action (those which take into account such factors as institutional budget, staffing levels, and physical facilities), it is possible to get quite a bit done. But without a well-designed and well-managed survey, there will be insufficient data upon which to base recommendations for action.

"There are people who think they're pack rats. And then there's Andy Warhol.

"The man apparently couldn't throw away a gun wrapper. Warhol saved everything: Not just letters, doodlings, and tchotchkes, but unopened bills and even a pizza. He also collected native-American art, Man Ray photographs, art-deco furniture, fancy jewelry, cookie jars, and tacky world's fair souvenirs....

"The [Andy Warhol] museum [in Pittsburgh] also holds his 608 cardboard-box 'time capsules,' into which he pitched all the ephemera of his life. The boxes are slowly being opened by museum archivists, who, like archaeologists, must laboriously catalog every item."

—*Christian Science Monitor*, March 29, 2002.

TO FURTHER A COLLECTING PROGRAM

Very often, furthering a collecting program is a goal of a non-repository survey. After surveying and identifying records, the archivist tries to convince records creators to transfer them to archival control. Sometimes records creators are relieved that the records they have cared for will now be properly preserved and made more widely available. Also, the creator often is flattered that an archival or manuscript repository thinks the records are of enduring value.

As mentioned previously, it requires a great deal of tact to balance surveying and acquisitions in such a way that the records creator is not threatened. The archivist must realize at the outset that many of the records identified in a non-repository survey will *not* be potential donations. Overzealousness for acquisitions may endanger the openness of respondents toward the survey.

TO IMPROVE PLANNING FOR ARCHIVAL PROGRAMS

Perhaps the key goal in any survey is to improve planning for archival programs. It is a goal, however, that does not receive enough emphasis. Even if a survey does not result in the immediate transfer of any records, it can be a valuable means of identifying priorities for the future and of marshaling resources to meet those priorities. To spend time on a survey without using the results for institutional planning is a squandering of resources. Similarly, to plan for an archival program without having an accurate survey of existing records and storage conditions is to risk failure of the entire effort.

"Chinese people once participated in the first World Exposition held in 1851 in London, the Shanghai Expo 2010 bidding committee and Shanghai Library discovered after careful studies on a batch of historical documents."

—Beijing People's Daily, March 18, 2002.

An example of using a survey as a planning tool is a project undertaken in 1982 by the United Negro College Fund (UNCF), a fund-raising consortium of private, predominantly black colleges and universities. With a grant from the National Historical Publications and Records Commission, UNCF developed a program to help its member colleges and universities establish or improve archival programs. The program consisted of a six-day training institute on the basics of archives followed by a survey of member institutions. Each college surveyed both archival records and institutional resources available to care for the records. After the survey, UNCF member institutions were eligible for consultant visits from recognized archival experts to help develop plans. Several UNCF institutions have built upon these plans in the intervening years to improve archival preservation.[9]

TO EDUCATE AND TRAIN

Education and training can be an important part of any survey. As part of the UNCF survey, for example, at least one person from each college was trained in the basics of archives. Not only can a survey educate the surveyors, but it can also educate the administrators within an institution. Reporting survey results can offer an entrée for the discussion of archival topics and issues. The firm foundation laid here can support the entire future archival program.

Figure 2.2 summarizes the above discussion. It shows the connection between survey types and survey goals.

Fig. 2.2 A Comparison of Survey Types and Survey Goals				
Survey Goals	**Survey Types**			
	Records Management Survey	Archival Records Survey	Multi-repository Survey	Non-repository Survey
Aid Researchers		X	X	X
Foster efficiency	X	X		
Promote preservation		X		X
Further collecting	X	X		X
Improve planning	X	X		
Educate and train	X	X	X	X

PLANNING A SURVEY

Since most beginning archivists will be involved first in surveying the records of their own institutions, this section and the next focus on planning and implementing such an in-house survey. Many of the techniques apply to both a records management and an archival records survey; therefore, they will be discussed together.[10]

In addition to defining the goals of a records survey, planning requires answering five basic questions:

- Who will coordinate the survey?
- Who will conduct the survey?

- How will you gather the information?
- What information will you collect?
- What will you do with the information gathered?

WHO WILL COORDINATE THE SURVEY?

The first order of business is to determine who will have administrative responsibility for the survey. Usually one person is the "project director" who will coordinate the day-to-day effort. Many projects also use an advisory board or committee to provide additional expertise, to involve those people being surveyed, and to receive guidance from researchers and other users of the survey results. The archival advisory committee is covered later in this chapter.

"'Titanic Sinks Four Hours After Hiting Iceberg.'

"With that banner headline on April 16, 1912, The New York Times informed the world about the 20th century's most epic disaster.

"Now, the venerable Gray Lady has digitally preserved its account of the Titanic sinking for future generations to see, exactly as it appeared to readers some 90 years ago....

"From the attack on Fort Sumter to Nixon's resignation, readers can trace watershed historical events from 1851 to 1999."

—*Wired*, July 29, 2002.

WHO WILL CONDUCT THE SURVEY?

Will your staff conduct the survey, or will you expect the staff of the surveyed departments to complete the assignment in addition to their regular duties? There will be more consistent results if a specialized project staff conducts the survey, because there are fewer people to train and monitor. Budgetary constraints, however, may not permit hiring additional staff. When that is the case, the archives will have to use the staff of the surveyed departments and design effective controls to ensure usable results. Another way to reduce costs—one that should not be overlooked—is to use archival students or volunteers to conduct the survey.

HOW WILL YOU GATHER THE INFORMATION?

This question is directly related to the previous one. The principal options for gathering information are:

- use field workers to visit each department or institution
- send a questionnaire to the departments for completion

Among the factors to consider in making this decision are: the complexity of the survey; the strain on the surveyed institution or department; the skill of the people in the surveyed institution or department; and the project budget.

If at all possible, it usually is better to have field workers visit all survey sites. The people in the surveyed institutions or departments have many other responsibilities; a questionnaire to complete independently will be low on their priority list. The best way to get good, consistent data—data on which one can base future decisions—is to have regular project staff conduct the survey through on-site visits. This initial consistency becomes even more important if a computer will be used to compile, summarize, and analyze data.

WHAT INFORMATION WILL YOU COLLECT?

The project director must select the appropriate level of detail for the survey. As chapter 5 on "Arrangement" discusses in much greater depth, archivists usually think in terms of five levels of detail. The levels and an example of each are as follows (terminology is defined in chapter 5).

Level of Detail	Example
Repository	North Fork University
Record Group	Comptrollers Department
Series	Check Vouchers
File Unit	File Folder of Vouchers Numbered 9600–9624
Item	Voucher 9617

The series is the most common level for a records survey. A records series is defined as materials used or filed together as a unit because of a relationship among them resulting from their creation, receipt, or use. In the earlier example, the NFU Comptrollers Department would contain many records series: accounts payable check vouchers, general and subsidiary ledgers, journal vouchers, financial statements, audit reports, and debit and credit advices, for example. A survey done at the series level would generate one survey form for each of these categories.

The survey form is the first link between the series and the researcher. The success or failure of the survey will depend in large measure upon the survey form used. Careful survey design is especially important if the survey takes the form of a questionnaire completed by the staff of the surveyed institution.

The general rule for survey forms is to *keep them as brief as possible*: the longer the survey form, the lower the response rate and the poorer the quality of the responses one receives. While there are numerous pieces of information that would be *nice* to collect about a records series, the person designing the form must determine which pieces of information are *essential* to the survey. Is the information so important that it merits inclusion on the form even if it lowers the response rate? Unless the answer is a resounding "yes," the question probably should be omitted. The ideal is a one-page survey form that follows a logical order and is easy to complete. An example appears in figure 2.3.

"Misplaced and long forgotten in a dirty underground storage room, the original accounting book of the Senate carries careful entries by the likes of John Adams, Thomas Jefferson, and Aaron Burr. The ledger, known as S-1, survived hundreds of years, escaping the torching of the Capitol in the War of 1812. But it was almost lost last week to an effort to modernize the building.

"Officials in the Senate historian's office said that a staff member in an out-of-the-way office and workers for the Architect of the Capitol, the agency supervising the construction, noticed the aged volume and 59 other ledgers dating from the 1800's to the 1950's and called Congressional curators, who rescued the books."

—*New York Times*, November 25, 2002.

Another advantage of using a one-page form is that instructions or guidelines for completion can be placed on the back of the form for easy reference. The inclusion of "check offs" for the most common responses will speed form completion; the use of such boxes also makes it easier to compile survey results. Most database software packages permit the creation of electronic forms: as each form is completed on the computer, responses are automatically entered into a database.

Most forms collect the following information for each records series:

- *Creator*. The department or individual that originated the records.
- *Title*. Both the formal title of the record series and any "slang" or abbreviated title. For example, audit reports might also be known as "red binder studies."

Fig. 2.3 Survey Form

SERIES INVENTORY FORM

1. DATE PREPARED	2. OFFICE MAINTAINING THE FILES *(Name and symbol)*

3. PERSON DOING INVENTORY *(Name, office, phone number)*	4. SERIES LOCATION

5. SERIES TITLE	6. INCLUSIVE DATES

7. SERIES DESCRIPTION

8. MEDIUM *(check all that apply)*

- ❏ Paper
- ❏ Microfoam
- ❏ Electronic *(use information system form)*
- ❏ Audiovisual *(use audiovisual form)*

9. ARRANGEMENT

- ❏ Subject file classification system
- ❏ Alphabetical by name
- ❏ Alphabetical by subject
- ❏ Geographical by *(specify)*
- ❏ Numerical by *(specify)*
- ❏ Chronological
- ❏ Other *(specify)*

10. VOLUME *(in cubic feet)*

11. ANNUAL ACCUMULATION *(in cubic feet or inches)*

12. CUTOFF *(e.g., end of FY)*

13. REFERENCE ACTIVITY *(after cutoff)*

- ❏ Current *(At least once a month per file unit)*
  For how long after cutoff?
- ❏ Semicurrent *(Less than once a month per unit file)*
- ❏ Noncurrent *(Not used for current agency business)*

14. VITAL RECORDS STATUS: ❏ Yes ❏ No
If yes, indicate type here; use entry 15 to show any duplication.)
___ Emergency-operating ___ Rights-and-interests ___ Both

15. DUPLICATION: Are documents in this series avail- in another place or medium? ❏ Yes ❏ No
(If yes, explain where and in what medium.)

16. FINDING AIDS *(if any)*

17. RESTRICTIONS ON ACCESS AND USE

18. CONDITION OF PERMANENT RECORDS
❏ Good ❏ Fair ❏ Poor
Comment:

19. DISPOSITION AUTHORITY Does the series have an approved disposition authority?
- ❏ Yes *(List the schedule and item number, give the current disposition instructions, and justify any proposed change.)*

- ❏ No *(Propose an appropriate retention period.)*

Disposition of Federal Records: A Records Management Handbook (Washington, D. C.: National Archives and Records Administration, 1992) III-11

- *Location.* Where the records currently are located. Some survey forms have several lines for listing records both in office areas and in storage. This permits completion of only one form per record series, no matter where the records are found.

- *Quantity.* What is the total volume of records found in each location? Quantity can be expressed by number of file drawers, number of boxes, or filing inches on open shelves, for example. Most forms, however, include space for conversion to the standard archival measure of cubic feet. This standard permits easier planning and better space management. The most common conversions are found in figure 2.4.

- *Inclusive dates.* The beginning and ending dates for the records in each location. In addition to the span dates, it also is helpful to note the dates of greatest concentration (the "bulk dates"). For example, the survey may uncover records dated from 1926 to 1985, with the bulk of the records dated from 1980 to 1985.

- *Description.* What the records series contains. Some examples are correspondence, minutes, photographs, bound volumes, and forms.

- *Current use.* A brief explanation of the purpose of the records series. Why was it created? What function or activity does it facilitate? How does the originating department use the records series? This information is important in assessing the value of the records series for preservation purposes.

- *Arrangement.* How the originating department organized the records. Typical arrangements are numerical, chronological, and alphabetical.

- *Form.* An assessment of such things as the size of the paper (letter or legal), its color, and whether or not both sides of the paper are used.

- *Medium.* Are the records on paper, microfilm, photographic media, or computer tape or disk?

- *Physical condition.* Is the paper torn or brittle? Is it badly yellowed? Are the records so far beyond salvaging that they are not worth saving?

- *Relationship to other records.* An important aspect of appraisal is whether or not the records are "unique." Is an exact physical duplicate of the records stored elsewhere?

(For example, is a second copy of the form filed by another department?) Is the intellectual content of the records series summarized elsewhere?

- *Frequency of use.* Usage is often difficult to gauge in a quick survey. People usually overestimate their use of a particular record. Short of a detailed user study, the best that may be possible is a range of reference: Do you use the records every day? Once a week? Once a month? Once a lifetime?
- *Annual accumulation.* How fast is the records series growing? This information is important for planning space in a records center.

A form that gathers the above information will enable the archivist to meet the specific goals of the records survey.

Fig. 2.4 Cubic Foot Equivalents[11]	
Item	Cubic Foot Equivalent
One letter-size file drawer	1.50
One legal-size file drawer	2.00
Seven reels of standard digital computer tape (2400 feet long, 1/2-inch wide)	1.00
One standard record center carton	1.00
Fifty 100-foot reels of 35mm microfilm	1.00
One hundred 100-foot reels of 16mm microfilm	1.00
One letter-size archives box	0.35
One legal-size archives box	0.43

WHAT WILL YOU DO WITH THE INFORMATION GATHERED?

The last consideration in planning a survey is to determine what you will do with the results. It is foolish to conduct a survey without planning for the dissemination of the findings; the survey form and procedures should be designed to facilitate reporting of the results.

The principal options for the product of a survey are

- to compile and file information
- to produce an internal report for management
- to publish a guide for external distribution

While the first option may seem facetious, it is the end product of too many surveys. After all the time and expense involved in a records survey, very often nothing is done with the results. The survey forms are filed away and quickly forgotten; in a few years it is necessary to conduct another survey to reassess the mess. The effort required for a survey is only justified if it leads to some action—a survey should be a means, not an end.

Most surveys result in internal reports to management recommending actions to improve the present situation. As stated before, a carefully crafted survey followed by reasonable recommendations for action often can achieve quite a bit. It is important to keep in mind, however, that years of neglect probably will take years to correct. Therefore, the survey results may lead to a plan of action for the next five or ten years, rather than just for the next six months.

"The space agency [NASA] was warned in 1990 that the protective tiles around the [space] shuttle's wheel wells were particularly vulnerable to damage and failure, inviting catastrophe because those tiles protect both fuel tanks and the shuttle's hydraulic system.

"The study, conducted by experts at Stanford University and Carnegie Mellon and financed by NASA, also identified ice that builds up on the supercold external fuel tank as a major source of debris that could fall on the tiles and trigger a cascade of failures that could doom the spacecraft."

—*New York Times*, February 5, 2003.

Survey projects intended to promote research usually publish a guide at the end of the project. A guide can take many forms: an elaborate hardcover volume; an inexpensively produced offset pamphlet; a computer printout; a computer tape or disk; a roll of microfilm; or a page on the World Wide Web. Whatever its form, the guide should meet the needs of the target audience of researchers. This is possible only if the design and format of the guide are considered at the earliest stages of planning the survey, and if they are reconsidered and revised as necessary throughout the project.

IMPLEMENTING A SURVEY

The bridge between planning and implementing a survey is a realistic action agenda. This document should list all the various activities of the survey along with target completion dates. The action plan should divide big projects into smaller units in order to make them easier to understand and achieve. It becomes the basic control document for monitoring the progress of the survey. Figure 2.5 provides an example of an action plan.

Fig. 2.5 Action Plan for North Fork University's Records Survey	
Activity	**Completion Date**
Select department liaisons	June 1
Train department liaisons	July 1
Design and test survey form	August 15
Survey departments • Accounting • Public Relations * Personnel	 • August 30 • September 15 • September 30
Issue report to management • first draft • final copy	 • October 31 • December 31

The activities involved in implementing a survey can be divided into two broad categories: activities before visiting departments and activities during the actual visits.

Before visiting the departments, it is important to have the project personnel structure in place—the project director, advisory committee (if any), and departmental liaisons. It is also important to have visible evidence of top management support in the form of an authorizing policy statement (which is discussed later in this chapter) or a management memorandum.

The management memorandum directs each department head to appoint a contact person, or liaison, to work with the survey team. The liaison should be someone with a thorough knowledge of the department files. While the liaison will not do the actual survey, he or she will be expected to be available to clarify the purposes of file series and to explain the various uses of the files. If the survey results in the transfer of records to lower-cost, inactive storage, the liaison will be the one to box and ship records and to request retrieval of the records as necessary.

Before conducting the full survey, it is a good idea to test the form on one or two departments. The time spent at this point may save a great deal of time later in the project. Since so much of the success of the survey depends upon the quality of the survey form, it is not unreasonable to review as many as four drafts of the form.

Both before and during the survey it is desirable to publicize the project using whatever internal media are available. Employee newsletters or Web sites, in particular, can help build interest in the project. Articles in such media should stress the value of the project to the surveyed departments, rather than focus on the intricacies of the survey. Orientation sessions, especially for departmental liaisons, are another common way of promoting the project.

When one is ready to begin the actual survey, it is crucial to consider the order in which to visit the departments. Careful selection of the first department to be surveyed is especially important, since the organizational grapevine will quickly spread word of your success or failure.

It is best to begin the survey with a visible, mid-level department. The archivist should avoid beginning with the highest administrative levels for two reasons. First, since the survey staff will be new to the game, it is best to make mistakes with someone other than the president. Second, beginning at such a high level may build unreasonable expectations for the completion time of the survey: it will take time to survey all other departments.

On the other hand, beginning with a department too low in the administrative hierarchy, such as the mailroom, can affect the "word of mouth" about the project. It may also reduce the "clout" carried to the next department on the survey schedule.

An example of a visible, mid-level department is public relations. This department often has valuable records; more important, however, are the organizational contacts of the department. Doing a good job with a department such as this will help with surveying other departments.

This is not to say that every survey should begin with public relations. Another item to consider is the "resistance factor." All things being equal, one should follow the path of least resistance. In terms of a records survey, this means beginning with friends or supporters, those enthusiastic about the project. Why begin with the reluctant and unenthusiastic? After all, you may be seen as a threat by some long-term custodians of records. It is better to save these people until the end of the survey, when you have built up momentum and have a track record for successfully surveying other departments. If necessary, you can then have senior management back up their authorizing memorandum with a friendly follow-up memo.

No matter where one begins the survey, it is important to pay an early visit to the big records creators. In most organizations, this means the accounting department. Though such a large department may seem daunting, it really is quite manageable. While accounting records series are large, they usually are straightforward: check vouchers, general ledgers, journal vouchers, and expense accounts. Also, guidelines often exist for the retention of such records. In this regard, the Internal Revenue Service has been very helpful. Because of these factors, it usually is easier to survey accounting records than to survey convoluted subject files in other departments.

There is another reason for visiting the large records creators early in the survey. If one of the survey goals is to save space by shifting inactive records to lower-cost storage, the transfer of accounting records may produce sufficient savings to justify the entire program. Studies have shown that the ten largest records series in an organization account for over 50 percent of the storage requirement. Several of these series may be found in the accounting department.

SURVEYING INDIVIDUAL DEPARTMENTS

Once the order of the departments has been set, it is time to develop a strategy for the actual survey of each department. The following strategy has proven successful:

1. Contact the department head in advance to schedule the visit. Send a copy of the authorizing memorandum and any other background materials you may have.

2. On the day of the survey, make a courtesy call on the department head, but plan on spending most of your time with the liaison.

3. First survey the active records still in the office files. This will make best use of the liaison. Later, when surveying the storage areas, you can try to match inactive records series with the active ones. To begin by plunging into an inactive storage area would take a great deal more time and lead to a considerable amount of confusion.

4. Sketch a floor plan of the department before beginning the survey. Identify and number all filing equipment. This will help with the subsequent transfer or destruction of records.

5. Systematically proceed around the department until you have surveyed all the files. Except for badly disorganized "miscellaneous" files, you will not need to review

in detail individual files. A series of questions and answers with the liaison will identify the files, their arrangement, and purpose.

6. Because of this give-and-take approach, some experienced records surveyors prefer not to attempt to complete forms while walking around the department. They prefer to jot down notes on a pad as the liaison speaks, saving until later the distillation of these notes onto the survey instrument. These surveyors find that the form sometimes constrains them and discourages rather than encourages an open exchange. It is best to use whatever style makes you most comfortable, as long as you obtain the information necessary for the form.

7. After completing the survey, send a draft copy of the floor plan and survey results to the liaison. The draft copy will serve as a future reference for answering questions and clarifying the nature of the records series. It also is an important statement of the partnership between you and the liaison. Remember that a survey is not just something you do *to* a department; a successful survey must be done *with* them. This partnership will be particularly valuable if you develop retention schedules for the various departments.

8. Throughout the survey project, issue regular reports to management. These reports should be frank and truthful. It is best not to wait until the end of the project to surprise management with problems. This can ruin your credibility and endanger the entire emerging archival program. Management is used to problems—every project has them. Hiding problems will not solve them. Often the opposite happens: a submerged problem gets worse. Reports should be easy and quick to read. In particular, a graphic presentation is helpful for giving an overview of progress to date. The report need not be elaborate: it could just be a restatement of your action plan along with an account of what has been accomplished.

9. Finally, be certain to thank both the department head and the liaison at the conclusion of the survey. Thank-yous are especially important if you will be working with the liaison to draft retention schedules and transfer records.

STARTING AN ARCHIVAL PROGRAM

While a well-designed and carefully implemented survey is a basic part of a beginning archival program, it is not the only part. There are a number of basic issues that the archivist must consider in establishing the program. As the previous sections of this chapter imply, many of these issues can be addressed as part of the records survey, especially at the planning stage. By way of summary, a nascent archival program should consider three items:

- issuance of an authorizing policy statement
- placement of the archives within the administrative hierarchy
- use of an advisory committee

AUTHORIZING POLICY STATEMENT

An authorizing policy statement, sometimes called a mission statement, is the foundation for all actions undertaken by the archivist. If possible, it should be approved by the highest governing body of the organization—the board of directors or the president—to make it clear that the archival program has the support of top management.

There are two strategies for getting a policy statement approved:

- Take a long time to work out every eventuality in writing before seeking administrative approval of the statement.
- Develop a very brief (one paragraph) statement that can be approved quickly. Revise and expand upon this statement at a later date, as circumstances require.

The choice of strategy will depend upon the prevailing circumstances within the parent institution. Are you likely to be able to go to the governing body only once for approval? If so, it is better to take a longer time to develop a more detailed policy statement. Do you have an immediate need for an indication of top management support? If so, then a brief policy statement that meets the present need may be preferable to a more detailed—but delayed—document.

Federal grants agencies have been instrumental in encouraging the development of archival policy statements. One factor in evaluating grant applications is to assess the level of institutional commitment to and support for the project. A policy statement approved by the highest governing body is one indication of such support. In some cases, the granting agency may require (rather than just recommend) the issuance of a policy statement.

Policy statements for archival programs typically cover the following points:

- purpose or mission
- responsibilities and duties of the archivist
- responsibilities of others throughout the institution
- scope of items the archives or manuscript repository will collect
- prohibition against the removal or destruction of records without prior approval of the archivist

Longer or more detailed policy statements may also discuss other areas. Some of the more common areas are:

- access to records
- records management
- copying or reproducing records[12]

Figure 2.6 is an example of a policy statement, one for the NFU Department of Archives and Special Collections.

Fig. 2.6 Policy Statement: NFU Department of Archives and Special Collections

The North Fork University Department of Archives and Special Collections exists to identify, preserve, and make available records and papers of enduring value. Its mission is twofold:

• *University Archives*. To collect and maintain records of enduring value created or received by the university and its employees.

• *Special Collections*. To collect and maintain non-university records and papers, which support the academic mission of the university. Areas of collecting interest are specified in a separate Collection Development Policy.

On behalf of the President and Board of Trustees, the Director of the Department of Archives and Special Collections is authorized to review all university records to identify those of enduring value. All university employees are directed to cooperate with the Director in the performance of this responsibility.

The Department of Archives and Special Collections provides access to its collections under a separate access policy that is available from the Director.

A good policy statement also can serve a public relations or outreach function. This brief statement can make both other staff members and the outside world aware of what the archives is and what it does. The policy statement can answer recurrent questions in a minimum amount of space. It can provide the clout necessary to back up a policy decision the archivist makes. And, most important, it can provide a context for all the detailed, day-to-day archival work.

PLACEMENT OF THE ARCHIVES

The placement of the archives within the administrative structure of the institution is another key consideration. The most common options in use today are:

- *Corporate Secretary*. The charters of most corporations assign responsibility for the "official records" to the secretary of the corporation. It is natural, therefore, for archives to be part of this department. Also, the corporate secretary usually creates a number of records series of permanent value, such as minutes of board of directors meetings. Establishing the archives as part of the secretary's function may make it easier to transfer these valuable records to archival custody.

- *Public Relations. Businesses*, in particular, favor this placement. One of the major values of an archives collection for a business is in projecting a positive image of the corporation—for example as a leader or innovator. Some businesses reproduce artifacts preserved in their archives and make them available to the public. In the absence of an archives collection, the public relations library might have preserved records of permanent value in order to answer questions and to provide background for speeches by executives; placing the archives within public relations may increase the visibility and influence of the archives program.

- *Office of the Chief Executive*. Since many archival programs owe their establishment and continued existence to the support of the chief executive of the institution, it is common to place the archives within that office. Naturally, this placement offers the ultimate in clout and visibility for the program. The disadvantage is that the archives may be seen as a personal project of the chief executive rather than as an integral part of the institution—the program may be endangered if the next chief executive does not support archival activities or wants to make a clear break with a predecessor's policies.

- *Administration.* Some archival programs, especially those involved with records management, are placed within the administrative services hierarchy. The rationale for this placement is that the records program improves efficiency and saves space. Depending upon the organization, this placement may offer less clout than some of the options outlined above. The advantage is the integration of active and inactive records within one program.

- *Library.* This is the most common administrative placement for college and university archives and manuscript repositories. The library is also the most common site for the physical placement of an archives collection on a college campus. Among the advantages are the following: researchers need only visit one building; archival finding aids can be integrated into the main library catalog; and it is possible to interchange library staff members to meet peak demands in the various areas. The major disadvantage is that many library administrators do not understand archival functions and how they differ from library functions. This can lead to tension, misunderstanding, and the possible underfunding of the archival program.

Photograph 2.2 A typical archival storage facility featuring acid-free boxes on open steel shelving Photograph courtesy of the Office of the County Clerk, Suffolk County (N.Y.).

Often the archivist will not have a choice in selecting administrative placement of the program. The archivist who does have a choice, however, should look beyond the structure to the individuals involved. The archives may do better as part of a lower-prestige department where the executive-in-charge believes in archives, actively promotes the program, and fights for the necessary organizational resources— such a placement is preferable to having the archives wither higher up on the organizational vine.[13]

ADVISORY COMMITTEE

An archival advisory committee may be one way to overcome some of the problems of organizational placement and visibility. An advisory committee can give the archival program added credibility and assist the archivist who lacks experience in specific areas.

An advisory committee differs from a governing board. The former has no real authority over the archival program, whereas the latter exercises administrative control. In order to avoid misunderstandings, it is important to understand which kind of body is present and to define clearly its purpose and scope of operations.

Therefore, the first step in creating an advisory committee is to draft a mission statement for the body (see figure 2.7 for an example). The statement should cover the following points:

- purpose of committee
- areas of responsibility (many organizations exclude such matters as personnel and budgets from the advisory committee's domain)
- composition of committee
- frequency of meetings (probably a minimum of one meeting per year)
- reporting relationship (where does the "advice" go?)

The archivist usually coordinates the meetings of the advisory committee, decides which topics will be discussed (in consultation with the chair of the advisory committee, if there is one), sets the agenda, prepares background materials for the committee members, keeps the discussion moving, and prepares minutes of the meeting. The archivist also makes certain that the recommendations of the advisory committee reach the proper ears.

The composition of the advisory committee can take several forms. One approach is to represent certain interests, such as outside researchers and community leaders. A second approach is to form a committee composed entirely of professional archivists with expertise in areas where the archives is heading, such as acquisitions, grant writing, and oral history. A third approach, especially in an institutional setting, is to involve administrators from key departments with which the archives must work, for example the legal and tax departments, public relations, and accounting.

Fig. 2.7 Mission Statement: NFU Advisory Committee

The Advisory Committee for the NFU Department of Archives and Special Collections was formed to assist the department in its mission of identifying, preserving, and making available records and papers of enduring value.

The committee will offer advice in all areas of departmental operations, as requested by the Director of the Department of Archives and Special Collections. Excluded from the committee's deliberations are matters of personnel and budget.

The committee is composed of six members—three from the university community and three from outside the university. All nominees to the committee must be approved by the President of the University, who also selects the chair of the committee. The Director of the Department of Archives and Special Collections will serve as the secretary of the Archives Advisory Committee.

The committee will meet at least twice per year and at other times by call of the chair. The committee will submit an annual report to the President of the University.

Whatever the composition of the committee, the archivist must make certain that this advisory group accomplishes what he or she has in mind. While some authors have urged an almost Machiavellian approach, I do not believe this extreme is necessary. In fact, it may be counterproductive. The members of an advisory committee will soon be able to tell if they are being manipulated or if their only role is to rubber-stamp decisions that the archivist has already made.

The most successful advisory committees are those where there is a feeling of openness and cooperation. The archivist must sincerely want the advice of the committee, must be willing to listen to what they have to say, and must be open to changing plans and policies to reflect the thinking of the advisors. Anything less makes the advisory committee a waste of time for all concerned.

A final consideration in establishing an advisory committee is the matter of financial reimbursement for committee members. In most cases, the archives should pay travel and a per diem for out of town members. Many archivists use local people in order to avoid such costs.

Honoraria are a different matter. If honoraria are paid, they should go to all members, no matter where they live. Small, nonprofit institutions may not be able to pay honoraria. There is no shame in this. It just means that the archivist has another factor to consider in selecting advisory committee members—those who are committed enough to the goals of the institution that they will be willing to donate time. Larger, better-funded institutions probably will want to offer honoraria in order to attract the people they desire. The size of the honorarium will depend upon the qualifications and reputation of the people sought. It should be noted, however, that some granting agencies have an upper limit on the size of any honorarium that may be paid with their funds. As with other aspects of the advisory committee, it is best to spell out the financial aspects at the beginning in order to avoid misunderstandings later.[14]

CONCLUSION

With a structure for the archives in place and the results of a records survey in hand, the archivist is ready to tackle one of the most difficult—and most important—aspects of the archival mission: deciding which records to keep and which to destroy. The items discussed in this chapter provide the context and background for appraisal decisions.

NOTES

1. A records survey is also called an "inventory," especially in government settings. I will not use this term, however, since I will use the term inventory when discussing an archival finding aid.

2. For some recent views of archives in the new century, see Jeannette Allis Bastian, "Taking Custody, Giving Access: A Postcustodial Role for a New Century," *Archivaria* 53 (spring 2002): 76–93; Clare Beghtol, "In Interesting Times: From the Twentieth Century to the Twenty-first," *American Archivist* 64, no. 1 (spring/summer 2001): 143–58; Chauncey Bell, "Re-membering the Future: Organizational Change, Technology, and the Role of the Archivist," *Archival Issues* 25, nos. 1–2 (2000): 11–33; Brien Brothman, "The Past that Archives Keep: Memory, History, and the Preservation of Archival Records," *Archivaria* 51 (spring 2001): 48–80; Bruno Delmas, "Archival Science Facing the Information Society," *Archival Science* 1, no. 1 (2001): 25–37; H. Thomas Hickerson, "Ten Challenges for the Archival Profession," *American Archivist* 64, no. 1 (spring/summer 2001): 6–16.

3. Records management is a closely related profession that grew out of archival work at the end of World War II. Records managers are responsible for the systematic control of all records of an organization, not just those of enduring value. Records managers control records throughout their "life cycle": creation or receipt, active use, semiactive use, and ultimate disposition (destruction or transfer to an archives).

4. The best source on surveys remains John Fleckner, *Archives and Manuscripts: Surveys* (Chicago: Society of American Archivists, 1977). Much of the discussion in this chapter is adapted from Fleckner.

5. For more on records management, see Gregory S. Hunter, "Thinking Small to Think Big: Archives, Micrographics and the Life Cycle of Records," *American Archivist* 49 (summer 1986): 315–20; and Mary F. Robek, et al., *Information and Records Management*, 4th ed. (Encino, Calif.: Glencoe Publishing, 1995).

6. One must be extremely careful, however, in making certain that the records are old enough that all fiscal and legal requirements are met. If there is any doubt, the archivist should not destroy the records without checking with professionals competent to make judgments in these areas.

7. This distinction between efficient and effective is taken from Peter F. Drucker, *The Effective Executive* (New York: Harper & Row, 1966). 1–24.

8. For more on this point, see Elsie T. Freeman, "In the Eye of the Beholder: Archives Administration from the User's Point of View," *American Archivist* 47 (spring 1984): 111–23.

9. For more on planning, see Gregory S. Hunter, "Filling the GAP: Planning on the Local and Individual Levels," *American Archivist* 50 (winter 1987): 110–15; and Thomas Wilsted and William Nolte, *Managing Archival and Manuscript Repositories* (Chicago: Society of American Archivists, 1991), 27–33. See also chapter 12 of this book.

10. This section also relies heavily on Fleckner, *Archives and Manuscripts*.

11. This table is taken from *Disposition of Federal Records* (Washington, D.C.: National Archives and Records Administration, 1992), III-10.

12. For more on policy statements, see Wilsted and Nolte, *Managing Archival and Manuscript Repositories*, 15–16.

13. See Wilsted and Nolte, *Managing Archival and Manuscript Repositories*, 16–18; also Karen M. Benedict, "Business Archives Reporting Structures: Is There an Ideal Placement?" *Archives and Manuscripts* 27, no. 2 (November 1999): 26–39.

14. For more on advisory committees, see Linda Henry, "Archival Advisory Committees: Why?" *American Archivist* 48 (summer 1985): 315–19; and Wilsted and Nolte, *Managing Archival and Manuscript Repositories*, 19–20.

3 SELECTION AND APPRAISAL

After conducting a records survey as discussed in the last chapter, the archivist now must decide which materials to add to the archives and which to destroy. As much as an archivist might like to acquire everything that is offered or available, space and other resources will not permit such a course of action. Like it or not, we have to make difficult decisions and choose to destroy some records identified in our survey.

Selection and appraisal are at the heart of archival work. To emphasize the point, some archivists call appraisal the profession's first responsibility.[1] Unless archivists do appraisal well, everything else is meaningless. While careful arrangement and expansive description are laudable goals, they are wasted effort on a collection with no enduring value.[2]

Because of the huge volume of modern records, appraisal currently is receiving much attention within the archival profession. This chapter summarizes appraisal theory and practice in the United States, while offering international perspectives from the United Kingdom, Canada, and Australia. As will be seen, archivists the world over are trying to discharge their first responsibility as professionally as possible.

In terms of a formal definition, appraisal is the process of determining the value, and thus the disposition, of records based upon

- their operating, administrative, legal, and fiscal values
- their evidential and informational value (research or historical value)
- their arrangement and physical condition
- their intrinsic value
- their relationship to other records[3]

The elements of this definition will be discussed at appropriate places throughout the present chapter. Suffice it to say at this point that the archivist tries to determine if the records in question have sufficient "value" to justify their continued retention in the archives.[4]

This process of determining value is similar to triage in medicine. In triage, a medical professional prioritizes patients, and allocates treatment based upon the resources at hand and the number of patients to treat. As anyone who has watched the 1980s television program "M*A*S*H" will recall, triage separates patients into three categories:

- those requiring immediate attention
- those who will not survive, even if treated
- those whose treatment is second priority, receiving attention as resources permit

The archival professional also uses three categories, sorting records into

- those definitely having enduring value
- those definitely not worth preserving
- those whose preservation will be a second priority if resources permit

---

"There is history and there is junk in Senator Robert T. Stafford's cartons of letters, newsletters, speeches, memorandums, reports, schedules, notes, statements, photographs, and press clippings. It is Connell B. Gallagher's job to decide which is which.

"Mr. Gallagher's mission is to spare Senator Stafford the burden that befalls most senators and their states: how to deal with senatorial records collected over years of public service."

—*New York Times*, August 16, 1988.

Appraisal decisions are so difficult because all records have *some* conceivable value. If one names any record series, it is possible to think of a person who might have some use for the records. The archivist's job, however, is to select those records with *sufficient* value to justify the costs of storage, arrangement, description, preservation, and reference. The scarcer the institution's resources, the more difficult are the appraisal decisions.

In judging value, possible research use is a key consideration. To quote Philip Bauer, one of the early leaders of the profession, "Prophecy is the essence of archival evaluation." The archivist must be aware of current research trends and interests, using this information to extrapolate what may be of interest to future researchers. This is a weighty responsibility: a wrong appraisal decision means always having to say you're sorry. The nature of the responsibility has led in the past to a conservative bias, with archivists keeping many records of limited value "just in case" someone might want to see them. The exploding volume of modern records combined with the imploding resources of many archival programs has forced a reevaluation of this conservative bias and even a reappraisal of records previously accepted into archival custody.

The appraisal (and reappraisal) process ends with a number of possible dispositions for non-current records. The options are:

- transfer to a records center for low-cost, temporary storage
- transfer to an archival repository within the agency or institution
- donation to a suitable outside repository
- reproduction on microfilm or other alternate media
- destruction

"Richard Nixon had a one-line retort on Monday when asked about the lesson of Watergate: 'Just destroy all the tapes.' That's what he told the annual luncheon of The Associated Press when asked what his presidential successors could learn from his experience."

—*Newsday,* April 22, 1986.

Many times, records managers use "disposition" as a synonym for "destruction." But this is only one choice, albeit the choice for the great majority of institutional or organizational records. In a typical business, only 1 or 2 percent of the records are worthy of archival preservation. In some government settings, the figure might approach 5 percent. And in a nonprofit institution very conscious of its history, 8 to 10 percent of the records might reach the archives. These figures contradict the view that we must keep "everything." Similarly, they also provide an argument against the view that nothing merits archival preservation.

THE VALUES OF RECORDS

Basic to the appraisal process is an understanding of the values of records. Value, in this sense, is not a monetary term, even though records may be bought and sold. Rather, value refers to the underlying reasons for retaining a record series. Archivists consider five reasons, or values, for retaining records:

- operating value
- administrative value
- fiscal value
- legal value
- archival value

The first four of these reasons are considered primary values, in that they are important mainly for the agency that originated the records. The concept of primary value reflects the fact that an organization creates records to accomplish some purpose—to pay bills, to sell products, or to care for patients, for example. At a later date, some records may have secondary value for others outside of the originating agency, such as scholars, genealogists, and lawyers. This secondary, or archival, value continues indefinitely, thus justifying preservation in a specialized facility.[5] Margaret Cross Norton, the former Illinois State Archivist, said it well: "The difference between a file clerk and an archivist is that an archivist has a sense of perspective. He knows that these documents have two phases of use: their present day legalistic use, and their potential historical value."[6]

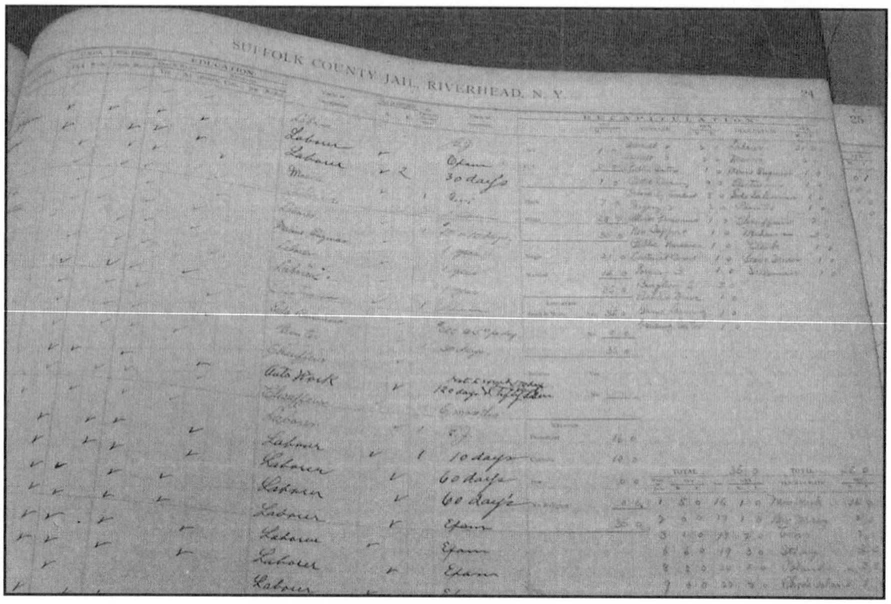

Photograph 3.1   Some archival records are found in large ledgers, as with this volume from the Suffolk County Jail. Photograph courtesy of the Office of the County Clerk, Suffolk County (N.Y.).

Let us now turn to a more detailed discussion of the five values of records. It should be noted that the retention period generally lengthens as records move through these five values.

OPERATING VALUE

Operating value is the value of the records for the current work of the organization or institution. To use an example, check vouchers have an operating value in paying bills and documenting payment when questioned by the vendor. Most operating value is short-term: in the case of check vouchers (and, indeed, most records of transactions), items have operating value for only a few weeks. If the records have no other value, they can be destroyed after that time.

ADMINISTRATIVE VALUE

After the records no longer are needed for current operations, they still may be valuable for some administrative reason. Perhaps management will use them to summarize operations or as the basis for a speech or written report. Administrative value often is difficult to judge, since "management" includes a wide variety of individuals with differing needs. In general, administrative values are in the range of one to two years.

FISCAL VALUE

It may be necessary to keep certain records as an "audit trail" to document financial transactions. The Internal Revenue Service and other agencies usually specify how long records must be retained for audit purposes. Once the originating organization clears the audit for the year in question, records being retained solely for their fiscal value may be destroyed. For example, most organizations destroy check vouchers after satisfying all audit requirements.

LEGAL VALUE

We weigh two distinct kinds of legal value:

- The organization may be required by statute or regulation to retain certain records for a specific period of time. For example, the Occupational Safety and Health Administration (OSHA) spells out how long organizations must retain records of employee exposure to hazardous materials.
- The records in question might document the legal rights or interests of individuals or corporate bodies. If so, the records need to be retained as long as the legal right or interest must be protected. An example is a patent or trademark file.

Unless there also is archival value, usually both categories of records are destroyed once the legal value has expired. As the corporate scandal involving Enron and Arthur Andersen illustrated, however, such destruction of records must not be taken lightly. Improper destruction can have major consequences for the organization as well as the individual involved.[7]

ARCHIVAL VALUE

The determination that records are worthy of "permanent" preservation in an archival repository is an assessment of archival value. Archival value is also known by other terms: historical, continuing, research, or enduring value. The remainder of this chapter further defines and applies archival value.

Figure 3.1 summarizes these five values of records and shows how they apply to three sample records series.

Fig. 3.1 Five Values of Records as Applied to Three Sample Series					
Series	Operating	Administrative	Fiscal	Legal	Historical
Check vouchers	Yes, 30–60 days	Yes, year-end summary reports	Yes, hold for audits	Yes, in case of claims	No, except perhaps for prominent individuals
Press releases	Yes, 30 days	Yes, annual reports	No	No	Yes, important source of information
Employee personnel folders	Yes, while an active employee	Yes, summary reports	No	Yes, in case of legal actions	No, too confidential to open

ARCHIVAL VALUE: CLASSIC APPRAISAL THEORY

It should not be surprising that archivists have spent a great deal of time developing and refining appraisal theory. While appraisal theory undoubtedly dates back to antiquity, most discussions of appraisal theory in the United States begin with Theodore R. Schellenberg, a former staff member at the National Archives.

Schellenberg developed the concepts of "evidential" and "informational" value and made them the core of appraisal theory. He wrote extensively on appraisal, thereby influencing an entire generation of archivists. As this chapter shows, subsequent authors have further refined Schellenberg's elements and applied them to new situations and types of records.[8]

"Thanks to the Enron scandal and the furor over Arthur Andersen's destruction of key documents sought by the government, businesses large and small are realizing they need formal policies for storing and deleting electronic data. Spelling out procedures and following them carefully will go a long way toward minimizing recordkeeping missteps that could otherwise cost firms dearly in a courtroom."

—*Kiplinger Washington Newsletter*, May 20, 2002.

EVIDENTIAL VALUE

By referring to items with evidential value, Schellenberg meant those records necessary to document the organization and functioning of the institution or department. The archivist, therefore, would preserve records of:

- *the origin of each entity*. Retain background on the problems or conditions that led to the establishment of the entity, as well as the actual documentation for its establishment, such as a charter.
- *the substantive programs of each entity*. Retain documentation for the development and execution of major programs, including such items as summary narrative accounts, policy documents, publications and publicity materials, and internal management records.

Before determining evidential value, it is important to do some preliminary research into the structure and function of the institution. What is the position of each office in the administrative hierarchy? What functions does each office perform? What types of decisions do the people in each office make?

In this regard, there is an important distinction between "substantive" and "facilitative" records. Substantive records are just what the name implies: the substance or core of the department's function. Facilitative records are those supporting records necessary to carry out the main activity. Most modern records fall into the facilitative category.

Preserving evidence of a department's activities most often will involve substantive rather than facilitative records. Very few petty cash forms will be of enduring value—except, perhaps, those that George Washington submitted to the Continental Congress. Facilitative records usually are of short-term value.

INFORMATIONAL VALUE

The second part of Schellenberg's formulation, informational value, shifts the appraisal emphasis. Instead of focusing on evidence about the organization itself, the archivist now considers the extent to which the records shed light upon:

- persons (both individuals and corporate bodies)
- things (places, buildings, and other objects)
- events (the interaction between persons and things)

The satisfied customer letter from Clyde Barrow to Henry Ford, which appeared at the beginning of this book, is an example of a record retained for its informational value. The letter was associated with a famous person; it was not retained because of the evidence it provided about how the Ford Motor Company dealt with customers.

"A team of archivists combing through the World Trade Center ruins has set aside fragments of the towers and the artwork and everyday artifacts that once filled them in a quest to preserve the memory of the horrific attack."

—*New York Post*, January 27, 2002.

Informational value can be difficult to determine. In order to help with the appraisal decision, Schellenberg provided three "tests" of informational value.

- *Uniqueness*. Is the information not physically duplicated elsewhere? Also, is the information not intellectually duplicated—is this the most complete and usable version of the information, or is it presented or summarized better elsewhere?
- *Form*. How concentrated is the information—is there a high ratio of research value to volume of the collection? Will the physical condition and arrangement lend themselves to archival preservation, or will they require a great deal of preliminary time and expense?

- *Importance*. How important are the persons, places, or events dealt with in the records? Are they likely to be the subject of future research?

Of the three tests, importance probably is the most difficult to assess. By definition, this test involves a subjective determination by the archivist of what is significant or noteworthy. Furthermore, recent historical and social science research, with their emphasis on ordinary men and women instead of such "Great White Fathers" as Washington and Jefferson, have turned importance on its head. Though Schellenberg recognized the difficulty of this third test, he could not have foreseen the extent to which the definition of importance would change.[9]

Schellenberg also could not have foreseen the way electronic records would change the above formulations. He assumed that concentrated information would be more desirable for research. With electronic records, however, raw data often have the greatest research value: they can be sorted and manipulated to answer new questions. We return to this issue again in chapter 10.

Very often informational value is either not recognized or not considered important by the creators of the records. This can be the case in private organizations or businesses that do not want to keep records "just to support research." The archivist in such a situation must be prepared to spend a great deal of time educating records creators about the secondary values of records.

CASE STUDY

In the previous chapter, I mentioned a situation where the NFU archivist had to survey records quickly and decide which had enduring value. The details of the situation are as follows:

One day you receive a call from NFU's Director of Plant Operations. He tells you that you "really should come down to the boiler room because there are a lot of boxes of old files down there." You ask if he mentioned this to your predecessor as archivist. He replies, "Nope, because space never was a problem. But now we need to move those boxes out in a week, because we're gonna replace the old boiler."

You immediately send your Assistant Archivist to the boiler room to make a list of records. When she returns, you decide what to save and what to destroy, using the concepts of evidential and informational value. Figure 3.2 summarizes your decisions.

Fig. 3.2 Evidential and Informational Value at NFU			
Record Series	**Evidential Value**	**Informational Value**	**Retain? (Yes/No)**
Employee time cards, 1960–72, 5 cubic feet (cu. ft.)	While the series provides evidence of how employees received paychecks, this part of the function does not have enduring value.	Would only be present if NFU had a famous employee	No
Minutes of the Board of Trustees (official copy signed by the University Secretary), 1939–50, 2 cu. ft.	Evidence of decisions and key actions	Might contain information about key persons, things, or events	Yes, this may need preservation work.
Vice President for Academic Affairs, Curriculum Development Files, 1925–40, 23 cu. ft.	Documentation for changes to the curriculum as well as the curriculum development process	Might be present, but is not the main reason for retention	Yes
Applications for Employment, 1953–58, 6 cu. ft.	As with time cards, evidence not worth preserving	Unlikely to be present; it would be too time-consuming to review all applications for fame of sender	No
Development Office, Daily Reports of Contributions Received,1940–53, 18 cu. ft.	While these provide detailed evidence of fundraising activities, the summary in the annual report should be sufficient	Unlikely to be present	No
University Bookstore, Annual Reports, 1976–80, 1 cu. ft.	Provides evidence of how the bookstore operated, but is this evidence worth preserving?	None	No, with space at a premium in the archives, there are higher priorities for preservation.
Library Daily Circulation Records (by Student), 1966–69, 50 cu. ft.	Documents a major activity of the library	Shows what individual students were reading during the Vietnam War era	No, privacy concerns would prevent the records from being opened for research.

BEYOND SCHELLENBERG: REFINEMENTS OF AMERICAN APPRAISAL THEORY

As the above case study indicated, even with Schellenberg's framework as a guide, appraisal decisions still are difficult to make. While evidential and informational value may be good starting points, they sometimes are inadequate as ending points. To borrow a concept from logic, evidential value and informational value are necessary but often are not sufficient for making a sound appraisal judgment.

Furthermore, there are two major problems with Schellenberg's approach.[10] The first problem stems from Schellenberg's background in government archives. In this setting, evidential value may assume greater importance than it would in the private sector: there is a desire to document for the citizenry how the government functioned. In effect, Schellenberg equated the records appraisal mandate with the statutory requirements of the National Archives.[11]

"Israel has given the United States a cache of documents that Israeli officials say were captured in raids in the West Bank and establish that Yasir Arafat financed and oversaw terrorist attacks by Palestinian militants.

"The documents were provided to Bush administration officials this week, apparently in an effort to reinforce Israel's contention that Mr. Arafat cannot be trusted and to blunt pressure from Washington for a halt to the Israeli military offensive....

"Palestinian officials have charged that the documents released by the Israelis are being taken out of context or are forgeries being used in an attempt to justify a military offensive in the West Bank that has drawn widespread criticism."

—*New York Times*, April 12, 2002.

The second problem flows from the first. Schellenberg advocated that archivists preserve a completeness of documentation for all government functions and activities. In the private sector, it is impossible to preserve evidence about every entity and substantive program in a large organization. Even if it were possible, would this be the best use of limited archival resources? Is it better to try to preserve evidence about everything rather than commit additional resources to the more significant entities or programs? As previously stated, archivists must consider the potential uses of records, as well as their evidential value, in making appraisal decisions.

A great deal has been written about appraisal, especially in the last fifteen years. Much of this literature has direct application for the working archivist facing appraisal decisions on a daily basis. To illustrate this, I will discuss five refinements of appraisal theory and show

how their insights would help with the NFU case study presented above. The refinements are:

- the "black box" concept
- intrinsic value
- sampling
- functional approach
- the "Minnesota method"[12]

"He was New York's original music man, and his name was Hill. Not Professor Harold Hill, the fast-talking brass-band huckster of 'The Music Man.' Ureli Corelli Hill, the violinist and conductor who founded the New York Philharmonic in 1842.

"Now the Philharmonic has landed a long-sought prize: a vast collection of Hill's papers and other effects that illuminate the origins of the Philharmonic Society of New York, as the nation's oldest continuing orchestra was then called, and the roots of classical music in the United States."

—*New York Times*, July 29, 2002.

THE BLACK BOX CONCEPT

For Frank Boles and Julia Marks Young, appraisal of modern records sometimes seemed like a "black box": archivists mixing together a variety of considerations and pulling out the determination of the record's value. Boles and Young analyzed university administrative records and developed an integrated system for their appraisal, one that made explicit the many factors archivists consider in making an appraisal judgment. The system is flexible enough, however, to apply to non-university settings. A grant from the National Historical Publications and Records Commission (NHPRC) enabled Boles and Young to test their system in other types of institutions.[13]

The core of the Boles and Young system is three closely related modules:

- the value of the information
- the cost of retention
- the implications of the appraisal recommendation

These three elements are considered together in reaching an appraisal decision. Depending on the repository, one element may be given greater weight than the others, but none of the three should be ignored.

This comprehensive scheme incorporates in a logical form all the significant parts of the appraisal process. The scheme includes both elements traditionally acknowledged by archivists (like evidential and informational value) and those often left unspoken (like the implications of the appraisal decision). An overview of the modules will illustrate this.

The value of information module contains much of Schellenberg's theory. It has three major subsections:

- *Circumstances of creation.* What is the position of the creating department within the organizational hierarchy? What are the principal functions and activities of the unit? To what extent do the records document these principal functions?

- *Analysis of content.* Are there practical limitations with the materials in terms of legibility and understandability? Does an exact physical duplicate exist elsewhere? Is there an intellectual duplication, with the information contained elsewhere? What topics do the records cover? What was the creator's relationship to the topic—a participant or an observer? What is the quality of the information about the topic?

- *Use of the records.* What is the extent of user interest in the records? Will the records be of interest to the repository's regular clientele? How do the records relate to present and future research trends and methodologies? Are there any restrictions on access imposed by either the donor or the repository?

The second module, cost of retention, raises a number of practical questions. It helps the repository determine if it has the staff and other resources to preserve the collection and make it available. By giving these monetary concerns equal consideration with the value of the records, Boles and Young acknowledge that archivists exist in a world of limited resources. Boles and Young identify costs in four areas:

- *Storage.* How much space will the records require? What type of storage is required? Are there any special environmental concerns? Are the present facility and shelving adequate?

- *Processing.* How much time and effort will it take to arrange and describe the records? Does the institution have sufficient expertise (both archival and subject area) to process the collection? How much will boxes, folders, and other supplies cost?

- *Preservation*. What quantity of preservation work will the collection require? Does the institution have, or can it acquire, the necessary preservation expertise? How much will preservation supplies cost?
- *Reference*. Can the institution provide adequate reference service for the collection? Is there sufficient staff and researcher space? Does the institution's staff have sufficient expertise in the subject matter to be able to answer researcher questions?

The third module, implications of the appraisal decision, is the area often left unarticulated by archivists and manuscript curators. Archivists like to think that they are serving posterity or scholarship, and therefore are above politics. But as anyone who works in an institution knows, programs of any type—not just archives—can be made or broken on this point.

"The deeds and deaths of the Alamo's defenders are the stuff of history, legend and mythology. But 166 years after a Mexican bugler sounded Deguello, the haunting declaration that no quarter would be given at the Alamo, exactly who fought there and who didn't is still open to debate.

"… a direct descendant of the Alamo's oldest known combatant and…an Austin researcher are working to correct the record. Poring over state archives and the musty probate records in county courthouses, they say they've found evidence of seven people, previously unidentified, who apparently died at the Alamo. And they have uncovered the names of at least 10 more who are likely candidates for that distinction."

—*Dallas Morning News*, March 1, 2002.

Boles and Young do a great service by specifically making two elements—political considerations and procedural precedents—part of the appraisal decision. Usually these elements come into play when an archivist believes the records do not have sufficient value to justify preservation, but he or she is worried that a person with "clout" might be offended by the decision. Specific questions to consider are:

- *Political considerations*. How important is the donor of the records? What kind of authority and influence does the donor have over the archival program? If the donor disagrees with the archivist's appraisal decision, is it because of a factual dispute or just an emotional attachment to the records? What kind of authority and influence do others such as potential users and affected third parties have? Do they carry sufficient weight to affect the appraisal decision?

- *Procedural precedents.* If the repository accepts the records, what precedent is it setting? In the future, will it have to accept records of similar value? Will the repository also have to commit itself to similar costs of storage, processing, preservation, and reference?

Let's apply the black box scheme to one of the records series that the NFU archivist is in the process of appraising. To do this, it is necessary to provide additional information about the series (see figure 3.3).

Fig. 3.3 Additional Detail on NFU Records Series

Vice President for Academic Affairs, Curriculum Development Files, 1925–40, 23 cubic feet

The records in this series document changes made to the curricula of the various schools and departments at NFU. Changes in curricula originate with the faculty of the school or department. The proposed change, along with detailed supporting documentation, is sent to the Vice President (VP) for Academic Affairs. The VP submits copies to all departmental chairpersons for their comments. The VP weighs these comments and decides whether or not to recommend approval by the President and Board of Trustees. In the case of programs approved by New York State, the VP is responsible for submitting copies to the state and following through with state approval.

The records are in letter-size file folders. All documents are typed, though some also have margin comments handwritten by the VP, departmental chairpersons, or others. Some of the older records are yellowed and brittle, ultimately requiring some preservation work.

The records series is arranged as follows: first, by department or school; second, by specific program within the department; and third, by date of change to the program. Copies of each proposed change are retained by the originating department. The state retains a copy of each change it considers.

Since the records contain detailed comments submitted to the VP, the current VP wants to consider this part of the collection "confidential" and to close it forever to outside researchers. You don't believe that these comments are as confidential as the VP believes—but you don't know if you'll be able to convince her of this.

In terms of the politics of the university, the library director (your boss) reports to the VP for Academic Affairs. There are three other vice presidents (Student Affairs, Financial Affairs, and Development), all of whom have similar types and volumes of program files that you might be asked to add to the archives. Accepting the records of the VP for Academic Affairs clearly would establish a precedent.

The NFU archivist can use the black box scheme to make certain that all appraisal factors receive consideration. In their subsequent NHPRC-funded project, Boles and Young attempted to develop weights and other measurements of the relative importance of the various factors. Even used qualitatively rather than quantitatively, the black box approach can be very helpful, as figure 3.4 illustrates.

Fig. 3.4 Application of the Boles and Young Scheme		
Module	**Element**	**Comments**
Value of the information	Circumstances of creation	The creating department is high in the organizational hierarchy (vice president). The records document a substantive function of the department: the development of academic programs.
	Analysis of content	The records are legible and understandable. While some parts of the records are duplicated elsewhere (originating departments and New York State), no other copy is as complete as this one. The vice president was a participant in the development of the programs. The information is of high quality.
	Use of the records	The records will be useful for university administrators. They also may be of interest to researchers of educational history or the development of the North Fork. If the restrictions on access stand, however, this will severely limit
Cost of retention	Storage	The archives has space at the moment for the records, though 23 cu. ft. is a sizeable commitment. There are no special environmental concerns.
	Processing	The archives has sufficient expertise to process the collection. It is not in a specialized subject matter unfamiliar to the staff.
	Preservation	The collection will require the usual acid-free boxes and folders. Some brittle items may require some additional preservation work.
	Reference	The archives should be able to provide reference service on the collection.

Fig. 3.4 (cont.)		
Implications of the appraisal recommedation	Public considerations	The donor of the records is very important to the archives (the archivist's boss's boss). The vice president has great influence over the archival program. She may have an emotional attachment to the records (she may think that her area of responsibility is a "natural" for archival preservation). Other parties (researchers, etc.) do not have the same kind of weight to influence the
	Procedural precedents	Accepting the records would set a precedent for the value of vice presidential program records. The other three vice presidents will expect their records to be preserved as well.

Taken as a whole, the Boles and Young framework provides a good working guide for appraisal decisions. It forces archivists to consider in a systematic way the many factors that should be a part of the decision. It also facilitates the creation of written appraisal documents explaining the decision (for future reference by archivists and researchers). This may be its greatest practical benefit for the working archivist.

INTRINSIC VALUE

As part of the appraisal decision, archivists must address the following question: even if the records have sufficient value to justify retention, must we preserve the records in their original form? The U.S. National Archives, in particular, grappled with this issue of "intrinsic value"— some records have physical qualities that make the original form of the records the only acceptable one in archival terms. For example, one would not microfilm the original Declaration of Independence and then throw out the document as a space-saving measure.

As facetious as this may sound, it is not that far removed from the situation faced by the National Archives in the late 1970s. At that time the head of the General Services Administration, then the parent body of the National Archives, advocated the microfilming of all records in the National Archives and the destruction of the original documents. The need to rebut the argument that all records were disposable forced the National Archives to articulate more clearly which records fell into the following categories:

- records that could be destroyed if an adequate copy were made
- records possessing qualities that would make disposal undesirable even if an adequate copy existed

At the heart of this distinction is that fact that records are composed of both "medium" and "message," to use Marshall McLuhan's terms. With records of intrinsic value, both the message and the medium merit preservation. By way of contrast, archival records without intrinsic value may have their message preserved in another medium: microfilm, optical disk, magnetic tape, or photographic film, for example. The decision to reformat is based on such factors as space savings, improved access, vital records protection, and permanence of the medium.

The National Archives published the results of its study in 1982 as a staff information paper. This paper identified nine qualities or characteristics of records with intrinsic value.[14] Figure 3.5 summarizes these characteristics.

Fig. 3.5 Characteristics of Records With Intrinsic Value	
Characteristic	**Example**
Example of a physical form which may be the subject of study	Glass plate photographic negatives
Aesthetic or artistic quality	Architectural drawings, watercolor sketches
Unique or curious physical features	Watermark, unusual binding
Age that provides a quality of uniqueness	Anything from before the Civil War
Value for use in exhibits	The first ledger book of a company
Questionable authenticity requiring physical examination	The Hitler Diaries
Substantial public interest, because of direct association with prominent people, things, or events	Anything connected with where George Washington slept
Documentation for legal status	Original corporate charter, signed copy of minutes
Documentation of the formulation of policy at the highest level	Cuban Missile Crisis memoranda

Using these categories as a basis, the staff of the National Archives surveyed the holdings in the main building in Washington, D.C. They concluded that only 20 percent of the textual records in the building held intrinsic value—the rest could be microfilmed and destroyed. The percentage would probably be lower in many other archival repositories across the country.[15] At NFU, only one of the records series under consideration has intrinsic value: the official, signed copy of the trustees' minutes should be retained for documentation of legal status.

The obvious conclusion is that archivists can be more aggressive than they have been in the past about reformatting records and destroying the paper. All too often, archivists reformat documents and still keep the originals even though they have no intrinsic value. As the bulk of records increases faster than the space and resources available for preservation, archivists must seriously rethink this practice.[16]

SAMPLING

Archivists have known about sampling techniques for decades, but such techniques have not been used to the fullest extent possible. This is due to two factors: confusion about the mathematics used in social science sampling, and fear of discarding a piece of paper crucial for future research. A more thorough understanding of sampling theory and practice should lead to its wider use by archivists in the future.[17]

As the name implies, sampling involves selecting only some of the records in question for preservation. It works best when the record series is homogeneous: for example, hundreds of boxes of invoices to customers. Sampling works less well when there is great variation within the record series, as with subject files or general reference files. It is important, therefore, for the archivist to analyze and understand the record series before deciding that sampling is the best solution.

Experience has shown that sampling is a viable option for record series with the following general characteristics:

- some research value, but not sufficient value to preserve the entire series
- too large a volume of records for the archives to store in hard copy
- prohibitively high cost to reformat the entire series

These characteristics are very common in records series created by modern organizations and institutions.

Depending on the type of information the archivist seeks to preserve, a number of different sampling techniques can be employed.

- probability or statistical sampling
  - random
  - systematic
- purposive or judgmental sampling
  - exemplary
  - exceptional[18]

In statistical sampling, the archivist selects a small portion of records with the intention of accurately reflecting all-important characteristics of the larger series. Mathematical formulas are used to determine the number of records required for a representative (statistically valid) sample. Social science researchers, in particular, favor statistical sampling, because conclusions about the sample can be applied to the entire records series. In order to reach such conclusions, the sample must be chosen in a rigorous way. The following paragraphs focus on reasons and theory, rather than mathematical formulas. Detailed discussions and explanations of such concepts as validity and sample size can be found in many of the statistics textbooks used in the social sciences.

There are two types of statistical sampling. The first, random sampling, has been considered the purest form of sampling because it is the freest of biases. To obtain a random sample, an archivist uses a random number table to identify which records to save. If the records are arranged numerically, this may be a relatively easy sample to pull. If the files are arranged alphabetically or in some other non-numerical sequence, however, they can be very difficult to pull—it first will be necessary to number the files. This is a slow, labor-intensive activity.

Systematic sampling, also a type of statistical sampling, is considerably faster and easier to manage. As the name implies, it involves selecting files according to some system—for example, every twentieth file, all files for years ending in 8, or all files for surnames beginning with M. Most authorities agree that if care is taken in obtaining the systematic sample, there is little mathematical difference between it and a random sample. A systematic sample, therefore, is the favored option among archivists for files that are not already numbered.

Either type of statistical sampling has a major disadvantage: while it is possible to preserve a microcosm of the entire records series, it is not possible to preserve the "unique" or "important" case (unless by chance it falls within the sample pulled).

Purposive sampling is used when the archivist is not concerned with obtaining a representative sample. Rather, the archivist makes a judgment about which individual items or cases merit retention. Such subjective sampling is very familiar to archivists; in fact, it is very similar to a standard archival appraisal decision.

The danger with any type of purposive sampling is that it is susceptible to bias. The judgment of a fallible human being is at the heart of the decision to retain or destroy an item. In order to make an informed decision, the archivist must have some expertise in the subject area and a familiarity with present research trends in the discipline. But no matter how careful the selection, there always will be some researcher upset that the files needed for a particular study were destroyed years earlier. Keeping this caveat in mind, let's turn to the two principal types of purposive samples.

With exemplary sampling, the archivist selects all items conforming to a particular "type." The goal of the sample is to document some characteristic, activity, or time period. A few examples will clarify this point:

- all files from one region to show how a typical field office operated
- all court cases of a particular type (e.g., felony convictions)
- all files from the years immediately before and after reorganization to show its impact on actual operations
- all files for faculty members reaching the rank of associate professor or above

In contrast, exceptional sampling seeks to identify and retain files on significant individuals and events, precedent-setting programs, and landmark cases. This type of sampling requires the greatest subject expertise on the part of the archivist. It also is the method most liable to second-guessing by researchers: they may not all consider the same items to be important.

One common way of selecting an exceptional sample, especially if the archivist is not confident of his or her expertise in a particular area, is the so-called fat file method. In this case, the archivist will retain all files measuring more than an agreed-upon thickness—one inch, or two inches, for example. The underlying assumption is that important or problem files are larger in volume than ordinary files. In reality, this is often the case; "fat" files often are the ones most in demand by researchers.

There is a problem, however, with the fat file method. Keeping all the thick files makes it extremely difficult to control the size of the sample and to plan space for the collection. In fact, depending on the record series, the fat file method may not even save very much space.

One of the records series discussed earlier at NFU might be a candidate for sampling. The library's daily circulation records (by student) totaled 50 cubic feet. They were dated 1966–1969, during the era of student protests and the Vietnam War. The records consist of call slips submitted by students to request books—at that time the NFU library stacks were closed to everyone but staff members. A request was given the next sequential number at the time the request was made. The slips are filed by request number. While it might not be worth keeping the entire series, a sample could be valuable for future researchers. Figure 3.6 compares the four sampling types as related to this records series.

Fig. 3.6 Sampling Possibilities: Library Daily Circulation Records	
Sampling Method	**Comments**
Random	It would be easy to use a random number table to pull a statistically valid sample. Any analysis of this sample would represent the entire NFU student population.
Systematic	It also would be easy to pull a systematic sample of every tenth or twentieth call slip.
Exemplary	This method seems less applicable, unless one wanted to keep only the call slips of a particular type of student—graduate students, for example.
Exceptional	To identify "significant" students (however defined) and locate their call slips would take a great deal of time. It also would raise the greatest privacy concerns.

Perhaps the most interesting example of sampling deals with records from the Federal Bureau of Investigation. In 1979 a group of social action organizations, historians, journalists, and others filed suit in U.S. District Court to stop the destruction of FBI field office records and to challenge the archival appraisal decision upon which the destruction was based. At the heart of the dispute was a National Archives practice dating back to 1945 that permitted the destruction of FBI field office records. The National Archives had not reviewed the files in question, originally because FBI director J. Edgar Hoover refused to permit anyone to see raw FBI files. As a result, archivists relied on FBI assurances that the field office files either were duplicated at FBI headquarters or were summarized in reports submitted to headquarters. At issue was a huge and steadily increasing volume of records. In 1979 it was estimated that the FBI field offices contained 300,000 cubic feet of records, even after destroying 710,000 cubic feet in the previous two years.

After a five-day trial in October 1979, Judge Harold H. Greene ruled in favor of the plaintiffs. He imposed a moratorium on the destruction of FBI files and ordered the National Archives to prepare a plan for handling the FBI's voluminous records.

The National Archives first undertook a lengthy and intensive study of FBI field office and headquarters records. Central to this study was the use of a stratified statistical sample to select items for appraisal. With stratification, some parts of the universe to be sampled are weighted differently from others, thereby increasing their odds of being selected. This differs from a straight statistical sample in which theoretically all parts of the universe have an equal chance of being selected. A stratified sample would be used when some parts of the universe are considered to be more valuable than others.

"A worker watches as about 15 tons of security files that had been kept on Greek citizens go up in flames in a blast furnace of a steel mill near Athens. The files were destroyed in a symbolic act marking the 40th anniversary of the end of the Greek civil war. Dossiers on the activities and political leanings of millions of Greeks considered threats to the state since 1944 were dropped into the furnace."

—*Newsday*, September 2, 1989.

At the conclusion of this study, the National Archives prepared a new retention schedule for the FBI's investigative case files. The schedule is a convenient summary for this section on sampling, since it incorporates many of the sampling types previously discussed. The schedule calls for

- retaining all exceptional cases (a list of which was developed in conjunction with researchers)
- retaining all files more than one folder thick
- judging remaining files by individual case type, such as auto theft, kidnapping, or espionage
  - In some case types, where the informational content is low, a small random sample will be retained.
  - In case types with greater informational content, a larger sample will be retained.[19]

While most archival situations will not be as complex as the FBI investigative case files, sampling still is a viable appraisal option in numerous settings.

FUNCTIONAL APPROACH

Archivists continue to search for new tools to assist with appraisal. Helen Willa Samuels of the Massachusetts Institute of Technology argues that archivists must start their selection activities not with a consideration of specific sets of records, but with an understanding of the context in which records are created. She recommends a functional approach to provide an understanding of the institution and its documentation. The emphasis would be on what organizations do, rather than who does it.[20]

Samuels believes that a functional approach can best achieve adequate documentation of an institution. Such documentation requires both official and nonofficial materials, as well as published, visual, and artifact materials. The basic approach is that analysis and planning must precede collecting.

Samuels identifies seven functions of colleges and universities that certainly apply to NFU:

- confer credentials
- convey knowledge
- foster socialization
- conduct research
- sustain the institution
- provide public service
- promote culture

For some of these functions, like sustaining the institution, the archivist's problem is an abundance of records—reams of accounting records, financial aid applications, and check vouchers. For some functions, like fostering socialization, the problem is a scarcity of records—there is little documentation for how students develop socially. Finally, in some areas we have plenty of documentation, but not of the proper type. For example, under conveying knowledge, we may know what courses were taught, but have few details of the educational experience—what actually happened in the classroom.

In the last section of her book, Samuels presents a six-step model for developing an institutional documentation plan:

1. Translate the functions so they describe a specific institution.
2. Draft documentary goals.
3. Apply a functional understanding to the preparation of administrative histories of individual units.
4. Evaluate the documentation already under curatorial care and the records still housed in offices.
5. Assess the resources (physical, financial, etc.) available to preserve the documentation

6. Confirm documentary goals and the process proposed to achieve them.

This is a promising methodology that will continue to be tested in a variety of archival settings.

THE MINNESOTA METHOD

The Minnesota Historical Society was involved in a multi-year effort to develop a pragmatic approach to the selection of twentieth-century business records. In the words of Mark A. Greene and Todd J. Daniels-Howell, "Our method borrows important concepts from various selection and appraisal literature, but it grew largely from our lack of success in applying most recent writing on appraisal to our daily work amidst archival reality as we know it." As such, the resulting "Minnesota Method" is important for any practical archivist.[21]

The basic approach of the Minnesota Method is as follows:

- Define the institution's mission and goals.
- Analyze its extant holdings.
- Survey the broader documentary universe, receiving input and advice from outside the repository.
- Define a set of criteria for organizing and prioritizing records creators into broad groups. These criteria should be based upon the repository's particular mission, resources and clientele.
- Establish a range of documentation levels to permit flexibility in accepting collections from creators of different priority status.
- Define, if necessary, further criteria ("decision points") for refining the prioritization of records creators.
- Link the priority group levels, the decision points, and the documentation levels.
- Use this framework to guide acquisition and appraisal decisions.
- Revise the framework over time to reflect the evolution of the repository's mission and goals, the success of past acquisitions, and economic considerations.[22]

Specific sections of the Minnesota Method derive from research discussed above, particularly functional analysis and the Boles and Young "black box." The prioritization steps draws heavily on the Canadian approach to macro-appraisal, which will be discussed below.

Finally, some steps draw upon approaches discussed in chapter 4 (collection policy and documentation strategy). Though the Minnesota Historical Society uses this methodology to guide acquisition of manuscripts, archivists have found it helpful in appraising records of their parent institutions as well.

Photograph 3.2 Corporate archives acquire products as well as other artifacts, as illustrated by the motorcycles displayed by the Harley-Davidson Archives. Photograph courtesy of the Harley-Davidson Motor Company Archives. Copyright Harley-Davidson.

The key for the institutional archivist is the setting of priorities. According to Greene and Daniels-Howell, "These priorities are the crucial step in moving from an unmanageable universe of potential documentation to a manageable one, and from a haphazard accumulation of records to a planned one."[23] The Minnesota Historical Society ultimately identified four "tiers," from high to low priority. Naturally, the tiers will differ in other repositories. What is important about the Minnesota Method, however, is the guidance it can give any archivist trying to establish appraisal priorities.[24]

INTERNATIONAL PERSPECTIVES ON APPRAISAL

Archivists in the United States have not been the only ones trying to refine appraisal theory and practice. The last half-century has been a fertile time in other countries, as well. While a comprehensive review is beyond the scope of this chapter, I will review appraisal theory in three countries that have had the most influence upon U.S. archivists: the United Kingdom, Canada, and Australia.[25]

UNITED KINGDOM

Appraisal theory in the United Kingdom derives from the writings of Sir Hilary Jenkinson, who lived from 1892 to 1961. Jenkinson was Deputy Keeper (chief administrative officer) of the Public Records Office from 1947 to 1954. His initial exposure to archives was through the handling of British medieval records. According to one article comparing Jenkinson with Schellenberg: "It is not surprising, then, that Jenkinson's archival writings concentrate on the development of rigid fundamentals with an emphasis on the legal character of archives. Moreover, Jenkinson's first years were free from the problem of dealing with huge masses of modern government records. Such a problem would not develop until later in the century when technological advancements and the business of fighting two major wars combined to produce a flood of administrative documents."[26]

Jenkinson also had a different beginning point than Schellenberg: the definition of archives. Jenkinson believed that only materials preserved for the creator's own information and in his or her own custody could be considered "archival." According to Jenkinson, the role of the archivist is not to make judgments about the "value" of records. Rather, the archivist is to be a passive recipient of records retained by the originator. This becomes the basis for the "impartiality" and "authenticity" of archives.

As discussed above, U.S. archival theory began at the National Archives at a time of abundance of records, rather than a shortage. Schellenberg and his colleagues believed it was the archivist's duty to enter actively into the appraisal arena. The fundamental differences between Jenkinson and Schellenberg remain the subject of discussion to the present day.[27]

CANADA

The Canadian archival community has made many contributions to archival theory and practice. Two of the most important contributions in the area of appraisal are "total archives" and "macro-appraisal."

Total Archives

From the establishment of the National Archives of Canada in 1872, it has had a mandate to acquire historical documents of all kinds, including copies from European sources. Only 100 years later was this approach given the name "total archives."

The total archives concept sees the National Archives of Canada with responsibilities for both public and private archives—the whole of Canadian society.[28] It is "A comprehensive archival system encompassing all types of archival material from any source and an intimate relationship between the producers and custodians of archives."[29]

Total archives at the National Archives of Canada has 4 elements:

1. Archival material appropriate to the jurisdiction of the archives are acquired from both public and private sources: from private individuals and organizations as well as government agencies.

2. All types of archival material may be acquired including manuscripts, maps, pictures, photographs, sound recordings, motion picture and other audio visual material and machine readable records; all records originating from the same source should be acquired and preserved in their totality rather than being divided among several repositories.

3. All subjects of human endeavor should be covered by a repository in accordance with its territorial jurisdiction rather than being assigned to different repositories on the basis of subject.

4. There should be a commitment by both the creator of the records and the archivist to ensure efficient management of records throughout the life cycle.[30]

The Canadian practice differs from the U.S., where there is a clear separation of government archives from private records and papers. The National Archives of Canada see the following advantages of the total archives approach:

- The consolidation of most relevant source materials in a single institution saves researchers time and money.

- There is consistent application of archival principles and techniques to all archival materials, both public and private. There are no separate professional practices for "manuscript curators."

- Consolidation prevents duplication of effort and expense. For example, there is no separate system of presidential libraries in addition to the National Archives.

- The integration of archives and records management benefits the archival program—it is difficult to get funding just for cultural purposes. Records management offers another advantage, efficiency.[31]

Macro-appraisal

In the early 1990s, the National Archives of Canada believed that it needed a new approach to appraisal. The result was "macro-appraisal"—a strategic approach to appraisal based upon an analysis of the archival value of the government's business rather than the archival value of its records.[32]

The National Archives of Canada no longer believed that assessing the value of information in records was sufficient, no matter how critically the value was assessed. Their reasoning was as follows:

1. Records evaluation assessments based on taxonomies of value are "both highly subjective and restrictive," insofar as they generally represent contemporary research interests which do not sustain user utility or historical value over time.
2. The sheer "superabundant volume" of information currently being created, accumulated, and managed by the federal government effectively prohibits any logical approach to appraisal that begins with an assessment of records.

The National Archives decided to provide Canadians with a "comprehensive documentary *picture* of government—how it operates and makes decisions, how it delivers programs and services, how it administers the public business, and how it interacts with citizens and groups—by analyzing and evaluating its business functions, processes, and activities." The new approach involves the following steps:

- Prioritize government's business *functions*.
- Link these functions to administrative *structures* (agencies and offices).
- Relate the structures to corresponding record-keeping *systems* and *records* in order to make appraisal decisions.

Macro-appraisal is a planned, research-based, top-down, functions-centered approach that focuses especially on the citizen's interaction with the state. According to Richard Brown, "The National Archives intends to offer Canadians a *complete* recorded *illustration* of government's history over time and to provide a comprehensive documentary means of assessing, evaluating, understanding and interpreting what has transpired."[33]

As noted above, macro-appraisal has influenced archivists south of the Canadian border. It is being tested in other countries as well. According to John Roberts, "Its advocates remain convinced that it provides the most defensible and practical approach to appraisal in a modern government environment. However, it waits to be seen how successful it will actually prove in the long run, both in its original Canadian setting and in other jurisdictions."[34]

AUSTRALIA

Contemporary Australian archival practice is founded upon an approach called the "records continuum." As developed during the mid-twentieth century by the National Archives of Australia and explained to the wider archival community by Ian Maclean, the records continuum rejects the life cycle concept developed in the United States.[35]

According to Sue McKemmish, "The life cycle model argues that there are clearly definable stages in recordkeeping, and creates a sharp distinction between current and historical recordkeeping. The records continuum, on the other hand, has provided Australian records managers and archivists with a way of thinking about the integration of recordkeeping and archiving processes."[36]

In the continuum model, records are both "current" and "historical" from the moment of their creation. Life cycle formulations suggest that records in the early stages of their lives serve organizational memory purposes (Schellenberg's primary values) and later come to serve collective memory purposes (secondary values). The records continuum embraces the view that records function simultaneously as organizational and collective memory from the time of their creation.

The continuum model also tries to do away with the distinction between *records manager* (responsible for the corporate memory) and *archivist* (responsible for the collective memory). Continuum theorists see the *recordkeeping profession* as being concerned with the multiple purposes of records. They take current, regulatory, and history perspectives on recordkeeping simultaneously, not sequentially.[37] Figure 3.7 summarizes the key differences between the life cycle and continuum approaches.

The Australian archivists draw this distinction quite sharply, making it a black-or-white proposition. In many archival settings, however, the differences are more apparent than real. For example, a "lone arranger" in an institutional archives is involved with records creators on a regular basis and probably has no records manager on which to delegate responsibility for "corporate memory." Even in larger institutions, archivists are breaking down barriers between themselves and records managers, often because of the challenges posed by electronic records. These archivists may be "acting life cycle" but they are "thinking continuum"—they are embodying the one world of records.

Fig. 3.7 Differences Between Life Cycle and Continuum	
Life Cycle Theory	**Continuum Theory**
Clearly definable stages in recordkeeping	No clearly definable stages in recordkeeping
Records serve "organizational memory" early in their life and "collective memory" later	Records are both "current" and "historical" from the moment of creation
Different professionals (records managers and archivists) responsible for different parts of the life cycle	No separation of responsibility among professionals

CONCLUSION

In 1951, an ad hoc committee of the American Historical Association issued a report on the problems associated with large, modern manuscript collections. The committee addressed the issue of how one locates the valuable information so often buried deep within these collections.

It is not surprising that they realized "practically any paper may conceivably be of some use, to somebody, at some time." This is what we would expect researchers to say. What is surprising is their sympathy for the task of the archivist and their encouragement for making hard choices. In the words of the committee, "the archivist must be wise enough, and bold enough, to take a calculated risk, and the historian and the biographer must recognize the difficulties, assist with conference and advice whenever possible, and finally, accept the situation."[37]

Appraisal decisions are not for the faint of heart. These decisions will shape the scholarship of the future and the view that subsequent generations have of our society. While they involve risk, however, they also offer opportunity: the exciting chance to apply archival theory, historical knowledge, and awareness of research trends in a way that will have a true impact on the future. No wonder appraisal is at the heart of all archival work.

NOTES

1. Richard J. Cox and Helen W. Samuels, "The Archivist's First Responsibility: A Research Agenda to Improve the Identification and Retention of Records of Enduring Value," *American Archivist* 51 (winter/spring 1988): 28–42.

2. The best one-volume work on archival appraisal still is F. Gerald Ham, *Selecting and Appraising Archives and Manuscripts* (Chicago: Society of American Archivists, 1993). For some recent articles, see: Peter Botticelli, "Records Appraisal in Network Organizations," *Archivaria* 49 (spring 2000): 161–91; Richard J. Cox, "Making the Records Speak: Archival Appraisal, Memory, Preservation, and Collecting," *American Archivist* 64, no. 2 (fall/winter 2001): 394–404; Barbara L. Craig, "The Archivist as Planner and Poet: Thoughts on the Larger Issues of Appraisal for Acquisition," *Archivaria* 52 (fall 2001): 175–83; Catherine Hobbs, "The Character of Personal Archives: Reflections on the Value of Records of Individuals," *Archivaria* 52 (fall 2001): 126–35; Russell Kelly, "The National Archives of Australia's New Approach to Appraisal," *Archives and Manuscripts* 29, no. 1 (May 2001): 72–85; Tony Newton, "Will the Tension Ever End? Some Observations and Suggestions from an Appraisal Archivist," *Archives and Manuscripts* 29, no. 1 (May 2001): 86–97; Riva A. Pollard, "The Appraisal of Personal Papers: A Critical Literature Review," *Archivaria* 52 (fall 2001): 136–50; John Roberts, "One Size Fits All? The Portability of Macro-Appraisal by a Comparative Analysis of Canada, South Africa, and New Zealand," *Archivaria* 52 (fall 2001): 47–68; Danielle Wickman, "Bright Specimens for the Curious or The Somewhat Imponderable Guided by the Unfathomable: Use, Users and Appraisal in Archival Literature." *Archives and Manuscripts* 28, no. 1 (May 2000): 64–79; Ian E. Wilson, "The Fine Art of Destruction Revisited," *Archivaria* 49 (spring 2000): 124–39; Stephen Yorke, "Great Expectations or None At All: The Role and Significance of Community Expectations in the Appraisal Function," *Archives and Manuscripts* 28, no. 1 (May 2000): 24–37.

3. Lewis J. Bellardo and Lynn Lady Bellardo, *A Glossary for Archivists, Manuscript Curators, and Records Managers* (Chicago: Society of American Archivists, 1992).

4. It is important to note, however, that some archivists, especially those trained in the European tradition exemplified by Sir Hilary Jenkinson, do not believe that archivists should be attributing "value" to records. See Duranti, Luciana. "The Concept of Appraisal and Archival Theory." *American Archivist* 57 (spring 1994): 328–44. This will be discussed further later in the chapter.

5. This distinction between primary and secondary values, as well as the fuller hierarchy of five values, is taken from Theodore R.

Schellenberg. For a statement of his views, see *The Appraisal of Modern Public Records, National Archives Bulletin* 8 (Washington, D.C.: National Archives and Records Service, 1956).

6. Margaret Cross Norton, "The Scope and Function of Archives," in *Norton on Archives: The Writings of Margaret Cross Norton on Archival and Records Management*, ed. Thornton W. Mitchell (Chicago: Society of American Archivists, 1975), 9.

7. Sources about the Enron/Arthur Andersen case are legion. The consequences are illustrated by a headline in the *New York Times*: "Andersen Guilty in Effort to Block Inquiry on Enron: Firm Informs U.S. It Will Give Up Auditing Public Companies." *New York Times*, 16 June 2002: p. 1.

8. Among Schellenberg's most influential works were, T*he Appraisal of Modern Public Records, National Archives*. Bulletin 8 (Washington, D.C.: National Archives and Records Service, 1956); and *Modern Archives: Principles and Techniques* (Chicago: University of Chicago Press, 1956).

9. For more on subjectivity versus objectivity in archival appraisal decisions and the entire concept of value, see Hans Booms, "Society and the Formation of a Documentary Heritage: Issues in the Appraisal of Archival Sources," *Archivaria* 24 (summer 1987): 69–107. For a discussion of social history and the changing notion of "importance" in history, see the nine articles in a special issue of *Archivaria* 14 (summer 1982).

10. These views on Schellenberg are taken from Frank Boles and Julia Marks Young, "Exploring the Black Box: The Appraisal of University Administrative Records," *American Archivist* 48 (spring 1985): 121–40.

11. This emphasis on evidence continues even today at the National Archives. Soon after John W. Carlin became Archivist of the United States, he shared with the archival profession his vision for the National Archives and Records Administration: "It enables people to inspect for themselves the record of what government has done. It enables officials and agencies to review their actions and helps citizens hold them accountable. It ensures continuing access to essential evidence that documents the rights of American citizens, the actions of federal officials, and the national experience." *Archival Outlook* [the newsletter of the Society of American Archivists] (November 1995), 26.

12. I will save another influential concept, documentation strategies, for the next chapter.

13. For the original article, see Frank Boles and Julia Marks Young, "Exploring the Black Box." For a report on the NHPRC project, see Frank Boles in association with Julia Marks Young, *Archival Appraisal* (New York: Neal-Schuman, 1991).

14. *Intrinsic Value*, Staff Information Paper 21 (Washington, D.C.: National Archives and Records Service, 1982). Reprinted in Maygene

F. Daniels and Timothy Walch, eds., *A Modern Archives Reader: Basic Readings on Archival Theory and Practice* (Washington, D.C.: National Archives, 1984).

15. Trudy Huskamp Peterson, "The National Archives and the Archival Theorist Revisited," *American Archivist* 49 (spring 1986): 125–33.

16. Gregory S. Hunter, "Thinking Small to Think Big: Archives, Micrographics and the Life Cycle of Records," *American Archivist* 49 (summer 1986): 315–20.

17. See Frank Boles, "Sampling in Archives," *American Archivist* 44 (spring 1981): 125–30; David R. Kepley, "Sampling in Archives: A Review," *American Archivist* 47 (summer 1984): 237–42; Paul Lewinson, "Archival Sampling," *American Archivist* 20 (October 1957): 291–312; Felix Hall, The Use of Sampling Techniques in the Retention of Records: A RAMP Study With Guidelines (Paris: UNESCO, 1981); and Ham, *Selecting and Appraising Archives and Manuscripts*, 75–79.

18. This categorization of sampling techniques is taken from an SAA case study prepared by Trudy Huskamp Peterson.

19. For more on this case, see James Gregory Bradsher, "The FBI Records Appraisal," *Midwestern Archivist* 13 (1988): 51–66; and Susan D. Steinwall, "Appraisal and the FBI Case Files: For Whom Do Archivists Retain Records?" *American Archivist* 49 (winter 1986): 52–63.

20. Helen Willa Samuels, *Varsity Letters: Documenting Modern Colleges and Universities* (Metuchen, N.J.: Scarecrow Press, 1992). Hans Booms discusses the functional approach in "Society and the Formation of a Documentary Heritage."

21. Mark A. Greene and Todd J. Daniels-Howell, "Documentation with an Attitude: A Pragmatist's Guide to the Selection and Acquisition of Modern Business Records," in *The Records of American Business*, ed. James O'Toole (Chicago: Society of American Archivists, 1997), 161–230.

22. Greene and Daniels-Howell, "Documentation," 171–72.

23. Greene and Daniels-Howell, "Documentation," 179–80.

24. Another interesting article compares appraisal methodologies to the decisions made by preservation administrators. See Tyler O. Walters, "Contemporary Archival Appraisal Methods and Preservation Decision-Making," *American Archivist* 59, no. 3 (summer 1996), 322–39.

25. For some other countries, see: Ole Kolsrud, "The Evolution of Basic Appraisal Principles: Some Comparative Observations," *American Archivist* 55 (winter 1992): 26–39; Luciana Duranti, "The Concept of Appraisal and Archival Theory," *American Archivist* 57 (spring 1994): 328–44; Angelika Menne-Haritz, "Appraisal or Documentation: Can We Appraise Archives by Selecting Content?" *American Archivist* 57 (summer 1994): 528–43.

26. Richard Stapleton, "Jenkinson and Schellenberg: A Comparison," *Archivaria* 17 (winter 1983–84): 75–86. Jenkinson's best-known work is *A Manual of Archive Administration* (London: Percy Lund, Humphries & Co., 1966).

27. Luciana Duranti, "The Concept of Appraisal and Archival Theory." *American Archivist* 57 (spring 1994): 328–44; Frank Boles and Mark A. Greene, "Et Tu Schellenberg? Thoughts on the Dagger of American Appraisal Theory," *American Archivist* 59, no. 3 (summer 1996): 298–311.

28. Roberts, "Portability," 52.

29. Wilfred I Smith, "'Total Archives:' The Canadian Experience," in *Canadian Archival Studies and the Rediscovery of Provenance*, ed. Tom Nesmith (Metuchen, N.J.: Scarecrow Press, in association with the Society of American Archivists and the Association of Canadian Archivists, 1993), 134. The Archives Act of 1912 established "a single archival agency to be responsible not only for the reception of government records which have archival value but also for the collection of historical material of all kinds from any source which can help in a significant way to reveal the truth about every aspect of Canadian life." Provincial and local archives also have similar mandates (see p. 137).

30. Smith, "Total Archives," 145–46.

31. Smith, "Total Archives," 146–47.

32. Richard Brown, "Back to the Strategic Roots: Appraisal Reform at the National Archives of Canada," *Archival Issues* 24, no. 2 (1999), 113–122.

33. Richard Brown, "Back to the Strategic Roots: Appraisal Reform at the National Archives of Canada," *Archival Issues* 24, no. 2 (1999): 113–22. Quotes from pages 114–15.

34. John Roberts, "One Size Fits All? The Portability of Macro-Appraisal by a Comparative Analysis of Canada, South Africa, and New Zealand," *Archivaria* 52 (fall 2001): 49..Roberts, "Portability," 68.

35. For the best discussion of the records continuum and its development, see - Frank Upward, "Structuring the Records Continuum. Part I: Postcustodial Principles and Properties" *Archives and Manuscripts* 24, no. 2 (1996), (http://www.sims.monash.edu.au/research/rcrg/publications/recordscontinuum/fupp1.html).

36. McKemmish, Sue. "Yesterday, Today and Tomorrow: A Continuum of Responsibility." *Proceedings of the Records Management Association of Australia, 14th National Convention, 15–17 September 1977.* (Perth: Records Management Association of Australia, 1997), (http://www.sims.monash.edu.au/research/rcrg/publications/recordscontinuum/smckp2.html).

37. McKemmish, "Yesterday, Today."

38 "Report of the Ad Hoc Committee on Manuscripts Set Up by the American Historical Association in December 1948," *American Archivist* 14 (July 1951): 229–32.

4 ACQUISITIONS AND ACCESSIONING

The previous chapter discussed appraisal of records generated by a parent agency or institution. For many archivists, fulfilling the "first responsibility" also involves acquiring records and papers not generated by the parent institution. In the United States, this is a common mission for historical societies and special collections departments of universities.[1]

An archival repository need not acquire records or papers from other institutions or individuals. The decision to do so must be made with the consent of the governing body of the archival repository. Acquisitions also should be in conformity with a collections policy approved at the highest levels. Only in this way can the institution build a unified collection that serves a variety of consituencies.[2]

Whatever the nature of an institution's holdings—records of the parent institution and/or records and papers acquired from other sources—the archivist must establish legal, physical, and intellectual control over the collection. This process begins with accessioning and continues through the detailed description of the holdings. Accessioning clarifies and documents the rights of the owner of the records as well as the archival repository.

Therefore this chapter will discuss two topics:

- acquisition of records and papers not generated by one's parent institution
- accession of records or papers, from whatever source, in order to establish control over them

ACQUISITIONS

In reality, both this and the previous chapter deal with acquisitions, and the distinction between the chapters is somewhat artificial. An accession is nothing more than an addition to the holdings of an archives, manuscript repository, or records center.

An acquisition of records or papers entails two related, but distinct, components: physical custody and legal title. Archives must deal with both of these elements.

- *Physical custody* involves *possession* of the records or papers. Usually the custody shifts from the creator or recipient of the item to the archives or manuscript repository. Custody, however, may not change. In the electronic environment, for example, several government archives are advising agencies about the long-term preservation of databases and other electronic records without ever transferring them into the archives.
- *Legal title* involves *ownership* of the records. As with most things legal, further distinctions pertain to this general heading. Legal title includes two elements reminiscent of Marshall McLuhan's saying about the "medium" and the "message." For an archives to "own" a record or paper completely, it must have legal title to both the physical and the intellectual property.

Ownership of the "message" involves the archives in the area of copyright: the right vested by law in the author of a document and his or her heirs or assignees to publish or reproduce the document or to authorize publication or reproduction of it.[3] Copyright later becomes a key issue in archival reference services—the archives must be careful not to violate the rights of the owners of the intellectual property.[4]

Transfers of both kinds of title must be stated explicitly—they cannot be presumed or assumed. In a subsequent section I will describe instruments that archives use to transfer title to the physical and intellectual property.

FIVE BASES FOR ACQUISITIONS

Archival institutions typically use five bases to justify the acquisition of materials.

- *Statute*. In many government settings, a statute passed by the legislature and signed by the chief executive of the jurisdiction forms the basis for the acquisition of records. This is the case with the U.S. federal government, where the Federal Records Act and other statutes not only define a record, but also empower the National Archives and Records Administration to acquire them on behalf of the people of the United States.

- *Administrative regulation.* Also in the government setting, there may be an administrative regulation rather than a statute that empowers an agency to acquire records. Regulations are issued by executive branch agencies or independent regulatory agencies in the discharge of their responsibilities authorized by statute.

- *Records retention schedule.* In both government and private sectors, many archives acquire records as the end result of a records retention program. Key to such a program is a records retention schedule, a listing of all series identified during an inventory along with the retention period for each series. Items identified as "permanent" are transferred to an archives, perhaps with an intermediate stop in a records center for more efficient retrieval during their semi-active life.

- *Permissive policy statement.* As noted previously, an archives policy statement usually authorizes the archives to acquire the records of the organization. The policy statement also may authorize the archives to acquire "other records and papers" related to the organization, but not generated by it. While this gives permission, it often does not sufficiently focus the collecting energies of the archivist.

- *Acquisition policy approved by a governing body.* If an archives or manuscript repository wishes to acquire records or papers systematically, it is best to develop an acquisition policy and have it approved by the governing body of the institution. This is discussed at some length below.

THREE METHODS OF ACQUISITION

Whatever the rationale for the acquisition, there are three principal methods for acquiring records or papers: transfer within an agency or institution, purchase, and gift. The type of institution will dictate which of these three methods is used most often. Figure 4.1 relates the three methods of acquisition to the previous discussion of custody and legal title.

Fig. 4.1 Relationship of Acquisition Type to Custody and Title		
Acquisition Type	**Transfer of Custody?**	**Transfer of Title?**
Transfer within agency	Yes	No
Purchase	Yes	Yes
Gift	Yes	Yes

For *transfers within an institution*, physical custody usually changes since the archives takes possession of the material records. The ownership, however, does not change: it is the institution itself, rather than the various departments, that owns both the physical and intellectual property—a concept called "dominion." As long as the records being preserved are from the parent institution, there is no change in ownership.[5]

Having said this, I must clarify that transfer to an archives involves different considerations than transfer to a records center. Once in an archives, records are governed by the access policies in place for the archives (see chapter 9). By contrast, a records center has responsibility for the physical safety of the materials but no control over use of the records, especially by outside researchers. Access to items in a records center is determined by the originating department. The records center, in effect, is nothing more than an extension of the filing equipment of the department; a records center is established for administrative efficiency rather than scholarly research.

For *purchases and gifts*, one transfers legal title as well as physical custody. Ideally, the title to both the physical item and the intellectual content of the item passes from one party to the other.

A *purchase* is the transfer of title for financial consideration. The primary concern of the archives should be with the legitimacy of the seller: does he or she have clear title to the property? If not, the archives may be forced to surrender the items at a later date to someone with a legal claim to the title.

While some manuscript repositories have built extensive collections through purchases, this method has several disadvantages, especially for the small repository. First and foremost, it is expensive. Most archives have limited budgets to begin with; using that small budget to purchase collections further limits the resources for essential archival activities. Secondly, once a repository begins purchasing manuscripts, there is a strong tendency to focus on individual items rather than entire collections. While isolated manuscripts containing autographs of prominent people may have monetary value, they may have little or no research value because they exist out of context. Finally, once money is involved, fraud rears its ugly head. While most autograph and manuscript dealers are honest, there still will be individuals willing to sell an unsuspecting repository the manuscript equivalent of the Brooklyn Bridge. The less knowledgeable an institution is about the ins and outs of the autograph business, the more it should heed the observation of P.T. Barnum that a sucker is born every minute. Does anyone want to buy the "authentic" Hitler diary?[6]

"Stanford University is getting hip—and hip-deep in Beat Generation memorabilia—after buying poet Allen Ginsberg's archives. Stanford wouldn't say yesterday how much it paid for the roughly 300,000 items in the Beat Generation poet's exhaustive and eclectic collection that ranges from original manuscripts to old electric bills."

—*Washington Post,* September 8, 1994.

A *gift* is a transfer of ownership without financial consideration. As with a purchase, the key question is: does the person really own what he or she is giving to the archives? If not, someone with a better claim to ownership may be able to force its return. Any gift has three characteristics:

- a clear offer
- acceptance of the offer
- delivery of the item(s)

Whether we are talking about a birthday present or the donation of historical manuscripts, these three elements apply. A deed of gift agreement, discussed below, attempts to document all three elements of the gift as well as the transfer of title to the physical and intellectual property.

Soliciting manuscript gifts requires patience and diplomacy. It sometimes takes years for a manuscript repository to receive a donation from a prospective donor. The repository must be interested but not obtrusive, solicitous but not sycophantic. Finding people who can achieve the right balance may be the key requirement for a successful manuscript gift program.

As important as interpersonal skills are, the best manuscript repositories do not rely on them alone. Repositories generate leads by keeping in touch with their constituents: researchers, benefactors, patrons, and previous donors. Staff members make the public aware of the repositories through speeches to community groups and interviews with the media. Brochures and flyers ensure that those contacted can review information about the repository at a later date.

Perhaps most important, successful manuscript repositories maintain good records of potential donors and the development of the prospect. While this practice should not be surprising in a profession that deals with records, it still is something that a repository can take for granted. Most curators establish "lead files" into which they place correspondence, notes on telephone conversations, and field reports. If a gift is made, transfer agreements and publicity about the donation become part of the "collection file" that may or may not be the same as the lead file.[7]

Potential donors often inquire about the monetary value of their collection and whether or not they can take a deduction for their donation. In the past, donors could take a tax deduction for the appraised value of the papers. The Tax Reform Act of 1969, however, changed this. To be a tax deductible contribution for an individual, the donated property must be a "capital asset" for the donor. Normally the papers cannot be a capital asset for the creator of the papers. The allowable deduction, therefore, is limited to the out-of-pocket costs of the creation of the material—such as the cost of paper and ink, typewriter ribbons, and floppy disks.

A second common donor question involves monetary appraisals. The Deficit Reduction Act of 1984 requires donors of property valued in excess of $5,000 to obtain a qualified appraisal of the property. The law prohibits the recipient of the donation, such as an archives, from providing the appraisal. As a general rule of thumb, it is safest for an archivist to refer all monetary appraisal questions to those best able to handle them—professional appraisers. Even better, the archivist should refer the donor to a professional association of appraisers—and not to an individual appraiser—so there is no hint of favoritism or collusion.[8]

DEVELOPING AN ACQUISITION POLICY

While an institutional archives documents the organization of which it is a part, a manuscript repository must establish a collecting focus or theme to guide its efforts. To use a formal definition, an acquisition policy is a written statement prepared by a specific repository to define the scope of its collection and to specify the subjects and formats of materials to be collected. Without such a focus, the repository runs several risks:

- The collection might be so scattered as to have no internal unity
- There might not be a critical mass of information in any one area to support research
- The repository might squander scarce resources on

collections it probably should not have acquired in the first place

- Several repositories might compete in one collecting area while neglecting other aspects of the human experience

An acquisition policy, however, must achieve a balance; while one wants definition, one also wants some flexibility so the collection has room to grow and evolve.

Maynard Brichford has outlined five ideals to guide the development of an acquisition policy. According to Brichford, an institution should collect in areas that

- extend research strengths, interests, and needs in a logical manner
- anticipate future research needs
- support the institution's extensive holdings of published or unpublished materials
- show a high ratio of use to volume and processing costs (high research value)
- do not directly compete with another major collector in the same region

Photograph 4.1 Archivists acquire materials in a variety of sizes, including oversized maps and drawings usually stored flat in map cabinets. Photograph courtesy of the Saint Benedict Center, Sisters of Saint Benedict of Madison, Wisconsin, Inc.

Focusing on these ideals enables an institution to maximize research interest in its collections while minimizing the inappropriate use of scarce resources.[9]

How does an institution actually draft an acquisition policy? It is best to involve the various constituencies of the repository, such as staff, administrators, researchers, donors, and volunteers. While the governing body will decide the ultimate policy, the input of all constituents guarantees that the acquisition policy will not lose touch with the people who care the most about the repository. If possible, convening a brainstorming session with key supporters is a good starting point. A helpful way to begin discussion is to have the assembled group answer questions in the following areas:

"To this day, Malcolm X remains one of America's most racially provocative icons."

"New generations have tapped his significance. Popular culture has co-opted his symbolism. Academics compete to decode him, to chart the trajectory his teachings would have taken, and they search, even still, for clues to the lingering mysteries of his 1965 murder.... Nearly 40 years after his death, the documentary legacy of Malcolm X is largely scattered and not controlled even by his family."

—*Washington Post*, March 20, 2002.

- *What are the financial resources of the institution?* What budget does it have for staff salaries, supplies, and other items? Based upon the financial resources, will the collecting program be modest or extensive? Some archivists consider it unethical to collect more materials than one can process and make available in a reasonable time.

- *How much space is available?* Are the shelves full or empty? Are you likely to collect in an area that will overwhelm storage capacity? Is there sufficient space for staff to process records and for researchers to access them? What is the likelihood of increasing repository space to accommodate new acquisitions (e.g., moving to new facilities, building a new repository)?

- *What is the quality of the staff?* For example, if the repository decides to collect items dealing with quantum physics, will it have staff members competent to process the materials and help researchers? If the repository is using volunteers, will they be able to handle the complexity of the anticipated collections?

- *Who are the patrons of the repository, both present and anticipated?* What types of collections interest them? If the repository is moving away from its traditional researcher base, how will it attract the new researchers to use the new collections?

- *What formats or types of materials would the institution like to collect?* Is the institution able to preserve and provide access to the items in question? Most repositories collect unpublished materials on paper; some also collect published materials. In addition to paper, there are other record media: photographs, videotapes and audiotapes, microfilm, magnetic disks and tapes, and optical disks. All of these media require special storage and handling that may be beyond the financial resources of some repositories.

"The widow of the Rev. Dr. Martin Luther King, Jr., is in Superior Court here [Boston] this week, fighting Boston University for possession of more than 83,000 of her husband's papers, including his letters, manuscripts and correspondence from American presidents.

"The papers, which Dr. King deposited at his alma mater in 1964 and 1965, at the height of the civil rights movement, are the crown jewel of the university's archives.

"But Coretta Scott King wants them turned over to the Martin Luther King, Jr., Center for Nonviolent Social Change in Atlanta. She maintains that this is in keeping with her husband's wishes that the papers find a permanent home in the South. The King Center houses the rest of Dr. King's work."

—*New York Times*, April 30, 1993.

- *What collecting themes or foci would the institution like to pursue?* Should the institution concentrate on a particular geographic area? This often makes sense for a local historical society. Should the focus be a particular time period? Most often, a repository will collect around one or more subjects: people, things, or events. No repository can reasonably collect in all the potential subject areas that vie for attention, so it becomes a question of priorities and selectivity.

This approach to developing an acquisition policy forces the institution to address resource issues before embarking on grandiose collecting projects. Usually there is no shortage of collecting ideas; however, often there is a shortage of institutional resources.

APPLYING AN ACQUISITION POLICY

Let us return to NFU, where the staff of the Department of Archives and Special Collections developed an acquisition policy by following the above suggestions. They assembled an advisory group composed of administrators, faculty, students, current researchers, and members of the local community. After several group meetings and numerous drafts, they agreed on an acquisition policy, which they forwarded to the university administration for review. The president and board of trustees made a couple of minor changes before approving the statement found in figure 4.2.

Fig. 4.2 NFU Department of Archives and Special Collections Acquisition Policy

In addition to University records, the Department of Archives and Special Collections wishes to identify, preserve, and make available for research, materials relating to the following major areas of life on the North Fork of Long Island:

- The *environment*. This area of interest includes the waters surrounding Long Island as well as the land use in the region. The department is particularly interested in documenting the impact of environmental changes on such industries as fishing, farming, and winemaking.
- *Social welfare*. The department seeks to document human and social conditions on the North Fork, particularly the life of the migrant worker.

The department will acquire unpublished records and papers, books, pamphlets, periodicals, maps, photographs, audiotapes, videotapes, films, microfilm, and magnetic disks and tapes related to the above areas.

The University wishes to work cooperatively with historical societies and local community groups to gather and preserve the history of the region without duplication or competition.

Materials may be added by gift, bequest, purchase, or any other transaction by which title passes to the University. In order to maintain and improve the quality of the collection, materials may be deaccessioned due to irrelevance, lack of space, duplication, or irreparable condition. This will be done only with the approval of the Director of the Library.[10]

With this acquisition policy in hand, the director of the Department of Archives and Special Collections opened a folder left by the previous director: "Offers to Donate Materials." Apparently, as soon as the previous director started interviewing for a job elsewhere, he suspended all acquisition decisions. A note in the front of the file said, "I wanted to give you a free hand to decide which collections to accept. Some of these may be difficult decisions. Good luck."

The new director decided to compare each of the possible donations with the recently approved acquisition policy. Figure 4.3 shows the worksheet used for this comparison.

Fig. 4.3 Evaluating Possible Acquisitions in Light of the NFU Acquisition Policy		
Collection Title	**Collection Description**	**Acquisition Notes**
Peconic Bay Yachting Association, 1899–1960, 30 cu. ft.	A voluntary association of people interested in boating. Collection contains minutes of meetings, membership rosters, photographs of members and events, general correspondence, and racing programs and publicity.	Fits acquisition policy. We are interested in uses of the water surrounding the North Fork.
Florence Kelly Papers, 1917–1989, 6 cu. ft.	Ms. Kelly was a teacher in the Orient Public Schools, a leader in the preservation of the Orient Point Lighthouse, and a local community activist. The collection includes correspondence, diaries, press clippings, and memorabilia.	Does not fit acquisition policy. Not primarily concerned with the environment, though it does relate tangentially. This collection is more appropriate for a local historical society.
South Shore Environmental Coalition, 1978–1988, 15 cu. ft.	A new group concerned especially with preservation of the pine barrens watershed recharge area. The collection contains lobbying records, press releases and clippings, correspondence with other environmental groups, records of contributions, and other financial information.	Fits acquisition policy, especially if we want to establish a strong regional collection. It is virtually impossible to separate the groups interested in the environment into "North" and "South" Fork.
Dr. Andrew Seligman papers, 1906–1968, 13 cu. ft.	Dr. Seligman was a graduate of NFU and a prominent social worker living in Riverhead. He was instrumental in establishing many of Suffolk County's social work programs. The collection includes correspondence, patient case files, reference files, and photographs.	Fits acquisition policy. A prominent person in the social welfare field as well as an alumnus.
Greenport Bakery, 1927–1980, 6 cu. ft.	A "Mom and Pop" bake shop, a fixture in Greenport until it closed in 1980. The collection contains financial data, letters from customers (some quite famous) and recipes.	Does not fit acquisition policy. While it would be heartbreaking to destroy the records of this piece of North Fork Life, we have no other choice. Try to interest a local historical society in the collection.

Fig. 4.3 (cont.)		
Collection Title	**Collection Description**	**Acquisition Notes**
Nancy Smith Papers, 1923–1980, 4 cu. ft.	Ms. Smith was president of the North Fork Gardening Association and vice president of the Southold Historical Society. Her main interest was historic houses. The collection includes correspondence, diaries, and records of both organizations.	Does not fit acquisition policy. More appropriate for a local historical society.
Nassau County Friends of the Environment, 1969–1980, 40 cu. ft.	The leading organization promoting environmental awareness on Long Island. The collection includes correspondence, financial information, membership data, reference files about environmental issues, and publications of the organization.	Fits acquisition policy, but only if we broaden our geographical focus to all of Long Island. Otherwise, we would not take the collection.
North Shore Literary Guild, 1955–1976, 18 cu. ft.	As association of authors, publishers, and other interested individuals who live on the North Fork. Collection includes correspondence with local and national authors, reviews of books, minutes of meetings, photographs of monthly meetings, and audiotapes of important lectures.	Does not fit acquisition policy. The arts fall outside of our collecting focus.
Mary Winthrop Papers, 1919–1986, 29 cu. ft.	Ms. Winthrop was a prominent local politician who served two terms in the State Senate. The collection includes constituent case files, legislative bill files, campaign materials, financial data, and personal correspondence.	Does not fit acquisition policy. Politics is outside of our collecting focus.
Long Island Winegrowers Association, 1975–1988, 15 cu. ft.	The trade association of Long Island vineyard owners. Collection includes correspondence, financial data, membership applications, and general reference materials about wines and vineyards.	Fits acquisition policy. Wine growing is one of the current uses of the land.

| **Fig. 4.3 (cont.)** | | |
Collection Title	Collection Description	Acquision Notes
Jonathan Redburn Papers, 1909–1975, 8 cu. ft.	Mr. Redburn was a prominent environmental leader from the Baltimore area. He made two speeches at NFU in the early 1970s. The collection includes correspondence, financial data, and reference files.	Does not fit acquisition policy, unless we broaden our interest in the environment into a national collecting focus. To do so would require more shelf space than we have.
James Anderson Papers, 1899–1972, 18 cu. ft.	Mr. Anderson owned one of the largest potato farms on Eastern Long Island. In addition to personal papers, the collection contains records from the farm itself.	Fits acquisition policy. Not only does it deal with the environment, but the collection might also document farm workers (social wel-

COOPERATIVE COLLECTING AND DOCUMENTATION STRATEGIES

As the above case study shows, North Fork University came to realize that it could not document the North Fork of Long Island by itself. The university had limited staff and other resources to devote to the task. But even with unlimited resources, the task would be too complex for any one institution to do well.

Some institutions work around resource shortages and other limitations by developing cooperative collecting programs. Such arrangements minimize wasteful competition while guaranteeing everyone a well-defined piece of the historical pie. For example, NFU might refer collections dealing with the arts and culture to another repository specializing in those areas.

Some archivists believe that even cooperative collecting programs do not go far enough. The focus, they say, is incorrect, because it still begins with the universe of records that exist rather than with the aspects of society that should be documented. This new approach, called a documentation strategy, attempts to channel energies into the *documentation of society* rather than into the *collection of existing records*. A diverse group of individuals—archivists, researchers, records creators, and community members—would determine the aspects of society that need documenting, identify institutions that may have records shedding light on these aspects, and work with those institutions to preserve and even create records, if necessary.[11]

For example, if one wished to document the AIDS epidemic in a particular community, one might identify several institutions whose records might have historical value. One organization targeted for preservation might be an advocacy and counseling group for gay men and lesbians. What if this organization purposely avoided creating records in order to guarantee the confidentiality of its clients? Should the archivist encourage the creation of records so they can be preserved? Once the records are in the archives, how will the archivist protect the rights and interests of the people who now—perhaps unbeknownst to them—have been made part of the historical record?

"When Michael Sullivan started the exterior renovation of the historic Catholic Center in downtown Buffalo, he figured somewhere in the 1930s era building was a time capsule. Sullivan, director of the Catholic Diocese of Buffalo's Buildings & Properties Department, was right.

"What surprised Sullivan was what he found when he opened the capsule. In it were newspapers including issues of the Buffalo Courier, the Buffalo Express and the Daily Star. Many of those dated from the late 1920s and early 1930s. There were a handful of photos taken during the building's construction, which began in 1929 and was finished the following year. Those were expected, especially since the building was the home to the former Courier-Express.

"The real surprise was the Buffalo Express, dated April 17, 1865. That's right, 1865, as in just two days after President Abraham Lincoln was assassinated. In it are detailed accounts of Lincoln's death. 'There's no way I though we'd ever find something like that,' Sullivan said.

"The papers and photos are being donated to the Courier-Express collection at Buffalo State College."

—*Buffalo Business First*, July 8, 2002.

If embraced fully, the documentation strategy concept would change the nature of the archivist from impartial evaluator of existing documents to empowered advocate for a consciously shaped historical record. Some would look at this change and say, "It's about time. If we're not more active, all we'll have is a disjointed series of historical artifacts that tell a partial story." I call this alternative the "Sleeper" syndrome, after the Woody Allen film of the same title. In Allen's film, the main character—played by Allen—is cryogenically preserved and thawed out in the future. He is then asked to comment on the few artifacts that have survived from the twentieth century. Scribes anxiously record his comments, for now they know the significance of the items they have been preserving. Unfortunately, the historical record as shaped by chance preservation and one person's interpretation, includes Richard Nixon as an obscure person who "did something wrong" and a pair of chattering novelty teeth as an indication of what Americans thought was funny.

There is nothing wrong with the documentation strategy theory. Putting it into practice, however, has been a challenge. Documentation strategies take time to develop and implement—they require the archivist to be in for the long haul. For the archivist willing to devote the time, Richard J. Cox has developed a practical five-step model based upon his experience documenting localities:

1. Assemble an advisory group and conduct a preliminary review of the locality's development and documentation.
2. Evaluate the documentation quality of the major aspects of the locality's historical development and present nature.
3. Prepare a report on priority actions for documenting the locality.
4. Establish working groups to analyze and plan for documenting priority topical areas.
5. Continue improving the locality's documentation.[12]

Whether archivists are collecting or documenting, the responsibility is great. We owe it to our repositories to expend their resources effectively. We owe it to present and future researchers to preserve a historical record that helps them understand our times. And we owe it to ourselves to fulfill this responsibility as professionally as possible.

> "When the East German Central State Archives were merged with the West German Federal Archives, Koblenz took over thousands of cardboard punch cards, magnetic disks and computer tapes. The electronic records from the East (about 30 percent were damaged) represented the digital memory of the ousted Communist administration....But the technology for reading them and the keys to the software that created them were often missing."
>
> —*New York Times*, March 2, 1998.

ACCESSIONS AND ACCESSIONING

Accessioning is defined as the act and procedures involved in a transfer of legal title and taking records or papers into the physical custody of an archival agency, records center, or manuscript repository. It is an attempt to establish three types of control over a collection: legal, physical, and intellectual.

LEGAL CONTROL

As noted earlier in this chapter, legal control of archives and manuscripts involves both intellectual and physical aspects—the medium and the message. The objective is to document clearly and unambiguously the transfer of both aspects. This can be done using one of six transfer instruments, some of which offer superior documentation to others. The six transfer instruments are

- oral agreement
- purchase agreement
- letter
- will
- deposit agreement
- deed of gift agreement (or contract)[13]

"As the nation's cultural institutions start to ponder what they will collect and preserve from the events of Sept. 11, the Internet is figuring largely in their strategies.

"Information from the Internet is being continually collected in a major undertaking spearheaded by the Library of Congress. A new Internet site, September11.archive.org, went online on Thursday and already contains more than 500,000 Internet pages related to the terrorist attacks and the United States reprisals, ranging from daily news reports to personal memorials."

—*New York Times*, October 15, 2001.

Oral Agreement

Though an oral agreement can be legally binding, it offers the poorest documentation of the six transfer instruments. For this reason, it can be a dangerous way of securing collections. If challenged in the future, especially by someone other than the donor, how will the archivist document the offer, acceptance, and actual transfer of the historical materials? Archivists should not accept oral agreements as binding, but use one of the five other options for legal transfer.

Even if an archivist or manuscript curator is painstaking in not entering into new oral agreements, often an invisible elephant lurks in the middle of the repository: all the collections now on the shelves, for which there are no transfer instruments except oral agreements with parties long deceased. What does an archivist or manuscript curator do about these "undocumented gifts"?

The best the archivist may be able to do is to document the collections as they now exist before memory dims any further. What is in the collection? As best we can determine, where did the collection come from, when, and by whose agency? A systematic way to capture this information is by using an accession form as described in the following section on control of intellectual property.

Purchase Agreement

As discussed earlier, a purchase involves a transfer of title for financial consideration. As long as the person offering the item has a clear title, that individual can enter into a sale. The documentation for a purchase may be as simple as a bill of sale or as complex as a formal contract. As with this and the following instruments, it is essential that legal counsel review them before signing, to protect the interests of the repository.

At the National Baseball Hall of Fame and Museum in Cooperstown, New York, "There are 36,000 three-dimensional items in the collection, and 130,000 baseball cards. In addition, the research library holds 2.6 million items, including a half a million photographs; 10,000 to 15,000 hours of audio recordings, film and video; 35,000 clip files, personal papers, scrapbooks, original manuscripts, scorecards, media guides, books and publications and assorted documents that would make serious scholars and baseball nuts salivate—like a promissory note from the Yankee owner Jacob Ruppert to the Boston Red Sox for partial payment for Babe Ruth.

"It is, in other words, a vast and idiosyncratic collection, the result of an acquisition policy affected by many factors, not the least of which is that the acquisition budget is in [the curator's] concise description, 'zilch.' The museum depends on cooperation from Major League Baseball and players and the generosity of donors, both of which are encouraged with active arm-twisting."

—*New York Times*, April 24, 2002.

Letter

Often a repository uses a letter to document the transfer of historical materials. It really is the *exchange* of letters, however, that is the key—the exchange documents the offer by the donor and the acceptance by the repository. While an exchange of letters is perfectly acceptable, the problem is that letters often do not go into enough detail. This can lead to problems later, especially in the areas of copyright and access. Did the donor want the repository to own the copyright—the intellectual property? Did the donor wish the collection or part of it to be restricted, and for how long? Can we discard duplicates or other items from the collection that do not interest us? Letters seldom go into such detail.

Will

A will transfers title upon the death of the donor. For prominent people, a lawyer usually consults with a repository while preparing the will, so the donation is to everybody's satisfaction. If a manuscript repository has been soliciting a collection for a number of years, a call from a lawyer preparing a will may be the first indication that the repository's persistence may pay off.

Sometimes an archives repository has no advance warning—it may just receive notice that it has been bequeathed a collection. If the collection does not relate to present holdings, or if there are serious restrictions on access, the archives can always refuse the donation. There is no obligation to accept the legacy.

"In a sort of homecoming for this country's most famous exile, the National Library of Ireland has acquired a sprawling collection of manuscripts by James Joyce, including, in a total of some 700 pages in six notebooks, 16 drafts from 'Ulysses' and typescripts and proofs of 'Finnegans Wake.' Discovered two years ago, they were kept secret until today."

—*New York Times*, May 31, 2002.

Deposit Agreement

A deposit is the placement of records or papers in the physical custody of a repository without transfer of title. This is similar to what we do with a bank account—the bank does not have legal title to our money, only physical custody. We control the money and how it is dispersed.

The deposit agreement is a statement of intent to transfer title at some (usually unspecified) date. In the meantime, the prospective donor deposits the physical property with the archives for safekeeping. Most archives try to avoid deposit arrangements unless the collection has great value and there is no other way to guarantee its preservation. With a deposit, the chance always exists that the archives will use its resources to process the collection, only to have the creator change his or her mind and demand the return of the items. In terms of individuals, it is best to try to have the title pass to the archives upon the individual's death, if not sooner.

If a repository chooses to enter into a deposit arrangement, it should be certain that the agreement answers the following questions:

- Is the archives responsible for accidental damage?
- Who insures the records from loss?

- What type of archival or preservation work may the repository undertake and who pays for this work?

- Is access permitted to the collection and, if so, who may grant and who may gain access?

- If the depositor removes the records before transferring title, must he or she reimburse the repository for direct or indirect costs previously incurred?

Deed of Gift Agreement

A deed of gift is a signed, written instrument containing a *voluntary* transfer of title to real or personal property *without a financial consideration*. This is the preferred method of documenting gifts to archives or manuscript repositories. The deed of gift should be a written contract governing the transfer of title and specifying any restrictions on access or use. It need not be verbose, nor does it require any magic legal words—but it should be clear and unambiguous, to avoid future problems. The repository's legal counsel also should review it in advance.

Many repositories use a standard deed of gift that they can modify to meet special situations. Using a standard form helps reassure donors that their materials are part of a professionally run repository and will be administered in the same way as other donations.

The basic elements of a typical deed of gift agreement are:

- the name of the donor as well as the donor's relationship to the creator of the records, if different

- the name of the recipient. For example, the receiving archives may be housed in a library on the campus of a branch of the state university. Is the donation to the archives, the library, the branch campus, the state university system, or the state?

- the date of the transfer of title

- detail on the materials conveyed by the deed of gift (such as the creator of the items, the volume, inclusive dates, and general description)

- the transfer of rights to the physical and intellectual property. In terms of copyright, it is important to stipulate the name of the person or institution holding copyright as well as the time period covered under copyright.

- a statement of restrictions on use. Typically there is a time restriction ("the entire collection is closed for ten years") or a content restriction ("confidential materials are closed"). The deed should specify who can impose restrictions, to whom the restrictions apply, who can lift restrictions, and how someone requests a temporary waiver of restrictions. Restrictions are discussed further in chapter 9.

- disposal criteria and authority. Under what circumstances can the repository dispose of materials? Can the archives dispose of them if they are duplicates, if they do not have historical value, or if they do not fit the acquisition policy or interests? If the repository does not want part of the collection, what are the options (return items to the donor, transfer them to other repositories, or destroy them)?
- signatures of both the donor and the recipient

Inclusion of all of these items may make the deed of gift appear very formal. This is precisely the point! The deed of gift agreement is a contract freely entered into by two parties and binding upon both of them. If the archives fails to meet its obligations, the contract can be voided and the items reclaimed by the donor. Also, the donor can sue for damages. Both parties must understand all parts of the agreement before committing to its provisions.

> "Those who write history in this city [New York] were aghast when former Mayor Rudolph W. Giuliani in his final days in office decided more or less on his own to move the public records out of City Hall and into a private warehouse. Mr. Giuliani has since promised public access to these documents but that, his critics argue, is not enough. The issue, they say, is not only about who has access, but also about who controls that access."
>
> —*New York Times*, February 24, 2002.

PHYSICAL CONTROL

Once legal control is established, the archives or manuscript repository can turn to physical control, especially shipping arrangements and the actual receipt of the collection.[14]

Shipping Arrangements

The most secure shipping arrangement is for the repository to pick up and transport the items itself. This will work for local collections, especially small ones. If small collections must be shipped by a third party, it is best to use one of the air express or parcel services known for their attention to detail, and which offer insurance. With large collections, there may be no choice but to use a freight handler or moving company.

If possible, have the repository staff box and label materials, carefully maintaining original order, and preparing a packing list. Care at this stage will make later processing of the collection easier (see chapter 5). When transporting fragile materials, especially photographic or magnetic media, the repository should try to avoid sizable temperature fluctuations inside shipping vehicles. If, for example, a company is shipping a photograph collection in the summer from Florida, they should not be left on a siding for a week in a boxcar without air-conditioning.

Documenting Receipt of Collections

Once a collection is received, the repository should document the transfer. An acknowledgment letter or memorandum usually suffices for statutory or regulatory transfers. For gifts, a thank-you letter from the staff member who had the most contact with the donor should be the minimum acknowledgment. For particularly important collections, a second letter from the head of the repository is appropriate.

At this point, the collection is on the repository's loading dock (or the archivist's desk). The archivist must know where to place the collection as well as what is in it. The archivist uses an "accession form" for this purpose. Since an accession form is the beginning of intellectual control, it is discussed below.

Photograph 4.2   Bound volumes stored flat on open shelving Photograph courtesy of the Office of the County Clerk, Suffolk County (N.Y.).

INTELLECTUAL CONTROL

An archivist must establish intellectual control—control over the contents of a collection—before researcher needs can be met. Accession records are an essential first step in this process for the following reasons:

- They provide a form of inventory control over total holdings by noting where each collection is located.
- They serve as temporary finding aids, providing intellectual control over collections until more detailed arrangement and description are completed.
- They provide worksheets for the control of work activities and help to establish priorities.

Accession records can be kept manually on paper or electronically in a database. If at all possible, it makes sense to establish a new accessioning system on a database since this will permit easier searching and updating as the collection grows in size.

"The [Gov. George] Pataki camp and the Republican State Committee continued to attack Mr. [H. Carl] McCall [the Democratic candidate for Governor of New York and State Comptroller] for retrieving several boxes of correspondence from the state archives late Friday. The letters in which Mr. McCall recommended his relatives for jobs were found in those boxes.

"Mr. McCall's aides said that his correspondence had been sent to the archives by mistake and that the boxes were taken back so that personal information about people, like Social Security numbers, could be deleted."

—*New York Times*, October 1, 2002.

Whether paper or electronic, an accession form or log should contain the following information for each collection:

- accession number
- record group number (defined in chapter 5) and name
- title of collection
- name and address of source/donor
- date of receipt
- description of collection (approximate volume, inclusive dates, and general subject matter)
- comments on restrictions

- temporary location
- preliminary plans for processing (identification of divisions within the collection, recommendations about arrangement and description, recommendations about scheduling, time and staff requirements, and preservation considerations)

The accession record is the first part of a repository's intellectual control system. This is probably its most important role. A descriptive system should take a building block approach. There should be no wasted effort and no need ever again to begin from scratch.[15] What an archivist learns about a collection at the accessioning stage should help with later arrangement and description. Until that arrangement and description are completed, the accession register will serve as the primary finding aid. Archives have too much to do with too few resources to squander any information about a collection.

CONCLUSION

To fulfill its mandate, an archives or manuscript repository requires focus and organization. The focus comes from a mission statement and acquisition policy. The organization comes from establishing legal, physical, and intellectual control over the materials added to the archives. Both of these elements enable an archives to begin to preserve and make available the records and papers of enduring value in its possession. Only then can an archives turn its energies outward, to the researchers that it serves.

NOTES

1. In the United States, "archives" and "special collections" often are managed in separate departments if not separate institutions (such as the National Archives and the Library of Congress). In Canada and some other countries, the premier national institution collects both archives and special collections. See Laura Millar, "Discharging Our Debt: The Evolution of the Total Archives Concept in English Canada," *Archivaria* 46 (fall 1998): 103-46.

2. For some recent articles on acquisitions, see: Robert Horton, "Cultivating Our Garden: Archives, Community, and Documentation," *Archival Issues* 26, no. 1 (2001): 27-40; Elisabeth Kaplan, "We Are

What We Collect, We Collect What We Are: Archives and the Construction of Identity," *American Archivist* 63, no. 1 (spring/summer 2000): 126-51; Myron Momryk, "'National Significance: The Evolution and Development of Acquisition Strategies in the Manuscript Division, National Archives of Canada," *Archivaria* 52 (fall 2001): 151-74; Cynthia K. Sauer, "Doing the Best We Can?: The Use of Collection Development Policies and Cooperative Collecting Activities at Manuscript Repositories," *American Archivist* 64, no. 2 (fall/winter 2001): 350-62; Michael E. Stevens, "Voices From Vietnam: Building a Collection from a Controversial War," *American Archivist* 64, no. 1 (spring/summer 2001): 115-20.

3. Lewis J. Bellardo and Lynn Lady Bellardo, *A Glossary for Archivists, Manuscript Curators, and Records Managers* (Chicago: Society of American Archivists, 1992).

4. For more on copyright, see Gary M. Peterson and Trudy Huskamp Peterson, *Archives and Manuscripts: Law* (Chicago: Society of American Archivists, 1985), 81-89; Kenneth D. Crews, *Copyright Essentials for Librarians and Educators* (Chicago: American Library Association, 2000).

5. Peterson and Peterson, *Archives and Manuscripts: Law*, 20. Much of the following discussion is based upon this book. The U.S. National Archives and Records Administration (NARA) defines custody in a slightly different manner: "Guardianship, or control, of records including both physical possession (physical custody) and legal responsibility (legal custody), unless one or the other is specified." While legal ownership still does not change, in NARA usage, legal responsibility does change. *Disposition of Federal Records: A Records Management Handbook* (Washington, D.C.: NARA, 1992), D-4.

6. A few years ago, the world was surprised by the discovery of Adolf Hitler's diaries. Several experts identified the diaries as authentic, only to be publicly humiliated when other experts proved the diaries to be fakes. For more information, see Joseph Henke, "Revealing the Forged Hitler Diaries," *Archivaria* 19 (winter 1984-85): 21-27.

7. For more on this topic, see F. Gerald Ham, *Selecting and Appraising Archives and Manuscripts* (Chicago: Society of American Archivists, 1993), 37-50.

8. Peterson and Peterson, *Archives and Manuscripts: Law*, 35-37.

9. Maynard J. Brichford, *Archives and Manuscripts: Appraisal and Accessioning* (Chicago: Society of American Archivists, 1977), 18-19. See also Ham, *Selecting and Appraising*, 15-24.

10. This acquisition policy is a modified version of one prepared by Candace Shuluk, a graduate student at the Palmer School of Library and Information Science, Long Island University, 1996.

11. For more on documentation strategies, see: Ham, *Selecting and Appraising*, 95-97; Philip N. Alexander and Helen W. Samuels, "The

Roots of 128: A Hypothetical Documentation Strategy," *American Archivist* 50 (fall 1987): 518-31; Helen W. Samuels, "Who Controls the Past," *American Archivist* 49 (spring 1986): 109-24; and Larry J. Hackman and Joan Warnow-Blewett, "The Documentation Strategy Process: A Model and Case Study," *American Archivist* 50 (winter 1987): 12-47. Not everyone thinks that the archivist should be shaping the historical record. For a view of the archivist as keeper rather than selector, see Sir Hilary Jenkinson, *A Manual of Archive Administration*, rev. 2d ed. (London: Percy, Lund, Humphries & Co., 1965).

12. Richard J. Cox, *Documenting Localities: A Practical Model for American Archivists and Manuscript Curators* (Lanham, Md.: Scarecrow Press and the Society of American Archivists, 2001), 120-28. For other reviews on the concept, see: Timothy L. Ericson, "'To Approximate June Pasture:' The Documentation Strategy in the Real World," *Archival Issues* 22, no. 1 (1997): 5-20; Jennifer A. Marshall, "Documentation Strategies in the Twenty-First Century?: Rethinking Institutional Priorities and Professional Limitations," *Archival Issues* 23, no. 1 (1998): 59-74.

13. The following discussion is drawn from Peterson and Peterson, *Archives and Manuscripts: Law*, 24-38. See especially the model deed of gift (pp. 28-34).

14. See Ham, *Selecting and Appraising*, 84-90.

15. Lydia Lucas, "Efficient Finding Aids: Developing a System for Control of Archives and Manuscripts," *American Archivist* 41 (winter 1981): 21-26.

5 ARRANGEMENT

At this point in the development of our archives, we have acquired records of value and documented the transfer of physical and intellectual property. The next step is to "process" the collection by arranging and describing it. This is the bridge between the records and their use by researchers of various types.

Arrangement is the process of organizing records and papers to reveal their contents and significance. The process usually includes packing, labeling, and shelving archives and manuscripts, and is intended to achieve physical or administrative control and basic identification of the holdings.[1]

The key point is that arrangement (and, later, description) is a *process*, not a product. We should never think of arrangement and description as ends in themselves. Rather, they are the means to an end—the ready accessibility of information for researchers.[2]

BASIC PRINCIPLES

Any discussion of archival arrangement usually begins with the terms *provenance* and *original order*. Not only are these important archival principles, they are essential terms to master before one's first archival cocktail party. An aspiring archivist on a buffet line is always safe talking about the weather, sports, and original order.

PROVENANCE

French archivists first articulated the principle of provenance in the 1840s. According to this principle, archives of a given records creator must not be intermingled with those of other records creators. Archivists always try to keep separate the records of different creating individuals or agencies. Provenance also is referred to by the French expression *respect des fonds* (lit. "respect for property"), especially at more prestigious archival cocktail parties.

The French did not immediately develop the principle of provenance upon their archival epiphany. Rather, after the French Revolution, the French archivists spent almost half a century arranging records primarily by subject. Only after trial and error did the French take the idea of provenance and elevate it to a guiding principle.

Someone from a library background might say, "A subject arrangement sounds pretty good to me." What archivists have found, however, is that while a subject arrangement makes it easier to answer *some* questions, it makes other equally valid questions almost impossible to answer. An example may make this clearer. Suppose a multinational bank decided to organize its archives by subject. Records received from the president, the public relations department, and the international finance department would all be broken apart by subject and intermingled with the records of other departments. This would make it easy for the bank's archivist to answer subject questions like "I need everything about our China branches." Other questions, however, would be difficult or impossible to answer: How did the public relations department function? What did the president know about the problems in Europe? How did information flow across departments? Archivists try to arrange collections in a way that answers the widest variety of potential questions.

"Henry A. Kissinger used his historic meeting with Prime Minister Zhou Enlai of China in 1971 to lay out in detail a radical shift in American policy toward Taiwan in exchange for China's help in ending the war in Vietnam, previously classified documents show.

"The account of the meeting in the newly released documents contradicts the one that Mr. Kissinger published in his memoirs.

"The documents also indicate that the Nixon administration was determined to withdraw from Vietnam—even unilaterally, and even if it led to the overthrow of the government of South Vietnam."

—*New York Times,* February 28, 2002.

ORIGINAL ORDER

Original order, the second fundamental principle of archival arrangement, was promulgated by the Prussian State Archives in the 1880s. Original order means that records should be maintained in the order in which they were placed by the organization, individual, or family that created them. Archivists restore and present to researchers, insofar as possible, the original order of the records as evidence of how the records were used by the creator.

A practical reason contributes to archivists' respect for original order: it is the only way to gain control over large, modern collections. When collections were small, archivists had the luxury of rearranging received collections in order to have them organizationally perfect.

Archivists no longer have this luxury, for modern organizations create records far faster than archivists can rearrange them. Original order also is referred to by the French expression *respect pour l'ordre primitif.*

As with provenance, original order sounds easy to implement. In practice, however, it is not so clear-cut. What was the office of origin for the records found in the North Fork University basement after twenty years of hibernation? Should the archivist maintain an original order that looks like it came from Mount Saint Helens rather than a file cabinet? If my predecessor as archivist completely destroyed provenance and original order, should I maintain this system or try to return to the archival ideal? Archivists face these decisions more often than they like to admit.[3]

FIVE LEVELS OF ARRANGEMENT

As archivists move from arrangement theory to practice, they have developed some helpful concepts and approaches. Perhaps the most useful is the concept of levels of arrangement articulated by Oliver Wendell Holmes of the U.S. National Archives.[4] No, this is not the Supreme Court justice—as versatile as Justice Holmes may have been, he was not also an archival theorist.

Holmes the archivist found it "elementary" that records have different levels of arrangement. Each level has an arrangement that can be coordinated with—but is still different from—the other four. Both archivists and manuscript curators have accepted this concept. It is effective with collections of historical materials of every size. The five levels are:

- repository
- record group (collection) and subgroup
- series
- file unit
- item

From a practical standpoint, Holmes's major contribution was in detailing the different activities archivists must perform at the five levels of arrangement. The following sections explain the levels and their associated archival activities.

REPOSITORY

A repository's total holdings usually are divided into a few major and distinct categories. Repository level decisions are not the kind that an archivist makes every day. Usually this is done at the highest administrative levels and, once determined, tends to remain in effect for a long time. For example, a university might divide its holdings into "institutional archives" generated by the university itself and "special collections" created by other organizations and individuals. The U.S. National Archives uses such repository level divisions as "civil archives" and "military archives," as well as special format divisions for electronic records and other special media.

RECORD GROUP AND SUBGROUP

Record group is a term unique to archivists and, therefore, confusing to almost everyone else. A record group is a body of organizationally related records established on the basis of provenance, with particular regard for the complexity and volume of the records and the administrative history of the record-creating institution or organization. An example is the records of the president's office. A subgroup is a subordinate administrative unit or a major division within the record group. To continue with the example, a subgroup might be the assistant to the president.

In establishing record groups, an archivist is concerned with both the *complexity* and *quantity* of the body of records. One must be able to manage the record group system physically. Archivists have tended to use one of the following strategies in establishing a record group system:

- Establish record groups *strictly according to provenance*. Records of each creating agency are kept together as a record group and assigned a unique number. The National Archives, for example, assigns each major federal agency or institution its own record group number. Manuscript repositories tend to use this approach since they assign each collection a unique number.
- Establish *general groups for records relating to an organization as a whole,* not merely one unit of it. An example would be one record group for the officers of an organization (each officer, in turn, would be considered a subgroup).
- Establish *collective groups* to bring together *like bodies of material.* This usually applies when an

institution has a large number of small entities. University archives, for example, might establish one record group for student organizations rather than have seventy-five separate record groups.[5]

The key to any record group system is that it be clear, unambiguous, and understandable. It is preferable, too, especially in a small archives setting, to have a system that is easy to remember without frequent references to a lengthy list of numbers.

Establishing a record group structure is a very personal decision—it reflects the personality of the archivist as well as his or her analysis of what is significant in the history of the institution. Whatever the system, there should only be one logical place to assign any collection or group of records; otherwise the system will appear to reflect a dysfunctional archival personality.

"Robert M. Gates, the Director of Central Intelligence, has ordered a sweeping overhaul of how the C.I.A. maintains its vast store of files, government officials said today.

"Mr. Gates's order is a result of the embarrassment suffered by the Central Intelligence Agency over its role in the criminal investigation of an Atlanta branch of an Italian Bank. The Justice Department complained in the summer that the nation's prime intelligence and espionage agency failed to pass on crucial information in the files about the bank Banca Nazionale del Lavoro....

"Computer-security experts said that the C.I.A.'s system of filing its secrets is so compartmentalized for security's sake that it is often difficult or impossible to track down all relevant information on a subject. At the same time, they said, the complicated system also provides a ready excuse for the agency when its officers want to withhold information."

—*New York Times,* January 1, 1993.

SERIES

A series is a group of files or documents maintained together *as a unit* because of some relationship arising out of their creation, receipt, or use. The records may relate to a particular subject or function, result from the same activity, or have a common form. Series usually are identified by common filing order, subject matter, or physical type. Some examples are: general correspondence, invoices, minutes, and patient case files. Subseries occur when the series is partitioned. For example, the originating department may have divided "general correspondence" into "incoming correspondence" and "outgoing correspondence," thereby making two subseries.

Record series is perhaps the most crucial archival arrangement level for a number of reasons:

- The archivist expresses the character of the collection by the divisions identified in it.
- Work on subordinate levels merely refines the order within each individual series.
- Description also focuses heavily on the series.
- Archivists usually direct researchers to series they believe may provide answers to their queries.

Series level arrangement actually involves two considerations: the order *within* a series (which file folder comes first in a series) and the order *among* series (which series comes before another series in the final collection arrangement). The creator of the records usually cares about order within a series, but not order among series. He or she established an original order based on intended use of the information. The creator seldom dictates which series should come first—the archivist decides this. In fact, when records are still active, the decision about which series comes before another is often based more on which drawer of a filing cabinet is free rather than any intellectual effort. The archivist's job, therefore, is to restore the order *within* series and to create an order *among* the series (see figure 5.1).

Fig. 5.1 Order at the Series Level		
	Within Series	**Among Series**
Who determines the order	The creator/originator of the series	The archivist
When is this order determined?	When the records are active in the originating department	When the inactive records are processed in the archives
What is the archivist's role?	Restore	Create

FILE UNIT

Records creators place individual items into units for ease of filing. These units may be file folders, bound volumes, magnetic disk packs, and countless other items. File folders are the most common unit that archivists face at this level. File folders tend to be arranged in one of several common schemes:

- alphabetical
- chronological
- geographical
- subject
- numerical

An archivist respecting original order would determine the filing sequence (alphabetical, let's say), and put the folders in proper order. Obvious misfiles would be corrected—they would not be preserved as a monument to someone's inability to alphabetize.

ITEM

The fifth level of arrangement is item level. An *item* is a letter or other document, regardless of length. Items are the letters, memoranda, and reports found within file folders. Usually items in folders are arranged chronologically or alphabetically. Once again, the archivist would retain the original order of items within file folders if at all possible.

THE FIVE LEVELS AT NORTH FORK UNIVERSITY

Figure 5.2 shows how Holmes's five levels apply to the North Fork University Department of Archives and Special Collections.

Photograph 5.1 The arrangement of individual items within an archival storage container. Photograph courtesy of the Harley-Davidson Motor Company Archives. Copyright Harley-Davidson.

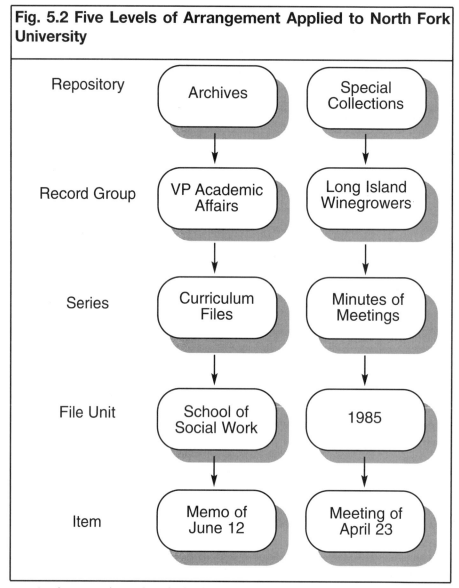

Fig. 5.2 Five Levels of Arrangement Applied to North Fork University

Repository — Archives / Special Collections

Record Group — VP Academic Affairs / Long Island Winegrowers

Series — Curriculum Files / Minutes of Meetings

File Unit — School of Social Work / 1985

Item — Memo of June 12 / Meeting of April 23

At the repository level, the holdings are divided into two major categories: university archives and special collections. This separation made sense to the university because of the differences in ownership and copyright that might apply. Official university records are placed in the Archives while all other records or papers become part of Special Collections.

The record group/collection level differs somewhat between Archives and Special Collections. Archives uses the term "record group" for its major holdings. Among the record groups are Board of Trustees, Vice President for Academic Affairs, Office of Financial Aid, and Student Organizations. Special Collections uses the term "collection" for its major holdings, the equivalent of record groups. Among the collections are the Long Island Winegrowers Association, the Dr. Andrew Seligman Papers, and the James Anderson Papers.

The remaining three levels will be less confusing if I work through the levels first for Archives and then for Special Collections. For the Archives, there are several series within the records of the Vice President for Academic Affairs: Curriculum Files; Correspondence with the President and Board of Trustees; University Departments; and Faculty Files. Within the Curriculum Files Series, there are individual file units (file folders) for each academic area. The School of Social Work, for example, has its own folder. Inside this folder are many items, including a memorandum dated June 12 of last year dealing with changes to the curriculum.

"University of Illinois physicist Albert Wattenberg didn't go to the Chicago branch of the National Archives last year looking for trouble. But when he could barely lift an 8-inch metal rod from a box containing artifacts used by nuclear physicist Enrico Fermi and his colleagues to build a nuclear pile under the University of Chicago football stadium, he knew something was wrong. 'There's only one metal that heavy,' says Wattenberg, who was part of Fermi's team in the 1940s. 'It was obviously uranium.'

"Wattenberg had literally put his fingers on a half-century of carelessness in preserving the beginnings of the nation's nuclear history. Thousands of artifacts contaminated by radionuclides during the testing and production of nuclear materials—laboratory notebooks, classified documents, components from experiments, and the like—were being stored along with nonradioactive material in files open to public inspection. Although the health hazards associated with these materials are small ... the contamination is presenting the Department of Energy and the National Archives with a major cleanup problem."

—*Science,* January 14, 1994.

In Special Collections, the Long Island Winegrowers Association Collection contains such series as Minutes of Meetings; Correspondence; Financial Data; Membership Applications; and General Reference. Within the Minutes series, there are file folders for each year. Finally, inside the 1985 folder one will find the minutes of the meeting of April 23, 1985.

RELATING THE FIVE LEVELS TO ARCHIVAL PROCESSING

Levels of arrangement is another modular concept. It is as valuable for establishing work priorities as it is for processing individual collections. Most nitty-gritty archival work involves arrangement at levels three, four, and five. Even here, however, archivists must make choices. If there is a large backlog of unprocessed collections, an archivist may opt not to work down to the item level. Taking this approach, an archivist first would process all collections down to the file unit level. Once caught up (if ever), the archivist would return to the collections and worry about the order of individual items within file folders.

Certainly there are trade-offs in this approach. Some archivists would cringe at the thought of having items within file folders not in perfect chronological or alphabetical order. Researchers might think that the person in charge was not a very careful archivist. While some researchers might think so, others would be pleased that archival processing time led to the availability of more collections rather than the precise micro-arrangement of just one collection. The bulk of modern collections forces archivists to balance time against resources at every step of the archival enterprise.

"The Pawtuxet River Valley [Rhode Island] is known for its interesting and important past. This is never more evident than through a visit to the Pawtuxet Valley Preservation and Historical Society.

"At the museum, which is located on Main Street in Crompton, a visitor can learn about those who lived in the Valley before them, and the historical significance these people had. Thanks to a dedicated staff, visitors can be entertained for hours by artifacts that cover generations.

"Included is a specific look at the mills that were located almost everywhere in the latter years of the 19th century. Other exhibits celebrate area war veterans, influential political and private citizens, firefighters, the police, and local sports teams."

—Kent County Daily Times, April 1, 2002.

ARRANGING A COLLECTION

How, then, do archivists arrange a collection? How do they make sense of a mass of boxes and folders? How do they approach this task without losing heart? To paraphrase the Marx Brothers, do archival job descriptions have a "sanity clause" or is this just a Christmas legend?

While there are different approaches to arranging a collection, the following nine steps have proven successful in a number of settings:

1 *Prepare to process the collection.* Make certain that there is sufficient workspace to spread records out during sorting. Place supplies (acid-free file folders, staple removers, erasers, etc.) in the same locations each day. This will relieve you of searching for supplies each time you need them.

2 *Review the accession register and other acquisitions documents.* Remember, the accession register serves as the interim finding aid until processing is completed. If prepared in sufficient detail, these documents should outline series and other major sections of the collection.

3 *Go through the entire collection without rearranging anything.* This initial pass is to confirm the information in the accession register, give you a feel for the collection, and allow you to come to some conclusions about series. It is best to take extensive notes during this stage. Some archivists use pads or even index cards so they can reshuffle entries and work out possible arrangements. Others prefer to use a personal computer or Personal Digital Assistant (PDA) for initial note-taking since computer technology facilitates sorting and reuse of entered data.

4 *Develop the processing plan.* Sketch out the order the final collection will have. Review this order with coworkers or superiors, especially if you are new to archival processing. Determine the appropriate level of detail for processing, including any preservation work that must happen at this stage.

5 *Sort the collection into series.* In this second pass through the collection, separate records into the series identified in the processing plan. Place the series in the order in which they will appear in the processed collection.

6 *Process each series to the filing unit level.* Take the series in order, "re-folder" them using acid-free materials, and place them in uniform-size boxes. The acid-free folders should be labeled but not numbered at this stage—there still may be some changes to filing sequence as the collection is processed. Placing the folders in uniform-size acid-free boxes not only helps one plan for the ultimate size of the collection (which usually is reduced during processing), but it gives a feeling of accomplishment as we see the collection move from unprocessed to processed. (Remember the sanity clause!)

7 *Proceed to the item level.* If resources permit, there are different types of item processing one can under-

take. The simplest is just removing paper clips, rubber bands, and other fasteners that will cause the collection to deteriorate. (Most archivists will remove these fasteners even if they can do nothing else at the item level.) More effort is required to place items in correct date order or other sequence. Many archives remove certain items (such as photographs or publications) from a collection for special handling. If such items are removed for storage elsewhere, it is customary to leave a "separation sheet" in the originating collection so that researchers will know where to look for the missing item. On the other side of the transaction, the removed item should contain or be labeled with enough information so that one can locate the collection from which it came.

8 *Lock in the final arrangement.* Place folders in final order. Do not overpack them into boxes. (Leave enough room to remove and return folders easily, but not so much room that items fall over and curl.) Place box and folder numbers on each folder.

"The chief executive of Global Crossing warned the company's chairman…as early as mid-2000 that the company was doomed to collapse, according to documents released yesterday by Congressional investigators.

"If publicly known, the warning from the chief executive…would have shocked investors. At the time, Global Crossing, the operator of a worldwide fiber optic network, seemed to have almost limitless potential."

—*New York Times,* October 1, 2002.

---

9 *Prepare a rough box and folder listing.* List all folders in box and folder order. Write down dates and any other information you will need to describe the collection (see chapter 6).

As one can see, archival arrangement is a labor-intensive process. It requires multiple passes through a collection. It also requires a great deal of discipline. Most archivists are interested in history to some degree, whether or not they majored in it in college, and they are tempted to read every word of every item, just because the story is so interesting and the contact with primary sources is so rewarding.

> "The document looks crisp, with a blue and purple line setting off the left margin of the white legal paper. The dark ink handwriting is clear and firm.
>
> "Belying the fresh look of the paper is the date: September 1876. The heading is Charge of the Court to the Jury. 'Gentlemen of the jury,' it begins, showing it derives from a period when only men could be jurors.
>
> "This was one of more than 80 documents relating to the trial of John D. Lee, the Mountain Meadows Massacre figure, discovered recently. They had been stashed away in the Beaver County Courthouse in Beaver.
>
> "Lee was executed in 1877 for the massacre, which took place in southwestern Utah. In the 1857 murders, carried out by members of the Iron County militia and local Indians, about 120 emigrants were killed. Although nine people were indicted, only Lee was convicted. He was executed in 1877 at the massacre site."
>
> —*Deseret News,* July 24, 2002.

Archivists must avoid the temptation if collections are ever to get processed. An archivist must read *just enough* to understand the nature and significance of the collection in order to make this known to researchers through finding aids. Any more than this is a waste of scarce archival resources.

TEN ARRANGEMENT HINTS

Even following the steps outlined above may not answer all of the questions that arise during arrangement. The following ten "Hunter's Hints" provide some additional insights:

1 *Box the records yourself prior to transfer.* As noted in chapter 4, this is the best way to understand and preserve the original order of the collection. The boxing procedure also offers the opportunity to identify series and processing priorities even before the collection reaches the repository door.

2 *When in doubt, chicken out.* If you have any doubt about the original order, or if there is an original order that does not make sense, be cautious before changing it. Order always can be changed and divisions made later; rarely can order be reconstituted, and divisions undone. (Even if they can be undone, this takes time and energy away from other activities.). Particularly troublesome are "Dewey-Decimal-type" filing systems where someone, long

dead, grouped files under a classification scheme now long forgotten and probably further hidden behind an array of file numbers. Archivists have been known to spend a great deal of time undoing an indecipherable system only to find the "cipher," or list of codes, in a subsequent file. Save yourself the headache.

3   *Remember the "test of creation."* You can distinguish one record group from another by asking, "who created these records?" Similarly, if you are unclear whether a body of records is a record group or series, try to focus on who created it. Multiple series can be part of a record group.

4   *Records follow function.* Functions usually remain constant in organizations, though department names and locations may change. The records of a predecessor department are maintained with the successor department, if that is the way the archives received them. Arrange the files under the name of the unit making the transfer. Consider, for example, an organization that once had a separate research department. It subsequently was closed and the research responsibility was transferred to public relations, along with all the extant records. Ten years later, the public relations department transferred its records to the archives. Intermingled throughout the public relations materials are files from the now-defunct research department. The archivist should not try to reassemble the records of the research department, because their integration into the public relations files tells a great deal about how the department functioned. The finding aid should explain the shift in responsibility and steer researchers to the public relations records for answers to their questions.

5   *What do you do if there is no original order,* or if there is an original order but it is an unserviceable one? Frank Boles argues that archivists should not be slaves to original order. He offers "simple usability" as a higher law than original order (like Hebrew National's "higher authority" for making hot dogs). Boles makes a great deal of sense: there is no point maintaining an unusable original order. The key is to do the least rearranging possible to make the collec-

tion serviceable. If there is no order at all, the archivist should use the simplest order possible.[6]

6 *What about manuscript collections?* Original order sometimes does not make as much sense with personal papers—the collection often arrives in a state of disarray. Imagine if someone took the contents of your desktop, shoveled them into a box, and shipped them to a manuscript repository. What was the original order of your desk? Perhaps it was an embodiment of the Big Bang Theory? Faced with such situations, manuscript curators often have to be more creative than their archival colleagues. Curators tend to divide personal papers in one of four ways:

- *Chronology.* Regardless of type of document, everything is placed in straight date order, since people (except perhaps Shirley MacLaine) only live once and do so in a chronological sequence. A chronological arrangement can be easy to implement, but likely will require extensive cross-referencing for subject access.

- *Topics.* The potential problem is who defines the topics. Will researchers be looking for the same topics as the curator who arranged the collection?

- *Types of materials.* The curator would establish separate series for such materials as correspondence, diaries, and minutes. Researchers find this arrangement very helpful since some types of materials tend to be more valuable for research than other types.

- *Functions of the creator.* The papers of a college professor active in professional and community affairs could have the following series: personal life, teaching and research, professional service, and community service.

7 *Avoid establishing more than one system within any one collection.* Such combinations create more than one proper place for some documents. This can lead to confusion and frustration for the staff, as well as for researchers. For example, if you begin dividing the collection by type of material, do not also have part of the collection divided by topic, or there will now be two logical places to file a particular item.

8 *Arrange series in order of the value of the information they contain.* This hint deals with the order among series in a collection. The series that provide the greatest insight and the fullest overview come first. If the series are ordered by types, then minutes, diaries, and correspondence usually come first. Indexes come before the records they illuminate. (There is nothing more frustrating for a researcher than to wade through a collection, only to find an index after the fact.) Archivists usually arrange records according to the administrative hierarchy: the president comes before the vice president, the main office comes before the field offices, records covering more than one function precede those documenting a single activity. Curators usually arrange manuscript collections from the most personal types of items (diaries and correspondence) to the least personal (newspaper clippings).

9 *Order within file folders.* Curators place the earliest items first, so the researcher may follow events as they developed. Archivists, following standard business practice, tend to put the most recent document on top. Naturally, if one does not get down to the individual item level, this point is moot.

10 *Create folder titles that are complete but terse.* Description will be based on information gathered during the arrangement stage. Folder titles are particularly important, since the archivist preparing a finding aid wants to avoid having to look inside folders once again. A concise list of folder titles is as much the end product of a thorough arrangement phase as a neat array of acid-free boxes.

CONCLUSION

Archival arrangement, once mastered, can be a very satisfying activity. Where once there was disorder and an inherently valuable collection inaccessible to researchers, there now is a body of records whose arrangement helps illuminate the significance of the collection. But arrangement is not the end of the story. Without carefully prepared descriptions, the best-arranged collection will remain a historical resource in potential only. The next chapter deals with description as a bridge to the use of archival collections.

NOTES

1. The best sources of further information are Fredric M. Miller, *Arranging and Describing Archives and Manuscripts* (Chicago: Society of American Archivists, 1990); David B. Gracy II, *Archives and Manuscripts: Arrangement and Description* (Chicago: Society of American Archivists, 1977); David W. Carmicheal, *Organizing Archival Records: A Practical Method of Arrangement and Description for Small Archives* (Harrisburg, Penn.: Pennsylvania Historical and Museum Commission, 1993); *Guidelines for Arrangement and Description of Archives and Manuscripts: A Manual for Historical Records Programs in New York State.* New York State Archives and Records Administration (Albany, N.Y.: University of the State of New York, 1991).

2. For recent articles about arrangement, see: Peter Horsman, "Dirty Hands: A New Perspective on the Original Order," *Archives and Manuscripts* 27, no. 1 (May 1999),): 42–53; Bob Krawczyk, "Cross Reference Heaven: The Abandonment of the Fonds as the Primary Level of Arrangement for Ontario Government Records," *Archivaria* 48 (fall 1999): 131–153; Laura Millar, "The Death of the Fonds and the Resurrection of Provenance: Archival Context in Space and Time," *Archivaria* 53 (spring 2002): 1–15.

3. For more on provenance and original order, see Miller, *Arranging and Describing Archives and Manuscripts,* 25–27.

4. Oliver W. Holmes, "Archival Arrangement: Five Different Operations at Five Different Levels," *American Archivist* 27 (January 1964): 21–41.

5. For more information on different types of record groups, see Lewis J. Bellardo and Lynn Lady Bellardo, *A Glossary for Archivists, Manuscript Curators, and Records Managers* (Chicago: Society of American Archivists, 1992).

6. Frank Boles, "Disrespecting Original Order," *American Archivist* 45 (winter 1982): 26–32. (Hebrew National uses the "higher authority" tag line in its television commercials. The company maintains its own standards for hot dog ingredients, rather than take example from the practices of other companies.)

6 DESCRIPTION

Description is the process of establishing administrative and intellectual control over archival holdings through the preparation of finding aids. The archivist takes what he or she has learned about a collection during the arrangement stage and translates it into a collection road map for the archival staff and researchers. Without adequate description, even the most historically valuable and best-arranged collection will remain unused and, hence, worthless from a research perspective.

Finding aids are the descriptive media, published and unpublished, created by an originating office, an archival agency, or a manuscript repository, to establish administrative and intellectual control over holdings. As noted in chapter 4, the accession register is the first finding aid created by an archives or manuscript repository; it is the beginning of a unified descriptive system.

OBJECTIVES OF A DESCRIPTION PROGRAM

As noted above, two objectives drive a description program: (1) to provide administrative control for the repository, and (2) to establish intellectual control for staff and researchers.

ADMINISTRATIVE CONTROL

Finding aids provide administrative control for the repository in a number of ways:

- Finding aids *give the location* of collections on the repository's shelves.
- Finding aids *identify the source,* or provenance, of the collections. This provides an important link in the "chain of custody" should it ever be necessary to document for legal reasons the administrative history of a collection.

- Finding aids *outline the general contents* of collections so that archivists can provide reference services from the moment the collection reaches the repository.

"In 1980, Texas Pacific Land Trust Certificate Number 390 surfaced in Wells Fargo's five-year-old archives in San Francisco. The most famous missing trust certificate in U.S. history was spotted by an alert archivist in a box of documents recovered from a Manhattan subbasement.

"Worth only a few hundred dollars when lost at the turn of the century, the certificate was worth $5 million when found. Wells Fargo's archivists also helped document transactions relating to it. Three medical schools and an elderly woman were the successful claimants to the money, and the company got good publicity for its frontier slogan, 'Wells Fargo never forgets!'"

—Wall Street Journal, January 16, 1989.

INTELLECTUAL CONTROL

Finding aids also establish intellectual control for staff and researchers in the following ways:

- Finding aids sketch the *general nature of a repository's holdings*. Is this the archives of an art museum or a special collection focusing on urban affairs?
- Finding aids identify the *general contents of individual collections*. What are the titles of all the collections and what do they contain?
- As the descriptive system develops, finding aids offer researchers *detailed information about individual collections*. What is in each box of the collection?
- Finding aids *summarize information on a specific topic* available in several collections. For example, what materials does the repository contain that would be useful for genealogical research?

THREE CATEGORIES OF FINDING AIDS

To meet the above objectives, most archives use three categories of finding aids: internal control tools, in-house reference aids, and external reference aids.[1] A well-rounded archival program will prepare at least one finding aid in each category, usually in the order presented below.

INTERNAL CONTROL TOOLS

As soon as a collection reaches a repository, an archivist or manuscript curator creates one or more finding aids. Accession worksheets, location registers, and checklists of various kinds are intended solely for the repository staff. While researchers never see these finding aids, they benefit from them nonetheless. Until other finding aids are created, these internal control documents provide the major access points for the collection.

IN-HOUSE REFERENCE AIDS

As arrangement and description proceed, and as the archival staff becomes familiar with the collections by answering reference requests, they create more detailed finding aids. These still are "in-house," in the sense that archives do not intend to publish and distribute finding aids to the research community. Unlike the previous category of finding aids, however, researchers are permitted to use these reference aids during visits to the repository. The three most common in-house reference aids are container lists, catalogs, and indexes.

Container Lists

Container lists have different names in different repositories: shelf lists, box lists, and folder lists, to name a few. Whatever the name, the finding aid usually takes the form of a columnar listing of box numbers, folder numbers, and folder titles.

During the arrangement stage, the processing archivist takes detailed notes on the final order of the collection. These notes, once typed in columns, become the container lists used by staff and researchers alike. Many repositories use three-ring binders to hold container lists. Some also make electronic versions of container lists available for searching, even if the list is nothing more than a word-processing document.

Since researchers will use the container lists, it is important to eliminate jargon and abbreviations. Some of the jargon comes from the subject matter of the collection; other jargon comes from the abbreviations used by archivists to save themselves time (for example, the abbreviation "mss" for manuscripts). Whatever the source of the jargon, the usefulness of the container list diminishes if a researcher must have an archivist present to translate the jargon.

Catalogs

Many archives use catalogs as in-house reference aids. This is true especially for archives located in library settings. Before wide-scale automation of archives, there probably was no better way to provide subject access to collections than through a card catalog.

Photograph 6.1   A typical card catalog Photograph courtesy of the University of Arizona Library, Special Collections.

Catalogs in an archival setting are used differently from in a traditional library setting. The inventory or register, to be discussed below, is the primary collection-level archival finding aid. Catalog entries, therefore, are not the primary finding aid; rather, they point researchers to relevant collections that are fully described in an inventory.

Indexes

The catalog also can serve as an index to archival collections. However, an index can take a number of other forms. In the electronic environment, it increasingly is a database or even a word-processing document that can be searched by keywords. Later in this chapter I will address in more detail the impact of computers on archival finding aids.

EXTERNAL REFERENCE AIDS

The last step in the description process is the creation of external reference aids. In a modular approach to description, external reference aids build upon internal control tools and in-house reference aids; there is no wasted effort in a well-planned descriptive system. Researchers are likely to encounter the following three external reference aids: calendars, inventories, and guides.

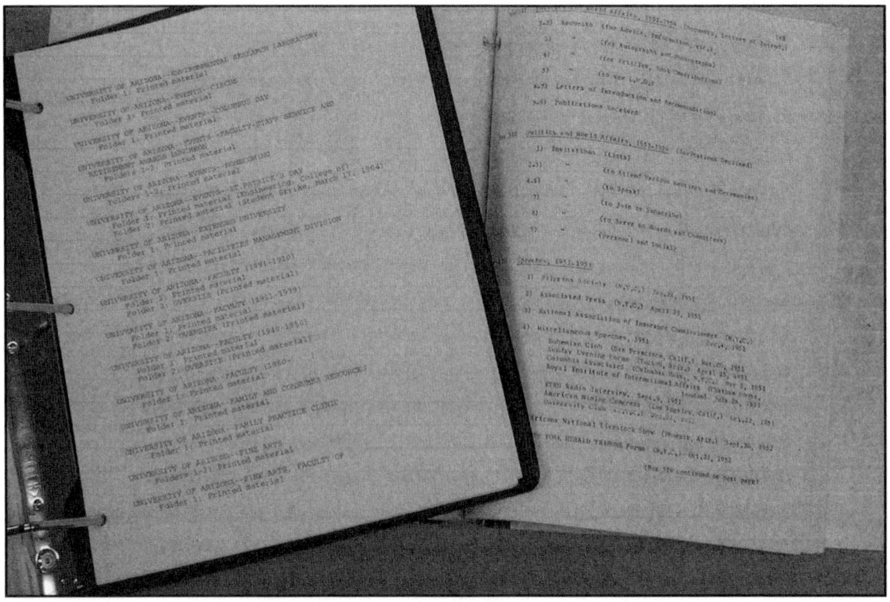

Photograph 6.2   Examples of archival finding aids Photograph courtesy of the University of Arizona Library, Special Collections.

Calendars

Today, calendars exist as archival artifacts. Earlier in the century, archivists created detailed, item-level descriptions of collections. These item-level descriptions were called calendars. It was common to create calendars for collections of the "Great White Fathers" (such as Washington and Madison).

One can imagine the time and effort involved in creating calendars for even a small collection. In some cases, the text in the description of an item may have been longer than the text in the item itself.

Although researchers probably would be pleased if archivists continued to produce calendars, it does not happen very often. Collections are too large to describe at the item level. Furthermore, if an archivist is describing one collection down to the item level, some other archival task is not being accomplished: another collection remains undescribed, fragile originals are not preserved, or the response to a reference request is delayed even longer. What is the best use of archival resources?

Inventories

An inventory (also called a register) is the basic archival finding aid. The National Archives developed the inventory after World War II. (The

National Archives also has "preliminary inventories," some of which have not been finalized in decades and probably never will be.) The Library of Congress has a similar finding aid, which it calls a register.

Inventories or registers provide detailed information about one collection or record group/subgroup. Inventories go beyond *content*, however, to provide *context*. Where did these records come from? What were the circumstances of their creation? How do these records relate to other records? Why are they significant for research now and in the future?

"Kuwait said Monday its looted national archive had not yet been returned by Iraq, despite a claim by Baghdad that it had fulfilled a promise to do so. Iraq said Sunday it had handed over 409 boxes of archives and documents which it took when it occupied its southern neighbor in 1990, triggering the Gulf War. But a Kuwaiti official involved in the U.N.-sponsored handover at the border said that the load did not include 20th century treaties, official diwan (court) documents of the emir and the crown prince that make up the national archive."

—*Reuters*, October 28, 2002.

A typical inventory is comprised of seven sections:

- preface
- introduction
- biographical sketch or agency history
- scope and content note
- series description
- container listing
- index or item listing[2]

Preface. A published inventory usually begins with a preface. A repository will use the same preface for all of its inventories, thereby providing continuity in its finding aids. A preface explains the institution's policies on access and restrictions. It also can provide information about photocopies and microfilm of collections. A well-written preface can be a welcoming experience to a potential researcher.

Introduction. The introduction provides an overview of the contents, provenance, and research strengths of the collection. It relates the contents of the collection to the history of the creating institution or the biography of the creator. It also includes information on restrictions that apply to this specific collection.

The sections of the inventory discussed below are specific to the collection in question. They are also modular; a researcher should be able to learn a little more about the collection in each section. An inventory should make it easier for the researcher to avoid reading a lengthy description of an irrelevant collection.

Biographical Sketch or Agency History. The next section of the inventory expands on the context of the collection. There is a brief overview, in either outline or narrative form, of the principal events in the history of the person or agency during the period encompassed by the collection. This is not a daily record included for its own sake. Rather, it is relevant detail included to illuminate events documented in the collection.

Focus is the key. A biographical sketch in a collection of personal papers might go on at great length about the person's Civil War exploits. In beautiful prose, it could wax eloquent about battle after battle. Is this the proper focus for a collection that does not begin until 1880? It would be better for the biographical sketch to focus on the time period covered by the collection of papers.

Scope and Content Note. The scope and content note discusses in narrative form the extent and depth of the collection—its strengths, weaknesses, and gaps. This and the series description are a dialog between the archivist and the researcher. At a minimum, the scope and content note mentions:

- types of materials
- dates (both "outside dates" that indicate the beginning and end of the collection, and "bulk dates" that let the researcher know where most of the material is concentrated)
- important divisions (usually series)
- significant correspondents and subjects

The best scope and content notes bring out what is hidden—what researchers would otherwise miss, because they did not process the collection. In order to identify these hidden treasures, the archivist must understand researchers and what they need.

Series Description. The series description builds upon the scope and content note. It lists each series in order and reviews the elements within each. In effect, each series description is an abbreviated scope and content note. After the series title, it includes five elements:

- inclusive dates
- quantity
- main types of material
- arrangement
- major subjects

The series description draws heavily upon the notes that the archivist takes while arranging the collection.

Container Listing. At this point in an inventory, the container list prepared as an in-house reference aid usually reappears. If not done previously, the list should be carefully edited for style and format. The container listing serves as a detailed table of contents providing specific information on the filing order and the contents of the collection, usually at the subseries or file unit level. The container list should be consistent and enumerate equivalent filing units.

"He was the Elvis of science. Women pursued him, celebrities sought him out, politicians courted him, and journalists followed him through the streets.

"But, as Einstein was well aware, there was a darker posse on his trail. For many years, the Federal Bureau of Investigation and other agencies spied on him, acting on suspicions as disturbing as a tip that he had been a Russian spy in Berlin; as vague as an unease with his support of civil rights and pacifist socialist causes; as goofy as claims that he was working on a death ray or that he was heading a Communist conspiracy to take over Hollywood.

"The broad outlines of this history have been known since 1993, when…a professor of English at Florida International University in Miami obtained a censored version of Einstein's 1,427-page F.B.I. file and wrote about it in The Nation magazine."

—*New York Times*, May 7, 2002.

Index or Item Listing. All published inventories, and larger unpublished ones, should include an index. As with card catalog entries, it is common for indexes to point the researcher to a particular series. If financing permits, the index may identify the relevant file folder. An item listing is rare, usually only for small and important manuscript collections. Literary collections, for example, may be listed at the item level because of the monetary value of individual documents.

Having outlined the order in which sections of an inventory appear, I must point out that it is very difficult to write the sections in that order. In fact, I usually write the sections of an inventory almost in reverse order. I always find it easier to start with the detail (the container listing) and to summarize and shorten the information for other sections. I write series descriptions and then condense them for the scope and content note. The biographical sketch or agency history also embodies what is fresh in my mind from the container listing. The scope and content note is further condensed for the introduction. I find it easier to edit and condense rather than to wait for a clear and concise introduction to pop into my head.

Figure 6.1 provides examples of sections of an inventory. These sections are considerably shorter than they would be in a typical inventory.

Fig. 6.1	Inventory to a Collection at NFU
	Peconic Bay Yachting Association Records, 1899–1960, 30 Cubic Feet

PREFACE

The North Fork University Department of Archives and Special Collections exists to identify, preserve, and make available records and papers of enduring value. Its mission is twofold:

- University Archives. To collect and maintain records of enduring value created or received by the university and its employees.

- Special Collections. To collect and maintain non-university records and papers that support the academic mission of the university. Areas of collecting interest are specified in a separate Collecting Policy.

The Department serves members of the NFU community and outside researchers. The Department provides access to its collections under a separate policy, which is available from the Director. It is recommended that researchers make an appointment before visiting the Department.

INTRODUCTION

The Records of the Peconic Bay Yachting association were received in the NFU Department of Archives and Special Collections in October 1995. The collection totals 30 cubic feet.

The collection documents the activities of a voluntary organization that was very prominent on the East End of Long Island. The organization's membership changed over time, reflecting the larger changes taking place in society. The collection, therefore, offers research possibilities outside the world of yachting.

The records are open for research without restrictions, under conditions of the Department's access policy. The suggested citation to the collection is: "Peconic Bay Yachting Association Records, North Fork University Department of Archives and Special Collections."

ORGANIZATIONAL HISTORY

The Peconic Bay Yachting Association was incorporated in 1899. Its original membership consisted of wealthy individuals who spent their summer on the East End of Long Island. During the Depression years, the nature of the yachting association changed as fewer people could afford to maintain sailboats. After the Second World War, the Yachting Association became an organization of middle-class individuals who shared a love of sailing. Its focus became families and the recreational use of the waters around Long Island. The organization disbanded in 1960, when many of its members moved west on Long Island to take jobs in the expanding defense industry.

SCOPE AND CONTENT NOTE

The collection is composed of six series: organizational documents, minutes, membership information, correspondence, racing programs, and photographs.

The collection is particularly strong in the membership area. Most of the correspondence is with individual members and reflects the full range of their interests. The Yachting Association prided itself on its involvement with the wider community; this involvement is reflected in the correspondence.

Fig. 6.1 (cont.)

The photographs are another unique source. Photographs of the East End of Long Island, especially during the 1940s and 1950s, are difficult to locate. The photographs in this collection would be useful in any number of historical projects.

SERIES DESCRIPTION

Organizational Documents
This series contains the Certificate of Incorporation as well as a list of charter members and notices of meetings that were published in the newspaper.

Minutes
There is a complete set of minutes of meeting of the association. The minutes for the early part of the century are especially rich in social commentary and include detail on the policy debates that took place at the meetings.

Membership Information
There are complete rosters of members as well as application forms completed by all members. Of particular interest are the essays that prospective members had to write as part of the application process. Applicants were asked to tell why the waters of Long Island were important to them. The essays, therefore, offer a grass roots look at the development of environmental consciousness.

Correspondence
The correspondence series is one of the strengths of the collection. As the largest series, it provides a detailed glimpse into the life of the members of the association. The correspondence documents the changing nature of communication as the membership shifted from wealthy to middle-class individuals. Because of the involvement of the association and its membership in many community activities, this series is an important source for anyone researching the history of the North Fork.

Racing Programs
The racing programs document the ebb and flow of interest in sailing. During the early years of the association, the Vanderbilts and Morgans were regular contestants in association races. Their yachts required large crew in order to race. By the end of the association's life, races were composed of "yachts" with crews of one or two.

Photographs
The members of the association kept very good photographic documentation. There are subseries of member photos and event photos. The event photos, in particular, are a rich historical research and offer beautiful views of Long Island and its environs.

Fig. 6.1 (cont.)

CONTAINER LISTING
[Note: This is an example which does not include the full 30 cubic feet]

Box	Folder	Contents
1	1	Certificate of incorporation, 1899
1	2	Minutes, 1899–1925
1	3	Minutes, 1926–1960
10	1	Membership Rosters, 1899–1960
18	1	Correspondence, 1899–1910
18	2	Correspondence, 1911–1920
25	1	Racing programs, 1945–1960
29	1	Photographs of members, 1950–1960
29	2	Photographs of events, 1954–1960

Guides

The third type of external finding aid is the guide. The reference section of almost any university library probably contains guides to several archival collections. Guides tend to fall into two categories: repository guides and subject guides.

Repository Guides. A repository guide briefly describes and indicates the relationships among holdings, with the record group or collection as the unit of entry. The guide used to be the epitome of archival description. A repository would spend years developing its guide. After lengthy editorial, typesetting, and printing steps, the guide would be issued—already out of date. Modern word processing has dramatically cut the time and effort involved in producing a guide. Other archives will never even issue a guide, relying instead on the World Wide Web to present and update collection information almost at will.

Entries in a repository guide should be similar in style and content, with an equivalent amount of text for each entry. The researcher rightfully expects all collections to be treated equally.

Entries are usually listed in alphabetical order and frequently are numbered. Indexing is keyed to the entry number of the collection or record group. This simplifies the indexing and shortens the final product.

Subject Guides. Subject guides describe the holdings of one or more repositories relating to particular subjects, time periods, or geographical areas. They offer researchers a different perspective on the holdings of the repository.

Many archives found that, beginning in the 1960s, they attracted new types of researchers or familiar researchers asking new questions. Interest in minority studies, women's studies, and gay and lesbian studies has led archivists to review their collections and describe them in new ways. Special subject guides often are the result.

Government archives find that genealogists are now their largest category of researchers. A subject guide can give researchers access to collections likely to contain genealogical information. Chapter 9 discusses in greater depth how to identify and meet the needs of archival researchers.

NETWORKED INFORMATION SYSTEMS

The spread of local and wide area networks has given archivists new opportunities to reach researchers. Archivists now are able to distribute collection-level information via library bibliographic systems. The World Wide Web makes it possible for researchers to review finding aids as well as digitized historical documents. Effective use of these and other networked information systems requires a clear statement of goals and a plan to meet these goals.

Archives exist within a larger context of information resources (for example, libraries, museums, and historic sites). Researchers seeking answers to questions often need to consult multiple sources within this information environment. In the last two decades, archivists have come to realize how important it is that archival records be part of the larger universe. This has involved two principle vehicles, which I discuss in detail below:

- The USMARC Format
- Encoded Archival Description

DESCRIPTIVE STANDARDS AND THE USMARC FORMAT

Beginning in the 1960s, archivists attempted to develop their own information system for sharing collection information. The first successful network for carrying archival data was called SPINDEX. It was a cooperative system initially developed in the largest repositories in the United States. According to Michael Cook, "The experiment ran for 20 years, had considerable success and spread quite widely before it was finally wound up as technologically outmoded." SPINDEX was limited by the technology of the time: input was on punched card or tape, the only output was printed indexes, and the system did not permit online searching.[3]

During this same time, the library community also was moving forward with information exchange. In 1968, the Library of Congress began developing a family of formats for "machine readable cataloging." Drawing upon a century of cataloging experience, each MARC format defined specific fields for use with particular media formats. The MARC formats—now integrated into one format called USMARC—had an important difference from archival automation efforts. MARC was a *format* for the exchange of information rather than being an information *system*. The MARC format simply provides a standard structure for arranging pieces of information—it does not require particular hardware or software.

"A lawsuit filed by a former high-level broker in Salomon's [Salomon Smith Barney's] office in Atlanta indicates that different, ostensibly independent, businesses within Salomon shared significant information about WorldCom employees' investing plans, putting Salomon in a position to profit at the expense of those customers. Notebooks and diaries kept by the broker also contain more examples of how Salomon's star research analyst ... served as a nexus through which privileged information flowed between telecommunications companies and Salomon, and among nominally distinct units within Citigroup.

"The notes also show the potential conflicts of interest that can arise at huge financial conglomerates and the perils that consumers may face when they entrust these companies with control over many aspects of their lives."

—*New York Times*, September 22, 2002.

By the mid-1970s, archivists saw the wisdom of including their records in the large library bibliographic systems then being developed. To do otherwise would relegate archival sources to an information backwater. The Society of American Archivists established a National Information Systems Task Force (NISTF), which developed a "Data Elements Dictionary" for archival materials. This dictionary influenced the design of the original MARC format for archives, MARC AMC. (The last three letters stood for "Archives and Manuscripts Control.") This was one of a number of MARC formats for specialized materials.

In order to use the MARC format, archivists have had to become familiar with various elements of library cataloging: standardized rules, subject classifications, and authority files. The most important of these are the *Anglo-American Cataloging Rules, 2d edition* (commonly called AACR2) and the *Library of Congress Subject Headings* (referred to as LCSH). A 1983 SAA publication, *Archives, Personal Papers and Manuscripts* (called APPM), provided descriptive rules for archives and manuscripts.[4] The revision of *APPM* in 1989 fully merged the data structure to the data content by applying extensive MARC examples for the cataloging rules.[5]

Canadian archivists also have been developing descriptive standards. In 1985, the Bureau of Canadian Archivists published *Toward Descriptive Standards: Report and Recommendations of the Canadian Working Group on Archival Descriptive Standards.* As a direct result, the *Rules for Archival Description (RAD)* were issued over several years beginning in 1990. "While the Canadians chose to focus on descriptive theory and content rather than on data output, and even though *RAD* follows closely the structure of *AACR2,* implementation of *RAD* to this point in time has focused primarily on finding aids, not catalog records."[6]

"Nearly 125 years after his death, residents can see more clearly than ever the man credited with being the first permanent white settler in the area that became Oshkosh.

"Working a combination of luck, timing and sleuthing, Oshkosh Public Museum archivist Scott Cross this month unearthed only the second known photograph of Webster Stanley, who came to Oshkosh from Ohio in 1836.

"The rare photograph has long been part of the museum's collection of 30,000 photographs, but until two weeks ago it was incorrectly identified ....

"'That's one of the neat things about being an archivist: You get to be a detective,' Cross said. 'These had been sitting here since 1930 and nobody really knew who it was. It's an earlier portrait of him and a much better photograph, too.'"

—*Post-Crescent*, April 28, 2002.

Archival repositories can use the USMARC format whether or not they have a computer, since it provides a standard set of information elements to be gathered on each collection. The format makes the most sense, however, if an archives plans to exchange information via national databases.

The USMARC format contains numbered "fields" that one uses in describing a collection. These fields are similar to the elements of archival finding aids previously discussed in this chapter. Figure 6.2 lists some of the most important fields for archival description. Learning to use these fields takes time and practice. Luckily, archival professional organizations regularly offer workshops in descriptive standards and the USMARC format.

Fig. 6.2 Selected USMARC Fields for Archival Description	
Field Name	**Field Number**
Personal name	100
Corporate name	110
Title statement	245a,b
Inclusive dates	245f
Bulk dates	245g
Physical description (volume)	300
Arrangement/organization	351
Biographical/historical note	545
Scope and content note	520
Restrictions on access	506
Terms governing use	540
Provenance	561
Subject added entry–topical term	650
Subject added entry–geographical	651
Personal name as added entry	700
Corporate name as added entry	710
Personal name as subject	600
Corporate name as subject	610

This is an exciting time for archival description. Generations of archivists had maintained that archival collections were so specialized that descriptive standards could not possibly apply. The current generation has proven otherwise.

THE INTERNET AND ENCODED ARCHIVAL DESCRIPTION

At the same time that archivists became part of the standardized information environment known as the library bibliographic utility, they also became part of the still chaotic information environment known as the Internet and World Wide Web.

The Internet had its roots in the U.S. Department of Defense. The military wanted to develop a computer network that was sufficiently distributed to survive an attack, either foreign or domestic. The original network was called ARPANET, after the Advanced Research Projects Agency, the research and development arm of the Department of Defense. The first two ARPANET sites were linked in late 1969.[7]

The World Wide Web was created at CERN, the European particle Physics laboratory in Switzerland. As explained by Eric Gagnon:

> Originally designed as a standardized method to help physicists organize and access their research data for international distribution online, the World Wide Web standards are essentially a text coding, or "markup" method, where selected elements in a text file, such as article headlines, subheads, images, and important words highlighted in the body of a text file can, by the insertion of special, bracketed codes (called HTML, or Hyper Text Markup Language codes), be turned into hotlinks that are easily and instantly accessible by anyone with a Web browser.[8]

Everyone, from children to computer experts, has discovered the World Wide Web, using it to "surf the net" on a regular basis. Archives are rushing to create Web pages and link them to other Internet sites, so as not to be left out of the surf.

Archivists are using the World Wide Web as part of their descriptive programs. They are providing information about their general holdings as well as their specific collections. The problem of out-of-date guides may be a thing of the past when finding aids can be revised and made available to millions at the blink of an eye.[9]

An approach that holds great promise is Encoded Archival Description (EAD)—the application of publishing standards to electronic finding aids. The underlying standard is called Standard Generalized Markup Language (SGML). SGML is an international standard (ISO 8879), which prescribes the rules used to define the logical structure of a class of documents. Those rules are expressed in a Document Type Definition (DTD) that describes the structural components of a type of document, how each component relates to the others, and how each is tagged. Jill Tatem defines tags as "codes inserted in digital documents to identify these components so that software can display, search, and navigate the document in ways not possible if the document's structure is not made explicit, i.e., if the document is simply a stream of characters or words."[10]

Encoded Archival Description is a Document Type Definition for archival inventories or registers. EAD's development began in 1993 at the University of California at Berkeley and proceeded through a series of reviews and modifications leading to the release of version 1.0 in the fall of 1998.[11]

In developing EAD, the goal was to go beyond just creating a USMARC record for each collection by offering more extensive electronic access points for researchers. As noted above, USMARC is used to create *cataloging records* while EAD is used for accessing the *full text* of inventories. MARC was determined to be unsuitable for inventories for three reasons:

- It was limited in length. (There are restrictions on the number of characters per record).
- It did not accommodate hierarchical structures, an essential for archival finding aids.
- The MARC user community was seen as too small and under-funded to support state-of-the-art hardware and software development.

SGML had a number of advantages when compared to MARC: there are unlimited levels of hierarchical structure, no size limitations, and a potentially large user community.[12]

In choosing SGML for EAD in 1993, the developers were consciously getting "ahead of the curve" with software. Why did they not just use HTML, the ubiquitous standard for the World Wide Web? The problem with HTML is that it is designed to provide only *procedural* encoding to facilitate improved layout and appearance; the intellectual *structure or content* of documents cannot be encoded meaningfully in HTML.[13]

Another option for EAD developers was to adopt a more general SGML scheme called the Text Encoding Initiative. This is an international cooperative effort to develop an SGML Document Type Definition for encoding literary and other texts as objects of study. Ultimately, EAD's developers concluded that the Text Encoding Initiative would not work for finding aids; nevertheless, EAD was made as consistent with TEI as possible.[14]

Implementing EAD in an archival repository usually involves three steps:

- converting old finding aids
- creating new finding aids
- publishing new finding aids on the Web[15]

Converting Old Finding Aids

Unfortunately, few archives can move directly from their existing finding aids into the world of EAD. As Dennis Meissner has noted, "before we try to convert our finding aids into EAD-encoded documents we ought to make certain that those finding aids are as well thought out as possible in terms of both their structure and their content." A number of common problems plague existing finding aids:

- Information elements are not clearly identified. This makes it difficult to determine where to place the EAD tags.

- Information elements are not optimally arranged. Even if all of the elements are present, they may be in an order that will make research more difficult.

- There can be inconsistent levels of description. Various series may be described to different levels. This inconsistency is a problem when converting to EAD.

- User instructions may be lacking. The finding aid may not help the researcher to find his or her way through the finding aid or collection.[16]

EAD need not be used only for creating Internet finding aids. EAD's stable yet flexible hierarchical structure is equally applicable to finding aids in any format. It can help in delivering intelligible, useful information about our collections to researchers.[17]

"An old wood box found in an attic of the Legislative Building might be the missing, second time capsule that was packed with historical materials but never buried during the state's territorial centennial celebration in 1953.

"A state research archivist…turned up a folder of materials Thursday that appears to identify the mysterious wooden box crews found as they cleaned the Capitol to prepare for a $100 million renovation."

—*The Olympian*, July 26, 2002

Creating New Finding Aids

Once an archivist decides to enter the world of EAD, she or he has four options for creating finding aids: text editors and word processors, native SGML/XML editors, text converters, and databases. Figure 6.3 summarizes these four options and their advantages and disadvantages.[18]

Fig. 6.3 Options for Creating EAD Finding Aids			
Option	**Description**	**Advantages**	**Disadvantages**
Text editors and word processors	Since SGML documents exist as simple text files, it is possible to key an EAD finding aid using any software that can output a document in ASCII format.	• low cost • ready availability • user familiarity	• no built-in knowledge of EAD DTD, hence no way to verify conformance with it
Native SGML/XML editors	Software packages designed specifically for authoring SGML/XML documents	• can validate a document during authoring • prompts and pull-down menus help in selecting elements and assigning attributes	• some knowledge of the DTD is required • software is not "commodity priced"
Text converters	Transform existing machine-readable text from its original format into an encoded document that conforms to a particular DTD	• leverages existing files • avoids the cost of a new suite of office software • eliminates the time to learn the new software	• source documents must be carefully formatted in advance to facilitate subsequent conversion • manual intervention may be required after conversion
Databases	Some archives store descriptive information in off-the-shelf relational database management software (DBMS).	• supports existing institutional investment in DBMS • permits exchange of data with other DBMS systems	• highly specialized programming may be needed • conversion of a "flat" database structure fails to exploit EAD's ability to express archival hierarchies

When EAD was in its early stages, encoding documents was a formidable task. While encoding finding aids in the EAD DTD has become much easier in recent years, James M. Roth still offers an important caveat: "Archivists implementing and delivering EAD-structured finding aids must give careful consideration to encoding activity, given its costs, steep learning curve, and little user evaluation and education." [19] As with most of the activities presented in *Practical Archives,* new initiatives must be balanced with other priorities of the institutions.[20]

Fig. 6.4 Example of an EAD-Encoded Document[21]

Container List

Container Nos.	*Contents*

LITERARY FILE, 1943-70, n.d.

Correspondence, manuscript drafts, royalty statements, printed matter, notes, outlines, research material, screenplays, and miscellaneous items and enclosures relating to books and short stories by Jackson. Organized alphabetically by type of material and arranged alphabetically by title or topic therein. Publication dates of books are given in parentheses.

46	Bibliographies and publishing lists, 1951-66
	Books
	Raising Demons (1957)
	Reviews, 1956-57, n.d.
	Royalty statements, 1956-69
47	*The Road Through the Wall* (1948), 1947-70, n.d.
	Short stories and other writings
	"The Lottery"
	Dramatic adaptations
	Correspondence, 1949-53, 1967-70
	Scripts and screenplays, n.d.
	Royalty statements, 1950-53, 1964-70
	"Lover's Meeting," n.d.

Tagged Example

```
<dsc type="combined"><head>Container List</head><thead><row valign="top"><entry colname="1">Container
Nos.</entry><entry colname="2">Contents</entry></row></thead>

<c01 level="series"><did><unittitle>Literary File, <unitdate>1943-70, n.d.</unitdate></unittitle></did>
<scopecontent><p>Correspondence, manuscript drafts, royalty statements, printed matter, notes, outlines,
research material, screenplays, and miscellaneous items and enclosures relating to books and short stories by
Jackson.</p><arrangement><p>Organized alphabetically by type of material and arranged alphabetically by title
or topic therein.  Publication dates of books are given in parentheses.</p></arrangement></scopecontent>

    <c02><did><container>46</container><unittitle>Bibliographies and publishing lists,
    1951-66</unittitle></did></c02>
    <c02><did><unittitle>Books</unittitle></did>
        <c03><did><unittitle><title render="italic">Raising Demons</title> (1957) </unittitle></did>
            <c04><did><unittitle>Reviews, 1956-57, n.d.</unittitle></did></c04>
            <c04><did><unittitle>Royalty statements, 1956-69</unittitle></did></c04></c03>
        <c03><did><container>47</container><unittitle><title render="italic">The Road Through the Wall</title>
        (1948), 1947-70, n.d.</unittitle></did></c03></c02>
    <c02><did><unittitle>Short stories and other writings</unittitle></did>
        <c03><did><unittitle><title render="quoted">The Lottery</title></unittitle> </did>
            <c04><did><unittitle>Dramatic adaptations</unittitle></did>
                <c05><did><unittitle>Correspondence, 1949-53, 1967-70</unittitle> </did></c05>
                <c05><did><unittitle>Scripts and screenplays, n.d.</unittitle> </did></c05></c04>
            <c04><did><unittitle>Royalty statements, 1950-53, 1964-70</unittitle> </did></c04></c03>
        <c03><did><unittitle><title render="quoted">Lover's Meeting,</title> n.d.
        </unittitle></did></c03></c02></c01> ... </dsc>
```

Publishing New Finding Aids on the Web

Once EAD finding aids are encoded, the archivist will need to work with the institution's information technology staff to publish the finding aids on the Web. Decisions will need to be made in at least three areas:

- choice of server (dedicated to EAD or shared with other services?)
- location and maintenance of servers (in IT or the archives?)
- security and access considerations (restricted to employees or open to anyone?)

The publishing of finding aids remains and area of concern for many archivists. According to Roth: After a few years of implementing the EAD structure and delivering EAD finding aids through various deployment methods, archivists have found that several problems or challenges remain. These include a steep learning curve for the entire EAD process, not having enough resources in the form of time and staff, and, most especially, difficulty with deployment software. While archivists are currently employing a variety of deployment methods, there has yet to be developed a single ideal deployment method. [22]

Many people hope that the widespread adoption of Extensible Markup Language (XML) will help with deployment. The Worldwide Web Consortium adopted XML as a Web standard in 1998. In order to be Web-deliverable, XML simplified some of SGML's complexities. Since EAD included few of these complexities, it was easily made XML-compliant. As researchers upgrade to XML-compliant Web browsers, they will no longer need separate software to read EAD and other SGML files. This will help bring EAD documents into the Web mainstream. [23]

EAD and the Future

Most of the EAD developers and early adopters were from the academic research library environment. Grant funding also heavily supported their work. EAD now must make the transition to the wider archival community. According to Jill Tatem, "Archives that primarily serve managers of parent institutions are unlikely to be swayed to EAD adoption by an emphasis on service to academic scholars."[24] For these administrators to be convinced, EAD will have to demonstrate sufficient return on the institution's investment of staff and other resources.

Up to this point, there have been few, if any, evaluation studies of EAD, making it difficult to assess the effectiveness of EAD. According to Roth, "Perhaps most troublesome is that few institutions are developing formal evaluations for monitoring the effectiveness of EAD, and, in fact, there is very little evaluation being conducted. Thus, archivists are basing their perceptions regarding end-user utilization of EAD finding aids on very little quantitative or systematic qualitative data." The meager information that has been gathered suggests that end-users do not care about the structure and format of the finding aids—they just are interested in the content.[25]

Jill Tatem has concluded that EAD's widespread adoption by archivists will depend upon two factors:

- *Changing current negative perceptions about EAD's complexity.* Advances in authoring and browsing software should address this.
- *Demonstrating EAD's advantages over other technologies for creating and delivering finding aids.* This will require user-centered research focusing on evaluating the effectiveness of EAD finding aids.[26]

The next few years will be crucial for seeing if Encoded Archival Description can live up to its promise of improving the creation of and access to archival finding aids.

FIVE CHARACTERISTICS OF A GOOD FINDING AID

Whatever form they take—whether on the World Wide Web or in a three-ring binder—good finding aids tend to share certain features. A good finding aid is

1. *Intended for the researcher,* not for the edification of the archivist (who may be a frustrated researcher). The focus should be on *use by others*, rather than on showcasing the literary abilities of the archivist. First and foremost, a finding aid must help the researcher to *find* materials.
2. *Objective about the collection.* Finding aids should have a professional tone. Whether one is describing a collection from the NAACP or the Ku Klux Klan, an archivist's personal sentiments should not cloud the description.
3. *Aware of the needs of a wide variety of researchers.* An archivist who knows the interests of current and

potential researchers can prepare finding aids useful to many people. A good finding aid anticipates how various researchers will approach the collection.

4. *Clear, concise, and consistent.* It avoids jargon and terms that make the finding aid inaccessible to researchers. There is a uniform level of description for each entry, thereby establishing consistency.

5. *Efficient.* It presents the maximum usable information in a minimum of space. It is easy for the researcher to scan: it uses headings, indentations, skipped lines, and an appropriate mix of fonts, to move the researcher through the finding aid. The researcher should be able to grasp the essence of the collection at a glance, and know where else to turn for more information.

FORGING A DESCRIPTIVE SYSTEM: FINAL CONSIDERATIONS

As with any system, a descriptive system takes planning. The archivist must define needs, analyze resources, and determine priorities in order to develop a realistic plan. Staff size and budget will affect the description program one can design.

Description follows (and proceeds along) the five levels of arrangement identified by Holmes and discussed in chapter 5. A descriptive system should provide basic bibliographic control. It is better to describe all collections *to the same level* than to focus all effort on one collection. The latter approach will result in a skewed descriptive program. One approach is first to describe everything at the collection/record group level. After this, one can establish priorities for further description. The staff can then proceed through the series level and the file unit level, if resources permit.

Efficient archivists take a "building block" approach to their descriptive system. There is no wasted effort; work on one finding aid is carried over to the next one. For example, in-house reference aids are the basis for published finding aids. Also, each section of an inventory builds upon the previous section. This can only happen if the system is planned from the very beginning rather than growing up like Topsy.[27]

A good descriptive program is also flexible. It allows the archivist to expand and emphasize different information as required. But the inventory remains the *key*; everything else builds upon it.

A final note concerning computers: as countless organizations have learned, computers are not magic boxes that solve all problems. I still remember the telephone call I received from a newly appointed archivist. He wanted to know which computer hardware and software to buy, as though this would solve everything. I talked at length about a descriptive program and the role of computers in it. We discussed staff and other resources that would be available for description. Only in this context could I begin to offer advice about automation. As a researcher, I still would prefer a well-thought-out manual system to a poorly designed automated one. The proof of the finding aid is in the finding.

NOTES

1. This distinction comes from David B. Gracy II, *Archives and Manuscripts: Arrangement and Description* (Chicago: Society of American Archivists, 1977).

2. The best source on inventories remains Gracy, *Archives and Manuscripts*. See also Fredric M. Miller, *Arranging and Describing Archives and Manuscripts* (Chicago: Society of American Archivists, 1990).

3. Michael Cook, *Information Management and Archival Data* (London: Library Association Publishing, 1993), 161.

4. See Steven L. Hensen, *Archives, Personal Papers, and Manuscripts: A Cataloging Manual for Archival Repositories, Historical Societies, and Manuscript Libraries*, 2d ed. (Chicago: Society of American Archivists, 1989); *Anglo-American Cataloging Rules*, 2d ed. (Chicago: American Library Association, 1988); Library of Congress, Subject Cataloging Division, *Library of Congress Subject Headings*, 10th ed. (Washington, D.C.: Library of Congress, 1986).

5. *Archives, Personal Papers, and Manuscripts (APPM)* "has been widely accepted by the American archival community as the standard for the cataloging of archives and manuscripts - especially in an automated environment." Steven L. Hensen, "'NISTF II' and EAD: The Evolution of Archival Description," *American Archivist* 60, no. 3 (summer 1997): 288.

6. Kris Kiesling, "EAD as an Archival Descriptive Standard," *American Archivist* 60, no. 3 (summer 1997): 345-46.

7. Peter H. Salus, *Casting the Net: From ARPANET to Internet and Beyond* (New York: Addison-Wesley, 1995).

8. Eric Gagnon, ed., *What's on the Web* (Fairfax, Va.: Internet Media Corp., 1995), 6.

9. For some examples, see: Burt Altman and John R. Nemmers. "The Usability of On-Line Archival Resources: The POLARIS Project

Finding Aid," *American Archivist* 64, no. 1 (spring/summer 2001): 121-31; Kathleen Feeney, "Retrieval of Archival Finding Aids Using World-Wide-Web Search Engines" *American Archivist* 62, no. 2 (fall 1999): 206-28; Helen R Tibbo and Lokman I. Meho, "Finding Finding Aids on the World Wide Web," *American Archivist* 64, no. 1 (spring/summer 2001): 61-78.

10. Jill Tatem, "EAD: Obstacles to Implementation, Opportunities for Understanding," *Archival Issues* 23, no. 2 (1998): 156. Jackie Dooley asks and answers one of the basic questions: "Why has the development of EAD captured the attention and enthusiasm of so many archivists, librarians, software designers, and other information professionals throughout the world? Within the U.S. archival community, surely this can be attributed to the inherent appeal of a *standard* for structuring and automating finding aids. Despite a somewhat traditional penchant within the profession for the development of unique solutions to common problems (and a concomitant resistance to various types of standardization), many archivists instinctively are attracted to a technique that promises to reduce the need to reinvent the finding aid wheel in every repository, or to rekey or edit data every time a software upgrade is necessary, and which also demonstrates clear potential to radically improve access to archival materials by facilitating structured access via the Internet." Jackie M. Dooley, "Introduction-Encoded Archival Description: Context and Theory." *American Archivist* 60, no. 3 (summer 1997): 264.

11. The basic "version 1.0" EAD documents are: Encoded Archival Description Working Group of the Society of American Archivists and the Network Development and MARC Standards Office of the Library of Congress, *Encoded Archival Description Tag Library, Version 1.0* (Chicago: Society of American Archivists, 1988). Encoded Archival Description Working Group of the Society of American Archivists, *Encoded Archival Description Application Guidelines, Version 1.0* (Chicago: Society of American Archivists, 1989).

12. James M. Roth, "Serving Up EAD: An Exploratory Study on the Deployment and Utilization of Encoded Archival Description Finding Aids," *American Archivist* 64, no. 2 (fall/winter 2001): 216-17. "MARC AMC provided a *data structure standard* for sharing cataloging information about archival and manuscript holdings, enabling their integration with library bibliographic data in online catalogs. The first edition of APPM, published at roughly the same time (1983), provided a companion *data content standard* for that same cataloging information" (*EAD Application Guidelines*, 4-5). According to Daniel Pitti, the initial developer of EAD: "The generalized descriptions found in AMC records can only lead a researcher to a collection which may have individual relevant items. The researcher must next consult the assortment of inventories, registers, indexes, and guides, generally

referred to as finding aids, with which libraries and archives have achieved administrative and intellectual control of archival materials in the form of in-depth, detailed descriptions of their collections" (Daniel V. Pitti, "Encoded Archival Description: The Development of an Encoding Standard for Archival Finding Aids," *American Archivist* 60, no. 3 [Summer 1997]: 272. For more on the advantages of SGML, see Steven J. DeRose, "Navigation, Access, and Control Using Structured Information." *American Archivist* 60, no. 3 (summer 1997): 308-9.

13. *EAD Application Guidelines*, 6; Pitti, "EAD," 277.

14. *EAD Application Guidelines*, 8.

15. *EAD Application Guidelines*, 249-52. For a series of case studies on implementing EAD, see the special issue of the *American Archivist* 60, no. 4 (fall 1997).

16. Dennis Meissner, "First Things First: Reengineering Finding Aids for Implementation of EAD." *American Archivist* 60, no. 4 (fall 1997): 373.

17. *EAD Application Guidelines*, v.

18. *EAD Application Guidelines*, 126-32.

19. Roth, "Serving Up EAD," 215.

20. Since EAD is only one descriptive option, some archivists "reuse" the tags in other information systems. To facilitate this, "crosswalks" have been developed to map fields among EAD, USMARC, and the Dublin Core metadata initiative. See *EAD Application Guidelines*, 235-42.

21. Janice E. Ruth, "Encoded Archival Description: A Structural Overview," *American Archivist* 60, no. 3 (summer 1997): 326.

22. Roth, "Serving Up EAD," 233.

23. *EAD Application Guidelines*, 10.

24. Tatem, "Obstacles," 161.

25. Roth, "Serving Up EAD," 234.

26. Tatem, "Obstacles," 155. Much of the archival literature assumes that EAD finding aids will be superior. For example: "Such distribution [of finding aids via the World Wide Web] enables finding aids to be searched with an effectiveness and thoroughness that was all but unthinkable a mere five years ago. Moreover, EAD enables digitized images of archival materials to be embedded in or linked to their corresponding finding aids, enabling a user to navigate successively more detailed layers of information." *EAD Application Guidelines*, v.

27. See Lydia Lucas, "Efficient Finding Aids: Developing a System for Control of Archives and Manuscripts," *American Archivist* 41 (winter 1981): 21-26.

7 PRESERVATION

When the general public thinks about archives (assuming they do think about archives at all), they generally equate archives with preservation. Unfortunately, the public often believes that "preservation" can take place in any location, even substandard ones. This is illustrated by the fact that it is almost impossible to find an article about archives without the word "dusty" preceding it.

As professionals use the term, preservation encompasses a wide variety of interrelated activities designed to prolong the usable life of archives and manuscripts. It is a broad term that covers protection, stabilization, and treatment of documents.[1] Preservation is one of the three core functions of the archivist, the other two being identification and use.[2]

Most preservation programs in small archives take a phased approach that emphasizes broad stabilizing actions to protect a repository's entire holdings, rather than concentrating resources solely on item-level treatment. Such an approach includes:

- understanding the nature of the preservation problem
- conducting preservation surveys to establish priorities
- controlling the storage environment
- planning for disasters
- performing holdings maintenance
- treating selected materials[3]

Except for disaster planning, which is covered fully in chapter 8, each of these activities is discussed below. This chapter deals with records on paper. Chapter 10 discusses the specific challenges posed by digital records, while chapter 11 covers audiovisual records in detail.

THE PRESERVATION PROBLEM

Before trying to address preservation problems, it is necessary to understand the nature of the materials in question and the causes of deterioration. Because most archival collections, by volume, consist of paper, the fragile nature of this medium is a major problem for archivists, as well as librarians. The materials and processes used to produce modern papers exacerbate this problem. The title of a popular article summarized the all-too-common sequence of events: pulp to paper, paper to dust.[4]

Modern paper, it turns out, contains the seeds of its own destruction; the very production of paper introduces elements, particularly sources of acid, which lead to physical deterioration. While raised consciousness bodes well for future paper production, archivists are left with almost one hundred years of deteriorating paper.[5]

Photograph 7.1 Bound volumes showing signs of deterioration. Photograph courtesy of the Saint Benedict Center, Sisters of Saint Benedict of Madison, Wisconsin, Inc.

First of all, just what is paper? It is a thin, flat sheet composed of fibers that have been reduced to pulp, suspended in water, and then matted. Paper is usually made of cellulose fibers, the lightweight material that forms the cell walls of plants. Cellulose fibers dissolve—breaking into shorter and shorter strands—when they come into contact with acid; hence, the problem with modern papers.

Paper was introduced into Europe from China in the twelfth century. It still is made the same basic way:

- Plant matter is beaten with water to produce a pulp.
- The pulp is shaped in a mold with a wire screen at

the bottom. It is this wire screen that produces a watermark.

• Water is drained off the mold and squeezed out of the paper.

• The paper is sized (coated) to prevent the absorption of water. Unsized paper acts like blotting paper or a paper towel—ink is absorbed into and spread throughout the fibers.[6]

"Rummaging through an old box of papers in your grandparents' attic, you come across an invitation to the 1953 inauguration of Dwight David Eisenhower and his not-yet disgraced running mate, Richard Milhous Nixon.

"Or browsing in a neighborhood antiques shop you spy a single ticket dated March 5, 1868, admitting the bearer to the U.S. Capitol where, in the Senate chamber, lawmakers debated whether to impeach President Andrew Johnson. (The effort failed.)…

"These objects are not merely pieces of American history. To collectors, curators and archivists, each is a bit of political 'ephemera,' from the Greek '*ephemeros*' meaning 'lasting a day' or 'daily.'"

—Washington *Post,* June 13, 2002.

If paper is still produced the same basic way, why are we having problems now? Until the nineteenth century, paper was made from cotton and flax plants, obtained from rags. These plants had long, strong fibers. The paper also was sized by hand—dipping it sheet by sheet in a gelatin or animal glue.

After 1840, trees replaced rags as the principal raw material for paper. Wood pulp was cheaper than rags and more widely available. Wood's cellulose fibers, however, are relatively short and contain impurities. In particular, lignin, which holds the cellulose fibers together, comprises 25 percent of most wood. When exposed to air, lignin's chemical structure changes: it turns brown and gives off acid.

To complicate matters further, sizing changed after 1836. Mass producers of paper began to add resin from pine trees while the paper was being beaten. It no longer was necessary to dip one sheet at a time. But in order to make the resin adhere to the pulp, manufacturers added alum (potassium aluminum sulphate). When alum comes into contact with moisture, it forms sulfuric acid, which attacks the cellulose fiber in pulp paper. Most paper even today has alum-resin sizing. Such paper will only last ten to fifty years, as opposed to the hundreds of years for handmade paper.

Figure 7.1 summarizes the slow and subtle forms of deterioration to which paper and other media are susceptible.

Fig. 7.1 Forms of Deterioration[7]

Form of Deterioration	Description	How Controlled
Inherent chemical	The material itself undergoes the reactions of decay. It does not need external pollutants or light; examples are: brittleness, discoloration, and fading.	Control rate of deterioration by controlling temperature and relative humidity in the storage environment.
Pollutant-induced	Since pollutants are external to objects, they are not always present. Pollutants can affect both organic and inorganic materials.	Use air purification systems and protective enclosures.
Light-induced	Light is a form of energy that breaks chemical bonds, thus causing decay. Damage depends on a number of factors: nature of the object, relative humidity, kind of light, intensity, and duration.	Keep illumination intensities down and store objects in dark places.
Biological	Primarily affect organic materials. Divided into three categories: bacterial, fungal, and insect-related. Involve a complex set of factors: temperature, relative humidity, light, ventilation, and housekeeping practices.	Tailor control measures to the particular circumstances of each collection.
Physical	Mechanical forms of deterioration like warping, cracking, or separation of layers. Changes in moisture content cause different materials to swell or shrink at different rates.	Keep relative humidity stable.

Preservation problems are compounded by the increasing volume of paper. It has been estimated that every four months, the federal government produces a stack of records equal to all those produced in the 124 years between George Washington and Woodrow Wilson. Paper still makes up most of this volume.[8] The impermanence of the physical medium of paper, combined with the huge volume of records stored on it, has even led some archivists to question the entire idea of preservation.[9] To know what is achievable within a particular institution requires accurate information about the scope of the preservation problem.

PRESERVATION SURVEYS

Planning even a modest preservation program begins with information about the situation as it now exists. Without this information, how can an archivist possibly determine the best use of limited preservation resources? For this planning to be effective, surveys or other data collection must happen at both the repository and collection levels.

"The archives of Radio Free Europe are to move to Budapest's Central European University. The archives' extensive collection of *samizdat* writings—the typed or hand-copied manuscripts of banned authors and dissidents that were circulated underground—needs the immediate attention of preservationists. Many of the documents are brittle or fading. 'A lot of the stuff only had 10 or 15 years left before it would have been un-photographable. People were writing with poor ink on poor-quality, high-acid paper, which was then circulated hand-to-hand, so the materials are very fragile. Part of our goal in this project is to save this world treasure and make it available to the citizens who produced it.'"

—*Chronicle of Higher Education,* November 2, 1994.

REPOSITORY LEVEL

Information gathered at the repository level is used to plan an integrated preservation program. It leads to policies and procedures that influence preservation of all the collections. This information also focuses attention on environmental shortcomings in storage and other areas.

The archivist should gather information about

- fire detection, alert, and suppression systems (such as sprinklers)
- water detection and alert systems
- environmental conditions in storage, processing, and reference areas
- recurring problems such as leaks or floods
- problems with insects or other infestations
- housing and storage equipment for records
- exhibition practices
- level of staff familiarity with preservation practices[10]

Once the information is gathered, it may be necessary to secure outside assistance with such technical areas as environmental monitoring and fire protection. Any expert advice, however, should be used in the context of the overall archival program. As noted throughout this book, balancing competing demands for resources is one of the toughest tasks facing an archivist.

COLLECTION LEVEL

Preservation planning cannot remain solely at the repository level. The archivist must look at individual collections, assess their preservation needs, and plan for the meeting of those needs within the overall context of the institution's budget.

An institution new to preservation planning will have a backlog of collections that need assessing. Even conducting the collection-level survey may be a daunting task in such a situation.

The best way to make the task less daunting is by using a form designed for the purpose. The form systematizes the collection of *necessary* information—and nothing more. Archivists are always tempted

---

"When Amy Braitsch thinks of Houston, she likely thinks of vinegar. And machine parts. And a black-and-white city of balloon-tired roadsters and crammed downtown sidewalks filled with people heading to the latest Clark Gable film.

"And then she probably thinks of vinegar again.

"Braitsch, a recent University of Texas graduate, spent much of last spring in a small room in Austin, tediously opening boxes and boxes filled with envelopes, envelopes that were filled with aging photographic negatives.

"Like all such negatives that are kept in less-than-optimal conditions, the film had long ago begun to deteriorate, shrinking and becoming brittle. As it did so, the film produced an acid that evaporates into the air with a sharp vinegar odor."

—Houston *Press,* May 23, 2002.

---

to collect every conceivable bit of information an archives may ever need. This presupposes that the archivist can define at this stage of program development all the preservation program possibilities for the future. Even if this were possible, such detail still might not be desirable, because of the time and expense it adds to the collection-level survey.

The advice, then, is: gather only information necessary for program planning at the present time. In addition, using closed-ended questions (in which the responses are predefined and one need only check or circle the answer) is faster than using open-ended questions (in which response choices are not provided). The goal is to gather the information as quickly as possible and move on to planning and program development.

Figure 7.2 presents some of the fields typically found on a collection-level survey form.

Fig. 7.2 Fields on a Collection Level Survey Form[11]	
Field	**Common Responses**
Primary housing	File drawer, records center carton, archives box
Secondary housing	File folders, envelopes, ring binders
Types of records	Loose papers, bound volumes, index cards, photographs, sound recordings, videotapes, electronic media
Condition of records	Folded, rolled, brittle, torn, molded, water damaged, taped, dirty
Special concerns	Impermanent media, faint text or images, colored media, use of fasteners, artifact value (seals, etc.)
Recommendations	Re-housing, duplication, treatment
Preservation priority	High, medium, low, none

If preservation is to become an integral part of an archival program, each collection should have a preservation assessment at the time of accessioning. This evaluation can be done by adding one or more fields to the accession form to gather some of the same information obtained in the collection-level survey described above. Preservation planning, as with all types of planning, is best done as an ongoing activity rather than according to the "locust model"—planning only once every seven years.

THE STORAGE ENVIRONMENT

In the film *The Graduate*, the youthful character played by Dustin Hoffman is pulled aside by an older man, who shares the one word that is the key to Hoffman's future: "plastics." If the relative had been an archivist, however, he would have whispered: "environment." The proper environment will prolong the life of the collections and reduce the repair and restoration activities the archives must undertake. In fact, without a proper environment, restoration activities are a waste of time and money. Why place a restored item back in an environment where it will deteriorate again?

First, it is necessary to determine as precisely as possible the environmental conditions. I recall a visit to a new colleague in the profession who gave me a tour of the archives he recently inherited. Although it was July, his facility was comfortably air-conditioned. I asked him if it was like this all the time. He responded that this was the temperature when he arrived in the morning, so he assumed the answer was "yes." At my suggestion he purchased a hygrothermograph, a device used to measure and record both relative humidity and temperature. The archivist was surprised to learn that the air-conditioning was turned off every evening at six o'clock and not reactivated until seven o'clock the next morning. On weekends, the air-conditioning was off from Friday night until Monday morning. In the interim, the hygrothermograph documented that the records were nice and toasty. Once the nature of the problem was understood (rather than assumed) it became possible to design appropriate environmental controls.[12]

An archivist should look at the following specific aspects of the storage environment:

- temperature
- relative humidity
- air quality
- light
- biological agents
- holdings maintenance practices

"The first Australian cricket team to embarrass England's bowlers and batsmen are the subject of a rediscovered archive expected to fetch £50,000 when it is auctioned in Melbourne this month.

"The team were their country's unsung heroes, an almost all-Aboriginal team who were originally brought to England in 1868 with the idea that they might make an attraction as circus freaks.

"In the event, the native Australians, playing barefoot, trounced the best teams in the land ten years before any white Australian team toured England."

—London *Times,* March 8, 2002.

TEMPERATURE

Temperature is important for preservation because higher temperatures speed up chemical reactions. It has been estimated that the useful life of paper is cut approximately in half with every ten degree Fahrenheit increase in temperature above 68 degrees. Conversely, for every ten-degree decrease, the expected life of paper is effectively doubled.[13]

Archival collections are complex, containing a variety of media. The proper temperature and humidity, therefore, will be a compromise. Each medium will have its own ideal conditions—but for an archives program to function, there must be a happy medium acceptable to the records as well as to the archives staff.

Many preservation administrators, therefore, recommend a compromise temperature of 68 degrees Fahrenheit, plus or minus two degrees.[14] While a colder environment might be better for preservation, it can be difficult to maintain relative humidity within an acceptable range. Furthermore, before items can be used, they must be gradually reconditioned to room temperature to avoid condensation. If one wishes to store records as cool as possible (to promote preservation) without having to recondition them before use, the temperature should not drop below 50 degrees Fahrenheit.

The range in which the temperature is permitted to vary is a very important consideration. Archivists try to avoid rapid cycling—dramatic shifts in temperature and humidity on a daily or weekly basis. It would be better to have a slightly higher constant temperature than one that varies greatly over a short period of time.

RELATIVE HUMIDITY

We talk about humidity as being relative—it relates to temperature. The warmer the air, the more water vapor it is capable of holding. The amount of moisture in the air contributes to chemical activity; high humidity accelerates some chemical reactions, including the formation of acids.

Humidity also affects organic materials. High humidity (above 65–70 percent) encourages the growth of mold and mildew; it also creates a resort environment preferred by some varieties of insects. On the other hand, low humidity (below 30 percent) causes materials to become dry and brittle.

Paper, vellum, and parchment all are hygroscopic; their moisture content changes as the environment around them changes. Rapid cycling of humidity causes these materials to shrink and expand—a workout that will not promote the physical fitness of the collection.

Over the course of a year, the relative humidity in a building may range from nearly 100 percent in summer (if no dehumidification is provided) to as low as 10 percent in winter (if heating is provided without humidification).[15]

As noted with temperature, each archival medium has an ideal humidity range. The target recommended for a collection of mixed media materials is 45 percent relative humidity, plus or minus 2 percent.[16]

Research conducted at the Image Permanence Institute of the Rochester Institute of Technology provides archivists and librarians with a framework for evaluating the effect of particular combinations of temperature and relative humidity on the rate of chemical deterioration in collections over time.[17] This new methodology can be a useful management tool, especially for determining cost-benefit ratios.

Archivists can now calculate how much longer a collection will last at improved temperature and humidity conditions. They then will be able to determine if this extra life is worth the cost of construction and annual operation—or if another option, such as microfilming, makes better economic sense.[18]

Fig. 7.3 Atmospheric Pollutants[20]		
Pollutant	**Source**	**Effect**
Sulfur dioxide	When sulfur-containing fuel (coal, natural gas, petroleum, or oil) is burned, the sulfur combines with water to form sulfur dioxide.	Sulfur dioxide combines with water in the air to form sulfuric acid, a strong corrosive.
Nitrogen dioxide	Nitrogen dioxide is a by-product of combustion and other chemical reactions.	Nitrogen dioxide combines with water in the air to form nitric acids, also strong corrosives.
Ozone	Ozone is a by-product of sunlight combining with nitrogen dioxide, especially from automobile exhausts. Some air conditioners and photocopy machines also produce ozone.	Ozone is a strong oxidizing agent that causes severe damage to organic materials.
Acetic acid	Acetic acid is generated by outgassing of wood, particularly oak, birch, and beech.	
Sulfides	Sulfides, used to produce vulcanized rubber, can be released when the rubber decomposes at high temperatures.	Sulfides are damaging especially to photographs.
Other gaseous pollutants	Smoking, cooking, cellulose nitrate film, paint finishes	These can cause chemical reactions and abrasion.
Solid particles (dirt, dust, carbon soot, tar)	Deposited on materials through the air	These cause abrasion. They may absorb moisture and other pollutants from the air, which they deposit on the records (not the kind of deposit arrangement archivist like to encourage). They may contain traces of metal, such as iron, which can become a focus for deterioration.

AIR QUALITY

Atmospheric pollutants also cause deterioration of archival materials. Some lead to the formation of acids that damage the records. Others break down the cellulose in paper fibers. Still others lead to abrasion, which damages materials over time. The main atmospheric challenges to archival materials are listed in figure 7.3.[19]

An ideal archival environment includes systems for air circulation and filtration. Some of the elements to look for are

- a dedicated system, rather than one shared with such sources of indoor pollution as kitchens, laboratories, and staff lounges
- sealed windows and gaskets on doors
- positive air pressure within the controlled area, to eliminate the introduction of contaminated air
- even circulation of a constant volume of air in and around stack ranges, including compact shelving
- filters in the air handling system to eliminate external pollutants
- air intakes situated away from loading docks, exhaust fans, or street traffic
- regular monitoring and replacement of filters

Achieving these system requirements will involve consultation with engineers and architects—and with the keepers of the institutional budget. Problems are particularly acute in urban areas, although virtually no region is immune from some of the conditions noted above.[20]

LIGHT

When God said, "Let there be light," a footnote might have been added: except in archives. Light speeds up the oxidation of paper and thus its chemical breakdown, resulting in a loss of strength. This oxidation of cellulose is accelerated by sulfur dioxide, nitrogen dioxide, and water. Light becomes the final ingredient in the bouillabaisse of deterioration.

Light also has a bleaching effect, causing some papers to whiten and some inks to fade. Lignin-containing papers can darken very quickly—just leave a newspaper in your car during a summer trip to the beach to try your own accelerated aging test.

Archival records must be protected from ultraviolet (UV) radiation, visible light, and infrared radiation. Ultraviolet radiation is a particularly damaging component, because of the way it accelerates photochemical decay.

Some of the ways archives can minimize the damaging effects of light are to

- box or otherwise protect records from direct exposure
- have no windows in stack areas (if windows are present, cover or block them in some way)
- treat windows in work or reference areas with UV-filtering glazes or films
- cover fluorescent lights with UV filters (tubes or sheets)
- keep light levels low by turning off unneeded lights and removing some bulbs
- design exhibit cases and rooms to minimize the amount of light exposure the records receive[21]

BIOLOGICAL AGENTS

Last but not least, archival records require a storage environment free of biological agents. In general, a warm and humid environment is more likely to attract these unwanted visitors. Figure 7.4 lists the major biological agents and the challenges they present.

Fig. 7.4 Biological Agents[22]		
Biological Agent	**Conditions They Prefer**	**Potential Damage**
Fungi (mold and mildew). ate	Warm (above 75 degrees), humid (above 65 percent relative humidity), dark, and little air circulation.	Feed on cellulose, starch adhesive, sizing, and gelatin. Can weaken, stain and obliterate material.
Insects (especially cockroaches, silverfish, termites, and beetles).	Dark, warm, and damp.	Eat away image-bearing materials (like gelatin emulsions); damage structures by boring through them.
Rodents (rats, mice, and squirrels).	Plentiful sources of food and materials to create "homes."	Nibble away at items; use shredded paper as nesting material; droppings are corrosive and can leave

Many of the above problems can be controlled by stabilizing the temperature and humidity. Good housekeeping practices are an important second step. Among the practices archives should adopt are to

- prohibit smoking, eating, or drinking in or near archival storage, processing, or reference areas
- remove garbage from the building on a daily basis
- keep stack and storage areas free of debris
- prohibit plants in areas where records are stored and used
- damp-mop or vacuum floors at least once per week
- dust shelves, boxes, and the exteriors of bound volumes on a regular basis

Most archives arrange to have cleaning services present during normal working hours. This is important for security reasons. It also is a way for the archivist to be certain that the cleaning staff neither inadvertently damages materials nor uses chemicals harmful to their long-term preservation. The archival heavy artillery of fumigation and extermination should be done by a trained professional aware of the particular preservation concerns in an archives.[23]

Fig. 7.5 Tips on Proper Handling[24]	
Medium or Type of Item	**Proper Handling**
Paper records	Support and protect records being moved; remove entire folder from box before looking for an individual item; do not lean on or write on top of records; do not use pressure-sensitive tape; avoid paper clips and staples that can rust.
Bound volumes	Do not pull volumes from the top —support volumes from the bottom when removing from shelves; be careful when turning pages, especially brittle ones; use book cradles and supports in reference areas.
Photographic media	Avoid bending or creasing; use two hands rather than picking up by one edge; wear white, lint-free gloves when handling.
Audiotapes, videotapes, magnetic tapes	Handle only by the housing supports (reels, cartridges, and cassettes); never touch tape surfaces; assure proper threading and mounting on playback equipment; rewind with even tension.

HOLDINGS MAINTENANCE PRACTICES

Holdings maintenance practices include unfolding or unrolling documents, removing or replacing harmful fasteners, reproducing unstable documents, placing materials in acid-free folders and boxes, and shelving them in environmentally controlled and secure storage.

In addition, staff and researchers must understand proper handling of various media. Some hints are found in figure 7.5.

"As if keeping track of 3 billion pieces of paper weren't enough trouble, the National Archives has discovered that most of its historic government documents dating from World War II and the cold-war period are rapidly disintegrating. Cheap, high-acid paper—a wartime austerity measure—is the major culprit. The acid eats the cellulose fibers of the paper, causing it to fall apart. Hundreds of millions of one-of-a-kind documents may be unreadable in 10 years."

—*U.S. News & World Report,* September 22, 1986.

TREATMENT OF MATERIALS

All archives reach a point where environment and holdings maintenance have done all they can do. Some materials may need conservation treatment, either by the archives staff or a professional conservator.

"Conservation" has replaced an earlier term, "restoration."[25] Conservation treatments attempt to stabilize materials in their original format by chemical and physical means. Among the main objectives are to

- return deteriorated or damaged items to stable and usable condition
- render archival materials capable of being duplicated safely
- reverse previous treatments that have proven unsuitable or have placed a document in jeopardy[26]

Conservators practice the rule of reversibility, which can be stated as follows: to the degree possible, no procedure or treatment should be undertaken that cannot later, if necessary, be undone without harm to the document. Materials and procedures used during the course of treatment must be stable and incapable of interacting with the item being treated in ways that alter its physical, chemical, aesthetic, or historical integrity.

Photograph 7.2 Some archives have unique preservation issues. At Harley-Davidson, the archives has to empty cardboard oil cans and old cans of "Harley-Davidson Beer." Photograph courtesy of the Harley-Davidson Motor Company Archives. Copyright Harley-Davidson.

Managing a practical archives program involves knowing which treatments can be done in-house and which should be sent to a conservator (either one who works for the same institution as the archivist or an independent professional). Naturally, the exact placement of the dividing line will depend upon the size and resources of the archival facility. For a small repository just beginning an archival program, I recommend the division of tasks outlined in figure 7.6.

Reformatting—onto paper, microfilm, or digital media—also is a preservation option. If a large collection needs item-level treatment, it would be more cost-effective to microfilm or digitize the entire collection rather than treat each item individually. This option becomes even more attractive if the documents lack intrinsic value, as defined in

Fig. 7.6 Recommended Specific Treatment of Archival Materials	
Place of Treatment	**Specific Treatment**
The archives itself	Surface cleaning, humidification and flattening, polyester film encapsulation, repairing simple tears.
Outside conservator	Fumigation, deacidification, repairing extensive tears and other paper strengthening.

Chapter 3. In this case, the original documents might be destroyed after reformatting. The microfilming or digitizing could be done by the repository's own staff or a service bureau.[27]

TREATMENTS HANDLED BY THE ARCHIVES

The following treatments should be simple and inexpensive enough that any archival program can perform them as needed:

- surface cleaning
- humidification and flattening
- polyester film encapsulation
- repairing simple tears

Remember, however, that even simple conservation treatments will take staff time away from the myriad other archival activities discussed in this book. Conservation treatment quickly can consume all available time and energy. This may currently be an appropriate focus in the life of the archives—or it may not. The only way to determine the appropriate amount of time to spend on conservation is to analyze needs and develop plans in the systematic way discussed in previous chapters.

The following sections present an overview of each technique. A more complete discussion, including diagrams of the steps for each technique, is found in Mary Lynn Ritzenthaler's book *Preserving Archives and Manuscripts.*

Surface Cleaning

Loose surface dirt, dust, and debris can be gently removed from paper strong enough to withstand moderate handling. Photographic materials and documents composed of more than one medium (a letter attached to a cardboard exhibit mount, for example) are much more complex and should be approached with healthy caution.

The following techniques for cleaning paper are listed in increasing order of potential damage:

- *Gently dust with a soft brush.* The brushing should proceed from the center to the edge.
- *Work eraser particles across non-text and non-image areas.* Work the eraser particles in a circular motion. As they become dirty, dust them away with a soft brush.
- *Clean with an eraser.* This must be done lightly—not with a scrubbing motion. The abrasive action can damage paper fibers.

Photograph 7.3 Many archives require staff and researchers to use gloves when handling artifacts, photographs, and valuable documents. Photograph courtesy of the Saint Benedict Center, Sisters of Saint Benedict of Madison, Wisconsin, Inc.

Humidification and Flattening

Humidification and flattening techniques are designed to introduce moisture into the paper so that it can be unrolled or flattened without tearing. It is important to understand the nature and structure of the paper in question. Coated papers and moisture-sensitive inks could be damaged by the introduction of moisture. It also takes an experienced eye to know just how much moisture is enough without being too much.

Archivists can use a passive humidification process to introduce moisture gently into the environment; the paper, in turn, will absorb the moisture. This process is done by using a humidification chamber constructed of an airtight, noncorrosive, rustproof enclosure. Some archives use a pair of plastic trash containers; others use an unplugged refrigerator devoid of rusting internal components.

The humidity in the closed chamber increases the moisture content of the paper, which should relax the fibers. The time required to accomplish this will vary according to the type and weight of the paper—anywhere from 30 minutes to several hours.

The humidified papers must be handled carefully to avoid tearing. They also must be dried between clean, dry blotters under moderate weight to complete the flattening. It may be necessary to change the blotter paper one or more times during the drying process.

Polyester Film Encapsulation

Polyester film encapsulation offers a way to support and protect fragile single sheets of paper. It involves sandwiching the paper between two layers of polyester. The sandwich is sealed on all sides, which offers increased security as well.[28]

A simpler option is just placing the item in a polyester sleeve. This is particularly appropriate if the item has not yet been deacidified (see below). Some items, however, would slip out of a sleeve; full encapsulation would thus be preferable, whether or not the items are deacidified.

"As of last week the company [Microsoft] has never had an e-mail policy, according to a Microsoft spokesman. Thus in its protracted investigation the government was able to get its hands on an estimated 3.3 million Microsoft documents, including megabytes of e-mail messages dating from the early 1990s—and is now using them to contradict Gates's own videotaped testimony in the most significant antitrust case of the decade."

—*Newsweek,* November 23, 1998.

There are different approaches to sealing the four edges of the polyester film capsule:

- stable, double-coated, pressure-sensitive adhesive
- ultrasonic welding
- electromagnetic radiation sealing
- sewing machine using a thread with non-bleeding dyes

The choice of sealing method depends upon such factors as staff time and capital budget levels. While encapsulating machines are expensive, they are cost-effective for institutions that require a large number of encapsulations.

Repairing Simple Tears

It is possible to mend documents using long-fiber Japanese paper and a starch adhesive. This is a tried-and-true approach to paper repairs. Though a time-consuming process, the end result is a strong, safe, long-lasting repair.

There are a number of pressure-sensitive mending tapes advertised as "archival quality," acid-free, non-yellowing, and reversible. Archivists are advised to use these products cautiously, if at all, until independent testing can either confirm or refute manufacturers' claims.[29]

TREATMENTS BEST REFERRED TO AN OUTSIDE CONSERVATOR

Practical archivists know when they are in over their heads. Though some archivists are comfortable with the following conservation treatments, many others are more than happy to refer the following treatments to outside experts:

- fumigation
- deacidification
- repairing extensive tears and other paper strengthening

> "One of the greatest ironies of the information age is that, while the late twentieth century will undoubtedly record more data than have been recorded at any other time in history, it will also almost certainly lose more information than has been lost in any previous era."
>
> —*The New Yorker,* March 8, 1999.

Fumigation

Fumigation and other chemical aspects of pest management certainly could be done by the archivist. However many archives, especially smaller ones, contract for these services, particularly in light of environmental and employee health and safety concerns.

The long-term effects of fumigants on archival materials still are unknown. Therefore fumigation should be seen as a last resort—only used when there are signs of an active infestation. It is better to improve the environment to make it less hospitable for our crawling friends.

Reading the literature about specific fumigation agents also leads to a "do not try this at home" mindset. Ethylene oxide, a commonly used fumigant, is flammable, toxic, and explosive. Carbon dioxide can be used as a fumigant if its concentration is high enough. Thymol, which was once used to treat mold-infested books and documents, is known to pose serious health hazards and is no longer recommended. Low-level gamma radiation (Cobalt-60) shows promise, although it appears to weaken the structure of cellulose. Freezing is an alternative to fumigation, but it must be done quickly and at a low enough temperature —otherwise some pests will continue to pester after their winter vacations.

Most local exterminators do not understand the particular needs of archival materials: to them, bugs are bugs. It may take a few telephone calls to neighboring archives, museums, or libraries to locate an exterminator for whom not all boxes are just boxes. There is no way around this exercise of archival caution.[30]

Deacidification

As noted previously, acid attacks the cellulose in paper, breaking down the strands and weakening the paper. Deacidification processes are intended to neutralize the paper's acidity and deposit an alkaline buffer to prevent the return to an acidic state—the cellulose equivalent of a long-lasting Tums.

Deacidification in archives is a labor-intensive process still done most often at the individual item level. Candidates for deacidification must be tested for solubility and color change prior to treatment. The two options are:

- *Aqueous deacidification.* Water-based treatments can only be done with loose papers—any bound volumes must be disassembled before immersion. Items usually are washed before treatment and then immersed in one or more baths. Documents often emerge with stains and discoloration removed, a bonus for a visit to the deacidification spa.
- *Nonaqueous deacidification.* This option is appropriate for the non-swimmers in the archival collection, usually because water would damage the paper or its inks. Organic solvents are used as a carrier for the chemicals. Using such solvents, however, requires a fume hood, protective clothing, and a breathing apparatus.

Archives and libraries have been trying to reach the promised land of low-cost mass deacidification. This appears to be the only way to treat the huge volume of deteriorating archival holdings effectively. Several processes have been used with books and other bound volumes. Conservators, however, remain skeptical of manufacturers' claims until they can be independently verified. Also, some initial experiments with mass deacidification at the Library of Congress ended ignominiously with an explosion and fire. Sadly, the Promised Land still is several hills away.[31]

I must interject one final point about deacidification: it will not *strengthen* the paper. While it will stabilize the paper and sometimes improve its appearance, there is no Lazarus, life-restoring effect. Following deacidification, weak papers must be strengthened or protected in polyester film.[32]

Repairing Extensive Tears and Other Paper Strengthening

While archives may do simple repairs, extensive repairs and paper strengthening are best left to professional conservators. Even simple repairs may be appropriate for referral if they involve records of high intrinsic value—the original charter of North Fork University, for example.

Experiments are under way to strengthen entire sheets of paper. At the present time, there are no standards in this area and little independent verification of manufacturers' claims. Reformatting onto microfilm is probably the preferred option for small archives with collections of embrittled documents.

CONCLUSION

A phased approach to preservation is the most appropriate approach for the small archives. Once the problems are identified, committing resources to stabilizing the environment will have the greatest preservation return for the dollar. Other aspects of preservation can be integrated into the archival program as funding and staff levels permit. In this way, a small archives program can achieve the proper balance between preservation and use.

NOTES

1. According to Paul Conway, "At one time, advocates for the protection of cultural artifacts, including books, primary source documents, and museum objects, used the terms 'conservation' and 'preservation' interchangeably. Today preservation is an umbrella term for the many policies and options for action, including conservation treatments. Preservation is the acquisition, organization, and distribution of resources to prevent further deterioration or renew the usability of selected groups of materials." Paul Conway, *Preservation in the Digital World* (Washington, D.C.: Commission on Preservation and Access, 1996), 5. For a preservation bibliography, see Robert E., Schnare, Jr., Susan G. Swatzburg, and George M. Cunha, *Bibliography of Preservation Literature, 1983–1996* (Lanham, Md.: Scarecrow Press, 2001).

2. For some recent literature on preservation, see: Paul N. Banks and Roberta Pilette, eds., *Preservation: Issues and Planning* (Chicago: American Library Association, 2000); Gregory S. Hunter, *Preserving Digital Information* (New York: Neal-Schuman, 2000); *Access to Information: Preservation Issues. Proceedings of the Thirty-Fourth International Conference of the Round Table on Archives, Budapest, 1999* (Paris: International Council on Archives, 2000); Barbra Buckner Higginbotham and Judith W. Wild, *The Preservation Program Blueprint*

(Chicago: American Library Association, 2001); Maggie Jones and Neil Beagrie, *Preservation Management of Digital Materials: A Handbook* (London: The British Library, 2001); Robert E. Schnare, Jr., Susan G. Swatzburg, and George M. Cunha, *Bibliography of Preservation Literature, 1983–1996* (Lanham, Md.: Scarecrow Press, 2001).

3. This framework is taken from Lewis J. Bellardo and Lynn Lady Bellardo, *A Glossary for Archivists, Manuscript Curators, and Records Managers* (Chicago: Society of American Archivists, 1992). The best one-volume discussion of preservation for archivists is Mary Lynn Ritzenthaler, *Preserving Archives and Manuscripts* (Chicago: Society of American Archivists, 1993). See also, Norvell M. M. Jones and Mary Lynn Ritzenthaler, "Implementing an Archival Preservation Program," in *Managing Archives and Archival Institutions*, ed. James Gregory Bradsher (Chicago: University of Chicago Press, 1989), 185–206. For an excellent review of preservation planning, see Paul N. Banks and Roberta Pilette, eds., *Preservation: Issues and Planning* (Chicago: American Library Association, 2000). For helpful checklists, see Barbra Buckner Higginbotham and Judith W. Wild, *The Preservation Program Blueprint* (Chicago: American Library Association, 2001).

4. Flora Skelly Johnson, "Pulp to Paper, Paper to Dust" *Newsday,* April 2, 1985.

5. Librarians have a similar problem with many of the "brittle books" on their shelves. For more information, see *Preserving the Intellectual Heritage: A Report of the Bellagio Conference, June 7–10, 1993* (Washington, D.C.: Commission on Preservation and Access, 1993). Not everyone believes that the situation is desperate. Nicholson Baker has denounced librarians' practice of microfilming newspapers and destroying the originals. See Nicholson Baker, *Double Fold: Libraries and the Assault on Paper* (New York: Random House, 2001).

6. For a more detailed description, see Mary Lynn Ritzenthaler, *Preserving Archives and Manuscripts,* 19–37. For an overview of reproduction technologies on paper and other media, see Gregory S. Hunter, "Reprography," *World Encyclopedia of Library and Information Services*, 3d ed. (Chicago: American Library Association, 1993), 711–15.

7. Adapted from James M. Reilly, Douglas W. Nishimura, and Edward Zinn, *New Tools for Preservation: Assessing Long-Term Environmental Effects on Library and Archives Collections* (Washington, D.C.: Commission on Preservation and Access, 1995), 2, 19–20.

8. Page Putnam Miller, *Developing a Premier National Institution: A Report from the User Community to the National Archives* (Washington, D.C.: National Coordinating Committee for the Promotion of History, 1989).

9. See James O'Toole, "On the Idea of Permanence," *American Archivist* 52 (winter 1989): 11–25. For recommendations on dealing with these limitations, see *The Preservation of Archival Materials: A Report of the Task Forces on Archival Selection to the Commission on Preservation and Access* (Washington, D.C.: Commission on Preservation and Access, 1993).

10. Ritzenthaler, *Preserving Archives and Manuscripts,* 8–11.

11. For another approach to a survey form, see Bruce W. Dearstyne, *The Archival Enterprise: Modern Archival Principles, Practices, and Management Techniques* (Chicago: American Library Association, 1993), 157–58.

12. For photographs and descriptions of hygrothermographs and other measuring devices, see Gregor Trinkaus-Randall, *Protecting Your Collections: A Manual of Archival Security* (Chicago: Society of American Archivists, 1995), 29–33. For a comprehensive discussion of environment issues, see Paul N. Banks, "Environment and Building Design," in, *Preservation Issues*, eds. Banks and Pilette, 114–44.

13. Ritzenthaler, *Preserving Archives and Manuscripts,* 46.

14. "Other things being equal, most objects would last longer at low temperatures. Higher temperatures of 60 or 70 degrees Fahrenheit are usually needed for human comfort, but not for the benefit of the collection. In almost all collections, the lower the temperature the better, with 65 to 68 degrees Fahrenheit a good compromise with human needs and other practical concerns. Due to their particular sensitivity to temperature, every attempt should be made to segregate any important photographic and film collections, particularly color, and keep them at temperatures below 55 degrees Fahrenheit." William P. Lull, with the assistance of Paul N. Banks, *Conservation Environment Guidelines for Libraries and Archives* (Albany, N.Y.: New York State Library, 1990), 4.

15. Lull, *Conservation Environment Guidelines,* 4.

16. Ritzenthaler, *Preserving Archives and Manuscripts,* 53. According to Paul Banks, "if RH can be maintained within plus or minus 3 percent, a set point between 33 percent and 47 percent should be selected, the set point varying with the season if necessary. If the RH cannot be maintained within 3 percent of the set point, the outer limits may have to be closer together." Banks, "Environment and Building Design," 122.

17. Reilly, Nishimura, and Zinn, *New Tools for Preservation.* This work built upon an earlier effort; see Donald K. Sebera, *Isoperms: An Environmental Management Tool* (Washington, D.C.: Commission on Preservation and Access, 1994).

18. For more information on temperature and humidity, see Barbara Appelbaum, *Guide to Environmental Protection of Collections* (Madison, Conn.: Sound View Press, 1991), 25–64. For excellent

advice on the design and implementation of improved preservation environments, see Lull, *Conservation Environment Guidelines,* 19–73.

19. Adapted from Ritzenthaler, *Preserving Archives and Manuscripts,* 47.

20. For more information, see Appelbaum, *Guide to Environmental Protection of Collections,* 97–116.

21. Appelbaum, *Guide to Environmental Protection of Collections,* 65–96.

22. Adapted from Ritzenthaler, *Preserving Archives and Manuscripts,* 48–49.

23. For more information, see Appelbaum, *Guide to Environmental Protection of Collections,* 117–44.

24. Adapted from Ritzenthaler, *Preserving Archives and Manuscripts,* 67–75. See also Appelbaum, *Guide to Environmental Protection of Collections,* 145–158.

25. As one might expect, terminology has changed over time. "Conservation" used to be the broadest term even a few years ago, the equivalent of the way we now use "preservation." Restoration was used to indicate one specific aspect of the conservation program.

26. Ritzenthaler, *Preserving Archives and Manuscripts,* 2.

27. For reformatting, see Eileen F. Usovicz and Barbara Lilley, "Preservation Microfilming and Photocopying," in *Preservation Issues and Planning,* eds. Banks and Pilette, 265–85; Paula De Stefano, "Digitization for Preservation and Access," in *Preservation Issues and Planning,* eds. Banks and Pilette, 307–22.

28. Usually one corner is left unsealed to permit some air circulation.

29. Ritzenthaler, *Preserving Archives and Manuscripts,* 149. For a discussion of book repairs, see Kenneth Lavender, *Book Repair.* 2nd ed. (New York: Neal-Schuman, 2001).

30. Ritzenthaler, *Preserving Archives and Manuscripts,* 140–43; and Appelbaum, *Guide to Environmental Protection of Collections,* 119–41.

31. The experiments at the Library of Congress used Diethyl Zinc (DEZ), which is also used as a rocket fuel and bomb material. DEZ is "pyrophoric," meaning that it bursts into flames upon contact with the air. See Baker, *Double Fold,* 111–35.

32. Ritzenthaler, *Preserving Archives and Manuscripts,* 144–47.

8 SECURITY AND DISASTER PLANNING

Security and disaster planning are not the stuff of pleasant archival dreams. Naturally, archivists prefer to think about the good times—a collection finally processed or a happy researcher leaving the reference room. Part of being responsible for an archival collection, however, is also trying to minimize or plan for the bad times through a security and disaster program. Especially in light of September 11, 2001, any information professional must address security and disaster planning.

The Society of American Archivists (SAA) defines security broadly enough to include disaster planning. According to SAA, security is "an archival and records management function concerned with the protection of documents from unauthorized access and/or damage or loss from fire, water, theft, mutilation, or unauthorized alteration or destruction."[1]

Although it is difficult to separate the two subjects, I will try to do so as follows:

- *Security* deals with potential human problems.
- *Disaster planning* deals with problems caused by natural elements as well as human beings.

Integrating both elements into a unified program for the protection of records is part of the archivist's mission.

SECURITY

Security presents archivists with a dilemma: how do we balance our desire to provide access with the responsibility for protecting records? (This dilemma is discussed in greater depth in chapter 9.) Archivists must balance present-day use of the records against long-term preservation. Part of that preservation is protection from human and natural catastrophes.

An archivist trying to address security issues needs to consider two aspects:

- physical security
- collection security

PHYSICAL SECURITY

Physical security deals with the repository and the building. Although most thefts take place during normal working hours, it is prudent to examine the building's after-hours security.

"When cuneiform stone tablets represented state-of-the-art printing, the best records retention policy was 'Don't drop them.' Each successive form of IT—printing press, filing cabinet, copier, e-mail and Internet—has made it harder to control information flow and access, and especially to reclaim freely disseminated material.

"Sept. 11 changed the rules, forcing government agencies to re-evaluate data they'd put online, such as infrastructure layouts.

"But anything available on the Internet—Web pages, Usenet newsgroup postings and even some e-mail—is difficult to remove from public view. You may not realize how widely replicated and long-lived content can be."

—Government Computer News, July 29, 2002.

The following six "Hunter's Hints" address the physical security of the repository. An archives program that is part of a larger institution may not have direct responsibility for all of these matters. A smaller archives program, however, will need to review all of these considerations.

- *Doors* should be strong and well made, including the frame. In most burglaries, the door is broken down.
- *Locks* should not be the key-in-the-knob type, because they can be pried open using a credit card—for this reason, most thieves "do not leave home" without one. Archivists should insist on a deadbolt lock, which has a bolt separate from the knob. Also, the bolt should extend well into the frame to provide extra protection against the breaking down of the door.
- *Windows* on the lower floor should be locked and secured. Depending on the local environment, gates and grills may be in order.
- *Alarms* to detect after-hour entry are highly recommended. If the archives does not have alarms, try to arrange for at least regular patrols by building guards.
- *Keys* should be carefully issued and monitored. Archives often remove themselves from the building

master. When cleaning or maintenance staff need to be in the archives, they must do so during normal working hours or after hours in the presence of a security guard.

- *Box labels* can be a security measure. I recommend that archives place only the minimum information on the box label: collection name and box number. Anything more than this is available from the finding aids—why make it easier for an unauthorized person to find items of interest?[2]

"Tucked away among miles of tree-covered slopes and pristine lakes 45 miles from Manhattan, the I.B.M. Business Continuity and Recovery Center is symbolic of the disaster recovery industry. Open since 1993, the Sterling Forest center was an afterthought for many people. It was referred to as 'the bunker' by those quasi-paramilitary emergency planning teams that were once the object of ridicule in some offices.

"On September 11, 2001, all of that changed. The unthinkable became real, and the bunker was a joke no more."

—*New York Times*, January 4, 2003.

COLLECTION SECURITY

Collection security involves making sure that documents do not disappear either during use or at other times. Anyone in the proximity of documents may be the source of a security problem.

Staff certainly have the opportunity to steal documents. An archival employer should carefully check the references of all applicants. It is important to contact previous employers, whether or not they are listed as references. It is not just that the archivist is looking for potential thieves; it is also necessary to know if the applicant will respect privacy and other aspects of administering archival collections.

There are certain patterns that emerge when employee thefts are involved. In particular, archivists should be alert to the following:

- materials consistently out of their usual locations
- the same person reporting items missing or always being the one to find missing items
- a staff member unconcerned about pursuing missing items
- regular inconsistencies or discrepancies in the repository's documentation and records

- a staff member's disregard for established rules and procedures
- a staff member's lifestyle that does not match salary and known assets[3]

Patrons are another cause of worry; there have been numerous cases of thefts by researchers. Archives can take a number of precautions to reduce the danger, some of which are discussed in greater detail in chapter 9.

- Require the researcher to present valid identification (driver's license or other photo ID). Note the identification on the form the researcher completes during the entrance interview. Some archives photocopy the identification and add it to the researcher's file.
- Establish and enforce some basic research room rules—require that all personal belongings be left at a checkpoint; limit the number of items used at any one time; recheck items when the researcher is done; inspect researchers' personal belongings before they leave.
- Close the stacks to researchers.
- Control access to the research room: have only one exit, past the reference desk.
- Supervise researchers' use of materials: always have one staff member in the research room; retain a clear field of vision to see all researchers all the time (don't let them build a "Berlin Wall" with manuscript boxes); make sure the researchers know you are watching them.
- Know what's in your collection, so you can tell if something is missing. Keep all call slips: they provide evidence of what a researcher requested, and they also document that a particular item was previously used by other researchers.
- Consider ways to protect valuable items in your collections, such as
  - remove originals and replace them with photocopies (keep the originals in a safe)
  - microfilm the entire collection if all of it is particularly valuable, and require researchers to use the microfilm

- mark valuable items with a property stamp and acid-free ink[4]

Despite all the precautions, there may come a time when an archives suspects a researcher of theft. Before getting to this point, it is imperative that all staff know what to do: remember that a false arrest or an improper detention might lead to a lawsuit. The archives should have security policies and procedures in which all staff members are trained. Role-playing often works well in this kind of training.

"Most of us know that millions disappeared into the vast frozen Siberian wilderness during Joseph Stalin's reign of terror in the Soviet Union. But the vast physical evidence of the atrocity has yet to be revealed to the same degree as that of the Holocaust.

"The multi-award-winning documentary Gulag charges into the story of the labor camps, where 20 million are believed to have perished.

"Along with providing rare footage of Norilsk, a huge city built by slave labor on the Siberian tundra, filmmakers interviewed survivors and former guards, KGB operatives, and camp commandants, now well-advanced in years, who recount what they saw and experienced.

"Archival footage and contemporary interviews are artfully intercut with Russian propaganda films of the 1930s. There are even interviews with a few who escaped Russia and fled to Britain."

—*Christian Science Monitor*, May 3, 2002.

The following guidelines will help archives facing the sensitive task of confronting a patron over a potential theft:

- Before detaining someone, make sure you have "probable cause" (such as seeing the person take an item). Do not rely on third-party witnesses.
- Notify security or the police, as dictated by the repository's written security plan.
- Make sure there is a credible witness for your upcoming discussion with the patron (to avoid "my word against your word.")
- Interrupt the researcher's activity—engage him or her in conversation.
- Take a quiet but firm approach.
- Try to avoid a scene, especially shouting and other displays of anger.
- Do not touch the patron, except in self-defense.

- Inform the patron that there appears to be a problem and ask the patron to go into an office to discuss it. The patron must go into the office voluntarily.
- Wait for security or the police, who will take over the investigation.
- If the patron denies there is a problem and leaves the building, one person should carefully follow the patron to get a license plate number and a description of the patron's car.[5]

Confronting a patron is not something archives should take lightly. It is a serious matter with legal implications for the patron as well as for archives. This is why most archives try to establish a research environment that minimizes the opportunity for theft and makes it easy to identify stolen materials. Archives minimize opportunity by having researchers check personal belongings and requiring that they work under staff observation. Consider using colored paper for photocopies and providing notepaper for researchers' use.

"The man in charge of archiving and maintaining electronic copies of Norway's most important historical documents is dead and so is access to those archives.

"So the director of the Norwegian cultural center is pleading for hackers to help him crack the center's password-protected database.

"The problem started when the technician responsible for the archives at Norway's National Center of Language and Culture never divulged the password before he died a few years ago.

"Since then, employees at the center have been unable to access some of the password-protected archives that contain data on a collection of thousands of documents and books. A national database that allowed researchers access to those documents is also partly inaccessible."

—*Wired*, June 5, 2002.

One major repository, for example, distributes notepaper with a hole in it. When researchers are ready to leave, they must stop at a security desk. The guard places a pencil or similar object into the stack of notepaper and shakes vigorously. Anything that falls out is examined very carefully—especially if it is signed by George Washington.

Will the precautions detailed above prevent all thefts? Of course not—even the best car alarm will not prevent all auto thefts. The prudent archivist attempts to raise the stakes for a potential thief so that the repository will not be viewed as an "easy mark." This, perhaps, is the best we can hope to accomplish.

DISASTER PLANNING

As if the above challenges were not enough, archives also face risks from natural events such as fires, floods, hurricanes, and earthquakes. An archivist can be consoled, however, that "acts of God" are not a "personal" thing—hurricanes usually do not have a vendetta against archives. On the other hand, a natural disaster will not avoid a repository just because it contains historically valuable records. The archivist must be prepared without being panicked.

Since September 11, 2001, the archivist also must consider the potential risks posed by regional and local terrorist acts. The potential impact is much larger than the thefts discussed above. In some cases, the archives may even be a terrorist target, because of its symbolic value as a cultural resource.

"NASA has recovered the data and voice recorders that investigators hope will provide valuable information about Challenger's 73-second flight that may not have been picked up by ground computers....The devices had been recovered in about 650 feet of water about 32 miles off shore, along with tons of other debris from the crew cabin....In a statement written before the recorders were recovered, NASA said they would be submerged in cool water until they can be cleaned and dried under controlled temperature and humidity conditions at a NASA facility."

—*Newsday*, March 14, 1986.

Disaster planning in an archival context can have either a narrow or a broad focus.

- The *narrow focus* plans only for the protection and restoration of records already in the archives. Other departments within the organization have to plan for themselves and be responsible for their own records.
- The *broad focus* involves planning for *all* the "vital records" of the organization, no matter who holds custody.[6]

I recommend that an archivist take the broad focus, especially in an organization where there is no other records professional. Such a void can have a negative impact on the organization in case of disaster. If the archivist does not fill the void, likely nobody will. While information systems professionals will deal with computer records, especially those on centralized systems, no one is likely to consider paper records.

DEFINING TERMS

First, we need to establish the meaning of vital records. These are records necessary for the maintenance of the functions, reasons, and objectives of the organization. Some archival records may be vital; others may not. Similarly, some records of short-term value will be vital but not archival.

According to the federal government, vital records fall into one or both of the categories presented in figure 8.1.[7]

Fig. 8.1 Categories of Vital Records		
Category	**Description**	**Examples of Records**
Emergency operating records	Essential to the continued functioning or reconstitution of an organization during and after an emergency	Emergency plans and directives; orders of succession; delegations of authority; staffing assignments; selected program records needed to continue the most critical organizational operations
Legal and financial rights records	Essential to protect the legal and financial rights of the organization and of the individuals directly affected by its activities	Accounts receivable; social security; payroll; retirement; insurance; binding contracts

The National Archives and Records Administration (NARA) makes a distinction between a disaster and an emergency[8] and defines them as follows:

- A *disaster* is an unexpected occurrence inflicting widespread destruction and distress and having long-term adverse effects on organization operations.
- An *emergency* is a situation or occurrence of a serious nature, developing suddenly and unexpectedly, and demanding immediate action. This is generally of short duration, like a power failure or minor flooding caused by broken pipes.

Using NARA terminology, an archivist in a small repository needs to plan for emergencies as well as disasters. In fact, the average archives is more likely to face a localized emergency than an extensive disaster. Certainly a disaster will receive more publicity and can completely devastate a repository, but the day-to-day survival of most archival records will depend on the way a repository plans for and responds to smaller emergencies.

Developing a vital records program involves four steps:

- identifying records that should be protected
- anticipating potential disasters and emergencies
- devising methods of protection
- planning responses[9]

IDENTIFYING RECORDS

An archivist taking the broad approach to disaster planning needs to look at all the records of the organization to determine

- the ability of the organization to continue in business without the record
- the cost of replacing or reconstructing the record

The entire process is similar to deciding whether or not to purchase an insurance policy. What are the risks? Do these risks justify protection that will cost a certain amount? Records exhibiting both high cost of replacement and high need for continuing operations are the prime candidates for the insurance policy of a vital records program.

It is best to identify vital records as part of a larger process: conducting a records inventory and developing a retention schedule for all of an organization's records. This process encourages an integrated approach to recordkeeping practices.

If such an integrated approach is not possible, however, one can identify vital records by asking the following questions:

- Do the records assure the collection of income due?
- Do the records protect against fraud or overpayment?
- Do the records provide information about real property or other assets?
- Do the records protect the rights or interests of employees, shareholders, customers, or other stakeholders?

Even within these broad categories of vital records, an archivist needs to establish priorities for protection and recovery. Are the payroll records "more vital" than the tax rolls? Does the fact that payroll records are duplicated in the payroll service bureau make them a lower priority for protection? How does the archivist make these choices?

Judith Fortson has developed a framework for determining vital records priorities. This framework is summarized in figure 8.2[10]

Fig. 8.2 Priorities for Protection	
Priority	**Types of Materials**
First priority	• difficult or impossible to replace or replicate, and are either essential for the ongoing operations of the institution or some larger body, such as a state agency • have prime research value • have significant monetary value
Second priority	• difficult to replace or replicate and provide significant operational or research resources
Last priority	• can be replaced, either in original or reprographic form • can be considered expendable, if necessary, to the institution and its constituents

In an archival setting, the finding aids should be a top priority, especially if only one copy of them exists. Without the finding aids, it would be difficult if not impossible even to determine what had been damaged in a disaster or emergency. The lowest-cost option is to duplicate the finding aids and store a copy off-site.

ANTICIPATING DISASTERS AND EMERGENCIES

Articles on disaster planning from the 1960s usually begin with a map, quite often of a metropolitan area, on which were superimposed a number of concentric circles. Those of us who grew up in major cities—and who were within the first or second ring—can remember school drills in which we hid under our desks to protect ourselves from a nuclear blast. In retrospect, organizational records certainly were better protected in their mines and vaults than we were under our desks and bookbags.

With the fall of the Soviet Union, Americans thought that the threats to our borders were a thing of the past. Sadly, we have learned the hard way that both domestic and foreign threats still do exist. From Oklahoma City to the World Trade Center, attacks have destroyed records as well as shattered families. Letters containing anthrax closed facilities for months, forcing organizations to function without their files. In these and other cases, vital records planning clearly demonstrated its value.

There also are regional natural disasters for which we must plan: hurricanes, tornadoes, major fires, and floods. The vivid images of the Mississippi River flooding a few years ago come quickly to mind, as well as the scenes of television reporters standing on the beach while an impending hurricane whips around them.

Often an archivist can guard against potential damage by understanding the nature of the likely types of disasters in the archives' location, examining the facility with an eye toward potential emergencies, implementing simple solutions, and advocating more extensive precautions. Figure 8.3 is North Fork University's assessment of potential major disasters.

Fig. 8.3 North Fork University: Assessment of Potential Major Disasters

TO: University President
FROM: Director, Department of Archives and Special Collections
RE: Potential Major Disasters

In addition to the localized disasters and emergencies like fires and floods, the university should prepare for major disasters that may affect the region as well as the campus.

Though we are in the New York Metropolitan Area, our distance from the city is sufficient to protect us from everything except a nuclear attack. A more immediate concern would be an attack upon or accident at a Connecticut nuclear power plant, since contamination easily would cross the Long Island Sound.

Located as we are on Long Island, NFU's vital records program must take into account the potential damage caused by a major hurricane. While high winds are a concern, all but the oldest buildings on campus have been constructed to withstand their force. At the present time, there are no vital records in these oldest buildings.

Massive flooding, however, is not so easy to address—especially with our location near Long Island Sound. Regional disaster impact studies have projected that a major hurricane hitting at high tide would submerge the campus under several feet of water. It could take days before the water recedes to normal levels.

For all of these reasons, I recommend that a copy of all university vital records be stored off Long Island. Storing these records in another building on campus, or even in a location a few miles away, would not prevent their destruction in a major disaster.

I will explore options for off-island storage as part of the disaster-planning program in which the university is engaged.

Fire

Two disasters for which all archivists need to plan are fire and water damage. In a fire, both flames and smoke are a cause for concern. Smoke, in fact, can be almost as damaging as flames, especially to sensitive items like records on magnetic media.

In planning for fires, it is essential to consult local building codes as well as the publications of the National Fire Protection Association dealing with libraries, archives and records centers. This is not an area where the archivist should learn by doing (especially by doing incorrectly).

Archivists can adopt certain practices, however, to reduce the risk of fire. Figure 8.4 presents a fire prevention checklist.[11]

Fig. 8.4 Fire Prevention Checklist

✔ Prohibit smoking in records storage areas.

✔ Keep food and trash away from records.

✔ Do not store flammable and combustible materials with records or in adjacent storage areas.

✔ Keep all chemical and solvent containers closed, even when in use.

✔ Ensure that air circulation is adequate throughout the building.

✔ Ensure that electrical appliances are operated at a safe distance from flammable materials and that they are kept off when not in use.

✔ Check electrical outlets, fixtures, equipment, and appliances regularly.

✔ Check fire suppression system/fire extinguishers regularly.

✔ Check security alarms regularly.

✔ Keep all fire doors closed.

✔ Keep aisles clear of impediments to fire fighters.

✔ Store as much as possible in boxes or other enclosures, rather than loose.

✔ Use fire-retardant furnishings as much as possible.

✔ Make certain that repair people, contractors, and others temporary workers are aware of and follow the above practices.

The main way to avoid extensive fire damage is to have a fire suppression system in the archives. While some archives rely exclusively on fire extinguishers, such an approach is dangerous: fire extinguishers are only appropriate for small fires and they offer no protection at all unless someone is there to operate them.

In the past, some archives installed a fire suppression system using Halon 1301 gas, a practice common in computer environments. Halon gas no longer is produced, however, because it proved damaging to the environment by depleting stratospheric ozone. Some archives have installed Halon substitutes, either the Inergen inert gaseous fire suppression agent[12] or the FM-200 fire suppression systems.[13] Other archives have just opted for sprinklers.

"The first clue that anything was amiss in the rare books collection of Columbia University came on a hot day last July. A librarian preparing a catalogue entry went to the shelves on the sixth floor, where medieval manuscripts are stored in boxes. But one of the boxes was empty. The head librarian ordered an inventory of the medieval manuscripts. By the time it was complete, it was clear that 22 were gone, including a papal bull written in 1202 and a French copy of the Book of Hours from the 14th century."

—*New York Times*, October 8, 1994.

But is the threat of water damage from malfunctioning sprinklers not a concern? While archivists would prefer not to introduce a source of water into the storage environment, the benefits outweigh the risks. As a subsequent section (Disaster Response and Recovery) of this chapter shows, water-damaged records can be restored at a reasonable cost; the same is not true of badly burned records. Furthermore, modern sprinkler systems are quite reliable—false discharges or leaks happen infrequently. The sprinkler systems are designed, moreover, to discharge water only in the immediate area of a fire. Unlike depictions in Hollywood films, the sprinkler heads usually do not all discharge and soak the entire facility.[14] New "water mist" systems use small water droplets to engulf even sheltered areas in a blanketing mist rather than a heavy stream of water.[15]

Water Damage

Water damage often happens as a result of a storm that brings wind and other damage. An engineer should examine the building's structure to be certain that the roof, foundation, and other components are able to withstand windstorm damage. Archives in areas subject to earthquakes face additional requirements for the building structure and such internal components as shelving.[16]

Water damage can also result from efforts to control fire. For this reason, an archivist should be prepared to cope with water-damaged materials after almost any kind of disaster.

Quick action is especially important with water-damaged records. Mold will develop within 48 to 72 hours when the temperature exceeds 75 degrees and the relative humidity exceeds 60 percent. Under these circumstances, the archivist must act quickly to prevent permanent damage to the records.

As with fire, certain practices will lessen potential water damage. Figure 8.5 presents these practices in a checklist.[17]

Fig. 8.5 Water Prevention Checklist

✔ Avoid basement storage as much as possible.

✔ Do not store records below pipes or restrooms.

✔ Do not store records near windows, skylights, or heating/cooling units.

✔ Do not store records on the floor. Records should be stored at least four inches off the floor (higher if flooding is more common).

✔ Locate all drains and check them regularly.

✔ Inspect the roof regularly for leaks.

✔ Do not install carpet in storage areas.

✔ Store records at least twelve inches from outside walls to prevent condensation.

✔ Keep plastic sheeting nearby to cover records quickly in case of water.

✔ Place drip pans under exposed pipes. Protect pipes vulnerable to freezing.

✔ Do not store particularly valuable records on the bottom or top shelves.

✔ Consider installing a sump pump with an alternate source of power.

DEVISING PROTECTION

A broad approach to disaster protection includes weighing three options for the protection of records:

- duplication and dispersal
- on-site protection
- off-site storage

Duplication and Dispersal

An effective way to protect records against disasters is to store a second copy at another location. Some records have a natural dispersal: additional copies are distributed elsewhere as part of the normal course of business. In case of disaster, it usually is possible to re-create the records, though the re-creation may involve some time and expense.

For other records, there is no natural dispersal. In certain instances, it may be desirable to create one or more additional copies specifically for remote storage. If copies must be made of a large volume of records, microfilm or digitization usually is more cost-effective than photocopying.

> "Swiss police have secretly tracked the whereabouts of mobile phone users via a telephone company computer that records billions of movements going back more than half a year, a Sunday newspaper reported.
> "The revelation ... triggered objections from politicians and the country's privacy ombudsman about high-tech snooping on citizens who like the convenience of a mobile phone."
>
> —*Reuters*, December 28, 1997.

An archives that has copied records onto preservation microfilm also has disaster protection, provided the original records or original microfilm are not stored in the same facility as the duplicate microfilm.

When choosing duplication and dispersal as a protection method, the copy of the vital record stored off-site is normally a duplicate of the original record. This facilitates the destruction of obsolete duplicates when replaced by an updated copy.

Computer backup tapes created in the normal course of systems maintenance, or other electronic copies routinely created in the normal course of business, may be used as a vital records copy. This natural dispersal is the simplest way to protect electronic vital records.

Archivists need to consider several factors when deciding where to store copies of vital records.

- Copies of emergency operating vital records, to use the federal term, must be accessible quickly for use in the event of a disaster or emergency.
- Copies of legal and financial rights records may not be needed as quickly. They can be stored far away from the institution.[18]

On-Site Protection

For some records, duplication and dispersal is not an option. For example, current accounting records may have to be kept on-site so they are available for immediate reference. There also are times when the most current version of a document is the vital record—when the document is updated tomorrow, today's document no longer is vital. The crucial time, in this case, is overnight.

On-site protection usually involves fireproof storage, either in cabinets or vaults. Such storage must be used on a daily basis if the organization's interests are to be protected adequately. As discussed above, however, fire is not the only disaster from which records must be protected. Records should be stored as far away from potential sources of water damage as possible.

Photograph 8.1 A vault door typical of that found in many archives Photograph courtesy of the Roman Catholic Diocese of Amarillo (Texas).

One important caveat with fireproof cabinets is in order: not all cabinets offer an equal level of protection. Before purchasing any cabinet, it is important to review the "fire rating" to determine the following:

- Will the cabinet protect the records for as long as it will take to extinguish the fire? The fire rating gives the protection in hours.
- Is the cabinet rated for the proper medium? Cabinets designed to protect paper records should *not* be used

for magnetic or photographic media; in the event of fire, their interior temperature and humidity will get too high for these fragile media.

Off-Site Storage

In some cases, the only copy of a record will be stored off-site. For example, archives may opt to store the original corporate charter off the premises. This option is only appropriate for records not needed for reference on a regular basis. If the record is needed for reference, it must be duplicated before being sent off-site.

"It was only an order for supplies, some latches and hinges, and a few other bits of hardware. But it was 232 years old and signed by Boston selectmen, including John Hancock. And this being a city that covets its history, a city archivist surfing the Internet blanched when she saw it for sale on eBay."

—*Boston Globe*, March 6, 2003.

Archives storing vital records off-site will need to evaluate the potential storage location carefully. Most archivists insist on a personal visit rather than just reviewing promotional materials. In conducting the visit, the archivist should try to answer the following questions:

- Is the facility secure? What does one need to do to gain access?
- Do they keep logs of visitors?
- Are there alarms, video monitors, and other security devices?
- Are temperature and humidity readings recorded? If so, what were the recent readings?
- Is the facility located beyond the area likely to be affected by a disaster that befalls your archives?
- How does the facility control records once entered into its system?
- How easy is it to retrieve records? What is the turn-around time?
- Are you willing to stake your reputation within your own organization on the adequacy of this off-site facility?

Of all these questions, the last is probably the most important one. If there is a problem with the off-site facility, others within the organization are likely to emphasize that the "archivist approved the off-site facility." The archivist must have a very high comfort level with any off-site facility before entrusting it with records.

PLANNING RESPONSES

Archives and libraries use disaster plans to summarize the above thinking, state it clearly, and provide a blueprint for use during an actual disaster or emergency. All the debating should happen at the planning stage—not at the time of a disaster, when minutes count.

Figure 8.6 presents the sections of a typical disaster plan.[19]

Fig. 8.6 Sections of a Disaster Plan	
Section	**Contents**
Introduction	Purpose or rationale; scope of the plan; references to related institutional documents or policies
Establishment of authority and assignment of responsibilities	List of names and recovery duties (especially the recovery manager); work and home phone numbers of key people
Recovery procedures	Step-by-step instructions for disaster response activities; sections dealing with each type of medium (paper, photographic, etc.); lists of necessary supplies for each procedure; names and phone numbers for consultants or vendors (vacuum freeze-drying, for example)
Appendices	Phone tree; additional contacts; supplies; floor plans; checklists.

Upon completion, the disaster plan should be submitted for approval by administrators at various levels, including the board of trustees in a small institution. Discussing and revising the plan becomes a way of educating administrators about the risks, how to minimize them, and how to deal with the disaster if it occurs.

Disaster plans should be tested regularly. I know of one business that tested its disaster plan by assuming that the entire facility had been destroyed. The recovery team was given a list of questions that they had to answer based upon information that was supposed to be duplicated off-site. Among the questions were:

- Who were the employees assigned to the facility at the time of the disaster?

- What was the current status of a major product then under development?
- What were the locations of the gas mains serving the facility?
- What was the current cash position of the facility?

Such rigorous tests are the only way to make certain that the plan will work when needed.

While it may seem obvious, the disaster plan itself is a vital record. Copies must be accessible outside the area in which the disaster occurs. Copies must also be accessible any time of the day or night—especially for the first people to respond to a disaster after hours (often the maintenance or security staff). After all the planning, it would be a shame to have the plan go unused because no one could find it.[20]

"After weathering the worst disaster in New York's history with no apparent loss of life, two federal agencies whose regional offices were located in the World Trade Center are now facing a different kind of loss. Both the Securities and Exchange Commission and the Equal Employment Opportunity Commission housed their regional operations in 7 World Trade Center. The building is now gone, along with all of the offices' records."

—*New York Law Journal*, September 14, 2001.

DISASTER RESPONSE AND RECOVERY

General

Once the archivist either discovers a disaster or is informed about one, it is time to implement the disaster plan. The following steps offer a general framework for disaster response:

1. *Assess the disaster situation.* It may be helpful to use an initial damage assessment form to record responses. In the chaos following a disaster, it would be easy to miss something important.
2. *Contact the insurer.* Insurance companies should be contacted immediately. It is helpful to begin taking photographs as soon as the disaster is discovered, for insurance and other purposes. A Polaroid, digital, or other instant camera should be part of the disaster response kit.

3. *Convene required staff and experts.* Once there is an initial assessment, it is time to call in staff members and relevant experts. All members of the team are working members—there are no honorary members. Furthermore, normal reporting relationships are suspended during the disaster: even a senior executive helping with recovery takes direction from a lower-ranking person identified in the plan as the disaster response coordinator.

4. *Set up a command post.* There must be a safe place that can be used to coordinate activities. Communication with the command post is important and may require the use of two-way radios or cellular telephones.

5. *Activate plans for supplies, additional staff, and volunteers.* Depending upon the severity of the disaster, other parts of the plan may be activated. If volunteers are needed, "on the job training" is necessary to ensure that well-meaning volunteers do not injure themselves or damage records.

6. *Make sure the building is safe.* Firefighters or other emergency personnel must certify that the building is safe before archivists can enter. Not only must the structure be sound, but also the area must be free of contamination from asbestos, PCBs, or other hazardous substances. A risk of electrical shock is present in any wet environment. An archivist needs to avoid the temptation of being a hero—rushing into an unsafe area can result in personal injury.

7. *Stop the source of the problem.* If there is a fire, it must be extinguished before recovery can begin. Similarly, if there is a flood, the flow of water must first be stopped. It is important to note that heat can cause delayed ignition of paper in file cabinets and vaults for up to three days.

8. *Stabilize the environment.* The archivist should try to keep the temperature in the room below 60 degrees and to reduce humidity by using dehumidifiers. It is important to keep air moving to prevent mold growth. Records should not be returned to an unstable environment.

9. *Protect or remove records.* Records can be covered with plastic sheeting for a short period of time to

protect them from imminent water damage. Also consider moving records to a higher location to protect them from rising water.

10. *Recover damaged records.* If records are damaged, they will need to be dealt with in a systematic way, from highest to lowest priority. The next two sections provide detail on recovery of fire- and water-damaged records.

11. *Conclude the initial response phase.* The initial response phase should end with a debriefing about what worked and what did not. This feedback should lead to revisions of the institution's disaster plan. Also, restored records remain more vulnerable than other records. They should be checked periodically for mold, fungus, or other deterioration.[21]

"At least 40,000 photographs of driver license applicants in Alabama were destroyed in a computer foul-up....The department learned the photographs were missing after repairing a software glitch that took the statewide system down December 13. The problem was fixed December 22, but the crash created a printing 'backlog' that will delay issuance of some 25,000 licenses."

—*Birmingham News*, January 17, 1998.

Recovering Fire-Damaged Records

In many instances, fire-damaged records are beyond recovery. The information they contain, however, might be found in other records stored elsewhere.

Charred paper can be trimmed and gently cleaned. It may be possible to return these records to the files. If the records are too fragile, extensively damaged, or contaminated, it is best to photocopy or microfilm the records and substitute the copies for the originals.

Photographic and magnetic media are likely to melt in a fire, making recovery even more difficult.

Recovering Water-Damaged Records

Water damage is common in most archival disasters. Every archivist, therefore, should be prepared to deal with water damage on a small or large scale. I can remember sacrificing more than one business suit to the recovery of records damaged by leaking pipes.

Photograph 8.2 It is common to use plastic to protect valuable parts of archival collections, including artifacts, from water as well as dust and atmospheric pollutants. Photograph courtesy of the Harley-Davidson Motor Company Archives. Copyright Harley-Davidson.

The following are some hints for the archivist facing water damage to collections and storage areas:

- Wear sturdy shoes when reentering the area, because of the possibility of broken glass and harmful debris.
- Resist the temptation to try to restore items on-site. First, get them out of the wet area, then worry about restoring them.
- Do not try to press water out of items. Also, do not stack wet items. Both practices are likely to damage the materials.
- It is possible to air-dry items, especially if they are merely damp or wet around the edges. In a well-ventilated area, stand books upright and fan them open slightly; at regular intervals they should be re-fanned and inverted. One can also interleave items with absorbent blotter paper or unprinted newsprint.
- Separate groups of soaked records with freezer or waxed paper.

- Use cubic-foot boxes or plastic milk crates for packing records.

- If items are severely soaked, or if large numbers are involved, freeze them. Freezing buys time by stopping mold growth and other deterioration.

- Frozen records can be dried in a self-defrosting freezer. Expect this to take several weeks to several months.

- Vacuum freeze-drying is another option. This process vaporizes ice crystals without permitting them to melt. Another benefit is that mud, dirt, and soot are lifted to the surface, facilitating later cleaning.

- Microfilm and other photographic media are more susceptible to water damage than is paper, and, as already noted, they are very sensitive to temperature and humidity. Because of the time and expense required for the recovery of these media (and the frequent need to consult outside experts) it is imperative that the archivist identify priorities for restoration and procedures to follow *before* a disaster occurs. In general, improper or sudden drying of these media may cause more damage than keeping them wet until an expert can restore them.[22]

Electronic Records Disasters

With electronic records, the best choice is to have backup files of records, so recovery can be done at a keyboard rather than in a flooded basement. If damaged magnetic records must be recovered, the archivist is well advised to seek professional assistance.

Many electronic records disasters, however, are of much smaller scale, involving everything from power surges to lost documentation. Some hints for minimizing electronic records disasters are:

- Use an uninterruptable power supply (UPS) for crucial systems.
- Use virus detection software.
- Implement a system of password-protected access to electronic files.
- Store copies of software and documentation off-site.
- Develop and implement a regular off-site backup schedule.

- Assess recoverability of information from other sources (such as paper or microfilm)
- Set up a cooperative recovery agreement with another institution possessing a similar computing infrastructure.[23]

"Backing up a computer ranks somewhere between cleaning the oven and checking the batteries in a smoke detector on most people's long-avoided to-do lists. They are all good ideas but, for some reason, you never follow through on any of them."

—*New York Times*, February 21, 2002.

CONCLUSION

This chapter began by equating security and disasters with archival nightmares. However, unlike nightmares that scare us in the dark, archivists can take some control during the day—by anticipating problems and planning for them. Moreover, archivists *must* anticipate and plan in order to fulfill the part of their mission that deals with preserving records of enduring value. Those records, once preserved and protected, are ready for use by researchers.

NOTES

1. Lewis J. Bellardo and Lynn Lady Bellardo, *A Glossary for Archivists, Manuscript Curators, and Records Managers* (Chicago: Society of American Archivists, 1992). Two helpful volumes on security are: Gregor Trinkaus-Randall, *Protecting Your Collection: A Manual of Archival Security* (Chicago: Society of American Archivists, 1995); and Timothy Walch, *Archives and Manuscripts: Security* (Chicago: Society of American Archivists, 1977). For an excellent one-volume treatment of disaster planning, see Judith Fortson, *Disaster Planning and Recovery: A How-To-Do-It Manual for Librarians and Archivists* (New York: Neal-Schuman, 1992).

2. For more on physical security systems, see Trinkaus-Randall, *Protecting Your Collections*, 43-59. This book contains photographs of locks, alarms, and detection devices.

3. Trinkaus-Randall, *Protecting Your Collections*, 63-64.

4. "The Office of Preservation of the Library of Congress advises repositories to use an ink that is nonfading, ineradicable with solvents

or bleaches, neutral or slightly alkaline in pH, essentially nonbleeding and nonmigratory, stable at heat up to 300 degrees Fahrenheit, resistant to light for at least one hundred years, and slow drying on the stamp pad but fast drying on the document. At the present time, inks with these requirements are not commercially available, but the Office of Preservation of the Library of Congress, in conjunction with the Government Printing Office, has formulated and tested such an ink that is available from the Library free of charge to all who request it. A single two-ounce bottle will last at least ten years if properly used. The Library will not divulge the ink's formula, since such knowledge might make it possible to develop an effective means of eradication." Trinkaus-Randall, *Protecting Your Collections*, 13.

5. For more on dealing with a suspected theft, see Trinkaus-Randall, *Protecting Your Collections*, 62-63.

6. For a general discussion, see Virginia A Jones and Kris E. Keyes, *Emergency Management for Records and Information Management Programs* (Prairie Village, Kans.: ARMA International, 1997); also Miriam B. Kahn, *Disaster Response and Planning for Libraries* (Chicago: American Library Association, 1998).

7. "Management of Vital Records," final rule issued by the National Archives and Records Administration, *Federal Register* 60, no. 109 (June 7, 1995): 29989-92.

8. *Vital Records and Records Disaster Mitigation and Recovery: An Instructional Guide*, (http://www.archives.gov).

9. For a book-length treatment of disaster planning developed in the Canadian context, see Johanna Wellheiser and Jude Scott, *An Ounce of Prevention: Integrated Disaster Planning for Archives, Libraries, and Records Centres*, 2d ed. (Lanham, Md.: Scarecrow Press and the Canadian Archives Foundation, 2002).

10. Adapted from Fortson, *Disaster Planning and Recovery*, 82.

11. This checklist was drawn from two sources: the New York State Archives and Records Administration (SARA) and Fortson's *Disaster Planning and Recovery*. The SARA information was prepared by its Local Government Records Advisory Services, and is accessible at the SARA Internet site (http://nyslgti.gen.ny.us:80/empireweb/SARA/home.html).

12. Inergen is a mixture of nitrogen, argon, and carbon dioxide. It extinguishes fires by reducing the oxygen level in the area to below 15 percent (the point at which most combustibles will no longer burn); see (http://www.inergen.com).

13. The FM-200 agent is stored in cylinders as a liquid and pressurized with nitrogen. It does not work by removing ambient room oxygen; rather, it chemically and physically interrupts the fire. See the FM-200 Web site for more detailed information (http://www.fm-200.com).

14. Trinkaus-Randall, *Protecting Your Collections*, 32-33.

15. See the brochure *Fire Suppression for Critical Areas*, (http://www.inergen.com).

16. For more on earthquakes, see Fortson, *Disaster Planning and Recovery*, 33-43.

17. This checklist comes from the New York State Archives and Fortson, *Disaster Planning and Recovery*.

18. "Management of Vital Records," NARA.

19. Fortson, *Disaster Planning and Recovery*, 88-95. See also "How to Design a Disaster Recovery Plan," News Digest, International Institute of Municipal Clerks (October 1992): 1-9; and Trinkaus-Randall, *Protecting Your Collections*, 33-36.

20. For more on disaster plans, see Mildred O'Connell, "Disaster Planning: Writing and Implementing Plans for Collections-Holding Institutions," *Technology and Conservation* (summer 1983): 18-25; Sally Buchanan, "Disaster: Prevention, Preparedness and Action," *Library Trends* (fall 1981): 241-52; *Hell and High Water: A Disaster Information Sourcebook* (New York: New York Metropolitan Reference and Research Library Agency [METRO], 1988); and Trinkaus-Randall, *Protecting Your Collections*, 33-36.

21. These steps were drawn from Sally A. Buchanan, *Resource Materials for Disaster Planning in New York Institutions* (Albany: New York State Library, 1988) and other documents found on the New York State Archives' Web site.

22. Adapted from Fortson, *Disaster Planning and Recovery*, 31-32, 45-75. See also *Western Association for Art Conservation Newsletter*, May 1988, and Peter Waters, *Procedures for Salvage of Water-Damaged Library Materials* (Washington, D.C.: Library of Congress, 1975).

23. Adapted from *Electronic Records Management: Checklist for Disaster Planning and Preparedness* (Albany: New York State Archives and Records Administration, 1995).

9 ACCESS, REFERENCE, AND OUTREACH

There is an old saying that "the proof of the pudding is in the eating." Despite our choice of ingredients and care in following the recipe, the only way to judge success is by sampling the final product. The same applies to the case in archives, where the "eating" involves use (but not consumption) of the collection.[1]

Archival records exist to be used. Identifying and preserving records, though laudable goals in themselves, are not enough to justify an archival program. This is not to say that all archives exist primarily to serve the general public. In many institutions (for example, businesses), the archives exists to serve the organization itself. In these cases, very few non-employees may ever gain access to archival records.

Whatever the organizational setting, the dual archival responsibility—preservation and use—introduces a tension. Archivists try to make materials available to the fullest extent possible, consistent with a reasonable regard for their preservation. The use of records can lead to deterioration, damage, and theft. If records were locked away in a "perfect" environment, they certainly would last longer. Every time someone uses a record, the lifetime of that record is shortened. Archivists must weigh the demands of present day researchers against the potential demands of posterity—use versus preservation.

Archives are not unique in this tension—it also applies to library materials. The tension is compounded, however, by the one-of-a-kind materials found in an archives. An archival program must constantly work to achieve the proper balance.[2]

ACCESS

Access is defined as the "right, opportunity, or means of finding, using, or approaching documents and/or information."[3] Access is the authority to obtain information from or perform research using archival materials. As will be noted below, granting *access* is not the same as granting permission to *duplicate* the materials in an archival repository. The latter involves archivists in the area of copyright.

ACCESS TRADITIONS

In the United States, there are two traditions in administering access: the historical manuscripts tradition and the public archives tradition. Elements of each tradition continue to influence contemporary archival practice.

"Images sent down by U.S. secret satellites in past decades are going up for public viewing.

"Later this month, the National Imagery and Mapping Agency (NIMA) is set to declassify Keyhole (KH) imagery from the KH-7 and KH-9 satellites, two highly hush-hush intelligence gathering spacecraft of Cold War vintage.

"The unveiling of the satellite snapshots is part of the U.S. government's Historical Imagery Declassification Program. Purpose of the program centers on three goals: Promote the spirit of open governance; demonstrate results of taxpayer investment in national security and ensure that researchers—from environmentalists to historians—have access to useful and unique sources of information."

—space.com, September 6, 2002.

Historical Manuscripts Tradition

The Library of Congress perhaps best exemplifies the historical manuscripts tradition. In this tradition, access is based upon an agreement between the repository and donor that exchanges ownership of the papers for restrictions on their use. In negotiating the deed of gift agreement, the donor is able to define access parameters, usually along one of the following lines:

- The donor or designee approves each application for access.
- The donor imposes an absolute restriction on access, usually for a fixed period of time.

In this tradition, ultimate preservation is viewed as more important than quick access. This viewpoint leads to a major disadvantage: the entire "forest" of a collection may be closed to protect a few sensitive "trees."

Public Archives Tradition

As exemplified by the National Archives, access policy in the public archives tradition is based upon the assumption that records with a high public policy content should be open. Since these records belong "to the people," the people should have access to them as quickly and as fully as possible.

In the public archives tradition, restrictions are regarded as a necessary evil. They usually are administered along the following lines:

- General restriction categories are established (such as national security).
- Archivists conduct a page-by-page review of the records against these categories, restricting records that fit each category.

This categorization leads to fast access to *most* of a collection, rather than restricting the entire collection. The forest is open quickly because the sensitive trees can be identified and segregated. There are disadvantages, however, to the page-by-page review:

- It is time-consuming, labor-intensive, and expensive.
- Since it relies on the judgment of the archivist, there is an element of subjectivity.

These traditions sometimes overlap. High-ranking public and private officials, for example, often consider their files to be personal papers rather than organizational records. If these are *personal* papers, then the high-ranking official would be able to negotiate access policies through a deed of gift agreement. If these are *archival* records, then

Photograph 9.1 This is an example of a well-designed archival reference room. Note how the staff members at the reference desk can observe all researchers. Photograph courtesy of the University of Arizona Library, Special Collections.

access would be governed by organizational policies rather than the wishes of the official. In this case, the two traditions would have dramatically different impacts on access to the materials.

"The heart of writer Alex Haley thumped. He was examining microfilmed census records in the National Archives Building in Washington, D.C.

""Suddenly in utter astonishment I found myself looking down there on "Tom Murray, black, blacksmith...." "Irene Murray, black, housewife..." followed by the names of Grandma's older sisters—most of whom I'd listened to countless times on Grandma's front porch. "Elizabeth, age 6"—nobody in the world but my Great Aunt Liz! At the time of that census, Grandma wasn't even born yet!' he has written.

"Haley had just discovered the first documentary evidence that led him to his past and to his best seller *Roots*."

—*Newsday*, March 31, 1985.

ADMINISTERING ACCESS

With these traditions as a foundation, the archivist faces the task of administering access on a daily basis. Four related concepts help the archivist meet the challenge:

- equal access
- full access
- competing rights
- restrictions

Equal Access

Archivists try to make materials available to researchers on equal terms. Archivists should neither permit access by only one researcher nor discriminate against particular types of researchers. These are basic tenets of the *Code of Ethics for Archivists* reprinted in Appendix B. Even such basic tenets, however, can be difficult to implement.

For example, the Director of the Department of Archives and Special Collections at North Fork University faced the following two situations:

- A faculty member in the political science department was instrumental in securing the donation of the papers of a local politician. As a way of "saying thank you," the professor asked that the archivist give her six months of exclusive access before the collection is opened to other researchers.

- An astrologer, considering sending his son to North Fork, visited the archives to examine the founding documents of the university. He wanted to know if the stars were favorable for his son's academic career at NFU.

How should the archivist handle these situations? Should the professor be given special treatment? The obvious answer may be "no," but how will the archivist then deal with a potential enemy within NFU, someone who may talk negatively about the archives within university circles?

What about the astrologer? Is this the kind of researcher that the university wishes to encourage? If the records are open, should they be open to everyone willing to abide by the rules and regulations? Is it the archivist's responsibility to determine the worthiness of a research request?

As these examples illustrate, the ethical challenges of granting equal access often involve shades of gray.

Full Access

Archivists try to grant access to *all* materials that may help a researcher, except those materials closed by law or other restrictions (either donor- or repository-imposed). Full access is not always easy to provide, however.

Some researchers are very secretive about their projects. A doctoral candidate embarking on dissertation research, for example, visited the North Fork University Archives. The archivist attempted to learn more about the dissertation topic in order to help the researcher. The researcher, however, would only discuss the topic in general terms; he was afraid that someone would "steal" the topic before he could finish the dissertation, thereby invalidating all his work.

On the other hand, assisting even a forthright researcher can be hindered by the nature of modern archives and manuscript collections. As collections get larger, it becomes more difficult to know their contents in detail. Archivists who do not know their collections will have a difficult time guiding researchers. The only solution is to rely on finding aids.[4] Full access implies that an archives has basic bibliographic control over *all* collections—both processed *and* unprocessed.

Competing Rights

Administering access places an archivist at the intersection of often-competing rights: the right to know and the right to privacy. Both are part of the American legal and cultural tradition. Archivists try to respect both rights, realizing that such respect may place the archivist in a difficult position.

Right to Know. Americans pride themselves in having an open society, especially as it relates to government actions. The Freedom of Information Act outlines specific procedures whereby citizens can request access to government records and information. Some states have "sunshine laws" and "open meeting laws" meant to prevent secret decision-making. Taken together, Americans expect to be able to get access to information, even information that once involved the nation's deepest secrets.

The right-to-know tradition also appears in the private sector. Genealogists and family researchers expect churches to provide information about their ancestors from sacramental records. Potential investors expect corporations to disclose information from their records that may affect share price. Patients expect to have access to their medical records to confirm a diagnosis or to monitor treatment. Therefore, all archivists, regardless of institutional setting, want information available and usable to the fullest extent possible while respecting the right to privacy.[5]

"A Nassau [County, N.Y.] judge yesterday refused to give the state permission to review confidential court records of divorce cases to gather statistical information on child support....

"[The judge] turned down the request from the state Department of Social Services after matrimonial lawyers argued that access to the records would be an unnecessary invasion of privacy. Before ruling, [the judge] said she was concerned about researchers reading files they might find 'titillating' and misinterpreting the financial information."

—*Newsday*, April 23, 1986.

Right to Privacy. Americans also cherish an individual's right to be left alone—to live free of unwanted publicity or intrusion. This is enshrined in legislation such as the Privacy Act and the Family Educational Rights and Privacy Act (FERPA). The latter act, dealing with student records, has changed the way educational institutions handle recommendations, transcripts, and other records.

Archivists respect the right to privacy partially out of a desire to prevent embarrassment. In these litigious times, however, archivists also are aware of the possibility of lawsuits and other legal actions. Whatever the motivation, understanding and respecting privacy is part of the archival consciousness.

At the time of donation or transfer, an archivist tries to determine the privacy issues inherent in the records and how to address these concerns. It is important to note that there is no privacy right for the dead. Heirs and other living relatives, however, *do* have a right to privacy that the archivist should consider when administering access.

Case files are the most difficult records to administer from a privacy standpoint. Case information usually is given as part of a confidential relationship with a doctor, social worker, clergyperson, or other professional. The information in the file is personal in the truest sense: it relates to a person at his or her deepest levels. Revealing the information certainly could be embarrassing for the subject.

A few years ago, the world witnessed a dramatic example of the conflict between these competing rights. After the fall of East Germany and other Communist regimes, once-secret police files were opened for research. On more than one occasion, people learned for the first time that the informant whose testimony condemned them to years in prison was none other than their spouse or other close relative. In these situations, much personal pain accompanied the move to an open society.

Restrictions

Restrictions are the way an archivist attempts to balance the competing rights. Restrictions usually flow from a desire to protect privacy, either of the donor or a third party. Restrictions should be noted on all finding aids, especially those distributed to researchers before they arrive at the archives. Imagine how frustrating it would be for a researcher to travel across the country to visit an archives, only to learn that all or most of the collection is restricted—"unhappy camper" would be an understatement.

There are three broad categories of restrictions:

- completely closed or sealed
- partially closed or restricted due to contents
- restricted for preservation or security reasons

Completely Closed or Sealed. If a collection is completely closed or sealed, no one—sometimes not even the archival staff—may see the contents. This drastic step is difficult to justify in light of the archivist's mission to make records available.

If complete closure *is* imposed, however, it is best to do so for a set time, rather than to leave the issue vague and open-ended. This guarantees that everyone, including the donor, knows that the collection will eventually be open for research.

It is common to close unprocessed collections completely—except, of course, to the archivists who must process them in order to lift the closure. How can an archivist administer privacy, copyright, or other concerns if relevant items remain unidentified in an unprocessed collection? Most archivists take the safer course of not granting access until the collection is processed.

Closed or Partially Restricted. In many cases, a collection is open, but researchers are permitted to use only some of the material. As with the previous category, it is best if restrictions are for a specific length of time rather than remaining in effect indefinitely. It is also best to avoid situations in which the archivist must approach the donor (or other designee) for permission each time a researcher wants to consult a collection. Not only is this a time-consuming process, but also it can pose questions about whether or not access is equal for all researchers.

Figure 9.1 lists the most common reasons for restricting access due to content. If only part of a collection exhibits these categories, the sensitive part would be removed from the collection prior to researcher use. It is customary to insert a separation sheet at the point of removal so researchers know that part of the collection was removed and why. Naturally, if an entire collection consists of sensitive material as defined in figure 9.1, the entire collection would be closed to researchers.

Fig. 9.1 Reasons for Restricting Access Due to Content

Reason	Description
Privacy	Information that would violate the right to privacy
Business information	Trade secrets and other proprietary business information
Personnel data	Salaries, performance reviews, and other employee data
Investigative information	Kept closed to protect both the individuals involved and the institutional investigative process
Statutory and other directed restrictions	National security restrictions, for example

In some cases, access is *conditional:* researchers may use the collection if they agree in advance to certain conditions. Usually this agreement with the researcher is made in writing to prevent future misunderstandings. Some typical conditions are

- the review of notes by the archives staff before the researcher leaves
- the prior review of any potential publication
- the limitation on or prohibition against quotation or publication

Some of these conditions may seem strange, especially to librarians accustomed to dealing with previously published materials. The unpublished nature of archival materials, however, means that an individual or organization—other than the archival repository—may hold the copyright, including the right to first publication. As noted in chapter 4, copyright *may* be transferred to the archives along with the transfer of the physical property—or the copyright holder may retain this right. The deed of gift agreement should be specific and unambiguous on this point.

Conditions placed on researcher access usually originate with the donor of the materials. Conditions are also common in archives that have had a negative experience with a researcher—either unauthorized publication of information or inaccurate citation of sources. The most important point is this: if conditions are imposed, they should be imposed equally upon all researchers.

Restricted for Preservation/Security Reasons. Access may be restricted for reasons other than the *content* of the collection. The *physical condition* of the items, or their market value, may also lead to restrictions. Fragile or deteriorated originals may suffer further damage if handled by researchers. Items with a monetary value may disappear in the course of research use.

"The Vatican announced today that it would partly open its prewar archives next year, but would not make available documents on Pius XII's controversial World War II pontificate for at least three more years. Jewish leaders and scholars expressed considerable disappointment, just as the Vatican itself predicted they would in the announcement."

—*New York Times*, February 16, 2002.

In such cases, it is common for the archivist to replace the original with a duplicate on paper or another medium. If only a few items are of concern, replacing the original with a photocopy is the usual practice. (The original is then stored in a secure environment.) If a larger number of items are of preservation or security concern, microfilm and digitizing become the preferred duplicating options.

Access and the Archival Repository

Administering access in an individual archival repository usually involves three steps:

1. *Prepare a general access policy for the repository.* This document should outline access and reference policies, indicate fees (if any), and detail searching and reference services. Some institutional archives also establish a default closure period for organizational records. The access policy should be approved by the governing body of the institution.[6]

2. *Determine specific restrictions for individual collections or parts of collections.* Some collections or parts of collections will be closed for longer or shorter periods than the default period. Board minutes, for example, may be closed longer, while press releases may be open immediately.

3. *Consistently apply the restrictions by developing a procedure manual and training staff in its use.* The larger the staff that administers access, the more important this third point becomes.

"The Supreme Court yesterday refused to allow publication of an unauthorized biography of J. D. Salinger that includes quotations from [unpublished] letters the novelist wrote. The justices, without comment, let stand a federal appeals court ruling that publication of J. D. Salinger: A Writing Life would violate federal copyright law....

"Ian Hamilton, a literary critic for The London Sunday Times... completed work on the Salinger biography in 1986.

"Hamilton located, and quoted from, letters sent to and from Salinger that had been placed in university libraries across the country."

—*Newsday*, October 6, 1987.

Once the access policies are established, the manuals are written, and the staff is trained, it is time for the archives to admit researchers.

REFERENCE

Reference service includes a range of activities to assist researchers in using archival materials. These activities make the past accessible to present and future generations. Effective reference service can make the difference in an archives fulfilling its mission. Such effective service does not happen by accident.

When providing reference services, archivists tend to deal with two broad categories of individuals: researchers of the interpretation and researchers of the fact.[7]

Researchers of the interpretation are the "traditional" archival users. These researchers—the stereotypical scholars on sabbatical—have weeks or months to spend wading through the collections in archives. They are "panning for gold" rather than "expecting a quick strike." Researchers of the interpretation want archivists to produce any bit of evidence that may relate; they are willing to make the links and connections, even if it takes a great deal of time. Contrary to popular opinion, this type of researcher no longer is the major user of archives.

Researchers of the fact now predominate. These researchers want a quick strike. They are looking for specific information and want to find it as soon as possible. Rather than developing a theory of immigration, they want to know if their ancestor was on a particular ship. Genealogists, journalists, and many in-house users fall into this category.

Why does this distinction matter? Because each type of researcher will have different expectations about and preferences toward the range of research services archives provides. Researchers of the interpretation may not mind the finding aids that offer only a general overview of a collection; in fact, they may not use the finding aids at all, preferring to locate their own nuggets of gold. Researchers of the fact, by contrast, may not be so tolerant of a finding aid system they believe fails to meet their specific needs.

It may seem obvious to say that archivists need to understand their researchers. Sometimes, however, the obvious does not happen. Studies have shown that much of archival administration has been *material-centered* rather than *client-centered*. Many archivists believe that they are oriented to users, yet they do not even know who their users are. In one user survey conducted by a major archives program, 30 percent of the users checked "other" as the best description of themselves—implying that the archives did not even know how to define the categories of its users, an important first step to meeting their needs.[8]

Archives offer a range of reference services to meet the needs of both types of researchers, including:

Photograph 9.2 Forms used in providing reference services Photograph courtesy of the University of Arizona Library, Special Collections.

- providing information about and from holdings
- assisting with research visits
- providing or making duplicates

PROVIDING INFORMATION

Archivists provide two types of information: information *about* their holdings and information *from* their holdings. As with all aspects of archival work, the trick is to achieve the proper balance.

Providing information *about* holdings is recognized universally as part of the archivist's mission. Potential researchers need to know what is contained in a particular archival repository. Archivists provide this information through the range of finding aids discussed in chapter 6: guides, inventories, entries in online catalogs, and World Wide Web sites, for example. As noted above, information about holdings should include statements about restrictions—both general restrictions applicable to all collections and specific restrictions relating to individual collections.

"The Supreme Court today upheld the 20-year extension that Congress granted to all existing copyrights in 1998, declaring that while the extension might have been bad policy, it fell clearly within Congress's constitutional authority.

"The 7-to-2 decision came in the court's most closely watched intellectual property case in years, one with financial implications in the billions of dollars. A major victory for the Hollywood studios and other big corporate copyright holders that had lobbied strenuously for the extension, the ruling had the effect of keeping the original Mickey Mouse as well as other icons of mid-century American culture from slipping into the public domain."

—*New York Times*, January 16, 2003.

Providing information *from* holdings is more controversial. It is common for archives to receive mail, telephone, or e-mail requests from researchers unable to visit the repository, but who still want information from the collections. This places the archivist, especially in a small institution, in a difficult position. Should we do the requested research? If so, how much time should we spend on it?[9]

The main problem is with providing equal access, one of the goals outlined above. An archives program will need to be consistent in the way it handles such requests in order to provide equal access to its collections. As in so many other areas, it is necessary to develop policies and implement them consistently.

Many archives set a time limit for how long they will spend researching a particular request. Typical time periods are anywhere from ten minutes to an hour. A distant researcher who needs more time than this will often be referred to professional researchers near the archives who are willing to work on a contract basis. In order to avoid any appearance of a conflict of interest, the archivist should never recommend only one person.

Service to internal users often is treated separately. Archivists in businesses and similar institutional settings find that they spend a great deal of time doing research for others in the institution. This is a fact of institutional life. The archivist provides a service, as other staff members do with legal research or library services. Employees of the institution do not expect to perform these services themselves—that is why the institution established a library or an archives in the first place. When a vice president calls looking for information from the archives, the best response probably is not, "We have dozens of boxes that may relate. Come down between 9:00 a.m. and 5:00 p.m. and we will bring them out for you to examine." Others in the organization would consider this the equivalent of a lawyer saying, "If you would like to know if we can be sued, I have shelves full of law books you are welcome to consult."

Some archives waive the time limit on research in the case of senior administrators. This waiver is a different kind of archival survival than that associated with preservation efforts. Once again, it all comes down to understanding one's patrons in general and the specific person we are trying to assist at the moment.

Archivists publicize their holdings through external and internal means. Externally, archivists use various outreach efforts: speeches before professional and community organizations, finding aids, exhibits, and sites on the Internet. Internally, contacts with researchers who visit the repository offer archivists opportunities to publicize holdings—through interviews with researchers, explanation of in-house finding aids, and other approaches. The next section discusses these efforts in more detail.

ASSISTING WITH RESEARCH VISITS

An effective research visit to an archives involves three steps:

- entrance interview
- reference room activities
- exit interview

At each of these steps, both the archivist and the researcher have specific things they wish to accomplish, as shown in figure 9.2. The trick is to achieve these differing purposes in a collegial rather than an adversarial way.

Fig. 9.2 Research Visit Goals: Archivist and Researcher Perspectives

Step	What the Archivist Wishes to Accomplish	What the ResearcherWishes to Accomplish
Entrance interview	• confirm the identity of the researcher • determine researcher interests • explain rules and regulations • explain the use of finding aids	• find out about relevant collections • learn how the research room operates • gain access to collections of interest
Reference room activities	• protect the records from damage or theft • efficiently retrieve and refile records	• find the information they want as quickly as possible • have someone available to answer questions
Exit interviews	• get feedback on the collections, finding aids, and procedures	• be certain that follow-up work by the archives (photocopies, etc.) will take place.

Unless there is clear communication between the archivist and the researcher, misunderstanding about these three steps will likely occur. In such cases, a chart of inaccurate perceptions and expectations might look like figure 9.3.

Fig. 9.3 Research Visit Goals: Inaccurate Perceptions and Expectations

Step	What the Researcher Thinks the Archivist Wishes to Accomplish	What the Archivist Thinks the Researcher Wishes to Accomplish
Entrance interview	• Tell the researcher how wonderful the archives is	• Get out of the room as quickly as possible
Reference room activities	• Put as many obstacles as possible in the way of the research visit • Make the researcher's life as miserable as possible	• Receive undivided attention • Have the rules changed if they are inconvenient for the researcher
Exit interviews	• Find one more way to delay the process	• Leave for home as soon as possible

Entrance Interview

An entrance interview is a key part of archival reference service. It gives both parties in the reference process (the researcher and the archivist) a chance to communicate their expectations, needs, and limitations. An entrance interview can save time and frustration for both parties.

The entrance interview has the following specific objectives:

- *Confirm the identity of the researcher.* Most archives have researchers complete a registration form that gives such information as name, address, institutional affiliation, and research topic. Many archives require the researcher to furnish identification. Sometimes a photocopy of the ID is made; in case of theft or another security problem, this identification can be very important. If identification is required, it should be consistently required of *all* researchers.

- *Determine the researcher's needs.* The archivist tries to clarify the researcher's topic and available time. The archivist also will suggest secondary sources the researcher should consult as well as other repositories holding related primary sources.

- *Discuss the exchange of researcher information.* Researchers have a right to the privacy of their research. The archives should not identify researchers or their topics to other researchers without permission. Some researchers are willing to have archives share this information, provided they also learn of related research. Such permission should be given in writing.

- *Explain the institution's rules and regulations.* The archivist will explain rules covering the use of materials, citation and quotation, and photocopying. Many archives have the researcher sign a copy of the rules as an acknowledgment that the rules have been discussed and understood.

- *Explain the use of finding aids.* In particular, the archivist describes in-house finding aids and suggests collections where the researcher may want to begin research.

- *Explain fees.* If the archives charges any fees, these should be clearly explained in the entrance interview. Charging for *use* of the archives is controversial (it is done by some historical societies); however, almost all archives charge for photocopies and other duplicates (such as photographs, videotape, and audiotape).

Reference Room Activities

With preliminaries out of the way, the researcher moves to the reference room to consult the archival records. Since the physical aspects of the reference room are discussed in chapter 8, "Security," this chapter only covers policies and procedures.

The following is a summary of reference room activities:

1. *Researchers check all personal belongings.* Hats, coats, briefcases and other belongings are placed in a secure area. Notepaper and writing instruments (including personal computers) are the only items permitted in the reference room.

2. *Researchers sign a logbook each day they are in the reference room.* While this may seem an unnecessary step, the log could be important in case of theft. It would demonstrate that a researcher *was* in the reference room on a particular day, with the notations made in the researcher's own handwriting.

3. *Researchers complete a call slip for each collection or part of a collection.* Staff members use these call slips to pull collections off the shelves. The slips are also important in case of theft—they document that a person used a particular collection.

"Joe Black's death this year occurred just days before he was scheduled to make a digital recording of his life story as the first African-American pitcher to win a World Series game.

"The sad timing of his passing was not lost on Camille Crosby and Renee Poussaint, who started the National Visionary Leadership Project this year to help preserve the voice of a generation of legendary and pioneering African Americans now in their 70s and older.

"'There's that sense of 'Oh my heavens, if we don't get an opportunity, so much is going to be lost,' said Poussaint, and Emmy Award-winning journalist, who was poised to interview Black in May.

"She and Cosby, an educator and wife of comedian Bill Cosby, felt it was important to give the elders an opportunity to have their life stories told in their own words, rather than have those histories interpreted and passed on by others."

—*New Haven Register*, July 21, 2002.

---

4. *A staff member retrieves the requested materials.* Since there are no open stacks, the researcher remains in the reference room while the records are retrieved.

5. *One staff member is always in the reference room to watch researchers.* The unique nature of archival

materials means that researchers should always be observed in the reference room. While this need not be *obtrusive*, it should be *apparent* to researchers.

6. *Researchers return the records to the archives staff.* A staff member checks the records for completeness and refiles the material when time permits.

7. *Researchers leave the reference room.* In some archives, researchers and their belongings are subject to search. This should be spelled out in the rules and regulations as well as posted on signs.[10]

Exit Interview

An exit interview is an important—but often overlooked—part of archival reference service. All too often, a researcher just leaves without any further contact with the archives staff. When this happens, some real opportunities are lost.

"Since January, The Defense Department has withdrawn more than 6,000 documents from government Web sites—including federal reports detailing how to make anthrax easier to inhale or how to grow smallpox."

—ABCNews.com, February 17, 2002.

The exit interview takes the form of a conversation with a colleague. Among the questions an archivist asks are

- How valuable were the collections to you? Did they contain what you thought they would contain?
- How helpful were the finding aids? What can the archives do to make them more helpful?
- Did you encounter any problems with the records? Were items out of order or missing?
- How helpful were archival staff members?
- Do you know of other repositories with related collections?

EAD and Reference Services

Chapter 6 discussed Encoded Archival Description (EAD), a standard for making inventories available on the World Wide Web. As EAD moves toward widespread implementation, it will affect reference services as much as it affects archival description. Richard Szary believes that EAD will transform the reference function in five ways:

1. *Increased standardization of finding aid information.* Researchers will find it easier to move from one finding aid to another because the information and presentation will be the same.

2. *Ability to search within and across finding aids.* Researchers will be able to search for a subject across finding aids or sections of a finding aid (scope and content note, series description, etc.).

3. *Integration of finding aids with the catalog.* The current system is a top-down model of information retrieval: researchers begin with summary catalog entries to identify records of possible interest, proceed to perusing a more detailed finding aid to identify subsets, and finally examine the materials. With EAD, researchers can move from summary to detail very easily.

4. *Increased user self-sufficiency and staff productivity.* In most archives, reference staffs have served as gatekeepers to help researchers through the labyrinth of finding aids. With EAD, researchers will be able to do much more on their own.

5. *Increased need to educate users.* Archivists will need to spend more time educating researchers about the new descriptive architecture, the intended function of the finding aid in that architecture, and the basics of primary source research.[11]

EAD promises to democratize archival finding aids and make the intricacies of archival research more transparent to users. This should help archivists achieve the goal of full and equal access to materials.

MAKING DUPLICATES

In the course of their visits, many researchers request copies of archival materials. Archives usually try to be as accommodating as time and staff will allow. The reproduction of archival materials, however, enmeshes the archivist in questions of copyright: can the archives duplicate or permit the duplication of the requested items?

General Considerations

Copyright is the right vested by law in the author of a document and his or her heirs or assignees to publish or reproduce a document, or to authorize publication or reproduction of a document. Copyright is a property right that pertains to original works of authorship. It is one part of what is known as intellectual property, which also includes patents and trademarks.[12]

The first question for the archivist is: Who is the copyright holder? It is not always the author, since a document may have been produced as a "work for hire" or as part of one's employment responsibilities. The determination of the copyright holder can be a complex matter best discussed with legal counsel. As noted in chapter 4, the resolution of copyright questions should be addressed in a deed of gift agreement.

Organizations or persons can only grant permission to duplicate items for which they possess the copyright. In general terms, institutions hold the copyright to their *outgoing* correspondence, but not their *incoming* correspondence. The same is true of individuals acting in a personal capacity. As one can see, a large collection of materials would contain items from numerous copyright holders.

"Among African-Americans, Denmark Vesey's plot to lead a slave rebellion in Charleston, S.C. in 1822 has always been a symbol of black resistance to oppression, proof that slaves did not docilely accept their fate. Along with slave rebellions like the Nat Turner uprising in 1831, the Vesey conspiracy has been held up as proof that the spirits of blacks were not broken by captivity. Had Vesey's plot succeeded, it would have been the largest slave rebellion in American history. But the conspiracy was thwarted by informers—or so historians have thought. Thirty-four slaves and Vesey, the one free black, were hanged as a result of the charges, making it probably the biggest execution ever in an American civilian judicial proceeding.

"But in an article in November in the William and Mary Quarterly, a leading journal of early American history, … a professor of history … has questioned whether a conspiracy took place. The paper has ignited a debate among scholars over what happened and how to interpret historical records."

—*New York Times*, February 23, 2002.

The Copyright Act of 1976, which took effect in 1978, eliminated a previous distinction between published and unpublished items. In the past, published items were governed by statutory law while unpublished items were governed by common law copyright. The intention of the new law is that eventually *all* published and unpublished materials, including those in archival institutions, will be in the public domain where they can be reproduced without infringing copyright.

Under the old law (prior to 1978), copyrights for *published works* lasted for twenty-eight years plus a renewal of another twenty-eight years. In the early 1960s, the renewal term was stretched to forty-seven years, for a total of seventy-five years of protection. In October 1998, Congress enacted the Sonny Bono Copyright Term Extension Act, which added another twenty years to the term of protection. Therefore, the rule today for works published before 1978 is that they are generally protected for a maximum of ninety-five years.[13]

Unpublished works—the kinds of documents that fill archives—also have copyright protection. Originally, an unpublished work created before 1978 was granted perpetual "common-law" copyright rather than statutory protection. The Copyright Act of 1976, however, rescinded all common-law copyright and subjected the older, unpublished work to a statutory term of protection (life of the author plus fifty years). As noted above, the Sonny Bono Copyright Term Extension Act added twenty years to the term or protection, meaning that the basic term today is the life of the author plus 70 years.[14]

One other consideration comes into play for unpublished works. To prevent abrupt termination of long-standing copyrights, the Copyright Act of 1976 provided that none of the former common-law rights would expire until after December 31, 2002. While the Term Extension Act did add twenty years to the duration of the copyrights, it did not alter the December 31, 2002 expiration date. Therefore, On January 1, 2003 unpublished works entered the public domain provided that the author was dead for 70 years or more. On each subsequent New Year's Day, the unpublished works of authors who died seventy years before will enter the public domain.[15]

"The [George W.] Bush administration has put a much tighter lid than recent presidents on government proceedings and the public release of information, exhibiting a penchant for secrecy that has been striking to historians, legal experts and lawmakers of both parties.

"Some of the Bush policies, like closing previously public court proceedings, were prompted by the September 11 terrorist attacks and are part of the administration's drive for greater domestic security. Others, like Vice President Dick Cheney's battle to keep records of his energy task force secret, reflect an administration that arrived in Washington determined to strengthen the authority of the executive branch, senior administration officials say."

—*New York Times*, January 3, 2003.

Until items enter the public domain, the archives must protect the rights of the copyright holder. Two sections of the Copyright Act most directly affect the way archives and libraries protect copyright holders and themselves.

Section 107 deals with "fair use" of materials. According to the law, if the use is fair, then duplicating it is permissible without authorization or payment of royalties. Fairness is determined by meeting four criteria:

- the purpose of the use
- the nature of the work used
- the substantiality of the use
- the effect of the use on the actual and potential market for the work used

The definition of fair use is an evolving one, especially in the electronic environment. A key determinant, however, is the purpose of the use. According to the Copyright Act, fair use of a copyrighted work "for purposes such as criticism, comment, news reporting, teaching (including multiple copies for classroom use), scholarship, or research, is not an infringement of copyright."

Section 108, titled "Limitations on Exclusive Rights: Reproduction by Libraries and Archives," is a special section dealing with the duplication of materials by archives and libraries. It goes beyond Section 107, which applies to everyone copying a work.

A scene in the Jedi Archives

JOCASTA NU (Jedi Archivist): "There are some inconsistencies here. Maybe the planet you're looking for was destroyed."

OBI-WAN KENOBI: "Wouldn't that be on record?"

JOCASTA NU: "It ought to be. Unless it was very recent. I hate to say it, but it looks like the system you're searching for doesn't exist."

OBI-WAN: "That's impossible. Perhaps the archives are incomplete."

JOCASTA NU: "The archives are comprehensive and totally secure, my young Jedi. One thing you may be absolutely sure of—if an item does not appear in our records, it does not exist!"

—*Star Wars, Episode II: Attack on the Clones*

According to Section 108, for an institution to copy a work without infringement, the institution

- must be open to the public or open to researchers in a specialized field;
- must not be copying for a commercial purpose;
- must include a notice of copyright in the copies produced.

Having met these tests, an institution can copy certain works as outlined in figure 9.4.[16]

The Digital Millennium Copyright Act of 1998 amended Section 108 of the Copyright Act to accommodate digital technologies and evolving preservation practices. Prior to DMCA, Section 108 permitted libraries and archives to make a single non-digital copy of a work for purposes of preservation or interlibrary loan. As amended by DCMA, Section 108 now permits a library or archives to make up to three copies, which may be digital, provided the digital copies are not made available to the public outside the premises of the library or archives. In addition, the amended section permits a library or archives to copy a work into a new format if the original format becomes obsolete.[17]

Fig. 9.4 Works for Which Copying is Permissible

Nature of Work	Copied For	Considerations
Unpublished work	The institution itself	Copying permitted for preservation or security purposes
Unpublished work	Another institution	Copying permitted for deposit for research use in another institution that is either open to the public or open to researchers in a specialized field
Published work	The institution itself or another research institution	Copying permitted to replace a damaged, deteriorating, lost, or stolen work if an unused replacement cannot be found at a fair price
Musical works, pictorial works, graphic works, sculptural works, or motion pictures	The institution itself	Copying permitted only for preservation, security or replacement of the work
Published or unpublished work	Researcher or other user	Before proceeding, the institution should have a reasonable belief that the copy will be used for private study, scholarship, or research. The notice (discussed below) must be posted at the place where the institution accepts copy orders and on any order forms.

Procedures for Duplication for Researchers

Archives use two approaches to comply with researcher requests for copies. Some archives make the copies for the researchers. Other archives permit researchers to make their own copies. In either case, the archives must make certain that it is protected from damages due to infringement of copyright.

If the archives makes copies for researchers, it is advisable to have the researcher complete a request form. This form should contain the warning printed in figure 9.5. The warning also should be posted in the area where the archives accepts copying orders. By signing the request form, the researcher acknowledges that he or she is aware of copyright issues and has assumed responsibility for complying with them.

If an institution has an unsupervised photocopying machine that is made available to researchers, the institution may escape liability if the equipment displays a notice that copying may be subject to the copyright law. A basic step, therefore, is to make certain that all photocopy machines display the notice in figure 9.5.

While these precautions may seem extreme, they are essential if an archives intends to protect itself from liability resulting from a researcher's infringement of copyright.[18]

Fig. 9.5 Warning from the Copyright Act of 1976

NOTICE
WARNING CONCERNING COPYRIGHT RESTRICTIONS

The copyright law of the United States (Title 17, United States Code) governs the making of photocopies and other reproductions of copyrighted material.

Under certain conditions specified in the law, libraries and archives are authorized to furnish a photocopy or other reproduction. One of these specified conditions is that the photocopy or reproduction is not to be "used for any purpose other than private study, scholarship or research." If a user makes a request for, or later uses, a photocopy or reproduction for purposes in excess of "fair use," that user may be liable for copyright infringement.

The institution reserves the right to refuse to accept a copying order if, in its judgment, fulfillment of the order would involve violation of copyright law.

OUTREACH AND PROMOTION

One of the most frustrating things for an archivist is to know that the collections have great research value, but that very few people are using them. Over the past decade, archivists have come to realize that outreach and promotion must be an integral part of archival work—not something done occasionally, as with an anniversary celebration.[19]

In an era of downsizing, rightsizing, reengineering, and plain-old-fashioned staff reductions, an unknown or underappreciated archives is likely to be closed. Outreach has moved from being an optional activity to one essential for survival.

Any outreach activity begins by defining the "publics" that the archives serves and the needs of those publics that the archives can meet. Defining publics depends on the nature of the organization of which the archives is a part. For example, North Fork University's Department of Archives and Special Collections defined the publics it served as follows:

- *NFU students*. The archives serves both undergraduate and graduate students, including all areas of the university.

- *NFU faculty*. While this includes all faculty, there will be a special emphasis on the needs of faculty in the university's areas of scholarly distinction: environmental studies and social work.
- *Alumni*. The NFU archives will try to use history as a way of keeping alumni connected with (and, the university hopes, contributing to) the university.
- *Local community*. NFU prides itself on its involvement with, and commitment to, the local community. NFU will try to make the resources of its archives available to all community members, not just to scholars.
- *News media*. NFU has defined news media, especially regional print and broadcast outlets, as an important group to serve.

An archives program in a different type of organization would have different publics to serve. State archives would define the citizens (and taxpayers) of the state as a key public. Archives in a religious congregation would serve the needs of members of the congregation. A small historical society might try to add services for genealogists and other family historians.

"Livingston County residents interested in their family history can visit an archive in the basement of the Howell Library.

"About a dozen or so visit the archive each week. When they do, they're usually searching for information on one of two topics.

"'Mainly it is either for family obituaries or for information about their houses. People want to know how old their houses are and who built them because they want to restore them,' said ... one of two full-time volunteers at the archive."

—*Detroit News*, May 22, 2002.

Once publics are defined, the archivist can design an outreach program that includes activities designed to meet their needs. Among the activities typically used by archives are

- exhibits
- public performances
- newsletters
- presentations at meetings and conferences
- tours

Photograph 9.3 An exhibit area can be a valuable addition to an archival program. Photograph courtesy of the University of Arizona Library, Special Collections.

- newspaper articles
- appearances on radio and television
- in-house receptions
- electronic publication on the World Wide Web[20]

Many archives find that a volunteer friends group can help with outreach and promotion. Individuals interested enough in the archives to accept the title of "friend" are a special resource not to be underestimated. Friends can spread the word about the archives and its services, often to circles that the archives otherwise never would reach. The friends group also provides a sounding board and a feedback mechanism for assessing the effectiveness of public programs. Finally, friends can become "angels" (either through their own fundraising or by the pressure they bring to bear on institutional administrators) if funding of the archives becomes a source of contention.

The North Fork University Department of Archives and Special Collections realized it needed to improve outreach. In consultation with administrators, users, and other stakeholders (to use a term popular in the management literature), the archives developed the plan for outreach and promotion printed in figure 9.6.

Any archivist involved with outreach and promotion activities usually asks: Are these activities effective? Are they worth the time and money I spend on them? Would my time be better spent elsewhere? At NFU, the archives is gathering information on a regular basis to help

Fig. 9.6 North Fork University Outreach and Promotion Audiences and Activities	
Target Audience	Activity
NFU Students	Write a regular column in the student newspaper: "This Week in NFU History."
NFU Faculty	Prepare packets of historical materials dealing with NFU during World War II for the U.S. History survey course.
Alumni	Prepare an historical calendar for next year that includes photographs from the NFU Archives and key dates in NFU history.
Local community	Prepare a traveling exhibit on the environment of the North Fork. Try to get the local wineries to take turns displaying the exhibit.
News media	Prepare press releases each time a new collection is received or a closed collection is opened for research.

answer these questions. Everyone who calls or visits the archives, for example, is asked how they heard about the archives. Over time, the archives will be able to devote more resources to effective strategies and to design other strategies to replace those found to be less effective.

CONCLUSION

This chapter began with a discussion of the tension that arises in archives due to the sometimes-competing goals of preservation and use. Detailed policies and procedures, like those outlined above, are a means for archives to keep this tension from leading to anxiety and paralysis. Policies and procedures also provide a sound foundation for the more extensive outreach and promotion efforts that are so necessary for archival survival. As the next chapter discusses, reference and access—and, indeed, all archival activities—must face the challenge posed by digital records.

NOTES

1. The best one-volume treatment of the subject is Mary Jo Pugh, *Providing Reference Services for Archives and Manuscripts* (Chicago:

Society of American Archivists, 1992). See also Sue Holbert, *Archives and Manuscripts: Reference and Access* (Chicago: Society of American Archivists, 1977); and David R. Kepley, "Reference Service and Access," in *Managing Archives and Archival Institutions*, ed. James Gregory Bradsher (Chicago: University of Chicago Press, 1988), 161-73.

2. For some recent literature on reference, access, and outreach, see: Tamar G. Chute, "Selling the College and University Archives," *Archival Issues* 25, nos. 1-2 (2000): 33-48; Elizabeth H Dow, et al., "The Burlington Agenda: Research Issues in Intellectual Access to Electronically Published Historical Documents," *American Archivist* 64, no. 2 (fall/winter 2001): 292-307; Wendy Duff and Catherine A. Johnson, "A Virtual Expression of Need: An Analysis of E-Mail Reference Questions," *American Archivist* 64, no. 1 (spring/summer 2001): 43-60; Kathleen Epp, "Telling Stories Around the 'Electric Campfire': The Use of Archives in Television Productions," *Archivaria* 49 (spring 2000): 53-83; Jay Gilbert, "Access Denied: The *Access to Information Act* and Its Effects on Public Records Creators," *Archivaria* 49 (spring 2000): 84-123; Herbert J. Hartsook, "By Fair Means If You Can: A Case Study of Raising Private Monies to Support Archival Programs," *Archival Issues* 25, nos. 1-2 (2000): 49-56; Gabrielle Hyslop, "For Many Audiences: Developing Public Programs at the National Archives of Australia," *Archives and Manuscripts* 30, no. 1 (May 2002): 48-59; Paul Macpherson, "Theory, Standards and Implicit Assumptions: Public Access to Post-current Government Records," *Archives and Manuscripts* 30, no. 1 (May 2002): 6-17; William J. Maher, "Between Authors and Users: Archivists in the Copyright Vise," *Archival Issues* 26, no. 1 (2001): 63-76; Kristin E. Martin, "Analysis of Remote Reference Correspondence at a Large Academic Manuscripts Collection," *American Archivist* 64, no. 1 (spring/summer 2001): 17-42; Angelika Menne-Haritz, "Access-the Reformulation of an Archival Paradigm," *Archival Science* 1, no. 1 (2001): 57-82; Catherine Nicholls, "The Role of Outreach in Australian Archive Programs," *Archives and Manuscripts* 29, no. 1 (May 2001): 62-71; Esther Robinson, "Archives in the Classroom: The Development and Evaluation of National Archives [of Australia] Teachers' Resources," *Archives and Manuscripts* 30, no. 1 (May 2002): 18-29; Andrea Rosenbusch, "Are Our Users Being Served? A Report on Online Archival Databases," *Archives and Manuscripts* 29, no. 1 (May 2001): 44-61; Elizabeth Yakel, "Thinking Inside and Outside the Boxes: Archival Reference Services at the Turn of the Century." *Archivaria* 49 (spring 2000): 140-60.

3. Lewis J. Bellardo and Lynn Lady Bellardo, compilers, *A Glossary for Archivists, Manuscript Curators, and Records Managers* (Chicago: Society of American Archivists, 1992).

4. For more on this point, see Mary Jo Pugh, "The Illusion of Omniscience: Subject Access and the Reference Archivist," *American Archivist* 45 (winter 1982): 33-44.

5. Luciana Duranti believes that archivists in the United States overemphasize potential use of records. This overemphasis leads archivists to assign "value" to records based largely on anticipated use. According to Duranti, the search for value in appraisal has taken U.S. archivists away from their traditional role—one still practiced in the rest of the world—of impartial selector of archival documents. Luciana Duranti, "The Concept of Appraisal and Archival Theory," *American Archivist* 57 (spring 1994): 328-44. For more on genealogists, see Gail R. Redmann, "Archivists and Genealogists: The Trend Toward Peaceful Coexistence," *Archival Issues* 18, no. 2 (1993): 121-32.

6. Pugh, *Providing Reference Services*, 55-64.

7. This distinction comes from Trudy Huskamp Peterson, "Archival Principles and Records of the New Technology," *American Archivist* 47 (fall 1984): 383-93.

8. Elsie T. Freeman, "In the Eye of the Beholder: Archives Administration from the User's Point of View," *American Archivist* 47 (spring 1984): 111-23. See also Pugh, *Providing Reference Services*, 11-24; Fredric Miller, "Use, Appraisal, and Research: A Case Study of Social History," *American Archivist* 49 (fall 1986): 371-92.

9. For more information, see Pugh, *Providing Reference Services*, 25-39.

10. Pugh, *Providing Reference Services*, 68-77.

11. Richard V. Szary, "Encoded Finding Aids as a Transforming Technology in Archival Reference Service," In *Encoded Archival Description on the Internet*, ed. Daniel V. Pitti and Wendy Duff (New York: Haworth Information Press, 2001), 187-98.

12. William Z. Nasri, "Copyright," *World Encyclopedia of Library and Information Services*, 3d ed., (Chicago: American Library Association, 1993), 228.

13. Kenneth D. Crews, *Copyright Essentials for Librarians and Educators* (Chicago: American Library Association, 2000), 21-22. Crews notes, however, a "twist" on this rule: Before Congress added twenty years to copyright protection in 1998, copyrights in works that had been published in 1922 and before already had expired. They remain expired. Those works received at most seventy-five years of protection and are now in the public domain."

14. Crews, *Copyright Essentials*, 24–25.

15. Crews, *Copyright Essentials*, 25. The Supreme Court subsequently upheld the Copyright Term Extension Act, declaring that it fell within Congress's constitutional authority. *New York Times*, 16 January 2003, A24.

16. Adapted from Gary M. Peterson and Trudy Huskamp Peterson, *Archives and Manuscripts: Law* (Chicago: Society of American Archivists, 1985), 81–89. For a review of recent court decisions that indicate a move toward narrowing the provisions of the Copyright Act, see Pugh, *Providing Reference Services*, 82–84. For the role of the archivist as mediator of competing rights, see William J. Maher, "Between Authors and Users: Archivists in the Copyright Vise." *Archival Issues* 26, no. 1 (2001): 63–76.

17. "Obsolete" means that the machine or device used to render the work perceptible is no longer manufactured or is no longer reasonably available in the commercial marketplace. *The Digital Millennium Copyright Act of 1998: U.S. Copyright Office Summary* (Washington, D.C.: U.S. Copyright Office, 1998), http://www.loc.gov/copyright/legislation/dmca.pdf.

18. For more information, see Pugh, *Providing Reference Services*, 79–91. For a discussion of copyright issues and digitization projects, see Melissa Smith Levine, "Overview of Legal Issues for Digitization," in *Handbook for Digital Projects*, ed. Maxine K. Sitts (Andover, Mass.: Northeast Document Conservation Center, 2000).

19. The best one-volume treatment is Elsie Freeman Finch, ed., *Advocating Archives: An Introduction to Public Relations for Archivists* (Metuchen, N.J.: Society of American Archivists and Scarecrow Press, 1994). Still useful is Ann E. Pederson and Gail Farr Casterline, *Archives and Manuscripts: Public Programs* (Chicago: Society of American Archivists, 1992). See also two articles in *Managing Archives* (Bradsher, ed.): Kathleen Roe, "Public Programs," 218–27; and James Gregory Bradsher and Mary Lynn Ritzenthaler, "Archival Exhibits," 218–40.

20. For the World Wide Web, see Kathleen Feeney, "Retrieval of Archival Finding Aids Using World-Wide-Web Search Engines," *American Archivist* 62, no. 2 (fall 1999), 206–228. Helen R. Tibbo and Lokman I. Meho, "Finding Finding Aids on the World Wide Web," *American Archivist* 64, no. 1 (spring/summer 2001), 61–78. William E. Landis, "Archival Outreach on the World Wide Web," *Archival Issues* 20, no. 2 (1995), 129–148. Jean-Stephan Piche, "Doing What's Possible with What We've Got: Using the World Wide Web to Integrate Archival Functions," *American Archivist* 61, no. 1 (spring 1998), 106–123. Elaine L. Westbrooks, "African-American Documentary Resources on the World Wide Web: A Survey and Analysis," *Archival Issues* 24, no. 2 (1999), 145–174. Daniel V. Pitti and Wendy Duff, editors, *Encoded Archival Description on the Internet* (New York: Haworth Information Press, 2001).

10 DIGITAL RECORDS

Digital information systems are much in the news these days. On the positive side are stories about the expanding capabilities of the World Wide Web, the increasing power of personal computer hardware and software, and the ability of organizations to network their information sources effectively. On the negative side are stories about Internet worms and viruses, fear of the dehumanization of work, and concern about the effects of such rapid changes on organizations and people.

Hollywood plays upon our greatest hopes and our deepest fears—as it always has done. In the 1950s, we had giant crabs and other mutations caused by nuclear fallout. By contrast, in the 1990s we had *The Net*, the tale of a computer expert whose personal information is systematically removed from all databases, effectively deleting her from existence.[1]

Moving from Hollywood to the real world, in 1995 Peter G. Neumann published a book called *Computer Related Risks*. The book chronicles hundreds of incidents involving computers and the risks of relying upon them.[2] Neumann reports several surprising incidents:

- An $18.5 million Atlas-Agena rocket, launching what was intended to be the first satellite to fly by Venus, had to be destroyed when it went off course. Subsequent analysis showed that the computer flight plan was missing a hyphen that was a symbol for a particular formula (p. 26).
- The Voyager 1 mission lost data over a weekend, because all five printers were not operational: four were configured improperly (including being offline) and one had a paper jam (p. 29).
- A woman on trial in Düsseldorf, Germany, used as her defense that she had been the victim of a computer error. She had been erroneously informed that medical test results showed that she had incurable syphilis and had passed it on to her daughter and son. As a result, she strangled her 15-year-old daughter and attempted to kill her son and herself. The woman was acquitted (p. 71).

- A physician reported that a ninety-nine-year-old man in the emergency room had a highly abnormal white-blood-cell count that the computer reported as being within normal limits. The computer, it turns out, was reporting results for an infant, assuming that the birth year of "89" was 1989 rather than 1889 (p. 72).

- The Air Force sold as surplus more than 1,200 used digital tapes and almost 2,000 used analog tapes, many with sensitive data that had not been erased (p. 145).

- The confidential files of a federal prosecutor in Lexington, Kentucky, remained on disks of a broken computer sold to a used equipment dealer for $45. The data included sealed federal indictments and confidential employee data. (p. 145).

"In the digital age, when information means money, many [state] agencies have come to recognize that they are sitting on potential gold mines. Whether it is driving records, tax assessments, liquor licenses or any of the other data that state and local governments gather at taxpayer expense , more and more of those governments see data base access as a new source of revenue."

—*New York Times*, July 14, 1997.

- An alleged cocaine dealer was released from Los Angeles County Jail in 1987 on the basis of a phony e-mail message ordering his release (p. 174).

- A Washington D.C. newspaper published computer records of video rentals by Supreme Court nominee Robert Bork (p. 186).

- Payroll printouts from a San Diego school accidentally wound up as Christmas gift-wrap in a local store (p. 188).

- The names of fourteen Americans were mistakenly carved on the Vietnam Memorial in Washington (p. 190).

- On July 18, 1989, an obsessed fan murdered actress Rebecca Schaeffer, having traced her home address through computer records at the California Department of Motor Vehicles (p. 184).

As an archivist reading these and other examples, I was struck by one major "risk" that does not appear in Neumann's book: the risk of not being able to use information over time. The above instances deal with access to current information. What about the person who in thirty years cannot collect a pension because no system exists to read today's computerized payroll records? What about the municipality that cannot renovate a deteriorating bridge in the future because all the Computer Assisted Design (CAD) drawings were created on a proprietary system by a vendor long defunct? What about an ill person whose digital X-rays deteriorated in an improper storage environment and are now unreadable for comparison with current images?

These and similar questions worry archivists who are already dealing with digital records.[3] Fulfilling the archival mission—identifying, preserving, and making records available—may have to change in this new environment. In the next few years, more and more archives will have to determine how they will face the challenge of digital records. To offer some guidance, this chapter will cover the following topics:

- the nature of the problem
- foundational research
- approaches to managing digital records
- suggestions for the practical archivist

Archival thinking in this area continues to evolve. Research studies now under way may change the future approach of archivists. But for now, the following sections summarize the way leading archivists are defining the problem and trying to solve it.

"Public employees in Tennessee are being taken to court in an attempt to force them into revealing the Internet sites they visit during working hours. A newspaper publisher has filed a lawsuit—believed to be the first of its type—claiming that taxpayers should have access to computer files that record the Net surfing habits of public servants."

—*New Scientist*, November 22, 1997.

THE NATURE OF THE PROBLEM

Digital records are more than information on a new medium—they are not the same old product in a "new and improved" package. Rather, there are dramatic shifts in the nature of the records themselves. Figure 10.1 summarizes these shifts.

Fig. 10.1 Shifts Caused by Digital Records[4]		
From	**To**	**Explanation**
Physical entities	Logical entities	We can no longer identify records from their physical characteristics.
Linear documents	Non-linear documents (hypermedia)	Documents are composed of images (still and moving), sound, and data—as well as text. These elements are combined in different ways by individual users.
Centralized information	Decentralized information	Not only are central paper files disappearing, the control offered by mainframe computing environments is diminishing.
Time and space dependent	Time and space independent	To use a record, a person previously had to go to the archives when it was open. People have access to electronic documents any time of the day and from almost any location (including the beach).
Vertical flow of organizational information	Horizontal flow of organizational information	Centralized files and reporting systems were designed to filter information, and reduce its volume, as it moved up the organizational hierarchy. Electronic document systems promote "organizational information democracy" by permitting direct access to a wider range of information sources.

At the heart of these changes is the following: paper records are tangible things, while digital records are often evolving processes. Different versions of digital records appear and disappear. Managers now make decisions based on snapshots of information combining text, data, and image. At a very basic level, it is even unclear when, if ever, a "record" appears.

We can begin to see the shape of a digital records spiral—some would call it a tornado. This spiral is gaining speed as a number of factors swirl around one another:

- cheaper information technology
- decentralized information systems
- downsized, leaner organizations
- process redesign and workflow improvements, especially among office workers

Into this vortex goes the archivist, often the only person in an organization concerned about, and trained in, long-term storage of and access to information.[5] The archivist's challenge is not only the records, but the organizations that are changing as well.

DEFINITION OF RECORD

In previous chapters of this book, identifying records seemed very straightforward. Since information was expensive to record (and duplicate) manually, organizations controlled what was recorded and were concerned about the information once it was committed to writing. With computers so plentiful, there is much more organizational flotsam and jetsam for the archivist to sift. We can no longer assume that, just because something is recorded, the value of the information is reflected by the cost of recording it.

There is even more confusion because terms like "document," "data," and "information" are used differently in various information professions. For the archivist, these terms have a very clear relationship to one another as outlined in figure 10.2.

Fig. 10.2 From Data to Archives	
Term	**Meaning**
Data	Content
Information	Data communicated or received
Document	Information in context
Record	Document preserved
Archives	Document preserved for enduring value

In both electronic and paper environments, a *record* has three characteristics:

- *Content*: that which conveys information (text, data, symbols, numerals, images, sound, and vision)
- *Structure*: the appearance and arrangement of the content (relationships between fields, entities, language, style, fonts, page and paragraph breaks, links, and other editorial devices)
- *Context*: the background information that enhances understanding of technical and business environments to which the records relate (application software, link to function or activity, provenance information)[6]

An *archival* record is one preserved because of its enduring value. When preserving digital records, the archivist must make certain that context and structure—as well as content—are accessible over time. Content alone is virtually useless, from an archivist's perspective.

"While more than 50 companies have expressed confidential interest in acquiring Global Crossing, their identities are no longer secret to one another, courtesy of an e-mail message from Global Crossing's lawyers.

"The e-mail message was sent to the potential bidders on March 28 by an employee of ... the New York law firm that is serving as Global Crossing's counsel in bankruptcy proceedings.

"Although the message included only routine information on bidding procedures for Global Crossing, it inadvertently named each of the more than 50 recipients by copying their e-mail addresses at the top of the message."

—*New York Times*, April 10, 2002.

At first glance, this discussion of what is or is not a record in the digital environment may seem esoteric. In fact, however, it has very practical applications—just ask Oliver North and Manuel Noriega. One of the central issues in the court case, *Armstrong* v. *Executive Office of the President* (nicknamed the "PROFS Case" after the Professional Office System that was in use), was whether or not electronic mail from the Reagan and Bush administrations is a federal record.[7] Documents from this e-mail system were used in the investigations of the Iran-Contra affair and Manuel Noriega.

In August 1993, the U.S. Court of Appeals ruled that electronic mail records were not the equivalent of extra copies of paper records. Furthermore, printouts of e-mail records are not sufficient for preservation unless the context and structure, as well as the content, are preserved.[8]

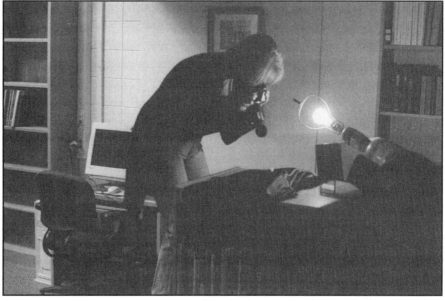

Photograph 10.1 Archives associate Crystal Gamradt preparing a digital exhibit of 4,000-year-old cuneiform "documents" Photograph courtesy of South Dakota State University Archives.

So, what constitutes a record in the digital environment? David Bearman defines a record as a document created to *conduct a transaction*, deliberately preserved as evidence of that transaction. A transaction can be between two people, between one person and a source of data (like a database), or between two sources of data. Furthermore, the organization, not individual employees, determines what should be preserved.

The changing nature of records has led to a new role that archivists are only now beginning to assume. The job description for this new archivist includes the following responsibilities:

- being involved in the design of electronic systems
- making certain that investments in records and information systems are worthwhile
- ensuring that organizations maintain accountability through the protection of their evidence captured in transactional records
- focusing on the organizationally created information that gives evidence of the organization's activities
- helping creators of digital records to maintain them, rather than taking custody of all records

The last point, in particular, is somewhat controversial. The traditional archival approach to records on any medium is to take custody of the records in order to guarantee their preservation and access. Some archival repositories, notably the U.S. National Archives and Records Administration, are using this approach with digital records—they will take custody of and responsibility for digital records of enduring value. Other archival repositories, including the National Archives of Australia, have taken another approach. They are working with the creators of digital records to assure preservation and access over time in the agencies themselves. In this case, the archives does not take custody of the digital records. David Bearman and Margaret Hedstrom have labeled this shift in thinking a change from a "rowing mentality" to a "steering mentality."[9] Thus, not only the definition of record, but also the definition of the record keeper, is changing.

"The Internet forgets. You'd think it wouldn't. After all, computers never forget, unless we tell them to. And we do.

"Every year, we draw up millions of Web pages and post billions of comments to Internet message boards. And every year, much of that information vanishes. We delete it to free up space on our servers, or maybe the company running the Internet site is driven out of business. Whatever the reason, the knowledge and opinions stored in these documents is gone forever.

"It's not a new issue. In the days before home video players, the TV networks figured there was no point archiving old programs. That's why the videotape of the first Super Bowl game was erased and NBC wiped out a decade's worth of Johnny Carson shows. Today, we wonder how TV executives could have been so stupid, even as we repeat the mistake."

—*Eugene, Oregon Register-Guard*, January 29, 2002.

STORAGE MEDIA

Archivists are quite concerned about storage media for digital records. Will information, once captured, last as long as needed? Is there anything archivists can do to address the fragility of storage media?

A study by the National Media Laboratory (NML) in St. Paul, Minnesota, highlighted the problems with magnetic tape used for audio and video recording as well as for digital records.[10] NML's best projection, based on current research, is that physical lifetimes for digital magnetic tapes are at least ten to twenty years, "a value commensurate with the practical life of the digital recording technology."

The study pointed out, however, that media life expectancies are like miles per gallon ratings on automobiles—your actual results may vary. In particular, life expectancy is highly dependent on media storage conditions. Controlled temperature and humidity will increase media life expectancies. A National Institute of Standards and Technology (NIST) publication recommended that magnetic tape be stored at sixty-five degrees Fahrenheit (plus or minus three degrees) and 40 percent relative humidity (plus or minus 5 percent).[11]

Optical media are another storage option. There are erasable and nonerasable optical media in various sizes and formats. To date, however, optical media have not been subjected to the same independent testing as magnetic media. As a result, there is no way to prove or disprove manufacturers' claims for life expectancy. It clearly is a case of *caveat emptor.*[12]

Optical media, particularly CD-ROMs, *are* being used as a *transfer medium* for digital records, if not a preservation medium. The U.S. National Archives, for example, will accept digital records on CD-ROM; NARA then transfers the information to magnetic media for storage and preservation.

"A conflict between a New York State prison regulation requiring that inmates be photographed clean-shaven and a religious belief that a man's beard must not be touched was resolved in Federal court yesterday through the latest computer technology.

"For the first time, New York State accepted a computer-generated image of what an inmate, in this case [a rabbi], would look like without a beard instead of making him shave for a conventional photograph. The state requires that a bearded inmate be photographed shaven so that he can be more easily identified if he escapes and shaves off his beard."

— *New York Times*, December 29, 1994.

SYSTEM DEPENDENCE

A bigger problem than the longevity of the physical media is the dependence on hardware and software that soon will be obsolete; technological obsolescence of digital recording systems is a greater concern than medium longevity. Scientists at the NML have concluded that "technological obsolescence of digital recording systems is a challenge for those individuals tasked with preserving digital archives. Digital archives should be transcribed every ten to twenty years to ensure that they will not become technologically obsolete. To realize lifetimes greater than this, one would be required to archive the recording system, system software, operating system, computer hardware, operations manuals, and ample spare parts along with the recorded media."[13] According to NML, the physical life of digital magnetic media may well exceed the lifetime of the recording technology.

An example of the problem of obsolescence is the 1960 U.S. federal census. In 1975, the National Archives learned that the Census Bureau still had 7,297 reels of tape readable only on a Univac II-A tape drive. The staff of the National Archives reviewed the files and determined that seven series, on 642 reels of tape, had enduring value. By this time, however, the Univac II-A drives were obsolete, thus presenting a major engineering challenge. The Census Bureau and NARA ultimately were successful in copying the tapes, though it took four years and a great deal of effort to do so.[14]

INTEGRITY OF RECORDS OVER TIME

A third issue to consider with digital records is how we will know that the digital records we use in the future have not been altered in some way. Archivists are concerned about this question since they are likely to be the individuals accountable for the integrity of the records over time.

Captain James T. Kirk faced this issue on the starship *Enterprise*. In a "Star Trek" episode called "The Court Martial," Kirk is on trial for causing the death of a crewmember, Ben Finney, who also happens to be the ship's records officer. The principal evidence against Kirk is the log of the *Enterprise,* an electronic record including full-motion images and sound. After the damning evidence is played in court, Kirk exclaims, "But that's not the way it happened!" The rest of the episode involves testing the integrity of the digital records system, with some surprising results.[15]

Researchers using archival records were concerned about integrity long before there were digital records. Researchers talk of two kinds of validity:

- *External validity.* Is this what it purports to be?
- *Internal validity.* Is the information accurate?

The famous (bogus) Hitler diaries of a few years ago were tested for external validity, and experts ultimately concluded that they may have belonged to Joe or Jim Hitler, but certainly not Adolf. Questionable internal validity means that a record is what it purports to be (a Civil War diary, for example), but the specific information (on the course of a battle) is just plain wrong as verified by other sources.

How will we test internal and external validity of digital records, even as the records themselves become more complex? For example, security concerns have led to the development of encryption and other devices to reassure anxious customers and clients. As a result, the archivist will inherit yet another layer of complexity in preserving records. Not only must we preserve hardware and software, but we must also preserve the encryption scheme (and the ability to read it) indefinitely. During the 1960s, a popular phrase was: "You're either part of the solution or part of the problem." In the world of digital records, a *solution* can become part of yet *another* problem.[16]

How extensive might the ultimate problem be? Rich Lysakowsi and Zahava Leibowitz anticipate a disaster on a major scale:

> While it is no wonder that Y2K inspired thoughts of a coming apocalypse, a much larger and very real crisis is on the horizon now—one we call "Titanic 2020."It has been brewing for a long time and grows larger everyday. Titanic 2020 results from software business practices that make new products quickly obsolete, cause major hassles for users, and put critical assets at risk. Comparing Titanic 2020 to Y2K, Y2K was the tip of an iceberg. Like the passengers on the Titanic on her maiden voyage, many of our most valuable records stored by the ship of computers will perish.[17]

Can we do anything now to prevent the apocalypse? As a first step, we must be alert to the danger. Next, we must have a map for navigating the treacherous digital waters. That map is being provided by three foundational research projects.

"It wasn't too long ago that technology idealists were predicting the advent of a paper-free world. Paper-thin electronic displays, they said, would take the place of wood pulp and ink, and civilized society would never again bear the indignities of dog ears and paper cuts. Perhaps that age is still to come, but for now, at least, paper is king."

—*Wired*, October 23, 2001.

FOUNDATIONAL RESEARCH

Much of the work on digital records in the last few years has built upon the foundation established by three key research projects: the University of British Columbia's research entitled, "The Preservation of the Integrity of Electronic Records;" the University of Pittsburgh's research into variables that affect the integration of recordkeeping requirements for evidence into electronic systems; and the InterPARES Project. Beginning in the mid-1990s, these three research projects explored the nature of digital records and the functional requirements for systems to manage them. The results have been tested and implemented in a wide variety of organizations and institutions around the world, from the U.S. Department of Defense (DoD) to the State of Victoria in Australia.

UNIVERSITY OF BRITISH COLUMBIA

The University of British Columbia's School of Library, Archival, and Information Studies conducted a research project entitled, "The Preservation of the Integrity of Electronic Records." The goal was to identify and define conceptually the nature of an electronic record and the conditions necessary to ensure its integrity (reliability and authenticity) during its active and semi-active life. The research team consisted of: Luciana Duranti, principal investigator; Terry Eastwood, co-investigator; and Heather MacNeil, research assistant. The Social Sciences and Humanities Research Council of Canada funded the project.[18]

The specific objectives of the research project were to

- establish what a record is in principle and how it can be recognized in an electronic environment;
- determine what kinds of electronic systems generate records;
- formulate criteria that allow for the segregation of records from all other types of information in electronic systems;
- define the conceptual requirements for guaranteeing the reliability and authenticity of records in electronic systems;
- assess these requirements against different administrative, juridical, cultural, and disciplinary points of view.

The UBC team took a deductive approach to the project—they began with a set of general premises and considered whether these premises held up in particular instances. The theoretical basis for the general premises was provided by the principles of diplomatics[19] and archival science.[20]

Central to the UBC research was the distinction between reliability and authenticity:

- *Reliability* refers to a record's authority and trustworthiness. This concept is tied to records creation and means that the record is able "to stand for the fact it is about."[21]
- *Authenticity* refers to a record's reliability over time. It is linked to the record's status, mode, and form of transmission and the manner of its preservation and custody.[22]

The findings of the research project fell into two categories. The first category involved specific methods for ensuring the reliability and authenticity of electronic records. This is best assured by three procedures:

- embedding procedural rules in the overall records system and integrating business and documentary procedures
- emphasizing the documentary context of the electronic records
- managing the electronic records together with all related records

The second category of findings involved management issues that are part of the maintenance and preservation of reliable and authentic records. With respect to management, the study came to two conclusions:

- There are two managerial phases, one involving active and semi active records, and the other involving inactive records.
- Entrusting the creating body with responsibility for their reliability and the preserving body with responsibility for their authenticity best preserves the integrity of electronic records.

The UBC team also collaborated with the U.S. Department of Defense. Because of its vast size and widespread use of computers, DoD needed to make certain that digital records remained readable for their full retention period. In addition to preservation, DoD also wanted to manage electronic documents as efficiently as possible.

The UBC and DoD teams used standard modeling techniques to relate archival and diplomatic concepts to DoD needs. The collaboration developed a series of rules that became the basis for the "Design Criteria Standard for Electronic Records Management Software Applications." This standard was given the number "DoD 5015.2-STD."[23]

The DoD standard established baseline functional requirements for Records Management Application (RMA) software. DoD defines a records management application as "software used by an organization to manage its records." Its primary management functions are categorizing and locating records and identifying records that are due for disposition. RMA software also stores, retrieves, and disposes of the electronic records that are stored in its repository. DoD tests and certifies vendor products that comply with the standard. The UBC-DoD collaborative is one of the best examples of moving digital records theory into practice.[24]

UNIVERSITY OF PITTSBURGH

In 1993, the University of Pittsburgh's School of Information Studies received a three-year grant from the National Historical Publications and Records Administration (NHPRC), a Division of the National Archives and Records Administration. This project researched variables that affect the integration of recordkeeping requirements for evidence into electronic systems. The project generated four main outcomes:

- recordkeeping functional requirements (defining records)
- production rules to support the requirements (making the functional requirements unambiguous and implementable)
- metadata specifications for recordkeeping (providing a software-independent way to encapsulate records)
- literary warrant (reflecting the professional and societal endorsement of the concept of recordkeeping functional requirements)[25]

The first project result, the recordkeeping functional requirements, addressed some of the same issues as those researched at the University of British Columbia. As Richard Cox stated, "In one sense both projects were part of a re-focusing on the fundamentals of what constitutes a record and how such a definition of *record* could better facilitate the management of electronic information systems increasingly being used to create and keep records."

The following is an abbreviated version of the "Functional Requirements for Evidence in Recordkeeping." This is a statement of the requirements for ensuring the preservation of evidence in electronic form. Although specifically related to electronic recordkeeping systems, the requirements are also applicable to manual or hybrid systems.[26]

Organization: Conscientious

1. *Compliant.* Organizations must comply with the legal and administrative requirements for recordkeeping within the jurisdictions in which they operate, and they must demonstrate awareness of best practices for the industry or business sector to which they belong and the business functions in which they are engaged.

Recordkeeping Systems: Accountable

2. *Responsible.* Recordkeeping systems must have accurately documented policies, assigned responsibilities and formal methodologies for their management.

3. *Implemented.* Recordkeeping systems must be employed at all times in the normal course of business.

4. *Consistent.* Recordkeeping systems must process information in a fashion that assures that the records they create are credible.

Records: Captured

5. *Comprehensive.* Records must be created for all business transactions.

6. *Identifiable.* Records must be bounded by linkage to a transaction that used all the data in the record and only that data.

7. *Complete.* Records must contain the content, structure, and context generated by the transaction they document.

8. *Authorized.* An authorized record creator must have originated all records.

Records: Maintained

9. *Preserved.* Records must continue to reflect content, structure, and context within any systems by which the records are retained over time.

10. *Removable.* It must be possible to delete records content and structure supporting the meaning of content.

Records: Usable

11. *Exportable.* It must be possible to transmit records to other systems without loss of information.

12. *Accessible.* It must be possible to output record content, structure, and context.

13. *Redactable.* Records must be masked when it is necessary to deliver censored copies and the version as released must be documented in a linked transaction.

These functional requirements were a significant step in the development of thinking about managing digital records. A number of projects have attempted to test and implement the functional requirements in different organizational settings, including the City of Philadelphia, Indiana University, and the Delaware Public Archives.[27] In Australia, the Public Records Office of the State of Victoria used the University of Pittsburgh functional requirements as the basis for their planning. They initiated the Victorian Electronic Records Strategy Project (VERS) to address the challenges of dealing with digital records. They have developed a test-bed system and are implementing digital archiving.[28]

What these tests and implementations have shown is that the functional requirements are not an "all or nothing" proposition. Rather, they are guidelines that an organization can use and adapt as necessary to meet its needs. This is the key point for any organization looking to manage digital records. The University of Pittsburgh Functional Requirements remain a succinct statement of what a digital records program is designed to achieve.

"Buried in bulging files and stored in computers in doctors' offices, drug stores, insurance companies and hospitals is information on nearly everything that the health care profession has done to or prescribed for Americans in recent years. To some, the records are a gold mine. To others, they are a minefield.

"But one thing is certain: the material is being unearthed. Insurers, drug companies and large health maintenance organizations are mounting an extensive effort to use medical data to decide which treatments are best, which doctors are best and which health plans keep people healthiest."

— *New York Times*, August 8, 1994.

INTERPARES

The most ambitious research initiative is also one of the most recent. It is called the InterPARES Project (International Research on Permanent Authentic Records in Electronic Systems). *Inter pares* is also Latin for "amongst peers," an appropriate name given the collaborative nature of the project.[29]

The project grew out of the research conducted at the University of British Columbia (discussed above). The second phase of the UBC Project was intended to address the long-term preservation of *inactive* electronic records. According to the project background document, "The immense scope and ubiquity of the issues surrounding the long-term preservation of authentic electronic records made evident the need for an interdisciplinary, international approach."

Led by the "International Team," the InterPARES Project is composed of several national and multinational research teams (Canadian, United States, Italian, Australian, Chinese, and Global Industry). These research teams are responsible for coordinating researchers, research partners, and related activities within their jurisdiction. Major funding has come from Canada's Social Science and Humanities Research Council, the U.S. National Historical Publications and Records Commission, and the Italian National Research Council.

The goal of the InterPARES Project is "to develop the theoretical and methodological knowledge essential to the permanent preservation of electronically generated records and, on the basis of this knowledge, to formulate model strategies, policies and standards capable of ensuring their preservation." In brief, InterPARES is studying the preservation of authentic digital records.

The first phase of the InterPARES Project is now complete. The various task forces and research teams have issued their reports. Most relevant are the findings of three task forces: authenticity, appraisal, and preservation. The principle findings of each task force are summarized below.[30]

Authenticity Task Force

- used both deductive and inductive approaches to profile the complexity of contemporary digital records
- identified the ways that digital records are embedded in their juridical-administrative, provenancial, procedural, documentary, and technological contexts
- concluded that most contemporary records systems are a hybrid of electronic and paper records
- determined that few explicit measures are employed to ensure the authenticity of digital records
- noted that authenticity is generally assured through procedural means
- developed a conceptual framework for establishing the requirements for preserving authentic digital records, but did not create a single, comprehensive typology of authenticity requirements for digital records

Appraisal Task Force

- concluded that appraisal is a knowledge- and research-intensive activity. Appraisers must be provided with the proper training, tools, information, support and resources to conduct the necessary research
- suggested that archivists need accurate and thorough documentation of the appraisal process in its various phases and outcomes
- determined that the appraiser needs to develop an interview protocol to gather information necessary to determine the records elements that need to be preserved

- recommended that the preserver set guidelines for the roles and responsibilities of monitoring appraised digital records and develop work flows to ensure smooth operation of this activity
- developed a functional model of the selection process, outlining the activities involved in the selection of authentic digital records for long-term preservation

Preservation Task Force

- developed a functional model of the process of preserving authentic digital records. This model provides a road map that institutions can use in designing, developing, and evaluating systems that address their specific requirements, objectives, and constraints. The model is based on the Open Archival Information System (OAIS) Reference Model, which will be discussed below
- concluded that solutions to the preservation of specific bodies of digital records should be inherently dynamic
- recommended that preservation systems need to be able to interface with evolving technologies for information discovery, retrieval, communication, and presentation

The InterPARES reports contain a great deal more information, including numerous flow charts and diagrams. The archival profession will be plumbing the depths of these reports for many years to come.

APPROACHES TO MANAGING DIGITAL RECORDS

How are archivists reacting to all of the challenges outlined above? As already noted, promising solutions are only now being developed and tested. Unlike other archival areas discussed in this book—arrangement, for example—in which methods have been tested for decades and even centuries, dealing with digital records is a work-in-progress.

At the moment, the following ten approaches are being developed, tested, and implemented:

- analog storage
- digital archaeology
- computer museums
- backward compatibility
- formulating policies
- standards
- conversion and migration
- emulation
- trustworthy information systems
- persistent digital archives[31]

ANALOG STORAGE

As organizations transition to digital records, they often opt for *analog storage*: printing a "record copy" on paper or microfilm and entering this copy into an existing recordkeeping system (usually paper files in cabinets). Such analog records tend to lack key information unless an organization plans the reformatting. For example, just printing the body of an e-mail message is not sufficient; an organization also must preserve transmission and receipt data.

Furthermore, preserving records in analog form does not always preserve their essence. Jeff Rothenberg of the Rand Corporation has identified a "unique collection of core digital attributes." According to Rothenberg, if we are to preserve digital records, we must preserve the ability to copy them perfectly; to access them without geographic constraint; to disseminate them at virtually no incremental cost; and to keep them machine-readable in all phases of their creation and distribution. In addition, documents that are "born digital" tend to be dynamic, hyperlinked, and interactive—additional attributes that may need to be preserved. Rothenberg considers managing an analog copy to be a "rear-guard action and not a true solution."[32]

I think, however, that generating a copy on microfilm can be an "archival hedge" (to paraphrase a famous article by F. Gerald Ham).[33] Computer Output Microfilm (COM) generates microfilm directly from a digital file without an intervening paper copy. Yes, there is a loss of the digital attributes noted above—but maintaining those attributes is an open-ended commitment to the future. Archivists have had so little experience with access to digital records that it is impossible to know which ones must be preserved in digital form for future research. Generating a "just-in-case" COM copy at the time of the transfer of the digital records to the archives gives us ultimate flexibility:

- If the records continue to warrant preservation in their digital form, they can be managed in this way.
- If at some future time, however, our successor archivists determine that the information still has enduring value but that the digital attributes no longer are worth the expense of preservation, they can destroy the digital file.[34]

The archival hedge of a COM copy may enable future archivists to conduct the kind of regular reappraisal advocated by Leonard Rapport.[35]

"The Secretary of State, Sam Reed, announced on Tuesday that the state is taking steps to create a Digital Archives building that will use storage area networks (SANs) to store electronic records from the various branches and levels of state government.

"'We've had a problem in the state, which I'm sure is generally found around the country, of actually losing some of our electronic records,' Reed said. 'We have e-mails from a previous governor's administration that have disappeared. We also have Wang disks from another governor's administration that we don't have the right equipment to read what is on those disks. We currently have a situation where there's a considerable amount of public policy discussion, and, frankly, development going on via e-mail, and we need to have a set up to be able to capture that for history.'"

—*Government Technology*, June 18, 2002.

DIGITAL ARCHAEOLOGY

Seamus Ross of the University of Glasgow has developed the concept of "digital archaeology." This is a "minimalist approach" whose primary focus is to convert digital records to a new technology only when future access to them is required. In this approach, the cost of moving digital records out of software dependency is shifted to some undefined point in the future.

This does not mean, however, that digital archaeology is without cost. The strategy calls for periodically transferring the records to new storage media. It also requires collecting and preserving documentation about operating systems and application software that would be used in the future to replicate the technology platform on which the digital records were originally created, used, and maintained. This documentation, in effect, will be our "digital Rosetta Stone." Charles Dollar has characterized digital archeology as "future reverse engineering."[36]

COMPUTER MUSEUMS

Another preservation approach suggested by some, possibly one of last resort, is to create computer museums. In this scenario, one or more institutions would gather and maintain the various versions of computer hardware and software. The institutions would need to have sufficient spare parts, manuals, and documentation for the indefinite future. Someone needing access to obsolete digital records would run them on the hardware and software preserved in the museum.

Photograph 10.2   Computers present both opportunities and challenges for the archivist. Photograph courtesy of the University of Arizona Library, Special Collections.

Computer museums raise a number of questions: Can we really hope to keep any machine running indefinitely? How many people in the future will have access to the resources of just a couple of computer museums? Doesn't this defeat one of the major advantages of digital technology, namely, distributed access?

Despite the long-term limitations of the computer museum approach, many institutions and individuals have an old personal computer tucked away in a closet as a last resort for reading digital files. As long as the PCs continue to work, some people refuse to discard them. It is hard to find fault with this as a short-term strategy.

BACKWARD COMPATIBILITY

One approach to managing digital records shifts responsibility to manufacturers and vendors. Organizations using backward compatibility as a strategy make certain that any new system can read old data, ideally through at least two previous generations.

In this approach, an organization makes a commitment that it will "leave no records behind." The organization maintains a window of backward compatibility through system upgrades and revisions.

The advantage of the backward compatibility strategy is that an organization always knows where its digital records are. By converting records as part of system upgrades, in theory there should be no orphaned records in the future. Also, the costs of managing digital records are spread out across the entire life cycle of the records.

"The sheer scope of the Enron case, believed to be the largest computer forensics case in history, dwarfs other financial probes. Investigators will pour through 10,000 computer backup tapes, 20 million sheets of paper and more than 400 computers and handheld devices, according to legal papers. The electronic data is up to 10 times the size of the Library of Congress."

—*USA Today*, February 19, 2002.

FORMULATING POLICIES

Policy statements were discussed earlier in this book—as part of acquisitions and reference services. In these cases, policy statements were part of building a consensus and offering consistent services. This also is true of digital records.

With digital records, however, policy statements are even more important. Without a policy defining digital records and authorizing the archivist to intervene, it is extremely difficult for an archivist to have an impact on the digital records of the organization—there are just too many other sources of power within the organization for the archivist to do battle alone.

In general, digital records policies should have the following features:

- capable of being generalized to the range of departments and problems being addressed
- pose clear alternatives with sufficient basis to support judgments
- be easily implemented, flexible, and cost effective

David Bearman outlined the issues associated with digital records that require policy formulation and determination. These issues, and brief explanations, are summarized in figure 10.3.

Fig. 10.3 Policy Issues Associated with Digital Records[37]	
Policy Issue	**Requirement**
Defining record and non-record	Define these concepts clearly enough so they can be implemented by people and systems
Assigning responsibility	Identify which organizational entities have what specific responsibilities for management of digital records
Adjusting to cultural change	Accommodate shifting behaviors and attitudes, as well as changing technologies
Assuring legality	Require the organization to take actions that will safeguard the legality of the electronic record
Scheduling for disposition	Ensure the retention of records for only as long as required by law, organizational objectives, and research needs
Appraising for enduring value	Be able to identify and preserve archival digital records
Integrating access	Require actions that prevent different formats of records from being a serious barrier to access
Documenting	Require consistent methods of describing records from their creation to their destruction, for intellectual control and documentation purposes
Storing	State who will have physical custody of archival electronic records
Preserving media	Establish standards for care and storage of digital records, and address the basis upon which storage media decisions are to be made
Preserving functionality	Define to what extent original functionality is to be replicated or documented when migration of data and systems are necessary to ensure continuing access
Ensuring security	Protect electronic information and preserve the rights of individuals and the confidentiality required of the organization
Providing for use	Dictate how the organization and others entitled to access will be enabled to use digital records
Controlling costs	Address how the organization will avoid unnecessary costs and target essential expenditures in the management of digital records

To show how policies are formed, let us return to North Fork University. Since NFU is a progressive institution, it has begun to address the policy issues identified by Bearman. A particularly contentious issue was assigning responsibilities in the area of digital records. After much debate, the NFU digital records policy assigned responsibilities to staff in the three major areas shown in figure 10.4.

Figure 10.4 North Fork University Staff Responsibilities for Digital Records[38]	
Functional Area	**Responsibilities**
NFU Archivist	• participate in planning for information systems and in reviewing their implementation to ensure that all digital records are appraised and scheduled • review existing information systems to ensure that disposition of records in the system has been authorized • oversee implementation of disposition instructions
Department heads, managers, and supervisors	• determine what information is needed to support the program or administrative function • identify the applications supported by automated systems by describing their purposes, informational content, and the main stages through which the data flow • work with the NFU Archivist to formulate retention periods for their digital records
Information systems manager	• identify all program and administrative activities that use or need digital records systems • ensure that information in electronic form is protected, preserved, and accessible for its full retention period • implement authorized disposition instructions for digital records that are maintained centrally

Cornell University conducted a research project involving policies for digital information. The PRISM Project focused on policy development and enforcement in several areas:

- long-term survivability of digital information
- reliability of information resources and services
- interoperability

- security
- privacy rights of users
- intellectual property rights of content creators
- metadata that ensures information integrity

The Cornell researchers concluded that few formal policies were in place for distributed resources and that as a result the level of trust about the preservation of digital content was low.[39]

This research reinforces an important point about relying on policies for managing digital records: Once the policies are in place, either the records manager or another person (such as the internal auditor) must monitor compliance. Having adequate policies usually is necessary but not sufficient—it is the foundation for digital preservation, but is not the entire solution.

STANDARDS

Policies usually have a requirement that the organization employ national and international *standards* as part of any digital records systems. Archivists have been among the leading advocates for standard approaches rather than proprietary vendor solutions. The long-term perspective does not always jibe with the latest software or hardware product. In the words of Carol King and Gerry Goffin, archivists always are asking a digital records system "Will you still love me tomorrow?"

The reason archivists advocate standards is that standards promote *interoperability* and *portability*. Interoperability means that different information systems can function together as a cohesive unit. Portability means that information can be carried to and used on different hardware and software platforms. Hardware and software may come and go, but data will always remain.

Standards develop in two ways. In some cases, a standard-setting organization—such as the American National Standards Institute (ANSI) in the United States or the International Organization for Standardization (ISO)—establishes criteria to which manufacturers and system designers adhere. These are called *de jure* standards. In other cases, a vendor product controls such a large market share that it becomes a *de facto* standard—Microsoft Windows, for instance.

While the list of applicable standards is growing all the time, archivists should be particularly aware of the following standards:

- *ASCII* (American Standard Code for Information Interchange): used for text files

- *JPEG* (Joint Photographics Expert Group): a standard for still-image compression
- *TIFF* (Tagged Image File Format): a standard for graphic files, especially in desktop publishing programs
- *SGML* (Standard Generalized Markup Language): a system of tags used for electronic publishing
- *XML* (Extensible Markup Language): a markup language for documents containing structured information—content (words, pictures, etc.) as well as some indication of the role the content plays (for example, content in a section heading or content in a footnote) XML provides a facility to define tags and the structural relationships among them. XML was created so that richly structured documents could be used over the Web. It is at the heart of some of the most promising research into preserving digital records.[40]
- *OSI* (Open Systems Interconnect): networking standards for computer communication
- *SQL* (Structured Query Language): the most common database language
- *TCP/IP* (Transmission Control Protocol/Internet Protocol): the communications standard that is the backbone of the Internet

Requiring that these and other standards be incorporated into digital records systems is the best guarantee of interoperability and portability over time.[41]

There is a tradeoff, however, with using standards. Standard formats, in particular, seldom contain the latest functions and components so desirable in the digital world. Vendors regularly implement features that go beyond the standards in order to secure market share. For example, the lowest common denominator standard format for text files, ASCII, does not retain such features as italics and boldface. Therefore, users face a difficult decision: if we use a standard format, we may not preserve all of the core digital attributes.

One of the most exciting developments on the standards front is the release of a standard model for digital archives systems. Called the "Reference Model for an Open Archival Information System" (OAIS), it was initially developed by NASA for archiving the large volume of data produced by space missions. The OAIS model defines the environment necessary to support a digital repository and the interactions within that environment.[42]

The OAIS model breaks the archiving system into six distinct functional areas:

1. *Ingest:* system accepts information submitted from outside the framework and prepares the contents for storage (including generating descriptive information)

2. *Archival storage:* system passes the information, now called archival information packages, into a storage repository, where it is maintained until the contents are requested and retrieved

3. *Data management:* system populates, maintains, and accesses both descriptive information about the archival holdings and administrative data used to manage the archives

4. *Administration:* function that provides services for the overall operation of the archives system

5. *Preservation planning:* system monitors the environment of the OAIS and provides recommendations to ensure that the information stored in the OAIS remains accessible, even if the original computing environment becomes obsolete

6. *Access:* system allows a user to determine the existence, description, location, and availability of information stored in the OAIS; subsequently, information products can be requested and received

In the words of the General Accounting Office:

The OAIS framework does not presume or apply any particular preservation strategy. This approach allows organizations that adopt the framework to apply their own strategies or combinations of strategies. The framework does assume that the information managed is produced outside the OAIS, and that the information will be disseminated to users who are also outside the system. Because the model is simplified to include only functions common to all repositories, it allows institutions to focus on the approaches necessary to preserve the information.[43]

A major research project in the United Kingdom is testing the OAIS Reference Model as well as other aspects of archiving digital records. The CEDARS Project (CURL Exemplars in Digital Archives) seeks to address strategic, methodological, and practical issues and provide best practices for digital preservation. CEDARS is a collaboration of librarians, archivists, publishers, authors, and institutions. The research team is evaluating different preservation strategies by

- conducting demonstration projects at test sites;
- developing recommendations and guidelines;
- developing practical, robust, and scaleable models for establishing distributed digital archives;
- considering the implications of rights management and metadata.[44]

The CEDARS project is developing a demonstrator system to recommend techniques for long-term storage of digital data primarily within the research library context. The demonstrator will try to implement the OAIS model.[45]

CONVERSION AND MIGRATION

The goal of conversion and migration is to translate documents into forms accessible by future generations of hardware and software. The translation takes place on a regular basis as hardware and software become obsolete.

Charles Dollar clarified the differences among four terms for media renewal often incorrectly used interchangeably: reformat, copy, convert, and migrate.

- *Reformatting* of electronic records means that there is a change to the underlying bit stream, but there is no change in the representation or intellectual content of the records. Typically, reformatting is associated with the transfer of a bit stream from one storage medium to a different one. For example, moving from nine-track computer tape to cassette would be reformatting, as would be transforming records from EDCDIC (the coding used on mainframe computers) to ASCII (the coding used on personal computers).
- *Copying* electronic records means transferring them from old storage media to new storage media with the same format specifications without any loss in structure, content, and context. In copying electronic records, the underlying bit stream pattern on one storage medium is replicated on a new but identical storage medium (e.g., old 3480 tape to new 3480 tape).

- *Converting* electronic records involves their export or import from one software environment to another without the loss of structure, content, and context, even though the underlying bit stream is likely to be altered. Conversion occurs when electronic records are moved from one software environment or application to another, for example when we convert a Word Perfect document to Microsoft Word.

- *Migrating* electronic records usually involves moving them from proprietary legacy systems that lack software functionality to open systems. The only way known at this time to migrate the records and their essential software functionality is to write custom, special-purpose, code or programs. For example, if the archivist found old magnetic tapes in storage from a long-obsolete computer system, the only option would be to write a special program to read the old data. This is more complex than is generally assumed, especially since archivists must preserve the integrity of the records during the migration.[46]

In some ways, conversion and migration are the opposite of a computer museum. The goal of conversion and migration is to keep the digital file readable as hardware and software change. Conversion, the less disruptive of the two approaches, involves the regular "rewriting" of digital files from older to newer computing environments. Anyone who has experienced a conversion, such as moving from Word Perfect to Microsoft Word, knows that this is not a seamless process. Migration, on the other hand, is usually a last-gasp attempt to move digital information from long-inactive legacy computer systems. Migration almost always requires the writing of special software that could call into question the intellectual integrity of the resulting records.

EMULATION

Emulation currently is the subject of research by archivists and records managers. Emulation means that one computer system will act like another. We regularly experience this when our personal computers emulate, or act like, a "dumb terminal" in a mainframe system.

According to Jeff Rothenberg, the emulation approach involves developing techniques for

- specifying emulators that will run on unknown future computers;

- saving in human-readable form the descriptive data needed to recreate digital documents;
- encapsulating documents along with their descriptive data, software, and emulator specifications.

Rothenberg believes that emulation is the "only reliable way to recreate a digital document's original functionality, look, and feel."[47]

Emulation currently is being testing through a project called CAMiLEON (Creative Archiving at Michigan & Leeds: Emulating the Old on the New). A joint project of the University of Michigan in the United States and the University of Leeds in the United Kingdom, CAMiLEON is investigating the viability of emulation as a preservation strategy that maintains the intellectual content, structure, and "look and feel" of software-dependent complex digital objects. Researchers are also assessing user preferences for different versions of emulators that vary considerably in how they reproduce those objects (running in native software environment, running under emulation, or delivered in migrated versions).[48]

Emulation might eventually prove to be the preferred long-term strategy. At the moment, however, it is a leap of faith for the archivist to rely only upon emulation. Most archives, especially smaller ones, probably will opt for conversion and migration. Though there is a potential loss of data with each conversion or migration, the loss should be apparent to the archivist. With emulation, we might not know for years or decades if someone has developed a successful emulator.

TRUSTWORTHY INFORMATION SYSTEMS

It does no good to have a digital archives if we cannot trust it. In 1996, the Commission on Preservation and Access and the Research Libraries Group formed a Task Force on Archiving of Digital Information. This Task Force identified five aspects of information integrity, a key component of trustworthiness:

- *Content.* The intellectual substance found in the information objects is its content.
- *Fixity.* The content must be fixed as a discrete object in order to be a record. If a digital object can be changed without notice, then its integrity may be compromised.
- *Reference.* For a digital object to maintain its integrity, one must be able to locate it definitively and reliably among other objects over time.
- *Provenance.* The integrity of an information object

is partly embedded in tracing its source.
- *Context.* Digital objects interact with other elements in the wider digital environment.[49]

Since this initial statement, archivists have continued to develop the concepts of integrity and authenticity.[50] Recently, the Minnesota Historical Society (MHS) codified the idea of a "trustworthy information system" and prepared a handbook to explain the concept to state agency officials.[51] According to MHS:

We chose the term *trustworthy* because it denotes integrity, ability, faith, and confidence. We use trustworthiness to describe information system accountability. We use the words *reliable* and *authentic* when we talk about the information and records that the information system creates. Reliability indicates a record's authority and is established when a record is created. Authenticity ensures that a record will be reliable throughout its life, whether that lifetime lasts six months, ten years, twenty years, or forever.

The handbook organizes criteria for trustworthy information systems into five categories:

- system documentation
- security measures
- audit trails
- disaster recovery plans
- record metadata

The handbook then assists state agencies in deciding what is reasonable and practical depending upon a variety of factors. The important point is "to make, justify, and document your choices in order to ensure consistent application and ... agency accountability for its decisions."[52] This handbook will be useful to archivists in almost any institutional setting.

PERSISTENT DIGITAL ARCHIVES

"Collection-Based Persistent Digital Archives" is the name given to a research project funded by the National Archives and Records Administration and other Federal sources. Working with the San Diego Supercomputer Center, NARA is trying to develop an operational system that captures, maintains, and provides access to digital records regardless of changes to the computing environment. The goal is to "wrap" in one package the record's contents with enough descriptive data and contextual information to permit its reading on other, future computer systems.

NARA has been managing digital archives since 1968, longer than almost anyone in the world.[53] Despite this long history, the current explosion of digital records forced NARA to re-think its policies and practices. NARA is calling its new approach, including the partnership with the San Diego Supercomputer Center, the Electronic Records Archives (ERA).[54]

The first phase of the San Diego project involved creating a one million-message persistent e-mail collection. During the test, the e-mail collection was ingested, archived, and dramatically rebuilt in just a single day—because all steps in the process were automated. Each message was tagged using Extensible Markup Language (XML), which was discussed earlier in this book in relation to Encoded Archival Description. The San Diego researchers state that they can scale the system to handle forty million messages in a month. Subsequent phases will test the ability to manage digital records in other formats.[55]

The Persistent Digital Archives has four components: ingestion, archival storage, information discovery, and presentation of the collection. The original plan also called for the development of an "archivist's workbench" that would provide tools for archives of all sizes. For budget reasons, it now appears that the workbench component will be delayed for years, at best.

CONCLUSION

In this section, I have briefly discussed ten strategies and approaches for managing digital archives. Some of the strategies can be implemented immediately by archives of all sizes (for example, policy formation and backward compatibility). Other strategies probably will only be reasonable for major institutions with large budgets (persistent digital archives and emulation, for example). Nevertheless, archivists in both large and small institutions will need to begin managing digital archives. The next section provides some practical advice based upon the current state of the art.

SUGGESTIONS FOR THE PRACTICAL ARCHIVIST

While there is much research in progress on digital records, what is the practical archivist to do in the meantime? The following are some suggestions for the archivist who must begin to deal with digital records *now*.

SUGGESTIONS FOR ORGANIZATIONS

An organization interested in improving the management and preservation of digital records should do the following:

- issue a policy that defines digital records and gives the archivist responsibility for their preservation
- establish rules for naming files and labeling disks and other digital media
- assemble system documentation and plan for its preservation
- let software and hardware vendors know that the management of electronic documents is important. Take this into account when choosing potential vendors and products

SUGGESTIONS FOR INDIVIDUALS

Archivists who raise the consciousness of individuals are often asked to provide specific guidance to employees. The following are suggestions that an archivist can propose to individuals within the organization:

- Attach meaningful descriptions to documents, if permitted by the software. At a minimum, fill in author, date, and subject matter.
- Record information about each document created. This will make it easier to match electronic and paper documents.
- Back up document storage media regularly, storing one copy off-site.
- If documents are stored in compressed format, retain the software required to expand documents to their original formats. Ensure that later versions of the compression software can still expand documents stored previously. The same considerations apply to encrypted documents.
- Only use password protection on documents when it is absolutely necessary, and ensure that there is always someone else who knows the password.
- Be particularly careful when storing compound documents (documents that incorporate information in different formats such as spreadsheets, databases, and images). All applications required to recreate the document must be maintained.[56]

IMPLEMENTATION: FUNDAMENTAL DECISIONS

Preservation solutions will continue to be developed and refined. In the meantime, archivists will need to make some decisions about implementation strategies—our organizations will not be able to wait until the "ideal" approach is developed (if it ever is).

The following three fundamental decisions will need to be part of any short- or long-term implementation plan:

- *Grand solution vs. trench warfare.* Will we work from the "top down," trying to establish universal rules, or will we work from the "bottom up," applying lessons learned from one case to another? The top-down deductive approach is exemplified by the InterPARES Project. The bottom-up inductive approach is being tested in such places as Indiana University.[57]

- *Build recordkeeping functionality into all systems vs. transfer records into a recordkeeping system.* Once we acknowledge that most information systems are not automatically designed to capture and maintain records, we face a choice: Do we want to try to make every information system a recordkeeping system or do we want to have a separate recordkeeping system attached to our computing infrastructure. Early efforts to implement the University of Pittsburgh Functional Requirements tended to focus on the former (for example, a project tested at the City of Philadelphia). Some recent initiatives have turned to the latter, particularly by adding a recordkeeping module to the portals that seem to be springing up like weeds in our Internet pastures.

- *In-house preservation vs. outsourced solution.* Some archivists will want to build their own preservation infrastructure, while others will contract for these services with third party providers. The decision will involve more than economics; it also will involve organizational dynamics and institutional priorities.

SEVEN-STEP APPROACH TO MANAGING DIGITAL ARCHIVES

Any organization needs a plan for managing digital archives. The plan, however, must take into account organizational realities as well as research possibilities. What follows is a seven-step approach for the archives with a limited budget. The approach focuses on partnering with others in the organization in order to develop incremental solutions.[58]

The seven steps are:

1. understand the organizational context
2. determine the role of the archives or preservation department
3. define issues and concerns
4. identify partners
5. design pilot projects
6. test approaches and solutions
7. roll out the program to the entire organization

Step 1: Understand the Organizational Context

As a first step, the archivist will need to understand the organization *in its entirety.* This will involve reading annual reports and other documents that state the current concerns of executives and administrators. The focus of the archivist must go beyond the care and feeding of inactive records on paper.

The archivist also will need to schedule one or more meetings with the information technology staff. This can be intimidating for archivists who may not feel technologically comfortable and may fear that they do not know the secret handshake that provides entrance into the IT community. Nevertheless, the archivist will need to understand, at least in broad brushstrokes, the IT landscape and architecture. This is something that can deepen over time, perhaps as the archivist works closely with a liaison appointed by IT.

At this point, it is also helpful to conduct one or more group meetings with electronic records creators and users. There is perhaps no more efficient way to obtain an overview of the entire organization than holding such group sessions. If the archivist provides coffee and Danishes, there usually is a dramatic increase in attendance at the group sessions.

It is important to note that, in this first step, the archivist is not proposing solutions to the groups. Rather, he or she is looking to let people express themselves about the nature of their jobs and the ways that they create and rely upon digital information. During subsequent steps the archivist again will assemble groups to discuss potential approaches and solutions.

Step 2: Determine the Role of the Archives

Once the archivist has an overall sense of the organization, he or she should try to state clearly the vision of the archives in the area of digital records. From this vision will flow the role that the digital archives will play in the life of the organization.

The possible roles are endless, limited mainly by resource requirements. However, what follows is a sampling of some of the roles that other archivists have established for their departments:

- *Advocate for historical concerns.* One obvious role is as an advocate for historical concerns. In many organizations, the archivist may be the only person focusing on the past and future, rather than the present. This is especially the case in an information systems environment where the focus is on meeting the current needs of users without worrying about what will happen to the data in the long term.

- *Internal consultant.* Another role for the archives is as an internal consultant on digital preservation. In order to fulfill this role, the staff may need additional training in information technologies. The staff will need to "speak the language" in order to have credibility as an internal consultant.

- *Voice at the table.* It is common for the archivist to try to get a seat at the table where information issues are discussed. This involves getting appointed to committees or task forces dealing with the design and implementation of new information systems. While this will take time away from other duties, it is time well spent to assure digital preservation.

- *Information locator.* Many archives are opting for the role of "information locator." In this model, the archives becomes a one-stop-shopping source for information resources, whether maintained by the archives or the originating department. In the government sphere, this role is called a Government Information Locator System (GILS) and is found at both the Federal and state levels.

- *Custodian of records.* As discussed previously, the archives can choose to take custody of all electronic records of long-term value. The alternate role is for the archives to opt to have custody remain in the originating department. Figure 10.5 summarizes arguments in favor of these two approaches to custody.

Fig. 10.5 Arguments in Favor of Different Approaches to Custody[59]	
Centralized Custody Approach	**Distributed Custody Approach**
Mission and competencies. It is not part of the mission of the creating agency, nor does its staff possess the necessary skills to safeguard the authenticity of non-current archival records. *Ability to monitor compliance.* There are not enough trained archivists available to monitor or audit records in a distributed custody environment. *Cost to monitor compliance.* Costs to manage records in a distributed environment are unknown, but it is likely to be more costly to monitor recordkeeping practices than to assume custody of the records. *Changes in work environment.* Changes in staffing and in departmental priorities can place records left with creating offices at great risk. *Vested interests.* Inactive records must be taken from those who have a vested interest in either corrupting or neglecting them.	*Costs.* It would be enormously expensive and a massive waste of resources to attempt to duplicate within the archival setting the technological environments already in place within the creating offices. *Changes in technology.* Rapid technological change and the reluctance of manufacturers to support old hardware make it extremely difficult for a centralized repository to manage an institution's digital records. *Skills required.* It would be difficult, if not impossible, for an archives staff to learn the skills and provide the expertise needed to access and preserve the wide variety of technologies and formats in use. *Loss of records.* Insisting on custody will result in some cases in leaving important records outside the recordkeeping boundary.

An approach that not enough archivists have considered is the "co-custodial" approach.

This approach recognizes that managing digital archives involves both "front office" and "back office" components:

- *Front Office.* These are the customer service functions, such as administration, acquisition, and access.
- *Back Office.* These are the collection management functions, such as: receipt of records in an approved format; copying onto preservation media; making a disaster protection copy and storing it off-site; storing records; monitoring the physical condition of stored media; refreshing the media as required; converting the information at regular intervals; and destroying the records in a secure fashion when possible.

A co-custodial approach means that the archives assumes *legal* custody of the records—the archives takes full responsibility for preservation of the records. However, the archives then delegates *physical* custody to a qualified third party, often the Information Technology Department of the parent organization. This permits the IT department to handle the back office functions under contract from the archives. In this scenario, the IT Department, rather than the archives, is responsible for purchasing new hardware and software as well as maintaining qualified technical staff.

"Last fall, Archivist [of the United States] John Carlin estimated that since 1972, [the National Archives and Records Administration] had taken in about 90,000 files of electronic records. But in this case the past is no guide to the future: Mr. Carlin estimated that the Treasury alone was generating 960,000 e-mail files every year that will need to be preserved. That is, just one federal agency created more than 10 times as many files in one year as Archives has received from the entire government over a quarter-century."

—*Wall Street Journal*, June 21, 1999.

Step 3: Define Issues and Concerns

The third step is to define the issues and concerns most relevant to the organization. For some organizations, they key issue will be the control of e-mail. For others, it will be the preservation of Web sites or the review of old computer tapes in inactive storage.

Once the issues are defined, I recommend summarizing current research on the issues. This brief document should be presented in clear, straightforward language suitable for wide distribution throughout the organization—it should be free of technical jargon and acronyms. The purpose of the summary is to place the organization's efforts within the larger professional context and to stimulate additional thinking by management and staff.

Step 4: Identify Partners

The next step involves "selling" the digital archives program to potential "partners" within the organization. Most archivists will not be able to go it alone; a successful digital archives program will have to flow from a partnership with others in the organization.

But how does one go about selecting partners? Let me review some key considerations:

- *Begin with your friends.* There is no point beginning with people who are resistant to the preservation initiative. Rather, it is better to begin with people who recognize the problem. At a later date, the program can be expanded to the entire organization, including the recalcitrant ones.

- *Try to address the concerns of the partners.* As tempting as it may be to try to focus exclusively on the concerns of the archives, this will not lead to a true partnership. The best way to build support within the organization is to listen to potential partners and give their concerns equal weight. Often during the course of discussion it will become clear how similar the interests of the archives and the partner department really are.

- *Try to find partners who can build positive word of mouth as the program progresses.* The ideal is to work with a partner who will enthusiastically tell others of your success. In this way, the "buzz" around the organization is positive rather than negative. Naturally, there only will be partner enthusiasm if we actually help partners solve their problems.

- *Be aware of organizational politics.* Sometimes the archivist must consider politics when choosing partners. For example, it may be unwise to exclude another department head, who also reports to your boss, or to appear to be taking sides in existing organizational struggles.

The main point in selecting partners, however, is to focus on projects with the greatest chance of meeting objectives on time and under budget. All the other considerations mean nothing if we do not accomplish what we set out to accomplish.

Step 5: Design Pilot Projects

The fifth step is to design one or more pilot projects in consultation with your partners. Each project should have the following components:

- *Objectives.* What do we hope to achieve in working with the partner?
- *Methodology.* How will we achieve the project objectives?
- *Time Frame.* When will the project begin and end?
- *Responsibilities.* Who will accomplish the objectives? Which responsibilities belong to the archives and the partner department?

An example from North Fork University may help clarify this step. Suppose that the NFU Public Relations Department has agreed to work with the archives on the transfer of quarterly reports now being created in electronic form. The answers to the above questions appear in figure 10.6.

Fig. 10.6 Elements of a Digital Archives Pilot Project	
Objectives	Eliminate the transfer and preservation of paper copies of quarterly reports and develop a seamless way of transferring digital copies
Methodology	Since the quarterly reports are posted to the organizational Web site, Public Relations will transfer this electronic copy rather than the one created by word processing software. This should cause the least interruption to departmental work processes.
Time Frame	The pilot project will begin on June 1. Within thirty days, the archives will be ready to test the digital transfer. We anticipate needing one more month to iron out the kinks and finalize the plans for ongoing transfer.
Responsibilities	The archivist will be responsible for securing space on a server where the files can be loaded. The Public Relations Department Webmaster will be responsible for writing a script to transfer the reports.

A clear statement of project objectives and methodologies, similar to the above, will go a long way toward assuring the success of the pilot project.

Step 6: Test Approaches and Solutions

The actual testing of approaches may take anywhere from a couple of days to several months. It is important to keep in mind that the partner is "lending" time and resources to the pilot project designed by the archivist—this project probably will not be the partner's primary concern. This means that crises may arise that force the partner to slow down work on the pilot. The archivist has to be ready for this. Usually adjusting the time frame for completion is enough to keep the partner involved in the project.

Remember that this is a pilot or experiment. Therefore, it is common to have to adjust expectations and refine solutions as work progresses. While this may be frustrating, it is precisely the reason why we opt for an incremental solution rather than trying to implement a program throughout the entire organization all at once. It is better to learn from our mistakes on a small scale than to try to repair large-scale damage to our department's reputation.

Near the end of the pilot it should become obvious if we need to write policies or procedures before implementing the program on a broader scale. Once again, these policies and procedures are best drafted in consultation with the partners we already have cultivated.

Near the end of the pilot phase, it is helpful to prepare written summaries of the projects, focusing on lessons learned and experience gained. These written summaries will bring the pilot phase to closure by forcing the archivist to reflect on project objectives and outcomes.

It is important to be honest in evaluating the pilot projects. Not everything will always go as planned, and sometimes what seemed like a good idea before the pilot turns out not to have been so well conceived. As long as we learn from the experience, the pilot phase will have been well worth the time.

Step 7: Roll Out the Program to the Entire Organization

The final step involves implementing the digital preservation program throughout the organization. Implementation requires four major activities:

- *Finalize policies and procedures.* If policies and procedures are in draft form, they need to be finalized before the program can be implemented broadly. Policies and procedures must be clear and consistent if the implementation is to be successful.

- *Prepare training and orientation materials.* The lessons learned during the pilot phase should be translated into training materials usable by all staff. This is the easiest way to institutionalize the program and to communicate its objectives to the entire staff. Training and orientation materials need to be appropriate for the organizational culture. In many cases, this will include written instructions, presentations using Microsoft PowerPoint, and educational Web pages.

- *Conduct staff training seminars.* The best way to move from policy to program is by conducting training for all staff members.

- *Follow up with departments.* After the training sessions, it is important to schedule time for meetings with attendees. There are bound to be questions about the nature and meaning of the program that the archives seeks to implement. The best way to deal with the uncertainties is by meeting face-to-face with staff members.

CONCLUSION

There is no shortage of issues when it comes to digital archives. In fact, the range of choices that we face and options to consider, sometimes lead to an avoidance reaction: we hope to be able to ignore digital preservation until we retire and then leave the problem to someone else. My dentist has been facing similar avoidance reactions for years. One of his favorite sayings is: "Ignore your teeth—they'll go away!" Unfortunately, the same thing will happen to our digital records unless we start acting now, even on a small scale. As professionals, we owe it to our institutions to confront head-on what may be our most difficult challenge over the next few decades.

NOTES

1. Computer records have played central roles in other fictional works. For example, Michael Crichton's *Rising Sun* hinges on the alteration of a digital video image. Also, Tom Clancy's *Debt of Honor* includes an attack on the world financial order through its computer system.

2. Peter G. Neumann, *Computer Related Risks* (New York: Addison-Wesley, 1995). Neumann collected the anecdotes as moderator of an Internet newsgroup, the "Forum on Risks to the Public in the Use of Computers and Related Systems."

3. I am consciously using the term "digital records" rather than "electronic records." The two terms have quite different meanings, even though they often are used interchangeably. "Electronic" refers to something produced by the action of electrons, specifically in an electrical current. "Digital" means that there are discrete states (like "on" and "off") with nothing in between. VHS movies, for example, are electronic but they are not digital. For more information see Gregory S. Hunter, *Preserving Digital Information* (New York: Neal-Schuman, 2000), 3.

4. This information is summarized from Charles M. Dollar, *Archival Theory and Information Technologies: The Impact of Information Technologies on Archival Principles and Methods* (Macerata, Italy: University of Macerata, 1992).

5. Long-term is, of course, relative. Information systems professionals believe they are addressing long-term needs when they plan information storage for a year or two.

6. This information is taken from "Keeping Electronic Records: Policy for Electronic Recordkeeping in the Commonwealth Government," published by the National Archives of Australia (http://www.naa.gov.au).

7. The best discussion of the archival issues in this case is David Bearman, "The Implications of *Armstrong v. the Executive Office of the President* for the Archival Management of Electronic Records," *American Archivist* 56 (fall 1993): 674-89. For an interesting perspective on the case, see Tom Blanton, ed., *White House E-Mail: The Top Secret Computer Messages the Reagan/Bush White House Tried to Destroy* (New York: Free Press, 1995).

8. The issue is likely to remain alive for a couple of hundred more years. In an episode of *Star Trek: The Next Generation*, Captain Jean-Luc Picard receives a transmission from another starship captain informing him of a suspected conspiracy within the Federation. The transmission is made using Star Fleet's most secure channel and the computer is instructed not to make a record of it. The episode, "Conspiracy," was first aired the week of May 8, 1988.

9. David Bearman and Margaret Hedstrom, "Reinventing Archives for Digital records: Alternative Service Delivery Options," in *Electronic Records Management Program Strategies*, ed. Margaret Hedstrom (Pittsburgh, Pa.: Archives and Museum Informatics, 1993), 82-98.

10. John W. C. Van Bogart, *Magnetic Tape Storage and Handling: A Guide for Libraries and Archives* (Washington, D.C.: Commission on Preservation and Access, 1995).

11. Taken from a John Van Bogart letter to the editor of *Scientific American* written in response to an article in the January 1995 issue (Jeff Rothenberg, "Ensuring the Longevity of Digital Documents"), which indicated that the physical lifetime of magnetic tape was only one to two years.

12. For an excellent summary of magnetic and optical media, see William Saffady, *Managing Electronic Records*, 3d ed. (Lenexa, Kans: ARMA International, 2003).

13. Van Bogart letter to *Scientific American*.

14. Narrative written by Margaret O. Adams of the National Archives and Records Administration, posted to the Digital Records Listserv (ERECS-L) on April 15, 1996.

15. The episode was first aired on February 2, 1967.

16. For more on the challenges of digital records, see David Bearman, ed., *Archival Management of Electronic Records* (Pittsburgh, Pa.: Archives and Museum Informatics, 1991); "Archives and Electronic Records," a special issue of the *Bulletin of the American Society for Information Science* 20 (October/ November 1993): 9-26; and Paul Conway, *Preservation in the Digital World* (Washington, D.C.: Commission on Preservation and Access, 1996).

17. Rich Lysakowski and Zahava Leibowitz , *Titanic 2020: A Call to Action* (Woburn, Mass.: Collaborative Electronic Notebook Systems Association [CENSA], 2000),(http://www.censa.org/html/Press-Releases/Titanic2020.htm).

18. For more on the project, see: University of British Columbia, *The Preservation of the Integrity of Electronic Records*, (http://www.interpares.org/UBCProject/intro.htm).

19. In the words of the project team, "Diplomatics is a body of concepts and methods, originally developed in the seventeenth and eighteenth centuries, 'for the purpose of proving the reliability and authenticity of documents.' Over the centuries it has evolved 'into a very sophisticated system of ideas about the nature of records, their genesis and composition, their relationships with the actions and persons connected to them, and with their organizational, social and legal context.'" (http://www.interpares.org/UBCProject/intro.htm.)

20. According to the InterPARES web site: "Whereas diplomatics studies records as individual entities, 'archival science studies them as aggregations, analyzes their documentary and functional interrelationships, and studies the ways in which the records with all their relations can be controlled and communicated.'" (http://www.interpares.org/ UBCProject/intro.htm).

21. A reliable record is "a record endowed with trustworthiness. Specifically, trustworthiness is conferred to a record by its degree of completeness and the degree of control on its creation procedure and/or its author's reliability." See "Template 3: What is a Reliable Record in the Traditional Environment," http://www.interpares.org/UBCProject/ tem3.htm.

22. An authentic record is one "whose genuineness can be established.... While a reliable record is one whose content you can trust, an authentic record is one whose provenance you can believe." See "Template 4: What is an Authentic Record in the Traditional Environment?" (http://www.interpares.org/UBCProject/tem4.htm).

23. A good place to begin a review of the standard is as the home page of the Department of Defense's Joint Interoperability Test Command, which is administering the certification testing program for Records Management Applications, http://jitc.fhu.disa.mil/recmgt/.

24. For more information, see Hunter, *Preserving Digital Information*, 33-37.

25. Richard C. Cox, "Electronic Systems and Records Management in the Information Age: An Introduction," *Bulletin of the American Society for Information Science* 23, no. 5 (June/July 1997): 8. This entire issue focuses on electronic recordkeeping issues. For a summary of the research on warrants, see Wendy M. Duff's article, "Compiling Warrant in Support of the Functional Requirements for Recordkeeping," pp. 12-13 of the same issue.

26. The full version can be found in *Bulletin of the American Society for Information Science* 23, no. 5 (June/July 1997): 10-11, see also http://web.archive.org/web/20000302194819/http://www.sis.pitt.edu/ ~nhprc/meta96.html.

27. For example, see Mark D. Giguere, "Automating Electronic Records Management in a Transactional Environment: The Philadelphia Story," *Bulletin of the American Society for Information Science* 23, no. 5 (June/July 1997): 17-19; Phillip Bantin, "NHPRC Project at the University of Indiana," *Bulletin of the American Society for Information Science* 23, no. 5 (June/July 1997): 24; the Indiana University Web site (http://www.indiana.edu/~libarch/ER/); Bantin, "Developing a Strategy for Managing Electronic Records-The Findings of the Indiana University Electronic Records Project," *American Archivist* 61, no. 2 (fall 1998): 328-64; Bantin, "The Indiana University Electronic Records Project Revisited," *American Archivist* 62, no. 1 (spring 1999): 153-63; Timothy A. Slavin, "Implementing Requirements for Recordkeeping:Moving From Theory to Practice," in *Effective Approaches for Managing Electronic Records and Archives*, ed. Bruce W. Dearstyne (Lanham, Md.: Scarecrow Press, 2002), 35-52.

28. *Victorian Electronic Records Strategy: Final Report*. South Melbourne: Public Record Office Victoria, 1998, http://www.prov.vic.gov.au/vers/published/final.htm.

29. The InterPARES Project Web site provides the most complete information (http://www.interpares.org).

30. InterPARES Project, *The Long-Term Preservation of Authentic Electronic Records: Findings of the InterPARES Project* (Vancouver: InterPARES Project and University of British Columbia, 2002), http://www.interpares.org/book/index.htm.

31. For a summary of some of these strategies, see Philip C. Bantin, "Electronic Records Management: A Review of the Work of a Decade and a Reflection on Future Directions," in *Encyclopedia of Library and Information Science* vol. 71, suppl. 34 (New York: Marcel Dekker, 2002), 62-66.

32. Jeff Rothenberg, *Avoiding Technological Quicksand: Finding a Viable Technical Foundation for Digital Preservation* (Washington, D.C.: Council on Library and Information Resources, 1999), 3.

33. F. Gerald Ham, "The Archival Edge," *American Archivist* 38 (January 1975): 5-13.

34. If we are going to generate an analog copy at some point, the legal admissibility of the records should be improved by generating the copy at the time of initial transfer rather than after several rounds of conversion and/or migration have taken place.

35. Leonard Rapport, "No Grandfather Clause: Reappraising Accessioned Records," *American Archivist* 44 (spring 1981): 143-150.

36. Charles M. Dollar, "Electronic Archiving in the 21st Century: Principles, Strategy, and Best Practices," *Of Significance* 2, no. 2 (2000): 13; Seamus Ross and Ann Gow, *Post-Hoc Rescue of Digital Material* (London: British Library and Joint Information Committee, 1998). The Rosetta Stone permitted archeologists to translate Egyptian hieroglyphics.

37. David Bearman, "Electronic Records Guidelines: A Manual for Policy Development and Implementation," in *Electronic Evidence*, ed. Bearman, 72-116. Reprinted with permission.

38. Adapted from *Managing Electronic Records* (Washington, D.C.: National Archives and Records Administration, 1990).

39. Cornell University, Project PRISM, http://www.library.cornell.edu/iris/research/prism/index.html.

40. For an introduction to XML, see Norman Walsh, "What is XML?" http://www.xml.com/pub/a/98/10/guide1.html#AEN58.

41. For more on standards see Bearman, *Electronic Evidence*, 210-20.

42. Consultative Committee for Space Data Systems. *Reference Model for an Open Archival Information System (OAIS)*. CCSDS 650.0-R-2, "Red Book." July 2001. http://wwwclassic.ccsds.org/documents/pdf/CCSDS-650.0-R-2.pdf.

43. General Accounting Office, "Information Management: Challenges in Managing and Preserving Electronic Records," Report GAO-02-586 (Washington, D.C.: General Accounting Office, 2002), 13-15, http://www.gao.gov/atext/d02586.txt.

44. Cedars Project, *Metadata for Digital Preservation*, http://www.leeds.ac.uk/cedars/documents/Metadata/cedars.html.

45. David Holdsworth and Derek M. Sergeant. "A Blueprint for Representation Information in the OAIS Model." <http://www.personal.leeds.ac.uk/~ecldh/cedars/ieee00.html>. Also available at <http://esdis-it.gsfc.nasa.gov/msst/conf2000/papers/d02pa.pdf>. For more on CEDARS, see Kelly Russell and Derek Sergeant, "The Cedars Project: Implementing a Model for Distributed Digital Archives," *RLG DigiNews 3*, no. 3 (1999). <http://www.rlg.ac.uk/preserv/diginews/diginews3-3.html>. The InterPARES Preservation Task Force also used OAIS as the basis for its report.<http://www.interpares.org>.

46. Charles M. Dollar, *Authentic Electronic Records: Strategies for Long-Term Access* (Chicago: Cohasset Associates, 1999), 26–32, 59–72; see also Hunter, *Preserving Digital Information*, 57–58.

47. Rothenberg, Avoiding Technological Quicksand, 30. David Bearman argues against Rothenberg and emulation, in "Reality and Chimeras in the Preservation of Electronic Records." *D-Lib Magazine* 5, no. 4 (April 1999), http://www.dlib.org/dlib/april99/bearman/04bearman.html.

48. University of Michigan and University of Leeds, CAMiLEON Project, http://www.si.umich.edu/CAMILEON. See also David Holdsworth and Paul Wheatley, "Emulation, Preservation and Abstraction," http://129.11.152.25/CAMiLEON//dh/ep5.html. The CAMiLEON Project also looked at migration as a strategy, on which see Paul Wheatley, "Migration—A CAMiLEON Discussion Paper" *Ariadne* 29 (2001), http://www.ariadne.ac.uk/issue29/camileon/intro.html.

49. John Garrett and Donald Waters, *Preserving Digital Information: Report of the Task Force on Archiving Digital Information* (Washington, D.C.: Commission on Preservation and Access and the Research Libraries Group, 1996), 11–19. See also Hunter, *Preserving Digital Information*, 5–10.

50. Luigi Sarno, editor, *Authentic Records in the Electronic Age: Proceedings from an International Symposium* (Vancouver, Canada: InterPARES Project, 2000); Heather MacNeil, *Trusting Records: Legal, Historical and Diplomatic Perspectives* (Boston: Kluwer Academic Publishers, 2000); *Authenticity in a Digital Environment* (Washington, D.C.: Council on Library and Information Resources, 2000),http://www.clir.org/pubs/abstract/pub92abst.html.

51. Minnesota Historical Society, *Trustworthy Information Systems Handbook* (St. Paul: Minnesota Historical Society, 2001), http://www.mnhs.org/preserve/records/tis/tableofcontents.html.

52. Minnesota Historical Society, "What are the Criteria for a Trustworthy Information System?" http://www.mnhs.org/preserve/records/tis/Section9.html.

53. Bruce Ambacher, "Preservation of Federal Electronic Records at the National Archives and Records Administration," *Of Significance* 2, no. 2 (2000): 20–27.

54. Daniel Jansen, "The National Archives and Records Administration's Electronic Records Archives Program and the Future Preservation and Use of Federal Electronic Records," *Of Significance* 2, no. 2 (2000): 43–49; National Archives and Records Administration, "Electronic Records Archives (ERA)," http://www.nara.gov/era/.

55. Moore, Reagan, et. al, "Collection-Based Persistent Digital Archives: Part 1," *D-Lib Magazine* 6, no. 3 (March 2000), http://www.dlib.org/dlib/march00/moore/03moore-pt1.html; Moore, et. al, "Collection-Based Persistent Digital Archives: Part 2." *D-Lib Magazine* 6, no. 4 (April 2000), http://www.dlib.org/dlib/april00/moore/04moore-pt2.html.

56. These hints are adapted from Commonwealth of Australia, "Draft Guidelines for Managing Electronic Documents in Australian Government Agencies," prepared by the Electronic Data Management Subcommittee of the Information Exchange Steering Committee, February 1995.

57. For more information, see the InterPARES Web site, http://www.interpares.org; for Indiana University's project, see http://www.indiana.edu/~libarch/ER/.

58. This is a modified version of the approach presented in *Preserving Digital Information*, ed. Hunter, 125–32.

59. Bantin, "Electronic Records Management," 66–68.

11 AUDIOVISUAL ARCHIVES

Audiovisual records are found in almost every archives or manuscript repository. Over the last hundred years, audiovisual records have become increasingly important in documenting contemporary society. One need only recall the sights and sounds of the collapse of the World Trade Center to appreciate that text alone could not convey the magnitude of the event.

According to the Society of American Archivists, audiovisual records are records "in pictorial and/or aural form, regardless of format."[1] Audiovisual records include photographs, films, videotapes, and sound recordings of various types. They also include both analog and digital records.

The variety of recording technologies and storage media make preservation and access to audiovisual records an ongoing challenge. Audiovisual records are among the most fragile record forms: adverse environmental conditions hasten their deterioration, contact with some materials causes harmful chemical reactions, and improper handling can damage them beyond repair. Any of the above can cause catastrophic loss of valuable information.[2]

In addition to managing the physical entities, archivists need to understand the intellectual issues associated with audiovisual records. In particular, archivists must become familiar with visual expression and interpretation, sometimes called "visual literacy." In the words of William H. Leary, "Visual literacy requires the same critical analysis as verbal literacy. Archivists and historians must learn to study a historical photograph with the same attention to detail that an archaeologist might devote to a single artifact."[3]

Elisabeth Kaplan and Jeffrey Mifflin illustrated this complexity by identifying three levels of visual content:[4]

1 *Superficial contents.* This describes what the material is. For example, a photograph of a dead Civil War soldier.

2 *Concrete subject matter.* This describes what the image is about. This requires historical knowledge of events and individuals. To continue with the

example, the photograph is of a young Union soldier at the Battle of Gettysburg.

3 *Abstract elements*. This involves both visual perception and visual awareness, including understanding the conventions of particular media in their particular context. For example, knowing that most photographs at the time were sold might explain why the dead soldier was posed in a way to make him look more heroic.

Understanding that there even *are* several levels of visual awareness is particularly useful for an archivist describing a collection of visual materials or providing reference services. According to Kaplan and Mifflin, "Archivists need to be able to describe visual materials in terms meaningful to researchers with various levels of sophistication."[5] As subsequent sections will show, description and access are even more closely connected with audiovisual records than with textual records.[6]

This chapter will discuss the primary categories of audiovisual records:

- photographs
- film
- videotape
- sound recordings

PHOTOGRAPHS

A photograph is defined as "an image produced on photosensitive material by exposure to light or other radiant energy with or without intermediate negative." Archivists responsible for photographic collections will have two specific media to manage:

- *Print*. "A copy of a photographic image on a light sensitive surface."
- *Negative*. "A photographic image with reversed polarity or, if colored, complementary tonal values to those of the original."[7]

Photographic media are composed of several elements. As a subsequent section will show, problems with any of the component elements can mean damage to or loss of the image.

Photograph 11.1 Archival collections can contain photographs as well as text documents. Photograph courtesy of the Joint Archives of Holland.

The first film base for commercial use was nitrate, introduced in 1889. It was employed for photographs until the early 1950s, when acetate (safety) film became popular. Nitrate film is inherently unstable and in a perpetual state of decomposition. It emits oxides of nitrogen that, in the presence of moisture, convert to nitric acid as the film deteriorates.[8]

Nitrate film also is highly flammable. Its chemical composition is similar to that of guncotton, which is used in the manufacture of explosives. Nitrate film burns twenty times faster than wood and contains sufficient oxygen to continue burning even underwater. It can self ignite at 300 degrees Fahrenheit or less, and the burning of nitrate film gives off a gas that can form nitric acid in the lungs, possibly fatal. In the words of Anthony Slide, "Nitrate film makes its own rules."[9]

Because of the condition of nitrate film, the photographic industry and preservation community had high hopes for acetate film. Acetate film also is called "safety film" because it does not self-combust. High heat and humidity, however, coupled with chemical contamination, can cause safety film base in any form (photographs, moving images, or microfilm) to decompose. Because decomposing safety film gives off a vinegar odor, this decomposition has come to be known as "vinegar syndrome."[10]

Vinegar syndrome was a new and unexpected hazard that only began to appear in Western countries in the late 1980s. Penelope Houston commented upon the impact of the problem with safety film:

"undoubtedly the discovery of the vinegar syndrome shifted the ground under the archivists' feet. It showed, if nothing else, how difficult it must always be to predict anything with certainty in an area where the materials themselves are less than a century old."[11] This lesson also should not be lost on electronic records archivists.

ARCHIVAL IMPLICATIONS AND APPLICATIONS

Photograph archivists stress the importance of organizing and identifying the collection, often down to the individual item level.[12] In particular, it is important to identify photos with captions or other markings: "Persons, places, dates, or circumstances that seem familiar today easily fade into obscurity tomorrow; unidentified audiovisual records become almost useless for research."[13]

A detailed inventory also promotes preservation. The handling of photographs is one of the greatest threats to their continued existence. If the collection is not properly arranged and described, the photographs must be handled much more by staff as well as researchers. As James Reilly has said, "In a real sense, to use photographs is to use them up."[14]

Collection Management

A photograph has a laminate structure composed of several layers. It is important to prevent photographs from bending or flexing, which can damage the emulsion and separate it from the base. Image surfaces also must be protected from scratches, abrasion, and fingerprints. For this reason, it is common to require staff and researchers to use lint-free cotton or nylon gloves when handling photographs.[15] If staff and budget permit, it is preferable to house each photograph in its own enclosure. This will provide maximum protection from dust, handling damage, and rapid changes in environmental conditions. James Reilly also recommends "armoring" the collection by providing three levels of packaging:

- Level 1: sleeve, envelope, or wrapper
- Level 2: box or drawer
- Level 3: shelf or cabinet[16]

Individual enclosures for photographs are made of either preservation-quality paper or one of several stable plastics (polyester, polypropylene, or polyethylene). The plastic should be free from surface coatings and not contain an excessive amount of plasticizer. Polyvinyl chloride (PVC), "shrink-wrap," and highly chlorinated or nitrated plastic also should be avoided. In addition, plastic should not be used with unstable materials (nitrate or acetate) since the plastic can trap gases and accelerate deterioration.[17] For these and other reasons, it is best to buy enclosures from an archival supplier.

Each choice has advantages and disadvantages from a collections management perspective. These considerations are outlined in figure 11.1[18]

Fig. 11.1 Options for Photographic Enclosures		
Option	**Advantages**	**Disadvantages**
Preservation-quality paper	• provides protection from light • can write on the outside	• photos must be removed to be viewed
Stable plastics	• permit immediate viewing without hands-on contact	• more expensive than paper • there can be moisture buildup within the sleeves • static electricity may lift damaged emulsions

Most archives store prints, negatives, and preservation copies separately. This offers a preservation advantage, since materials of dissimilar chemical stability are not stored together. This practice also provides protection from a localized disaster, like a leaky pipe in the storage area or a theft from the reference room.[19]

Several other points should be kept in mind when storing photographs:

- Once enclosed individually, photos should be stored in boxes with low lignin and alkaline reserves.
- It is important to minimize curling or slumping by using spacer boards in the boxes.
- Photos of the same size should be housed together so they support one another.
- Oversized photos should be stored flat.
- Glass plate negatives should be individually sleeved in paper enclosures and stored upright resting on a long edge in strong boxes.[20]

Preservation

As noted above, photographic images are formed by the action of light on chemical compounds. Photographs are composed of a number of layers, each of which responds differently to environmental conditions. Figure 11.2 is a generic model of layers in photographic images.

Fig. 11.2 Layers in Photographic Images[21]	
Layer	**Comments**
Final image material	A finely divided metallic silver is the most common image material, especially in archival photographs. Other final image materials have included platinum, pigments, and dyes.
Binder	The most common binder has been gelatin, though albumen and collodion were common nineteenth-century binders.
Support	Supports have included paper, metal, glass, and plastic film (cellulose nitrate, cellulose acetate esters, and polyester).
Surface treatments, adhesives and other layers	There can be anti-curl and anti-abrasion layers; coatings such as wax or varnish; adhesives; and applied colors.

The failure of any of these layers can lead to the loss of the image. Accordingly, the long-term preservation of photographic materials involves a number of interrelated factors:

- the inherent stability of the component materials
- the quality of original processing, including proper or improper fixing and washing
- exposure to an uncontrolled environment, including high temperature and relative humidity, light, and pollutants
- physical and chemical suitability of enclosure materials
- handling and use procedures

Balancing all these factors can be a very complex task.[22]

How should an archivist deal with disintegrating photographs? While archivists can do many things themselves, there are some problems that should receive priority treatment by a photographic conservator:

- daguerreotypes with deteriorating glass covers
- photographs on broken glass or corroded metal
- photographs with mold
- photographs with visible flaking
- photographs with lifting emulsions
- photographs adhered with pressure-sensitive tape or rubber cement
- photographs that are stuck to their framing.[23]

Most deterioration, however, is not so obvious. One of the leading experts on photographic preservation, James Reilly, noted that deterioration often is "imperceptibly slow." On a daily basis, we fail to appreciate the effect that the storage environment is having on the collection. According to Reilly, "This subtle pace of deterioration tends to obscure the long-term importance of coordinated preservation policies and can foster a stubborn inertia about initiating such policies."[24]

"Having organized and received some basic training, the Kailua Historical Society has begun collecting oral histories from dozens of residents whose memories will become the foundation of the organization's historic collection. But the task is difficult, and witnesses to Kailua's earlier years get fewer with each passing year, prompting the group to seek more people to conduct interviews."

—Honolulu *Advertiser,* February 11, 2002.

Relative humidity is the single most important environmental agent and the key to the preservation (or destruction) of photographs. Relative humidity measures how saturated the air is with water. Depending upon the humidity level, photographs and other water-absorbing materials will gain or lose moisture. In particular, high humidity and pollutants affect the silver in images. Over time, the images fade, discolor, or produce a metallic surface sheen known as "mirroring."[25]

High temperature increases the rate of nearly all chemical reactions, including those that cause the deterioration of photographs. Therefore, the storage temperature for photographic prints should be kept as low as possible, consistent with the practical considerations of limiting the cost of temperature control and allowing access to the collection. According to Reilly, "The combination of high temperature and high RH is one of the worst environmental calamities that can befall a collection."[26]

The American National Standards Institute (ANSI) has issued the following standards for the storage of black-and-white prints:

- maximum temperature of 65 degrees Fahrenheit
- relative humidity ranging from 30 percent to 50 percent.[27]

The fading of color film images also is of great concern. Color dyes, made of organic materials, are not permanent. Heat, humidity, and exposure to light accelerate color dye fading, resulting in the discolored images that may be found in many older collections.

"The world's first dolphin movie, 'Training Flippy,' has turned into a pile of vile-smelling gunk, and other important films have also crumbled into oblivion here [Marineland]....

"Shot from 1938 until the mid 1980s, only a few are first-run movies. Most are stock footage containing some of the world's first underwater photography....

"'We're doing this [restoring the films] because we want to save this library.... When you see these films destroyed, you want to break down and cry.'"

—St Augustine *Record,* May 2, 2002.

ANSI recommends that color prints be stored at a temperature of 36 degrees Fahrenheit with a relative humidity of between 30 and 40 percent. The National Archives and Records Administration noted that "Cold storage below freezing combined with low relative humidity effectively retards color fading."[28]

As complex as the issues are with photographs, moving images present even greater challenges, especially when soundtracks are introduced into the equation. As a result, in the past few decades, film preservation has developed into its own specialization within the archival community.

FILM

On one level, films and motion pictures are easy to categorize. Film is defined as "a flexible sheet or strip of transparent plastic upon which images can be recorded." In addition to moving images, microfilm is recorded on this medium. Similarly, a motion picture is defined as "a sequence of images on roll film or videotape that as the film or tape is advanced, presents the illusion of motion or movement. Motion pictures are also called moving images and, in Canada, cinefilm."[29]

But anyone who has lived through the twentieth century knows that film is much more than a recording medium. In the words of Penelope Houston, who has written extensively about film preservation: "[I]t is useful to be reminded occasionally of what film basically is. It's everything we always say it is: the entertainment medium which sometimes entertains, and the commercial property; on rare occasions the work of art; a significant part of the historical record.... Film makes up a major and enduring part of the collective memory of the century."[30]

"A hundred years from now, the world will have plenty of photos of presidents, kings and football games. But unless you document everyday life in 1999, your descendants and historians won't have a picture of you....

"Photos of you and your family at the end of the 20th Century will someday be historical and cultural souvenirs. Photos of your hobbies, cars and computers will fascinate folks three centuries from now. Pictures of your family watching the Super Bowl, eating bagels with cream cheese or playing Nintendo 64 aren't trite. They're tomorrow's history."

—Detroit *Free Press,* January 17, 1999.

Preserving this collective film memory involves two closely related groups of professionals. Some major institutions have archivists who specialize in films. These institutions work with motion picture studios and others in the film industry to identify and preserve theatrical releases. The second group is composed of archivists with general responsibilities who manage film as well as other media. These archivists seldom will deal with theatrical releases. Rather, they will manage films produced by the parent institution or films acquired as part of a manuscript repository's collecting program. Both groups of archivists are essential if we are to have an adequate record of contemporary society.

HISTORY

Since the introduction of movies in the 1890s, there have been many motion picture formats. Outside of specialized film archives, however, only a few formats are likely to be found:

- standard theatrical releases on 35 mm
- most educational films on 16 mm
- amateur films on 16 mm, 8 mm or super-8 mm formats

The archival situation is complicated, however, by several related factors:

- different sound systems (monaural, stereo, surround-sound)
- audio elements (magnetic sound recordings on sprocketed 16mm, 17.5mm or 35 mm celluloid; 1/2-inch or 1/4-inch magnetic tape recordings; Vitaphone discs used for early sound films in the late 1920s).
- other formats used abroad (9 mm and 28 mm)
- wide-screen formats (70 mm, VistaVision, Cinemascope, etc.)
- various film production elements that may find their way into archival collections (negatives, answer prints, "full-coat" magnetic film, etc.)[31]

It is often claimed that 75 percent of all American silent films are lost and that 50 percent of all films made prior to 1950 are gone. But according to Anthony Slide, "such figures, as archivists admit in private, were thought up on the spur of the moment, without statistical information to back them up."[32] Even without statistics, however, we know that much of our collective memory never reached the film archives.

"Digital technology is so ephemeral that an artwork created using a G4 Mac, Flash 4.0 software and C++ coding today may no longer be viewable 10, 20 or even 200 years from now.

"Film canisters are collecting dust after 75 years of nonuse, video formats from the 1980s are becoming unreadable and Web projects created just minutes ago are already becoming stale.

"That's why it's critical that these artworks are documented and preserved now, before they are lost indefinitely, observers say."

—*Wired*, July 23, 2002.

But why did early films not survive as part of the copyright registration process? Originally, there was no provision in the Copyright Act for films to be registered for protection. This is an issue that has surfaced again and again as new media, including digital media, have appeared. To deal with the copyright omission, motion pictures were deposited in the Library of Congress on paper strips beginning in 1894 (printing films onto rolls of paper meant that they could be copyrighted as photographic images). It was not until 1912 that motion pictures could be copyrighted in their own right.[33]

TECHNOLOGY

As noted above, nitrate film was first used in the late 1800s as roll film for still photography. Nitrate also was used for film production for fifty years. The earliest form of safety film, diacetate, dates from 1909 but did not receive widespread use. Triacetate, introduced in 1949, was the most widely used type of safety-base film until recently. Polyester, an extremely tough and long lasting film base invented in 1941, is resistant to shrinkage and has greater chemical stability than other forms of safety film. Polyester film predominates today.[34]

Nitrate movie film is subject to the same deterioration as photographs. Decomposition starts with the discoloration of the picture image. The film gets sticky and blisters, gooey bubbles appear and form a brown, frothy film, and when the foam dries, all that is left is a fine powder.[35]

One major difference exists between film and photographs: since the amount of nitrate is more concentrated in film, fire is a very real problem. The most cited example is from the National Archives and Records Administration. On December 7, 1978, there was a disastrous fire in NARA's nitrate vaults in Suitland, Md. As later reported, unsupervised construction workers were using electric power tools within the vaults. Heat from the tools started a fire, which spread quickly because the vault doors had been left open while the workers were at lunch. The fire ultimately destroyed almost 13 million feet of film.[36]

Color film technology also presents problems. The dyes used for both negatives and prints fade relatively quickly. The prints eventually become one color—pink. The solution—storage at low temperature and humidity—will be discussed below.[37]

ARCHIVAL IMPLICATIONS AND APPLICATIONS

According to Anthony Slide, the major problem facing film preservationists is one of selectivity: "It is easy to garner public enthusiasm and funding for the preservation of familiar titles, but these are not the films in need of preservation."[38] The films produced by the wide range of organizations and individuals will require appraisal before preservation can begin.

It is interesting that the first film industry trade paper, *Views and Film Index,* realized the potential historical importance of film. On December 1, 1906, only nine months after it first began publishing, the following comments appeared in the paper:

> We often wonder where all the films that are made and used
> a few times go to, and the questions come up in our minds,

again and again: Are the manufacturers aware that they are making history? Do they realize that in fifty or one hundred years the films now being made will be curiosities? In looking through the maker's catalogues, we observe specially important subjects of great public interest, such as President Roosevelt at gatherings, Veterans processions, Scenes in busy streets, Political meetings, Prominent senators, and a host of other subjects too numerous to mention, all of which are of value to the present generation; but how much more so will they be to the men and women of the future? ... Perhaps the day will come when motion pictures will be treasured by governments in their museums as vital documents in their historical archives. Our great universities should commence to gather in and save for future students films of national importance.[39]

These comments from a century ago could just as easily be written about today's new communications medium, the World Wide Web.

"On the lowest floor of the Miami-Dade Public Library, through a series of blue doors, in a room defined by nothingness, the black experience in South Florida is abundantly realized.

"A compilation of news clips plays—amateur footage and rare home movies, 41 minutes long—snapshots both momentous and humdrum of blacks over more than 75 years. A much longer version of the story is available, in the stacks of the chilly room just down the hall, where the Florida Moving Image Archive folks labor to preserve and reclaim our visual past."

—Miami *Herald,* March 2, 2003.

North Fork University considered what films to acquire in the Department of Archives and Special Collections. In making the decision, NFU assessed its own resources as well as the collecting interests of other repositories. NFU came to the following decisions:

The University Archives will acquire all films produced by the university. It also will seek to acquire any films about the university, its staff members, or students.
The Special Collections Department has two acquisition priorities: the environment and social welfare. Therefore, the department has decided to collect films that document the impact of environmental changes on such industries as fishing, farming, and winemaking. The department also collects films that document human and social conditions on the North Fork, particularly the life of the migrant worker.

Access

Just as there are some specific appraisal issues with films, there also are access considerations that will be different than those of textual records. Many of the differences reflect the fact that films have a "recycle value"—they can be reused in different contexts almost indefinitely. According to Penelope Houston, "Access is the watchword, one might almost say the talisman, for the modern film archives. They talk about it all the time, practice it, worry about the ways in which they can make themselves and their services more available to the public.... Now, the mood has become almost one of exploit or die. The image of the mere passive preserver had to be discarded."[40]

Copyright always is a factor that influences decisions about access. Some older films already are in the public domain, including such classics as *It's a Wonderful Life*. But even if a film is in the public domain because its copyright has expired, there still can be restrictions on use. For example, actors who are members of the Screen Actors Guild must be paid residuals for their work in television from 1952 onwards and in motion pictures from 1960 onwards, regardless of the copyright status of the production in which they appeared. Similarly, there are requirements for composers, musicians, and others involved in the film. Furthermore, laws in many states require that celebrities be paid if their images are used to promote a product; most such laws also apply to the heirs up to fifty years after the death of the personality.[41]

One might think that these concerns only apply if the archives is collecting feature films. On the contrary, if an organization has produced an instructional film, promotional film, or commercial, there may be acting or musical talent with residual rights that the archives must protect.

Access to film also has some practical deterrents. As Anthony Slide noted, "It is more expensive to study films than to read books, takes more time and is more difficult. Unless the researchers know their way quite well about the archives, they are up against the problem that they often can't estimate the usefulness of the film without looking at it— by which time there will probably be a bill to be paid."[42]

Despite these limitations, preservation without access is insufficient. Archivists must balance physical preservation, the rights of copyright holders, and access to the films. In achieving this balance, archivists provide access through screening programs, museum exhibitions, educational distribution, and on-site study. In addition, materials unrestricted by copyright, donor agreements, or residual talent rights can be made more widely available through sale or licensing. For a creative archivist, the possibilities are endless.[43]

Preservation

As with photographs, the key to preserving films is regulating the storage environment. The Library of Congress called this "the film preservation equivalent of preventive medicine." Prolonging the life of original films reduces the need for emergency duplication and buys time for the collection.[44]

Most film archivists are trying to achieve a cost-effective strategy combining improved storage with selective copying. The current ANSI standards for storage environments are as follows:

- *Black-and-white films*: maximum seventy degrees Fahrenheit and 20-30 percent relative humidity
- *Color negatives and transparencies*: thirty-six degrees Fahrenheit and 20–30 percent relative humidity.[45]

Many archivists are storing films at temperatures lower than the ANSI standards. According to the research, even degraded film will last longer under cooler and drier conditions.[46] However, cold storage can present its own problems with film, as it does with paper—there must be a gradual warming of film from cold storage to prevent condensation. Rapid removal from cold storage can result in moisture seeping into the emulsion and lifting the image from the film.[47]

"A Warsaw gallery is marking the anniversary of martial law in Poland with a display of pictures communist censors deemed too realistic to show. 'Some of the pictures are funny, some of them are terrifying but all of them are truthful,' said Piotr Rogacz, who helped trawl the archives for images the communist authorities refused to show to Poles."

—Reuters, December 13, 1998.

Among film archivists, there is a difference between "preservation" and "restoration." Preservation involves storing the master film under the best possible conditions and duplicating the film as the stock deteriorates. "In comparison, restoration of a film can be a long and complex task, often involving the matching of incomplete negatives and prints, and a reworking of the film's soundtrack. Restoration demands both technical and artistic decisions from the restorer." In brief, restoration tries to return the film to its "definitive form."[48]

As we move into the future, a question of increasing importance emerges: Will there *be* a "definitive version" of any contemporary film to preserve in an archives? In addition to the original theatrical release and edited-for-television versions, there are "director's cuts," DVDs with added footage, and reissues of "restored" films.[49] Are all of these versions of equal archival value? Should all of them be preserved? If not, who decides what gets preserved?

In recent years, the definitive version question also has related to black-and-white films. Many classic films have been "colorized" to increase their marketability. "Colorization" converts black-and-white motion picture film into color videotape; it cannot be projected as colorized motion picture film. In preservation terms, colorization does not affect the original negative of a film or any other master elements. Its retention is a separate issue that the archivist must address.[50]

While some of the above considerations only will apply to archives preserving theatrical films, archives of all types need to handle their film collections properly. Here is a list of some basic guidelines:

- Handle motion picture film carefully by its edges.
- Wear gloves to protect the film from fingerprints and abrasion.
- Keep projectors clean and in good working order.
- Never project film masters; use copies should be made.
- Wind film evenly onto cores.
- Place the wound cores within canisters that are free of plasticizers, chlorine, and peroxides. Acceptable materials include polyethylene or polypropylene, low lignin paperboard, or noncorrosive and nonferrous metal.
- Never use pressure-sensitive tape.
- Use alkaline paper or polyester film bands to secure the free end of the film and keep it tightly wound.
- Stack canisters horizontally, with a maximum of 6–10 containers of the same size per stack.
- Safety or color film may be placed in polyethylene bags before being placed in canisters. Nitrate film should not be placed in bags; they should be in cans with the lids loose to permit deterioration by-products to escape.[51]

Just as archivists were beginning to understand film and its preservation, moving image technology shifted under their feet and changed the nature of their collections.[52] Since its introduction in 1956, videotape has become the predominant moving image format for both commercial television and amateur recordings. As the next section will show, it also presents particular challenges for archivists.

VIDEOTAPE

Videotape is defined as "a magnetic tape on which visual images are electronically recorded, with or without sound." As with all magnetic tapes, data are stored by selectively magnetizing portions of the surface. This is basically the same technology that computers use to store information in the form of electromagnetic signals [53]

Much of the history of the second half of the twentieth century was recorded on videotape. From the assassination of John F. Kennedy, through the moon landings and Vietnam, to the fall of the Berlin Wall and the World Trade Center, images on videotape have defined our lives. The Library of Congress noted both the promise and the peril of our video heritage: "Archival holdings of television and video materials have enormous educational and cultural value .... Our heritage would be diminished if this vast record of our culture is allowed to vanish. Inaction will eventually take its toll."[54]

Magnetic tapes are composed of a support coated with a binder layer in which magnetic particles (primarily ferric oxide but also chromium dioxide) are suspended. Support materials were initially paper followed by cellulose acetate and, since the 1960s, polyethylene terepthalate film (i.e., polyester).

Videotape was developed by the Ampex Corporation in 1956. The first practical videotape recorder was the two-inch Quadruplex, which was used to record network television programs for re-broadcast across time zones. Other significant milestones in the history of videotape technology are worth mentioning, as well:

- In 1969, several Japanese companies produced ½-inch reel-to-reel videotape recorders.
- In 1971, Sony introduced the first successful cassette recorder, the ¾-inch U-matic.
- The first successful home VCR was Sony's ½-inch Betamax, which was introduced in 1975.
- In 1976, JVC introduced the VHS format, which eventually became the preferred consumer videotape format over Betamax.
- The 1-inch reel-to-reel (Type C) professional format was introduced in 1978.[55]

Videotape history has been one of new formats replacing older ones. This affects archives in two ways. First, archives often become custodians of inactive videotapes in all of the above formats. Second, archivists have no choice but to pick one or more "preservation" formats onto which they will copy images from discontinued technologies.

One of the most popular analog archival formats is Sony's Betacam SP ("Superior Performance"). Some archivists fear, however, that Sony soon will discontinue the format. In terms of digital media, archivists have several options. According to the Association of Moving Image Archivists:

> Many archives use Digital Betacam as an archival format. However, the lossy compression and weak physical structure inherent in digital videotape formats makes many archivists wary of converting analog video to digital tape for preservation. Optical disk media, such as DVD, is also considered risky as an archival format. It is possible, however, to convert analog video into digital file formats which can be stored on hard drive disks in either uncompressed form or using acceptable (open source, non-proprietary) lossless compression schemes. The files can be managed by digital asset management systems and protected from loss by redundant back-up copies.[56]

Many of these media questions first were faced by archivists preserving the history of television. In particular, these archivists have seen the problems caused by the obsolescence of older formats. Our television heritage is too important, however, just to throw up our hands in despair.

"You're dependent on the machine. The machines are constantly changing, and the software is constantly changing and the media on which the information is stored is constantly changing. In the good old days, when man was deciphering hieroglyphics on rocks, at least the rocks just stayed right there."

—Maine State Archivist Jim Henderson quoted in the *Boston Globe,* December 26, 1997.

TELEVISION

In the words of Anthony Slide, "The first problem which television archivists face is the constantly changing technology. Every time a new tape standard comes in to replace an older one, the video transfer and postproduction houses dispose of the old equipment. Similarly, the operators are only familiar with the newest equipment, and cannot handle what might appear on the surface to be a simple transfer operation."[57]

Early television programs from the late 1940s and early 1950s were broadcast live. For many of these programs, no record exists—except for the occasional "lost episode" which always seem to be discovered in a trunk in Secaucus, N.J. Such lost episodes tended to be made selectively and sometimes were retained by accident. The copies were made using a "kinescope"—usually a 16mm (but occasionally a 35mm) film copy made directly from a cathode ray tube with a motion picture camera.[58]

Once videotape recording became the norm in television, there was a new challenge to the historical record. Since videotapes could be erased and reused, economic pressures led many television stations to record over previous programs or raw footage. Unfortunately, this practice is particularly common in local television news, even to this day.[59]

Television therefore offers a microcosm of the challenges all archivists face. There is an abundance rather than a scarcity of material available for possible inclusion in the archives. Recording technologies, driven by market forces rather than preservation concerns, change quickly. Each new recording technology seems less stable than its predecessors, despite initial manufacturers' claims to the contrary. And reference and access often must be redefined because of the new materials and new researchers in the archives. A fuller discussion of these archival implications follows.

ARCHIVAL IMPLICATIONS AND APPLICATIONS

Selection and Appraisal

Most new moving image material will be on videotape rather than film. In fact, virtually all non-theatrical, non-fiction material is now on video.[60] This increasing volume presents a selection problem for archivists.

Television is a prime example. From 1948 to 1974, ABC, CBS, and NBC broadcast over 360,000 hours of programming. Only 60 percent of this programming is believed to have survived, but even that amount is too much for any television archives to preserve. Of necessity, most television archives must be selective. The three major archives—the Library of Congress, the Museum of Broadcasting, and UCLA Film and Television Archives—concentrate on collecting at the national level. Regional archives, in turn, concentrate on regional programming, usually news broadcasts.[61] This cooperative approach, while imperfect, is preserving much of contemporary television broadcasting. As Penelope Houston observes, "Television comes at the archivist from every direction at once, and has to be caught on the wing. How much of it is netted, collected and stored—or how much should be—remains partly a matter of luck, with practicalities defying the archivists' taste for order."[62]

Institutional archivists also have to make appraisal decisions, though most tend to be conservative in terms of materials generated by the parent institution. The institutional archivist's selection process often is complicated by an inability to play some of the older video materials. Under these circumstances, proper labeling and identification of the physical media become essential.[63]

"In a temperature-controlled laboratory in the bowels of the vast new National Archives Building, outside Washington—nearly two million square feet of futuristic steel-and glass construction—an engineer cranks up an old Thomas A. Edison phonograph. A cylinder disk begins to turn, and from the phonograph's large metal horn we suddenly hear the scratchy oompah-pah of a marching band, striking up a tune at a Knights of Columbus parade in July of 1902. Nearby sits an ancestor of the modern reel-to-reel tape recorder: it's the very machine that recorded President Harry Truman's famous whistlestop speeches as he traveled around the country by train in 1948 to win an extraordinary come-from-behind election victory. Instead of capturing sound on magnetic tape, the device stored its data on spools of thin steel wire as fine as fishline. Now some of the wire has rusted, and it occasionally snaps when it is played back through the machine."

—*The New Yorker,* March 8, 1999.

Archives are starting to show interest in amateur videos and home movies as supplements to collections of textual records. According to Houston, "Archivists are prepared to sift through the footage of babies on beaches, nervously posed wedding groups, jokey dashings about suburban gardens, for the nuggets of authentic social history which might otherwise go unrecorded, the story of life through the years of a family or a town."[64]

As noted above, North Fork University established a collecting focus for films. NFU decided to collect videos in the same general areas. What has caused the staff the most difficulty is selecting videos that "document human and social conditions on the North Fork, particularly the life of the migrant worker." Once the NFU Special Collections Department reached out to the community to seek videos, it was overwhelmed with potential acquisitions. Home videos arrived from various sources. While most did document "human and social conditions," few dealt with the life of the migrant worker (for obvious economic reasons). The NFU staff has decided to accession a few "typical" home videos now and to make similar appeals once every ten years in order to document changes to individual and family life on the North Fork.

Preservation

I already have discussed one of the major preservation problems with videotape—the ease of erasure and reuse. In particular, television networks have tried to save money by recording over videotapes rather than purchasing new ones. Perhaps the most egregious example comes from the 1950s. On March 31, 1957, CBS broadcast *Cinderella,* a new musical written for television by Richard Rodgers and Oscar Hammerstein II. The cast featured several notables, including Julie Andrews in the title role. For some unexplainable reason, the videotape of the performance was erased and reused at a later date. The only thing that survives is a recording of the musical numbers made for Columbia Records.[65]

Even when we do not intend to erase a videotape, the simple process of playing it can cause damage: "During playback, magnetic tapes ride against playback heads and are thus slightly degraded after each use; with repeated use the sound or image can noticeably deteriorate. If dust is present or if decoding heads are dirty, the damage and loss is greatly exacerbated."[66]

As an archival preservation medium, videotape is highly unstable. There is an oxide-binder problem that can separate the emulsion from the base. There also are inherent problems with print-through and magnetic debris.[67] Videotape just will not last.

Ultimately, the only way to preserve videotape is to transfer it to another videotape. How frequently this transfer should take place is a subject of some debate. The literature says that videotape only will last for ten years, yet many of us have older home videos that still play without difficulty. The seeming contradiction comes from the fact that our eyes can "fill in" some of the lost analog data; in the digital world, similar losses might make the tape unreadable.

One might think that the solution to video deterioration is to copy it onto safety-based polyester film. The Association of Moving Image Archivists, however, does not recommend this approach. (Similarly, they do not recommend that film be copied to videotape for preservation.) According to AMIA, "The two media have different color spectra and frame rates, so a transfer from one medium to the other will not result in a faithful reproduction. Cross-media transfers should only be done for distribution purposes, for particular viewing situations (such as a special event), or as a last resort for preservation."[68]

The realm of digital videotape introduces its own concerns. With digital media, it is possible to transfer picture and sound from one tape to another without a loss of quality. Digital technologies also would permit us to "enhance" the original material, through colorization, time compression, false 'stereo' sound, panning, or more subtle means." The film archivist should avoid these practices.[69]

Once again, the preservation environment becomes important in making videotapes last as long as possible. Currently AMIA recommends the following precautions:

- *Extended-term storage conditions for polyester-based magnetic tape*: sixty-eight degrees Fahrenheit and 20–30 percent relative humidity or fifty-nine degrees Fahrenheit and 20–40 percent relative humidity.
- *Long-term storage conditions*: forty-six degrees Fahrenheit and 25 percent relative humidity.

Humidity variation should be less than 5 percent plus or minus and the temperature variation should be less than four degrees Fahrenheit plus or minus within a twenty-four-hour period. Magnetic tapes should be handled at temperatures between sixty-four and seventy-seven degrees Fahrenheit with a relative humidity between 15 and 50 percent. Above 65 percent relative humidity, the possibility of fungus growth increases substantially.[70]

Tapes require certain types of space for physical storage. The following list delineates additional requirements for the physical space in which tapes are stored:

- The space should be well insulated and sealed in order to maintain proper temperature and humidity as well as keep out pests and animals.
- There should be no windows, in order to keep out ultraviolet light.
- Tapes should be stored off the floor on shelves. Shelving should provide air circulation around the tapes.
- Reels should be stored within closed containers and oriented vertically on shelves.
- All work and handling surfaces should be elevated off the floor.
- Minimize any water incursion due to condensation, floods, leaks, or faulty sprinklers.
- There should be no carpeting—it retains moisture and traps insects and dust. Floors should be tiled and provide drainage.
- The room must be fireproof and should not contain combustible materials (wood, cardboard).

Fig. 11.3 Tips for Handling Videotapes	
Do	**Don't**
• Learn to use correct procedures for operating equipment. • Handle tapes gently. • Keep tapes in protective cases when not in use. • Keep tapes vertical when not in use. • Make sure machine alignment is correct before use. • Clean tapes before playback if they show any evidence of dirt or contamination. • Ensure that the tape is properly seated in the machine before use. • Wind tape at low speed entirely onto one reel after each use. • Secure tape ends on open reel tapes. • Package tapes adequately for protection before shipment or transport. • Use only new tapes when recording a tape for long-term storage. • Activate the records protection feature of all master cassettes immediately after they have been recorded. • Inspect tapes for damage or contamination before use. • Seek experienced help as soon as possible in the case of a disaster. • Protect both tapes and machinery from dust and debris. • Keep tapes in a stable environment. • Acclimatize tapes before use if they are hot or cold. • Store tapes in a cool and dry place.	• Touch tape surfaces with bare hands. • Put pressure on reel flanges. • Stack or place objects on top of unprotected tapes. • Force tapes into cases or machines. • Drop or throw tapes. • Splice any portion of a videotape. • Place tapes on or near sources of magnetic fields. • Play or spool tapes that are dirty, contaminated, or wet. • Play or spool tapes on a dirty, misaligned, or malfunctioning machine. • Store tapes in an area subject to dampness or possible pipe leaks. • Expose tapes to food or beverages. • Expose tapes to temperature extremes. • Expose tapes to ultraviolet radiation, including the sun, for extended periods. • Attempt to clean tapes contaminated with adhesives, fungus, or unknown substances unless you have the necessary training or experience.

- A sticky floor mat, like those used in "clean rooms", should be placed in the entrance doorway to prevent debris from being tracked in.

- Walls, floor, and ceiling should be made of a dust-free, easy to clean material.

- The floors should be cleaned with either a "water" vacuum cleaner, a vacuum with a hose that diverts the exhaust out of the immediate area, or a vacuum cleaner equipped with a HEPA filter rated 95 percent or better.

- If possible, maintain positive air pressure in use and handling areas relative to adjacent hallways to minimize contamination from outside sources.[71]

Beyond storage, a number of other "dos and don'ts" apply to handling magnetic tapes. These hints are summarized in figure 11.3 Observing proper care and handling can extend the life of the videotapes.[72]

Some of these dos and don'ts may seem to be common sense. Nevertheless, any archivist can attest to the fact that he or she has found videotapes in their "native habitat" that violate most if not all of the above guidelines. Proper care and handling begin with the creators of the videotapes; part of the archivist's responsibility is getting this message out early and often.

SOUND RECORDINGS

There is only one remaining audiovisual format for the archivist to handle—sound recordings. Like photographs, this technology dates from the nineteenth century and has undergone a number of major transformations since then. In recent years, digital technologies have also come to predominate in this area.

A sound recording is a disc, tape, filament, or other medium on which sound has been recorded. Another common term, audiotape, is defined as a sound recording on magnetic tape.[73]

But just what is "sound?" According to the International Association of Sound and Audiovisual Archives, sound is "a continuous variation in air pressure which may be represented by means of a signal that may be stored as the primary information on a carrier using a particular recording format. The signal representation may be analog or digital."[74] The speakers on our stereos convert the signal back to variations in air pressure that our ears can perceive.

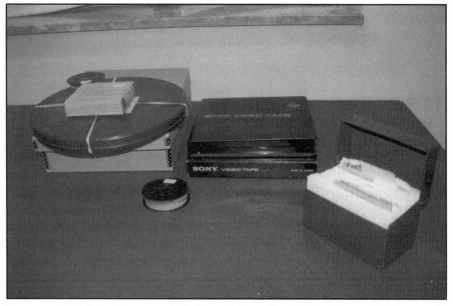

Photograph 11.2 Archives can include a variety of audiovisual formats Photograph courtesy of the Saint Benedict Center, Sisters of Saint Benedict of Madison, Wisconsin, Inc.

Finally, a "sound archives" is an institution created to "preserve, make available and develop a documentary heritage through concentration on deliberately structured interviews and performances made by recording devices."[75] In addition to the dedicated sound archives, many institutional archivists and manuscript curators will have sound recordings as part of their general collections.

Contemporary archivists commonly encounter eight types of sound recordings in their collections:

- *Commercial recordings*: training materials, educational materials, etc.
- *Recordings of events*: conferences, meetings, speeches, etc.
- *Dictation recordings*: made for the purpose of preparing correspondence, minutes, etc.
- *Field recordings*: live recordings of people, such as those done by anthropologists
- *Musical, theatrical, and artistic works*: includes albums and compact discs produced commercially
- *Broadcast industry recordings*: music, spoken word, news broadcasts, etc.

- *Home recordings*: various recordings of events and activities
- *Oral histories*: structured interviews to gather historical reminiscences[76]

These types reflect the many uses of sound recordings throughout history. They mirror almost all aspects of contemporary society.

"Concerned that history may be dying along with 1,500 American war veterans every day, archivists are launching an urgent effort to get their stories down in video and audio tapes for future reference.

"The Veterans History Project was to be formally announced on Thursday, the 58th anniversary of the D-Day invasion of France, at the USS Intrepid sea-air-space museum in New York."

—Army Times, June 6, 2002.

HISTORY AND TECHNOLOGY

The official date for the invention of sound recording by Thomas Edison is July 18, 1877. The earliest recordings were made on cylinders using a wide variety of materials—including tin foil, wax, celluloid, and synthetic resins—as the surfaces into which grooves were mechanically inscribed. The surfaces of all cylinders are vulnerable to damage (such as scratches and fingerprints) during handling and playback, but wax in particular is not very durable. Cylinder core materials range from cardboard to plaster of Paris. Most cylinders tend to become hard and brittle as they age and are thus susceptible to cracking and chipping.[77]

Using discs for recordings also has a long history. During the 1880s, Emil Berliner began the first mass production of phonodiscs. A major technological change occurred in 1925 when Joseph P. Maxwell and Henry C. Harrison of Bell Laboratories adapted the vacuum-tube amplifier to electrically record on discs. Earlier recordings had been acoustic rather than electric.

Electrical recording today still involves the same basic steps:

- Sound waves are converted into electrical energy, called the "signal."
- The signal is captured on sound carriers in one of several forms: grooves on a disk, magnetic patterns on tape, or "pits" on a laser disc.

- During reproduction (playback), a reading device (phono cartridge and stylus, tape playback head, or laser) recovers the signal from the sound carrier.
- The signal is converted back into electrical energy and sent to the loudspeaker or headphones through an amplifier so that the recorded sounds can be heard again.

The recorded sounds are referred to as the "signal," and it is the signal that archivists preserve when copying (transferring) the information from a failing sound carrier to a new medium.[78]

Audio discs have remained a popular storage medium. Discs have been fabricated from many materials, principally shellac, acetate, and vinyl. Disc cores have been made from cardboard, resins, glass, and metal. Like all composite materials, discs are subject to physical and chemical stresses and instability.[79]

In the 1930s, records used an acetate or nitrate lacquer cover over a thin core of aluminum, glass, or cardboard. According to Frederick Stielow, "While producing high-quality sound duplication, the malleable nature of the acetate or nitrate covers did present significant problems for preservation."[80] Unlike other disk types that are "pressed" or molded in multiple copies, "acetates" are instantaneous recordings that are engraved directly. The chemical makeup of these discs had to be a compromise between ease of engraving and the quality of the recording that resulted.[81]

Acetate discs are the least stable type of sound recording. Acetate direct recordings have limited life expectancies even when stored and handled properly. Shrinkage of the lacquer coating is the primary destructive force. The gradual loss of plasticizer causes progressive embrittlement and the irreversible loss of sound information. Because the coating is bonded to a core that cannot shrink, internal stresses result, which in turn cause cracking and peeling of the coating.[82]

ARCHIVAL IMPLICATIONS AND APPLICATIONS

As with other types of audiovisual records, the major archival issues involve selection and preservation. The two are inextricably linked: the audiovisual records we decide to acquire will require preservation resources on a regular basis.

Selection and Appraisal

Christopher Ann Paton has summarized the importance of appraisal decisions: "Given that the quantity of media materials in archives will undoubtedly continue to grow in coming years, the number of obsolete formats will increase, and the costs and complexity of preservation will not decrease any time soon, the appraisal and reappraisal of recorded sound holdings becomes more important."[83]

In acquiring sound collections, an archives needs to consider its own resources. Frederick Stielow asks the key question: "If the archive cannot afford to process, cannot legally offer access, or cannot hear the contents—why bring the donation into the archive?" Despite this logical question, many archives seem to keep whatever sound recordings come in the door. Stielow continues, "Yet, there are considerations that should lead anyone to reject deposits: in particular, the probable continued absence of legal releases, restrictions that would make the donation all but useless, and tapes in very poor or unplayable condition."[84]

Paton has developed an "audio appraisal checklist" to assist the archivist with potential acquisitions. This checklist includes many of the points previously discussed in chapter 3 on selection and appraisal:

- relevance to institutional mission or collecting policy
- uniqueness/rarity
- duplication, both internal and external
- medium specificity
- form
- age
- condition
- quality/legibility
- completeness
- documentation
- use potential
- use limitations
- costs of retention[85]

It is especially worth noting that "use limitations" and "costs of retention" are among the factors to weigh when acquiring sound recordings. As will be seen, preservation can be one of the more significant costs.

Preservation

Since the audio signal resides on a physical carrier, preservation must begin with an assessment of the condition of the carrier and a plan for the maintenance of the signal. Furthermore, carriers cannot be read without a suitable apparatus—hardware. Therefore, items of hardware in archives cannot be regarded as museum pieces. Rather, archivists need to keep outdated equipment in a functioning condition, even if it means destroying the machine's value as an artifact.

The combination of carrier and hardware constitutes a system. Obsolescence of a system is frequently caused by a market-driven discontinuation in the manufacture and support of the hardware rather than a problem with a carrier. Because of this limited lifetime, safeguarding the audio heritage can only be accomplished by copying the recorded contents from old to new carriers.[86] A discussion of some of the carriers and their preservation concerns follows.

Cylinders

While the surfaces of all cylinders are vulnerable to damage, wax in particular is very fragile. This medium is especially vulnerable to damage (such as scratches and fingerprints) during handling and playback. Celluloid cylinder recordings are subject to fungal attack if stored under humid conditions.

Core materials for cylinders range from cardboard to plaster of Paris. Most cylinders tend to become hard and brittle as they age and thus are susceptible to cracking and chipping.

Cylinders should be handled only on the inside and at the top and bottom edges. The grooves on cylinders should never be touched.[87] Audio cylinders should be stored on edge in an upright position rather than resting on their grooved surfaces.[88]

Discs

Discs are subject to physical and chemical stresses and instability, just like other composite materials. They must be handled carefully to prevent surface damage or breakage. Discs should be lifted using the fingers of both hands on the outer edges; grooved playing surfaces should not be touched.[89]

Audio disc recordings should be shelved in a fully vertical position at all times. Discs should not be allowed to lean or slant, because they might warp. Discs of the same size should be shelved together for protection. The archives will need heavy-duty shelves, because the discs are heavy.[90]

"Shellacs" (roughly corresponding to 78-rpm recordings), and "vinyl LPs" (including 45-rpm recordings) all have reasonable life expectancy if properly stored and handled. Shellacs, however, are especially vulnerable to mishandling as they become more brittle with age. Vinyl LPs sometimes distort spontaneously from relaxation of stresses molded in at the time of manufacture. They also are subject to damage from leaning on the shelf or imprinting by irregular surfaces, such as wrinkled album liners.[91]

According to Mary Lynn Ritzenthaler, "Repositories that maintain collections of cylinder and disc sound recordings have difficulty with playback if compatible equipment of the appropriate type and vintage is not available." Because of differences in styluses, construction and recording grooves, modern equipment is often unable to reproduce sounds accurately from older recordings. Damage during playback is also a real possibility if needles are too sharp or accidentally skid across grooved surfaces. Repeated playback results in wear and mechanical damage due to friction contact between the stylus and the grooves. Ritzenthaler's solution "that alleviates the need to maintain a museum of phonograph equipment is to transfer the contents of cylinders and discs to master reel-to-reel tape, from which use copies can be made."[92]

Tapes

Archivists preserve audiotapes to make them available, yet each play destroys a little bit of the tape's contents. Frederick Stielow has said that this tension represents the basic dilemma in sound archives: "how can we listen and still preserve our collections?" Stielow recommends that archivists use commonsense practices, such as the production of master and user copies, and the employment of modern air-conditioning and filtering devices.[93]

Stielow believes that archivists can "put to rest" many of the "apocryphal horror tales of accidental erasures" of magnetic tapes. While he recommends that care be taken not to introduce strong magnetic fields, "actual danger is almost nonexistent." With three inches of separation, even quite powerful source fields produce no adverse consequences. In fact, in an experiment, a powerful junkyard magnet capable of lifting 800 pounds of metal had no effect on stored signals at a distance of five feet and only a 5 percent degradation as close as sixteen inches.[94]

However, there *is* another "horror" that awaits. Audiotapes, as well as other types of magnetic tapes, are subject to "hydrolysis." This is a chemical reaction whereby the binder resin "consumes" water drawn from humidity in the air to liberate carboxylic acid and alcohol. According to Gilles St-Laurent, "Hydrolysis in magnetic tape results in the binder shedding a gummy and tacky material which causes tape layers to stick together and inhibits playback when it is deposited onto the tape recorded heads. Hydrolysis also causes a weakening in the bond holding the binder to the backing, which results in shedding or possible detachment." Another name for this is "sticky-shed syndrome."[95]

There are further preservation problems with cassette tapes. This format should not be relied upon for long-term storage of historical information. Cassettes use a very thin tape, which is more susceptible to damage and failure than reel-to-reel tapes. This thin tape produces recorded tracks with relatively small dimensions. Finally, the cassette mechanisms themselves are prone to problems. Cassettes can be used as service copies, though original records received on cassette tapes should be transferred to reel tape for long-term storage.[96]

Good Housekeeping

Good housekeeping can go far in maintaining a sound archives. Barbra Buckner Higginbotham and Judith W. Wild provide some hints for maintaining sound recordings, especially in a library setting. They recommend several practices:

- House sound recordings vertically.
- Keep sound recordings clean.
- Maintain playback equipment on a regular basis.
- Favor mediated (staff-assisted) versus self-service playback.
- Label equipment with instructions on how to operate it and how to handle the collection.
- Prepare a flyer or broadside about collection care.[97]

As noted above, foreign matter deposits can be particularly damaging to sound recordings. St-Laurent recommends the following precautions to minimize damaging deposits:

- Never touch the surface of a recording. Use white, lintless cotton gloves and handle by the edges.
- Do not leave recordings exposed to air. Return items to their containers when not in use and keep containers closed.
- Do not place recordings near sources of paper or cardboard dust.
- Keep the surrounding area clean.
- Do not permit food or beverages in the areas where recordings are handled.
- Keep storage facilities as dust-free as possible.
- Install dust-filtering equipment on the air conditioning system.
- Keep labels to a minimum.
- Keep equipment clean and in good working order.[98]

Beyond surface deposits, there is the threat of surface deformations such as warping of discs and stretching of tape. The following practices will help prevent deformation:

- Avoid sources of heat and light (especially ultraviolet light).

- Do not place heavy objects on top of recordings.
- Never place recordings on top of one another.
- Shelve recordings vertically.
- Do not use shelving units where supports put uneven pressure on recordings.
- Do not use shelving units where supports are more than four to six inches apart.
- Do not interfile recordings of different sizes: smaller items may get lost while larger items may be subjected to uneven pressure.[99]

Even with the "Good Housekeeping Seal of Approval," some parts of our audio collection will require rerecording. Since this is both expensive and time-consuming, preservation rerecording must be planned rather than haphazard.

Preservation Rerecording

A preservation rerecording plan must be based on a clear understanding of the problems to be addressed, the strengths and weaknesses of the available preservation options, and the types of personnel, equipment, and administrative support necessary for success.[100]

The first step is to examine the collection to identify vulnerable types of recordings. The International Association of Sound and Audiovisual Archives has identified the following analog carriers that are "inherently unstable" and should be copied:

- cylinders
- instantaneous discs of all types, especially lacquer discs
- acetate tapes
- all long/double/triple play open reel tapes
- all cassette tapes of any type
- any carrier that shows obvious signs of decay or deterioration[101]

Once the audio archivist has identified at-risk recordings, there are a number of other decisions to make as part of the preservation rerecording plan. One question is, should archivists enhance the signal as part of preservation rerecording? Most sound archivists in the U.S. are trying to "transfer, or copy, the signal from the original source to the new medium as accurately as possible, neither 'improving' the original nor allowing the introduction of new distortion or flaws." It is common practice, however, to employ filtering, noise suppression, and other enhancements for service copies.[102]

A second question is, should preservation rerecording be done on analog or digital media? Christopher Paton provides a number of insights for decision-makers, which are summarized in figure 11.4[103]

Fig. 11.4 Considerations for Preservation Rerecording		
Option	**Advantages**	**Disadvantages**
Analog	• fully mature technology • formats are standardized and well known • can capture and reproduce sounds with good fidelity	• presence of "tape hiss," a form of noise • gradual loss of quality in successive generations of rerecording • discontinuance of analog equipment by vendors
Digital	• less noisy than analog systems • easier to edit • can make many generations of identical copies	• technology evolving rapidly • obsolescence is a concern • longevity of digital storage media unknown

Analog reel-to-reel tape has been the preferred preservation option for archivists. While it now appears that reel-to-reel tape will become outmoded in the near future, it is impossible to predict the nature of its replacement.[104]

To date, none of the digital audio recording systems has achieved a proven stability in the market place, let alone become an "archival" format. The International Association of Sound and Audiovisual Archives believes that the rapid development of audiovisual data carriers makes it unlikely that a digital audio format will ever achieve the depth of penetration in the market place of formats such as the LP or the analog quarter-inch tape. According to the International Association of Sound and Audiovisual Archives, "It is also likely that in some arenas there will be no physical carrier to distribute, in which event the issues of format obsolescence applies to the file format itself."[105]

Previously in this chapter, when talking about videotape, I discussed the issue of compression and "lost" digital data. These concerns apply to sound recordings, as well. It generally has become accepted that a digital preservation format should not use "lossy" compression, since the further use of the data-reduced signal will be severely restricted. As an additional archival hedge, whenever possible, the original carriers, together with suitable replay equipment, should be placed in storage for potential future use.[106]

"To mark the eleventh anniversary of Nelson Mandela's release from jail, the British Library has issued audio recordings of the trial that led to his 26-year jail term."

—BBC News, February 10, 2001.

CONCLUSION

Maintaining audiovisual archival collections involves a variety of knowledge and skills. One component is the technical knowledge about media, formats, and their deterioration. A second component is an understanding of research trends and an appreciation of the possible uses of audiovisual collections by current and future clients. Finally, the archivist must be able to manage the audiovisual holdings, juggling this responsibility with the other areas of archival practice. Chapter 12 deals with management issues and techniques in greater detail.

NOTES

1. Lewis J. Bellardo and Lynn Lady Bellardo, *A Glossary for Archivists, Manuscript Curators, and Records Managers* (Chicago: Society of American Archivists, 1992), 4.

2. *Managing Audiovisual Records: An Instructional Guide,* 1999 Web Edition (Washington, D.C.: National Archives and Records Administration, 1999), http://www.archives.gov/records_management/publications/managing_audiovisual_records.html.

3. William H. Leary, *The Archival Appraisal of Photographs: A RAMP Study with Guidelines* (Paris: UNESCO, 1985), 4.

4. Elisabeth Kaplan and Jeffrey Miflin, "'Mind and Sight:' Visual Literacy and the Archivist," *American Archivist* 21, no. 2 (1996): 107–27. For insights about the "truth" of photographs, see Peter Robertson, "More than Meets the Eye," *Archivaria* 1, no. 2 (summer 1976): 33–43.

5. Kaplan and Mifflin, "Visual Literacy," 119.

6. For a good overview of audiovisual records, see Helen P. Harrison, ed., *Audiovisual Archives: A Practical Reader* (Paris:

UNESCO, 1997), http://www.unesco.org/webworld/ci_publications/ Archives/. For forms to use in managing audiovisual records (especially collection assessment, rerecording, and other preservation treatments), see *Sample Forms for Archival and Records Management Programs* (Chicago: Society of American Archivists and Lenexa, KS: ARMA International, 2002). For a discussion of audiovisual records in corporate archives, see Ernest J. Dick, "Corporate Memory in Sound and Visual Records," in *The Records of American Business*, ed. James O'Toole (Chicago: Society of American Archivists, 1997), 275–96.

7. Bellardo and Bellardo, *Glossary.* The definitions of photograph, print, and negative are found on pages 26, 27, and 23, respectively.

8. Ritzenthaler, *Preserving Archives and Manuscripts*, 38.

9. Anthony Slide, *Nitrate Won't Wait: Film Preservation in the United States* (Jefferson, N.C.: McFarland & Company, 1992), 1–3.

10. Slide, *Nitrate Won't Wait,* 5.

11. Penelope Houston, *Keepers of the Frame: The Film Archives* (London: British Film Institute, 1994), 4.

12. See chapter 5 of this book for information about the five levels of arrangement.

13. *Managing Audiovisual Records.* For an extensive discussion of archival implications, see the nine articles in a special issue of *Archivaria* dealing with "Photographs and Archives," *Archivaria* 5 (winter 1977–78). For an example of possible use of government photographs, see Janice Sandomirsky, "Toronto's Public Health Photography," *Archivaria* 10 (summer 1980): 145–56. For a discussion of amateur photographs, see the three articles "Private Realms of Light: Canadian Amateur Photography, 1839–1940." *Archivaria* 17 (winter 1983–84): 106–44. See also Diana Pedersen, "The Photographic Record of the Canadian YWCA, 1890–1930: A Visual Source for Women's History," *Archivaria* 24 (summer 1987): 10–35.

14. Reilly, *Care and Identification,* 74–75. "Policies for access, housekeeping, handling, loan, and exhibition should be developed and implemented to reduce the effects of use on photographs. These policies should include such things as requiring users to wear cotton gloves when handling photographs, prohibiting the use of pens in the reading room, establishing guidelines for processing newly acquired collections (removing damaging enclosures and paper clips; segregating different types of photographs; and providing suitable protective enclosures), and restricting exhibition length of exposure and quality of illumination to reduce fading." Eleanore Stewart and Paul N. Banks, "Preservation of Information in Nonpaper Formats," in *Preservation: Issues and Planning*, ed. Paul N. Banks and Roberta Pilette (Chicago: American Library Association, 2000), 332. Reilly, *Care and Identification,* 333. Providing a reference/ service copy also reduces wear and tear, though it can be expensive.

15. Ritzenthaler, *Preserving Archives and Manuscripts*, 72.

16. Reilly, *Care and Identification,* 92. On individual enclosures, see also Ritzenthaler, *Preserving Archives and Manuscripts*, 93–94.

17. Reilly, *Care and Identification,* 94.

18. Ritzenthaler, *Preserving Archives and Manuscripts*, 94–96.

19. Ibid., 94.

20. Ibid., 96–98.

21. James M. Reilly, *Care and Identification of Nineteenth-Century Photographic Prints* (Rochester, N.Y.: Eastman Kodak Company, 1986).

22. For more information, see Barbara Applebaum, *Guide to Environmental Protection of Collections* (Madison, Conn.: Sound View Press, 1991), 198–200.

23. Stewart and Banks, "Preservation of Nonpaper Formats," 334.

24. Reilly, *Care and Identification,* 73.

25. Stewart and Banks, "Preservation of Nonpaper Formats," 83.

26. Reilly, *Care and Identification,* 89. See also Stewart and Banks, "Preservation of Nonpaper Formats," 332.

27. Stewart and Banks, "Preservation of Nonpaper Formats," 332. The Standard is ANSI/NAPM IT9.20–1996. Reilly recommends the following conditions for nineteenth-century photographic prints: relative humidity, 30–50 percent (ideally 30–40 percent); temperature not to exceed sixty-five degrees Fahrenheit; air filtration for particulates; and air purification to remove oxidant gases. Reilly, *Care and Identification,* 91.

28. *Managing Audiovisual Records.*

29. Bellardo and Bellardo, *Glossary,* 14, 23.

30. Houston, *Keepers of the Frame*, 1. See also Barrie E. King, "Film Archives: Their Purpose and Problems," *Archives and Manuscripts* 4, no. 2 (May 1970): 8–16.

31. Stewart and Banks, "Preservation of Nonpaper Formats," 334. Slide, *Nitrate Won't Wait,* 102.

32. Slide, *Nitrate Won't Wait,* 5.

33. Slide, *Nitrate Won't Wait,* 36, 38.

34. Slide, *Nitrate Won't Wait*, 1, 102.

35. Slide, *Nitrate Won't Wait,* 3. Houston, *Keepers of the Frame,* 81.

36. Slide, *Nitrate Won't Wait,* 29–30.

37. Slide, *Nitrate Won't Wait,* 106–8. See also Richard Hincha, "Crisis in Celluloid: Color Fading and Film Base Deterioration," *Archival Issues* 17, no. 2 (1992): 125–36.

38. Slide, *Nitrate Won't Wait,* 6. For a Canadian perspective on the archival issues surrounding film, see K.M. Larose, "Preserving the Past on Film: Problems for the Archivist," *Archivaria* 6 (summer 1978): 137–50.

39. Quoted in Slide, *Nitrate Won't Wait,* 10–11.

40. Houston, *Keepers of the Frame,* 95.

41. Slide, *Nitrate Won't Wait,* 135.

42. Houston, *Keepers of the Frame,* 112–14.

43. Library of Congress, National Film Preservation Board, *Film Preservation 1993: A Study of the Current State of American Film Preservation* (Washington, D.C.: Library of Congress, 1993), http://lcweb.loc.gov/film/study.html.

44. Library of Congress, National Film Preservation Board, "Film Storage White Paper. Keeping Cool and Dry: A New Emphasis in Film Preservation" (Washington, D.C.: Library of Congress, 1994), http://lcweb.loc.gov/film/storage.html.

45. Stewart and Banks, "Preservation of Nonpaper Formats," 332. The standard is ANSI/NAPM IT9.11–1993. "Research shows that film needs better storage to survive, and that film in all stages of decay can have a longer useful life with small improvements to its environment." Library of Congress, "Film Storage White Paper."

46. Library of Congress, "Film Storage White Paper." See also Library of Congress, National Film Preservation Board, "Redefining Film Preservation: A National Plan. Recommendations of the Librarian of Congress in Consultation wit the National Film Preservation Board" (Washington, D.C.: Library of Congress, 1994), http://lcweb.loc.gov/film/plan.html.

47. Slide, *Nitrate Won't Wait,* 106–8.

48. Slide, *Nitrate Won't Wait,* 110. Houston, *Keepers of the Frame,* 126–27.

49. Houston, *Keepers of the Frame,* 126.

50. Slide, *Nitrate Won't Wait,* 122, 128.

51. Ritzenthaler, *Preserving Archives and Manuscripts,* 72, 98.

52. Anthony Slide is pessimistic about film preservation: "The manifold problems of selection, retention, conservation, and preservation are insoluble. Never will enough money, staff time or technological facilities be available, and future archivists must accept the inevitability that the sheer quantity of films in need of preservation will override the requirement that moving images must be preserved in their original format to the highest standard of quality." Slide, *Nitrate Won't Wait,* 159.

53. Bellardo and Bellardo, *Glossary,* 37, 21.

54. Library of Congress, National Film Preservation Board, *Television and Video Preservation 1997. A Report on the Current State of American Television and Video Preservation* (Washington, D.C.: Library of Congress, 1997), http://lcweb.loc.gov/film/tvstudy.html.

55. Association of Moving Image Archivists, "Video Preservation fact Sheets: A Very Brief History of Videotape," http://www.amianet.org/11_Information/Information.html

56. Association of Moving Image Archivists, "Videotape Preservation Fact Sheets: Reformatting for Preservation," http://www.amianet.org/11_Information/Information.html. "Lossy" compression means that some "unessential" bits are discarded in order to reduce file size. These discarded bits can never be recovered.

57. Slide, *Nitrate Won't Wait,* 115. See also Houston, *Keepers of the Frame,* 144.

58. Slide, *Nitrate Won't Wait,* 114–15. The time differences between the East and West coasts eventually made it necessary to record live programming systematically for later broadcast.

59. Library of Congress, *Television and Video Preservation.*

60. Houston, *Keepers of the Frame,* 117.

61. Slide, *Nitrate Won't Wait,* 115–16.

62. Houston, *Keepers of the Frame,* 152. See also Paul Rutherford, "Researching Television History: Prime-Time Canada, 1952–1967," *Archivaria* 20 (summer 1985): 79–93.

63. For detailed information about describing video materials, see Ingrid Hiseh-Yee, *Organizing Audiovisual and Electronic Resources for Access: A Cataloging Guide* (Englewood, Colo.: Libraries Unlimited, 2000) and Abigail Leab Martin, ed., *AMIA Compendium of Moving Image Cataloging Practice* (Chicago: Society of American Archivists, and Beverly Hills: Association of Moving Image Archivists, 2001).

64. Houston, *Keepers of the Frame,* 118.

65. Slide, *Nitrate Won't Wait,* 116.

66. Ritzenthaler, *Preserving Archives and Manuscripts*, 74.

67. Slide, *Nitrate Won't Wait,* 115. For information about such common tape problems as sticky-shed syndrome, poor playback signal, demagnetization, edge damage, and warped tape, see: Association of Moving Image Archivists, "Videotape Preservation Fact Sheets: Common Tape Problems," http://www.amianet.org/11_Information/Information.html.

68. Association of Moving Image Archivists, "Videotape Preservation Fact Sheets: Reformatting for Preservation," http://www.amianet.org/11_Information/Information.html.

69. Slide, *Nitrate Won't Wait,* 115.

70. Association of Moving Image Archivists, "Videotape Preservation Fact Sheets: Environmental Conditions," http://www.amianet.org/11_Information/Information.html.

71. Association of Moving Image Archivists, "Videotape Preservation Fact Sheets: Environmental Conditions," http://www.amianet.org/11_Information/Information.html. See also Slide, *Nitrate Won't Wait,* 115.

72. Association of Moving Image Archivists, "Videotape Preservation Fact Sheets: Minimum Requirements," http://www.ami-anet.org/11_Information/Information.html.

73. Bellardo and Bellardo, *Glossary,* 33, 4.

74. International Association of Sound and Audiovisual Archives, *The Safeguarding of the Audio Heritage: Ethics, Principles and Preservation Strategy,* ver. 2 (September 2001), http://www .iasa-web.org/iasa0013.htm.

75. Frederick J. Stielow, *The Management of Oral History Sound Archives* (New York: Greenwood Press, 1986), 31. See also David Roberts, "Archives and Sound Archives: What's the Difference?" *Archives and Manuscripts* 12, no. 2 (November 1984): 116–26.

76. Christopher Ann Paton, "Appraisal of Sound Recordings for Textual Archivists," *Archival Issues* 22, no. 2 (1997): 122–24. For a summary of the situation in Canada, see Josephine Langham, "Tuning In: Canadian Radio Resources," *Archivaria* 9 (winter 1979–80): 105–24.

77. Ritzenthaler, *Preserving Archives and Manuscripts*, 73.

78. Christopher Ann Paton, "Preservation Re-Recording of Audio Recordings in Archives: Problems, Priorities, Technologies, and Recommendations," in *American Archival Studies: Readings in Theory and Practice,* ed. Randall C. Jimerson (Chicago: Society of American Archivists, 2000), 533. See also Stielow, *Oral History Sound Archives,* 112.

79. Ritzenthaler, *Preserving Archives and Manuscripts*, 73.

80. Stielow, *Oral History Sound Archives,* 111.

81. Gilles St-Laurent, *The Care and Handling of Recorded Sound Materials* (Washington, D.C.: Commission on Preservation and Access, 1991), 4.

82. Stewart and Banks, "Preservation of Nonpaper Formats," 334. .St-Laurent, *Care and Handling,* 4.

83. Paton, "Appraisal", 118.

84. Stielow, *Oral History Sound Archives,* 59–60.

85. Paton, "Appraisal," 128–31.

86. International Association of Sound and Audiovisual Archives, *Safeguarding.*

87. Ritzenthaler, *Preserving Archives and Manuscripts*, 73.

88. Ritzenthaler, *Preserving Archives and Manuscripts*, 98.

89. Ritzenthaler, *Preserving Archives and Manuscripts*, 73.

90. Ritzenthaler, *Preserving Archives and Manuscripts*, 98.

91. Stewart and Banks, "Preservation of Nonpaper Formats," 336.

92. Ritzenthaler, *Preserving Archives and Manuscripts*, 73.

93. Stielow, *Oral History Sound Archives,* 109.

94. Stielow, *Oral History Sound Archives,* 126–27.

95. St-Laurent, *Care and Handling,* 13.

96. Ritzenthaler, *Preserving Archives and Manuscripts*, 75. Paton, "Preservation Re-Recording," 527.

97. Barbra Buckner Higginbotham and Judith W. Wild, *The Preservation Program Blueprint* (Chicago: American Library Association, 2001), 95–98.

98. St-Laurent, *Care and Handling,* 9.

99. Ibid., 11.

100. Paton, "Preservation Re-Recording," 520.

101. International Association of Sound and Audiovisual Archives, *Safeguarding.* Paton, "Preservation Re-Recording," 521–22.

102. Paton, "Preservation Re-Recording," 534–35. International Association of Sound and Audiovisual Archives, *Safeguarding.*

103. Paton, "Preservation Re-Recording," 536–40.

104. Ibid.," 540.

105. International Association of Sound and Audiovisual Archives, *Safeguarding.*

106. Ibid.

12 MANAGEMENT

Like it or not, most archivists wear the hat of a manager. Certainly, the archivist working alone, the "lone arranger," by default will have to be a manager. Even when arrangers are not alone, however, staffs still tend to be small, requiring hands-on management by the person in charge.[1] Therefore, it is important for every archivist to know enough about management to administer the program successfully. As Michael J. Kurtz points out, "Effective archival administration requires successful integration of the principles and practices of archival administration with the management techniques of business or public administration."[2]

Many books have been written about management in general[3] and managing archives in particular.[4] This chapter cannot possibly cover management in as much detail as those volumes. However, I will briefly discuss ten topics that I consider essential for all archival managers:

- management basics
- management and leadership
- organizational culture
- planning
- leading people
- managing finances
- managing facilities
- managing technology
- fundraising and development
- public relations and marketing[5]

James Gregory Bradsher makes an important point about the nature of archival institutions and the challenge facing their managers:

Archivists, faced with change, the ever-increasing volume and complexity of records, and reference demands, are encountering difficulties in managing their institutions and administering their archives. To some degree these difficulties arise because archival institutions lack the financial resources to cope adequately with the problems facing them. However, many of them also arise from the way in which archival institutions are managed and led. Most such institutions are designed for stability and predictability, places where routine and repetition are organized efficiently through standard operating procedures. Under current conditions of rapid change and increased complexity, uncertainty often leads to ambiguity, confusion, and disarray as archivists experience the frustrations of dealing with conditions for which their institutions were never designed.[6]

In summary, managing an archival institution requires knowledge of management theory and practice, an understanding of the traditional ways to organize and control the archival enterprise, and a willingness to go beyond the theory and tradition when new circumstances warrant.

MANAGEMENT BASICS

The most fundamental of management basics is the definition of the term. There are almost as many definitions of management are there management consultants trying to sell books. For purposes of this chapter, I will use the definition furnished by Thomas Wilsted and William Nolte in *Managing Archival and Manuscript Repositories*: "Management is the exercise of responsibility for the effective use of human, financial, and other resources available to meet an organization's objectives."[7] I prefer this definition because it stresses responsibility and effectiveness, two aspects not always emphasized in contemporary practice, but at the heart of management.

"The computerized medical records of millions of Americans are vulnerable to misuse and abuse, but few people recognize the extent of the problem and little is being done to improve the security of these personal files, a National Research Council panel said today.

"The committee said numerous steps could be taken immediately to increase the privacy and security of electronic patient records. But it said there were few incentives to encourage those practices."

—*New York Times*, March 6, 1997.

Sometimes it seems that management is nothing more than a series of "fads," buzzwords, and catchphrases that ebb and flow in a predictable pattern. A few years ago, *Business Week* traced many of the fads that American organizations have survived since the 1960s: intrapreneuring, demassing, Theory Z, and one-minute managing, to name just a few.[8]

Managers of archives sometimes are forced to implement such new approaches because senior executives in the parent organization become enamored of the latest trend. Those who have managed archives for a number of years have their share of war stories in this regard.

Rather than focusing on the latest trend, archival managers would do well to stay with a proven approach. One classic statement of management responsibilities includes five functions:

- *Planning*: developing and implementing both short- and long-term plans
- *Organizing*: marshaling financial and other resources according to the plan
- *Staffing*: selecting, training, and motivating employees
- *Directing*: using meetings, and written and oral communications to move the organization forward
- *Controlling*: using performance reviews, budgets, and other measures to achieve objectives[9]

These five functions grew from the formalization of the management profession in the late nineteenth century. Modern bureaucratic structures also date from this time and developed in tandem with professional managers.[10] We still are feeling the effects of this intertwined legacy.

In the twenty-first century, we are seeing fundamental changes in the nature of bureaucracies: there is a shift away from hierarchical organizations to flatter, team structures; ad hoc, multi-discipline task forces are being assembled to solve problems that cross organizational lines; and direct communication through e-mail has eliminated some of the more formal report-generating functions. How management theory and practice will respond to these changes remains to be seen, but it will be important to keep both responsibility and effectiveness at the heart of any new approach. In the meantime, archivists will have to manage their departments by drawing upon the best of contemporary practice. It will take leaders to deal with the change and uncertainty.

MANAGEMENT AND LEADERSHIP

It has been said that the problem with American organizations is that we have too much *management* and not enough *leadership*. Viewed in this way, *leaders* are visionaries who can develop and transmit a sense of purpose and direction; people follow leaders because they want to. In contrast, some *managers* are bereft of inspiration and treat people like office equipment; people obey these managers because they have to.

Bruce W. Dearstyne perceptively highlighted the differences between leaders and managers:

Leaders are change agents; they envision a better future for their programs, articulate goals, inspire employees, represent needs clearly, advocate passionately, and have a flair for program building. They gaze out at the horizon, yearn for the future, and think in terms of change. They have a sense of *destiny*. Managers, by contrast, are well organized, focus on the work at hand, are performance-and-outcome oriented by nature, and pride themselves in getting the work done. They are more likely to gaze at the annual workplan (or the clock) than at the horizon, yearn for finishing a particular project on time and within budget, and think in terms of concrete deliverables and products. They have a sense of *let's get it done*. In Warren Bennis's memorable phrase, the leader *does the right thing* while the manager *does things right*.[11]

In an archival setting, we have a mission and purpose that are easy to communicate to staff members. As noted in chapter 1, the mission of the archives is to identify, preserve, and make available records and papers of enduring value. People tend to work in archives because they believe in this mission—it certainly is not to get rich. Therefore, the person in charge of an archives may find it easier to be a leader than the people in charge of other types of organizations, where the sense of mission and purpose is not so easy to articulate.

I do not mean to imply, however, that a managerial vision is automatic in an archives. The leader first must develop his or her own vision—inspiring the staff comes later. Since, unfortunately, not all archival leaders take the time to form a personal vision, "it is not surprising…to find that many archival institutions are overmanaged and underled."[12]

Leaders come in many styles, from Mother Theresa to George Patton. It is important to understand your own leadership style before trying to inspire others. Only if we are true to ourselves can we be effective leaders. According to Frank G. Burke, "A true leader excels in personal attributes that expand the Golden Rule, and true leaders have been with us for millennia, most frequently working within organizational systems that demanded skills, innovation, foresight, empathy, equitability, maturity of mind, abnegation of self, and, perhaps, a touch of panache. True leaders are not new, and we can find them in institutions large and small."[13]

One aspect of the "organizational systems" to which Burke alluded is the culture of the institution. The archival leader will need to understand and work within the larger institutional culture. Only in this way can the archives hope to achieve its mission.

ORGANIZATIONAL CULTURE

As with management itself, there are many definitions or organizational or institutional culture. I prefer Edgar H. Schein's definition of organizational culture: "A pattern of basic assumptions—invented, discovered, or developed by a given group as it learns to cope with its problems of external adaptation and internal integration—that has worked well enough to be considered valid and, therefore, to be taught to new members as the correct way to perceive, think, and feel in relation to those problems."[14]

To some people, organizational culture is just another of the business fads discussed above. *Business Week* told the story of a corporate executive who, upon hearing a presentation about organizational culture, said to his staff: "This corporate culture stuff is great. I want a culture by Monday."[15]

Obviously, organizational cultures cannot be invented overnight or even over a weekend. Furthermore, organizational cultures arise with or without the approval and direction of senior managers. The culture is a factor of organizational life, part of the infrastructure in which the archival manager must work.

Organizational cultures also are not monolithic. Often individual departments have their own cultures, sometimes radically different from the main organizational culture. For example, an old-line manufacturing

Photograph 12.1: Motorcycles, one of the main elements of the corporate culture at Harley-Davidson, are much in evidence in the archives. Photograph courtesy of the Harley-Davidson Motor Company Archives. Copyright Harley-Davidson.

company may have a bureaucratic culture that emphasizes completing the right forms and acting deliberately to avoid mistakes. Within the manufacturing company, however, might be a research and development unit with a much looser attitude and a more risk-taking worldview.

At whatever level, we can think of an organization's culture as having two components:

- *Guiding beliefs:* the values and principles that the organization espouses
- *Daily practices:* the patterns of organizational behaviors and activities

In a healthy culture, the guiding beliefs and daily practices are in conformity: the organization does what it believes and believes what it does. For example, the organization both says that it values customers and shows this in its daily activities. In an unhealthy culture, there is discontinuity between guiding beliefs and daily practices: the organization says that it values customers but treats them shabbily.

Furthermore, in the best organizations, employees have internalized the culture's guiding beliefs in such a way that they know how to act without having to consult lengthy procedural manuals. For example, if the culture of a business emphasizes customer satisfaction, front-line employees are authorized and encouraged to act in a way that meets the customer's needs without having to check with supervisors or consult written documentation.

Turning specifically to archives, there are several ways that organizational culture relates:

- *The archives documents the culture of the organization.* The archivist must be aware of the need to document both guiding beliefs and daily practices. This is not always an easy thing to do, since the documentation may include informal as well as formal sources. For example, one university archivist is documenting the culture of the campus by saving samples of bulletin board flyers or a regular schedule. In another case, a local historical society sends staff members into the street to collect flyers distributed to pedestrians on their way to work. Archivists in many institutional settings regularly use oral history interviews to document culture.
- *The archives helps transmit the culture of the organization.* Many archivists are involved in employee orientation sessions and other presentations where

they talk about the values and traditions of the company. The transmission of culture also happens through articles in employee publications, exhibits, and Web pages.

- *The daily practices of the archives must be in conformity with the guiding beliefs of the organization.* If the archives is to survive and prosper, it must be supportive of the basic beliefs and values of the organization. For example, in a consumer products corporation, a successful archives makes basic historical information accessible to the customers of the organization. In a university, a successful archives will support the research mission of the institution, its faculty and students.

The question of the "bottom line" is left unspoken in many discussions of institutional culture and archives Almost by definition, a guiding belief of any for-profit organization is a fair financial return to its investors. In the contemporary non-profit sector as well, the bottom line drives many institutional decisions. If the archives supports the bottom line of the organization, perhaps by justifying its existence by the revenues it generates, is this "selling out" history? Should an archives be above such mundane concerns?

"Exactly which parts of an agency's Web site constitute federal records, subject to rules governing retention and disposition, depends on the agency in question.

"Officials of the National Archives and Records Administration and other agencies reached no consensus at last week's FedWeb 2002 conference at the National Institutes of Health in Bethesda, Md.

"The debate over maintenance of Web records was just one of the hot-button issues at the annual gathering. Other workshops tackled such topics as Web site design and performance, security requirements and the Government Paperwork Elimination Act."

—*Government Computer News,* May 28, 2002.

In the abstract, we may say that we are "preserving history for history's sake" or documenting society for "future generations," but, in reality, we cannot achieve these long-term goals if the archives does not exist in the here and now. Relating the archives to the organization's culture, as well as implementing the other aspects of management discussed in this chapter, are not just necessary evils, but are essential for the continued existence of a program. The planning process helps facilitate this.

PLANNING

Peter F. Drucker, one of the leading management theorists, once stated that "[e]ach member of the enterprise contributes something different, but all must contribute to a common goal. Their efforts must all pull in the same direction, and their contributions must fit together to produce a whole."[16] The planning process is central to this common effort. It has three distinctive features: planning is anticipatory in character; it is a series of related decisions; and it looks to the future.[17]

Despite the importance of planning, many archivists feel ambivalent toward it. According to Michael J. Kurtz:

> Many archival managers and their staffs remain reluctant to engage in detailed planning efforts. They seem to feel that the time "wasted" on planning could be better spent on doing actual work. There is some truth in this if planning becomes an end in itself, and results in "tending" an overly complicated and rigid plan by means of an elaborate reporting system. Despite these concerns, though, a modern archival program cannot survive without a creative planning process that results in well-defined written goals and objectives.[18]

Kurtz is correct that any plan must be in proportion to the staff and other resources available to the archival program. If it requires twenty hours to plan for ten hours of work, the process is complicated beyond reason. Balance and proportion must be part of any plan.

Whether we are from a large or small repository, planning offers a number of benefits for archival repositories:

- *Planning forces managers to define program goals and objectives.* The beginning point is to establish what it is we wish to accomplish. Planning also requires the manager to share these goals and objectives with all staff members.
- *Planning provides a clear way to justify the archival program to outsiders.* The plan can serve as an outreach vehicle for various constituencies.
- *Planning enables managers to achieve and maintain direction and control.* The plan becomes the means for allocating and monitoring resources.
- *Planning insures that the archival program will not just respond to day-to-day crises.* Planning certainly will not eliminate daily crises. However, it does keep the crises from becoming the entire focus of archival activity.

- *Planning furnishes a framework for accountability.* Once we outline our goals and objectives, we then can monitor how well we achieve the elements in our plan.[19]

The key point is that planning is not a one-time exercise to create a document and then file it away. Any archival plan must be a living document that is revised as situations change. As Philip F. Mooney has stated, "Too often such documents become stone tablets that are periodically dusted off and reissued without ever asking a key series of questions: Is the work we are doing the right work? Could we be doing it better? Can we do it differently? Should we be doing other things?"[20]

Bruce Dearstyne has outlined six steps to the planning process:

1 *Prepare to plan.* This involves answering such questions as: Who supports the process? Who will lead the process? How will staff be involved? Will we produce a long-range (strategic) or a short-range (operational) plan? When will the planning process be completed?

2 *Develop a program mission statement.* As discussed earlier, a mission statement answers such questions as: Why was the program established? What does the program seek to document or collect? Who can use the collection?

3 *Carry out a self-analysis of program services and resources.* This is similar to what a university does before an accreditation team visits the campus.

4 *Formulate goals, objectives, and activities.*

   - *Goals* are broad statements of desired outcomes.

   - *Objectives* are clear, measurable, and attainable targets intermediate to the goal.

   - *Activities* are specific, distinguishable work units that must be performed in order to meet the objective. Examples are given below.

5 *Implement the plan.* At this point, we begin to carry out the activities for which we have been planning.

6 *Revise the plan, as necessary.* Every plan must be a living document subject to revision as the plan unfolds. As Philip Mooney noted above, no plan is carved in stone.[21]

The greatest confusion usually involves the creation of goals, objectives, and activities. *Goals* provide the basic sense of direction for an institution's activities. In the final analysis, an archives has three goals: (1) identifying records of archival value, (2) preserving them, and (3) making them available for research.[22] Beyond these overarching goals, there usually are a number of smaller goals developed during the planning process. These goals are action oriented and grow from the mission statement. They provide general direction for the repository and should take a number of years to achieve.[23]

As part of goal setting, Mooney recommends that archivists create a "destination document" that outlines where the program is going and what the desired results will be. In Mooney's words:

> Rather than focusing on past achievements, [the destination document] takes a more futuristic approach to the results that management can expect to see from an allocation of resources. For the archivist, such a document can place proper emphasis on a "return on investment" and can make strategic thinking a paramount part of work plans, annual reports, and budget submissions. While data on research requests, reference questions answered, and collections processed are meaningful to compile and demonstrate levels of activity, there must be business-related results to generate long-term support in terms of both personnel and finances.[24]

Objectives are more specific actions in an archival plan and must be achieved to reach the goals. Objectives should be measurable and should be attainable within a limited period of time. Objectives are more specific than goals and can be broken down into a number of smaller parts.[25]

In setting objectives, it is important to be selective and realistic. James C. Worthy emphasized these points a number of years ago:

> Resources are always limited. There is never enough money or enough people or enough space or enough time to do all of the things that would be well worth doing—or, indeed, all of the things there might well be an urgent need to do. Aside from the danger of failing to establish the archives' relevance to the host organization, the greatest menace to successful archival administration is failure to establish realistic priorities.... If anything significant is to be accomplished in any area—archival or other–there must be a concentration of resources on a few well-defined ends. Activities that do not contribute meaningfully to those ends must be forsworn, no matter how important or appealing they may be from a personal or professional viewpoint.[26] *Activities* are the smallest units of the plan. They are

finite projects that are carried out over a specific period of time, typically one year or less. Activities should be measurable and generally are assigned to one staff member to complete.[27]

An example from North Fork University may help clarify goals, objectives, and activities. Suppose that the NFU Archives has established the goal of "increasing awareness of our archives among school-age children." Two possible objectives and their related activities are presented in figure 12.1:

Fig. 12.1 Objectives and Activities		
Objective	Have ten more schools visit than last year.	Get archival materials into the fourth grade curriculum.
Activity	Call all schools in the NFU area and invite them to the archives.	Prepare a curriculum packet that includes primary source materials and teacher lesson plans.

As presented above, the planning process forces one to address some fundamental questions:

- *Why* does this archival program exist?
- *What* do we want it to accomplish?
- *How* can we make certain it will accomplish these things?[28]

Answering these questions implies a willingness to disrupt the status quo, the way things were done up to now. This can be very threatening and may lead to resistance. Dealing with the disruption and resistance requires strategies for leading the staff of the archival repository, the next topic in this chapter.

LEADING PEOPLE

Management theorists rightly have stressed the importance of leading people in an organization of any size. Peter Drucker notes that "Executives spend more time on managing people and making people decisions than on anything else—and they should. No other decisions are so long lasting in their consequences or so difficult to unmake."[29] Douglas McGregor emphasizes the role of the leader in the process.

According to McGregor, there is a need for "creation of an environment which will encourage commitment to organizational objectives and which will provide opportunities for the maximum exercise of initiative, ingenuity, and self-direction in achieving them."[30]

These comments are even more relevant in archives, which have smaller staffs than other organizations. Just how small are archival staffs? While there is much anecdotal evidence, it is difficult to find documentation in the professional literature about the average staff size in archives. An article from 1987 published the data presented in figure 12.2:[31]

Fig. 12.2 Statistics on Archival Staffs

Type of Archives	Total Staff (Median)	Total Staff (Average)	Professional Staff (Median)	Professional Staff (Average)
Federal	9.1	17.0	3.3	6.2
State	11.5	25.0	5.4	10.6
Local	3.1	5.6	2.0	3.1
Academic	3.9	6.7	1.4	2.4
Business	2.6	2.7	1.5	1.8
Religious	2.0	3.7	1.4	2.3
Subject	3.6	7.4	1.9	3.6
Museum	2.6	8.1	2.2	3.8
All	3.5	8.6	1.8	3.7

The above chart indicates that while government archives may be larger, every other segment has a median[32] staff size of two or fewer people. In departments of this size, there is no place to hide people problems.

SELECTING AND DEVELOPING STAFF

Michael Kurtz discusses the importance of personnel management in an archival setting: "The finest organizational structure and planning process will be to no avail without a quality archival staff. Personnel management is a major element in the success of an archival program. The essential elements of personnel management include personnel selection, performance evaluation, and professional development."[33]

Since most archives are part of larger organizations, usually basic personnel policies and procedures already are in place. This is an advantage for the archivist who is new to management, especially the archivist who needs to recruit staff.

"It's like putting together pieces to a puzzle. Old photographs, historic documents, and artifacts that can take your breath away.

"'It makes me feel really good inside to see old pictures that are so well preserved,' says ... a member of Seattle's Black Heritage Society.

"Every Friday, a small group of volunteers meets to learn as much as they can, and to add to the growing archive of Seattle's black history."

—Seattle KOMO Television, February 18, 2002.

Personnel selection involves a number of steps:

- *Prepare a position description.* The position description should flow from the mission of the archives. It should clearly state the responsibilities of the position as well as educational and other requirements.
- *Advertise the position.* While some archives continue to advertise in newspapers, it is more cost-effective to advertise these specialized positions through professional organizations and Internet discussion groups and listservs.
- *Screen the applicants.* After an initial screening of the applicants, one or more are brought to the archives for personal interviews. The nature and content of interviews usually is governed by organizational policies and procedures.
- *Make the final selection.* The archives extends an offer to the most suitable candidate.

Position titles often have a symbolic as well as a practical value. An organization's label for a position, and how this name relates to other positions in the organization, reflects the esteem in which the archival program is held. Philip F. Mooney thinks this is especially important with managerial positions: "Positions and job grades in the [archives] department should be parallel to other managerial roles that entail responsibilities for knowledge management, resource allocation, and interface with internal and external audiences." Mooney believes that comparisons with libraries or records management programs do not go far enough. "The wider the base of comparison, the more elevated the job grades and pay scales become for the archivist."[34]

Once the staff is hired, the archival manager must provide effective supervision on a daily basis. Effective supervision involves the following:

- *written performance plan and standards*: It is important for employees to understand what is expected of them within a certain period of time. A written performance plan, developed in consultation with the employee, is the best way to clarify the situation. The plan should also include standards or measures so that both the supervisor and the employee can monitor performance regularly.

- *performance reviews*: At least annually, the supervisor should conduct a formal review, comparing actual performance to the plan developed earlier. According to Wilsted and Nolte, "A performance review should include three elements: an assessment of the employee's performance during the rating period being reviewed, an evaluation of the employee's potential for development within the organization, and consideration of a plan to permit the employee to obtain the additional skills, education, or experience needed to realize that potential."[35] This need not be an adversarial process. If the plan was developed collegially, the review should be in the same spirit. The main objective is to keep the archival program moving toward its goals.

- *professional development plan*: Every employee should have a professional development plan. During the planning and review cycle, gaps in knowledge or skills may be identified. The effective leader will develop a plan to help employees improve in this area. Such a plan often includes attending seminars, workshops, or formal courses.

In preparing a professional development plan, it is useful to keep in mind that employees, including archival employees, go through a series of stages in their professional life. The task of the leader is to nurture the growth of his or her staff through the four stages presented in figure 12.3.

Fig. 12.3 Stages of Professional Growth				
	Stage 1	**Stage 2**	**Stage 3**	**Stage 4**
Central activity	• helping • learning • following directions	working as an independent contributor	training	shaping direction
Primary relationship	apprentice	colleague	mentor	sponsor
Major psycho-logical issues	dependence	independence	assuming responsibility for others	exercising power

Employees begin as *apprentices*, where they are "learning the ropes" and are dependent upon other, more senior staff. In the second stage, the employee becomes a *colleague,* an independent professional who can contribute as an equal member of the team. Employees next progress to the role of *mentor,* in which they assume responsibility for others and help with the professional development of staff. Finally, the employee becomes a *sponsor,* responsible for shaping direction and exercising power.

The supervisor's contact with staff goes beyond evaluation and development. On a daily basis, the supervisor will need to look at existing work processes and try to improve them. Any change to the status quo can be a source of tension and stress. Frank Burke has outlined the best approach for minimizing negative consequences:

> A good supervisor will not initiate new processes without at least some consultation with affected staff, and at best only after a joint effort to test a new procedure against the old, prove its effectiveness, and in the end have the staff members understand why the change is being made, and embrace it. If a supervisor can look at the assignment as a collegial process with an intellectual (and perhaps social) challenge, the atmosphere is an office or a stack area can be modified positively. The process can also change how such a person is perceived—as just another supervisor, or as a leader.[36]

The collegial process also should extend to other frequent members of the archival staff: volunteers, interns, and contractors.

VOLUNTEERS, INTERNS AND CONTRACTORS

Volunteers are part of many archival programs. The nature of archival materials and the personal connection with the past encourages members of the public to offer their services to an archives. This is particularly so with people interested in genealogy or local history.

Volunteers bring background and interests that can be especially useful for an archives. In fact, some archives would not be able to function were it not for their volunteers. It is important to realize, however, that volunteers also require an expenditure of resources, at a minimum, for staff to select, train, and monitor the performance of volunteers. For this reason, some archives decide that volunteers are not worth the required care and feeding.

For the archives that wants to use volunteers, Bruce W. Dearstyne has outlined seven aspects of a successful program:

- Designate a volunteer program administrator or coordinator.
- Develop and plan for the role of volunteers in the program.
- Establish an organizational climate that is conducive to volunteers.
- Carefully match volunteer interest and experience to the work at hand.
- Provide for orientation, training, and development opportunities.
- Establish a supervisory system.
- Evaluate the program periodically.[37]

A common question with volunteers is: how much responsibility should they be given? According to Wilsted and Nolte, "Volunteers gain a measure of independence from their status that only a foolish manager would overlook. While recognizing that volunteers may be exempt from some rules that apply to the permanent staff, management needs to make clear which apply to one and all. For instance, volunteers should be expected to work the hours for which they are scheduled."[38] The alternative is to abdicate management control to a major segment of archival personnel.

Student interns have a similar special status. Generally, interns are only with the repository for a brief, fixed time. This is unlike volunteers who may be with the repository for a longer period. How much training are you willing to give an intern who will only be available for a few months? The investment in training and supervision must not exceed the benefit the institution derives from the presence of the intern.

The main benefit that interns bring is the ability to make progress on some discreet projects that the regular staff never seem able to address. It is common for interns to process collections or perform similar tasks. Both the intern and the archives benefit from the relationship. The intern receives real-world archival experience and the host institution makes headway on its processing backlog.

An additional factor relates to interns but does not apply to volunteers: the archives will have to comply with policies established by the student's academic institution. Since the student receives academic credit, the internship usually has to meet certain requirements. Also, some interns may receive pay, while other academic institutions require that interns not receive compensation.

If the requirements are not clearly stated and understood by all parties, the internship can be a negative experience. One way to clarify matters is to draft a "learning contract" among the three parties (student, archives, and academic institution). The learning contract should cover such matters as:

- *Contact information.* This should include all three parties.
- *Learning objectives.* What does the student hope to learn from the experience?
- *Project supervision.* Who will supervise the intern?
- *Project details.* With which projects will the student be involved? If the student is involved in more than one project, it is helpful to indicate the number of hours the intern will spend on each project.
- *Evaluation.* How will the internship be evaluated and by whom?

Independent contractors are the third category of additional staff resources. Such contractors can be of three types:

- *Short-term consultants.* If an archives needs specialized assistance for a short time, there are consultants available with a wide range of expertise. In particular demand are consultants who can assist with descriptive systems (such as Encoded Archival Description) and digital archives.
- *Long-term on-site contractors.* Some organizations limit the number of regular employees but are willing to pay almost indefinitely for services by outside contractors. In the last decade, this has become

particularly common in corporate archives. Contractors enable important work to get done while maintaining the flexibility of the employing institution to add or decrease total staff. The use of contract employees, however, can also have negative consequences: contractors can resent the full-time employees who often have better benefit packages and more security; full-time employees, especially in a unionized situation, can feel that the contractors are reducing the number of union employees; and both sides can resent the fact that management often is willing to spend more for contractors than for regular employees.

• *Off-site, fee-based services.* A number of companies maintain archival collections for their customers. These companies store, process, preserve, and provide reference services for records. In effect, the entire archival staff is outsourced to a third party.

LEADING ARCHIVAL STAFFS

Whatever the composition of the archival staff, the bottom line is that it still is a team that must be led to achieve its goals. The following five hints can help in leading archival staffs:

• *If possible, let your employees completely process collections.* Do not have one person arrange the records and another person describe them. Having one person process the entire collection offers a number of advantages: improved morale, a sense of accomplishment and achievement, a view of the total picture, and the creation of a "subject specialist" in that particular collection.

• *Involve as many people as possible in the appraisal decisions.* In particular, ask the reference staff (if they are separate), about the use of similar records. This helps to keep appraisal archivists close to your patrons.

• *Make certain that everyone clearly understands his or her job.* Clear and concise position descriptions are an essential part of this. It is best to develop the position description in consultation with staff members.

- *Try to find some objective measures to evaluate employee performance.* Avoid relying completely on subjective data. Some of the information used to quantify costs also can be used to evaluate performance.
- *Understand that some employees are "locals" and others are "cosmopolitans" in outlook.* Locals primarily identify with the institution employing them at the moment. Their preferred career path would involve a series of promotions within this one institution. Cosmopolitans, on the other hand, identify primarily with their profession. The preferred career path would involve increasing professional responsibility, probably at a number of different institutions. It is not that one approach is right and the other is wrong. Rather, the point is that these different worldviews can lead to misunderstandings in the workplace.

While managing people is the most important leadership responsibility, a close second is managing financial resources. Even a lone arranger who has no staff to lead will need to manage finances. It is an area in which many archivists feel inadequate.

MANAGING FINANCES

Almost every archivist will need to prepare and monitor a budget at some point in his or her career. According to Michael J. Kurtz, "Accurate, realistic budget projections provide an aura of legitimacy for the archival program in the competition for resources within a larger organization or from an appropriating body. In addition, the budget is a key element in effective internal management."[39]

There is nothing mysterious about a budget: it is simply a plan expressed in monetary terms. Viewed in this way, a budget need not be a source of anxiety. In beginning the process, it is important to keep in mind the words of Evans, Ward, and Rugass: "Budgets serve three interrelated purposes: planning, coordinating, and control."[40] These are three of the essential functions of management.

Budgets fall into two main categories:

- *Operating budget*: a statement of the requirements to operate a program for a defined period of time[41]

- *Capital budget*: a statement of the requirements for long-term projects such as construction or major equipment

At the heart of any budget is an estimate of income and expenses. In most archives, however, expenses are the key factor to estimate. The archival manager then tries to secure the necessary resources to meet projected expenses.

Managers take two approaches to operating budgets. The first approach, *consolidated budgeting*, assigns income and expenses to "lines" such as salaries and supplies. The second approach, *program budgeting,* does not consolidate costs for the entire organization. Rather, costs such as salaries, materials, equipment, and building maintenance, are charged to various programs (general administration, acquisition and appraisal, collection maintenance, preservation, user services, and outreach).

Budgets also are affected by the way income and expenses are booked. Wilsted and Nolte discuss the differences between cash accounting and accrual accounting:

> For many institutions, *cash accounting,* familiar to everyone as the accounting procedure used with a checkbook, should be sufficient. Income is credited at the time it is received or made available for use, and costs are noted when bills are paid. A more complicated process, known as *accrual accounting,* may be required in larger repositories and in those that are part of larger operations, where accrual accounting is the norm. An accrual system records income when it is earned by sales or services, even if this precedes actual receipt of money owed. It accounts for expenses when they are incurred, even if payment takes place somewhat later.[42]

Archival processing is a major expense component in any budget. Arrangement and description break down into two basic costs, supplies and staff time.

- *Supply costs* are the easier ones to estimate. The major archival supplies are acid-free boxes and folders. Boxes are available both in "records center size" (1 cu. ft.) and "manuscript size" (approximately one-third of a cubic foot). A standard, letter-size file drawer equals 1.5 cubic feet.
- *Staff costs* can be more difficult to determine. Archival work is very labor-intensive. The time required to process a collection can vary greatly

depending upon the nature of the materials (organizational records, photographic negatives, etc.) and the condition before processing (i.e., out of order, brittle, yellowed, folded). One study concluded that, on average, it took over twenty-five hours to process completely one cubic foot of records.[43] Even at a modest cost of fifteen dollars per hour for salary and benefits, this would equal $375 to process an average cubic foot of records. This same article concluded that photographs could take forty-seven hours per cubic foot to process, for a total cost of $705 per cubic foot.

Processing archival collections for preservation and use does not come cheaply. This is why appraisal decisions are so important: it costs a great deal of money to process junk. This also is why we must consider if the records we so laboriously are processing will ever be used by anyone. Archivists have limited-enough resources without squandering them on records of questionable value.

"The Library of Congress is charged with collecting the creative work of the American people. This has come to include such varied output as the papers of Thomas Jefferson and the Wright brothers, the original compositions of Leonard Bernstein and the video archives of the Martha Graham Dance Company.

"But now the nation's creativity extends to Web sites, electronic journals and magazines, and CD-ROMs of every sort. And the library is lagging in collecting and archiving that digital material, according to a report released yesterday by the National Academy of Sciences. Unless its administrators act swiftly, the report says, the library risks diminishing in relevance."

—*New York Times,* July 27, 2000.

MANAGING FACILITIES

An archival program needs an adequate facility for processing and other activities. The primary role of the manager is to plan this space, either by using existing space or building new space. The facility can be difficult to plan, however, because it has both "front office" and "back office" components:

- The *front office* component includes space intended for the public, such as research rooms and exhibit halls.

- The *back office* space is for archival staff and functions. This includes secure storage, processing, conservation, and reformatting.

The two types of space have symbolic and fiscal implications. Symbolically, the public spaces present the image of the archives to its constituents. The best example is the rotunda of the National Archives Building in Washington, D.C., where the "charters of freedom" are displayed in a cathedral-like setting. While other archival facilities will not rise to this level, each manager must consider the face that the archival program will present.

Photograph 12.2 Many archival facilities include "compact" or "movable" shelving for the storage of boxes. Photograph Courtesy of the SBC Archives and History Center, San Antonio, TX

One fiscal implication is that such a public facelift can be expensive—it can significantly increase the cost of a building project. A second implication involves back office operations. Some of the non-public areas are expensive to build and maintain. In particular, controlled temperature and humidity, as discussed in previous chapters, are costly endeavors. Conservation laboratories and reformatting departments (microfilm, digital scanning) also are more expensive to build than standard office areas. In the future, as more archives begin to acquire digital records, back office costs will increase even more.

Planning an archival facility becomes an even greater challenge when the front and back offices are one and the same space. This can be the case in small archives, where processing space doubles as reference space when researchers are present. Though this is far from ideal, it is a reality in many archives that are not yet able to renovate or build new space.

"If you've been sued, you know that pretrial 'discovery' can disrupt your business and potentially damage your case. Bad news: As lawyers increasingly demand discovery of computer as well as paper records, this particular form of legal torture is getting even worse.

"Particularly dangerous are careless notes dashed off by executives who treat E-mail like a water-cooler session."

—*Forbes,* January 13, 1997.

If an archival manager should be fortunate enough to plan new space, Wilsted and Nolte identify four factors to consider:

1 the size of the collection

2 the number of staff members

3 the number of tasks for which the archives is responsible

4 the number of researchers and other clients who are served[44]

In such space planning, the archival manager has certain key responsibilities. According to Michael Kurtz:

> Only the archivist can determine program needs through identifying the kind of storage space required for the particular holdings of the archives, projecting the growth of holdings, and documenting the most effective workflow patterns. The last point is important in providing direction to architects on which functions need to be performed near one another. Archivists must also be familiar with the literature and with issues relating to matters such as environmental standards and archival storage media. When archival program requirements are clearly defined, then the archivist can begin working with other professionals in constructing, renovating, or maintaining facilities.[45]

One particular area in which archival program requirements need to be clearly defined is the management of technology.

MANAGING TECHNOLOGY

According to Thomas Wilsted and William Nolte, "Technology will present archival managers with the most volatile component of their external environment."[46] This volatility comes from the increasing speed of technological change in society, not just in the archival world.

Managing technology in an archives is not the same as managing digital records, which I discussed in chapter 10. This chapter covers the managerial aspects of selecting and maintaining information technology within the archives itself. As Edward Evans, Patricia Layzell Ward, and Bendik Rugaas note:

> Ever-growing dependence on technology requires a surprising amount of management. Issues range from specialized support staff to planning for ongoing replacement as new generations of hardware and software make compatibility with existing technology too complex to maintain. In addition to planning for constant upgrading technology, there is the need to provide constant staff training.[47]

To further complicate matters, not all of the change involves hardware and software. Information Technology (IT) departments experience rapid turnover in staff as well as technology. Good IT professionals tend to move to greater responsibilities, often in other institutions. This leaves the archival manager in a position of having to educate new IT liaisons on a regular basis.

This education is necessary for two reasons:

- *Archival issues and concerns are not well understood by the general public; there is no reason to think that IT professionals would be any different.* Archivists face a constant task of educating almost anyone with whom they come into contact.
- *Some archival systems are outside of the institutional mainstream supported by the IT department.* In particular, some description and space management software is from niche vendors outside of the usual IT circles. The IT department may not want to support the systems.

As the archival manager surveys his or her IT landscape, it may be helpful to keep in mind a hierarchy developed by the IT department of one major corporation. The IT staff in this corporation divides technology into three categories:

- *Core*. This is comprised of the hardware and software that the IT department currently supports.
- *Declining Core*. This includes the hardware and software that the IT department considers to be past their prime. IT makes a commitment to maintain the systems for a limited time, usually one to two years, so departments can convert data to newer systems.
- *Emerging Core*. These are the technologies with which IT is experimenting; some may eventually be added to the core. This is where IT sees the future of technology within the corporation.

This tripartite division has another advantage for the archivist. By staying in contact with IT, the archivist can identify other departments with records in declining core systems. The archivist then can try to preserve these records before they are stranded in technological backwaters. On the other side, being aware of emerging core technologies may enable the archivist to influence system selection and design. As noted in chapter 10, this is one of the recommended practices for identifying electronic records of archival value.

FUNDRAISING AND DEVELOPMENT

The cost of information technology is one of the factors driving archivists to seek outside financial support. This can take the form of either one-time grant applications or an integrated development campaign.

The development process usually involves several components:

- *Definition of needs*. What are the funding priorities? Which individuals or institutions are potential sources of funding?
- *Advisory board*. Will our fundraising activities be enhanced by having prominent names on an advisory board? Do we expect the advisory board members to contribute themselves?
- *Annual campaign*. How do we expand our base of support to meet regular operating needs?
- *Capital campaign*. Do we have building or equipment needs that only can be met with a separate capital campaign?

Many organizations decide to hire development professionals, either in-house staff or outside consultants, to manage the development process. These development professionals are another group that will require education about archival needs and concerns.

Grant funds are available from a variety of sources: Federal government, state government, and private foundations. Even within for-profit corporations, there sometimes are pools of internal funds that require the equivalent of a grant proposal.

"We often view the Internet as a communications medium or an information-retrieval tool, but it's also a powerful archiving technology that makes snapshots of our digital lives—and can store those fleeting images forever.

"Not only are official documents and consumer profiles accumulating, but the very essence of our daily online existence—our political opinions, prejudices, religious beliefs, sexual tastes and personal quirks—are all becoming part of an immense, organic media soup that is congealing into a permanent public record. What is different about the digital archiving phenomenon is that our beliefs, habits and indiscretions are being preserved for anyone to see—friends, relatives, rivals, lovers, neighbors, bosses, landlords, even obsessed stalkers."

—*Salon Magazine,* November 25, 1998.

A typical grant proposal contains the following sections:[48]

- *Purpose:* a brief statement of what the project hopes to accomplish
- *Need for the project*: Why is the project worthy of outside funding? Why can the applicant not complete the project without additional resources?
- *Relationship to previous work*: How does this project relate to other projects, especially those previously funded by the granting agency?
- *Plan of work and timetable*: How will the proposed work be accomplished within the period of the grant?
- *Staff*: Which professional and support staff will be used throughout the project? What are their qualifications?
- *Budget*: What is the total project budget? How much is requested from the granting institution? How much will the applicant institution cost-share?

The importance of outside grants extends beyond the financial assistance. Since many grant programs involve peer reviewers, securing a grant is an affirmation of the professional expertise of the applicant institution and the archivist, as well as the importance of the collection. The increased visibility also can assist with a public relations or marketing initiative.

"The melodic voice of Marianne Moore echoed from a reel-to-reel tape recorder at the American Poetry Archives here [San Francisco] on a recent morning. She was reading her poems to an enthusiastic audience in 1957, and the tape offered delights quite different from those that come from reading a printed page....

"As the tape wound on, the archives manager ... hovered nearby, watching a computer screen. He was turning the Moore reading into a digital recording, since the tape on which it was originally recorded was starting to disintegrate.

"This process is being repeated at poetry centers around the United States. Three of the largest—in San Francisco, New York and Boulder, Colo.—have recordings of many of the greatest 20th-century poets. Often these tapes were made in casual settings where the poets felt free to muse, explain and joke as well as read. But the recordings, many of them decades old, are in poor condition."

—*New York Times,* May 16, 2002.

PUBLIC RELATIONS AND MARKETING

Throughout this chapter, a recurring theme has been the importance of effective communications. The planning process was designed, in part, to develop goals and communicate them to various constituents. Leading an archival staff is a constant exercise in listening and communicating. Effective fundraising also presupposes effective communication. This section takes the discussion further by exploring two related concepts: public relations and marketing.

Despite being closely related, public relations and marketing often are confused. According to Evans, Ward, and Rugass, public relations is the "planned and sustained effort to establish and maintain goodwill and mutual understanding between an organization and its public." Marketing, on the other hand, "tends to focus on identifying and meeting customer needs for services or products."[49] While the purposes are different, some techniques (exhibits, brochures, speeches, etc.) can be used for both.

PUBLIC RELATIONS

Goodwill and mutual understanding can be established and maintained in a number of ways. Among the most common ways that archives try to establish a positive public image are

- press releases
- press kits
- articles for newspapers and journals
- annual reports
- guides to the repository
- pamphlets
- newsletters
- event flyers
- exhibits
- tours
- orientation and training programs for employees
- speeches to local organizations
- education kits and curriculum packets
- audiovisual presentations
- internet and Intranet sites and pages

According to Michael Kurtz, "All such communication should address current societal needs through the information contained in the archives. Continually reinforcing this message is one way to gain a broader base of support in the community for archives."[50]

In particular, archivists actively seek out events that can be used to improve the public image of the archives. As Philip F. Mooney has noted, all organizations "have anniversaries and milestones that mark key events in their history—events that can generate books, pamphlets, brochures, calendars, and other commemorative items that draw from the archival collection. These special events also create opportunities for producing oral histories and audio-visual productions to mark the events."[51] As important as these special events are, sometimes a more formal marketing program is required.

MARKETING

As defined above, marketing focuses on identifying and meeting customer needs for services or products. According to Evans, Ward, and

Fig. 12.4 Steps in North Fork University's Marketing Program

Step	Explanation	North Fork University
1. Generic product definition	Define the general product or services that you offer.	The NFU Archives and Special Collections Department provides historical information about NFU and its environs.
2. Target group definition	Divide the large market into smaller units with common needs or wants.	NFU's target groups are scholars, students, genealogists, and community members.
3. Differential marketing analysis	Determine the marketing approaches likely to resonate with different market segments.	Genealogists are likely to be interested in family-related activities and events. Therefore, NFU's marketing should look for these kinds of community events. (For this and subsequent steps, I only will use genealogists as an example.)
4. Customer behavior analysis	Try to understand customer needs and lifestyles.	Genealogists tend to travel great distances if they think a particular collection will provide information, so NFU can market it's archives nationally.
5. Differential advantages analysis	Once you understand each customer segment, then you can seek out differential advantages for each segment. "A differential advantage is one that exploits the reputation, services, or programs by creating or enhancing a special value in the minds of potential customers."	Since genealogists are willing to travel, we can market NFU's location in a highly desirable vacation area for the genealogists and their families.
6. Multiple marketing approaches	Employ several different marketing tools (newsletters, flyers, etc.) selected to meet the lifestyles of the target segment.	Prepare a vacation-type brochure to mail to various lists of genealogists.
7. Integrated market planning	It is important not to have components of the program working at cross-purposes. An integrated program is the best insurance against ineffective use of marketing funds.	The NFU Archives will coordinate its genealogist's brochure with other university marketing efforts and programs, particularly to parents of prospective students, or potential Elderhostel participants.

Fig. 12.4 (Cont)		
Step	**Explanation**	**North Fork University**
8.Continuous feedback	Continuous monitoring will help assure the maximum results for the funds available.	The NFU Archives will ask each genealogist how they heard about the collection.
9.Marketing audit	Look at what worked and what did not. Assess the resources available and expended.	At year-end, the NFU Archives will determine whether or not the campaign to genealogists achieved the desired results.

Rugass, a marketing program involves nine steps.[52] These steps progress from defining your product or service to auditing the effectiveness of the marketing program. In order to make these nine steps concrete, figure 12.4 explains the steps and relates them to North Fork University.

Philip F. Mooney points out that the key elements in marketing an archives are creativity and flexibility. "Marketing is a continual process that adjusts to a changing work environment. It is pro-active and targeted towards specific measurable objectives."[53] Moreover, creativity and flexibility are the hallmarks of the best archival leaders.

CONCLUSION

The ten elements of management presented above offer both challenges and opportunities for the archivist. The true leader is the one who can maximize the opportunities in support of the goals of the archives.

Bruce W. Dearstyne has stated that "Strong, well-led [archival] programs feature adequate support, sufficient (and rising) funding, clear direction, appropriate staffing, and secure facilities." Successful programs have seven characteristics:

- clear sense of purpose and mission
- evolution and change
- dynamic, balanced expansion
- high visibility
- customer focus
- peer recognition
- professional engagement[54]

These seven characteristics offer a useful checklist for the archival leader. To reinforce a point made earlier in this chapter, the characteristics promote leadership rather than management. They keep the archives focused on the big picture, looking at the forest rather than the trees. This is where the vision of the archival leader should reside.

NOTES

1. According to Frank Burke, "Most archives have a staff of fewer than five people; in many cases there is only one salaried member on the staff, and that person is perhaps a part-time employee. Many, if not most of the remaining archival staffs are composed of students who may or may not be paid an hourly wage, or of volunteers." Frank G. Burke, "The Art of the Possible: The Archivist as Administrator," in *Leadership and Administration of Successful Archival Programs*, ed. Bruce W. Dearstyne (Westport, Conn.: Greenwood Press, 2001), 19–36.

2. Michael J. Kurtz, "Archival Management," in *Managing Archives and Archival Institutions*, ed. James Gregory Bradsher (Chicago: University of Chicago Press, 1988), 242.

3. For example, see G. Edward Evans, Patricia Layzell Ward, and Bendik Rugaas, *Management Basics for Information Professionals* (New York: Neal-Schuman, 2000).

4. Some titles are: Thomas Wilsted and William Nolte, *Managing Archival and Manuscript Repositories* (Chicago: Society of America Archivists, 1991); Bryce W. Dearstyne, ed., *Leadership and Administration of Successful Archival Programs* (Westport, Conn.: Greenwood Press, 2001); Richard J. Cox, *Managing Institutional Archives: Foundational Principles and Practices* (Westport, Conn.: Greenwood Press, 1992); James Gregory Bradsher, ed., *Managing Archives and Archival Institutions* (Chicago: University of Chicago Press, 1988). Michael Kurtz is completing an update of the Wilsted and Nolte manual for the Society of American Archivists, which was not available at the time of publication.

5. Several related organizational issues (institutional placement, mission statement, and use of an advisory board) were previously discussed in chapter 2.

6. James Gregory Bradsher, "Archival Effectiveness," in *Managing Archives*, ed. Bradsher, 254.

7. Wilsted and Nolte, *Managing Archival and Manuscript Repositories,* 3–4. A second definition claims that management "is the process of accomplishing things through people," Evans, Ward, and Rugaas, *Management Basics,* 3.

8. "Business Fads: What's In—And Out," *Business Week*, 20 January 1986, 52–61.

9. This is covered in Wilsted and Nolte, *Managing Archival and Manuscript Repositories,* 4–5.

10. See JoAnne Yates, "Internal Communication Systems in American Business Structures: A Framework to Aid Appraisal," *American Archivist* 48 (spring 1985): 141–58; Michael A. Lutzker, "Max Weber and the Analysis of Modern Bureaucratic Organization: Notes Toward a Theory of Appraisal," *American Archivist* 45 (spring 1982): 119–30.

11. Bruce W. Dearstyne, "Leadership of Archival Programs," in *Leadership and Administration,* ed. Dearstyne, 112–13. Bradsher has said something similar: "To manage is to direct the daily operations, to oversee the effectiveness of the routine, and to ensure the efficiency of the existing system. But leadership involves much more than management. To lead is to grasp the wider picture, to understand relationships, to clarify choices, to recognize both needs and opportunities, to encourage agreement, to inspire cooperation, and to instill confidence." Bradsher, "Archival Effectiveness," 260–61.

12. Bradsher, "Archival Effectiveness," 255.

13. Frank G. Burke, "The Art of the Possible,", 33.

14. Edgar H. Schein, *Organizational Culture and Leadership* (San Francisco: Jossey-Bass Publishers, 1985), 9.

15. "Business Fads," 52.

16. Peter F. Drucker, *Management Tasks, Responsibilities, Practices* (New York: Harper & Row, 1973), 430.

17. Evans, Ward, and Rugass, *Management Basics,* 162.

18. Kurtz, "Archival Management," 244. According to James Gregory Bradsher, "Planning, that is, determining what, when, how, and by whom work is to be carried out, is fundamental to an archival institution because it gives the institution its goals and sets up a procedure for reaching them…. Planning helps archivists focus their attention on institutional goals and makes it easier to apply and coordinate institutional resources more efficiently. It provides benchmarks against which accomplishments can be measured and allows managers and institutions to minimize risk and uncertainty, helping them prepare for and deal with change." Bradsher, "Archival Effectiveness," 255–56.

19. Bruce W. Dearstyne, *Planning for Archival Programs: An Introduction*, MARAC Technical Leaflet No. 3 (New York: Mid-Atlantic Regional Archives Conference, 1983).

20. Philip F. Mooney, "Corporate Culture in the Archives," in *Leadership and Administration,* ed. Dearstyne, 92.

21. Dearstyne, "Planning for Archival Programs." Dearstyne does not include the sixth step presented above. For a slightly different version, see Dearstyne's later work: Bruce W. Dearstyne, *Managing*

Historical Records Programs: A Guide for Historical Agencies (Walnut Creek, Calif.: AltaMira Press, 2000), 49–50.

22. Bradsher, "Archival Effectiveness," 256.

23. Wilsted and Nolte, *Managing Archival and Manuscript Repositories,* 30–32.

24. Mooney, "Corporate Culture and the Archives," 87–88.

25. Wilsted and Nolte, *Managing Archival and Manuscript Repositories,* 30–32.

26. James C. Worthy, "Management Concepts and Archival Administration," in *A Modern Archives Reader: Basic Readings on Archival Theory and Practice*, eds. Maygene F. Daniels and Timothy Walch (Washington, D.C.: National Archives and Records Service, 1984), 304.

27. Wilsted and Nolte, *Managing Archival and Manuscript Repositories,* 30–32.

28. Dearstyne, "Planning for Archival Programs."

29. Peter F. Drucker, "Getting Things Done: How to Make People Decisions," *Harvard Business Review* 63, no. 4 (July-August 1985): 22.

30. Douglas McGregor, *The Human Side of Enterprise* (New York: McGraw Hill, 1960), 132.

31. Paul Conway, "Perspectives on Archival Resources: The 1985 Census of Archival Institutions," *American Archivist* 50 (spring 1987), 182.

32. In this case, median is a better measure than arithmetic average. Using the median allows us to exclude atypically large archival institutions like the National Archives and Records Administration and the Smithsonian Institution.

33. Kurtz, "Archival Management," 248.

34. Mooney, "Corporate Culture in the Archives,", 89. The symbolism of the position title also is something to consider. According to Mooney, "Terms like 'manager,' 'director,' and 'vice president' establish a clear hierarchy of rank, but the 'archivist' designation has no meaning and consequently little respect." Mooney, "Corporate Culture," 89.

35. Wilsted and Nolte, *Managing Archival and Manuscript Repositories,* 39–40.

36. Frank G. Burke, "The Art of the Possible," 27.

37. Dearstyne, *Managing Historical Records Programs,* 59–60. See also, Rhonda Huber Frevert, "Archives Volunteers: Worth the Effort?" *Archival Issues* 22, no. 2 (1997): 147–62.

38. Wilsted and Nolte, *Managing Archival and Manuscript Repositories,* 43.

39. Kurtz, "Archival Management," 248.

40. Evans, Ward, and Rugass, *Management Basics,* 432.

41. Wilsted and Nolte, *Managing Archival and Manuscript Repositories,* 49.

42. Ibid., 53.

43. Terry Abraham, Stephen E. Balzarini, and Anne Frantilla, "What is Backlog is Prologue: A Measurement of Archival Processing," *American Archivist* 48 (winter 1985): 31–44. A rule of thumb from reviewing grant proposals is that a processor of archival collections can complete ten cubic feet per month. Therefore, another way to estimate cost per cubic foot would be to divide the monthly salary of a full-time processor by ten.

44. Wilsted and Nolte, *Managing Archival and Manuscript Repositories,* 57.

45. Kurtz, "Archival Management," 251.

46. Wilsted and Nolte, *Managing Archival and Manuscript Repositories,* 89.

47. Evans, Ward, and Rugass, *Management Basics,* 481.

48. This is based in part on Wilsted and Nolte, *Managing Archival and Manuscript Repositories,* 73.

49. Evans, Ward, and Rugass, *Management Basics,* 90.

50. Kurtz, "Archival Management," 250.

51. Mooney, "Corporate Culture in the Archives,", 97.

52. Evans, Ward, and Rugass, *Management Basics,* 97–101.

53. Mooney, "Corporate Culture in the Archives,", 97–98.

54. Dearstyne, "Leadership of Archival Programs,", 115–18.

13 THE ARCHIVAL PROFESSION

Individual archivists are not alone in performing the responsibilities discussed in the previous chapters. They are part of a larger community of professionals with shared values, traditions, and specialized knowledge. In North America, this community has developed rapidly in the last half century, forming professional organizations, issuing educational guidelines, and promulgating a code of ethics. These developments bode well for the future. As Richard Cox stated in 1986, "Archivists are literally at a crossroads, celebrating the golden anniversary of their professional association and facing a new world of information technology and new vocations."[1] It is an exciting time to be a member of the archival profession.

THE DEVELOPMENT OF THE ARCHIVAL PROFESSION

The American archival profession traces its roots to the beginning of the twentieth century. The first public archives was founded in 1901. Eight years later, the American Historical Association sponsored the first Conference of Archivists. According to Richard Cox, at that meeting Waldo G. Leland "charted a course in which the archivist would emerge as an independent professional with standardized methodologies and specialized education."[2]

Within three decades, archivists would realize some of their dreams. The National Archives was established in 1934. The Conference of Archivists the following year called for an autonomous professional association, which was established in 1936 as the Society of American Archivists. One of the three main objectives of the new organization was the "development of a genuine archival profession in the United States."[3]

Since the 1930s, there have been three principal routes into the archival profession:

- *History.* The first American archivists were educated as historians. Some of these historians consciously chose archives; others were steered toward archives because of shortages of teaching positions.

- *Library and information science.* In recent decades, more and more library and information science schools have established archival education programs. Since LIS programs emphasize knowledge organization, reference services, and an understanding of information technologies, they have become congenial homes for archival education.

- *Other.* Some people are appointed archivists after working for years in the institution. These long-time employees embody the organizational memory and are natural choices for archival programs. They then have to acquire archival knowledge once on the job, either through a graduate archival education program or through continuing professional education.

However people come to archival work, they quickly learn that they are part of a larger professional community.

"It's been online only about three months, and not all of its records are accessible on Paula Fraser's classroom Macintosh.

"Still, the Bellevue elementary-school teacher says that the Web site developed by the Densho Project—an effort to record and archive video interviews of Japanese American internment survivors—is the next-best thing to personal contact.

"'I really like to bring history alive for students,' said Fraser, a fifth-grade teacher at Stevenson Elementary School. But many who lived through the internment are now too old for class visits.

"Densho, Fraser said, opens 'a different dimension' that allows people to 'climb into the skins' of Japanese Americans."

—Seattle Times, May 4, 2002.

THE NATURE OF "PROFESSION"

In the previous section, I briefly discussed the development of the archival profession without clarifying just what makes a profession. Is every "occupation" a "profession," or do only some occupations rise to this status? Into which category do archivists fall?

The oldest professions, in a positive sense, are law and medicine. They are well established and respected by society at large. A career in such a profession is often the dream of a parent of a newborn son or daughter.

But what makes these professions special? Abraham Flexner articulated the classic model of a profession in 1915. Called the "taxonomic model," it summarizes the characteristics of an "ideal" profession and provides a yardstick for measuring any would-be professionals.

"A nonprofit organization based in Vienna called Centropa—Central Europe Center for Research and Documentation—has just opened a Web site offering a new combination of oral histories and photographs of 20th-century Jewish history in Central and Eastern Europe.... Centropa claims to have the largest online library of privately owned pre- and post-Holocaust family pictures and oral histories ever assembled in this region, as well as more photographs of contemporary Jewish life than anywhere on the Internet."

—*New York Times*, September 15, 2002.

According to Flexner, an ideal profession has five characteristics:

1. *Specialized knowledge or systematic theory.* This knowledge is intellectual rather than practical. An understanding of the theory is required to enter the profession. This research is developed through research at professional schools.
2. *Community sanction.* The public recognizes the members of the profession and sanctions their independence on technical judgments. The public permits the profession to control entry via certification and accreditation.
3. *Professional cohesion or organization.* Practitioners feel part of the profession and participate actively in professional associations.
4. *Professional culture.* There are values, norms, and symbols that transform "work" into a "calling."
5. *Institutionalized altruism.* Professionals realize that their behavior can benefit or hurt others. The responsibility to protect clients comes with the profession's monopoly of knowledge and control over it use.[4]

How well does the archives profession meet Flexner's ideal characteristics? As with many professions, archivists do better on some elements than on others. Figure 13.1 presents an assessment of the archival profession.

Fig. 13.1 Assessment of Archives as a Profession	
Flexner's Characteristic	**Assessment of the Archival Profession**
Specialized knowledge or systematic theory	Until recently, archival theory was more practical than theoretical. The expansion of graduate archival education in the last ten years has created more opportunities for pure research. Several universities even offer doctoral studies in archival science. The need to manage electronic records also has sparked a great deal of theoretical research.
Community sanction	It is difficult for the public to *sanction* archivists when so few members of the public even understand what archivists do. Since 1989, there has been a certification program for individual archivists, though this certainly does not *control* entry into the profession.
Professional cohesion or organization	Professional cohesion is one of the strengths of the archival profession. There are national, regional, and local archival organizations that offer a variety of meetings, publications, and other services.
Professional culture	Archivists share a commitment to the mission of managing the nation's documentary heritage. This and other aspects of the professional culture are quite strong.
Institutionalized altruism	Since the archival profession does not control entry via licensing, it is difficult to impose penalties for poor professional practice. As a result, archivists must rely upon persuasion rather than enforceable standards.

To summarize, archivists are on the road to becoming a profession with public acceptance. There is a strong culture, high level of cohesion, and an emerging theoretical foundation. What is lacking (in comparison to law and medicine) is the ability of archivists to control entry into the profession and enforce standards for professional practice. Some would say, however, that such standards and control are not necessarily desirable additions to the archival profession. As reflected by its roots, the archival profession remains diverse in perspective.

THE PROFESSIONAL COMMUNITY

As noted above, one of the strengths of the archival profession is the community of common purpose embodied in professional organizations.

Wherever an archivist lives or works, there is a regional or national archival organization nearby.

In North America, there are three principal archival organizations:

- the Society of American Archivists, established in 1936[5]
- the Association of Canadian Archivists, established in 1975 and incorporated in 1978[6]
- the Academy of Certified Archivists, established in 1989[7]

The Society of American Archivists (SAA) and the Association of Canadian Archivists each hold an annual meeting, publish a scholarly journal (*The American Archivist* and *Archivaria,* respectively), provide a range of member services, and are involved in archival advocacy and outreach. The Academy of Certified Archivists, which exists for the sole purpose of certifying individual archivists, is discussed below.

"Secretary of State Matt Blunt today launched a World War I Service Record Data Base on the Internet, based on Missouri National Guard records.

"More than 145,000 Missourians who served during World War I are listed in the new database, which was created by the State Archives."

—Jefferson City *News Tribune*, May 28, 2002.

In addition, there are several other national archival organizations that serve particular groups within the larger profession. Among the national organizations are:

- Archivists of Religious Institutions
- Association of Catholic Diocesan Archivists
- Association of Moving Image Archivists
- National Association of Government Archives and Records Administrators
- National Episcopal Historians and Archivists[8]

Regional and local archival organizations usually are smaller and closer to their membership. While only the larger organizations publish scholarly journals, almost all have newsletter and hold regular meetings, sometimes meeting as often as once a month. The organizations vary in size from a couple of dozen members to more than a thousand.

Canada has eleven provincial and local archival organizations:

- Archives Association of British Columbia
- Archives Association of Ontario
- Archives Council of Prince Edward Island
- Canadian Council of Archives/Conseil canadien des archives
- Archives Society of Alberta
- Association des Archivistes du Québec, Inc.
- Association of Manitoba Archives
- Association of Newfoundland and Labrador Archives (ANLA)
- Council of Nova Scotia Archives
- Réseau des Archives du Québec
- The Saskatchewan Council of Archives[9]

The United States has an even larger number of regional, state, and local organizations. According to a directory published by SAA, there are forty-three local organizations:

- Arizona Paper and Photograph Conservation Group (100 members)
- Association of Hawaii Archivists (52 members)
- Association of St. Louis Area Archivists (30 members)
- Austin Archivists Associated
- Bay Area Archivists
- Capital Area Archivists of New York (90 members)
- Charleston Archives, Libraries and Museums Council (CALM) (44 members)
- Chicago Area Archivists (100 members)
- Chicago Area Business Archivists
- Cleveland Archival Roundtable (75 members)
- Conference of Inter-Mountain Archivists (CIMA) (125 members)
- Connecticut River Archives Group (150 members)
- Delaware Valley Archivists Group (145 members)
- Greater New Orleans Archivists (55 members)

- Kansas City Area Archivists (110 members)
- Kentucky Council on Archives (100 members)
- Lake Ontario Archives Conference
- Library Council of Metropolitan Milwaukee Archives Committee (36 members)
- Louisiana Archives and Manuscripts Association
- Maine Archives & Museums
- Miami Valley Archives Roundtable
- Michigan Archival Association (243 members)
- Mid-Atlantic Regional Archives Conference (MARAC) (1,172 members)
- Midwest Archives Conference (MAC) (1,100 members)
- New England Archivists (NEA) (653 members)
- New England Archivists of Religious Institutions (NEARI) (110 members)
- New Hampshire Archives Group (82 members)
- New York Archivists Round Table (NY-ART) (350 members)
- Northwest Archivists, Inc.
- Pametto Archives, Libraries and Museum Council on Preservation (PALMCOP) (70 members)
- Saint Louis Area Religious Archivists (50 members)
- Seattle Area Archivists (50 members)
- Society of Alabama Archivists (68 members)
- Society of California Archivists (400 members)
- Society of Florida Archivists (120 members)
- Society of Georgia Archivists
- Society of Indiana Archivists (100 members)
- Society of North Carolina Archives (163 members)
- Society of Ohio Archivists (150 members)
- Society of Rocky Mountain Archivists (180 members)
- Society of Southwest Archivists (400 members)
- Society of Tennessee Archivists (210 members)
- Twin Cities Archives Roundtable (TCART) (150 members)[10]

It is important to note that local and regional archival organizations are completely independent. They are neither "chapters" of SAA nor affiliated with SAA in any official capacity. This differs from some other professions, where local organizations are subsidiaries of the national organizations. Archivists have never embraced this kind of hierarchy.

These local and regional archival organizations are especially receptive to new archivists. Countless professionals will tell you that they first became involved through a local archival organization—it is here that they first experienced the "professional cohesion" identified by Flexner.

"The Declaration of Independence, written two centuries ago, can be read by a child. The Dead Sea Scrolls are a bit tougher, but scholars can still decode words written on parchment two millennia ago. But if you were to dig up a computer disk formatted on a PC just two decades ago, you'd be hard-pressed to read it. Even if the magnetically coded information is undisturbed, the 5-inch floppy won't fit in today's disk drive, your CD-ROM won't read it and any computer that could is probably in a museum."

—*Sacramento Bee*, December 26. 1998.

Local organizations tend to have more open committee structures than national organizations. If someone is willing to work, almost every local archival organization will have work just waiting to be done. In particular, the more frequent meetings mean that program and local arrangement committees always are looking for new members.

Local organizations also are the venue where most archivists give their first professional presentations. While some new archivists burst directly onto the national scene, most begin speaking at smaller local meetings. Once the archivist feels more confident, he or she can approach the national organizations to speak at their meetings.

Finally, local organizations are among the principal providers of continuing archival education, especially at the basic level. Workshops and seminars at local archival organizations also tend to be more affordable than those at the national level, especially when one factors in the lower travel costs for staying local.

As valuable as are the workshops and seminars offered by local and national organizations, many new archivists find that the complexity of their responsibilities requires a more integrated educational experience in a university graduate program. Such formal archival education has expanded and developed over the last fifty years.

ARCHIVAL EDUCATION

Once the National Archives was established in 1934, systematic and standardized training for archivists was seriously discussed for the first time. When the Society of American Archivists formed in 1936, one of its first committees dealt with education and training. This committee issued a report in 1938 that recommended historical training for archivists.[11]

The library science tradition also began early. In 1936, Margaret Cross Norton, the Director of the Illinois State Library, proposed the establishment of a two-year Master of Library Science in Archives degree program. The first year would be a traditional library science program and the second year would be devoted to archival methods. This program, however, never went beyond the proposal stage.[12]

"Long before politicians were routinely suspected of committing crimes while in office, a future president was indicted in Madison County for assault and battery.

"A grand jury sitting in Edwardsville in 1814 indicted Zachary Taylor, who was elected the 12th president 34 years later, on charges he assaulted a Frenchman, Simon Bartrane, a recently discovered document revealed."

—*The Telegraph*, July 22, 2002.

The first course in archival administration was taught at Columbia University in 1938–39 but was only offered once. Beginning in 1939, American University partnered with the National Archives in offering coursework that combined theory with practice. This program was designed primarily for employees of the National Archives and lasted for many years.

It was not until 1977 that SAA issued its first guidelines for archival education. These guidelines were advisory and differed from *standards* that other professions have established as the basis for accreditation of educational programs. The 1977 guidelines recommended what became know as the "three-course sequence": an introductory course, a special topics course, and an internship. SAA revised its guidelines in 1988 and 1994, each time trying to define more clearly what archivists needed to know and how best to offer that education.

In January 2002, the SAA Council approved revised "Guidelines for a Graduate Program in Archival Studies." These guidelines establish minimum standards for archival education programs in terms of mission, curriculum, faculty, and infrastructure. The guidelines serve as a benchmark against which graduate programs in archival studies may be measured.[13]

Among the main points in the guidelines are:

- The curriculum should be composed of both "core archival knowledge" and "interdisciplinary knowledge."
- Core archival knowledge should comprise at least eighteen credits that cover: knowledge of archival functions (appraisal, arrangement, etc.); knowledge of the profession (historical development, ethics, etc.); and contextual knowledge (social and cultural systems, legal and financial systems, records and information management, and digital records and access systems).
- Interdisciplinary knowledge is drawn from the following fields: information technology; conservation; research design and execution; history and historical methods; management; organizational theory; liberal arts and sciences; and other allied professions.
- A program must have at least one full-time, tenure-track faculty member. Furthermore, the faculty must be sufficient in number and diversity of specialties to carry out the major share of the teaching, research, and service activities required for the archival studies program.
- The graduate program should combine coursework, practical experience, and scholarly research.

These guidelines set a high standard for graduate archival education programs. Nevertheless, they should be considered a living document that undoubtedly will evolve as the profession grows and changes.[14]

CERTIFICATION

As noted above, archivists have not been able to define and enforce professional standards in the same way as lawyers and doctors. Almost from the very beginning of the archival profession in the United States, there has been a desire to address this in the three ways used by other professions:

1. *Accreditation of educational programs.* Librarians, among others, have standards for professional

education programs and accredit institutions that meet those standards.

2. *Accreditation of institutions.* Museum professionals accredit individual institutions that meet agreed-upon standards. The museums must continue to meet the standards to retain accreditation.

3. *Certification of individual professionals.* Some professions take the approach of certifying individual practitioners who demonstrate sufficient knowledge, skills, and attitudes. For example, doctors with specialized knowledge are able to be "board certified" in such specializations as cardiology and dermatology.

The 1980s was a period of great professional development for archivists. Graduate education blossomed after the 1977 publication of the Society of American Archivists' first graduate education guidelines. Archival research was advanced by a multi-year grant-funded program at the Bentley Historical Library of the University of Michigan that gave practitioners a summer away from their jobs. SAA's publications program also expanded in breadth and depth as the profession faced new challenges.

"The U.S. Justice Department today announced the indictment of embattled accounting firm Arthur Andersen on one count of obstruction of justice relating to the collapse of former energy giant Enron Corp.... 'The firm sought to undermine our justice system by destroying evidence,' said Deputy Attorney General Larry Thompson at an afternoon news conference, adding: 'At the time, Andersen knew full well that these documents were relevant.'"

—ABCNews.com, March 14, 2002.

In this heady atmosphere, archivists hoped to move forward on all three professional fronts. They hoped to keep the "stool" in balance by keeping all three "legs" level. Such balance, however, soon proved impossible. Accreditation of educational institutions stalled on such substantive issues as cost of the process and acceptance of another accrediting agency by already-overburdened colleges and universities. Accreditation of individual institutions advanced to the point of developing voluntary self-study criteria as a precursor to a hoped-for (but never realized) full-scale accreditation program.

This left certification of individual archivists as a goal that could be achieved in a reasonable period of time—a first step with the other two steps to follow. The step was not unanimously hailed, however; the profession was divided about the desirability and advisability of certifying archivists.[15]

To move matters forward, SAA established an Interim Board for Certification (IBC) that set criteria and administered a "certification by petition" process. During the first year only, archivists with sufficient education and experience were grandparented into the new Academy of Certified Archivists (ACA), which was formed in 1989. Since then, the designation of Certified Archivist can only be awarded upon passing an examination. At present, the examination is a 100 question multiple-choice exam, developed with the assistance of a professional testing company.[16]

"A set of historic maps, usually relegated to archival drawers, will soon be available for study virtually anywhere. A collection of 18 maps from the estate of Robert Tobin is being converted to digital images on an Internet site for the Alamo's library."

—*San Antonio Express-News*, June 4, 2002.

One of the most important professional contributions of IBC and ACA was the development of a "role delineation" for archivists, which is included in its entirety as Appendix C. The role delineation describes seven "domains" or areas of archival practice:

1. selection
2. arrangement and description
3. reference services and access
4. preservation and protection
5. outreach, advocacy, and promotion
6. managing archival programs
7. professional, ethical, and legal responsibilities

Within each domain are a series of tasks with related knowledge statements. In ACA's words, "Together, these elements encompass commonly accepted duties and responsibilities that professional archivists perform in the course of their work."[17]

The role delineation also serves as the test specifications for the Certified Archivist's examination. Each question must be related to a specific domain, task, and knowledge statement. In addition, every question in the test item bank has a citation to the archival literature to support the correct answer.

Membership in the Academy of Certified Archivists has grown steadily since 1989. There is a growing appreciation of having an objective measure of archival knowledge, skills, and attitudes. Eventually archivists may add the other two legs of the stool, but for now the certification of individual archivists remains the only professional standard for archival practice.

PROFESSIONAL ETHICS

As noted above, professionals recognize that the actions they take have implications for society at large. Therefore, professions eventually reach a point in their development where they address these societal implications by issuing a code of ethical practice. The archival profession is no different.

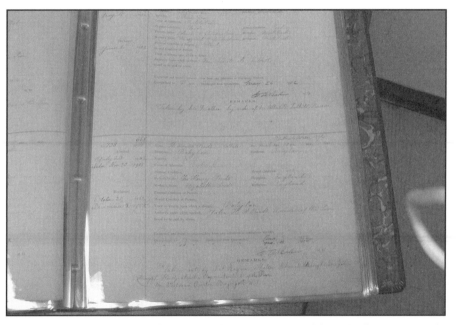

Photograph 13.1 Archives often deal with sensitive or confidential information, such as this ledger from the Suffolk County Orphan's Home. Photograph courtesy of the Office of the County Clerk, Suffolk County (N.Y.).

In 1992, the Society of American Archivists published a new "Code of Ethics for Archivists," which is reprinted in Appendix B. According to this document, "Codes of ethics in all professions have several purposes in common, including a statement of concern with the most serious problems of professional conduct, the resolution of problems arising from conflicts of interest, and the guarantee that the special expertise of the members of a profession will be used in the public interest."

SAA thought that the archival profession needed a code of ethics for three reasons:

1. to inform new members of the profession of the high standards of conduct in the most sensitive areas of archival work

2. to remind experienced archivists of their responsibilities, challenging them to maintain high standards of conduct in their own work and to promulgate those standards to others

3. to educate people who have some contact with archives, such as donors of material, dealers, researchers, and administrators, about the work of archivists and to encourage them to expect high standards

I believe the best way to look at the code of ethics is to relate it directly to the archival functions and responsibilities discussed throughout this book. While I previously covered some of these points in other chapters, it is convenient to put them all together in one place. This also can serve as a summary of some of the main points presented in the book.

With regard to *appraisal and acquisitions*, an ethical archivist

- does not compete for records when such competition would endanger the records
- does not denigrate a competing repository
- only acquires records if they can be processed within a reasonable period of time
- does not give monetary appraisal of collections for donors
- tries to avoid unreasonable restrictions on records
- faithfully observes all agreements made at the time of transfer or acquisition
- does not personally collect the same materials collected by the repository

With regard to *arrangement and description,* an ethical archivist

- processes records in accordance with standard archival principles and practices
- processes records as rapidly as resources permit

With regard to *preservation and security,* an ethical archivist

- protects the integrity of records or papers in his or her custody
- guards the collections against defacement, alteration, theft, and physical damage
- ensures that the evidentiary value of the records is not impaired in the archival work of preservation, arrangement, and use

With regard to *reference and access,* an ethical archivist

- neither reveals nor profits from information gained through work with restricted holdings
- respects the privacy of the individuals who created the records or who are the subject of the records
- courteously answers all reasonable inquiries
- encourages the greatest use of the records consistent with the institutional policies, preservation of holdings, legal considerations, individual rights, and donor agreements
- applies restrictions equitably and uniformly
- tries to inform researchers of parallel research by others, while still respecting the privacy of researchers
- conducts research into his or her collections only with the prior approval of the employing institution

This may seem to be a great deal to expect of archivists. Indeed, this is precisely the point. The archival mission—the identification, preservation, and use of records and papers of historical value—brings with it a responsibility to the past, present, and future. Accepting such responsibility is the hallmark of a professional.

CONCLUSION

One of the most elegant reflections on the nature of the archival profession came at the 1990 annual meeting of the Society of American Archivists. In his presidential address, John A. Fleckner of the Smithsonian Institution's National Museum of American History read a series of letters that he wrote to a student intern named Mary Jane.

These letters reflected on the nature of the profession and what it means to be an archivist.

Fleckner ended his address with the following paragraphs:

Mary Jane, I would like to tell you much more about my profession: about the sense of shared commitment to the archival mission; about the spirit of generosity and collegiality; about the lifelong friendships. I would tell you, too, about the Society of American Archivists, which embodies so much of the profession and through which we have accomplished so much on its behalf. And, lastly, I would tell you of my hopes for the profession: that we will overcome centrifugal forces and embrace all who care for the historical record in all its forms; that we will articulate the public interest in preservation of the record; and that we will increase public understanding and support for our essential mission.

I would like to tell you all this, but perhaps better, I invite you to

---

"Hoping to uncover what the LDS Church knew about a high priest convicted of sexually abusing an 11-year-old boy, a Multnomah County judge ordered the church to release internal records of sex-abuse complaints and discipline actions."

—Portland, Oregon *Daily Herald*, February 10, 2001.

---

join me in this profession, to share in our commitments, and to discover for yourself the larger (and smaller) meanings in what we do. If this is your calling, I assure you lifelong challenges, a sense of community through participation, good friends, and more than a few god times. Let me know; I expect to follow this path for a good while longer. I hope you will come and walk with us.[18]

Yes, archival work is challenging, but it is very rewarding. My hope is that this book will help provide the foundation for a successful career as a professional archivist.

NOTES

1. Richard J. Cox, "Professionalism and Archivists in the United States," *American Archivist* 49 (summer 1986): 231.

2. Cox, "Professionalism," 230.

3. Ibid.

4. Cox, "Professionalism," 232-33. Cox also discusses a second model, the "professionalism process model." Developed in the 1960s, this model examines an occupation's ability to gain authority from soci-

ety over a period of time. The level of an occupation's professionalism is determined by the degree of autonomy society grants it.

5. See http://www.archivists.org.

6. See http://archivists.ca.

7. See http://www.certifiedarchivists.org.

8. For the complete list, see http://www.archivists.org/assoc-orgs/directory/directory_us.asp.

9. For more information, see http://www.archivists.org/assoc-orgs/directory/directory_canada.asp.

10. See http://www.archivists.org/assoc-orgs/directory/directory_us.asp.

11. Jacqueline Goggin, "That We Shall Truly Deserve the Title of 'Profession:' The Training and Education of Archivists, 1930-1960," *American Archivist* 47, no. 3 (summer 1984): 245-47.

12. Goggin, "That We Shall Truly Deserve," 248.

13. "Guidelines for a Graduate Program in Archival Studies," http://www.archivists.org/prof-education/ed_guidelines.asp. For a discussion of the first Master of Archival Studies program in North America, see Terry Eastwood, "The Origins and Aims of the Master of Archival Studies Programme at the University of British Columbia," *Archivaria* 16 (summer 1983): 35-52.

14. For more on graduate archival education, see Fredric M. Miller, "The SAA as Sisyphus: Education Since the 1960s," *American Archivist* 63, no. 2 (fall/winter 2000): 224-36; Luciana Duranti, "The Society of American Archivists and Graduate Archival Education: A Sneak Preview of Future Directions," *American Archivist* 63, no. 2 (fall/winter 2000): 237-42; Terry Eastwood, "Archival Research: The University of British Columbia Experience," *American Archivist* 63, no. 2 (fall/winter 2000): 243-57; Anne J. Gilliland-Swetland, "Archival Research: A 'New' Issue for Graduate Education," *American Archivist* 63, no. 2 (fall/winter 2000): 258-70; Peter J. Wosh, "Research and Reality Checks: Change and Continuity in NYU's Archival Management Program," *American Archivist* 63, no. 2 (fall/winter 2000): 271-83; David A. Wallace, "Survey of Archives and Records Management Graduate Students at Ten Universities in the United States and Canada," *American Archivist* 63, no. 2 (fall/winter 2000): 284-300; Elizabeth Yakel, "The Future of the Past: A Survey of Graduates of Master's-Level Archival Education Programs in the United States," *American Archivist* 63, no. 2 (fall/winter 2000): 301-21; Angelika Menne-Haritz, "Archival Training in a Changing World," *American Archivist* 63, no. 2 (fall/winter 2000): 341-52; Richard J. Cox, "The Society of American Archivists and Graduate Education: Meeting at the Crossroads," *American Archivist* 63, no. 2 (fall/winter 2000): 368-79; Terry Cook, "'The Imperative of Challenging Absolutes' in Graduate Archival Education Programs: Issues for Educators and the

Profession," *American Archivist* 63, no. 2 (fall/winter 2000): 380-91.

15. Actually, the first proposal to certify individual archivists was made by Dolores C. Renze in 1953. See Goggin, "That We Shall Truly Deserve," 251. For a discussion of certification of archivists in Australia in the 1960s, see M.F.F. Lukis, "Archives in Australia: 1966-1965: Retrospect and Prospect," *Archives and Manuscripts* 3, no. 1 (November 1965): 6-7.

16. See Gregory S Hunter, "Ten Years After: Reflections of the Academy's First Year," http://www.certifiedarchivists.org/html/newsltr/declook.html. See also, "History of the Academy of Certified Archivists," http://www.certifiedarchivists.org/html/history.html.

17. The role delineation was recently revised by the Academy of Certified Archivists.

18. John A. Fleckner, " 'Dear Mary Jane:' Some Reflections on Being an Archivist," *American Archivist* 54 (winter 1991): 8-13.

APPENDIX A
NORTH FORK UNIVERSITY: INSTITUTIONAL BACKGROUND

INTRODUCTION

North Fork University (NFU) is a private institution founded in 1892. It is located on the rural North Fork of Long Island, approximately fifteen miles west of the Orient Point lighthouse. It is the only institution of higher education on the entire North Fork.

THE AREA

The North Fork of Long Island is known for its tranquil country environment and New England-like lifestyle. Once an area dominated by large farms growing potatoes and other vegetables, it is now on the verge of potentially major changes. In place of the potato farms is an increasing number of world-class vineyards, drawn by the similarity of the North Fork's climate to that of the wine-growing regions of France. In recent years, another traditional industry, fishing, has been hurt by the pollution of local waterways.

While much of the North Fork remains undeveloped, there is increasing pressure to speed the pace of change. On one side of the debate are developers and their allies, who see great opportunities for profit in the broad expanses of the North Fork. On the other side are environmentalists and long-term residents who fear that the North Fork will become as crowded as the South Fork, sacrificing its distinctive lifestyle and culture in the process.

In spite of, or perhaps because of, these challenges, the North Fork retains a strong sense of history. A friendly rivalry exists between Southold (on the North Fork) and Southampton (on the South Fork) over which town was settled earlier (ca. 1640). The North Fork has several small local historical societies, but no one institution preserves the overall history of the area. A strong community of genealogists also lives on the North Fork.

THE INSTITUTION

North Fork University is located on two hundred acres bordering the Long Island Sound. It is a resident campus with an enrollment of over three thousand full- and part-time students.

In addition to undergraduate programs, NFU offers masters degrees in public administration, social work, journalism, and environmental studies. Most of the North Fork's leaders in these four disciplines are graduates of NFU. In addition, NFU's graduates hold positions of national and international importance, especially in the area of environmental studies.

NFU is known for its involvement with the local community. Faculty and administrators have provided expertise and support to local groups concerned with environmental issues. The School of Social Work runs a nationally renowned program of assistance to migrant workers who toil on the farms and vineyards of the island. This program also is known for the active participation of both graduate and undergraduate students.

As one might expect from its waterfront location, the university's two major intercollegiate sports are crew and sailing. These programs attract student athletes from across the nation.

ARCHIVES AND MANUSCRIPTS AT NFU

North Fork University has a Department of Archives and Special Collections located within the library. The archives was founded two years ago, largely through the initiative of then newly appointed president, Dr. Mary Swanson. Dr. Swanson was born and raised on the North Fork, studied at Harvard and Cambridge, and had a distinguished career as a political scientist at the University of North Carolina before returning to Long Island.

The archives is located on the second floor of the library. In addition to areas for work and research, the archives has shelving that can accommodate approximately 500 cubic feet of records. Half of the shelving is now full.

As a recently established department, the archives has a considerable backlog of materials waiting to be processed. The shelves contain both archival records (materials generated or received by the parent institution in the normal course of business) and special collections (records generated by other institutions, or papers generated by individuals and families with or without connections to NFU).

The Department of Archives and Special Collections has been receiving favorable publicity, on campus and off. Both the student newspaper and alumni quarterly have carried articles about the archives. In addition, *Newsday*, the local newspaper, featured the archives on the cover of its "Features" section, and the local cable television channel had an extensive report on "News 12 Long Island." Much of this interest was generated by the anniversary celebrations held by Southold and Southampton to commemorate their 1640 foundings.

As a result of all this publicity, the archives has been inundated with offers to donate materials. On-campus offices, as well as alumni from across the country, have contacted the archives about donating NFU records. The campus has never had a records management program, so there is a considerable volume of inactive records taking up valuable space in the various offices. Many campus officials, eyeing the empty shelves in the archives, see this as a solution to their space problems. The alumni, in turn, care deeply about NFU and its history. Some have been holding materials, particularly records of the student organizations in which they were involved, since they left the university—until two years ago, the university itself never seemed committed to its history. Several former faculty members also have inquired about donating their papers to the archives.

The local community seems to have been energized by the formation of the archives. A wide variety of organizations and institutions (fraternal, business, social welfare, environmental) have said that they now see NFU as the logical place to donate their records. The same is true of several prominent individuals who live on the North Fork.

While most of the community is supporting NFU's efforts in archives and special collections, the university has heard some grumbling from the local historical societies and their supporters. Understandably, they feel left out of the process to date and fear NFU's competition for local history collections.

The Department of Archives and Special Collections has two full-time professional archivists, one clerical assistant, and the possibility for student assistants during the academic year. With its reasonable though modest budget for supplies and equipment, the department has adequate resources to do archiving, such as utilizing personal computers for preparing archival finding aids.

You recently have been appointed University Archivist and department head, replacing the person who initially established the archives. Your predecessor was just hired as archivist at Temple University and has relocated to Philadelphia.

In addition to the factors summarized above, you note that the department does not have a mission statement or collecting policy. In your experience, this is a common occurrence: new archivists are often so busy dealing with day-to-day concerns that they do not step back to set overall goals for the program. You resolve to correct this problem as soon as possible.

You also determine that your immediate focus will have to be on the area of appraisal. You will have to assess the value of the various materials being offered to the department from both internal and external sources. Also, you want to look carefully at the materials already on the shelves: you suspect that "extra" shelf space over the past two years may have led to the acquisition of some materials of questionable value.

Moreover, you decide that you will try to mend fences with the local historical societies. You hope to convince them that cooperation, not competition, will mark your tenure at NFU. Your underlying assumption is that no single institution, even one like NFU, can document all aspects of local life and culture.

Once you have determined what you will and will not gather, you will have to turn your attention to other aspects of the archival program. How long will it take to process your existing holdings? How will you balance processing time against the increasing volume of reference requests? What are the preservation needs of the collection and how will you meet these needs within the university's tight budget? How will you deal with the emerging problem of electronic records and their long-term preservation and use?

You have just returned from a meeting with President Swanson and the University Librarian (your boss). At this meeting, you presented your preliminary findings and short-term priorities, receiving a generally favorable response. You leave the president's office on a positive note and return to your department to begin work in earnest. It is time to put the archival theory you have learned into practice.

APPENDIX B
CODE OF ETHICS FOR ARCHIVISTS

Archivists select, preserve, and make available documentary materials of long-term value that have lasting value to the organization or public served by the archivist. Archivists perform their responsibilities in accordance with statutory authorization or institutional policy. They subscribe to a code of ethics based on sound archival principles and promote institutional and professional observance of these ethical and archival standards.

Archivists arrange transfers of records and acquire documentary materials of long-term value in accordance with their institutions' purposes, stated policies, and resources. They do not compete for acquisitions when competition would endanger the integrity or safety of documentary materials of long-term value, or solicit the records of an institution that has an established archives. They cooperate to ensure the preservation of materials in repositories where they will be adequately processed and effectively utilized.

Archivists negotiating with transferring officials or owners of documentary materials of long-term value seek fair decisions based on full consideration of the following: authority to transfer, donate, or sell; financial arrangements and benefits; copyright; plans for processing; and conditions of access. Archivists discourage unreasonable restrictions on access or use, but may accept as a condition of acquisition clearly stated restrictions of limited duration and may occasionally suggest such restrictions to protect privacy. Archivists observe faithfully all agreements made at the time of transfer or acquisition.

Archivists establish intellectual control over their holdings by describing them in finding aids and guides to facilitate internal controls and access by users of the archives.

Archivists appraise documentary materials of long-term value with impartial judgment based on thorough knowledge of their institutions' administrative requirements or acquisitions policies. They maintain and protect the arrangement of documents and information transferred to their custody to protect its authenticity. Archivists protect the integrity of documentary materials of long-term value in their custody, guarding

Reprinted with permission from the Society of American Archivists (www.archivists.org)

them against defacement, alteration, theft, and physical damage, and ensure that their evidentiary value is not impaired in the archival work of arrangement, description, preservation, and use. In cases of theft, archivists cooperate with other archivists and law enforcement agencies in the apprehension and prosecution of thieves.

Archivists respect the privacy of individuals who created, or are the subjects of, documentary materials of long-term value, especially those who had no voice in the disposition of the materials. They neither reveal nor profit from information gained through work with restricted holdings.

Archivists answer courteously and with a spirit of helpfulness all reasonable inquiries about their holdings, and encourage use of them to the greatest extent compatible with institutional policies, preservation of holdings, legal considerations, individual rights, donor agreements, and judicious use of archival resources. They explain pertinent restrictions to potential users, and apply them equitably.

Archivists endeavor to inform users of parallel research by others using the same materials, and, if the individuals concerned agree, supply each name to the other party.

As members of a community of scholars, archivists may engage in research, publication, and review of the writings of other scholars. If archivists use their institutions' holdings for personal research and publication, such practices should be approved by their employers and made known to others using the same holdings. Archivists who buy and sell manuscripts personally should not compete for acquisitions with their own repositories, should inform their employers of their collecting activities, and should preserve complete records of personal acquisitions and sales.

Archivists avoid irresponsible criticism of other archivists or institutions and address complaints about professional or ethical conduct to the individual or institution concerned, or to a professional archival organization.

Archivists share knowledge and experience with other archivists through professional associations and cooperative activities and assist the professional growth of others with less training or experience. They are obligated by professional ethics to remain informed about standards of good practice and to follow the highest level possible in the administration of their institutions and collections. They have a professional responsibility to recognize the need for cooperative efforts and support the development and dissemination of professional standards and practices.

Archivists work for the best interests of their institutions and their profession and endeavor to reconcile any conflicts of interest by encouraging adherence to archival standards and ethics.

CODE OF ETHICS FOR ARCHIVISTS AND COMMENTARY

The code is a summary of guidelines in the principal areas of professional conduct. A longer Commentary explains the reasons for some of the statements and provides a basis for discussion of the points raised. The Code of Ethics is in italic bold face; the Commentary is in modern type.

I. THE PURPOSE OF THE CODE OF ETHICS

The Society of American Archivists recognizes that ethical decisions are made by individuals, professionals, institutions, and societies. Some of the greatest ethical problems in modern life arise from conflicts between personal codes based on moral teachings, professional practices, regulations based on employment status, institutional policies, and state and federal laws. In adopting a formal code of professional ethics for the Society, we are dealing with only one aspect of the archivist's ethical involvement.

Codes of ethics in all professions have several purposes in common, including a statement of concern with the most serious problems of professional conduct, the resolution of problems arising from conflicts of interest, and the guarantee that the special expertise of the members of a profession will be used in the public interest.

The archival profession needs a code of ethics for several reasons: (1) to inform new members of the profession of the high standards of conduct in the most sensitive areas of archival work; (2) to remind experienced archivists of their responsibilities, challenging them to maintain high standards of conduct in their own work and to promulgate those standards to others; and (3) to educate people who have some contact with archives, such as donors of material, dealers, researchers, and administrators, about the work of archivists and to encourage them to expect high standards.

A code of ethics implies moral and legal responsibilities. It presumes that archivists obey the laws and are especially familiar with the laws that affect their special areas of knowledge; it also presumes that they act in accord with accepted moral principles. In addition to the moral and legal responsibilities of archivists, there are special professional concerns, and it is the purpose of a code of ethics to state those concerns and give some guidelines for archivists. The code identifies areas where there are or may be conflicts of interest, and indicates ways in which these conflicting interests may be balanced; the code urges the highest standards of professional conduct and excellence of work in every area of archives administration.

This code is compiled for archivists, individually and collectively. Institutional policies should assist archivists in their efforts to conduct themselves according to this code; indeed, institutions, with the assistance of their archivists, should deliberately adopt policies that comply with the principles of the code.

II. INTRODUCTION TO THE CODE

Archivists select, preserve, and make available documentary materials of long-term value that have lasting value to the organization or public served by the archivist. Archivists perform their responsibilities in accordance with statutory authorization or institutional policy. They subscribe to a code of ethics based on sound archival principles and promote institutional and professional observance of these ethical and archival standards.

Commentary: The introduction states the principal functions of archivists. Because the code speaks to people in a variety of fields—archivists, curators of manuscripts, records managers—the reader should be aware that not every statement in the code will pertain to every worker. Because the code intends to inform and protect non-archivists, an explanation of the basic role of archivists is necessary. The term "documentary materials of long-term value" is intended to cover archival records and papers without regard to the physical format in which they are recorded.

III. COLLECTING POLICIES

Archivists arrange transfers of records and acquire documentary materials of long-term value in accordance with their institutions' purposes, stated policies, and resources. They do not compete for acquisitions when competition would endanger the integrity or safety of documentary materials of long-term value, or solicit the records of an institution that has an established archives. They cooperate to ensure the preservation of materials in repositories where they will be adequately processed and effectively utilized.

Commentary: Among archivists generally there seems to be agreement that one of the most difficult areas is that of policies of collection and the resultant practices. Transfers and acquisitions should be made in accordance with a written policy statement, supported by adequate resources and consistent with the mission of the archives. Because personal papers document the whole career of a person, archivists encourage donors to deposit the entire body of materials in a single archival institution. This section of the code calls for cooperation rather than wasteful competition, as an important element in the solution of this kind of problem.

Institutions are independent and there always will be room for legitimate competition. However, if a donor offers materials that are not within the scope of the collecting policies of an institution, the archivist should tell the donor of a more appropriate institution. When two or more institutions are competing for materials that are appropriate for any one of their collections, the archivists must not unjustly disparage the facilities or intentions of others. As stated later, legitimate complaints about an institution or an archivist may be made through proper channels, but giving false information to potential donors or in any way casting aspersions on other institutions or other archivists is unprofessional conduct.

It is sometimes hard to determine whether competition is wasteful. Because owners are free to offer collections to several institutions, there will be duplication of effort. This kind of competition is unavoidable. Archivists cannot always avoid the increased labor and expense of such transactions.

IV. RELATIONS WITH DONORS, AND RESTRICTIONS

Archivists negotiating with transferring officials or owners of documentary materials of long-term value seek fair decisions based on full consideration of the following: authority to transfer, donate, or sell; financial arrangements and benefits; copyright; plans for processing; and conditions of access. Archivists discourage unreasonable restrictions on access or use, but may accept as a condition of acquisition clearly stated restrictions of limited duration and may occasionally suggest such restrictions to protect privacy. Archivists observe faithfully all agreements made at the time of transfer or acquisition.

Commentary: Many potential donors are not familiar with archival practices and do not have even a general knowledge of copyright, provision of access, tax laws, and other factors that affect the donation and use of archival materials. Archivists have the responsibility for being informed on these matters and passing all pertinent and helpful information to potential donors. Archivists usually discourage donors from imposing conditions on gifts or restricting access to collections, but they are aware of sensitive material and do, when necessary, recommend that donors make provision for protecting the privacy and other rights of the donors themselves, their families, their correspondents, and associates.

In accordance with regulations of the Internal Revenue Service and the guidelines accepted by the Association of College and Research Libraries, archivists should not appraise, for tax purposes, donations to their own institutions.

Some archivists are qualified appraisers and may appraise records given to other institutions.

It is especially important that archivists be aware of the provisions of the copyright act and that they inform potential donors of any provision pertinent to the anticipated gift.

Archivists should be aware of problems of ownership and should not accept gifts without being certain that the donors have the right to make the transfer of ownership.

Archivists realize that there are many projects, especially for editing and publication, which seem to require reservation for exclusive use. Archivists should discourage this practice. When it is not possible to avoid it entirely, archivists should try to limit such restrictions; there should be a definite expiration date, and other users should be given access to the materials as they are prepared for publication. This can be done without encouraging other publication projects that might not conform to the standards for historical editing.

V. DESCRIPTION

Archivists establish intellectual control over their holdings by describing them in finding aids and guides to facilitate internal controls and access by users of the archives.

Commentary: Description is a primary responsibility and the appropriate level of intellectual control should be established over all archival holdings. A general descriptive inventory should be prepared when the records are accessioned. Detailed processing can be time-consuming and should be completed according to a priority based on the significance of the material, user demand and the availability of staff time. It is not sufficient for archivists to hold and preserve materials; they also facilitate the use of their collections and make them known. Finding aids, repository guides, and reports in the appropriate publications permit and encourage users in the institution and outside researchers.

VI. APPRAISAL, PROTECTION AND ARRANGEMENT

Archivists appraise documentary materials of long-term value with impartial judgment based on thorough knowledge of their institu-

tions' administrative requirements or acquisitions policies. They maintain and protect the arrangement of documents and information transferred to their custody to protect its authenticity. Archivists protect the integrity of documentary materials of long-term value in their custody, guarding them against defacement, alteration, theft, and physical damage, and ensure that their evidentiary value is not impaired in the archival work of arrangement, description, preservation, and use. In cases of theft, archivists cooperate with other archivists and law enforcement agencies in the apprehension and prosecution of thieves.

Commentary: Archivists obtain material for use and must ensure that their collections are carefully preserved and therefore available. They are concerned not only with the physical preservation of materials but even more with the retention of the information in the collections. Excessive delay in processing materials and making them available for use would cast doubt on the wisdom of the decision of a certain institution to acquire materials, though it sometimes happens that materials are acquired with the expectation that there soon will be resources for processing them.

Some archival institutions are required by law to accept materials even when they do not have the resources to process those materials or store them properly. In such cases, archivists must exercise their judgment as to the best use of scarce resources, while seeking changes in acquisitions policies or increases in support that will enable them to perform their professional duties according to accepted standards.

VII. PRIVACY AND RESTRICTED INFORMATION

Archivists respect the privacy of individuals who created, or are the subjects of, documentary materials of long-term value, especially those who had no voice in the disposition of the materials. They neither reveal nor profit from information gained through work with restricted holdings.

Commentary: In the ordinary course of work, archivists encounter sensitive materials and have access to restricted information. In accordance with their institutions' policies, they should not reveal this restricted information, they should not give any researchers special access to it, and they should not use specifically restricted information in their own research. Subject to applicable laws and regulations, they weigh the need for openness and the need to respect privacy rights to determine whether the release of records or information from records would constitute an invasion of privacy.

VIII. USE AND RESTRICTIONS

Archivists answer courteously and with a spirit of helpfulness all reasonable inquiries about their holdings, and encourage use of them to the greatest extent compatible with institutional policies, preservation of holdings, legal considerations, individual rights, donor agreements, and judicious use of archival resources. They explain pertinent restrictions to potential users, and apply them equitably.

Commentary: Archival materials should be made available for use (whether administrative or research) as soon as possible. To facilitate such use, archivists should discourage the imposition of restrictions by donors.

Once conditions of use have been established, archivists should see that all researchers are informed of the materials that are available, and are treated fairly. If some materials are reserved temporarily for use in a special project, other researchers should be informed of these special conditions.

IX. INFORMATION ABOUT RESEARCHERS

Archivists endeavor to inform users of parallel research by others using the same materials, and, if the individuals concerned agree, supply each name to the other party.

Commentary: Archivists make materials available for research because they want the information on their holdings to be known as much as possible. Information about parallel research interests may enable researchers to conduct their investigations more effectively. Such information should consist of the previous researcher's name and address and general research topic and be provided in accordance with institutional policy and applicable laws. Where there is any question, the consent of the previous researcher should be obtained. Archivists do not reveal the details of one researcher's work to others or prevent a researcher from using the same materials that others have used. Archivists are especially sensitive to the needs of confidential research; such as research in support of litigation, and in such cases do not approach the user regarding parallel research.

X. RESEARCH BY ARCHIVISTS

As members of a community of scholars, archivists may engage in research, publication, and review of the writings of other scholars. If archivists use their institutions' holdings for personal research and publication, such practices should be approved by their employers and made known to others using the same holdings. Archivists who buy and sell manuscripts personally should not compete for acquisitions with their own repositories, should inform their employers of their collecting activities, and should preserve complete records of personal acquisitions and sales.

Commentary: If archivists do research in their own institutions, they introduce the potential for serious conflicts of interest—an archivist might be reluctant to show to other researchers material from which he or she hopes to write something for publication. On the other hand, the archivist might be the person best qualified to research an area represented in institutional holdings. The best way to resolve these conflicts is to clarify and publicize the role of the archivist as researcher.

At the time of their employment, or before undertaking research, archivists should have a clear understanding with their supervisors about the right to research and to publish. The fact that archivists are doing research in their institutional archives should be made known to patrons, and archivists should not reserve materials for their own use. Because it increases their familiarity with their own collections, this kind of research should make it possible for archivists to be more helpful to other researchers. Archivists are not obliged, any more than other researchers are, to reveal the details of their work or the fruits of their research. The agreement reached with an employer should include in each instance a statement as to whether the archivists may or may not receive payment for research done as part of the duties of their positions.

XI. COMPLAINTS ABOUT OTHER INSTITUTIONS

Archivists avoid irresponsible criticism of other archivists or institutions and address complaints about professional or ethical conduct to the individual or institution concerned, or to a professional archival organization.

Commentary: Disparagement of other institutions or of other archivists seems to be a problem, particularly when two or more institutions are seeking the same materials, but it can also occur in other areas of archival work. Distinctions must be made between defects due to lack of funds, and improper handling of materials resulting from unprofessional conduct. In either case, these concerns should be directed to the appropriate parties.

XII. PROFESSIONAL ACTIVITIES

Archivists share knowledge and experience with other archivists through professional associations and cooperative activities and assist the professional growth of others with less training or experience. They are obligated by professional ethics to remain informed about standards of good practice and to follow the highest level possible in the administration of their institutions and collections. They have a professional responsibility to recognize the need for cooperative efforts and support the development and dissemination of professional standards and practices.

Commentary: Archivists may or may not choose to join local, state, regional, and national professional organizations, but they must be well informed about changes in archival functions and practices. Contact with colleagues is an indispensable way to stay current. They should share their expertise by participation in professional meetings and by publishing on topics relevant to archival work. By such activities, in the field of archives, in related fields, and in their own special interests, they continue to grow professionally.

XIII. CONCLUSION

Archivists work for the best interests of their institutions and their profession and endeavor to reconcile any conflicts of interest by encouraging adherence to archival standards and ethics.

Commentary: The code has stated the "best interest" of the archival profession—such as proper use of archives, exchange of information, and careful use of scarce resources. The final statement urges archivists to pursue these goals. When there are apparent conflicts between such goals and either the policies of some institutions or the practices of some archivists, all interested parties should refer to this code of ethics and the judgment of experienced archivists.

APPENDIX C
ACADEMY OF CERTIFIED ARCHIVISTS: ROLE DELINEATION STATEMENT FOR PROFESSIONAL ARCHIVISTS

PREAMBLE

These specifications for the certified archivist examination delineate the major domains of archival practice. Within each domain a series of tasks and related knowledge statements are defined. Together these elements encompass commonly accepted duties and responsibilities that professional archivists perform in the course of their work. This document assumes that individuals seeking certification recognize that (a) their professional practice is performed within the context of an institutional mission and is directed to the achievement of goals consistent with that mission, and (b) their professional practice has an ongoing effect on the emergence and evolution of that overall mission and its associated goals, as well as the development of the archival profession.

In addition, although those seeking certification do not necessarily control how archival policies are set that relate to activities such as acquisition, access, preservation, and security, it is assumed that archivists understand that the elements contained in such policies are important in carrying out in a professional manner the tasks specified below.

Each of the seven major domains is comprised of task statements which outline the duties included within each domain, as well as knowledge statements that describe generally what archivists need to know in order to complete each of the tasks. Preceding the domains is a listing of General Knowledge Statements applicable to several or all of the seven areas.

The ACA Role Delineation uses the definitions and distinctions found in the Society of American Archivists' Guidelines for a Graduate Program in Archival Studies: "Archival records and papers are recorded information, regardless of physical format or type of creator (public or private), that is created or received by an individual or organization carrying out its activities and that is set aside for preservation and future use. Archival records and papers are instrumental for evidence and accountability as well as for social and cultural memory. The phrase 'records and papers' will be used to encompass documentary evidence produced by organizations and individuals in all media (paper, digital, audio, and visual) and in any format."

GENERAL KNOWLEDGE STATEMENTS

Archivists know and can apply knowledge about:

K-1   the impact of social, cultural, economic, political, and technological factors on the evolution and characteristic of records and papers and their management.

K-2   the origins, development, and definitions of archival concepts, terms, principles, practices and methods.

K-3   the development of archival institutions and programs in society.

K-4   the similarities and differences between the nature and administration of organizational records and personal papers.

K-5   the physical and technological characteristics of records and papers and how these characteristics influence their appraisal, acquisition, preservation, and use.

K-6   archival theory, methodology, and practice appropriate for records and papers on all media: paper, digital, audio, and visual.

K-7   the standards and accepted professional best practices that apply to archival work, including their rationale and implications.

K-8   the concepts of the life cycle of records and the records continuum.

K-9   the relationship between accepted professional policies and practices and institutional applications of these policies and practices.

K-10 how the core archival functions (selection, appraisal, and acquisition; arrangement and description; reference services and access; preservation and protection; and outreach, advocacy and promotion) relate to each other and influence the administration of records and papers.

K-11 the different institutional settings in which archival programs may exist and the implications of placement within a particular institution.

K-12 how the administration of archives is related to, different from, and draws upon the theory, methodology, and practice of such allied professions and disciplines as: history, library and information science, records management, museology, historic preservation, historical editing, and oral history.

K-13 how archival theory, methodology, and practice have been influenced and affected by computer technologies and applications such as electronic communication, including e-mail; and online information exchange, including the World Wide Web.

DOMAIN 1: SELECTION, APPRAISAL, AND ACQUISITION

Task 1 Identify sources of archival records and papers by applying knowledge about subjects, individuals, organizations, and others that create, receive, and accumulate records and papers appropriate for acquisition.

Task 2 Establish, maintain, and keep a record of communication(s) with creators and/or potential donors of records and papers.

Task 3 In determining the acquisition of records and papers, identify and evaluate record characteristics.

Task 4 Appraise records and papers for their long term retention.

Task 5 Implement disposition recommendations or decisions through legal instruments of transfer such as schedules, deed of gift, purchase contracts, and deposit agreements.

Task 6 Promote cooperative acquisition and disposition strategies when appropriate.

Knowledge Statements

Archivists know and can apply knowledge about:

K-101   how the mission and holdings of archival repositories relate to selection, appraisal and acquisition.

K-102   techniques for locating and surveying potential acquisitions.

K-103   the evolution, nature, and variety of recordkeeping systems and practice.

K-104   the history of record-creating and record-accumulating sources.

K-105   factors that should be considered when defining collecting or accessioning areas and developing an acquisition policy.

K-106   solicitation and negotiating techniques, including ways of educating document creators about the importance of preserving records and papers.

K-107   laws, policies, regulations, procedures, legal instruments, and ethical standards relating to acquisitions.

K-108   the values of records such as evidential, informational, administrative, legal, fiscal, and intrinsic.

K-109   the past, current, and potential uses of records and papers.

K-110   inventorying, scheduling, appraisal, and disposition techniques.

K-111   selection, sampling, weeding, and other techniques to reduce volume.

K-112   methods of deaccessioning and other techniques of internal disposal.K-113   impact of technology on traditional methods of inventorying, scheduling, appraisal, and disposition.

K-114   selection and appraisal methodologies, including documentation strategy and functional analysis, on all media: paper, digital, audio.

K-115   the characteristics of records and papers such as trustworthiness, authenticity, reliability, usability, and comprehensiveness, as well as form, uniqueness, and quantity.

DOMAIN 2: ARRANGEMENT AND DESCRIPTION

Task 1   Analyze the existing arrangement and description of records and papers and make decisions about any further arrangement and description that may be necessary.

Task 2   Design and implement an arrangement plan to either perfect the existing arrangement or establish a new one.

Task 3   Design and implement a descriptive plan to identify and explain the structure, context and content of records and papers to promote their accessibility.

Knowledge Statements

Archivists know and can apply knowledge about:

K-201   the complementary principles of provenance and original order.

K-202   the history and variety of recordkeeping systems and practices for all media.K-203   the role of access and retrieval in making arrangement and description decisions.

K-204   the concept of hierarchical levels of arrangement.

K-205   the distinctions and relationships between physical and intellectual control of records and papers.

K-206   the impact of technology on policies, practices, and methods for archival arrangement and description.

K-207   the levels, types, and components of finding aids within an overall description program.

K-208   the applicability of such standards as the MARC format, Encoded Archival Description (EAD), Anglo-American Cataloging Rules (AACR2), and Library of Congress Subject Headings (LCHS), SGML, XML, HTML/XHTML, and Dublin Core.

K-209   the use of descriptive standards for records and papers stored in any form or medium.

K-210   how the descriptive process may begin at or before records creation and continue throughout the life of the records and papers.

DOMAIN 3: REFERENCE SERVICES AND ACCESS

Task 1   Define the informational needs of users by such techniques as customer surveys, analysis of user requests, and keeping abreast of current research trends and strategies.

Task 2   Develop policies and procedures designed to serve the information needs of various user groups, based on evaluation of institutional mandates and constituencies, the nature of the collections, relevant laws and ethical considerations, and appropriate technologies.

Task 3   Make an appropriate response to user requests by: providing information about records and papers, providing information from records and papers, providing access to records and papers, making copies, referring to other sources, or denying the requests for information.

Task 4   Create, maintain, and periodically review, for self-evaluation and planning purposes, records of user requests.

Knowledge Statements

Archivists know and can apply knowledge about:

K-301   issues and elements of archives user services, including policies and procedures governing access, reference services, and reproduction.

K-302   laws, regulations, and ethical principles governing copyright, freedom of information, privacy, confidentiality, security, and equality of access.

K-303   research strategies, needs, and past and current research interests and trends of genealogists, scholars, journalists, and other major users of records and papers.

K-304   reference strategies based on varying holdings, formats, media, and user needs.

K-305   the subject areas of an institution's holdings, and how they relate to holdings in other repositories.

K-306   accepted best practices for safeguarding records and papers while in use and accommodating researcher-owned technical equipment in research rooms.

K-307 techniques for expediting the handling of repeated requests on the same or similar topics through such tools as reference files, reference reports, frequently asked question pages on web sites, or surrogates of actual documents.

DOMAIN 4: PRESERVATION AND PROTECTION

Task 1 Analyze the current physical condition of records and papers, and determine appropriate preservation priorities and actions.

Task 2 Make and implement decisions about reformatting (e.g., digitization or microfilming), handling techniques, data migration, data conversion, appropriate laboratory treatments, phased conservation, and referral to technical experts.

Task 3 Ensure the correct long-term storage of records and papers by such techniques as using proper containers and encasements, using acceptable shelving, and maintaining acceptable environmental controls.

Task 4 Ensure the security of records and papers in all media and formats from damage, destruction, theft, and other forms of loss.

Task 5 Prepare and implement procedures for disaster prevention, response, and recovery.

Knowledge Statements
Archivists know and can apply knowledge about:

K-401 research on the nature of materials' treatment and current preservation techniques.

K-402 the causes and consequences of the deterioration of various media and formats.

K-403 the elements of preservation management and preservation planning, including environmental monitoring, disaster planning, inhouse conservation, reformatting, data migration, data conversion, and services available through outside vendors.

K-404 the elements of security management and risk assessment.

K-405 when to preserve records and papers in their original format or structure, and when to replace originals with reproductions in the same and/or different media or format.

K-406 the range of preservation options and the application of each to records and papers on different media.

DOMAIN 5: OUTREACH, ADVOCACY, AND PROMOTION

Task 1 Promote the use of records and papers by identifying potential users and uses, by analyzing and describing the benefits of use, and through public and educational programs.

Task 2 Develop an understanding of, and support for, the archival program among resource allocators, key constituents, potential donors, allied professionals, and within related functional areas (IT, library, etc.) of the archives' parent organization.

Task 3 Participate in programs that draw directly on records and papers to support such activities as exhibitions, conferences, publications, and editorial projects.

Task 4 Participate in efforts to publicize archival collections and repositories through print, electronic, and broadcast media.

Knowledge Statements
Archivists know and can apply knowledge about:

K-501 the variety of uses of records and papers, the benefits of such uses, and methods of imparting this information to potential users.

K-502 the range of approaches that might be taken to advance public understanding of archival work and programs, such as news releases, websites, exhibitions, press kits, and curriculum packages.

K-503 methods of presenting archival records and papers, or information from or about them, in a user-friendly manner that reduces the need for on-site visitation to the repository.

K-504 methods of articulating to resource allocators the benefits of establishing and supporting the continued operation of an archival program in an organization.

K-505   methods of collaborating with functional units within the archives' parent organization to enhance or further archival work.

DOMAIN 6: MANAGING ARCHIVAL PROGRAMS

Task 1   Participate in the development of a strategic vision for an archival program, establish priorities, continually assess progress toward that vision, and make adjustments as environments and resources change.

Task 2   Assess staffing needs, recruit appropriate personnel, and train staff; support professional development; and ensure that the staff works together to fulfill the archives' mission.

Task 3   Plan, gain approval of, and administer a budget; assess financial performance; and monitor progress.

Task 4   Identify facility and equipment needs and prepare and implement plans to meet those needs.

Task 5   Create policies, standards, and procedures that facilitate the range of activities in archival programs.

Task 6   Use appropriate technologies to manage an archival program.

Knowledge Statements

Archivists know and can apply knowledge about:

K-601   planning models and assessment tools and their role in an archival program.

K-602   institutional structures, cultures, and values; and the role of archival programs within these institutions and structures.

K-603   basic principles and procedures in human resource management appropriate for an archival program.

K-604   current archival education standards for graduate and continuing education as well as other professional development options and certification programs.

K-605   basic financial planning techniques appropriate for an archival program.

K-606   legal requirements that affect the management of archival programs.

K-607   space and resource management techniques.

K-608   the application and impact of evolving technologies and information systems on the overall archival program.

K-609   methodologies for gathering and evaluating data about archival functions within one's own program and programs at other institutions.

K-610   sources of professional and technical advice and assistance, internal and external funding agencies, and other forms of potential program assistance.

DOMAIN 7: PROFESSIONAL, ETHICAL, AND LEGAL RESPONSIBILITIES

Task 1   Keep abreast of current issues in the field of archival history, theory, and practice through such activities as reading professional literature, attending conferences, and participating in continuing education programs.

Task 2   Contribute to the development of the archival profession through such means as conducting research, making public presentations, and participating in professional organizations.

Task 3   Respect all statutory and regulatory requirements relating to records and papers.

Task 4   Conform to professional standards.

Knowledge Statements
Archivists know and can apply knowledge about:

K-701 the variety of international, national, regional, and local organizations whose activities include archival concerns.

K-702   research and literature relating to archival history, theory, methodology, and practice.

K-703   the influence of social, cultural, economic, and legal systems upon the responsibilities of archivists.

K-704   laws, regulations, and ethical considerations governing loans, deposits, exchanges, and gifts to institutions, including tax consequences.

K-705   laws, regulations, and ethical considerations governing reference services and access to records and papers, including copyright, freedom of information, privacy, confidentiality, security, and equality of access.

K-706   the uses of records and papers as legal evidence in courts, and the standards applied for legal admissibility.

K-707   laws and regulations defining public records and governing their retention, accessibility, integrity, and disposition.

K-708   laws, regulations, and ethical considerations governing personal papers.

K-709   archival and information professional codes and standards, such as the Code of Ethics of the Society of American Archivists and the SAA/ALA joint statement on Standards for Access to Research Materials in Archival and Manuscript Repositories.

Revised 2003

BIBLIOGRAPHY

GENERAL

Adam, Dawne. "The Tuol Sleng Archives and the Cambodian Genocide." *Archivaria* 45 (spring 1998): 5–26.

Adkins, Elizabeth W. "The Development of Business Archives in the United States: An Overview and a Personal Perspective." *American Archivist* 60, no. 1 (winter 1997): 8–33.

Alegbeleye, G.B.O. "Archives Administration and Records Management in Nigeria: Up the Decades from Amalgamation." *ARMA Records Management Quarterly* 22 (July 1988): 26–31.

Allen, Marie. "Crossing Boundaries: Intergovernmental Records Cooperation, 1987–1997." *American Archivist* 60, no. 2 (spring 1997): 216–33.

Alonso, P.A.G. "Archival Map Preservation and Documentation." *Archives and Manuscripts* 5, no. 1 (November 1972): 8–13.

Alsberg, Paul. "The Israel State Archives." *Archivaria* 7 (winter 1978): 70–75.

Andrews, Patricia A. and Bettye J. Grier, comps. *Writings on Archives, Historical Manuscripts, and Current Records, 1979–82.* Washington, D.C.: National Archives and Records Service, 1985.

Andrews, Patricia A., comp. "Writings on Archives, Historical Manuscripts, and Current Records: 1983." *American Archivist* 49 (summer 1986): 277–303.

Archival Forms Manual. Chicago: Society of American Archivists, 1981.

Archives Journals: A Study of Their Coverage by Primary and Secondary Sources. Paris: UNESCO, 1981.

Arena, Franca. "Ethnic Archives." *Archives and Manuscripts* 8, no. 1 (June 1980): 22–26.

Atchison, J.F. "Archives of a Joint-Stock Company: The Australian Agricultural Company: Its System of Administration and Its Records, 1824–1970." *Archives and Manuscripts* 4, no. 3 (November 1970): 21–32.

Atherton, Jay. "From Life Cycle to Continuum: Some Thoughts on the Records Management-Archives Relationship." *Archivaria* 21 (winter 1985–86): 43–51.

Averill, Harold. "The Church, Gays, and Archives." *Archivaria* 30 (summer 1990): 85–90.

Ayres, Marie-Louise. "Evaluating the Archives: 20th Century Australian Literature." *Archives and Manuscripts* 29, no. 2 (November 2001): 32–47.

Baker, Kathryn Hammond. "The Business of Government and the Future of Government Archives." *American Archivist* 60, no. 2 (spring 1997): 234–53.

Banks, Brenda S. "Seeing the Past as a Guidebook to Our Future." *American Archivist* 59, no. 4 (fall 1996): 392–99.

Barata, Kimberly J. "Managing Intellectual Assets: The Identification, Capture, Maintenance, and Use of the Records of Federally Sponsored Scientific Research." *Archival Issues* 21, no. 2 (1996): 129–44.

Barbiche, Bernard. "Diplomatics of Modern Official Documents (Sixteenth-Eighteenth Centuries): Evolution and Perspectives." *American Archivist* 59, no. 4 (fall 1996): 422–37.

Barnickel, Linda. "Spoils of War: The Fate of European Records During World War II." *Archival Issues* 24, no. 1 (1999): 7–20.

Barr, Debra. "Religious Archives: Lifting Up Our Eyes." *Archivaria* 30 (summer 1990): 39–41.

Barritt, Marjorie Rabe. "Coming to America: Dutch *Archivistiek* and American Archival Practice." *Archival Issues* 18, no. 1 (1993): 43–54.

Barritt, Marjorie Rabe, and Nancy Bartlett, eds. "European Archives in an Era of Change." Special issue of *American Archivist* 55 (winter 1992): 4–223.

Bastian, Jeannette Allis. "A Question of Custody: The Colonial Archives of the United States Virgin Islands." *American Archivist* 64, no. 1 (spring/summer 2001): 96–14.

———. "Taking Custody, Giving Access: A Postcustodial Role for a New Century." *Archivaria* 53 (spring 2002): 76–93.

Baumann, Roland M., ed. *A Manual of Archival Techniques,* rev. ed. Harrisburg, Pa.: Pennsylvania Historical and Museum Commission, 1982.

Beghtol, Clare. "In Interesting Times: From the Twentieth Century to the Twenty-first." *American Archivist* 64, no. 1 (spring/summer 2001): 143–58.

Bell, Chauncey. "Re-membering the Future: Organizational Change, Technology, and the Role of the Archivist." *Archival Issues* 25, nos. 1–2 (2000): 11–33.

Bellardo, Lewis J. and Lynn Lady Bellardo. *A Glossary for Archivists, Manuscript Curators, and Records Managers.* Chicago: Society of American Archivists, 1992.

Belton, Tom. "By Whose Warrant? Analyzing Documentary Form and Procedure." *Archivaria* 41 (spring 1996): 206–20.

Benedict, Karen M., ed. *A Select Bibliography on Business Archives and Records Management.* Chicago: Society of American Archivists, 1981.

———. "Business Archives Reporting Structures: Is There an Ideal Placement?" *Archives and Manuscripts* 27, no. 2 (November 1999): 26–39.

Berner, Richard C. "Archival Management and Librarianship: An Exploration of Prospects for their Integration." *Advances in Librarianship* 14 (1986): 253–83.

Blouin, Francis X., Jr. "Archivists, Mediation, and Constructs of Social Memory." *Archival Issues* 24, no. 2 (1999): 101–12.

Boberach, Heinz. "Archives in the Federal Republic of Germany." *Archivaria* 7 (winter 1978): 62–69.

Boccaccio, Mary, ed. *Constitutional Issues and Archives.* New York: Mid-Atlantic Regional Archives Conference, 1988.

Bolotenko, George. "Archivists and Historians: Keepers of the Well." *Archivaria* 16 (summer 1983): 5–25.

Booms, Hans. "*Uberlieferungsbildung:* Keeping Archives as a Social and Political Activity." *Archivaria* 33 (winter 1991–92): 25–33.

Bordin, Ruth B. and Robert M. Warner. *The Modern Manuscript Library.* New York: Scarecrow Press, 1966.

Bradsher, James Gregory. "A Brief History of the Growth of Federal Government Records, Archives, and Information, 1789–1985." *Government Publications Review* 13 (July/August 1986): 491–505.

Brazier, Jan. "The Archivist: Scholar or Administrator?" *Archives and Manuscripts* 16, no. 1 (May 1988): 9–14.

Brichford, Maynard J. "Academic Archives: *Uberlieferungsbildung.*" *American Archivist* 43 (fall 1980): 449–60.

———. "Seven Sinful Thoughts." *American Archivist* 43 (winter 1980): 13–16.

Bridges, Edwin C. "Can State Archives Meet the Challenges of the Eighties? Four Recent Views on the Condition of American State Archives." *ARMA Records Management Quarterly* 20 (April 1986): 15, 21, 52.

Bridges, Edwin C., et al. "Historians and Archivists: A Rationale for Cooperation." *Journal of American History* 80 (June 1993): 179–86.

Brooks, Philip C. *Research in Archives: The Use of Unpublished Primary Sources.* Chicago: University of Chicago Press, 1969.

Brothman, Brien. "Declining Derrida: Integrity, Tensegrity, and the Preservation of Archives from Deconstruction." *Archivaria* 48 (fall 1999): 64–88.

———. "The Past that Archives Keep: Memory, History, and the Preservation of Archival Records." *Archivaria* 51 (spring 2001): 48–80.

———. "Some Themes in American Historical Writing During the 1990s." *American Archivist* 64, no. 1 (spring/summer 2001): 159–88.

Brown, Richard. "The Death of a Renaissance Record-Keeper: The Murder of Tomasso da Tortona in Ferrara, 1385." *Archivaria* 44 (fall 1997): 1–43.

Brown, William E., Jr., and Elizabeth Yakel. "Redefining the Role of College and University Archives in the Information Age." *American Archivist* 59, no. 3 (summer 1996): 272–87.

Bucknall, Brian. "The Archivist, the Lawyer, the Clients and Their Files." *Archivaria* 33 (winter 1991–92): 181–87.

Burckel, Nicholas C. and J. Frank Cook. "A Profile of College and University Archives in the United States." *American Archivist* 45 (fall 1982): 410–28.

Burke, Frank G. "The Future Course of Archival Theory in the United States." *American Archivist* 44 (winter 1981): 40–46.

———. "Letting Sleeping Dogmas Lie." *American Archivist* 55 (fall 1992): 530–37.

———. "The Beginnings of the NHPRC Records Program." *American Archivist* 63, no. 1 (spring/summer 2000): 18–42.

———. *Research and the Manuscript Tradition.* Lanham, Md.: Scarecrow Press and Chicago: Society of American Archivists, 1997.

Burke, J.L., and C.M. Shergold. "What are Archives?" *Archives and Manuscripts* 6, no. 6 (February 1976): 235–40.

Butlin, S.J. "Australian Bank Archives and Research." *Archives and Manuscripts* 4, no. 8 (August 1972): 1–6.

Cadin, Martine. "Archives in 3D." *Archivaria* 51 (spring 2001): 112–36.

Cameron, Richard A. "The Concept of a National Records Program and Its Continued Relevance for a New Century." *American Archivist* 63, no. 1 (spring/summer 2000): 43–66.

Chamberlain, David R. "The Description of Cartographic Archives Using the *Anglo-American Cataloging Rules,* Second Edition." *Archivaria* 13 (winter 1981–82): 41–46.

Child, Margaret S. "Reflections on Cooperation Among Professions." *American Archivist* 46 (summer 1983): 286–92.

Clanchy, M.T. "'Tenacious Letters': Archives and Memory in the Middle Ages." *Archivaria* 11 (winter 1980–81): 115–26.

Clow, Barbara. "Essiac: The Secret Life of a Document." *Archivaria* 41 (spring 1996): 221–33.

Cole, Arthur H. "Business Manuscripts: Collection, Handling, and Cataloging." *Library Quarterly* 8 (January 1938): 93–114.

College and University Archives: Selected Readings. Chicago: Society of American Archivists, 1979.

College and University Guidelines. Chicago: Society of American Archivists, 1979.

Colvin, H.M. "Architectural History and its Records." *Archives: Journal of the British Records Association* 2, no. 14 (1955): 300–11.

Conway, Paul. "Perspectives on Archival Resources: The 1985 Census of Archival Institutions." *American Archivist* 50 (spring 1987): 174–91.

The Concept of Record: Second Stockholm Conference on Archival Science and the Concept of Record, 30–31 May 1996. Sweden: Riksarkivet, 1998.

Cook, Michael. *The Management of Information from Archives.* Brookfield, Vt.: Gower, 1986.

———. *Information Management and Archival Data.* London: Library Association Publishing, 1993.

Cook, Terry. "What is Past is Prologue: A History of Archival Ideas Since 1898, and the Future Paradigm Shift." *Archivaria* 43 (spring 1997): 17–63.

———. "Archival Science and Postmodernism: New Formulations for Old Concepts." *Archival Science* 1, no. 1 (2001): 3–24.

———. "The Tyranny of the Medium: A Comment on 'Total Archives.'" *Archivaria* 9 (winter 1979–80): 141–50.

———. "From Information to Knowledge: An Intellectual Paradigm for Archives." *Archivaria* 19 (winter 1984–85): 28–49.

———. "Fashionable Nonsense or Professional Rebirth: Postmodernism and the Practice of Archives." *Archivaria* 51 (spring 2001): 14–35.

Cox, Richard J. "American Archival History: Its Development, Needs, and Opportunities." *American Archivist* 46 (winter 1983): 31–41.

———. *An Annotated Bibliography of Basic Readings on Archives and Manuscripts.* Technical Leaflet No. 130. Nashville, Tenn.: American Association for State and Local History, 1980.

———. "Archivists and Public Historians in the United States." *Public Historian* 8 (summer 1986): 29–45.

———. *Managing Institutional Archives: Foundational Principles and Practices.* New York: Greenwood Press, 1992.

———. "On the Value of Archival History in the United States." *Libraries and Culture* 23 (spring 1988): 135–51.

———. *Managing Records as Evidence and Information.* Westport, Conn.: Quorum Books, 2001.

———. *American Archival Analysis: The Recent Development of the Archival Profession in the United States.* Metuchen, N.J.: Scarecrow Press, 1990.

———. *Closing an Era: Historical Perspectives on Modern Archives and Records Management.* Westport, Conn.: Greenwood Press, 2000.

———, comp. *Archives and Manuscript Administration: A Basic Annotated Bibliography.* Nashville, Tenn.: American Association for State and Local History, 1990.

Craig, Barbara L. "Hospital Records and Record-keeping, c. 1850–c. 1950: Part I: The Development of Records in Hospitals." *Archivaria* 29 (winter 1989–90): 57–87.

———. "Hospital Records and Record-keeping, c. 1850–c. 1950: Part II: The Development of Record-Keeping in Hospitals." *Archivaria* 30 (summer 1990): 21–38.

———. "Batson's Trust for the Royal London Hospital: Records Management 1820s Style." *Archivaria* 41 (spring 1996): 188–205.

———. "Medical Archives: Answers...and Questions." *Archivaria* 43 (spring 1997): 174–79.

Craig, Barbara L., and James M. O'Toole. "Looking at Archives in Art." *American Archivist* 63, no. 1 (spring/summer 2000): 97–125.

Crew, Spencer R. and John A. Fleckner. "Archival Sources for Business History at the National Museum of American History." *Business History Review* 60 (autumn 1986): 474–86.

Crush, Peter. "Archives and Historians." *Archives and Manuscripts* 16, no. 1 (May 1988): 15–24.

Daniels, Maygene. "Computer-Aided Design and Drafting Systems and the Records of Architecture." *Janus* 1 (1992): 31–33.

———. "On Being an Archivist." *American Archivist* 59, no. 1 (winter 1996): 6–13.

Daniels, Maygene F., and Timothy Walch, eds. *A Modern Archives Reader: Basic Readings on Archival Theory and Practice.* Washington: National Archives and Records Service, 1984.

Dearstyne, Bruce W. *The Archival Enterprise: Modern Archival Principles, Practices, and Management Techniques.* Chicago: American Library Association, 1993.

———. *Managing Historical Records Programs: A Guide for Historical Agencies.* Walnut Creek, Calif.: AltaMira Press, 2000.

Deiss, William A. *Museum Archives: An Introduction.* Chicago: Society of American Archivists, 1983.

Dellheim, Charles. "Business in Time: The Historian and Corporate Culture." *Public Historian* 8 (spring 1986): 9–22.

Delmas, Bruno. "Archival Science Facing the Information Society." *Archival Science* 1, no. 1 (2001): 25–37.

———. "Manifesto for a Contemporary Diplomatics: From Institutional Documents to Organic Information. *American Archivist* 59, no. 4 (fall 1996): 438–53.

———. "What is the Status of Archival Science in France Today?" In *The Concept of Record: Second Stockholm Conference on Archival Science and the Concept of Record, 30–31 May 1996.* Sweden: Riksarkivet, 1998, 27–36.

DeLottinville, Peter. "Life in the Age of Restraint: Recent Developments in Labour Archives in English Canada." *Archivaria* 27 (winter 1988–89): 8–24.

Densmore, Christopher. "Understanding and Using Early Nineteenth Century Account Books." *Midwestern Archivist* 5, no. 1 (1980): 5–19.

Derrida, Jacques. *Archive Fever: A Freudian Impression.* Chicago: University of Chicago Press, 1995.

Dicken, Judy. "Twentieth-Century Literary Archives: Collecting Policies and Research Initiatives," In *New Directions in Archival Research*, edited by Margaret Procter and C.P. Lewis, 49–82. Liverpool: Liverpool University Centre for Archive Studies, 2000.

"Documenting Twentieth Century Architecture: Problems and Issues." *American Archivist* 59, no. 2 (spring 1996). Special issue.

Dodds, Gordon. "Canadian Archival Literature: A Bird's-Eye View." *Archivaria* 17 (winter 1983–84): 18–40.

Dodge, Bernadine. "Places Apart: Archives in Dissolving Space and Time." *Archivaria* 44 (fall 1997): 118–31.

———. "Across the Great Divide: Archival Discourse and the (Re)presentations of the Past in Late-Modern Society." *Archivaria* 53 (spring 2002): 16–30.

Duckett, Kenneth W. *Modern Manuscripts: A Practical Manual for Their Management, Care and Use.* Nashville, Tenn.: American Association for State and Local History, 1975.

Duffy, Mark J. "The Archival Bridge: History, Administration, and the Building of Church Tradition." *Historical Magazine of the Protestant Episcopal Church* 55 (December 1986): 275–87.

Duranti, Luciana. "The Odyssey of Records Managers: Part I." *ARMA Records Management Quarterly* 23 (July 1989): 3–11.

———. "The Odyssey of Records Managers: Part II." *ARMA Records Management Quarterly* 23 (October 1989): 3–11.

———. "Diplomatics: New Uses for an Old Science (Part I)." *Archivaria* 28 (summer, 1989).

———. "Diplomatics: New Uses for an Old Science (Part II)." *Archivaria* 29 (winter 1989–90): 4–17.

———. "Diplomatics: New Uses for an Old Science (Part III)." *Archivaria* 30 (summer, 1990): 4–20.

———. "Diplomatics: New Uses for an Old Science (Part IV)." *Archivaria* 31 (winter 1990–91): 10–25.

———. "Diplomatics: New Uses for an Old Science (Part V)." *Archivaria* 32 (summer 1991): 6–24.

———. "Diplomatics: New Uses for an Old Science (Part VI)." *Archivaria* 33 (winter 1991–92): 6–24.

———. *Diplomatics: New Uses for an Old Science.* Lanham, Md.: Scarecrow Press (in association with the Society of American Archivists and the Association of Canadian Archivists), 1998.

———. "Medieval Universities and Archives." *Archivaria* 38 (fall 1994): 37–44.

———. "Reliability and Authenticity: The Concepts and Their Implications." *Archivaria* 39 (spring 1995): 5–10.

———. "The Impact of Digital Technology on Archival Science." *Archival Science* 1, no. 1 (2001): 39–55.

———. "The Records: Where Archival Universality Resides." *Archival Issues* 19, no. 2 (1994): 83–94.

Eastwood, Terry. "What is Archival Theory and Why is it Important? " *Archivaria* 37 (spring 1994): 122–30.

Edgerly, Linda. "The Present and Future of Corporate Archives: A Golden Age?" *Business and Economic History,* 2d series. 15 (1986): 197–203.

Ehrenberg, Ralph E. "Administration of Cartographic Materials at the Library of Congress and National Archives of the United States." *Archivaria* 13 (winter 1981–82): 23–40.

Ellis, Judith, ed. *Keeping Archives.* 2d ed. Port Melbourne, Australia: D.W. Thorpe, 1993.

———. "Consulting into Business Archives." *Archives and Manuscripts* 27, no. 2 (November 1999): 16–25.

Erlandsson, Alf. "The United Nations Archives." *Archivaria* 7 (winter 1978): 5–15.

Eulenberg, Julia Neibuhr. "The Corporate Archives: Management Tool and Historical Resource." *Public Historian* 6 (winter 1984): 21–37.

Evans, Frank B., et al. *A Basic Glossary for Archivists, Manuscript Curators, and Records Managers.* Chicago: Society of American Archivists, 1974.

———. *Modern Archives and Manuscripts: A Select Bibliography.* Chicago: Society of American Archivists, 1975.

———. "Promoting Archives and Research: A Study in International Cooperation." *American Archivist* 50 (winter 1987): 48–65.

———. *Writings on Archives Published by and with the Assistance of UNESCO: A RAMP Study.* Paris: UNESCO, 1983.

Fischer, G.L. "The Clock of History." *Archives and Manuscripts* 7, no. 5 (November 1979): 240–51.

Fisher, Simon. "The Archival Enterprise, Public Archival Institutions and the Impact of Private Law." *Archives and Manuscripts* 26, no. 2 (November 1998): 328–67.

Fleckner, John A. "Archives and Museums." *Midwestern Archivist* 15 (1990): 67–76.

Fode, Henrik, and Jorgen Fink. "Business Archives in Scandinavia." *Archives and Manuscripts* 27, no. 2 (November 1999): 54–67.

———. "The Business Records of a Nation: The Case of Denmark." *American Archivist* 60, no. 1 (winter 1997): 72–87.

Fogerty. James E. "Archival Brinksmanship: Downsizing, Outsourcing, and the Records of Corporate America." *American Archivist* 60, no. 1 (winter 1997): 44–55.

Foote, Kenneth E. "To Remember and Forget: Archives, Memory, and Culture." *American Archivist* 53 (summer 1990): 378–93.

Fournier, Frances. "'For They Would Gladly Learn and Gladly Teach'—University Faculty and Their Papers: A Challenge for Archivists." *Archivaria* 34 (summer 1992): 58–74.

Fraser, Maryna. "Profile of a South African Company Archive." *Archivaria* 7 (winter 1978): 95–103.

Freckelton, Ian. "Records as Reliable Evidence: Medico-legal Litigation." *Archives and Manuscripts* 26, no. 2 (November 1998): 270–93.

Gaffield, Chad. "Theory and Methodology in Canadian Historical Demography." *Archivaria* 14 (summer 1982): 123–36.

Gartrell, Ellen G. "'Some Things We Have Learned…': Managing Advertising Archives for Business and Non-Business Users." *American Archivist* 60, no. 1 (winter 1997): 56–71.

Gerachty, Isabel. "Telephone Historical Collection." *Archivaria* 7 (winter 1978): 118–24.

Gillis, Peter. "Of Plots, Secrets, Burrowers and Moles: Archives in Espionage Fiction." *Archivaria* 9 (winter 1979–80): 3–14.

Giusti, Martino. "The Vatican Secret Archives." *Archivaria* 7 (winter 1978): 16–27.

Goerler, Raimund E. "Archives in Controversy: The Press, the Documentaries, and the Byrd Archives." *American Archivist* 62, no. 2 (fall 1999): 307–24.

Golder, Hilary. "History and Archives." *Archives and Manuscripts* 27, no. 2 (November 1999): 8–15.

Gracy, David B., II. "Archives and Society: The First Archival Revolution." *American Archivist* 47 (winter 1984): 7–10.

———. *An Introduction to Archives and Manuscripts.* New York: Special Libraries Association, 1981.

Grady, K., D. McRostie, and S. Papadopoulos. "Hunters and Gatherers: From Research Practice to Records Practice." *Archives and Manuscripts* 25, no. 2 (November 1997): 242–65.

Grant, Hugh. "Bookkeeping in the Eighteenth Century: The Grand Journal and Grand Ledger of the Hudson's Bay Company." *Archivaria* 43 (spring 1997): 143—57.

Gray, Carolyn. "Business Structures and Records: The Dominion Power and Transmission Company, 1896–1930." *Archivaria* 19 (winter 1984–85): 152–61.

Gray, Peter R.A. "Saying It Like It Is: Oral Traditions, Legal Systems and Records." *Archives and Manuscripts* 26, no. 2 (November 1998): 248–69.

Green, Edwin. "Multi-National, Multi-Archival: The Business Records of the HSBC Group." *American Archivist* 60, no. 1 (winter 1997): 100–11.

Greene, Mark A. "The Power of Meaning: The Archival Mission in the Postmodern Age." *American Archivist* 65, no. 1 (spring/summer 2002): 42–55.

Grimsted, Patricia Kennedy. "*Glasnost* in the Archives? Recent Developments on the Soviet Archival Scene." *American Archivist* 52 (spring 1989): 214–36.

Grover, Ray. "The National Archives of New Zealand." *Archivaria* 18 (summer 1984): 232–40.

Guidelines for Archives and Manuscript Repositories. New York: Mid-Atlantic Regional Archives Conference, 1983.

Guyotjeanin, Olivier. "The Expansion of Diplomatics as a Discipline." *American Archivist* 59, no. 4 (fall 1996): 414–21.

Hackman, Larry J. "From Assessment to Action: Toward a Usable Past in the Empire State." *Public Historian* 7 (summer 1985): 23–34.

———. "A Perspective on American Archives." *Public Historian* 8 (summer 1986): 10–28.

———. "State Government and Statewide Archival Affairs: New York as a Case Study." *American Archivist* 55 (fall 1992): 578–99.

———. "Toward the Year 2000." *Public Historian* 8 (summer 1986): 92–98.

Hackman, Larry J., et al. "Case Studies in Archives Program Development." *American Archivist* 53 (fall 1990): 548–61.

Hall, Roger. "Minding Our Own Business." *Archivaria* 3 (winter 1976–1977): 73–78.

Ham, F. Gerald. "Archival Choices: Managing the Historical Record in an Age of Abundance." *American Archivist* 47 (winter 1984): 11–22.

———. "The Archival Edge." *American Archivist* 38 (January 1975): 5–13.

———. "Archival Strategies for the Post-Custodial Era." *American Archivist* 44 (summer 1981): 207–16.

Hamer, Philip M. *A Guide to Archives and Manuscripts.* New Haven, Conn.: Yale University Press, 1961.

Hande, D'Arcy, and Erich Schultz. "Struggling to Establish a National Identity: The Evangelical Lutheran Church in Canada and Its Archives." *Archivaria* 30 (summer 1990): 64–70.

Hardenberg, H. "Archives in the Netherlands." *Archives and Manuscripts* 5, no. 3 (May 1973): 51–64.

Harris, Verne. "Redefining Archives in South Africa: Public Archives and Society in Transition, 1990–1996." *Archivaria* 42 (fall 1996): 6–27.

————. "Claiming Less, Delivering More: A Critique of Positivist Formulations on Archives in South Africa." *Archivaria* 44 (fall 1997): 132–41.

————. "The Archival Sliver: Power, Memory, and Archives in South Africa." *Archival Science* 1, no. 2 (2001): 63–86.

————. *Exploring Archives: An Introduction to Archival Ideas and Practice in South Africa.* Pretoria: National Archives of South Africa, 2000.

Haury, David A. "The Research Potential of Religious Archives: The Mennonite Experience." *Midwestern Archivist* 11 (1986): 135–40.

Haworth, Kent M. "Local Archives: Responsibilities and Challenges for Archivists." *Archivaria* 3 (winter 1976–1977): 28–39.

Heald, Carolyn. "Is There Room for Archives in the Postmodern World?" *American Archivist* 59, no. 1 (winter 1996): 88–101.

Heaps, Jennifer Davis. "Tracking Intelligence Information: The Office of Strategic Services." *American Archivist* 61, no. 2 (fall 1998): 287–308.

Hedlin, Edie. *Business Archives: An Introduction.* Chicago: Society of American Archivists, 1978.

————. "*Chinatown* Revisited: The Status and Prospects of Government Records in America." *Public Historian* 8 (summer 1986): 46–59.

Hedstrom, Margaret. "Archives, Memory, and Interfaces with the Past." *Archival Science* 1, no. 2 (2001): 21–43.

————. "Cohesion and Chaos: The State of Archival Science in the United States." *In The Concept of Record: Second Stockholm Conference on Archival Science and the Concept of Record, 30–31 May 1996.* Sweden: Riksarkivet, 1998, 37–56.

Hefner, Loretta L. "Lawrence Berkeley Laboratory Records: Who Should Collect and Maintain Them?" *American Archivist* 59, no. 1 (winter 1996): 62–87.

Henke, Josef. "Revealing the Forged Hitler Diaries." *Archivaria* 19 (winter 1984–85): 21–27.

Hesselager, Lise. "Fringe or Grey Literature in the National Library: On 'Papyrolatry' and the Growing Similarity Between the Materials in Libraries and Archives." *American Archivist* 47 (summer 1984): 255–70.

Hickerson, H. Thomas. "Ten Challenges for the Archival Profession." *American Archivist* 64, no. 1 (spring/summer 2001): 6–16.

Higgs, Edward. "Record and Recordness: Essences or Conventions?" In *The Concept of Record: Second Stockholm Conference on Archival Science and the Concept of Record, 30–31 May 1996.* Sweden: Riksarkivet, 1998, 101–14.

Higham, Robin. "Military Archives and Military History: A Matter of Perspective." *Archivaria* 35 (spring 1993): 270–72.

Hildebrand, Suzanne, ed. *Women's Collections: Libraries, Archives, and Consciousness.* New York: Haworth Press, 1986.

Hine, Janet. "How Librarians Need Archivists." *Archives and Manuscripts* 5, no. 1 (November 1972): 14–17.

Hives, Christopher L. "Business Archives: Historical Developments and Future Prospects." M.A. thesis, University of British Columbia, 1985.

————. "History, Business Records, and Corporate Archives in North America." *Archivaria* 22 (summer 1986): 40–57.

Hodson, J.H. *The Administration of Archives.* Oxford: Pergamon Press, 1972.

Holmes, Oliver Wendell. "The Evaluation and Preservation of Business Archives." *American Archivist* 1 (1938): 171–85.

————. "Some Reflections on Business Archives in the United States." *American Archivist* 17 (October 1954): 291–304.

Hornabrook, Judith. "New Zealand's Archives." *Archivaria* 7 (winter 1978): 82–85.

Howse, Janet. "The Preservation of Local Government Records in New South Wales: Historical and Current Legislative Requirements. Part I." *Archives and Manuscripts* 11, no. 1 (May 1983): 38–46.

————. "The Preservation of Local Government Records in New South Wales: Historical and Current Legislative Requirements. Part II." *Archives and Manuscripts* 11, no. 2 (November 1983): 162–71.

Hoyle, Michael. "Review, Restructure, and Reform: Recordkeeping Standards in the New Zealand State Sector." *Archivaria* 48 (fall 1999): 44–63.

Hunter, Gregory S. "Archival Management: The 1980's and Beyond." *Records and Retrieval Report* 2 (October 1986): 9–12.

————. "Thinking Small to Think Big: Archives, Micrographics and the Life Cycle of Records." *American Archivist* 49 (summer 1986): 315–20.

Hurley, C. "Personal Papers and the Treatment of Archival Principles." *Archives and Manuscripts* 6, no. 8 (February 1977): 351–65.

Iacovino, Livia. "The Nature of the Nexus Between Recordkeeping and the Law." *Archives and Manuscripts* 26, no. 2 (November 1998): 216–47.

————. "Common Ground, Different Traditions: An Australian Perspective on Italian Diplomatics, Archival Science, and Business Records." *Archives and Manuscripts* 29, no. 1 (May 2001): 118–38.

Inkster, Carole M. "Geographically Misplaced Archives and Manuscripts: Problems and Arguments Associated With Their Restitution." *Archives and Manuscripts* 11, no. 2 (November 1983): 113–24.

International Council on Archives, Architectural Records Section. *A Guide to the Archival Care of Architectural Records: 19th-20th Centuries.* Paris: International Council on Archives, 2000.

International Council on Archives, Committee on Business Archives. *Business Archives: Studies on International Practices.* New York: K.G. Saur, 1983.

Iwakura, Norio. "The Archives of Japan." *Archivaria* 7 (winter 1978): 76–81.

Jacobs, Sally J. "How and When We Make the News: Local Newspaper Coverage of Archives in Two Wisconsin Cities." *Archival Issues* 22, no. 1 (1997): 45–60.

Jenkinson, Hilary. *A Manual of Archive Administration.* London: Percy Lund, Humphries and Co., 1965.

Jimerson, Randall C., ed. *American Archival Studies: Readings in Theory and Practice.* Chicago: Society of American Archivists, 2000.

———. "Margaret C. Norton Reconsidered." *Archival Issues* 26, no. 1 (2001): 41–62.

Jones, H.G. *The Records of a Nation: Their Management, Preservation and Use.* New York: Atheneum, 1969.

Jury, Francesca. "Invisible Boundaries: A Paradigm Shift." *Archives and Manuscripts* 27, no. 1 (May 1999): 62–73.

Kane, Lucille. *A Guide to the Care and Administration of Manuscripts.* 2d ed. Nashville, Tenn.: American Association for State and Local History, 1966.

Kantrow, Alan M., ed. "Why History Matters to Managers." *Harvard Business Review* 64 (January-February 1986).

Ketelaar, Eric. *Archival and Records Management Legislation and Regulations: A RAMP Study with Guidelines.* Paris: UNESCO, 1985.

———. "Archival Theory and the Dutch Manual." *Archivaria* 41 (spring 1996): 31–40.

———. "The Difference Best Postponed? Cultures and Comparative Archival Science." *Archivaria* 44 (fall 1997): 142–48.

———. "Archivalisation and Archiving." *Archives and Manuscripts* 27, no. 1 (May 1999): 54–61.

———. "Tacit Narratives: The Meanings of Archives." *Archival Science* 1, no. 2 (2001): 131–41.

———. *The Archival Image: Collected Essays.* Hilversum: Verloren, 1997.

Kidd, Betty. "A Brief History of the National Map Collection in the Public Archives of Canada." *Archivaria* 13 (winter 1981–82): 3–22.

Kinniburgh, Ian A.G. "The Cartography of the Recent Past." *Archivaria* 13 (winter 1981–82): 91–98.

Klippenstein, Lawrence. "Mennonite Archives in Canada." *Archivaria* 31 (winter 1990–91): 36–49.

Knight, James. "Architectural Records and Archives in Canada: Toward a National Programme." *Archivaria* 3 (winter 1976–1977): 62–72.

Kousser, J. Morgan. "Ignoble Intentions and Noble Dreams: On Relativism and History with a Purpose [Litigation Support]." *Public Historian* 15 (summer 1993): 15–28.

Laberge, Danielle. "Information, Knowledge, and Rights: The Preservation of Archives as a Political and Social Issue." *Archivaria* 25 (winter 1987–88): 44–50.

Ladeira, Caroline Durant, and Maryellen Trautman, comps. "Writings on Archives, Historical Manuscripts, and Current Records: 1984." *American Archivist* 49 (fall 1986): 425–54.

Laine, Edward. "Archival Resources Relating to Finnish Canadians." *Archivaria* 7 (winter 1978): 110–17.

Lambert, James. "Public Archives and Religious Records: Marriage Proposals." *Archivaria* 1, no. 1 (winter 1975–76): 48–67.

———. "Toward a Religious Archives Programme for the Public Archives of Canada." *Archivaria* 3 (winter 1976–1977): 40–61.

Lasewicz, Paul C. "Strangers in a Strange Land: Archival Opportunities in a Multinational Corporation." *Archival Issues* 19, no. 2 (1994): 131–42.

———. "Riding Out the Apocalypse: The Obsolescence of Traditional Archivy in the Face of Modern Corporate Dynamics." *Archival Issues* 22, no. 1 (1997): 61–76.

Lemieux, Victoria L. "Let the Ghosts Speak: An Empirical Exploration of the 'Nature' of the Record." *Archivaria* 51 (spring 2001): 81–111.

Littlejohn, M. "Archives and Australian Universities." *Archives and Manuscripts* 4, no. 3 (November 1970): 1–4.

Love, John. "What Are Records?" *Archives and Manuscripts* 14, no. 1 (May 1986): 54–60.

Lowe, Graham S. "'The Enormous File': The Evolution of the Modern Office in Early Twentieth-Century Canada." *Archivaria* 19 (winter 1984–85): 137–51.

Lowell, Howard P. "Elements of a State Archives and Records Management Program." *ARMA Records Management Quarterly* 21 (October 1987): 3–14.

———. "The Quiet Crisis in State Archives." *ARMA Records Management Quarterly* 22 (April 1988): 23–27.

———. "Building a Public Archives in Delaware for the Twenty-First Century." *American Archivist* 60, no. 2 (spring 1997): 152–65.

Lukenbill, W. Bernard. "Historical Resources in the Local Church: A Field Report on a Largely Gay and Lesbian Congregation." *American Archivist* 61, no. 2 (fall 1998): 384–99.

Lukis, M.F.F. "Archives in Australia: 1966–1965: Retrospect and Prospect." *Archives and Manuscripts* 3, no. 1 (November 1965): 3–9.

MacNeil, Heather. "Weaving Provenancial and Documentary Relations." *Archivaria* 34 (summer 1992): 192–98.

———. "Archival Theory and Practice: Between Two Paradigms." *Archivaria* 37 (spring 1994): 6–20.

———. "Trusting Records in a Postmodern World." *Archivaria* 51 (spring 2001): 36–47.

———. *Trusting Records: Legal, Historical and Diplomatic Perspectives.* Boston: Kluwer Academic Publishers, 2000.

Maher, William J. *The Management of College and University Archives*. Chicago: Society of American Archivists and Scarecrow Press, 1992.

———. "Ensuring Continuity and Preservation Through Archival Service Agreements." *Archival Issues* 19, no. 1 (1994): 5–18.

———. "Archives, Archivists, and Society." *American Archivist* 61, no. 2 (fall 1998): 252–65.

Managing Cartographic and Architectural Records. Washington, D.C.: National Archives and Records Administration, 1989.

Mason, Karen M. and Tanya Zanish-Belcher. "A Room of One's Own: Women's Archives in the Year 2000." *Archival Issues* 24, no. 1 (1999): 37–54.

Mayer, Dale C. "The New Social History: Implications for Archivists." *American Archivist* 48 (fall 1985): 388–99.

Maynard, Steven. "'The Burning Wilful Evidence': Lesbian/Gay History and Archival Research." *Archivaria* 33 (winter 1991–92): 195–201.

McCarthy, Paul. "Insights from the Outside: The NHPRC Records Program at Twenty-Five." *American Archivist* 63, no. 1 (spring/summer 2000): 90–96.

McCrank, Lawrence, ed. *Archives and Library Administration: Divergent Traditions and Common Concerns*. New York: Haworth Press, 1986.

McDonald, John. "Managing Records in the Modern Office: Taming the Wild Frontier." *Archivaria* 39 (spring 1995): 70–79.

McDonald, Robert A.J. "Acquiring and Preserving Private Records: Cultural Versus Administrative Perspectives." *Archivaria* 38 (fall 1994): 162–63.

McDowall, Duncan. "'Wonderful Things': History, Business, and Archives Look to the Future." *American Archivist* 56 (spring 1993): 348–57.

McKemmish, Sue. "Yesterday, Today and Tomorrow: A Continuum of Responsibility." *Proceedings of the Records Management Association of Australia, 14th National Convention, 15–17 September 1977*. Perth: Records Management Association of Australia, 1997. http://www.sims.monash.edu.au/research/rcrg/publications/recordscontinuum/smckp2.html.

McIntosh, Robert. "The Great War, Archives, and Modern Memory." *Archivaria* 46 (fall 1998): 1–31.

McPherson, Kathryn. "Nurses, Archives, and the History of Canadian Health Care." *Archivaria* 41 (spring 1996): 108–20.

McRanor, Shauna. "Maintaining the Reliability of Aboriginal Oral Records and Their Material Manifestations: Implications for Archival Practice." *Archivaria* 43 (spring 1997): 64–88.

Menne-Haritz, Angelika. "What Can Be Achieved with Archives?" In *The Concept of Record: Second Stockholm Conference on Archival Science and the Concept of Record, 30–31 May 1996*. Sweden: Riksarkivet, 1998, 11–26.

Menninger, W. Walter. "Memory and History: What Can You Believe?" *Archival Issues* 21, no. 2 (1996): 97–106.

Merz, Nancy M. "Archives and the One World of Records." *Inform* 2 (April 1988): 30–36.

Mifflin, Jeffrey. "'Clothing Facts in Words': Archivists and the Holocaust." *American Archivist* 61, no. 2 (fall 1998): 453–74.

Millar, Laura. "Discharging Our Debt: The Evolution of the Total Archives Concept in English Canada." *Archivaria* 46 (fall 1998): 103–46.

———. "The Spirit of Total Archives: Seeking a Sustainable Archival System." *Archivaria* 47 (spring 1999): 46–65.

Mitchell, Thornton W., ed. *Norton on Archives: The Writings of Margaret Cross Norton*. Chicago: Society of American Archivists, 1975.

Montgomery, Bruce P. "Archiving Human Rights: The Records of Amnesty International USA." *Archivaria* 39 (spring 1995): 108–31.

———. "The Iraqi Secret Police Files: A Documentary Record of the Anfal Genocide." *Archivaria* 52 (fall 2001): 69–99.

Morrison, James. "Archives and Native Claims." *Archivaria* 9 (winter 1979–80): 15–32.

Mortensen, Preben. "The Place of Theory in Archival Practice." *Archivaria* 47 (spring 1999): 1–26.

Moss, William W. "Tibetan Archives: A Report From China." *American Archivist* 59, no. 3 (summer 1996): 350–55.

Muller, Samuel, John A. Feith, and Robert Fruin. *Manual for the Arrangement and Description of Archives*. 2d ed. New York: H. W. Wilson, 1940.

Nelson, Michael. "Records in the Modern Workplace: Management Concerns." *Archivaria* 39 (spring 1995): 80–87.

Nesmith, Tom. "Still Fuzzy, But More Accurate: Some Thoughts on the 'Ghosts' of Archival Theory." *Archivaria* 47 (spring 1999): 136–50.

———. "Archives From the Bottom Up: Social History and Archival Scholarship." *Archivaria* 14 (summer 1982): 5–26.

———. "Seeing Archives: Postmodernism and the Changing Intellectual Place of Archives." *American Archivist* 65, no. 1 (spring/summer 2002): 24–41.

———, ed. *Canadian Archival Studies and the Rediscovery of Provenance*. Metuchen, N.J.: Scarecrow Press, in association with the Society of American Archivists and the Association of Canadian Archivists, 1993.

O'Brien, Jerome. "Archives and the Law: A Brief Look at the Canadian Scene." *Archivaria* 18 (summer 1984): 38–46.

Ogawa, Chiyoko. "Archives in Japan: The State of the Art." *American Archivist* 54 (fall 1991): 546–55.

Ormsby, William G. "The Public Archives of Canada, 1948–1968." *Archivaria* 15 (winter 1982–83): 36–46.

O'Toole, James M. "Commendatory Letters: An Archival Reading of the Venerable Bede." *American Archivist* 612 (fall 1998), 266–86.

———. "Cortes's Notary: The Symbolic Power of Records." *Archival Science* 1:2 (2001), 45–61.

———. "Democracy and Documents in America." *American Archivist* 65, no. 1 (spring/summer 2002): 107–15.

———. "Herodotus and the Written Record." *Archivaria* 33 (Winter 1991-92), 148-160.

———. "On the Idea of Uniqueness." *American Archivist* 57 (fall 1994): 632–59.

———. "The Symbolic Significance of Archives." *American Archivist* 56 (1993): 234–55.

———. *Understanding Archives and Manuscripts.* Chicago: Society of American Archivists, 1992.

O'Toole, James M., ed. *The Records of American Business.* Chicago: Society of American Archivists, 1997.

Pacifico, Michelle F. "Founding Mothers: Women in the Society of American Archivists, 1936–72." *American Archivist* 50 (summer 1987): 370–89.

Page, Don. "Whose Handmaiden?: The Archivist and the Institutional Historian." *Archivaria* 17 (winter 1983–84): 162–72.

Panitch, Judith M. "Liberty, Equality, Posterity? Some Archival Lessons from the Case of the French Revolution." *American Archivist* 59, no. 1 (winter 1996): 30–47.

Parezo, Nancy J. "Preserving Anthropology's Heritage: CoPAR, Anthropological Records, and the Archival Community." *American Archivist* 62, no. 2 (fall 1999): 271–306.

Park, Eun G. "Understanding 'Authenticity' in Records and Information Management: Analyzing Practitioner Constructs." *American Archivist* 64, no. 2 (fall/winter 2001): 270–91.

Patkus, Ronald D. "Religious Archives and the Study of History and Religion: An Essay Review of Recent Titles." *American Archivist* 60, no. 1 (winter 1997): 112–23.

Peace, Nancy E. and Nancy Fisher Chudacoff. "Archivists and Librarians: A Common Mission, a Common Education." *American Archivist* 42 (October 1979): 456–62.

Peterson, Gary M. and Trudy Huskamp Peterson. *Archives and Manuscripts: Law.* Chicago: Society of American Archivists, 1985.

Peterson, Trudy Huskamp. "An Archival Bestiary." *American Archivist* 54 (spring 1991): 192–205.

———. "The National Archives and the Archival Theorist Revisited, 1954–1984." *American Archivist* 49 (spring 1986): 125–33.

Pomeroy, Robert W., ed. "Business and History." Special issue of the *Public Historian* 3 (summer 1981). 6–159.

Posner, Ernst. *American State Archives.* Chicago: University of Chicago Press, 1964.

———. *Archives in the Ancient World.* Cambridge, Mass.: Harvard University Press, 1972. Reprint, Chicago: Society of American Archivists, 2002.

Powell, Graeme T. "Archival Principles and the Treatment of Private Papers." *Archives and Manuscripts* 6, no. 7 (August 1976): 259–68.

Prasad, S.N. "Archives in India." *Archivaria* 7 (winter 1978): 56–61.

Preservation Needs in State Archives. Albany, N.Y.: National Association of Government Archives and Records Administrators, 1986.

Procter, Margaret, and C.P. Lewis. *New Directions in Archival Research.* Liverpool: Liverpool University Centre for Archive Studies, 2000.

Proffitt, Kevin. "The Archival Bridge." *Midwestern Archivist* 16 (1991): 115–20.

Pylypchuk, Mary Ann. "The Value of Aboriginal Records as Legal Evidence in Canada: An Examination of Sources." *Archivaria* 32 (summer 1991): 51–77.

Rabchuk, Gord. "Life After the 'Big Bang': Business Archives in an Era of Disorder." *American Archivist* 60, no. 1 (winter 1997): 34–43.

Reaume, Geoffrey and Barbara L. Craig. "Medical Archives: An Update of the Spandoni Bibliography, 1986–1995." *Archivaria* 41 (spring 1996): 121–57.

Redmann, Gail R. "Archivists and Genealogists: The Trend Toward Peaceful Coexistence." *Archival Issues* 18, no. 2 (1993): 121–32.

Reilly, Jan. "Integrating Archival Programs into the Core Business of the Independent School." *Archives and Manuscripts* 25, no. 1 (May 1997): 50–61.

Rhoads, James B. *The Applicability of UNISIST Guidelines and ISO International Standards to Archives Administration and Records Management: A Records and Archives Management Program (UNESCO) Study.* Paris: UNESCO, 1982.

———. *The Role of Archives and Records Management in National Information Systems: A RAMP Study.* Paris: UNESCO, 1983.

Richmond, Lesley. "Securities, Whisky, Tourism, and Co-operation: Business Archives in Scotland at the End of the Twentieth Century." *Archives and Manuscripts* 27, no. 2 (November 1999): 68–75.

Roberts, John W. "Archival Theory: Much Ado About Shelving." *American Archivist* 50 (winter 1987): 66–74.

———. "Archival Theory: Myth or Banality." *American Archivist* 53 (winter 1990): 110–20.

———. "Practice Makes Perfect, Theory Makes Theorists." *Archivaria* 37 (spring 1994): 111–21.

Roberts-Moore, Judith. "Establishing Recognition of Past Injustices: Uses of Archival Records in Documenting the Experience of Japanese Canadians During the Second World War." *Archivaria* 53 (spring 2002): 64–75.

Rosenberg, William G. "Politics in the (Russian) Archives: The 'Objectivity Question,' Trust, and the Limitations of Law." *American Archivist* 64, no. 1 (spring/summer 2001): 78–95.

Russell, Peter A. "The Manx Peril: Archival Theory in Light of Recent American Historiography." *Archivaria* 32 (summer 1991): 124–37.

Russell, Mattie U. "The Influence of Historians on the Archival Profession in the United States." *American Archivist* 46 (summer 1983): 277–85.

Sample Forms for Archival and Records Management Programs. Chicago: Society of American Archivists and Lenexa, Kans.: ARMA International, 2002.

Sanders, Robert L. "Archivists and Records Managers: Another Marriage in Trouble?" *ARMA Records Management Quarterly* 23 (April 1989): 12–20.

Schellenberg, Theodore R. *The Management of Archives.* New York: Columbia University Press, 1965.

———. *Modern Archives: Principles and Techniques.* Chicago: University of Chicago Press, 1956.

Schmuland, Arlene. "The Archival Image in Fiction: An Analysis and Annotated Bibliography." *American Archivist* 62, no. 1 (spring 1999): 24–73.

Schwartz, Joan M., and Terry Cook. "Archives, Records, and Power: The Making of Modern Memory." *Archival Science* 2, nos. 1–2 (2002): 1–19.

Schwirtlich, Anne-Marie. "Archives in the Roman Republic." *Archives and Manuscripts* 9, no. 1 (September 1981): 19–29.

Seeff, Judy. "Archives as Museum Objects." *Archives and Manuscripts* 13, no. 1 (May 1985): 39–48.

Seton, Rosemary E. *The Preservation and Administration of Private Archives: A RAMP Study.* Paris: UNESCO, 1984.

Sharman, R.C. "The Archivist and the Historian." *Archives and Manuscripts* 4, no. 6 (February 1972): 8–20.

———. "Australian Archives in Lamb's Clothing." *Archivaria* 1, no. 2 (summer 1976): 20–32.

———. "Public Archives and National Information Policy." *Archives and Manuscripts* 11, no. 1 (May 1983): 14–21.

Shaw, Gareth. "Nineteenth Century Directories as Sources in Canadian Social History." *Archivaria* 14 (summer 1982): 107–22.

Shepard, C.J. "Court Records as Archival Records." *Archivaria* 18 (summer 1984): 124–34.

Shkolnik, Leon. "The Role of the Archive in the Corporate Structure." *ARMA Records Management Quarterly* 24 (October 1990): 18–25.

Sickinger, James. "Literacy, Documents, and Archives in the Ancient Athenian Democracy." *American Archivist* 62, no. 2 (fall 1999): 229–46.

Simmons, Joseph M. "The Special Librarian as Company Archivist." *Special Libraries* 56 (1965): 647–50.

Skemer, Don C. and Geoffrey P. Williams. "Managing the Records of Higher Education: The State of Records Management in American Colleges and Universities." *American Archivist* 53 (fall 1990): 532–47.

Smith, Clive. "The Australian Archives." *Archives and Manuscripts* 8, no. 1 (June 1980): 33–40.

Smith, Colin. "Australian Archives Through a Looking Glass." *Archives and Manuscripts* 17, no. 1 (May 1989): 51–65.

Smith, David R. "An Historical Look at Business Archives." *American Archivist* 45 (summer 1982): 273–78.

Smith, George David. "Dusting Off the Cobwebs: Turning the Business Archives Into a Managerial Tool," *American Archivist* 45 (summer 1982): 287–90.

Spragge, Shirley. "The Abdication Crisis: Are Archivists Giving Up Their Cultural Responsibility?" *Archivaria* 40 (fall 1995): 173–81.

———. "'One Parchment Book at the Charge of the Parish....' A Sample of Anglican Record Keeping." *Archivaria* 30 (summer 1990): 55–63.

Stadick, Anna. "Saint Patrons: The Role of Archives in the Roman Catholic Process of Canonization." *Archival Issues* 24, no. 2 (1999): 123–44.

Stark, Marie Charlotte. *Development of Records Management and Archives Services Within United Nations Agencies: A RAMP Study.* Paris: UNESCO, 1983.

Stewart, Bob. "Nurturing the Spirit: Reflections on the Role of a Church Archivist." *Archivaria* 30 (summer 1990): 110–13.

Storch, Susan E. "Diplomatics: Modern Archival Method or Medieval Artifact?" *American Archivist* 61, no. 2 (fall 1998): 365–83.

Stout, Leon J. "Reimagining Archives: Two Tales for the Information Age." *American Archivist* 65, no. 1 (spring/summer 2002): 9–23.

Strengthening New York's Historical Records Programs: A Self-Study Guide. Albany, N.Y.: State Archives and Records Administration, 1989.

Strong-Boag, Veronica. "Raising Clio's Consciousness: Women's History and Archives in Canada." *Archivaria* 6 (summer 1978): 70–82.

Suelflow, August. *Religious Archives: An Introduction.* Chicago: Society of American Archivists, 1980.

Swancott, Leigh. "Origins and Development of the University of Melbourne Archives." *Archives and Manuscripts* 27, no. 2 (November 1999): 40–53.

Sweeney, Shelley. "Sheep That Have Gone Astray?: Church Record Keeping and the Canadian Archival System." *Archivaria* 23 (winter 1986–87): 54–68.

Swift, Michael D. "The Canadian Archival Scene in the 1970s: Current Developments and Trends." *Archivaria* 15 (winter 1982–83): 47–57.

Symons, T.H.B. "Archives and Canadian Studies." *Archivaria* 15 (winter 1982–83): 58–69.

Taylor, Hugh. "Recycling the Past: The Archivist in the Age of Ecology." *Archivaria* 35 (spring 1993): 203–13.

———. "'Heritage' Revisited: Documents as Artifacts in the Context of Museums and Material Culture." *Archivaria* 40 (fall 1995): 8–20.

———. "The Archivist, the Letter, and the Spirit." *Archivaria* 43 (spring 1997): 1–16.

———. "Canadian Archives: Patterns from a Federal Perspective." *Archivaria* 1, no. 2 (summer 1976): 3–19.

———. "The Collective Memory: Archives and Libraries as Heritage." *Archivaria* 15 (winter 1982–83): 118–30.

———. "Information Ecology and the Archives of the 1980s." *Archivaria* 18 (summer 1984): 35–37.

————. "Transformation in the Archives: Technological Adjustment or Paradigm Shift?" *Archivaria* 25 (winter 1987–88): 12–28.

Taylor, Priscilla S., ed. *Manuscripts: The First Twenty Years.* Westport, Conn.: Greenwood Press, 1984.

Trace, Ciaran B. "What is Recorded is Never Simply 'What Happened': Record Keeping in Modern Organizational Culture." *Archival Science* 2, nos. 1–2 (2002): 137–59.

Tryon, Roy. "The South Carolina Archives: A Decade of Change and Program Development." *American Archivist* 60, no. 2 (spring 1997): 166–83.

Turner, Janet. "Experimenting With New Tools: Special Diplomatics and the Study of Authority in the United Church of Canada." *Archivaria* 30 (summer 1990): 91–103.

Tyacke, Sarah. "Archives in a Wider World: The Culture and Politics of Archives." *Archivaria* 52 (fall 2001): 1–25.

Ulfsparre, Anna-Christina. "Archival Science in Sweden." In *The Concept of Record: Second Stockholm Conference on Archival Science and the Concept of Record, 30–31 May 1996.* Sweden: Riksarkivet, 1998, 57–66.

Upward, Frank. "Structuring the Records Continuum. Part I: Postcustodial Principles and Properties." *Archives and Manuscripts* 24, no. 2 (1996). http://www.sims.monash.edu.au/research/rcrg/publications/recordscontinuum/fupp1.html.

———— "Structuring the Records Continuum. Part II: Structuration Theory and Recordkeeping." *Archives and Manuscripts* 25, no. 1 (May 1997): 10–35. http://www.sims.monash.edu.au/research/ rcrg/publications/recordscontinuum/fupp2.html.

Upward, Frank and Sue McKemmish. "Somewhere Beyond Custody." *Archives and Manuscripts* 22, no. 1 (May 31994): 136–49.

Vaughn, Stephen, ed. *The Vital Past: Writings on the Uses of History.* Athens, Ga.: University of Georgia Press, 1985.

Wagner, Stephen C. "Integrated Archives and Records Management Programs at Professional Membership Programs: A Case Study and a Model." *American Archivist* 62, no. 1 (spring 1999): 95–129.

Walch, Timothy, ed. *Guardian of Heritage: Essays on the History of the National Archives.* Washington, D.C.: National Archives and Records Administration, 1985.

Walch, Victoria Irons. "State Archives in 1997: Diverse Conditions, Common Directions." *American Archivist* 60, no. 2 (spring 1997): 132–51.

Walichnowski, Tadeusz. "The Polish State Archives." *Archivaria* 7 (winter 1978): 42–55.

Walker, Bill. "Records Managers and Archivists: A Survey of Roles." *ARMA Records Management Quarterly* 23 (January 1989): 18–21.

Wallot, Jean-Pierre. "Archival Oneness in the Midst of Diversity: A Personal Perspective." *American Archivist* 59, no. 1 (winter 1996): 14–29.

Ward, Peter. "Family Papers and the New Social History." *Archivaria* 14 (summer 1982): 63–75.

Wareham, Evelyn. "'Our Own Identity, Our Own Taonga, Our Own Self Coming Back': Indigenous Voices in New Zealand Record-Keeping." *Archivaria* 52 (fall 2001): 26–46.

Warkentin, Germaine. "Who Was the Scribe of the Radisson Manuscript?" *Archivaria* 53 (spring 2002): 47–63.

Warner, Sam Bass, Jr. "The Shame of the Cities: Public Records of the Metropolis." *Midwestern Archivist* 2, no. 2 (1977): 27–34.

Wehner, Monica, and Ewan Maidment. "Ancestral Voices: Aspects of Archives Administration in Oceania." *Archives and Manuscripts* 27, no. 1 (May 1999): 22–41.

Weinberg, David M. "The Impact of Grantsmaking: An Evaluation of Archival and Records Management Programs at the Local Level." *American Archivist* 62, no. 2 (fall 1999): 247–70.

Weldon, Edward. "Archives and the Challenge of Change." *American Archivist* 46 (spring 1983): 125–34.

Wheeler, D. "Business Records, and the Sole Archivist Creating an Archives." *Archives and Manuscripts* 7, no. 3 (August 1978): 101–9.

Wilson, Ian E. "Canadian University Archives." *Archivaria* 3 (winter 1976–1977): 17–27.

————. "'A Noble Dream': The Origins of the Public Archives of Canada." *Archivaria* 15 (winter 1982–83): 16–35.

Wilsted, Thomas. "Face to Face Across the Counter: Archivists and Historians in New Zealand." *Archives and Manuscripts* 7, no. 1 (August 1977): 3–18.

Wilson, Ian E., and William Nolte. *Managing Archival and Manuscript Repositories.* Chicago: Society of American Archivists, 1991.

Wood, Helen. "The Fetish of the Document: An Exploration of Attitudes Towards Archives." In *New Directions in Archival Research,* edited by Margaret Procter and C.P. Lewis, 20–48. Liverpool: Liverpool University Centre for Archive Studies, 2000.

Wosh, Peter J. "Bibles, Benevolence, and Bureaucracy: The Changing Nature of Nineteenth Century Religious Records." *American Archivist* 52 (spring 1989): 166–78.

Wright, Steven L. "Love Me Or Leave Me: Getting Businesses Interested in Archives." *Archival Issues* 21, no. 2 (1996): 159–68.

Yakel, Elizabeth. "The Way Things Work: Procedures, Processes, and Institutional Records." *American Archivist* 59, no. 4 (fall 1996): 454–65.

Yates, JoAnne. "From Press Book and Pigeonhole to Vertical Filing: Revolution in Storage and Access Systems for Correspondence." *Journal of Business Communication* 19 (summer 1982): 5–26.

Yax, Maggie. "Arthur Agarde, Elizabethan Archivist: His Contributions to the Evolution of Archival Practice." *American Archivist* 61, no. 1 (spring 1998): 56–69.

Yorke, Stephen. "Management of Petroleum Data Records in the Custody of Australian Archives." *Archives and Manuscripts* 25, no. 1 (May 1997): 62–73.

Young, Rod. "Labour Archives: An Annotated Bibliography." *Archivaria* 27 (winter 1988–89): 97–110.

CONDUCTING A SURVEY AND STARTING AN ARCHIVES PROGRAM

Baumann, Roland M. "Oberlin College and the Movement to Establish an Archives, 1920–1966." *Midwestern Archivist* 13 (1988): 27–38.

Christian, John F. and Shonnie Finnegan. "On Planning an Archives." *American Archivist* 37 (1974): 573–78.

Eddy, Henry H. "Surveying for Archives Buildings." *American Archivist* 24 (1961): 75–79.

Evans, Frank B. and Eric Ketelaar. *A Guide for Surveying Archival and Records Management Systems and Services: A RAMP Study.* Paris: UNESCO, 1983.

Fleckner, John. *Archives and Manuscripts: Surveys.* Chicago: Society of American Archivists, 1977.

———, ed. "Records Surveys: A Multi-Purpose Tool for the Archivist." *American Archivist* 42 (July 1979): 293–311.

Frye, Dorothy T. "Linking Institutional Missions to University and College Archives Programs: The Land-Grant Model." *American Archivist* 56 (winter 1993): 36–53.

Gracy, David B., II. "Starting an Archives." *Georgia Archive* 1 (1972): 20–29.

Gross, John W. "Inventorying and Scheduling Records." *ARMA Records Management Quarterly* 7 (1973): 28–31.

Henry, Linda J. "Archival Advisory Committees: Why?" *American Archivist* 48 (summer 1985): 315–19.

Koplowitz, Bradford. "The Oklahoma Historical Records Survey." *American Archivist* 54 (winter 1991): 62–68.

Ling, Ted. *Solid, Safe, Secure: Building Archives Repositories in Australia.* Canberra: National Archives of Australia, n.d.

Somers, Dale A., et al. "Surveying the Records of a City: The History of Atlanta Project." *American Archivist* 36 (July 1973): 353–59.

Starting an Archives. Problems in Archives Kit No. 3. Chicago: Society of American Archivists, 1980.

Thomson, Robert P. "The Business Records Survey in Wisconsin." *American Archivist* 14 (July 1951): 249–55.

Yakel, Elizabeth. "Institutionalizing an Archives: Developing Historical Records Programs in Organizations." *American Archivist* 52 (spring 1989): 202–7.

Zitmore, Irving. "Planning a Records Management Survey." *American Archivist* 18 (April 1955): 133–40.

SELECTION, APPRAISAL, ACQUISITIONS, AND ACCESSIONING

Abraham, Terry. "Collection Policy or Documentation Strategy: Theory and Practice." *American Archivist* 54 (winter 1991): 44–53.

Alexander, Philip N. and Helen W. Samuels. "The Roots of 128: A Hypothetical Documentation Strategy." *American Archivist* 50 (fall 1987): 518–31.

Allen, Marie B. and Roland M. Baumann. "Evolving Appraisal and Accessioning Policies of Soviet Archives." *American Archivist* 54 (winter 1991): 96–111.

Anderson, R. Joseph. "Managing Change and Chance: Collecting Policies in Social History Archives." *American Archivist* 48 (summer 1985): 296–303.

Annemat, Louise. "Documenting Secret/Sacred (Restricted) Aboriginal History." *Archives and Manuscripts* 17, no. 1 (May 1989): 37–50.

Baer, Christopher T. "Strategy, Structure, Detail, Function: Four Parameters for the Appraisal of Business Records." In *The Records of American Business,* edited by James O'Toole, 75–136. Chicago: Society of American Archivists, 1997.

Bailey, Catherine. "From the Top Down: The Practice of Macro-Appraisal." *Archivaria* 43 (spring 1997): 89–128.

Barritt, Marjorie Rabe. "The Appraisal of Personally Identifiable Student Records." *American Archivist* 49 (summer 1986): 263–75.

Bassett, T. D. Seymour. "Documenting Recreation and Tourism in New England." *American Archivist* 50 (fall 1987): 550–69.

Bauer, G. Philip. *The Appraisal of Current and Recent Records.* Staff Information Circular 13. Washington, D.C.: National Archives, 1946.

Bearman, David. "Documenting Documentation." *Archivaria* 34 (summer 1992): 33–50.

Beaven, Brian P.N. "Macro-Appraisal: From Theory to Practice." *Archivaria* 48 (fall 1999): 154–98.

Becker, Ronald L. "On Deposit: A Handshake and a Lawsuit." *American Archivist* 56 (winter 1993): 320–29.

Benedict, Karen. "Invitation to a Bonfire: Reappraisal and Deaccessioning of Records as Collection Management Tools in an Archives: A Reply to Leonard Rapport." *American Archivist* 47 (winter 1984): 43–50.

———. "Collecting Repositories and Corporate Archives: Variations on a Theme?" In *The Records of American Business*, edited by James O'Toole, 349–68. Chicago: Society of American Archivists, 1997.

Blouin, Francis X., Jr. "A New Perspective on the Appraisal of Business Records: A Review." *American Archivist* 42 (July 1979): 312–20.

Boadle, Don. "Documenting 20th Century Rural and Regional Australia: Archival Acquisition and Collection Development in Regional University Archives and Special Collections." *Archives and Manuscripts* 29, no. 2 (November 2001): 64–81.

Bodem, Dennis R. "The Use of Forms in the Control of Archives at the Accessioning and Processing Level." *American Archivist* 31 (October 1968): 365–69.

Boles, Frank. *Archival Appraisal.* New York: Neal-Schuman, 1991.

———. "'Just a Bunch of Bigots': A Case Study in the Acquisition of Controversial Materials." *Archival Issues* 19, no. 1 (1994): 53–66.

———. "Mix Two Parts Interest to One Part Information and Appraise Until Done: Understanding Contemporary Record Selection Processes." *American Archivist* 50 (summer 1987): 356–68.

———. "Sampling in Archives." *American Archivist* 44 (spring 1981): 125–30.

Boles, Frank and Julia Marks Young. "Exploring the Black Box: The Appraisal of University Administrative Records." *American Archivist* 48 (spring 1985): 121–40.

Boles, Frank and Mark A. Greene. "Et Tu Schellenberg? Thoughts on the Dagger of American Appraisal Theory." *American Archivist* 59, no. 3 (summer 1996): 298–311.

Booms, Hans. "Society and the Formation of a Documentary Heritage: Issues in the Appraisal of Archival Sources." *Archivaria* 24 (summer 1987): 69–107.

Botticelli, Peter. "Records Appraisal in Network Organizations." *Archivaria* 49 (spring 2000): 161–91.

Bradsher, James Gregory. "The FBI Records Appraisal." *Midwestern Archivist* 13 (1988): 51–66.

Breton, Arthur J. "The Critical First Step: *In Situ* Handling of Large Collections." *American Archivist* 49 (fall 1986): 455–58.

Brichford, Maynard. *Archives and Manuscripts: Appraisal and Accessioning.* Chicago: Society of American Archivists, 1977.

Brooks, Philip C. "The Selection of Records for Preservation." *American Archivist* 3 (October 1940): 221–34.

Brothman, Brien. "Orders of Value: Probing the Theoretical Terms of Archival Practice." *Archivaria* 32 (summer 1991): 78–100.

———. "Where's Home? Documenting Locality at the Dawn of the Electronic Age." *Archivaria* 47 (spring 1999): 151–57.

Brown, Richard. "The Value of 'Narrativity' in the Appraisal of Historical Documents: Foundations for a Theory of Archival Hermeneutics." *Archivaria* 32 (summer 1991): 152–56.

———. "Records Acquisition Strategy and Its Theoretical Foundation: The Case for a Concept of Archival Hermeneutics." *Archivaria* 33 (winter 1991–92): 34–56.

———. "Macro-Appraisal Theory and the Context of the Public Records Creator." *Archivaria* 40 (fall 1995): 121–72.

———. "Back to the Strategic Roots: Appraisal Reform at the National Archives of Canada." *Archival Issues* 24, no. 2 (1999): 113–22.

Bruemmer, Bruce H. "Avoiding Accidents of Evidence: Functional Analysis in the Appraisal of Business Records." In *The Records of American Business*, edited by James O'Toole, 137–60. Chicago: Society of American Archivists, 1997.

Burton, Shirley J. "Documentation of the United States at War in the Twentieth Century: An Archivist's Reflection on Sources, Themes, and Access." *Midwestern Archivist* 13 (1988): 17–26.

Carleton, Don E. "'McCarthyism Was More than McCarthy': Documenting the Red Scare at the State and Local Level." *Midwestern Archivist* 12 (1987): 13–19.

Chestnut, Paul I. "Appraising the Papers of State Legislators." *American Archivist* 48 (spring 1985): 159–72.

Coker, Kathy Roe. "Records Appraisal: Practice and Procedure." *American Archivist* 48 (fall 1985): 417–21.

Colman, Gould P. "Documenting Agriculture and Rural Life." *Midwestern Archivist* 12 (1987): 21–27.

Connors, Thomas. "Appraising Public Television Programs: Toward an Interpretive and Comparative Evaluation Model." *American Archivist* 63, no. 1 (spring/summer 2000): 152–74.

Cook, Terry. "'Many Are Called But Few Are Chosen': Appraisal Guidelines for Sampling and Selecting Case Files." *Archivaria* 32 (summer 1991): 25–50.

———. "Documentation Strategy." *Archivaria* 34 (summer 1992): 181–91.

———. "'Another Brick in the Wall': Terry Eastwood's Masonry and Archival Walls, History, and Archival Appraisal." *Archivaria* 37 (spring 1994): 96–103.

Cox, Richard J. "A Documentation Strategy Case Study: Western New York." *American Archivist* 52 (spring 1989): 192–200.

———. "The Documentation Strategy and Archival Appraisal Principles: A Different Perspective." *Archivaria* 38 (fall 1994): 11–36.

———. "The Archivist and Collecting: A Review Essay." *American Archivist* 59, no. 4 (fall 1996): 496–512.

———. "Making the Records Speak: Archival Appraisal, Memory, Preservation, and Collecting." *American Archivist* 64, no. 2 (fall/winter 2001): 394–404.

———. *Documenting Localities: A Practical Model for American Archivists and Manuscript Curators.* Lanham, Md.: Scarecrow Press and the Society of American Archivists, 2001.

———, and Helen W. Samuels. "The Archivist's First Responsibility: A Research Agenda to Improve the Identification and Retention of Records of Enduring Value." *American Archivist* 51 (winter/spring 1988): 28–51.

Craig, Barbara L. "The Acts of the Appraisers: The Context, the Plan and the Record." *Archivaria* 34 (summer 1992): 175–80.

———. "The Archivist as Planner and Poet: Thoughts on the Larger Issues of Appraisal for Acquisition." *Archivaria* 52 (fall 2001): 175–83.

Crawford, Miriam I. *A Model for Donor Organizations and Institutional Repository Relationships in the Transfer of Organizational Archives.* Philadelphia: National Federation of Abstracting and Information Services, 1987.

Daniels-Howell, Todd. "Reappraisal of Congressional Records at the Minnesota Historical Society: A Case Study." *Archival Issues* 23, no. 1 (1998): 35–40.

Davis, Richard Carter. "Getting the Lead Out: The Appraisal of Silver-Lead Mining Records at the University of Idaho." *American Archivist* 55 (summer 1992): 454–63.

Day, Deborah Cozort. "Appraisal Guidelines for Reprint Collections." *American Archivist* 48 (winter 1985): 56–63.

Denham, Elizabeth. "Dealing With the Records of Closing Hospitals: The Calgary Area Health Authority Plan." *Archivaria* 41 (spring 1996): 78–87.

Disposition of Federal Records: A Records Management Handbook. Washington, D.C.: National Archives and Records Administration, 1992.

Dozois, Paulette. "Beyond Ottawa's Reach: The Federal Acquisition of Regional Government Records." *Archivaria* 33 (winter 1991–92): 57–65.

Duranti, Luciana. "The Concept of Appraisal and Archival Theory." *American Archivist* 57 (spring 1994): 328–44.

Elzy, Martin I. "Scholarship vs. Economy: Records Appraisal at the National Archives." *Prologue* 6 (1974): 183–88.

Endelman, Judith E. "Looking Backward to Plan for the Future: Collection Analysis for Manuscript Repositories." *American Archivist* 50 (summer 1987): 340–55.

Ericson, Timothy L. "At the 'Rim of Creative Dissatisfaction': Archivists and Acquisition Development." *Archivaria* 33 (winter 1991–92): 66–77.

———. "Beyond Business: External Documentation and Corporate Records." In *The Records of American Business*, edited by James O'Toole, 297–326. Chicago: Society of American Archivists, 1997.

———. "'To Approximate June Pasture': The Documentation Strategy in the Real World." *Archival Issues* 22, no. 1 (1997): 5–20.

Evans, Max J. "The Visible Hand: Creating a Practical Mechanism for Cooperative Appraisal." *Midwestern Archivist* 11 (1986): 7–13.

Fishbein, Meyer. "Appraisal of Twentieth Century Records for Historical Use." *Illinois Libraries* 52 (1970): 154–62.

———. "Reflections on Appraising Statistical Records." *American Archivist* 50 (spring 1987): 226–34.

Frost, Eldon. "A Weak Link in the Chain: Records Scheduling as a Source of Archival Acquisition." *Archivaria* 33 (winter 1991–92): 78–86.

Gilfoyle, Timothy J. "Prostitutes in the Archives: Problems and Possibilities in Documenting the History of Sexuality." *American Archivist* 57 (summer 1994): 514–27.

Gilliland-Swetland, Anne J. "Archivy and the Computer: A Citation Analysis of North American Archival Periodical Literature." *Archival Issues* 17, no. 2 (1992): 95–112.

———. "Health Sciences Documentation and Networked Hypermedia: An Integrative Approach." *Archivaria* 41 (spring 1996): 45–60.

Gillis, Peter. "The Case File: Problems of Acquisition and Access from the Federal Perspective." *Archivaria* 6 (summer 1978): 32–39.

Gray, David P. "A Technique for Manuscript Collection Development Analysis." *Midwestern Archivist* 12 (1987): 91–104.

Greene, Mark. "Appraisal of Congressional Records at the Minnesota Historical Society: A Case Study." *Archival Issues* 19, no. 1 (1994): 31–44.

———. "From Village Smithy to Superior Vacuum Technology: Modern Small-Business Records and the Collecting Repository." *Archival Issues* 23, no. 1 (1998): 41–58.

———. "Store Wars: Some Thoughts on the Strategy and Tactics of Documenting Small Business." *Midwestern Archivist* 16 (1991): 95–104.

———. "'The Surest Proof': A Utilitarian Approach to Appraisal." *Archivaria* 45 (spring 1998): 127–69.

Greene, Mark and Todd J. Daniels-Howell. "Documentation with an Attitude: A Pragmatist's Guide to the Selection and Acquisition of Modern Business Records." In *The Records of American Business*, edited by James O'Toole, 161–230. Chicago: Society of American Archivists, 1997.

Haas, Joan K., Helen Willa Samuels, and Barbara Trippel Simmons. "The MIT Appraisal Project and Its Broader Applications." *American Archivist* 49 (summer 1986): 310–14.

Hackman, Larry J. and Joan Warnow-Blewett. "The Documentation Strategy Process: A Model and a Case Study." *American Archivist* 50 (winter 1987): 12–47.

Hall, Kathy. "Archival Acquisitions: Legal Mandates and Methods." *Archivaria* 18 (summer 1984): 58–69.

Ham, F. Gerald. *Selecting and Appraising Archives and Manuscripts.* Chicago: Society of American Archivists, 1993.

Heald, Carolyn. "Are We Collecting The 'Right Stuff?'" *Archivaria* 40 (fall 1995): 182–88.

———. "Documenting Disease: Ontario's Bureaucracy Battles Tuberculosis." *Archivaria* 41 (spring 1996): 88–107.

Henry, Linda J. "Collecting Policies of Special-Subject Repositories." *American Archivist* 43 (winter 1980): 57–63.

Hinding, Andrea. "Inventing a Concept of Documentation." *Journal of American History* 80 (June 1993): 168–78.

Hite, Richard W., and Daniel J. Linke. "A Statistical Summary of Appraisal During Processing: A Case Study With Manuscript Collections." *Archival Issues* 17 (1992): 23–30.

Hobbs, Catherine. "The Character of Personal Archives: Reflections on the Value of Records of Individuals." *Archivaria* 52 (fall 2001): 126–35.

Horton, Robert. "Cultivating Our Garden: Archives, Community, and Documentation." *Archival Issues* 26, no. 1 (2001): 27–40.

Hull, Felix. *The Use of Sampling Techniques in the Retention of Records: A RAMP Study with Guidelines.* Paris: UNESCO, 1981.

Hyry, Tom, Diane Kaplan, and Christine Weideman. "'Though this be madness, yet there is a method in 't': Assessing the Value of Faculty Papers and Defining a Collecting Policy." *American Archivist* 65, no. 1 (spring/summer 2002): 56–69.

Iacovino, Livia. "The Development of the Principles of Appraisal in the Public Sector and Their Application to Business Records (Part I)." *Archives and Manuscripts* 17, no. 2 (November 1989): 197–218.

Intrinsic Value. Staff Information Paper 21. Washington, D.C.: National Archives and Records Service, 1982.

Janzen, Mary E. "Pruning the Groves of Academe: Appraisal, Arrangement and Description of Faculty Papers." *Georgia Archive* 9 (fall 1981): 31–41.

Jung, Maureen A. "Documenting Nineteenth-Century Quartz Mining in Northern California." *American Archivist* 53 (summer 1990): 406–19.

Kaplan, Diane E. "The Stanley Milgram Papers: A Case Study on Appraisal of and Access to Confidential Data." *American Archivist* 59, no. 3 (summer 1996): 288–97.

Kaplan, Elisabeth. "We Are What We Collect, We Collect What We Are: Archives and the Construction of Identity." *American Archivist* 63, no. 1 (spring/summer 2000): 126–51.

Kelly, Russell. "The National Archives of Australia's New Approach to Appraisal." *Archives and Manuscripts* 29, no. 1 (May 2001): 72–85.

Kemp, Edward C. *Manuscript Solicitation for Libraries, Special Collections, Museums, and Archives.* Littleton, Colo.: Libraries Unlimited, 1978.

Kepley, David R. "Sampling in Archives: A Review." *American Archivist* 47 (summer 1984): 237–42.

Klaassen, David J. "Achieving Balanced Documentation: Social Services from a Consumer Perspective." *Midwestern Archivist* 11 (1986): 111–24.

Kolish, Evelyn. "Sampling Methodology and Its Application: An Illustration of the Tension Between Theory and Practice." *Archivaria* 38 (fall 1994): 61–73.

Kolsrud, Ole. "The Evolution of Basic Appraisal Principles: Some Comparative Observations." *American Archivist* 55 (winter 1992): 26–39.

Krizack, Joan D. "Hospital Documentation Planning: The Concept and the Context." *American Archivist* 56 (winter 1993): 16–35.

Kuhn, Clifford M. "A Historian's Perspective on Archives and the Documentary Process." *American Archivist* 59, no. 3 (summer 1996): 312–21.

Kula, Sam. *The Archival Appraisal of Moving Images: A RAMP Study with Guidelines.* Paris: UNESCO, 1983.

Lamoree, Karen M. "Documenting the Difficult or Collecting the Controversial." *Archival Issues* 20, no. 2 (1995): 149–54.

Leary, William H. *The Archival Appraisal of Photographs: A RAMP Study with Guidelines.* Paris: UNESCO, 1985.

Lemieux, Victoria. "Archival Solitudes: The Impact on Appraisal and Acquisition of Legislative Concepts of Records and Archives." *Archivaria* 35 (spring 1993): 153–61.

———. "Applying Mintzberg's Theories on Organizational Configuration to Archival Appraisal." *Archivaria* 46 (fall 1998): 32–85.

Lewinson, Paul. "Archival Sampling." *American Archivist* 20 (October 1957): 291–312.

———. "Toward Accessioning and Standards: Research Records." *American Archivist* 23 (July 1960): 297–309.

Lockwood, Elizabeth. "'Imponderable Matters': The Influence of New Trends in History on Appraisal at the National Archives." *American Archivist* 53 (summer 1990): 394–405.

Loewen, Candace. "From Human Neglect to Planetary Survival: New Approaches to the Appraisal of Environmental Records." *Archivaria* 33 (winter 1991–92): 87–103.

Lutzker, Michael A. "Max Weber and the Analysis of Modern Bureaucratic Organization: Notes Toward a Theory of Appraisal." *American Archivist* 45 (spring 1982): 119–30.

Marshall, Jennifer A. "Documentation Strategies in the Twenty-First Century?: Rethinking Institutional Priorities and Professional Limitations." *Archival Issues* 23, no. 1 (1998): 59–74.

Mattern, Carolyn J. "Documenting the Vietnam Soldier: A Case Study in Collection Development." *Midwestern Archivist* 15 (1990): 99–107.

Maxwell-Stewart, Hamish, and Alistair Tough. "Cutting the Gordian Knot: Or How to Preserve Non-Current Clinical Records Without Being Buried in Paper." *Archivaria* 41 (spring 1996): 61–77.

McCausland, Sigrid. "Voices of Opposition: Documenting Australian Protest Movements." *Archives and Manuscripts* 29, no. 2 (November 2001): 48–63.

McCree, Mary Lynn. "Good Sense and Good Judgment: Defining Collections and Collecting." *Drexel Library Quarterly* 2 (1975): 21–32.

McRanor, Shauna. "A Critical Analysis of Intrinsic Value." *American Archivist* 59, no. 3 (summer 1996): 400–11.

McReynolds, Samuel A. "Rural Life in New England." *American Archivist* 50 (fall 1987): 532–48.

Menne-Haritz, Angelika. "Appraisal or Documentation: Can We Appraise Archives by Selecting Content?" *American Archivist* 57 (summer 1994): 528–43.

Miller, Fredric M. "Social History and Archival Practice." *American Archivist* 44 (spring 1981): 113–24.

———. "Use, Appraisal, and Research: A Case Study of Social History." *American Archivist* 49 (fall 1986): 371–92.

Mills, Thomas E. *Appraisal of Social Welfare Case Files*. Technical Leaflet No. 1. New York: Mid-Atlantic Regional Archives Conference, 1982.

Momryk, Myron. "'National Significance: The Evolution and Development of Acquisition Strategies in the Manuscript Division, National Archives of Canada." *Archivaria* 52 (fall 2001): 151–74.

Newton, Tony. "Will the Tension Ever End? Some Observations and Sugestions from an Appraisal Archivist." *Archives and Manuscripts* 29, no. 1 (May 2001): 86–97.

O'Toole, James M. "On the Idea of Permanence." *American Archivist* 52 (winter 1989): 10–25.

———. "Things of the Spirit: Documenting Religion in New England." *American Archivist* 50 (fall 1987): 500–17.

Peace, Nancy A. *Archival Choices: Managing the Historical Record in an Age of Abundance*. Lexington, Mass.: Lexington Books, 1984.

Peterson, Trudy Huskamp. "The Gift and the Deed." *American Archivist* 42 (January 1979): 61–66.

Phillips, Faye. "Developing Collecting Policies for Manuscript Collections." *American Archivist* 47 (winter 1984): 30–42.

Piche, Jean-Stephen. "Macro-Appraisal and Duplication of Information: Federal Real Property Management Records." *Archivaria* 39 (spring 1995): 39–50.

Piche, Jean-Stephen and Sheila Powell. "Counting Archives In: The Appraisal of the 1991 Census of Canada." *Archivaria* 45 (spring 1998): 27–43.

Pinkett, Harold T. "Accessioning Public Records: Anglo-American Practices and Possible Improvements." *American Archivist* 41 (October 1978): 413–21.

———. "Identification of Records of Continuing Value." *Indian Archives* 16 (January 1965): 54–61.

———. "Selective Preservation of General Correspondence." *American Archivist* 30 (January 1967): 33–43.

Pollard, Riva A. "The Appraisal of Personal Papers: A Critical Literature Review." *Archivaria* 52 (fall 2001): 136–50.

Powell, Sheila. "Archival Reappraisal: The Immigration Case Files." *Archivaria* 33 (winter 1991–92): 104–16.

Pylypchuk, Mary Ann. "A Documentation Approach to Aboriginal Archives." *Archivaria* 33 (winter 1991–92): 117–24.

Quinn, David. "Documenting Canada's Early White History." *Archivaria* 7 (winter 1978): 86–94.

Rapport, Leonard. "In the Valley of Decision: What to Do About the Multitude of Files of Quasi Cases." *American Archivist* 48 (spring 1985): 173–89.

———. "No Grandfather Clause: Reappraising Accessioned Records." *American Archivist* 44 (spring 1981): 143–50.

Reed-Scott, Jutta. "Collection Management Strategies for Archivists." *American Archivist* 47 (winter 1984): 23–29.

Roberts, John. "One Size Fits All? The Portability of Macro-Appraisal by a Comparative Analysis of Canada, South Africa, and New Zealand." *Archivaria* 52 (fall 2001): 47–68.

Robinson, Catherine. "Records Control and Disposal Using Functional Analysis." *Archives and Manuscripts* 25, no. 2 (November 1997): 288–303.

Ruller, Thomas J. "Dissimilar Appraisal Documentation as an Impediment to Sharing Appraisal Data: A Survey of Appraisal Documentation in Government Archival Repositories." *Archival Issues* 17 (1992): 65–74.

Samuels, Helen Willa. "Drinking From the Fire Hose: Documenting Education at MIT." *Archives and Manuscripts* 25, no. 1 (May 1997): 36–49.

———. "Improving Our Disposition: Documentation Strategy." *Archivaria* 33 (winter 1991–92): 125–40.

———. *Varsity Letters: Documenting Modern Colleges and Universities.* Chicago: Society of American Archivists and Scarecrow Press, 1992.

———. "Who Controls the Past?" *American Archivist* 49 (spring 1986): 109–24 [re: documentation strategies].

Sanders, Robert L. "Accessioning College and University Publications: A Case Study." *American Archivist* 49 (spring 1986): 180–83.

Sauer, Cynthia K. "Doing the Best We Can?: The Use of Collection Development Policies and Cooperative Collecting Activities at Manuscript Repositories." *American Archivist* 64, no. 2 (fall/winter 2001): 350–62.

Schaeffer, Roy C. "Transcendent Concepts: Power, Appraisal, and the Archivist as 'Social Outcast.'" *American Archivist* 55 (fall 1992): 608–19.

Scheinberg, Ellen. "Case File Theory: Does It Work In Practice?" *Archivaria* 38 (fall 1994): 45–60.

Schellenberg, Theodore R. *The Appraisal of Modern Public Records.* Bulletin No. 8. Washington, D.C.: National Archives, 1956.

Schrock, Nancy Carlson. "Images of New England: Documenting the Built Environment." *American Archivist* 50 (fall 1987): 474–98.

Sigmond, J. Peter. "Form, Function and Archival Value." *Archivaria* 33 (winter 1991–92): 141–47.

Sink, Robert. "Appraisal: The Process of Choice." *American Archivist* 53 (summer 1990): 452–59.

Skelton, Robin. "The Acquisition of Literary Archives." *Archivaria* 18 (summer 1984): 214–19.

Smith, Wilfred I. "Archival Selection: A Canadian View." *Society of Archivists Journal* 3 (1967): 275–80.

Stapleton, Richard. "Jenkinson and Schellenberg: A Comparison." *Archivaria* 17 (winter 1983–84): 75–86.

Steinwall, Susan D. "Appraisal and the FBI Case Files: For Whom Do Archivists Retain Records?" *American Archivist* 49 (winter 1986): 52–63.

Stevens, Michael E. "Voices From Vietnam: Building a Collections from a Controversial War." *American Archivist* 64, no. 1 (spring/summer 2001): 115–20.

Strachan, Stuart. "The Acquisition of Business Records: A New Zealand Approach." *Archives and Manuscripts* 6, no. 5 (November 1975): 177–84.

Straw, John. "From Classrooms to Commons: Documenting the Total Student Experience in Higher Education." *Archival Issues* 19, no. 1 (1994): 19–30.

Sturgeon, Stephen. "A Different Shade of Green: Documenting Environmental Racism and Justice." *Archival Issues* 21, no. 1 (1996): 33–46.

Suderman, Jim. "Appraising Records in the Expenditure Management Function: An Exercise in Functional Analysis." *Archivaria* 43 (spring 1997): 129–42.

Taylor, R.J. "Field Appraisal of Manuscript Collections." *Archivaria* 1, no. 2 (summer 1976): 44–48.

Thompson, Teresa. "Ecumenical Records and Documentation Strategy: Applying 'Total Archives.'" *Archivaria* 30 (summer 1990): 104–9.

Turnbaugh, Roy. "Plowing the Sea: Appraising Public Records in an Ahistorical Culture." *American Archivist* 53 (fall 1990): 562–65.

Turner, Jane. "Theoretical Dialectics: A Commentary on Sampling Methodology and its Application." *Archivaria* 38 (fall 1994): 74–78.

Walden, David. "Stretching the Dollar: Monetary Appraisal of Manuscripts." *Archivaria* 11 (winter 1980–81): 101–14.

Walters, Tyler O. "Contemporary Archival Appraisal Methods and Preservation Decision-Making." *American Archivist* 59, no. 3 (summer 1996): 322–39.

Wertheimer, Jack, Debra Bernhardt, and Julie Miller. "Toward the Documentation of Conservative Judaism." *American Archivist* 57 (spring 1994): 374–79.

Whyte, Doug. "The Acquisition of Lawyers' Private Papers." *Archivaria* 18 (summer 1984): 142–53.

Wickman, Danielle. "Bright Specimens for the Curious or the Somewhat Imponderable Guided by the Unfathomable: Use, Users and Appraisal in Archival Literature." *Archives and Manuscripts* 28, no. 1 (May 2000): 64–79.

Wilson, Ian E. "The Fine Art of Destruction Revisited." *Archivaria* 49 (spring 2000): 124–39.

Wrathall, John D. "Provenance as Text: Reading the Silences Around Sexuality in Manuscript Collections." *Journal of American History* 79 (June 1992): 165–78.

Yates, JoAnne. "Internal Communication Systems in American Business Structures: A Framework to Aid Appraisal." *American Archivist* 48 (spring 1985): 141–58.

Young, Julia Marks, comp. "Annotated Bibliography on Appraisal." *American Archivist* 48 (spring 1985): 190–216.

Yorke, Stephen. "Great Expectations or None At All: The Role and Significance of Community Expectations in the Appraisal Function." *Archives and Manuscripts* 28, no. 1 (May 2000): 24–37.

ARRANGEMENT

Abraham, Terry. "Oliver W. Holmes Revisited: Levels of Arrangement and Description in Practice." *American Archivist* 54 (summer 1991): 370–77.

Bearman, David A., and Richard Lytle. "The Power of the Principle of Provenance." *Archivaria* 21 (winter 1985–86): 14–24.

Berner, Richard C. "Arrangement and Description: Some Historical Observations." *American Archivist* 41 (April 1978): 169–81.

Boles, Frank. "Disrespecting Original Order." *American Archivist* 45 (winter 1982): 26–32.

Carmicheal, David W. *Organizing Archival Records: A Practical Method of Arrangement and Description for Small Archives.* Harrisburg, Pa.: Pennsylvania Historical and Museum Commission, 1993.

Cook, Terry. "The Concept of the Archival Fonds in the Post-Custodial Era: Theory, Problems and Solutions." *Archivaria* 35 (spring 1993): 24–37.

Duchein, Michel. "Theoretical Principles and Practical Problems of *Respect des fonds* in Archival Science." *Archivaria* 16 (summer 1983): 64–82.

Evans, Frank B. "Modern Methods of Arrangement of Archives in the United States." *American Archivist* 29 (April 1966): 241–63.

Evans, Max J. "Authority Control: An Alternative to the Record Group Concept." *American Archivist* 49 (summer 1986): 249–61.

Gracy, David B., II. *Archives and Manuscripts: Arrangement and Description.* Chicago: Society of American Archivists, 1977.

Haller, Uli. "Processing for Access." *American Archivist* 48 (fall 1985): 400–15.

———. "Variations in the Processing Rates on the Magnuson and Jackson Senatorial Papers." *American Archivist* 50 (winter 1987): 100–9.

Hite, Richard W. and Daniel J. Linke. "Teaming Up with Technology: Team Processing." *Midwestern Archivist* 15 (1990): 91–98.

Holmes, Oliver W. "Archival Arrangement: Five Different Operations at Five Different Levels." *American Archivist* 27 (January 1964): 21–41.

Horsman, Peter. "Dirty Hands: A New Perspective on the Original Order." *Archives and Manuscripts* 27, no. 1 (May 1999): 42–53.

Krawczyk, Bob. "Cross Reference Heaven: The Abandonment of the Fonds as the Primary Level of Arrangement for Ontario Government Records." *Archivaria* 48 (fall 1999): 131–53.

The Lone Arranger. Problems in Archives Kit. Chicago: Society of American Archivists, 1983.

McGregor, Lee. "Arrangement and Description of Records at Queensland State Archives." *Archives and Manuscripts* 6, no. 5 (November 1975): 147–53.

Millar, Laura. "The Death of the Fonds and the Resurrection of Provenance: Archival Context in Space and Time." *Archivaria* 53 (spring 2002): 1–15.

Miller, Fredric M. *Arranging and Describing Archives and Manuscripts.* Chicago: Society of American Archivists, 1992.

Polden, Kenneth A. "The Record Group—A Matter of Principle." *Archives and Manuscripts* 3, no. 6 (May 1968): 3–6.

———. "Preserving the Principle of Provenance: Archives Practices at the Reserve Bank of Australia." *Archives and Manuscripts* 4, no. 4 (May 1971): 12–15.

Roe, Kathleen. *Guidelines for Arrangement and Description of Archives and Manuscripts.* New York: New York State Archives and Records Administration, 1991.

Slotkin, Helen W. and Karen T. Lynch. "An Analysis of Processing Procedures: The Adaptable Approach." *American Archivist* 45 (spring 1982): 155–63.

Smith, Colin. "A Case for Abandonment of 'Respect.'" *Archives and Manuscripts* 14, no. 2 (November 1986): 154–68.

Vincent, Carl. "The Record Group: A Concept in Evolution." *Archivaria* 3 (winter 1976–1977): 3–15.

Zelenyj, Dan. "Linchpin Imperilled: The Functional Interpretation of Series and the Principle of Respect des Fonds." *Archivaria* 42 (fall 1996): 126–36.

DESCRIPTION

Altman, Burt, and John R. Nemmers. "The Usability of On-Line Archival Resources: The POLARIS Project Finding Aid." *American Archivist* 64, no. 1 (spring/summer 2001): 121–31.

Baumann, Karen. "Archival Finding Aids: An Essay Review of Recent Titles." *American Archivist* 60, no. 3 (summer 1997): 355–62.

Bearman, David. "Archives and Manuscript Control with Bibliographic Utilities: Opportunities and Challenges." *American Archivist* 52 (winter 1989): 26–39.

Berner, Richard C. and M. Gary Bettis. "Description of Manuscript Collections: A Single Network System." *College and Research Libraries* 30 (1969): 405–16.

Berner, Richard C. and Uli Haller. "Principles of Archival Inventory Construction." *American Archivist* 47 (spring 1984): 134–55.

Bouche, Nicole L. "Implementing EAD in the Yale University Library." *American Archivist* 60, no. 4 (fall 1997): 408–19.

Brown, Charlotte B., and Brian E.C. Schottlaender. "The Online Archive of California: A Consortial Approach to Encoded Archival Description." In *Encoded Archival Description on the Internet,* edited by Daniel V. Pitti and Wendy Duff, 97–112. New York: Haworth Information Press, 2001.

Burrows, Toby. "Using Encoded Archival Description with Manuscript Collections: The Guide to Australian Literary Manuscripts." *Archives and Manuscripts* 30, no. 2 (November 2002): 82–95.

Carson, James G. "The American Medical Association's Historical Health Fraud and Alternative Medicine Collection: An Integrated Approach to Automated Collection Description." *American Archivist* 54 (spring 1991): 184–91.

Cloud, Patricia. "RLIN, AMC, and Retrospective Conversion." *Midwestern Archivist* 11 (1986): 125–34.

Cook, Michael. "Description Standards: The Struggle Toward the Light." *Archivaria* 34 (summer 1992): 50–57.

Coombs, Leonard. "A New Access System for the Vatican Archives." *American Archivist* 52 (fall 1989): 538–46.

Dack, Diana. "Encoded Archival Description in the National Library of Australia." *Archives and Manuscripts* 30, no. 2 (November 2002): 60–71.

Davis, Richard Carter. "Adventures with MicroMARC: A Report on Idaho's Centennial Database." *American Archivist* 55 (fall 1992): 600–7.

DeRose, Steven J. "Navigation, Access, and Control Using Structured Information." *American Archivist* 60, no. 3 (summer 1997): 298–309.

Diamond, Elizabeth. "The Index of the Diefenbaker Speech Collection: An Experiment in Computer-Assisted Indexing of Archives." *Archivaria* 31 (winter 1990–91): 50–59.

Dooley, Jackie M. "Subject Indexing in Context." *American Archivist* 55 (spring 1992): 344–54.

Dow, Elizabeth H. "EAD and the Small Repository." *American Archivist* 60, no. 4 (fall 1997): 446–55.

Duff, Wendy M. "Will Metadata Replace Archival Description? A Commentary." *Archivaria* 39 (spring 1995): 33–38.

Duff, Wendy M., and Kent M. Haworth. "Advancing Archival Description: A Model for Rationalising North American Descriptive Standards." *Archives and Manuscripts* 25, no. 2 (November 1997): 194–217.

———. "The Reclamation of Archival Description: The Canadian Perspective." *Archivaria* 31 (winter 1990–91): 26–35.

Durance, Cynthia J. "Authority Control: Beyond a Bowl of Alphabet Soup." *Archivaria* 35 (spring 1993): 38–46.

Duranti, Luciana. "Origin and Development of the Concept of Archival Description." *Archivaria* 35 (spring 1993): 47–54.

Encoded Archival Description Working Group of the Society of American Archivists and the Network Development and MARC Standards Office of the Library of Congress. *Encoded Archival Description Tag Library, Version 1.0.* Chicago: Society of American Archivists, 1988.

Encoded Archival Description Working Group of the Society of American Archivists. *Encoded Archival Description Application Guidelines, Version 1.0.* Chicago: Society of American Archivists, 1989.

Feeney, Kathleen. "Retrieval of Archival Finding Aids Using World-Wide-Web Search Engines." *American Archivist* 62, no. 2 (fall 1999): 206–28.

Fox, Michael. "Implementing Encoded Archival Description: An Overview of Administrative and Technical Considerations." *American Archivist* 60, no. 3 (summer 1997): 330–43.

———. "Stargazing: Locating EAD in the Descriptive Firmament." In *Encoded Archival Description on the Internet*, Daniel V. Pitti and Wendy Duff, 61–74. New York: Haworth Information Press, 2001.

Garrison, Ellen. "Neither Fish Nor Fowl Nor Good Red Meat: Using Archival Descriptive Techniques for Special Format Materials." *Archival Issues* 21, no. 1 (1996): 61–72.

Gilliland-Swetland, Anne J. "Popularizing the Finding Aid: Exploring EAD to Enhance Online Discovery and Retrieval in Archival Information Systems by Diverse User Groups." In *Encoded Archival Description on the Internet*, edited by Daniel V. Pitti and Wendy Duff, 199–226. New York: Haworth Information Press, 2001.

Gracy, David B. "Finding Aids Are Like Streakers." *Georgia Archive* 4 (1976): 39–47.

Hamburger, Susan. "Life With Grant: Administering Manuscripts Cataloging Grant Projects." *American Archivist* 62, no. 1 (spring 1999): 130–52.

Haworth, Kent M. "Archival Description: Content and Context in Search of Structure." In *Encoded Archival Description on the Internet*, edited by Daniel V. Pitti and Wendy Duff, 7–26. New York: Haworth Information Press, 2001.

———. "The Development of Descriptive Standards in Canada: A Progress Report." *Archivaria* 34 (summer 1992): 75–90.

———. "The Voyage of *RAD*: From the Old World to the New." *Archivaria* 35 (spring 1993): 55–63.

Hensen, Steven, "Archival Cataloging and the Internet: The Implications and Impact of EAD." In *Encoded Archival Description on the Internet*, edited by Daniel V. Pitti and Wendy Duff, 75–96. New York: Haworth Information Press, 2001.

———., ed. *Archives, Personal Papers, and Manuscripts: A Cataloging Manual for Archival Repositories, Historical Societies, and Manuscript Libraries.* 2d ed. Chicago: Society of American Archivists, 1989.

———. "The First Shall Be First: *APPM* and Its Impact on American Archival Description." *Archivaria* 35 (spring 1993): 64–70.

———. "'NISTF II' and EAD: The Evolution of Archival Description." *American Archivist* 60, no. 3 (summer 1997): 284–97.

———. "The Use of Standards in the Application of the AMC Format." *American Archivist* 49 (winter 1986): 31–40.

Hives, Christopher, and Blair Taylor. "Using Archival Descriptive Standards as a Basis for Cooperation: The British Columbia Archival Union List Project." *Archivaria* 35 (spring 1993): 71–85.

Hodges, Martha. "Using the MARC Format for Archives and Manuscripts Control to Catalog Published Microfilms of Manuscript Collections." *Microform Review* 18 (winter 1989): 29–35.

Holmes, William M., Jr., Edie Hedlin, and Thomas E. Weir, Jr. "MARC and Life Cycle Tracking at the National Archives: Project Final Report." *American Archivist* 49 (summer 1986): 305–9.

Holyoke, Francesca, and Marlene Power. "The Anatomy of a Record: How Descriptive Standards Provide Building Blocks." *Archivaria* 34 (summer 1992): 152–65.

Honhart, Frederick L. "MicroMARC:AMC: A Case Study in the Development of an Automated System." *American Archivist* 52 (winter 1989): 80–86.

Hoyer, Timothy P., Stephen Miller, and Alvin Pollock. "Consortial Approaches to the Implementation of Encoded Archival Description (EAD): The American Heritage Virtual Archive Project and the Online Archive of California (OAC)." In *Encoded Archival Description on the Internet*, edited by Daniel V. Pitti and Wendy Duff, 113–36. New York: Haworth Information Press, 2001.

Hurley, Chris. "The Making and the Keeping of Records: (1) What Are Finding Aids For?" *Archives and Manuscripts* 26, no. 1 (May 1998): 58–77.

———. "The Making and the Keeping of Records: (2) The Tyranny of Listing." *Archives and Manuscripts* 28, no. 1 (May 2000): 8–23.

Hutchinson, Tim. "Strategies for Searching Online Finding Aids: A Retrieval Experiment." *Archivaria* 44 (fall 1997): 72–101.

International Council on Archives. "ISAD(G): General International Standard Archival Description." *Archivaria* 34 (summer 1992): 17–32.

———. "Statement of Principles Regarding Archival Description." *Archivaria* 34 (summer 1992): 8–16.

Inventories and Registers: A Handbook of Techniques and Examples. Chicago: Society of American Archivists, 1976.

Isaac, Glen, and Derek Reimer. "Right From the Start: Developing Predescriptive Standards at the British Columbia Archives and Records Service." *Archivaria* 35 (spring 1993): 86–98.

Kiesling, Kris. "EAD as an Archival Descriptive Standard." *American Archivist* 60, no. 3 (summer 1997): 344–54.

Lacy, Mary A., and Anne Mitchell. "EAD Testing and Implementation at the Library of Congress." *American Archivist* 60, no. 4 (fall 1997): 420–35.

Larade, Sharon P., and Johanne M. Pelletier. "Mediating in a Neutral Environment: Gender-Inclusive or Neutral Language in Archival Description." *Archivaria* 35 (spring 1993): 99–109.

Lucas, Lydia. "Efficient Finding Aids: Developing a System for Control of Archives and Manuscripts." *American Archivist* 44 (winter 1981): 21–26.

Lyandres, Natasha, and Olga Leontieva. "Developing International Cataloging Standards for Archival Holdings: Rosarkhiv-RLG-Hoover Project, 1994–1997." *American Archivist* 61, no. 2 (fall 1998): 441–52.

MacNeil, Heather. "Metadata Strategies and Archival Description: Comparing Apples to Oranges." *Archivaria* 39 (spring 1995): 22–32.

MARC Format and Life Cycle Tracking at the National Archives: A Study. Washington, D.C.: National Archives and Records Administration, 1986.

McInerny, Carmel. "Implementation of Encoded Archival Description at the Australian War Memorial: A Case Study." *Archives and Manuscripts* 30, no. 2 (November 2002): 72–81.

McKemmish, Sue, et al. "Describing Records in Context in the Continuum: The Australian Recordkeeping Metadata Schema." *Archivaria* 48 (fall 1999): 3–43.

McKemmish, Sue, and Dagmar Parer. "Towards Frameworks for Standardizing Recordkeeping Metadata." *Archives and Manuscripts* 26, no. 1 (May 1998): 24–45.

Meissner, Dennis. "First Things First: Reengineering Finding Aids for Implementation of EAD." *American Archivist* 60, no. 4 (fall 1997): 372–87.

———. "Online Archival Cataloging and Public Access at the Minnesota Historical Society." *Archival Issues* 17 (1992): 31–48.

Michelson, Avra. "Description and Reference in the Age of Automation." *American Archivist* 50 (spring 1987): 192–208.

Morris, Leslie A. "Developing a Cooperative Intra-Institutional Approach to EAD Implementation: The Harvard/Radcliffe Digital Finding Aids Project." *American Archivist* 60, no. 4 (fall 1997): 388–407.

Morton, Katharine D. "The MARC Formats: An Overview." *American Archivist* 49 (winter 1986): 21–30.

Pederson, Ann. "Unlocking Hidden Treasures Through Description: Comments on Archival Voyages of Discovery." *Archivaria* 37 (spring 1994): 47–63.

Pitti, Daniel V. "Encoded Archival Description: The Development of an Encoding Standard for Archival Finding Aids." *American Archivist* 60, no. 3 (summer 1997): 268–83.

Pitti, Daniel V. and Wendy M. Duff, eds. *Encoded Archival Description on the Internet.* New York: Haworth Information Press, 2001.

Preparation of Preliminary Inventories. Staff Information Circular 14. Washington, D.C.: National Archives, 1950.

Pugh, Mary Jo. "The Illusion of Omniscience: Subject Access and the Reference Archivist." *American Archivist* 45 (winter 1982): 33–44.

Rabins, Joan. "Redescription Reconsidered: Current Issues in Description and Their Applications for Labour Archives." *Archivaria* 27 (winter 1988–89): 57–66.

Reed, Barbara. "Metadata: Core Record or Core Business?" *Archives and Manuscripts* 25, no. 2 (November 1997): 218–41.

Reid, Elspeth. "The Presbyterian Church in Canada Archives Recataloguing Project." *Archivaria* 34 (summer 1992): 91–108.

Rinehart, Richard. "Cross-Community Applications: The EAD in Museums." In *Encoded Archival Description on the Internet*, edited by Daniel V. Pitti and Wendy Duff, 169–86. New York: Haworth Information Press, 2001.

Roe, Kathleen. "Enhanced Authority Control: Is It Time?" *Archivaria* 35 (spring 1993): 119–29.

Roth, James M. "Serving Up EAD: An Exploratory Study on the Deployment and Utilization of Encoded Archival Description Finding Aids." *American Archivist* 64, no. 2 (fall/winter 2001): 214–37.

Russell, Beth M., and Robin L. Brandt Hutchison. "Official Publications at Texas A&M University: A Case Study in Cataloging Archival Material." *American Archivist* 63, no. 1 (spring/summer 2000): 175–84.

Ruth, Janice E. "The Development and Structure of the Encoded Archival Description (EAD) Document Type Definition." In *Encoded Archival Description on the Internet*, edited by Daniel V. Pitti and Wendy Duff, 27–60. New York: Haworth Information Press, 2001.

———. "Encoded Archival Description: A Structural Overview." *American Archivist* 60, no. 3 (summer 1997): 310–29.

Sahli, Nancy. "Finding Aids: A Multi-Media, Systems Perspective." *American Archivist* 44 (winter 1981): 15–20.

———. "Interpretation and Application of the AMC Format." *American Archivist* 49 (winter 1986): 9–20.

Seaman, David. "Multi-Institutional EAD: The University of Virginia's Role in the American Heritage Project." *American Archivist* 60, no. 4 (fall 1997): 436–45.

Shawcross, Nancy M. "Cataloging: A Case Study of Practices at the University of Pennsylvania." *Archival Issues* 18, no. 2 (1993): 133–44.

Smiraglia, Richard, ed. *Describing Archival Materials: The Use of the MARC AMC Format.* New York: Haworth, 1990.

Spindler, Robert P. and Richard Pearce-Moses. "Does AMC Mean 'Archives Made Confusing'? Patron Understanding of USMARC AMC Catalog Records." *American Archivist* 56 (spring 1993): 330–41.

"Standards for Archival Description." Special issues of *American Archivist* 52 (fall 1989): 432–537 and 53 (winter 1990): 24–109.

Stibbe, Hugo. "Implementing the Concept of Fonds: Primary Access Point, Multilevel Description and Authority Control." *Archivaria* 34 (summer 1992): 109–37.

Sweet, Meg, et al. "EAD and Government Archives." In *Encoded Archival Description on the Internet*, edited by Daniel V. Pitti and Wendy Duff, 147–68,. New York: Haworth Information Press, 2001.

Szary, Richard V. "Encoded Finding Aids as a Transforming Technology in Archival Reference Service." In *Encoded Archival Description on the Internet*, edited by Daniel V. Pitti and Wendy Duff, 187–98. New York: Haworth Information Press, 2001.

Tatem, Jill. "EAD: Obstacles to Implementation, Opportunities for Understanding." *Archival Issues* 23, no. 2 (1998): 155–70.

Thibodeau, Sharon. "Archival Context as Archival Authority Record: The ISAAR (CPF)." *Archivaria* 40 (fall 1995): 75–85.

Tibbo, Helen R., and Lokman I. Meho. "Finding Finding Aids on the World Wide Web." *American Archivist* 64, no. 1 (spring/summer 2001): 61–78.

Van Camp, Anne. "Providing Unified Access to International Primary Research Resources in the Humanities: The Research Libraries Group." In *Encoded Archival Description on the Internet*. edited by Daniel V. Pitti and Wendy Duff, 137–46. New York: Haworth Information Press, 2001.

Vargas, Mark A. "Do We Need Authority Control? Investigations at the Milwaukee Urban Archives." *Archival Issues* 19, no. 1 (1994): 45–52.

Vargas, Mark A. and Janet Padway. "Catalog Them Again for the First Time." *Archival Issues* 17 (1992): 49–64.

Wallace, David. "Managing the Present: Metadata as Archival Description." *Archivaria* 39 (spring 1995): 11–21.

Walters, Tyler O. "Adapting Library Bibliographic Utilities and Local System Software for Use in Archival Information Systems: The Case of NOTIS 5.0." *Archival Issues* 19, no. 2 (1994): 107–18.

Zboray, Ronald J. "dBase III Plus and the MARC AMC Format: Problems and Possibilities." *American Archivist* 50 (spring 1987): 210–25.

PRESERVATION

Access to Information: Preservation Issues. Proceedings of the Thirty-Fourth International Conference of the Round table on Archives, Budapest, 1999. Paris: International Council on Archives, 2000.

Allen, Barbara Ann. *A Guide to Bibliotherapy.* Chicago: Association of Specialized and Cooperative Library Agencies, 1982.

Appelbaum, Barbara. *Guide to Environmental Protection of Collections.* Madison, Conn.: Sound View Press, 1991.

Archival Preservation of Motion Pictures: A Summary of Current Findings. Technical Leaflet No. 126. Nashville, Tenn.: American Association for State and Local History.

Baker, Nicholson. *Double Fold: Libraries and the Assault on Paper.* New York: Random House, 2001.

Banks, Paul N. *Preservation of Library Materials.* Chicago: Newberry Library, 1978.

———. *A Selective Bibliography on the Conservation of Research Library Materials.* Chicago: Newberry Library, 1981.

Banks, Paul N. and Roberta Pilette, eds. *Preservation: Issues and Planning.* Chicago: American Library Association, 2000.

Batterham, I.H., W.S. Hamilton, and M.L. Weightman. "A Comparative Study of Six Writing Papers After Artificial Aging." *Archives and Manuscripts* 10, no. 2 (December 1982): 115–35.

Bigelow, Susan. "Duels or Dialogues? The Relationship Between Archivists and Conservators." *Archivaria* 29 (winter 1989–90): 51–56.

Book Longevity: Reports of the Committee on Production Guidelines for Book Longevity. Washington, D.C.: Council on Library Resources, 1982.

Brittle Books. Washington, D.C.: Council on Library Resources, 1986.

Bruce, James. "Restoration and Preservation of Documents, Part I." *Archives and Manuscripts* 5, no. 7 (May 1974): 179–82.

——— "Restoration and Preservation of Documents, Part II." *Archives and Manuscripts* 5, no. 8 (August 1974): 215—20.

——— "Restoration and Preservation of Documents, Part III." *Archives and Manuscripts* 6, no. 1 (November 1974): 20–23.

Bruce, Jim, Jill Caldwell, and Lee McGregor. "The Conservation of Archives in Australia." *Archives and Manuscripts* 7, no. 2 (February 1978): 63–71.

Calmes, Alan. "To Archive and Preserve: A Media Primer." *Inform* 1 (May 1987): 14–17, 33.

Carey, Kathryn M. "Preservation of Colonial Court Records: Treating a Vast Collection of Historic Documents." *Technology and Conservation* 6 (spring 1981): 42–45.

Clapp, Verner W. "The Story of Permanent/Durable Book-Paper, 1150–1970." *Restaurator* 3 (1972): 1–51.

Conway, Paul. *Preservation in the Digital World.* Washington, D.C.: Commision on Preservation and Access, 1996.

Corbett, N.J. "Damage to Records in Darwin Caused by Cyclone Tracy." *Archives and Manuscripts* 6, no. 3 (May 1975): 91–95.

Cribbs, Margaret A. "Photographic Conservation: An Update." *ARMA Records Management Quarterly* 22 (July 1988): 17–19.

Cunha, George, and Dorothy Cunha. *Library and Archives Conservation: 1980's and Beyond.* 2 vols. Metuchen, N.J.: Scarecrow Press, 1983.

Cunningham, Veronica Colley. "The Preservation of Newspaper Clippings." *Special Libraries* (winter 1987): 41–46.

D'Arienzo, Daria, Anne Ostendarp, and Emily Silverman. "Preservation Microfilming: The Challenges of Saving a Collection at Risk." *American Archivist* 57 (summer 1994): 498–513.

Dimitroff, Michael, and James W. Lacksonen. "The Diffusion of Sulfur Dioxide in Air Through Stacked Layers of Paper." *Journal of the American Institute for Conservation* 25 (spring 1986): 31–37.

Eaton, George. *Conservation of Photographs.* Rochester, N.Y.: Eastman Kodak, 1985.

Environmental Controls Resource Packet. Albany, N.Y.: New York State Library, 1991.

Field, Jeffrey. "The NEH Office of Preservation, 1986–1988." *Microform Review* 17 (October 1988): 187–89.

Fox, Lisa L. "A Two Year Perspective on Library Preservation: An Annotated Bibliography." *Library Resources and Technical Services* 30 (July/September 1986): 290–318.

Geller, L.D. "In-House Conservation and the General Practice of Archival Science." *Archivaria* 22 (summer 1986): 163–67.

Grimard, Jacques. "Mass Deacidification: Universal Cure or Limited Solution?" *American Archivist* 57 (fall 1994): 674–79.

Gwinn, Nancy E. "The Fragility of Paper: Can Our Historical Records Be Saved?" *Public Historian* 13 (summer 1991): 33–54.

Haines, John H. and Stuart A. Kohler. "An Evaluation of Ortho-Phenyl as a Fumicidal Fumigant for Archives and Libraries." *Journal of the American Institute for Conservation* 25 (spring 1986): 49–55.

Hendriks, Klaus B. *The Preservation and Restoration of Photographic Materials in Archives and Libraries: A RAMP Study with Guidelines.* Paris: UNESCO, 1984.

Higginbotham, Barbra Buckner, and Judith W. Wild. *The Preservation Program Blueprint.* Chicago: American Library Association, 2001.

Hirst, Warwick. "Salvaging Flood Damaged Records." *Archives and Manuscripts* 13, no. 1 (May 1985): 24–29.

Hunter, Gregory S. *Preserving Digital Information.* New York: Neal-Schuman, 2000.

———. "Reprography." *World Encyclopedia of Library and Information Services.* 3d ed. Chicago: American Library Association, 1993.

Jones, Maggie, and Neil Beagrie. *Preservation Management of Digital Materials: A Handbook.* London: The British Library, 2001.

Kaebnick, Gregory E. "Slow Fires: A National, NEH-Funded Microfilming Program Seeks to Rescue Civilization." *Inform* 3 (November 1989): 12–14.

Kaplan, Hilary A., Maria Holden, and Kathy Ludwig, comps. "Archives Preservation Resource Review." *American Archivist* 54 (fall 1991): 502–45.

Kathpalia, Y.P. *Conservation and Preservation of Archives.* Paris: UNESCO 1973.

———. *A Model Curriculum for the Training of Specialists in Document Preservation and Restoration: A RAMP Study With Guidelines.* Paris: UNESCO, 1984.

Krasnow, Lawrence L. "Legal Aspects of Conservation: Basic Considerations of Contracts and Negligence." *Technology and Conservation* 7 (spring 1982): 38–40.

Lavender, Kenneth. *Book Repair.* 2d ed. (New York: Neal-Schuman, 2001).

Lull, William P., with the assistance of Paul N. Banks. *Conservation Environment Guidelines for Libraries and Archives.* Albany, N.Y.: New York State Library, 1990.

Mathey, Robert. *Air Quality Criteria for Storage of Paper-Based Archival Records.* Washington, D.C.: National Bureau of Standards, 1983.

McGregor, Lee, and Jim Bruce. "Recovery of Flood Damaged Documents by the Queensland State Archives." *Archives and Manuscripts* 5, no. 8 (August 1974): 193–99.

Morrison, Robert. "Conservation Notes." *Archives and Manuscripts* 8, no. 1 (June 1980): 55–61.

Nielsen, T.F. "Deacidification, Lamination and the Use of Polyester Film." *Archives and Manuscripts* 6, no. 8 (February 1977): 379–81.

——— "The Effects of Air Pollution on Stored Paper." *Archives and Manuscripts* 7, no. 2 (February 1978): 72–77.

O'Toole, James M. "On the Idea of Permanence." *American Archivist* 52 (winter 1989): 10–25.

——— "Do Not Fold, Spindle, or Mutilate: *Double Fold* and the Assault on Libraries." *American Archivist* 64, no. 2 (fall/winter 2001): 385–93.

Petherbridge, Guy, ed. *Conservation of Library and Archive Materials and the Graphic Arts.* London: Butterworths, 1987.

Poole, Frazer G. "Some Aspects of the Conservation Problem in Archives." *American Archivist* 40 (April 1977): 163–71.

"Preservation." Special issue. *American Archivist* 53 (spring 1990): 184–369.

Preservation of Archival Materials: A Report of the Task Forces on Archival Selection to the Commission on Preservation and Access. Washington, D.C.: Commission on Preservation and Access, 1993.

Preservation of Historical Records. Washington, D.C.: National Research Council, 1986.

"Preservation: Old and New Technologies Save Books for Future Use." *Journal of Information and Image Management* 18 (November 1985): 22–27.

Preserving the Intellectual Heritage: A Report of the Bellagio Conference, June 7–10, 1993. Washington, D.C.: Commission on Preservation and Access, 1993.

Pursell, Carroll. "Preservation Technologies: As Answers Get Easier, Questions Remain Hard." *Public Historian* 13 (summer 1991): 113–16.

Rare Book and Paper Repair Techniques. Technical Leaflet No. 13. Nashville, Tenn.: American Association for State and Local History.

Reilly, James M. *Care and Identification of Nineteenth-Century Photographic Prints.* Rochester, N.Y.: Eastman Kodak Company, 1986.

Reilly, James M., Douglas W. Nishimura, and Edward Zinn. *New Tools for Preservation: Assessing Long-Term Environmental Effects on Library and Archives Collections.* Washington, D.C.: Commission on Preservation and Access, 1995.

Ritzenthaler, Mary Lynn. *Archives and Manuscripts: Conservation.* Chicago: Society of American Archivists, 1983.

———. *Preserving Archives and Manuscripts.* Chicago: Society of American Archivists, 1993.

Schmidt, J. David. "Freeze-Drying of Historic/Cultural Properties: A Valuable Process in Restoration and Documentation." *Technology and Conservation* 9 (spring 1985): 20–26.

Schnare, Robert E., Jr., Susan G. Swatzburg, and George M. Cunha. *Bibliography of Preservation Literature, 1983–1996.* Lanham, Md.: Scarecrow Press, 2001.

Schur, Susan E. "Conservation Profile: The Northeast Document Conservation Center." *Technology and Conservation* 7 (fall 1982): 32–39.

———. "Conservation Profile: The Preservation Office of the Library of Congress." *Technology and Conservation* 7 (summer 1982): 26–35.

Sebera, Donald K. *Isoperms: An Environmental Management Tool.* Washington, D.C.: Commission on Preservation and Access, 1994.

Story, Keith O. *Approaches to Pest Management in Museums.* Washington, D.C.: Conservation Analytical Laboratory, Smithsonian Institution, 1985.

Trinkaus-Randall, Gregor. *Protecting Your Collections: A Manual of Archival Security.* Chicago: Society of American Archivists, 1995.

Tuttle, Craig A. *An Ounce of Preservation: A Guide to the Care of Papers and Photographs.* Highland City, Fla.: Rainbow Books, 1995.

Waegemann, C. Peter. "Preservation of Information." *Records and Retrieval Report* 2 (March 1986): 1–15.

Walker, Gay. "Advanced Preservation Planning at Yale." *Microform Review* 18 (winter 1989): 20–28.

———. "Storing Paper." *Records and Retrieval Report* 3 (September 1987): 1–12.

Walsh, T.C. "Archival Conservation: An Annotated Bibliography." *Archives and Manuscripts* 7, no. 3 (August 1978): 137–40.

Walsh, Timothy. "A Typical Conservation Laboratory." *Archives and Manuscripts* 7, no. 5 (November 1979). 268–75.

——— and Neville Corbett. "Fumigation Chamber and Airing Room at Villawood." *Archives and Manuscripts* 6, no. 8 (February 1977): 376–78.

——— and Deborah Keane. "Technical Note: The Dangers of Fumigation of Archives with Ethylene Oxide." *Archives and Manuscripts* 8, no. 1 (June 1980): 62–63.

Watson, A.J. "Manufacturing and Environmental Factors Affecting the Permanence of Paper." *Archives and Manuscripts* 6, no. 7 (August 1976): 285–91.

White, John R. "An Introduction to the Preservation of Information on Paper, Film, Magnetic, and Optical Media." Silver Spring, Md.: Association for Information and Image Management.

Woodhouse, A.J. "The Queensland State Archives Fumigation Unit: Ethylene Oxide/Vacuum Fumigation as an Aid for the Preservation of Archives and Manuscripts." *Archives and Manuscripts* 4, no. 3 (November 1970): 14–20.

Wright, Sandra, and Peter Yurkiw. "The Collections Survey in the Federal Archives and Manuscript Divisions of the Public Archives of Canada: A Progress Report on Conservation Programme Planning." *Archivaria* 22 (summer 1986): 58–74.

SECURITY AND DISASTER PLANNING

Anderson, Hazel. *Planning Manual for Disaster Control in Scottish Libraries and Records Offices.* Edinburgh: National Library of Scotland, 1985.

Archives and Records Centers. Leaflet 232AM. Quincy, Mass.: National Fire Protection Association, 1986.

Balon, Brett J. and H. Wayne Gardner. "Disaster Contingency Planning: The Basic Elements." *ARMA Records Management Quarterly* 21 (January 1987): 14–16.

Barton, John P. and Johanna G. Wellheiser, eds. *An Ounce of Prevention: A Handbook on Disaster Contingency Planning for Archives, Libraries, and Records Centers.* Toronto: Toronto Area Archivists, 1986.

Bohem, Hilda. *Disaster Prevention and Disaster Preparedness.* Berkeley, Calif.: University of California, 1978.

Buchanan, Sally. "Disaster: Prevention, Preparedness and Action." *Library Trends* (fall 1981): 241–52.

———. *Resource Materials for Disaster Planning in New York Institutions.* Albany, N.Y.: New York State Library, 1988.

Bulgawicz, Susan, and Charles E. Nolan. "Disaster Planning and Recovery: A Regional Approach." *ARMA Records Management Quarterly* 21 (January 1987): 18–20, 44.

Disaster Planning Kit. Andover, Mass.: Northeast Document Conservation Center, 1982.

Disaster Prevention and Preparedness. Problems in Archives Kit. Chicago: Society of American Archivists, 1982.

Eulenberg, Julia N. *Handbook for the Recovery of Water Damaged Business Records.* Prairie Village, Kans.: Association of Records Managers and Administrators, 1986.

Fortson, Judith. *Disaster Planning and Recovery.* New York: Neal-Schuman, 1992.

Fuss, Eugene L. "Security in Cultural Institutions: Advances in Electronic Protection Techniques." *Technology and Conservation* 4 (winter 1979): 34–37.

Galvin, Theresa. "The Boston Case of Charles Merrill Mount: The Archivist's Arch Enemy." *American Archivist* 53 (summer 1990): 442–51.

Griffith, J. W. "After the Disaster: Restoring Library Service." *Wilson Library Bulletin* 58 (December 1983): 258–65.

Hell and High Water: A Disaster Information Sourcebook. New York: New York Metropolitan Reference and Research Library Agency (METRO): 1988.

Hendriks, Klaus B. and Brian Lesser. "Disaster Preparedness and Recovery: Photographic Materials." *American Archivist* 46 (winter 1983): 52–68.

Hoffman, Annie, and Bryan Baumann. "Disaster Recovery: A Prevention Plan for Northwestern National Life Insurance." *ARMA Records Management Quarterly* 20 (April 1986): 40–44.

Hunter, John E. "Museum Disaster Planning." *Museums, Archives, and Library Security.* Woburn, Mass.: Butterworth Publishers, 1983.

Jones, Virginia A., and Kris E. Keyes. *Emergency Management for Records and Information Management Programs.* Prairie Village, Kans.: ARMA International, 1997.

Kahn, Miriam B. *Disaster Response and Planning for Libraries.* Chicago: American Library Association, 1998.

Kemp, Toby. "Disaster Assistance Bibliography: Selected References for Cultural/ Historic Facilities." *Technology and Conservation* 8 (summer 1983): 25–27.

Langelier, Gilles and Sandra Wright. "Contingency Planning for Cartographic Archives." *Archivaria* 13 (winter 1981–82): 47–58.

Marrelli, Nancy. "Fire and Flood at Concordia University Archives, January 1982." *Archivaria* 17 (winter 1983–84): 266–74.

Mathieson, David F. "Hurricane Preparedness: Establishing Workable Policies for Dealing with Storm Threats." *Technology and Conservation* 8 (summer 1983): 28–29.

Morris, John. *The Library Disaster Preparedness Handbook.* Chicago: American Library Association, 1986

Murray, Toby. "Bibliography on Disasters, Disaster Preparedness and Disaster Recovery," *ARMA Records Management Quarterly* 21 (April 1987): 18–30, 41.

———. "Don't Get Caught with Your Plans Down." *ARMA Records Management Quarterly* 21 (April 1987): 12–17.

O'Connell, Mildred. "Disaster Planning: Writing and Implementing Plans for Collections-Holding Institutions." *Technology and Conservation* 8 (summer 1983): 18–24.

Purcell, Aaron D. "Abstractions of Justice: The Library of Congress's Great Manuscripts Robbery, 1896–1897." *American Archivist* 62, no. 2 (fall 1999): 325–45.

Protection of Records. Leaflet 232. Quincy, Mass.: National Fire Protection Association, 1986.

Tiszkus, Alphonse T. and E. G. Dressler. "Fire Protection Planning for Cultural Institutions: Blending Risk Management, Loss Prevention, and Physical Safeguards." *Technology and Conservation* 5 (summer 1980): 18–23.

Totka, Vincent A., Jr. "Preventing Patron Theft in the Archives: Legal Perspectives and Problems." *American Archivist* 56 (fall 1993): 664–73.

Trinkaus-Randall, Gregor. *Protecting Your Collections: A Manual of Archival Security.* Chicago: Society of American Archivists, 1995.

Vital Records. Prairie Village, Kans.: Association of Records Managers and Administrators, 1984.

Vossler, Janet L. "The Human Element of Disaster Recovery." *ARMA Records Management Quarterly* 21 (January 1987): 10–12.

Waegemann, C. Peter. "Disaster Prevention and Recovery." *Records and Retrieval Report* 1 (March 1985).

Walch, Timothy. *Archives and Manuscripts: Security.* Chicago: Society of American Archivists, 1977.

Walters, Tyler O., in association with Ivan E. Hanthorn. "Special Collections Repositories at Association of Research Libraries Institutions: A Study of Current Practices in Preservation Management." *American Archivist* 61, no. 1 (spring 1998): 158–87.

Waters, Peter. *Procedures for Salvage of Water-Damaged Library Materials.* Washington, D.C., Library of Congress, 1975.

Welch, Edwin. "Security in an English Archives." *Archivaria* 1, no. 2 (summer 1976): 49–55.

Wellheiser, Johanna, and Jude Scott. *An Ounce of Prevention: Integrated Disaster Planning for Archives, Libraries, and Records Centres.* Second Edition. Lanham, Md.: Scarecrow Press and the Canadian Archives Foundation, 2002.

Wolff, Richard E. "Snap, Crackle and Pop." *ARMA Records Management Quarterly* 19 (April 1985): 3–7.

Zeidberg, David S. "We Have Met the Enemy: Collection Security in Libraries." *Rare Book and Manuscript Librarianship* 2 (spring 1987): 19–26.

ACCESS, REFERENCE, AND OUTREACH

Armstrong-Ingram, R. Jackson. "The Giveness of Kin: Legal and Ethical Issues in Accessing Adoption Records." *Archival Issues* 22, no. 1 (1997): 21–36.

Aubitz, Shawn, and Gail F. Stern. *Developing Archival Exhibitions.* Mid-Atlantic Regional Archives Conference Technical Leaflet No. 5. Mid-Atlantic Regional Archives Conference, 1990.

Bain, George W. "Archives Week and the Power of Intersecting Ripples." *Archival Issues* 23, no. 1 (1998): 5–16.

Barnett, LeRoy. "Standing on the Other Side of the Reference Desk." *Archival Issues* 19, no. 2 (1994): 119–30.

Baumann, Roland M. "The Administration of Access to Confidential Records in State Archives: Common Practices and the Need for a Model Law." *American Archivist* 49 (fall 1986): 349–69.

Beattie, Diane L. "An Archival User Study: Researchers in the Field of Women's History." *Archivaria* 29 (winter 1989–90): 33–50.

Blais, Gabrielle, and David Enns. "From Paper Archives to People Archives: Public Programming in the Management of Archives." *Archivaria* 31 (winter 1990–91): 101–13.

Blouin, Francis X., Jr. "A Case for Bridging the Gap: The Significance of the Vatican Archives Project for International Archival Information Exchange." *American Archivist* 55 (winter 1992): 182–91.

Bradsher, James Gregory. "Researchers, Archivists, and the Access Challenge of the FBI Records in the National Archives." *Midwestern Archivist* 11 (1986): 95–110.

Brauer, Carl M. "Researcher Evaluation of Reference Services." *American Archivist* 43 (winter 1980): 77–79.

Burke, John. "Archives and Reader Services: A Statistical Survey." *Archives and Manuscripts* 6, no. 8 (February 1977): 325–42.

Campbel, Madeline. "Government Accountability and Access to Information on Contracted-Out Services." *Archives and Manuscripts* 26, no. 2 (November 1998): 294–327.

Casterline, Gail Farr. *Archives and Manuscripts: Exhibits.* Chicago: Society of American Archivists, 1980.

Chute, Tamar G. "Selling the College and University Archives." *Archival Issues* 25, nos. 1–2 (2000): 33–48.

Conway, Paul. "Facts and Frameworks: An Approach to Studying the Users of Archives." *American Archivist* 49 (fall 1986): 393–408.

———. "Research in Presidential Libraries: A User Survey." *Midwestern Archivist* 11 (1986): 35–56.

Cook, Sharon Anne. "Connecting Archives and the Classroom," *Archivaria* 44 (fall 1997): 102–17.

Cook, Terry. "Viewing the World Upside Down: Reflections on the Theoretical Underpinnings of Archival Public Programming." *Archivaria* 31 (winter 1990–91): 123–34.

Craig, Barbara L. "What Are the Clients? Who Are the Products? The Future of Archival Public Service in Perspective." *Archivaria* 31 (winter 1990–91): 135–41.

———. "Old Myths in New Clothes: Expectations of Archives Users." *Archivaria* 45 (spring 1998): 118–26.

Crawford, Michael J. "Copyright, Unpublished Manuscript Records, and the Archivist." *American Archivist* 46 (spring 1983): 135–47.

Crews, Kenneth D. *Copyright Essentials for Librarians and Educators.* Chicago: American Library Association, 2000.

Czech, Rita L.H. "Archival MARC Records and Finding Aids in the Context of End-User Subject Access to Archival Collections." *American Archivist* 61, no. 2 (fall 1998): 426–40.

Danielson, Elena S. "The Ethics of Access." *American Archivist* 52 (winter 1989): 52–62.

Dearstyne, Bruce W. "What is the *Use* of Archives? A Challenge for the Profession." *American Archivist* 50 (winter 1987): 76–87.

Delgado, David J. "The Archivist and Public Relations." *American Archivist* 30 (October 1967): 557–64.

DeWitt, Donald L. "The Impact of the MARC AMC Format on Archival Education and Employment During the 1980s." *Midwestern Archivist* 16 (1991): 73–86.

Diamond, Sigmund. "Archival Adventure Along the Freedom of Information Trail: What Archival Records Reveal About the FBI and the Universities in the McCarthy Period." *Midwestern Archivist* 12 (1987): 29–42.

Dow, Elizabeth H., et al. "The Burlington Agenda: Research Issues in Intellectual Access to Electronically Published Historical Documents." *American Archivist* 64, no. 2 (fall/winter 2001): 292–307.

Dowler, Lawrence. "The Role of Use in Defining Archival Practice and Principles: A Research Agenda for the Availability and Use of Records." *American Archivist* 51 (winter/spring 1988): 74–95.

Dryden, Jean E. "Copyright in Manuscript Sources." *Archivaria* 1, no. 1 (winter 1975–76): 39–47.

Duchein, Michel. *Obstacles to the Access, Use, and Transfer of Information from Archives: A RAMP Study.* Paris: UNESCO, 1983.

Duff, Wendy, and Penka Stoyanova. "Transforming the Crazy Quilt: Archival Displays from a User's Point of View." *Archivaria* 45 (spring 1998): 44–79.

Duff, Wendy, and Catherine A. Johnson. "A Virtual Expression of Need: An Analysis of E-Mail Reference Questions." *American Archivist* 64, no. 1 (spring/summer 2001): 43–60.

Epp, Kathleen. "Telling Stories Around the 'Electric Campfire': The Use of Archives in Television Productions." *Archivaria* 49 (spring 2000): 53–83.

Ericksen, Paul A. "Letting the World in: Anticipating the Use of Religious Archives for the Study of Nonreligious Subjects." *Midwestern Archivist* 12 (1987): 83–90.

Ericson, Timothy L. "'Preoccupied With Our Own Gardens': Outreach and Archivists." *Archivaria* 31 (winter 1990–91): 114–22.

Ericson, Timothy L. and Joshua P. Ranger. "'The Next Great Idea': Loaning Archival Collections." *Archivaria* 47 (spring 1999): 85–113.

Eutick, Mal. "On the Display of Archives." *Archives and Manuscripts* 12, no. 1 (May 1984): 17–23.

Finch, Elsie Freeman, ed. *Advocating Archives: An Introduction to Public Relations for Archivists.* Metuchen, N.J.: Society of American Archivists and Scarecrow Press, 1994.

———. "Archival Advocacy: Reflections on Myths and Realities." *Archival Issues* 20, no. 2 (1995): 115–28

———. "Making Sure They Want It: Managing Successful Public Programs." *American Archivist* 56 (winter 1993): 70–75.

Freedom and Equality of Access to Information: A Report to the American Library Association. Chicago: American Library Association, 1986.

Freeman, Elsie T. "Buying Quarter Inch Holes: Public Support Through Results." *Midwestern Archivist* 10, no. 2 (1985): 89–97.

———. "In the Eye of the Beholder: Archives Administration from the User's Point of View." *American Archivist* 47 (spring 1984): 111–23.

———. "Soap and Education: Archival Training, Public Service, and the Profession: An Essay." *Midwestern Archivist* 16 (1991): 87–94.

Freivogel, Elsie Freeman. "Education Programs: Outreach as an Administrative Function." *American Archivist* 41 (April 1978): 147–53.

Garay, K.E. "Access and Copyright in Literary Collections." *Archivaria* 18 (summer 1984): 220–27.

Geselbracht, Raymond H. "The Origins of Restrictions on Access to Personal Papers at the Library of Congress and the National Archives." *American Archivist* 49 (spring 1986): 142–62.

Gilardi, Ronald L. "The Archival Setting and People with Disabilities: A Legal Analysis." *American Archivist* 56 (fall 1993): 704–13.

Gilbert, Jay. "Access Denied: The *Access to Information Act* and Its Effects on Public Records Creators." *Archivaria* 49 (spring 2000): 84–123.

Gilliland-Swetland, Anne J. and Carol Hughes. "Enhancing Archival Description for Public Computer Conferences of Historical Value: An Exploratory Study." *American Archivist* 55 (spring 1992): 316–30.

Gilliland-Swetland, Anne J., Yasmin B. Kafai, and William E. Landis. "Integrating Primary Sources into the Elementary School Classroom: A Case Study of Teachers' Perspectives." *Archivaria* 48 (fall 1999): 89–116.

Goerler, Raimund E. "Play It Again, Sam: Historical Slide Presentations in Archivists' Public Programming." *American Archivist* 54 (summer 1991): 378–88.

Goggin, Jacqueline. "The Indirect Approach: A Study of Scholarly Users of Black and Women's Organizational Records in the Library of Congress Manuscript Division." *Midwestern Archivist* 11 (1986): 57–67.

Gracy, David B., II. "Is There a Future in the Use of Archives?" *Archivaria* 24 (summer 1987): 3–9.

Gray, Edward. "Copyright and the Right to Copy: Thoughts on the Betamax Case." *Journal of Information and Image Management* 17 (December 1984): 48–49.

Greene, Mark A. "Moderation in Everything, Access in Nothing?: Opinions About Access Restrictions on Private Papers." *Archival Issues* 18, no. 1 (1993): 31–42.

Hanlon, David. "The Chill of History: The Experience, Emotion and Changing Politics of Archival Research in the Pacific." *Archives and Manuscripts* 27, no. 1 (May 1999): 8–21.

Harris, Verne, and Christopher Merrett. "Toward a Culture of Transparency: Public Rights of Access to Official Records in South Africa." *American Archivist* 57 (fall 1994): 680–93.

Hartsook, Herbert J. "By Fair Means If You Can: A Case Study of Raising Private Monies to Support Archival Programs." *Archival Issues* 25, no. 1–2 (2000): 49–56.

Hay, Douglas. "Archival Research in the History of the Law: A User's Perspective." *Archivaria* 24 (summer 1987): 36–46.

Hayward, Robert J. "Federal Access and Privacy Legislation at the Public Archives of Canada." *Archivaria* 18 (summer 1984): 47–57.

Herzstein, Robert Edwin. "The Recently Opened United Nations War Crime Archives: A Researcher's Comments." *American Archivist* 52 (spring 1989): 208–13.

Hodson, Sara S. "Freeing the Dead Sea Scrolls: A Question of Access." *American Archivist* 56 (fall 1993): 690–703.

Hoff-Wilson, Joan. "Access to Restricted Collections: The Responsibility of Professional Historical Organizations." *American Archivist* 46 (fall 1983): 441–47.

Holbert, Sue E. *Archives and Manuscripts: Reference and Access.* Chicago: Society of American Archivists, 1977.

Humphries, Shirley. "Copyright and Related Issues Affecting Original Research Materials." *Archives and Manuscripts* 11, no. 2 (November 1983): 125–41.

Hyslop, Gabrielle. "For Many Audiences: Developing Public Programs at the National Archives of Australia." *Archives and Manuscripts* 30, no. 1 (May 2002): 48–59.

Jackson, William J. "The 80/20 Archives: A Study of Use and Its Implications." *Archival Issues* 22, no. 2 (1997): 133–46.

Jacobsen, Phebe R. " 'The World Turned Upside Down': Reference Priorities and the State Archives." *American Archivist* 44 (fall 1981): 341–45.

Jordan, Philip D. "The Scholar and the Archivist: A Partnership." *American Archivist* 31 (January 1968): 57–65.

Joyce, William L. "Archivists and Research Use." *American Archivist* 47 (spring 1984): 124–33.

Kearsey, Irene. "Some Problems in Placing Modern Medical Records in Public Archives." *Archives and Manuscripts* 17, no. 2 (November 1989): 183–96.

Kepley, Brenda Beasley. "Archives: Accessibility for the Disabled." *American Archivist* 46 (winter 1983): 42–51.

Keon, Jim. "The Canadian Archivist and Copyright Legislation." *Archivaria* 18 (summer 1984): 91–98.

Kirby, M.D. "Access to Information and Privacy: The Ten Information Commandments." *Archivaria* 23 (winter 1986–87): 4–15.

Klaassen, David J. "Achieving Balanced Documentation: Social Services from a Consumer Perspective." *Midwestern Archivist* 11 (1986): 111–24.

LaForce, Gina. "Archives and Copyright in Canada: An Outsider's View." *Archivaria* 11 (winter 1980–81): 37–52.

Landis, William E. "Archival Outreach on the World Wide Web." *Archival Issues* 20, no. 2 (1995): 129–48.

Lathrop, Alan K. "Copyright of Architectural Records: A Legal Perspective." *American Archivist* 49 (fall 1986): 409–23.

Library Reproduction of Copyrighted Works (17 U.S.C. 108): Report of the Register of Copyrights. Washington, D.C.: Library of Congress, 1988.

Linard, Laura, and Brent M. Sverdloff. "Not Just Business as Usual: Evolving Trends in Historical Research at Baker Library." *American Archivist* 60, no. 1 (winter 1997): 88–99.

Long, Linda J. "Question Negotiation in the Archival Setting: The Use of Interpersonal Communication Techniques in the Reference Interview." *American Archivist* 52 (winter 1989): 40–51.

Looking to the Past, Teaching for the Future: Recommendations for the Improvement of Teaching Using Historical Records. Albany, N.Y.: New York State Council for the Social Studies, 1989.

Lutton, Nancy. "Researchers, Permits and Archival Sources in Papua, New Guinea." *Archives and Manuscripts* 7, no. 1 (August 1977): 19–27.

MacDougall, Heather. "Researching Public Health Services in Ontario, 1882–1930." *Archivaria* 10 (summer 1980): 157–72.

MacNeil, Heather. "Defining the Limits of Freedom of Inquiry: The Ethics of Disclosing Personal Information Held in Government Archives." *Archivaria* 32 (summer 1991): 138–44.

Macpherson, Paul. "Theory, Standards and Implicit Assumptions: Public Access to Post-current Government Records." *Archives and Manuscripts* 30, no. 1 (May 2002): 6–17.

Maher, William J. "Between Authors and Users: Archivists in the Copyright Vise." *Archival Issues* 26, no. 1 (2001): 63–76.

———. "The Use of User Studies." *Midwestern Archivist* 11 (1986): 15–26.

Martin, Kristin E. "Analysis of Remote Reference Correspondence at a Large Academic Manuscripts Collection." *American Archivist* 64, no. 1 (spring/summer 2001): 17–42.

Martin, Lyn M. "Viewing the Field: A Literature Review and Survey of the Use of U.S. MARC AMC in U.S. Academic Archives." *American Archivist* 57 (summer 1994): 482–97.

McAdam, Rhona. "AIDS and Confidentiality: The Records Manager's Dilemma." *ARMA Records Management Quarterly* 23 (July 1989): 12–16, 28.

McCall, Nancy, and Lisa A. Mix. "Scholarly Returns: Patterns of Research in a Medical Archives." *Archivaria* 41 (spring 1996): 158–87.

Menne-Haritz, Angelika. "Access—the Reformulation of an Archival Paradigm." *Archival Science* 1, no. 1 (2001): 57–82.

Miller, Fredric. "Use, Appraisal, and Research: A Case Study of Social History." *American Archivist* 49 (fall 1986): 371–92.

Miller, Harold L. "Will Access Restrictions Hold Up in Court? The FBI's Attempt to Use the Braden Papers at the State Historical Society of Wisconsin." *American Archivist* 52 (spring 1989): 180–90.

Miller, Page Putnam. "Archival Issues and Problems: The Central Role of Advocacy." *Public Historian* 8 (summer 1986): 60–73.

Montgomery, Bruce P. "Nixon's Legal Legacy: White House Papers and the Constitution." *American Archivist* 56 (fall 1993): 586–613.

Nicholls, Catherine. "The Role of Outreach in Australian Archive Programs." *Archives and Manuscripts* 29, no. 1 (May 2001): 62–71.

Nixon, Diane S. "Providing Access to Controversial Public Records: The Case of the Robert F. Kennedy Assassination Files." *Public Historian* 11 (summer 1989): 29–44.

Nokes, Jane. "The Value of Archives/Selling the Program." *Archives and Manuscripts* 16, no. 1 (May 1988): 33–41.

Orbach, Barbara C. "The View from the Researcher's Desk: Historians' Perceptions of Research and Repositories." *American Archivist* 54 (winter 1991): 28–43.

Osborn, Deborah. "Copyright and Access to Archives." *Archives and Manuscripts* 12, no. 1 (May 1984): 45–49.

Osborne, Ken. "Archives in the Classroom." *Archivaria* 23 (winter 1986–87): 16–40.

Patry, William F. *The Fair Use Privilege in Copyright Law.* Washington, D.C.: Bureau of National Affairs, 1985.

Pedersen, Ann E. and Gail Farr Casterline. *Archives and Manuscripts: Public Programs.* Chicago: Society of American Archivists, 1980.

Peterson, Trudy Huskamp. "After Five Years: An Assessment of the Amended U.S. Freedom of Information Act." *American Archivist* 43 (spring 1980): 161–68.

———. "Reading, 'Riting, and 'Rithmetic: Speculations on Change in Research Processes." *American Archivist* 55 (summer 1992): 414–19.

Preston, Jean. "Problems in the Use of Manuscripts." *American Archivist* 28 (July 1965): 367–80.

Pugh, Mary Jo. *Providing Reference Services for Archives and Manuscripts.* Chicago: Society of American Archivists, 1992.

Ress, Imre. "The Effects of Democratization on Archival Administration and Use in Eastern Middle Europe." *American Archivist* 55 (winter 1992): 86–93.

Robertson, Gordon. "Confidentiality in Government." *Archivaria* 6 (summer 1978): 3–12.

Robbin, Alice. "State Archives and Issues of Personal Privacy: Policies and Practices." *American Archivist* 49 (spring 1986): 163–75.

Robinson, Esther. "Archives in the Classroom: The Development and Evaluation of National Archives [of Australia] Teachers' Resources." *Archives and Manuscripts* 30, no. 1 (May 2002): 18–29.

Rosenbusch, Andrea. "Are Our Users Being Served? A Report on Online Archival Databases." *Archives and Manuscripts* 29, no. 1 (May 2001): 44–61.

Rumm, John C. "Working Through the Records: Using Business Records to Study Workers and the Management of Labour." *Archivaria* 27 (winter 1988–89): 67–96.

Saclier, Michael. "Archivists, Users, and the Copyright Act, 1968." *Archives and Manuscripts* 6, no. 3 (May 1975): 72–86.

Sawer, Geoffrey. "Copyright in Letters Unpublished at Writer's Death." *Archives and Manuscripts* 3, no. 2 (November 1966): 27–28.

———. "Copyright in Letters Not Published at the Author's Death." *Archives and Manuscripts* 4, no. 5 (November 1971): 1–3.

Schwarz, Judith. "The Archivist's Balancing Act: Helping Researchers While Protecting Individual Privacy." *Journal of American History* 79 (June 1992): 179–89.

Shortt, Samuel. "The New Social History of Medicine: Some Implications for Research." *Archivaria* 10 (summer 1980): 5–22.

Smart, John. "The Professional Archivist's Responsibility as an Advocate of Public Research." *Archivaria* 16 (summer 1983): 139–49.

Speakman, Mary N. "The User Talks Back." *American Archivist* 47 (spring 1984): 164–71.

Stephenson, Mary Sue. "Deciding Not to Build the Wall: Research and the Archival Profession." *Archivaria* 32 (summer 1991): 145–51.

Stewart, Virginia R. "Problems of Confidentiality in the Administration of Personal Case Records." *American Archivist* 37 (July 1974): 387–98.

Summerrell, Richard. "Improving the Education and Professional Development of Reference Archivists." *Archives and Manuscripts* 27, no. 1 (May 1999): 74–95.

Sweeney, Shelley. "An Act of Faith: Access to Religious Records in English-Speaking Canada." *Archivaria* 30 (summer 1990): 42–54.

Synnott, Marcia G. "*The Half-Opened Door*: Researching Admissions Discrimination at Harvard, Yale, and Princeton." *American Archivist* 45 (spring 1982): 175–87.

Taylor, Hugh A. *Archival Services and the Concept of the User: A RAMP Study.* Paris: UNESCO, 1984.

———. "Clio in the Raw: Archival Materials and the Teaching of History." *American Archivist* 35 (July/October 1972): 317–30.

Tener, Jean. "Accessibility and Archives." *Archivaria* 6 (summer 1978): 16–31.

Tibbo, Helen R. "The Epic Struggle: Subject Retrieval from Large Bibliographic Databases." *American Archivist* 57 (spring 1994). 310–26

Turnbaugh, Roy C. "Archival Mission and User Studies." *Midwestern Archivist* 11 (1986): 27–33.

Van Camp, Anne. "Access Policies for Corporate Archives." *American Archivist* 45 (summer 1982): 296–98.

Walters, Tyler O. "Automated Access Practices at Archival Repositories of Association of Research Libraries Institutions." *Archival Issues* 23, no. 2 (1998): 171–90.

Warnow-Blewett, Joan. "Work to Internationalize Access to the Archives and Manuscripts of Physics and Allied Sciences." *American Archivist* 55 (summer 1992): 484–89.

Weinberg, David M. "The Other Side of the Human Experience: Providing Access to Social Service Case Study Files." *American Archivist* 53 (winter 1990): 122–29.

Welch, Todd. "'Green' Archivism: The Archival Response to Environmental Research." *American Archivist* 62, no. 1 (spring 1999): 74–94.

Whalen, Lucille, and Bill Katz, eds. *Reference Services in Archives.* New York: Haworth Press, 1986.

Wilson, Ian E. "Towards a Vision of Archival Services." *Archivaria* 31 (winter 1990–91): 91–100.

Winn, Karyl. "American Archivists' Experience With Copyright." *Archivaria* 18 (summer 1984): 99–104.

Yakel, Elizabeth. "Pushing MARC AMC to Its Limits: The Vatican Archives Project." *American Archivist* 55 (winter 1992): 192–201.

————. "Thinking Inside and Outside the Boxes: Archival Reference Services at the Turn of the Century." *Archivaria* 49 (spring 2000): 140–60.

Yakel, Elizabeth and Laura L. Bost. "Understanding Administrative Use and Users in University Archives." *American Archivist* 57 (fall 1994): 596–615.

Yoxall, Helen. "Privacy and Personal Papers." *Archives and Manuscripts* 12, no. 1 (May 1984): 38–44.

DIGITAL RECORDS

Adelstein, Peter Z. "Permanence of Digital Information." In *Access to Information: Preservation Issues. Proceedings of the Thirty-Fourth International Conference of the Round table on Archives, Budapest, 1999.* Paris: International Council on Archives, 2000, 149–57.

Ahlgren, Dorothy, and John McDonald. "The Archival Management of a Geographical Information System." *Archivaria* 13 (winter 1981–82): 59–66.

Ambacher, Bruce. "Preservation of Federal Electronic Records at the National Archives and Records Administration." *Of Significance* 2, no. 2 (2000): 20–27.

"Archival Issues Raised by Information Stored in Electronic Form." Position statement issued by Society of American Archivists, 1995.

Authenticity in a Digital Environment. Washington, D.C.: Council on Library and Information Resources, 2000. http://www.clir.org/pubs/abstract/pub92abst.html.

Bailey, Catherine. "Archival theory and Electronic Records." *Archivaria* 29 (winter 1989–90): 180–96.

Bantin, Philip C. "Developing a Strategy for Managing Electronic Records—The Findings of the Indiana University Electronic Records Project." *American Archivist* 61, no. 2 (fall 1998): 328–64.

————. "Electronic Records Management: A Review of the Work of a Decade and a Reflection on Future Directions." *Encyclopedia of Library and Information Science,* Volume 71, Supplement 34. New York: Marcel Dekker, 2002, 47–80.

————. "The Indiana University Electronic Records Project Revisited." *American Archivist* 62, no. 1 (spring 1999): 153–63.

————. "Strategies for Managing Electronic Records: A New Archival Paradigm? An Affirmation of Our Archival Tradition?" *Archival Issues* 23, no. 1 (1998): 17–34.

Barry, Richard E. "Technology and the Transformation of the Workplace: Lessons Learned Traveling Down the Garden Path." In *Effective Approaches for Managing Electronic Records and Archives*, edited by Bruce W. Dearstyne, 1–22. Lanham, Md.: Scarecrow Press, 2002.

Bearman, David. "Diplomatics, Weberian Bureaucracy, and the Management of Electronic Records in Europe and America." *American Archivist* 55 (winter 1992): 168–81.

————. *Electronic Evidence.* Pittsburgh, Pa.: Archives and Museum Informatics, 1995.

————. "The Implications of *Armstrong v. Executive Office of the President* for the Archival Management of Electronic Records." *American Archivist* 56 (fall 1993): 674–89.

————. "Managing Electronic Mail." *Archives and Manuscripts* 22, no. 1 (May 1994): 28–51.

————. "Reality and Chimeras in the Preservation of Electronic Records." *D-Lib Magazine* 5, no. 4 (April 1999). http://www.dlib.org /dlib/april99/bearman/04bearman.html.

————, ed. "Archival Management of Electronic Records." *Archives and Museum Informatics Technical Report No. 13.* Pittsburgh: Archives and Museum Informatics, 1991.

Bellinger, Meg. "Understanding Digital Preservation: A Report from OCLC." In *The State of Digital Preservation: An International Perspective.* Washington, D.C.: Council on Library and Information Resources, 2002, 38–48. http://www.clir.org/pubs/abstract/ pub107abst.html.

Bikson, Tora K. "Organizational Trends and Electronic Media: Work in Progress." *American Archivist* 57 (winter 1994): 48–69.

————. *Preserving the Present: Toward Viable Electronic Records.* The Hague: Sdu Publishers, 1993.

Blouin, Francis. "A Framework for a Consideration of Diplomatics in the Electronic Environment." *American Archivist* 59, no. 4 (fall 1996): 466–79.

Brindley, Lynne. "Research-Library Directions in the 1990s." In *History and Electronic Artefacts*, edited by Edward Higgs, 229–42. Oxford: Clarendon Press, 1998.

Brogan, Mark. "Frontiers in Recordkeeping: Internet Service Providers." *Archives and Manuscripts* 28, no. 1 (May 2000): 38–51.

Brown, Thomas Elton. "Myth or Reality: Is There a Generation Gap Among Electronic Records Archivists?" *Archivaria* 41 (spring 1996): 234–43.

————. "The Society of American Archivists Confronts the Computer." *American Archivist* 47 (fall 1984): 366–82.

Building and Sustaining Digital Collections: Models for Libraries and Museums. Washington, D.C.: Council on Library and Information Resources, 2001.

Campbell. Laura. "Update on the National Digital Infrastructure Initiative." In *The State of Digital Preservation: An International Perspective.* Washington, D.C.: Council on Library and Information Resources, 2002, 49–53. http://www.clir.org/pubs/abstract/ pub107abst.html.

Campbell-Kelly, Martin. "Information in the Business Enterprise." In *History and Electronic Artefacts*, edited by Edward Higgs, 59–67. Oxford: Clarendon Press, 1998.

Chamberlin, Brewster, Marilyn Courtot, and Lawrence F. Karr. "Holocaust Memorial Museum: New Approaches for an All-in-One Resource Center." *Journal of Information and Image Management* 19 (July 1986): 35–40.

Chasse, Kenneth L. "The Legal Issues Concerning the Admissibility in Court of Computer Printouts and Microfilm." *Archivaria* 18 (summer 1984): 166–201.

Cloonan, Michele V., and Shelby Sanett. "Preservation Strategies for Electronic Records: Where We Are Now—Obliquity and Squint." *American Archivist* 65, no. 1 (spring/summer 2002): 70–106.

Cloud, Patricia. "RLIN, AMC, and Retrospective Conversion." *Midwestern Archivist* 11 (1986): 125–34.

Congress Online Project. "E-mail Overload in Congress: Managing a Communications Crisis." http://www.congressonlineproject.org.

Consultative Committee for Space Data Systems. *Reference Model for an Open Archival Information System (OAIS)*. CCSDS 650.0-R-2, "Red Book." July 2001. http://www.ceds.org/documents/pdf/ CSSDS-650.0-R-2.pdf.

Conway, Paul. *Preservation in the Digital World*. Washington, D.C.: Commission on Preservation and Access, 1996.

Conway, Paul and Shari Weaver. *The Setup Phase of Project Open Book*. Washington, D.C.: Commission on Preservation and Access, 1994.

Cook, Michael. *Archives and the Computer*. 2d ed. Boston: Butterworth, 1986.

———. *Information Management and Archival Data*. London: Library Association Publishing, 1993.

Cook, Terry. "Easy to Byte, Harder to Chew: The Second Generation of Electronic Records Archives." *Archivaria* 33 (winter 1991–92): 202–16.

———. "Rites of Passage: The Archivist and the Information Age." *Archivaria* 31 (winter 1990–91): 171–76.

Building and Sustaining Digital Collections: Models for Libraries and Museums. Washington, D.C.: Council on Library and Information Resources, 2001.

Couture, Carol. "Is the Concept of a Record Still Relevant in the Information Age?" In *The Concept of Record: Second Stockholm Conference on Archival Science and the Concept of Record, 30–31 May 1996*. Sweden: Riksarkivet, 1998, 77–100.

Cox, Richard J. "Blown to Bits: Electronic Records, Archivy, and the Corporation." In *The Records of American Business*, James O'Toole, 231–50. Chicago: Society of American Archivists, 1997.

Cullen, Charles T. "Authentication of Digital Objects: Lessons from a Historian's Research." In *Authenticity in a Digital Environment*. Washington, D.C.: Council on Library and Information Resources, 2000, 1–7. http://www.clir.org/pubs/abstract/pub92abst.html.

Cunningham, Adrian. "The Archival Management of Personal Records in Electronic Form: Some Suggestions." *Archives and Manuscripts* 22, no. 1 (May 1994): 94–105.

———. "Waiting for the Ghost Train: Strategies for Managing Electronic Personal Records Before It Is Too Late." *Archival Issues* 24, no. 1 (1999): 55–64.

Dacey, Robert F. "Computer Security: Progress Made, But Critical Federal Operations and Assets Remain at Risk." Testimony Before the Subcommittee on Government Efficiency, Financial Management and Intergovernmental Relations, Committee on Government Reform, House of Representatives. Washington: General Accounting Office, 2002. http://www.gao.gov/new.items/ d03303t.pdf.

Davidson, Jenni, and Louisa Moscato. "Towards an Electronic Records Management Program: The University of Melbourne." *Archives and Manuscripts* 22, no. 1 (May 1994): 124–35.

Dearstyne, Bruce W. "Riding the Lightning: Strategies for Electronic Records and Archives Programs." In *Effective Approaches for Managing Electronic Records and Archives*, edited by Bruce W. Dearstyne, 139–60. Lanham, Md.: Scarecrow Press, 2002.

———. , ed. *Effective Approaches for Managing Electronic Records and Archives*. Lanham, Md.: Scarecrow Press, 2002.

Deegan, Marilyn, and Simon Tanner. *Digital Futures: Strategies for the Information Age*. New York: Neal-Schuman, 2002.

de Zwart, Melissa. "Information Wants to be Free: How Cyberspace Challenges Traditional Legal Concepts of Information Use and Ownership." *Archives and Manuscripts* 26, no. 2 (November 1998): 368–89.

DLM-Forum. *Guidelines on Best Practices for Using Electronic Information: How to Deal With Machine-Readable Data and Electronic Documents*. Luxembourg: Office for Official Publications of the European Communities, 1997.

Dollar, Charles M. "Appraising Machine-Readable Records." *American Archivist* 41 (October 1978): 423–30.

———. *Archival Preservation of Smithsonian Web Resources: Strategies, Principles, and Best Practices*. Washington, D.C.: Smithsonian Institution, 2001. http://www.si.edu/archives/archives/ dollar%report.html.

———. "Archival Preservation of Web Sites and Web Pages: Strategy, Principles, and Guidelines." Unpublished paper, November 22, 2000.

———. *Archival Theory and Information Technologies*. Macerata, Italy: University of Macerata Press, 1992.

———. "Electronic Archiving in the 21st Century: Principles, Strategy, and Best Practices." *Of Significance* 2, no. 2 (2000): 10–19.

Dollar, Charles M. and Carolyn L. Geda, eds. "Archivists, Archives, and Computers: A Starting Point." *American Archivist* 42 (April 1979): 149–93.

Doorn, Peter. "Electronic Records and Historians in the Netherlands." In *History and Electronic Artefacts*, edited by Edward Higgs, 304–16. Oxford: Clarendon Press, 1998.

Dryden, Jean E. "Archival Description of Electronic Records: An Examination of Current Practices." *Archivaria* 40 (fall 1995): 99–108.

Duff, Wendy. "Ensuring the Preservation of Reliable Evidence: A Research Project Funded by the NHPRC." *Archivaria* 42 (fall 1996): 28–45.

———. "Harnessing the Power of Warrant." *American Archivist* 61, no. 1 (spring 1998): 88–105.

Duranti, Luciana "The Impact of Digital Technology on Archival Science." *Archival Science* 1, no. 1 (2001): 39–55.

———. "The Impact of Technological Change on Archival Theory." Paper delivered at the International Congress of Archives, Seville, September 2000. http://www.interpares.org/papers.htm.

———. "Meeting the Challenge of Contemporary Records: Does It Require a Role Change for the Archivist." *American Archivist* 63, no. 1 (spring/summer 2000): 7–15.

Duranti, Luciana and Heather MacNeil. "The Protection and Integrity of Electronic Records: An Overview of the UBC-MAS Research Project." *Archivaria* 42 (fall 1996): 46–67.

Duranti, Luciana, Terry Eastwood, and Heather MacNeil. *The Preservation of the Integrity of Electronic Records.* University of British Columbia, 1997. http://www.interpares.org/UBCProject/ intro.htm.

Durr, W. Theodore. "Some Thoughts and Designs about Archives and Automation, 1984." *American Archivist* 47 (summer 1984): 271–89.

Ellis, Judith A., editor. *Selected Essays in Electronic Recordkeeping in Australia.* Australian Society of Archivists, 2000.

Effects of Electronic Recordkeeping on the Historical Record of the U.S. Government. Washington, D.C.: National Academy of Public Administration, 1989.

Florian, Doris. "The Impact of Artificial Intelligence on Information Management: Questions and Answers." *International Information Management Congress Journal* 24 (1988): 18–21.

Forsyth, Richard. *Machine Learning: Applications in Expert Systems and Information Retrieval.* New York: Halsted, 1986.

Gardner, Martin. "Secondary Use of Computerized Patient Records." In *History and Electronic Artefacts*, edited by Edward Higgs, 120–37. Oxford: Clarendon Press, 1998.

Geda, Carolyn, Eric W. Austin, and Francis X. Blouin, Jr. *Archives and Machine-Readable Records.* Chicago: Society of American Archivists, 1980.

General Accounting Office. "Assessing the Reliability of Computer-Processed Data." Washington: General Accounting Office, 2002. http://www.gao.gov/new.items/d03273g.pdf.

———. "Information Management: Challenges in Managing and Preserving Electronic Records." Washington: General Accounting Office, 2002. http://www.gao.gov/new.item/d02586.pdf.

———. "National Archives: Preserving Electronic Records in an Era of Rapidly Changing Technology." Washington: General Accounting Office, 1999.

Gildemeister, Glen A. "Automation, Reference, and the Small Repository, 1967–1997." *Midwestern Archivist* 13 (1988): 5–16.

Gill, Tony. "3D Culture on the Web." *RLG DigiNews* 5, no. 3 http://www.rlg.org/preserv/diginews/diginews5-3.html.

Gilliland-Swetland, Anne J. "Digital Communications: Documentary Opportunities Not to be Missed." *Archival Issues* 20, no. 1 (1995): 39–50.

———. *Enduring Paradigm, New Opportunities: The Value of the Archival Perspective in the Digital Environment.* Washington: Council on Library and Information Resources, 2000. http://www.clir.org/pubs/abstract/pub89abst.html.

———. "An Exploration of K-12 User Needs for Digital Primary Source Materials." *American Archivist* 61, no. 1 (spring 1998): 136–57.

Gilliland-Swetland, Anne J. and Greg Kinney. "Uses of Electronic Communication to Document an Academic Community: A Research Report." *Archivaria* 38 (fall 1994): 79–96.

Goerler, Raimund E. "Towards 2001: Electronic Workstations and the Future of Academic Archives." *Archival Issues* 17 (1992): 11–22.

Government of Western Australia. *Guidelines for State Government Websites.* Draft for comment. Version 3, Document Number 120605. West Perth: Department of Industry and Technology, Government of Western Australia, 2002. http://www.egov.dpc.wa.gov.au/ index.cfm?fuseaction=projects.policy.

Granstrom, Claes. "Swedish Society and Electronic Data." In *History and Electronic Artefacts*, edited by Edward Higgs, 317–30. Oxford: Clarendon Press, 1998.

Green, Ann, JoAnn Dionne, and Martin Dennis. *Preserving the Whole: A Two-Track Approach to Rescuing Social Science Data and Metadata.* Washington: Digital Library Federation, Council on Library and Information Resources, 1999.

Greenberg, Jane. "The Applicability of Natural Language Processing (NLP) to Archival Properties and Objectives." *American Archivist* 61, no. 2 (fall 1998): 400–25.

Greenstein, Daniel. "Electronic Information Resources and Historians: A Consumer's View." In *History and Electronic Artefacts*, edited by Edward Higgs, 68–84. Oxford: Clarendon Press, 1998.

Greenstein, Daniel and Gerald George. "Digital Reproduction Quality: Benchmark Recommendations." *RLG DigiNews* 5, no. 4. http://www.rlg.org/pre-serv/diginews/diginews5-4.html.

Greenstein, Shane. "Tape Story Tapestry: Historical Research with Inaccessible Digital Information Technologies." *Midwestern Archivist* 15 (1990): 77–85.

Guercio, Maria. "Principles, Methods, and Instruments for the Creation, Preservation and Use of Archival Records in the Digital Environment." *American Archivist* 64, no. 2 (fall/winter 2001): 238–69.

Harrison, Donald Fisher. "Computers, Electronic Data, and the Vietnam War." *Archivaria* 26 (summer 1988): 18–32.

Harrison, Donald F., ed. *Automation in Archives.* Washington, D.C.: Mid-Atlantic Regional Archives Conference, 1993.

Heazlewood, Justine. "Management of Electronic Records Over Time." In *Selected Essays in Electronic Recordkeeping in Australia*, edited by Judith A. Ellis, 97–118. Australian Society of Archivists, 2000.

Heazlewood, Justine et al. "Electronic Records: Problem Solved?" *Archives and Manuscripts* 27, no. 1 (May 1999): 114–27.

Hedstrom, Margaret L. "Applications of the Pittsburgh Functional Requirements for Evidence in Recordkeeping: A Review of Testing and Implementation." *Archives and Manuscripts* 25, no. 1 (May 1997): 84–87.

———. *Archives and Manuscripts: Machine-Readable Records.* Chicago, Society of American Archivists: 1984.

———. "Building Record-Keeping Systems: Archivists Are Not Alone on the Wild Frontier." *Archivaria* 44 (fall 1997): 44–71.

———. "The Digital Preservation Research Agenda." In *The State of Digital Preservation: An International Perspective.* Washington, D.C.: Council on Library and Information Resources, 2002, 32–37. http://www.clir.org/pubs/abstract/pub107abst.html.

———. "How Do Archivists Make Electronic Archives Usable and Accessible?" *Archives and Manuscripts* 26, no. 1 (May 1998): 6–23.

———. "Understanding Electronic Incunabula: A Framework for Research on Electronic Records." *American Archivist* 54 (summer 1991): 334–54.

———, ed. *Electronic Records Management Program Strategies.* Pittsburgh, Pa.: Archives and Museum Informatics, 1993.

Hendley, Tony. *The Archival Storage Potential of Microfilm, Magnetic Media, and Optical Data Disks.* Hertford, England: National Reprographic Centre for Documentation, 1983.

Henry, Linda J. "Schellenberg in Cyberspace." *American Archivist* 61, no. 2 (fall 1998): 309–28.

Hensen, Steven L. "The Use of Standards in the Application of the AMC Format." *American Archivist* 49 (winter 1986): 31–40.

Hickerson, Thomas H. *Archives and Manuscripts: An Introduction to Automated Access.* Chicago: Society of American Archivists, 1980.

Higgs, Edward. "Historians, Archivists, and Electronic Record-Keeping in British Government." In *History and Electronic Artefacts*, edited by Edward Higgs, 138–52. Oxford: Clarendon Press, 1998.

———. "The Role of Tomorrow's Electronic Archives." In *History and Electronic Artefacts*, edited by Edward Higgs, 184-194. Oxford: Clarendon Press, 1998.

———, ed. *History and Electronic Artefacts.* Oxford: Clarendon Press, 1998.

Hirtle, Peter B. "Archival Authenticity in a Digital Age." *Authenticity in a Digital Environment.* Washington, D.C.: Council on Library and Information Resources, 2000, 8–23. http://www.clir.org/pubs/ abstract/pub92abst.html.

Hodge, Gail M. "Best Practices for Digital Archiving: An Information Life Cycle Approach." *D-Lib Magazine* 6, no. 1 (January 2000). http://www.dlib.org/dlib/january00/01hodge.html.

Hodges, Martha. "Using the MARC Format for Archives and Manuscripts Control to Catalog Published Microfilms of Manuscript Collections." *Microform Review* 18 (winter 1989): 29–35.

Hofman, Hans. "Lost in Cyberspace: Where Is the Record?" In *The Concept of Record: Second Stockholm Conference on Archival Science and the Concept of Record, 30–31 May 1996.* Sweden: Riksarkivet, 1998, 115–30.

———. "Towards a United but Distributed Archives of Europe?" In *History and Electronic Artefacts*, edited by Edward Higgs, 331–38. Oxford: Clarendon Press, 1998.

Holdsworth, David, and Derek M. Sergeant. "A Blueprint for Representation Information in the OAIS Model." http://www.personal.leeds.ac.uk/~ecldh/cedars/ieee00.html. http://esdis-it.gsfc.nasa. gov/msst/conf2000/papers/d02pa.pdf.

Holdsworth, David, and Paul Wheatley. "Emulation, Preservation and Abstraction." http://129.11.152.25/CAMiLEON//dh/ep5.html.

Holmes, William M., Jr.; Edie Hedlin; and Thomas E. Weir, Jr. "MARC and Life Cycle Tracking at the National Archives: Project Final Report." *American Archivist* 49 (summer 1986): 305–9.

Honhart, Frederick L. "MicroMARC:AMC: A Case Study in the Development of an Automated System." *American Archivist* 52 (winter 1989): 80–86.

Hopkins, Mark. "Computerizing a Government Records Archives: The FEDDOCS [Federal Archives Division of the Public Archives of Canada] Experience." *ARMA Records Management Quarterly* 20 (July 1986): 36–39.

Hornfeldt, Torbjorn. "The Concept of Record: On Being Digital." In *The Concept of Record: Second Stockholm Conference on Archival Science and the Concept of Record, 30–31 May 1996.* Sweden: Riksarkivet, 1998, 67–76.

Horton, Robert. "Obstacles and Opportunities: A Strategic Approach to Electronic Records." In *Effective Approaches for Managing Electronic Records and Archives*, edited by Bruce W. Dearstyne, 53–72. Lanham, Md.: Scarecrow Press, 2002.

Hunter, Gregory S. "Appraisal and Retention of Digital Records." *History News* 57, no. 4 (Autumn 2002): 17–20.

———. "The Digital Future: A Look Ahead." *Information Management Journal* 36, no. 1 (January February 2002): 70—72

———. *Preserving Digital Information.* New York: Neal-Schuman, 2000.

Hyry, Tom, and Rachel Onuf. "The Personality of Electronic Records: The Impact of New Information Technology on Personal Papers." *Archival Issues* 22, no. 1 (1997): 37–44.

InterPARES Project. *The Long-Term Preservation of Authentic Electronic Records: Findings of the InterPARES Project.* Vancouver: InterPARES Project and University of British Columbia, 2002. http://www.interpares.org/book/index.htm.

Jansen, Daniel. "The National Archives and Records Administration's Electronic Records Archives Program and the Future Preservation and Use of Federal Electronic Records." *Of Significance* 2, no. 2 (2000): 43–49.

Jones, Maggie, and Neil Beagrie. *Preservation Management of Digital Materials: A Handbook.* London: The British Library, 2001.

Jordahl, Gregory. "NARA Takes Steps to Protect the [Electronic] Historical Record." *Inform* 4 (July/August 1990): 10–11.

Kansas State Historical Society. "Digital Imaging Guidelines for State Agencies." http://www.kshs.org/government/records/electronic/digitalimagingguidelines.htm.

———. "Kansas Electronic Records Management Guidelines." http://www.kshs.org/government/records/electronic/electronicrecordsguidelines.htm

Katz, Richard N. and Victoria A. Davis. "The Impact of Automation on Our Corporate Memory." *ARMA Records Management Quarterly* 20 (January 1986): 10–14.

Kaufhold, Penny. "The Rough Edges of the Learning Curve." *ARMA Records Management Quarterly* 21 (April 1987): 33–34, 39.

Kesner, Richard. *Automation for Archivists and Records Managers: Planning and Implementation Strategies.* Chicago: Society of American Archivists, 1984.

———. "Automated Information Management: Is There a Role for the Archivist in the Office of the Future?" *Archivaria* 19 (winter 1984–85): 162–72.

———. "Computers, Archival Administration, and the Challenges of the 1980's." *Georgia Archive,* 9 (fall 1981): 1–18.

———. *Information Management, Machine-Readable Records, and Administration: An Annotated Bibliography.* Chicago: Society of American Archivists, 1983.

———. "Information Resource Management in the Electronic Workplace: A Personal Perspective on 'Archives in the Information Society.'" *American Archivist* 61, no. 1 (spring 1998): 70–87.

———. *Information Systems: A Strategic Approach to Planning and Implementation.* Chicago: American Library Association, 1988.

———. "Microcomputer Archives and Records Management Systems: Guidelines for Future Development." *American Archivist* 45 (summer 1982): 299–311.

Kesner, Richard and Don Hurst. "Microcomputer Applications in Archives: A Study in Progress." *Archivaria* 12 (summer 1981): 3–20.

Koltun, Lilly. "The Promise and Threat of Digital Options in an Archival Age." *Archivaria* 47 (spring 1999): 114–35.

Kowlowitz, Alan S. "Playing the Electronic Angles and Working the Digital Scams: The Challenges and Opportunities State Electronic Government Initiatives Present to State Archival and Records Management Programs." In *Effective Approaches for Managing Electronic Records and Archives*, edited by Bruce W. Dearstyne, 89–108. Lanham, Md.: Scarecrow Press, 2002.

Kula, Sam. "Optical Memories: Archival Storage Systems of the Future, or More Pie in the Sky?" *Archivaria* 4 (summer 1977): 43–48.

Landis, William E. "Archival Outreach on the World Wide Web." *Archival Issues* 20, no. 2 (1995): 129–48.

Landis, William E. and Robert Royce. "Recommendations for an Electronic Records Management System: A Case Study of a Small Business." *Archival Issues* 20 (1995): 7–21.

Lawrence, Gregory W., et al. *Risk Management of Digital Information: A File Format Investigation.* Washington: Council on Library and Information Resources, 2000. http://www.clir.org/pubs/abstract/ pub93abst.html.

Levy, David M. "Where's Waldo? Reflections on Copies and Authenticity in a Digital Environment." *Authenticity in a Digital Environment.* Washington, D.C.: Council on Library and Information Resources, 2000, 24–31. http://www.clir.org/pubs/ abstract/pub92abst.html.

Lievesley, Denise. "Increasing the Value of Data." In *History and Electronic Artefacts*, edited by Edward Higgs, 253–64. Oxford: Clarendon Press, 1998.

Lubar, Steven. "Information Culture and the Archival Record." *American Archivist* 62, no. 1 (spring 1999): 10–23.

Lynch, Clifford. "Authenticity and Integrity in the Digital Environment: An Exploratory Analysis of the Central Role of Trust." *Authenticity in a Digital Environment.* Washington, D.C.: Council on Library and Information Resources, 2000, 32–50. http://www.clir.org/pubs/abstract/pub92abst.html.

Lysakowski, Rich, and Zahava Leibowitz. *Titanic 2020: A Call to Action.* Woburn, Mass.: Collaborative Electronic Notebook Systems Association (CENSA): 2000. http://www.censa.org/html/Press-Releases/Titanic2020.htm.

Maher, William J. "Administering Archival Automation: Development of In-House Systems." *American Archivist* 47 (fall 1984): 405–17.

Mallinson, John C. "On the Preservation of Human and Machine-Readable Records." *Information Technologies and Libraries* 7 (March 1988): 19–22.

———. "Preserving Machine-Readable Archival Records for the Millenia." *Archivaria* 22 (summer 1986): 147–52.

Managing Electronic Records. Washington, D.C.: National Archives and Records Administration, 1990.

MARC Format and Life Cycle Tracking at the National Archives: A Study. Washington, D.C.: National Archives and Records Administration, 1986.

Marker, Hans-Jorgen. "Data Conservation at a Traditional Data Archive." In *History and Electronic Artefacts*, edited by Edward Higgs, 294–303. Oxford: Clarendon Press, 1998.

Marsden, Paul. "When is the Future? Comparative Notes on the Electronic Recordkeeping Projects of the University of Pittsburgh and the University of British Columbia." *Archivaria* 43 (spring 1997): 158–73.

Martin, Julia, and David Coleman. "The Archive as an Ecosystem." *Journal of Electronic Publishing* 7, no. 3 (April 2002). http://www.press.umich.edu/jep/07-03/martin.html.

McClure, Charles and Timothy Spreh. *Analysis and Development of Model Quality Guidelines for Electronic Records Management on State and Federal Websites.* http://istweb.syr.edu/~mcclure/nhprc/ nhprc_title.html.

McDonald, John. "Archives and Cooperation in the Information Age." *Archivaria* 35 (spring 1993): 110–18.

———. "Government On-line and Electronic Records: The Role of the National Archives of Canada." In *Effective Approaches for Managing Electronic Records and Archives*, edited by Bruce W. Dearstyne, 73–88. Lanham, Md.: Scarecrow Press, 2002.

McKemmish, Sue. "Understanding Electronic Recordkeeping Systems: Understanding Ourselves." *Archives and Manuscripts* 22, no. 1 (May 1994): 150–63.

Michelson, Avra. "Description and Reference in the Age of Automation." *American Archivist* 50 (spring 1987): 192–208.

Michelson, Avra and Jeff Rothenberg. "Scholarly Communication and Information Technology: Exploring the Impact of Changes in the Research Process on Archives." *American Archivist* 55 (spring 1992): 236–315.

Middleton, Michael, and Baiba Irving. "Archives and Computers: Description and Retrieval." *Archives and Manuscripts* 9, no. 1 (September 1981): 53–65.

Minnesota Historical Society. *Trustworthy Information Systems Handbook.* St. Paul: Minnesota Historical Society, 2001. http://www.mnhs.org/preserve/records/tis/tableofcontents.html.

Mohlhenrich, Janice, ed. *Preservation of Electronic Formats and Electronic Formats for Preservation.* Fort Atkinson, Wis.: Highsmith Press, 1993.

Moore, Reagan, et. al. "Collection-Based Persistent Digital Archives: Part 1." *D-Lib Magazine* 6, no. 3 (March 2000). http://www.dlib.org/ dlib/march00/moore/03moore-pt1.html.

———, "Collection-Based Persistent Digital Archives: Part 2." *D-Lib Magazine* 6, no. 4 (April 2000). http://www.dlib.org/dlib/april00/ moore/04moore-pt2.html.

Moiseenko, Tatyana. "The Russian Archive System Under Pressure in the Information Age." In *History and Electronic Artefacts*, edited by Edward Higgs, 277–93. Oxford: Clarendon Press, 1998.

Morelli, Jeffrey D. "Defining Electronic Records: Problems of Terminology." In *History and Electronic Artefacts*, edited by Edward Higgs, 169–83. Oxford: Clarendon Press, 1998.

Morris, R.J. "Electronic Documents and the History of the Late Twentieth Century: Black Holes or Warehouses?" In *History and Electronic Artefacts*, edited by Edward Higgs, 31–48. Oxford: Clarendon Press, 1998.

Morton, Katharine D. "The MARC Formats: An Overview." *American Archivist* 49 (winter 1986): 21–30.

Motz, Arlene. "Applying Records Management Principles to Magnetic Media." *ARMA Records Management Quarterly* 20 (April 1986): 22–26.

National Archives and Records Administration. "Electronic Records Archives (ERA)." http://www.nara.gov/era/.

————. *Records Management Guidance for Agencies Implementing Electronic Signature Technologies.* Washington, D.C.: National Archives and Records Administration, 2000.

National Archives of Australia. *Managing Electronic Messages as Records.* Canberra: National Archives of Australia, 1997. http://www.naa.gov.au/record-keeping/er/elec_messages/summary.html.

————. *A Policy for Keeping Records of Web-based Activity in the Commonwealth Government.* Canberra: National Archives of Australia, 2001. http://www.naa.gov.au/recordkeeping/er/ web_records/intro.html.

————. *Guidelines for Keeping Records of Web-based Activity in the Commonwealth Government.* Canberra: National Archives of Australia, 2001. http://www.naa.gov.au/recordkeeping/er/ web_records/intro.html.

————. Managing Electronic Records. Canberra: National Archives of Australia, 1995. http://www.naa.gov.au/recordkeeping/er/ manage_er/foreward.html.

National Library of Australia. "Safeguarding Australia's Web Resources: Guidelines for Creators and Publishers." Canberra: National Library of Australia, 2002. http://www.nla.gov.au/guidelines/webresources.html.

————. "Guidelines for the Selection of Online Australian Publications Intended for Preservation by the National Library of Australia." Canberra: National Library of Australia, 1999.http://pandora.nla.gov.au/selectionguidelines.html.

National Research Council. *Preservation of Historical Records.* Washington: National Academy Press, 1986.

Neumann, Peter G. *Computer Related Risks.* New York: Addison-Wesley, 1995.

Newhall, Ann Clifford. "The NHPRC in the New Records Age." *American Archivist* 63, no. 1 (spring/summer 2000): 67–89.

Nicholls, Catherine, and Jon-Paul Williams. "Identifying Roadkill on the Information Superhighway: A Website Appraisal Case Study." *Archives and Manuscripts* 30, no. 2 (November 2002): 96–111.

Nowicke, Carole Elizabeth. "Managing Tomorrow's Records Today: An Experiment in Archival Preservation of Electronic Mail." *Midwestern Archivist* 13 (1988): 67–76.

Olson, David. "'Camp Pitt' and the Continuing Education of Government Archivists: 1989–1996. *American Archivist* 60, no. 2 (spring 1997): 202–15

O'Shea, Greg. "The Medium is *not* the Message: Appraisal of Electronic Records by Australian Archives." *Archives and Manuscripts* 22, no. 1 (May 1994): 68–93.

Paquet, Lucie. "Appraisal, Acquisition and Control of Personal Electronic Records: From Myth to Reality." *Archives and Manuscripts* 28, no. 2 (November 2000): 71–91.

Parer, Dagmar, and Keith Parrott. "Management Practices in the Electronic Records Environment." *Archives and Manuscripts* 22, no. 1 (May 1994): 106–23.

Peterson, Trudy Huskamp. "Archival Principles and Records of the New Technology." *American Archivist* 47 (fall 1984): 383–93.

Phillips, Margaret E. "Ensuring Long-Term Access to Online Publications." *Journal of Electronic Publishing* 4, no. 4 (June 1999). http://www.press.umich.edu/jep/04-04/phillips.html.

Piche, Jean-Stephan. "Doing What's Possible with What We've Got: Using the World Wide Web to Integrate Archival Functions." *American Archivist* 61, no. 1 (spring 1998): 106–23.

Picot, Anne. "Electronic Record Systems in the Roads & Traffic Authority, NSW." *Archives and Manuscripts* 22, no. 1 (May 1994): 52–67.

Prietto, Carole. "Automating the Archives: A Case Study." *American Archivist* 57 (spring 1994): 364–73.

Prochaska, Alice. "Special Collections in the British Library and Electronic Media." In *History and Electronic Artefacts*, edited by Edward Higgs, 243–52. Oxford: Clarendon Press, 1998.

Puglia, Steven. "The Costs of Digital Imaging Projects." *RLG DigiNews* 3, no. 5 (October 1999). http://www.rlg.org/preserv/diginews/diginews3-5.html.

Rayward, W. Boyd. "Electronic Information and the Functional Integration of Libraries, Museums, and Archives." In *History and Electronic Artefacts*, edited by Edward Higgs, 207–26. Oxford: Clarendon Press, 1998.

Reed, Barbara. "Electronic Records Management in Transition." *Archives and Manuscripts* 22, no. 1 (May 1994): 164–71.

Reed, Mervin. "Archivists and Computers." *Archives and Manuscripts* 9, no. 1 (September 1981): 49–52.

Relf, Fiona Ash. "PANDORA: Towards a National Collection of Australian Electronic Publications." Paper Delivered at the 10th National Library Technicians' Conference, Fremantle, September 8–10, 1999. http://www.nla.gov.au/nla/staffpaper/ ashrelf1.html.

"Reviews: Computer Applications Programs." *Midwestern Archivist* 11 (1986): 69–83.

Rhodes, Steven B. "Archival and Records Management Automation." *ARMA Records Management Quarterly* 25 (April 1991): 12–17.

Roberts, David. "Defining Electronic Records, Documents and Data." *Archives and Manuscripts* 22, no. 1 (May 1994): 14–27.

————. "Disposal and Appraisal of Machine Readable Records—From the Literature." *Archives and Manuscripts* 13, no. 1 (May 1985): 30–38.

————. "The Disposal of Electronic Records in Office Automation Systems in the Australian Public Service." *Archives and Manuscripts* 17, no. 2 (November 1989): 219–31.

Ross, Seamus. "The Expanding World of Electronic Information and the Past's Future." In *History and Electronic Artefacts*, edited by Edward Higgs, 5–28. Oxford: Clarendon Press, 1998.

Ross, Seamus and Ann Gow. *Post-Hoc Rescue of Digital Material.* London: British Library and Joint Information Committee, 1998.

Rothenberg, Jeff. *Avoiding Technological Quicksand: Finding a Viable Technical Foundation for Digital Preservation.* Washington, D.C.: Council on Library and Information Resources, 1999.

———. "Ensuring the Longevity of Digital Documents." *Scientific American* 22, no. 1 (January 1995). 42–47.

———. *An Experiment in Using Emulation to Preserve Digital Publications.* The Hague: National Library of the Netherlands, 2000. http://www.kb.nl/coop/nedlib/results/emulationpreservationreport.pdf.

———. "Preserving Authentic Digital Information." In *Authenticity in a Digital Environment.* Washington, D.C.: Council on Library and Information Resources, 2000, 51–68. http://www.clir.org/pubs/ abstract/pub92abst.html.

Russell, Kelly, and Derek Sergeant. "The Cedars Project: Implementing a Model for Distributed Digital Archives." *RLG DigiNews* 3, no. 3 (1999). http://www.rlg.ac.uk/preserv/diginews/ diginews3-3.html.

Saffady, William. *Managing Electronic Records,* 3d ed. Lenexa, Kansas: ARMA International, 2002.

Sahli, Nancy A. "Interpretation and Application of the AMC Format." *American Archivist* 49 (winter 1986): 9–20.

Samuel, Jean. "Electronic Mail: Information Exchange or Information Loss?" In *History and Electronic Artefacts*, edited by Edward Higgs, 101–19. Oxford: Clarendon Press, 1998.

Sanders, Robert M. "The Company Index: Information Retrieval Thesauri for Organizations and Institutions." *ARMA Records Management Quarterly* 20 (April 1986): 3–14.

———. "While Waiting for the Real Computerization of Your Archives: A Lo-Tech Recipe." *ARMA Records Management Quarterly* 18 (October 1984): 5–11.

Sarno, Luigi, ed. *Authentic Records in the Electronic Age: Proceedings from an International Symposium.* Vancouver, Canada: InterPARES Project, 2000.

Scalera, Nicholas. "Public-Key Encryption and the Clipper Chip: Implications for the Archival Administration of Electronic Records." *Archival Issues* 20, no. 1 (1995): 65–78.

Schurer, Kevin. "The Implications of Information Technology for the Future Study of History." In *History and Electronic Artefacts*, edited by Edward Higgs, 155–68. Oxford: Clarendon Press, 1998.

Sellen, Abigail J., and Richard H.R. Harper. *The Myth of the Paperless Office.* Cambridge: MIT Press, 2002.

Shankar, Kalpana. "Towards a Framework for Managing Electronic Records in Scientific Research." *Archival Issues* 24, no. 1 (1999): 21–36.

Shervington, Christine. "Automation Records Management." *Archives and Manuscripts* 14, no. 2 (November 1986): 129–43.

Simpson, Helen. "The Management of Electronic Information Resources in a Corporate Environment." In *History and Electronic Artefacts*, edited by Edward Higgs, 87–100. Oxford: Clarendon Press, 1998.

Sitts, Maxine, Editor. *Handbook for Digital Projects: A Management Tool for Preservation and Access.* Andover, Mass.: Northeast Document Conservation Center, 2000.

Skillman, Juanita, and April Dmytrenko. "A Comparison of PC Based Records Management Software." *ARMA Records Management Quarterly* 23 (April 1989): 21–33.

Skupsky, Donald S. "Establishing Retention Periods for Electronic Records." *ARMA Records Management Quarterly* 27 (April 1993): 40–43.

Slavin, Timothy A. "Implementing Requirements for Recordkeeping: Moving From Theory to Practice." In *Effective Approaches for Managing Electronic Records and Archives*, edited by Bruce W. Dearstyne, 35–52. Lanham, Md.: Scarecrow Press, 2002.

Smith, Abby. "Authenticity in Perspective." In *Authenticity in a Digital Environment.* Washington, D.C.: Council on Library and Information Resources, 2000, 69–75. http://www.clir.org/pubs/ abstract/pub92abst.html.

———. *Strategies for Building Digitized Collections.* Washington, D.C.: Digital Library Federation, Council on Library and Information Resources, 2001.

Smith, Colin. "Our Problems with Machine-Readable Records." *Archives and Manuscripts* 11, no. 2 (November 1983): 160–61.

Smith, Helen, and Chris Hurley. "Developments in Computerized Documentation Systems at the Public Records Office, Victoria." *Archives and Manuscripts* 17, no. 2 (November 1989): 165–82.

Smither, Roger. "Formats and Standards: A Film Archive Perspective on Exchanging Computerized Data." *American Archivist* 50 (summer 1987): 324–37.

Sprehe, J. Timothy. "Archiving Electronic Databases: The NAPA [National Academy of Public Administration] Report." *Inform* 6 (March 1992): 28–31.

The State of Digital Preservation: An International Perspective. Washington, D.C.: Council on Library and Information Resources, 2002. http://www.clir.org/pubs/abstract/pub107abst.html.

Stielow, Frederick J. "Archival Theory and the Preservation of Electronic Media: Opportunities and Standards Below the Cutting Edge." *American Archivist* 55 (spring 1992): 332–43.

————. "The Impact of Information Technology on Archival Theory: A Discourse on the Automation Pedagogy." *Journal of Education for Library and Information Science* 34 (winter 1993): 48–65.

Stout, Leon J. and Donald A. Baird. "Automation in North American College and University Archives: A Survey." *American Archivist* 47 (fall 1984): 394–404.

Strickland, Lee S. "The Law of Electronic Information: Burgeoning Mandates and Issues." In *Effective Approaches for Managing Electronic Records and Archives*, edited by Bruce W. Dearstyne, 109–38. Lanham, Md.: Scarecrow Press, 2002.

Stuckey, Steve, and Anne Liddell. "Electronic Business Transactions and Recordkeeping: Serious Concerns—Realistic Responses." *Archives and Manuscripts* 28, no. 2 (November 2000): 92–109.

Suderman, Jim. "Defining Electronic Series: A Study." *Archivaria* 53 (spring 2002): 31–46.

Sundin, Jan, and Ian Winchester. "Towards Intelligent Databases: Or the Database as Historical Archivist." *Archivaria* 14 (summer 1982): 137–58.

Swade, Doron. "Preserving Software in an Object-Centered Culture." In *History and Electronic Artefacts*, edited by Edward Higgs, 195–206. Oxford: Clarendon Press, 1998.

Taylor, Hugh. "Chip Monks at the Gate: The Impact of Technology on Archives, Libraries and the User." *Archivaria* 33 (winter 1991–92): 173–80.

————. "Information Ecology and the Archives in the 1980's." *Archivaria* 18 (summer 1984): 25–37.

————. "'My Very Act and Deed': Some Reflections on the Role of Textual Records in the Conduct of Affairs." *American Archivist* 51 (fall 1988): 456–69.

Thibodeau, Kenneth. "Overview of Technological Approaches to Digital Preservation and Challenges in Coming Years." In *The State of Digital Preservation: An International Perspective.* Washington, D.C.: Council on Library and Information Resources, 2002, 4–31. http://www.clir.org/pubs/abstract/pub107abst.html.

Turnbaugh, Roy. "Information Technology, Records, and State Archives." *American Archivist* 60, no. 2 (spring 1997): 184–201.

————. "What is an *Electronic* Record?" In *Effective Approaches for Managing Electronic Records and Archives*, edited by Bruce W. Dearstyne, 23–34. Lanham, Md.: Scarecrow Press, 2002.

"Uniform Electronic Transactions Act." National Conference of Commissioners on Uniform State Laws, 1999. http://www.law.upenn.edu/bll/ulc/uecicta/uetast84.htm.

Van Bogart, John. *Magnetic Tape Storage and Handling: A Guide for Libraries and Archives.* Washington, D.C.: Commission on Preservation and Access, 1995.

van der Werf, Titia. "Experience of the National Library of the Netherlands." In *The State of Digital Preservation: An International Perspective.* Washington, D.C.: Council on Library and Information Resources, 2002 54–64. http://www.clir.org/pubs/abstract/ pub107abst.html.

Victorian Electronic Records Strategy: Final Report. South Melbourne: Public Record Office Victoria, 1998. http://www.prov.vic.gov.au/vers/published/final.htm.

Waters, Donald. *From Microfilm to Digital Imagery: On the Feasibility of a Project to Study the Means, Costs and Benefits of Converting Large Quantities of Preserved Library Materials from Microfilm to Digital Images.* Washington: Commission on Preservation and Access, 1991.

————. "Good Archives Make Good Scholars: Reflections on Recent Steps Toward the Archiving of Digital Information." In *The State of Digital Preservation: An International Perspective.* Washington, D.C.: Council on Library and Information Resources, 2002, 78–95. http://www.clir.org/pubs/abstract/pub107abst.html.

Waters, Donald and John Garrett. *Preserving Digital Information: Report of the Task Force on Archiving of Digital Information.* Washington: Commission on Preservation and Access, and Mountain View, Calif.: Research Libraries Group, 1996).

Watson, Andrea, with P. Toby Graham. "CSS Alabama Digital Collection: A Special Collections Digitization Project." *American Archivist* 61, no. 1 (spring 1998): 124–35.

Webb, Colin. "Digital Preservation—A Many-Layered Thing: Experience at the National Library of Australia." In *The State of Digital Preservation: An International Perspective.* Washington, D.C.: Council on Library and Information Resources, 2002, 65–77. http://www.clir.org/pubs/abstract/pub107abst.html.

Weber, Lisa. "Electronic Records: Too Ephemeral?" *Inform* 6 (February 1992): 32–36.

Weissman, Ronald F. E. "Archives and the New Information Architecture of the Late 1990s." *American Archivist* 57 (winter 1994): 20–35.

Westbrooks, Elaine L. "African-American Documentary Resources on the World Wide Web: A Survey and Analysis." *Archival Issues* 24, no. 2 (1999): 145–74.

Wettengel, Michael. "German Unification and Electronic Records." In *History and Electronic Artefacts*, edited by Edward Higgs, 265–76. Oxford: Clarendon Press, 1998.

———. "Old Traditions and New Uncertainties: The German Archival Concept of a Record and Electronic Environments." In *The Concept of Record: Second Stockholm Conference on Archival Science and the Concept of Record, 30–31 May 1996.* Sweden: Riksarkivet, 1998, 131–44.

Whaley, John H., Jr. "Digitizing History." *American Archivist* 57 (fall 1994): 660–74.

Wheatley, Paul. "Migration—A CAMiLEON Discussion Paper." *Ariadne* 29 (2001). http://www.ariadne.ac.uk/issue29/camileon/ intro.html.

Wheaton, Bruce R. "A Computer Database System to Store and Display Archival Data on Correspondence of Historical Significance." *American Archivist* 45 (fall 1982): 455–66.

Williams, Robert F. "Electronic Document Management: The Coming Revolution in Records Management." *International Information Management Congress Journal* 21 (fourth Quarter 1985): 33–37.

Wilson, P.D. "Computers and Archives—Some Random Thoughts." *Archives and Manuscripts* 4, no. 8 (August 1972): 11–18.

Yen, David, and Huang-Lian Tang. "Future Trends of Computer-Based Information Systems." *ARMA Records Management Quarterly* 22 (October 1988): 12–19.

Zboray, Ronald J. "dBase III Plus and the MARC AMC Format: Problems and Possibilities." *American Archivist* 50 (spring 1987): 210–25.

Zelenyj, Dan. "Archivy *Ad Portas:* The Archives-Records Management Paradigm Re-visited in the Electronic Information Age." *Archivaria* 47 (spring 1999): 66–84.

Zimmerman, Ann. "Partnership and Opportunity: The Archival Management of Geographic Information Systems." *Archival Issues* 20, no. 1 (1995): 23–38.

Zweig, Ronald W. "Beyond Content: Electronic Fingerprints and the Use of Documents." In *History and Electronic Artefacts*, edited by Edward Higgs, 49–58. Oxford: Clarendon Press, 1998.

AUDIOVISUAL ARCHIVES

Adelstein, Peter Z., C. Loren Graham, and Lloyd E. West. "Preservation of Motion-Picture Color Film Having Permanent Value." *Journal of the Society of Motion Picture and Television Engineers* 79, no. 11 (November 1970): 1011–18.

Allen, Barbara. "Story in Oral History: Clues to Historical Consciousness." *Journal of American History* 79 (September 1992): 606–11.

Association of Moving Image Archivists. "Video Preservation Fact Sheets." http://www.amianet.org/11_Information/11g_VidPres/ intro.html.

Bartlett, Nancy. "Diplomatics for Photographic Images: Academic Exoticism?" *American Archivist* 59, no. 4 (fall 1996): 486–95.

Baum, Willa, and David Dunaway. *Oral History: An Interdisciplinary Anthology.* Nashville: American Association for State and Local History, 1984.

Bergeron, Rosemary. "The Selection of Television Productions for Archival Preservation." *Archivaria* 23 (winter 1986–87): 41–53.

Birrell, Andrew. "Private Realms of Light: Canadian Amateur Photography, 1839–1940: From Acquisition to Exhibition." *Archivaria* 17 (winter 1983–84): 106–14.

Birrell, Andrew, Peter Robertson, Lilly Koltun, Andrew Rodger, and Joan Schwartz. "Private Realms of Light: Canadian Amateur Photography, 1839–1940: On View: The Evolution of Amateur Photography." *Archivaria* 17 (winter 1983–84): 115–35.

The Book of Film Care. Rochester, N.Y.: Eastman Kodak Company, 1983.

Bowser, Eileen, and John Kuiper. *A Handbook for Film Archives.* Brussels: FIAF, 1980.

Borwick, John, ed. *Sound Recording Practice.* London: Oxford, 1976.

Bruemmer, Bruce H. "Access to Oral History: A National Agenda." *American Archivist* 54 (fall 1991): 494–501.

Burant, Jim. "The Visual World in the Victorian Age." *Archivaria* 19 (winter 1984–85): 110–21.

Calhoun, J.M. "The Preservation of Motion-Picture Film." *American Archivist* (July 1967): 517–25.

Campbell, Fiona. "Apparat: A Computer Cataloguing System for Sound Recordings." *Archives and Manuscripts* 8, no. 2 (December 1980): 33–40.

Charlton, Thomas. "Videotaped Oral Histories." *American Archivist* 47 (1984): 228–36.

Collins, Karen. "Providing Subject Access to Images: A Study of User Queries." *American Archivist* 61, no. 1 (spring 1998): 36–55.

Connors, Thomas. "Appraising Public Television Programs: Toward an Interpretive and Comparative Evaluation Model." *American Archivist* 63 (spring/summer 2000): 152–74.

Dick, Ernest J. "An Archival Acquisition Strategy for the Broadcast Records of the Canadian Broadcast Corporation." *Historical Journal of Film, Radio and Television* 11, no. 3 (1991): 253–68.

———. "Corporate Memory in Sound and Visual Records." In *The Records of American Business*, edited by James O'Toole, 275–96. Chicago: Society of American Archivists, 1997.

Epp, Kathleen. "Telling Stories Around the 'Electric Campfire': The Use of Archives in Television Productions." *Archivaria* 49 (spring 2000): 53–83.

Filippelli, R.L. "Oral History and the Archives." *American Archivist* 39 (1976): 479–83.

Fogerty, James E. "Facing Reality: Oral History, Corporate Culture, and the Documentation of Business." In *The Records of American Business*, edited by James O'Toole, 251–74. Chicago: Society of American Archivists, 1997.

Harrison, Helen. "Selection and Audiovisual Collections." *IFLA Journal* 21, no. 3 (1995): 185–90.

———, ed. Audiovisual Archives: A Practical Reader. Paris: UNESCO. http://www.unesco.org/webworld/audiovis/reader/preface.htm.

Haynes, Kathleen J.M., Lynda Lee Kaid, and Charles E. Rand. "The Political Commercial Archive: Management of Moving Image and Sound Recordings." *American Archivist* 59, no. 1 (winter 1996): 48–61.

Hendriks, Klaus B. "The Preservation of Photographic Records." *Archivaria* 5 (winter 1977–78): 92–100.

———. *The Preservation and Restoration of Photographic Materials in Archives and Libraries: A RAMP Study with Guidelines.* Paris: UNESCO, 1984.

Hincha, Richard. "Crisis in Celluloid: Color Fading and Film Base Deterioration." *Archival Issues* 17, no. 2 (1992): 125–36.

Honniball, Jack. "Australia and the World's Film Archives." *Archives and Manuscripts* 11, no. 2 (November 1983): 156–59.

Houston, Penelope. *Keepers of the Frame: The Film Archives.* London: British Film Institute, 1994.

Hiseh-Yee, Ingrid. *Organizing Audiovisual and Electronic Resources for Access: A Cataloging Guide.* Englewood, Colo. Libraries Unlimited, 2000.

Huyda, Richard J. "Photographs and Archives in Canada." *Archivaria* 5 (winter 1977–78): 3–16.

International Association of Sound and Audiovisual Archives. *The Safeguarding of the Audio Heritage: Ethics, Principles and Preservation Strategy.* Version 2, September 2001. http://www.iasa-web.org/iasa0013.htm.

Johnson, Linda. "Yukon Archives Visual Photograph Finding Aid." *Archivaria* 5 (winter 1977–78): 112–23.

Kaplan, Elisabeth, and Jeffrey Mifflin. "'Mind and Sight': Visual Literacy and the Archivist." *Archival Issues* 21, no. 2 (1996): 107–27.

King, Barrie E. "Film Archives: Their Purpose and Problems." *Archives and Manuscripts* 4, no. 2 (May 1970): 8–16.

———. "The International Federation of Film Archives." *Archives and Manuscripts* 9, no. 1 (September 1981): 87–91.

Koltun, Lilly, *et al.* "The Photograph: An Annotated Bibliography for Archivists." *Archivaria* 5 (winter 1977–78): 124–40.

Kula, Sam. *The Archival Appraisal of Moving Images: A RAMP Study with Guidelines.* Paris: UNESCO, 1983.

Lambert, Phyllis. "Photographic Documentation and Buildings: Relationships Past and Present." *Archivaria* 5 (winter 1977–78): 60–77.

Langham, Josephine. "Tuning In: Canadian Radio Resources." *Archivaria* 9 (winter 1979–80): 105–24.

Larose, K.M. "Preserving the Past on Film: Problems for the Archivist." *Archivaria* 6 (summer 1978): 137–50.

Leary, William H. *The Archival Appraisal of Photographs: A RAMP Study with Guidelines.* Paris: UNESCO, 1985.

Library of Congress, National Film Preservation Board. *Film Preservation 1993: A Study of the Current State of American Film Preservation.* Washington, D.C.: Library of Congress, 1993. http://lcweb/loc.gov/film/study.html.

———. "Film Preservation White Paper. Keeping Cool and Dry: A New Emphasis in Film Preservation." Washington, D.C.: Library of Congress, 1994. http://lcweb.loc.gov/film/storage.html.

———. "Redefining Film Preservation: A National Plan." Recommendations of the Librarian of Congress in Consultation with the National Film Preservation Board. Washington, D.C.: Library of Congress, 1994. http://lcweb.loc.gov/film/plan.html.

———. Television and Video Preservation 1997: A Report on the Current State of American Television and Video Preservation. Washington, D.C.: Library of Congress, 1997. http://lcweb.loc.gov/ film/tvstudy.html.

Managing Audiovisual Records: An Instructional Guide. 1999 Web Edition. Washington, D.C.: National Archives and Records Administration, 1999. http://www.archives.gov/records_management/publications/managing_audiovisual_records.html.

Managing Cartographic and Architectural Records. Washington, D.C.: National Archives and Records Administration, 1989.

Martin, Abigail Leab, ed. *AMIA Compendium of Moving Image Cataloging Practice*. Chicago: Society of American Archivists, and Beverly Hills: Association of Moving Image Archivists, 2001.

Mattison, David, and Saundra Sherman. "Cataloguing Historical Photographs with ISBD(NBM)." *Archivaria* 5 (winter 1977–78): 101–11.

McWilliams, Jerry. *The Preservation and Restoration of Sound Recordings*. Nashville: American Association for State and Local History, 1979.

Moss, William. *An Oral History Program Manual*. New York: Praeger, 1974.

O'Donnell, Lorraine. "Towards Total Archives: The Form and Meaning of Photographic Records." *Archivaria* 38 (fall 1994): 105–18.

Pare, Richard. "Creating the Photographic Record: The United States Court House Project." *Archivaria* 5 (winter 1977–78): 78–91.

Parinet, Elisabeth. "Diplomatics and Institutional Photos." *American Archivist* 59, no. 4 (fall 1996): 480–85.

Paton, Christopher Ann. "Annotated Selected Bibliography of Works Relating to Sound Recordings and Magnetic and Optical Media." *Midwestern Archivist* 16 (1991): 31–48.

———. "Appraisal of Sound Recordings for Textual Archivists." *Archival Issues* 22, no. 2 (1997): 117–32.

———. "Preservation Re-Recording of Audio Recordings in Archives: Problems, Priorities, Technologies, and Recommendations." In *American Archival Studies: Readings in Theory and Practice*, edited by Randall C. Jimerson, 519–46. Chicago: Society of American Archivists, 2000.

Pedersen, Diana. "The Photographic Record of the Canadian YWCA, 1890–1930: A Visual Source for Women's History." *Archivaria* 24 (summer 1987): 10–35.

Pruter, Robert. "Words and Music: Understanding the Value of Textual Content on Commercial Sound Recording Labels." *Archival Issues* 25, nos. 1–2 (2000): 57–70.

Reilly, James M. *Care and Identification of 19th-Century Photographic Prints*. Rochester, N.Y.: Eastman Kodak Company, 1986.

———. *The IPI Storage Guide for Acetate Film*. Rochester, N.Y.: Image Permanence Institute, 1993.

Roberts, David. "Archives and Sound Archives: What's the Difference?" *Archives and Manuscripts* 12, no. 2 (November 1984): 116–26.

Robertson, Peter. "More Than Meets the Eye." *Archivaria* 1, no. 2 (summer 1976): 33–43.

Rodger, Andrew C. "Amateur Photography by Soldiers of the Canadian Expeditionary Force." *Archivaria* 26 (summer 1988): 163–68.

Roman, D. "Restoration of Old Faded Photographs." *Archives and Manuscripts* 4, no. 8 (August 1972): 7–10.

Ross, David. "Military Dress and the Cataloguing of Photographs." *Archivaria* 26 (summer 1988): 173–75.

Rutherford, Paul. "Researching Television History: Prime-Time Canada, 1952–1967." *Archivaria* 20 (summer 1985): 79–93.

Sandomirsky, Janice. "Toronto's Public Health Photography." *Archivaria* 10 (summer 1980): 145–56.

Sargent, Ralph. *Preserving the Moving Image*. Washington, D.C.: Corporation for Public Broadcasting/National Endowment for the Arts, 1974.

Schwartz, Joan. "The Photographic Record of Pre-Confederation British Columbia." *Archivaria* 5 (winter 1977–78): 17–44.

———. "'We Make Our Tools and Our Tools Make Us': Lessons From Photographs for the Practice, Politics, and Poetics of Diplomatics." *Archivaria* 40 (fall 1995): 40–74.

Slide, Anthony. *Nitrate Won't Wait: Film Preservation in the United States*. Jefferson, North Carolina: McFarland & Company, 1992.

Sprinkle, Matthew. "Lasers and the Fate of Phonographic Recordings." *American Archivist* 58, no. 4 (fall 1995): 458–63.

Spurgeon, Greg. "Pictures and History: The Art Museum and the Visual Arts Archives." *Archivaria* 17 (winter 1983–84): 60–74.

St-Laurent, Gilles. *The Care and Handling of Recorded Sound Materials*. Washington, D.C.: Commission on Preservation and Access, 1991.

Stewart, Eleanore, and Paul N. Banks. "Preservation of Information in Nonpaper Formats." In *Preservation: Issues and Planning*, edited by Paul N. Banks and Roberta Pilette, 323–42. Chicago: American Library Association, 2000.

Stewart, John. "Oral History and Archivists." *American Archivist* 36 (July 1973): 361–65.

Stielow, Frederick J. *The Management of Oral History Sound Archives*. New York: Greenwood Press, 1986.

Thomas, Ann. "Private Realms of Light: Canadian Amateur Photography, 1839–1940: Reflections of an Exhibition." *Archivaria* 17 (winter 1983–84): 136–44.

Thompson, Paul. *The Voice of the Past: Oral History*. New York: Oxford University Press, 1978.

Thornton, Robert. "Rose-tinted Images: The Photographic Archives of the City of Adelaide." *Archives and Manuscripts* 28, no. 2 (November 2000): 46–57.

Trevelen, Dale. "Oral History and the Archival Community: Common Concerns About Documenting Twentieth-Century Life." *International Journal of Oral History* 10 (February 1989): 50–58.

Tuttle, Craig A. *An Ounce of Preservation: A Guide to the Care of Papers and Photographs*. Highland City, Fla.: Rainbow Books, 1995.

Vansina, Jan. *Oral Tradition: A Study in Historical Methodology*. Chicago: Aldine, 1965.

Walsh, Timothy. "The Conservation of Photographic Records: A Select Bibliography." *Archives and Manuscripts* 9, no. 1 (September 1981): 77–82.

Weinstein, Robert A., and Larry Booth. *Collection, Use, and Care of Historical Photographs.* Nashville, Tenn.: American Association for State and Local History, 1977.

MANAGEMENT

Abraham, Terry, Stephen E. Balzarini, and Anne Frantilla. "What is Backlog is Prologue: A Measurement of Archival Processing." *American Archivist* 48 (winter 1985): 31–44.

Archival Processing Costs. Problems in Archives Kit. Chicago: Society of American Archivists, 1981.

Atherton, Jay. "Emphasizing the *Management* in Time Management." *ARMA Records Management Quarterly* 20 (October 1986): 26–29.

Bailey, Martha J. *The Special Librarian as Supervisor or Middle Manager.* New York: Special Libraries Association, 1977.

Berzins, Baiba. "The Australian Society of Archivists Survey of Salaries and Conditions of Employment." *Archives and Manuscripts* 10, no. 1 (May 1982): 53–63.

Bradsher, James Gregory, ed. *Managing Archives and Archival Institutions.* Chicago: University of Chicago Press, 1988.

Bridges, Edwin C. "Can State Archives Meet the Challenges of the Eighties? Four Recent Views on the Condition of American State Archives." *ARMA Records Management Quarterly* 20 (April 1986): 15–21, 52.

Burke, Frank G. "Archival Cooperation." *American Archivist* 46 (summer 1983): 293–305.

Carmicheal, David W. *Involving Volunteers in Archives.* Mid-Atlantic Regional Archives Conference Technical Leaflet No. 6. Mid-Atlantic Regional Archives Conference, 1990.

Conway, Paul. "Perspectives on Archival Resources: The 1985 Census of Archival Institutions." *American Archivist* 50 (spring 1987): 174–91.

Cox, Richard J. *Managing Institutional Archives: Foundational Principles and Practices.* Westport, Conn.: Greenwood Press, 1992.

Davis, W.N., Jr. "Budgeting for Archival Processing." *American Archivist* 43 (spring 1980): 209–11.

Dearstyne, Bruce W. *Managing Historical Records Programs: A Guide for Historical Agencies.* Walnut Creek, Calif.: AltaMira Press, 2000.

———. *Planning for Archival Programs: An Introduction.* Technical Leaflet No. 3. New York: Mid-Atlantic Regional Archives Conference, 1983.

———, ed. *Leadership and Administration of Successful Archival Programs.* Westport, Conn.: Greenwood Press, 2001.

Drucker, Peter F. *Management Tasks, Responsibilities, Practices,* New York: Harper & Row, 1973.

Evaluation of Archival Institutions: Services, Principles, and Guide to Self-Study. Chicago: Society of American Archivists, 1982.

Evans, G. Edward, Patricia Layzell Ward, and Bendik Rugaas. *Management Basics for Information Professionals.* New York: Neal-Schuman, 2000.

Ewing, Susan E. "Using Volunteers for Special-Project Staffing at the National Air and Space Museum Archives." *American Archivist* 54 (spring 1991): 176–83.

Francis, James, Cynthia L. Sutton, and Bill Cox. "New Tools for the Information Manager [Quality Circles and Nominal Grouping Technique]." *ARMA Records Management Quarterly* 21 (April 1987): 3–8.

Grabowski, John J. "Keepers, Users, and Funders: Building an Awareness of Archival Value." *American Archivist* 55 (summer 1992): 464–72.

Hackman, Larry J. "Historical Documentation in the United States: Archivists—and Historians?" *Organization of American Historians Newsletter* (August 1985): 17–18.

Haller, Uli. "Variations in the Processing Rates on the Magnuson and Jackson Senatorial Papers." *American Archivist* 50 (winter 1987): 100–9.

Ham, F. Gerald. "Planning for the Archival Profession." *American Archivist* 48 (winter 1985): 26–30.

Hefner, Loretta L. "The Change Masters: Organizational Development in a State Archives." *American Archivist* 51 (fall 1988): 440–54.

Henry, Linda J. "Archival Advisory Committees: Why?" *American Archivist* 48 (summer 1985): 315–19.

Hunter, Gregory S. "Filling the GAP: Planning on the Local and Individual Levels." *American Archivist* 50 (winter 1987): 110–15.

Klein, Phyllis A. *Our Past Before Us: A Five-Year Regional Plan for METRO's Archives and Historical Records Program.* New York: New York Metropolitan Reference and Research Library Agency [METRO], 1989.

Long-Range Planning for Academic Archives. Problems in Archives Kit. Chicago: Society of American Archivists, 1983.

Maher, William J. "The Importance of Financial Analysis in Archival Programs." *Midwestern Archivist* 3 (1978): 3–24.

McCarthy, Paul H. "The Management of Archives: A Research Agenda." *American Archivist* 51 (winter/spring 1988): 52–73.

McGregor, Douglas. *The Human Side of Enterprise.* New York: McGraw Hill, 1960.

McShane, Stephen G. "Planning is Prologue: The Planning Process and the Archival Profession." *Midwestern Archivist* 15 (1990): 109–16.

Planning for the Archival Profession: A Report of the SAA Task Force on Goals and Priorities. Chicago: Society of American Archivists, 1986.

Schein, Edgar H. *Organizational Culture and Leadership.* San Francisco: Jossey-Bass Publishers, 1985.

Scott, P.J., and G. Finlay. "Archives and Administrative Change: Some Methods and Approaches (Part 1)." *Archives and Manuscripts* 7, no. 3 (August 1978): 115–27.

Scott, P.J., C.D. Smith, and G. Finlay. "Archives and Administrative Change: Some Methods and Approaches (Part 2)." *Archives and Manuscripts* 7, no. 4 (April 1979): 151–65.

Scott, Peter. "Archives and Administrative Change: Some Methods and Approaches (Part 5)." *Archives and Manuscripts* 9, no. 1 (September 1981): 3–18.

Scott, Peter, Gail Finlay, and Clive Smith. "Archives and Administrative Change: Some Methods and Approaches (Part 3)." *Archives and Manuscripts* 8, no. 1 (June 1980): 41–54.

———. "Archives and Administrative Change: Some Methods and Approaches (Part 4)." *Archives and Manuscripts* 8, no. 2 (December 1980): 51–69.

Strengthening New York's Historical Records Programs: A Self-Study Guide. New York: State Archives and Records Administration, 1989.

Swift, Michael. "Management Techniques and Technical Resources in the Archives of the 1980s." *Archivaria* 20 (summer 1985): 94–104.

Virgo, Julie. *Principles of Strategic Planning in the Library Environment.* Chicago: Association of College and Research Libraries, 1984.

Waegemann, C. Peter. "Cost Management in Records Management." *Records and Retrieval Report* 1 (February 1985). 21–36.

Wilsted, Thomas. *Computing the Total Cost of Archival Processing.* Technical Leaflet No. 2. New York: Mid-Atlantic Regional Archives Conference, 1982.

Wilsted, Thomas and William Nolte. *Managing Archival and Manuscript Repositories.* Chicago: Society of American Archivists, 1991.

EDUCATION, PROFESSIONAL DEVELOPMENT, AND ETHICS

Albada, Joan Van. "The Identity of the American Archival Profession: A European Perspective." *American Archivist* 54 (summer 1991): 398–402.

Ambacher, Bruce. "The Modern Archives Institute: A History and Profile of Recent Students." *Archival Issues* 18, no. 2 (1993): 109–20.

Bearman, Toni Carbo. "The Education of Archivists: Future Challenges for Schools of Library and Information Science." *Journal of Education for Library and Information Science* 34 (winter 1993): 66–72.

Bennett, George E. *Librarians in Search of Science and Identity: The Elusive Profession.* Metuchen, N.J.: Scarecrow Press, 1988.

Boles, Frank. "Making Hard Choices: Continuing Education and the Archival Profession." *Archival Issues* 21, no. 1 (1996): 7–24.

Bower, Peter. "Reflections of Early *Archivaria:* Intimations of Polyphony." *Archivaria* 49 (spring 2000): 1–19.

Brichford, Maynard. "Who Are the Archivists and What Do They Do?" *American Archivist* 51 (winter/spring 1988): 106–10.

Bridges, Edwin, et al. "Toward Better Documenting and Interpreting of the Past: What History Graduate Programs in the Twenty-First Century Should Teach about Archival Practices." *American Archivist* 56 (fall 1993): 730–49.

Brumm, Eugenia K. "Graduate Education in Records Management: The University of Texas Model." *Journal of Education for Library and Information Science* 33 (fall 1992): 333–37.

Burckel, Nicholas C. "The Society [of American Archivists]: From Birth to Maturity." *American Archivist* 61, no. 1 (spring 1998): 12–35.

"A Code of Ethics for Archivists." *American Archivist* 43 (summer 1980): 414–18.

Conway, Paul. "Archival Education and the Need for Full-Time Faculty." *American Archivist* 51 (summer 1988): 254–65.

———. "Effective Continuing Education for Training the Archivist." *Journal of Education for Library and Information Science* 34 (winter 1993): 38–47.

Cook, Michael. *The Education and Training of Archivists: Status Report of Archival Training Programs and Assessment of Manpower Needs.* Paris: UNESCO, 1979.

———. *Guidelines for Curriculum Development in Records Management and the Administration of Modern Archives: A RAMP Study.* Paris: UNESCO, 1982.

———. "Professional Training: International Perspectives." *Archivaria* 7 (winter 1978): 28–41.

Cook, Terry. "'The Imperative of Challenging Absolutes' in Graduate Archival Education Programs: Issues for Educators and the Profession." *American Archivist* 63, no. 2 (fall/winter 2000): 380–91.

Corbett, Bryan E. "Archival Education: The Experience of the Association of Canadian Archivists." *Archival Issues* 18, no. 2 (1993): 97–108.

Corbett, Bryan E., and Margery Hadley. "Post-Appointment and Continuing Education: Alberta's Five-Year Plan." *Archivaria* 29 (winter 1989–90): 142–48.

Cox, Richard J. "American Archival Literature: Expanding Horizons and Continuing Needs, 1901–1987." *American Archivist* 50 (summer 1987): 306–23.

———. "Archives and Archivists in the Twenty-First Century: What Will We Become?" *Archival Issues* 20, no. 2 (1995): 97–114.

———. "Archivists and Public Historians in the United States." *Public Historian* 8 (summer 1986): 29–45.

———. "Educating Records Professionals in a Hostile Age." In *Closing an Era: Historical Perspectives on Modern Archives and Records Management*, edited by Richard Cox, 159–96. Westport, Conn.: Greenwood Press, 2000.

———. "Our Disappearing Past." *Organization of American Historians Newsletter* 15 (February 1987): 8–9.

———. "Professionalism and Archivists in the United States." *American Archivist* 49 (summer 1986): 229–47.

———. "The Society of American Archivists and Graduate Education: Meeting at the Crossroads." *American Archivist* 63, no. 2 (fall/winter 2000): 368–79.

———, ed. "Educating the American Archivist for the Twenty-First Century." *Journal of Education for Library and Information Science* special issue 34 (winter 1993).

Couture, Carol. "Education and Research in Archival Science: General Tendencies." *Archival Science* 1, no. 2 (2001): 157–82.

———. "Today's Students, Tomorrow's Archivists: Present-Day Focus and Development as Determinants of Archival Science in the Twenty-First Century." *Archivaria* 42 (fall 1996): 95–104.

Craig, Barbara L. "A Look at the Bigger Picture: the Demographic Profile of Archivists in Canada Based on a National Survey." *Archivaria* 49 (spring 2000): 20–52.

———. "Outward Visions, Inward Glance: Archives History and Professional Identity." *Archival Issues* 17, no. 2 (1992): 113–24.

———. "Serving the Truth: The Importance of Fostering Archives Research in Education Programmes, Including a Modest Proposal for Partnrships With the Workplace." *Archivaria* 42 (fall 1996): 105–17.

Cunningham, Adrian. "What's in a Name?: Broadening Our Horizons in the Pursuit of a Recordkeeping Profession that Cherishes Unity and Diversity." *Archives and Manuscripts* 29, no. 1 (May 2001): 110–17.

Danielson, Elena S. "The Ethics of Access." *American Archivist* 52 (winter 1989): 52–62.

Davis, Susan E. "Continuing Education for Archivists." *Journal of Education for Library and Information Science* 34 (winter 1993): 79–81.

———. "Development of Managerial Training for Archivists." *American Archivist* 51 (summer 1988): 278–85.

Delmas, B. *The Training of Archivists: Analysis of the Study Programmes of Different Countries and Thoughts on the Possibilities of Harmonization.* Paris: UNESCO, 1979.

Diamond, Elizabeth. "The Archivist as Forensic Scientist: Seeing Ourselves in a Different Way." *Archivaria* 38 (fall 1994): 139–54.

Duchein, Michel. "The History of European Archives and the Development of the Archival Profession in Europe." *American Archivist* 55 (winter 1992): 14–25.

Duff, Wendy M. "Integrating New Paraprofessionals into an Old Profession." *Archivaria* 38 (fall 1994): 97–104.

Duranti, Luciana. "The Archival Body of Knowledge: Archival Theory, Method, and Practice, and Graduate and Continuing Education." *Journal of Education for Library and Information Science* 34 (winter 1993): 8–24.

———. "The Society of American Archivists and Graduate Archival Education: A Sneak Preview of Future Directions." *American Archivist* 63, no. 2 (fall/winter 2000): 237–42.

Eastwood, Terry. "Archival Research: The University of British Columbia Experience." *American Archivist* 63, no. 2 (fall/winter 2000): 243–57.

———. "Nailing a Little Jelly to the Wall of Archival Studies." *Archivaria* 35 (spring 1993): 232–52.

———. "Nurturing Archival Education in the University." *American Archivist* 51 (summer 1988): 228–52.

———. "The Origins and Aims of the Master of Archival Studies Programme at the University of British Columbia." *Archivaria* 16 (summer 1983): 35–52.

———. "Reforming the Archival Curriculum to Meet Contemporary Needs." *Archivaria* 42 (fall 1996): 80–88.

Education Committee, Association of Canadian Archivists. "Guidelines for the Development of a Two-Year Curriculum for a Master of Archival Studies Programme (December 1988)." *Archivaria* 29 (winter 1989–90): 128–41.

———. "Guidelines for the Development of Post-Appointment and Continuing Education and Training Programmes (December 1990)." *Archivaria* 31 (winter 1990–91): 60–89.

Edwards, R. Dudley, and Ailsa C. Holland. "Teaching Archival Studies in an Irish University." *Archivaria* 4 (summer 1977): 20–33.

Endelman, Judith E. and Joel Wurl. "The NHPRC/Mellon Foundation Fellowship in Archives Administration: Structured Training on the Job." *American Archivist* 51 (summer 1988): 286–97.

Enderby, A. "Practical Training for Archivists." *Archives and Manuscripts* 3, no. 5 (November 1967): 9–12.

Ericson, Timothy L. "'Abolish the Recent': the Progress of Archival Education." *Journal of Education for Library and Information Science* 34 (winter 1993): 25–37.

———. "Forming 'Structures of Exquisite Beauty': Archivists and Education." *Archivaria* 42 (fall 1996): 118–25.

———. "Professional Associations and Archival Education: A Different Role, or a Different Theater?" *American Archivist* 51 (summer 1988): 298–311.

Eso, Elizabeth, and Robin G. Keirstead. "A Survey of Students of the Master of Archival Studies Program at the University of British Columbia, 1981–88." *Archivaria* 29 (winter 1989–90): 104–27.

Fleckner, John A. "'Dear Mary Jane': Some Reflections on Being an Archivist." *American Archivist* 54 (winter 1991): 8–13.

Frevert, Rhonda Huber. "Archives Volunteers: Worth the Effort?" *Archival Issues* 22, no. 2 (1997): 147–62.

Gabehart, Alan D. "Qualifications Desired by Employers for Entry-Level Archivists in the United States." *American Archivist* 55 (summer 1992): 420–39.

Geller, Lawrence D. "Joseph Cuvelier, Belgian Archival Education, and the First International Congress of Archivists, Brussels, 1910." *Archivaria* 16 (summer 1983): 26–34.

Gibbney, H.J. "The Trials of Training." *Archives and Manuscripts* 4, no. 4 (May 1971): 9–11.

Gilliland-Swetland, Anne J. "Archival Research: A 'New' Issue for Graduate Education." *American Archivist* 63, no. 2 (fall/winter 2000): 258–70.

———. "Graduate Archival Education and the Professional Market: Perspectives on Data and Data Gathering." *Archival Issues* 23, no. 2 (1998): 91–116.

Gilliland-Swetland, Luke J. "The Provenance of a Profession: The Permanence of the Public Archives and Historical Manuscripts Tradition in American Archival History." *American Archivist* 54 (spring 1991): 160–75.

Goggin, Jacqueline. "That We Shall Truly Deserve the Title of 'Profession': The Training and Education of Archivists, 1930–1960." *American Archivist* 47 (summer 1984): 243–54.

Gracy, David B., II "Archivists, You Are What People Think You Keep." *American Archivist* 52 (winter 1989): 72–78.

Ham, F. Gerald, et al. "Is the Past Still Prologue? History and Archival Education." *American Archivist* 56 (fall 1993): 718–29.

Helmuth, Ruth W. "Education for American Archivists: A View from the Trenches." *American Archivist* 44 (fall 1981): 295–303.

Henry, Linda J. "Women Archivists in the Federal Government: A Glass Ceiling?" *Archival Issues* 19, no. 2 (1994): 95–106.

Hopkins, Mark. "'There's a Hole in the Bucket, Dear Liza, Dear Liza': Archivists' Responsibilities Reviewed." *Archivaria* 16 (summer 1983): 134–38.

Horn, David E. "The Development of Ethics in Archival Practice." *American Archivist* 52 (winter 1989): 64–71.

———. "Education for Archivists: Hard Choices and Hard Work." *Archival Issues* 21, no. 1 (1996): 25–32.

Hurley, Chris. "Recordkeeping, Document Destruction, and the Law (Heiner, Enron and McCabe)." *Archives and Manuscripts* 30, no. 2 (November 2002): 6–25.

Iacovino, Livia. "Teaching Law in Recordkeeping Courses: The Monash Experience." *Archives and Manuscripts* 25, no. 2 (November 1997): 266–87.

Joyce, William L. "Archival Education: Two Fables." *American Archivist* 51 (winter/ spring 1988): 16–22.

Ketelaar, Eric. "Archivistics Research Saving the Profession." *American Archivist* 63, no. 2 (fall/winter 2000): 322–40.

Kigongo-Bukenya, I.M.N. "Education and Training of Archivists at the East African School of Librarianship in the 1990s and Beyond." *American Archivist* 56 (spring 1993): 358–65.

Klumpenhouwer, Rick. "The MAS and After: Transubstantiating Theory and Practice Into an Archival Culture." *Archivaria* 39 (spring 1995): 88–95.

Lemieux, Victoria. "An Archival Practitioner's Views on Archival Literature: Where We Have Been and Where We Are Going." *Archivaria* 40 (fall 1995): 199–209.

Locker, Anne. "Should Archivists Be Professionals?" In *New Directions in Archival Research*, edited by Margaret Procter and C.P. Lewis, 188–43. Liverpool: Liverpool University Centre for Archive Studies, 2000.

Lytle, Richard H. "Ethics of Information Management." *ARMA Records Management Quarterly* 4 (October 1970): 5–8.

MacNeil, Heather. *Without Consent: The Ethics of Disclosing Personal Information in Public Archives.* Chicago: Society of American Archivists and Scarecrow Press, 1992.

Maher, William J. "Contexts for Understanding Professional Certification: Opening Pandora's Box?" *American Archivist* 51 (fall 1988): 408–27.

———. "Cooperative Competitors: Local, State, and National Archival Associations." *Midwestern Archivist* 16 (1991): 105–14.

Martin, Robert Sidney. "The Development of Professional Education for Librarians and Archivists in the United States: A Comparative Essay." *American Archivist* 57 (summer 1994): 544–59.

McAdam, Rhona. "AIDS and Confidentiality: The Records Manager's Dilemma." *ARMA Records Management Quarterly* 23 (July 1989): 12–16, 28.

McKemmish, Sue. "Collaborative Research Models: A Review of Australian Initiatives." *American Archivist* 63, no. 2 (fall/winter 2000): 353–68.

Menne-Haritz, Angelika. "Archival Training in a Changing World." *American Archivist* 63, no. 2 (fall/winter 2000): 341–52.

———. "Archival Training in Germany: A Balance Between Specialization in Historical Research and Administrative Needs." *American Archivist* 57 (spring 1994): 400–9.

Miller, Fredric M. "The SAA as Sisyphus: Education Since the 1960s." *American Archivist* 63, no. 2 (fall/winter 2000): 224–36.

Mirandi, Paul J., Jr. "Associationalism, Statism, and Professional Regulation: Public Accountants and the Reform of the Financial Markets, 1896–1940." *Business History Review* 60 (autumn 1986): 438–68.

Moss, Michael S. "The Scent of the Slow Hound and the Snap of a Bull-Dog: The Place of Research in the Archival Profession." In New Directions in Archival Research, edited by Margaret Procter and C.P. Lewis, 7–19. Liverpool: Liverpool University Centre for Archive Studies, 2000.

Museum Ethics. Washington, D.C.: American Association of Museums, 1978.

Neal, Kathryn M. "The Importance on Being Diverse: The Archival Profession and Minority Recruitment." *Archival Issues* 21, no. 2 (1996): 145–58.

Nesmith, Tom. "'Professional Education in the Most Expansive Sense': What Will the Archivist Need to Know in the Twenty-First Century?" *Archivaria* 42 (fall 1996): 89–94.

Olson, David. "'Camp Pitt' and the Continuing Education of Government Archivists: 1989–1996." *American Archivist* 60, no. 2 (spring 1997): 202–15

Orlovich, Peter. "Some Basic Assumptions Underlying the Education and Training of Archivists." *Archives and Manuscripts* 6, no. 6 (February 1966): 204–25.

O'Toole, James M. "The Archival Curriculum: Where Are We Now?" *Archival Issues* 22, no. 2 (1997): 103–16.

———. "Curriculum Development in Archival Education: A Proposal." *American Archivist* 53 (summer 1990): 460–66.

Pacifico, Michelle F. "Founding Mothers: Women in the Society of American Archivists, 1936–72." *American Archivist* 50 (summer 1987): 370–89.

Peace, Nancy E. and Nancy Fisher Chudacoff. "Archivists and Librarians: A Common Mission, a Common Education." *American Archivist* 42 (October 1979): 456–62.

Peters, Evelyn. "Measures of Success: Evaluating University of British Columbia's Master of Archival Studies Program." *Archivaria* 45 (spring 1998): 80–103.

Piggott, Michael. "At the Drawing Board: Problems in the Professional Education of the Archivist." *Archives and Manuscripts* 4, no. 5 (November 1971): 25–32.

Rees, Anthony L. "Masters in Our Own House?" *Archivaria* 16 (summer 1983): 53–59.

Rene-Bazis, Paule. "The Future of European Archival Education." *American Archivist* 55 (winter 1992): 58–65.

Robyns, Marcus C. "The Archivist as Educator: Integrating Critical Thinking Skills into Historical Research Methods Instruction." *American Archivist* 64, no. 2 (fall/winter 2001): 363–84.

"Roundtable: Ethics and Public History." *The Public Historian* 8 (winter 1986): 5–68.

Rumschottel, Hermann. "The Development of Archival Science as a Scholarly Discipline." *Archival Science* 1, no. 2 (2001): 143–55.

Russell, E.W. "Archival Ethics." *Archives and Manuscripts* 6, no. 6 (February 1976): 226–34.

———. "Archival Training in London: Some Experiences, 1972–73." *Archives and Manuscripts* 6, no. 1 (November 1974): 3–10.

Ruth, Janice E. "Educating the Reference Archivist." *American Archivist* 51 (summer 1988): 266–76.

Schaeffer, Roy. "From Craft to Profession: The Evolution of Archival Education and Theory in North America." *Archivaria* 37 (spring 1994): 21–34.

Skupsky, Donald S. "Legal Liability of the Records and Information Management Professional." *ARMA Records Management Quarterly* 21 (April 1987): 36–39.

Stephenson, Mary Sue. "The Function and Content of Research Methods in Graduate Archival Studies Education." *Archivaria* 35 (spring 1993): 175–89.

Stielow, Frederick. "Archival Theory Redux and Redeemed: Definition and Context Toward a General Theory." *American Archivist* 54 (winter 1991): 14–26.

Summerrell, Richard. "Improving the Education and Professional Development of Reference Archivists." *Archives and Manuscripts* 27, no. 1 (May 1999): 74–95.

Taylor, Hugh A. "From Dust to Ashes: Burnout in the Archives." *Midwestern Archivist* 12 (1987): 73–82.

Thurston, Anne. "The Training of Archivists From Developing Countries: A Commonwealth Perspective." *Archivaria* 20 (summer 1985): 116–26.

Waegemann, C. Peter. "Careers in Records Management." *Records and Retrieval Report* 2 (December 1986): 1–10.

Wallace, David A. "Survey of Archives and Records Management Graduate Students at Ten Universities in the United States and Canada." *American Archivist* 63, no. 2 (fall/winter 2000): 284–300.

Wallot, Jean-Pierre. "Free Trade in Archival Ideas: The Canadian Perspective on North American Archival Development." *American Archivist* 57 (spring 1994): 380–99.

———. "Limited Identities for a Common Identity: Archivists in the Twenty-First Century." *Archivaria* 41 (spring 1996): 6–30.

Walters, Tyler O. "Creating a Front Door to Archival Knowledge in the United States: Guidelines for a Master of Archival Studies Degree." *Archival Issues* 18, no. 2 (1993): 77–96.

———. "Possible Educations for Archivists: Integrating Graduate Archival Education with Public History Education Programs." *American Archivist* 54 (fall 1991): 484–92.

Welch, Edwin. "Archival Education." *Archivaria* 4 (summer 1977): 49–59.

Wheeler, D. "Archival Training: A Canberra Experiment Dies." *Archives and Manuscripts* 6, no. 7 (August 1976): 275–80.

White, Brenda. *Directory of Audio-Visual Materials for Use in Records Management and Archives Administration Training.* Paris: UNESCO, 1982.

Wiegand, Wayne A. *The Politics of an Emerging Profession: The American Library Association, 1876–1917.* Westport, Conn.: Greenwood Press, 1986.

Wosh, Peter J. "Research and Reality Checks: Change and Continuity in NYU's Archival Management Program." *American Archivist* 63, no. 2 (fall/winter 2000): 271–83.

Wosh, Peter J., and Elizabeth Yakel. "Smaller Archives and Professional Development: Some New York Stories." *American Archivist* 55 (summer 1992): 474–82.

Yakel, Elizabeth. "The Future of the Past: A Survey of Graduates of Master's-Level Archival Education Programs in the United States." *American Archivist* 63, no. 2 (fall/winter 2000): 301–21.

INDEX

ABOUT THE AUTHOR

Gregory S. Hunter is a Professor in the Palmer School of Library and Information Science, Long Island University. He also is president of his own consulting firm, Hunter Information Management Services, Inc. He earned a doctorate in American History at New York University and is both a Certified Archivist and a Certified Records Manager. In 1989, Dr. Hunter was elected the first president of the Academy of Certified Archivists. He also has served as chair of the Society of American Archivists' Committee on Education and Professional Development and treasurer of the Mid-Atlantic Regional Archives Conference. Dr. Hunter is the author of four other books, including the award-winning *Preserving Digital Information* (also published by Neal-Schuman). He is a frequent author and lecturer on archives, records management, electronic imaging systems, digital records, and organizational change issues.